CRIMINAL JUSTICE

By

STEVE UGLOW
Senior Lecturer in Law,
Kent Law School at the
University of Kent

with Lisa Dickson,
Deborah Cheney
and Katherine Doolin

LONDON
SWEET & MAXWELL
2002

Published in 2002 by
Sweet & Maxwell Limited of
100 Avenue Road, Swiss Cottage,
London NW3 3PF
www.sweetandmaxwell.co.uk
Typeset by YHT Ltd, London
Printed in England by
MPG Books, Bodmin

No natural forests were destroyed to make this product.
Only farmed timber was used and re-planted.

A catalogue record for this book is
available from the British Library.

ISBN 0 421 738405

For Jenny

Preface

The first edition of this book was completed in 1995. At that time, I wrote that the preceding five years had seen unprecedented turbulence throughout the criminal justice system and successive Home Secretaries had alienated professionals in almost every part of the service. Much the same could be written five years later. In 1995 it was the repercussions from the reorganisation of the police resulting from the *Sheehy Report*—now it is the passage of the Police Reform Act 2002. In 1995 sentencing policy had been radically changed (for the better!) by the Criminal Justice Act 1991 but was immediately turned on its head in 1993 with the abolition of unit fines and the prospect (and actuality) of still more crowded jails—now sentencing policy will be thrown into the melting pot again if the recommendations of the *Halliday Report* on sentencing are carried through. In 1995, new police powers were introduced to criminalise partygoers and hunt protestors and civil liberty lawyers were dismayed by the cavalier overturning (against Royal Commission advice) of a right to silence, which went back centuries. The labour administration has done nothing to reduce, let alone, reverse the steady accretion of police powers and in 2001, extended powers still further through the Police and Criminal Justice Act.

There has been an unremitting flow of legislation. In 2001, Liberty estimated that there had been some 85 statutes dealing with crime and criminal justice promulgated since the beginning of the 1980s. A flood of government reports and white papers has driven this tidal wave—*Glidewell* on the prosecution service, *Halliday* on sentencing, *Auld* on the criminal courts and a comprehensive policy document, *Justice for All*, in July 2002. It has been a period when the government has stressed efficiency and effectiveness in public services—perhaps it should now mirror that concern by commissioning an evaluative study of that mass of legislation—how much of it was necessary? how much was based on research evidence? how much was cost effective? how much was ever used? This latter point is illustrated well by s.48 of the Police and Criminal Justice Act 2001, which extends local child curfew schemes to include children under 16. But in the three years since curfews were introduced in the Crime and Disorder Act 1998, as yet no local authority has applied for such an order—logic seems to dictate repeal rather than expansion?

There is one crucial counter-balance to this sense that the criminal justice system is being used as a political football. That is the passage of the Human Rights Act 1998 and its implementation some two years later. The extent of its impact on the criminal process waits to be seen but its provisions already inform both the textbooks and the practice. We can only applaud the idea that the system must be led by fundamental principles of human rights and not by technical legal rules. We must welcome the slightly heterodox concept that the British policeman and the British criminal trial are not wonderful solely because they are British and accept that we must measure and evaluate our procedures alongside other European jurisdictions and the jurisprudence of the European Court of Human Rights. The authors of this book have sought to introduce the Convention perspective wherever relevant. But there have proved to be significant limits to the Convention, which permits governments considerable latitude in their actions, as long as they act 'in accordance with law'. And in that law, the Court also permits a wide 'margin of appreciation'.

This book grew out of my experiencing of teaching in law schools. Although a teacher of criminal law, the day-to-day reality and, for me, the fascination lies in the interstices of enforcement: the processes which precede the accused's appearance in court, the problems of establishing facts at the trial or the operation of the penal system. Doctrinal niceties of appellate decisions had less appeal. Perhaps I share that relative lack of interest with some members of the House of Lords whose lack of concern with principle and with coherence in criminal jurisprudence should give cause for concern. No doubt criminal appeals may be seen as of marginal importance when compared with other weightier matters competing for judicial attention. But in any society one of the acid tests of 'fairness' rests is the manner in which we deal with those embroiled in the criminal justice system. Getting the substantive criminal law and procedure right should be regarded as a basic requirement. For students, substantive law should always be placed in their context. At one level this can be simply a procedural context, for example ensuring knowledge of the powers of arrest or the rules for drafting indictments. But more importantly (and to the students' dismay) it is necessary to grapple with the historical and cultural aspects of 'justice'. Equally important is knowledge of how the police, prosecutors and prisons operate and an understanding of how governmental policies affect these. This book is the result of seeking to teach criminal law in context.

This edition is the result of some collaboration—whereas I have revised the first eight chapters, I have been able to call on the specialist skills of my colleagues and friends, Lisa Dickson, Deborah Cheney and Kate Doolin to undertake the updates of the chapters on sentencing, imprisonment and youth justice. The edition has been delayed and all of us would like to thank the editorial staff at Sweet and Maxwell for their forbearance and assistance. The revision was undertaken in the summer of 2002 and we have endeavoured to state the law as it is on July 1st 2002.

Steve Uglow
August 2002

Contents

Chapter Eleven

Table of Cases

Table of Statutes

Paragraph numbers in **bold** indicate that the section is reproduced in full.

Table of Statutory Instruments

Frequently Used Acronyms

ACPO—Association of Chief Police Officers
ADP—Average Daily Population
BCS—British Crime Survey
BCU—Base Command Unit
BOV—Board of Visitors
CCP—Code for Crown Prosecutors
CNA—Certified Normal Accommodation
CPS—Crown Prosecution Service
CRO—Criminal Record Office
CSO—Community Service Order
DPP—Director of Public Prosecutions
ENM—Ecole Nationale de la Magistrature
HMCIP—Her Majesty's Chief Inspector of Prisons
HMI(C)—Her Majesty's Inspectorate (of Constabulary)
JP—Justice of the Peace
LPA—Local Police Authority
LRC—Local Review Committee
MCC—Magistrates' Courts Committee
NCIS—National Crime Intelligence Service
PACE—Police and Criminal Evidence Act 1984
PCA—Police Complaints Authority
PICA—Public Interest Case Assessment Schemes
PII—Public Interest Immunity
PSR—Pre-Sentence Report
RCCP—Royal Commission on Criminal Procedure
RCS—Regional Crime Squad
SIR—Social Inquiry Report
TIC—Offences Taken Into Consideration
YOI—Young Offenders' Institution

A System of Criminal Justice?

1.1 INTRODUCTION

The aim of this book is to describe and analyse the processes of the criminal justice system—from the making of the laws, through their enforcement by the police and the courts to the penal system. As a nation, we devote significant public resources on a criminal justice system that is aimed at reducing crime as well as prosecuting and punishing offenders. But this is not just a mechanistic process—detaining people against their will and punishing them brings into sharp relief the beliefs and principles about how we live with one another. Any examination of the criminal justice system requires consideration of the extent of individual freedom, the nature of common interests and the problems of fair treatment.

Crime and disorder issues impinge on our lives on most days: we read newspapers which rely on police investigation and court cases to fill their pages; we watch television which provides a diet of crime fiction and documentary programmes; on the street we are aware of the presence of the police or, if there is no patrolling officer, the CCTV camera as we walk down the high street, enter a shop or park the car. These penetrate everyday life to a greater extent than other social issues such as housing, poverty, education or health, although those who suffer from poor housing, bad health and low incomes are also likely to be the victims of crime.

Is our criminal justice system efficient, effective, just? We live in a society that imprisons 71,000 of its citizens, approximately 126 per hundred thousand of the population.[1] In 1998, that was the highest proportion in the E.U. with the sole exception of Portugal.[2] To interfere with such a fundamental right[3] requires clear

---

[1] The prison population in England and Wales at the end of June 2002 was 71,218 (Home Office—Research, Development and Statistics Directorate: Offenders and Corrections Unit).

[2] Barclay G. and Tavares C., *International comparisons of criminal justice statistics 2000* (Home Office: Briefing Note 05/02).

[3] The right to liberty is guaranteed by Art. 5 of the European Convention on Human Rights.

principles about why we should make certain sorts of conduct criminal but not others,[4] about whose behaviour requires investigation and prosecution, about the limits of state investigation of private life and about the objectives of any punishment. This book aims to explore the criminal process, in its procedural and legal aspects and to analyse its dynamic qualities in its day-to-day operations and its social significance. There are no simple answers and criminal justice is a complex process with many dimensions, ethical, political, constitutional and economic, all of which affect criminal justice policy-making.

But what are the building bricks of criminal justice?

- **substantive criminal law**—by this is meant laws that forbid particular conduct and lay down punishments. It is the existence of such laws that provides a basis of legitimacy for state agencies to investigate, prosecute and punish individuals for the commission of an offence. Originally the courts were able to create criminal offences and some crimes, such as murder and manslaughter, are still based on common law. The courts no longer regard themselves as having the capacity to create new crimes[5] and the vast majority of offences are created and defined by Acts of Parliament. The courts still affect the scope of any offence through their interpretation of the language used in the statute. Furthermore many defences raised by the accused are common law in origin and the courts are able to affect the scope of offences by widening or narrowing such defences—for example, the dismissal of the defence of spousal immunity in rape.[6] Until 1998, only Parliament and the courts could affect this body of criminal law but, since the Human Rights Act, the rights guaranteed under the European Convention on Human Rights and the jurisprudence developed by the Court of Human Rights in Strasbourg will also influence its boundaries, albeit indirectly.[7]

- **procedural criminal law**—procedural structures perform a range of functions. They may empower and constrain law enforcement agencies in their investigation of crime, providing them with the legal basis for arrest, detention and trial of suspects but also ensuring that suspects are treated with due respect. Pre-trial procedures that affect the investigation and prosecution of crime are primarily statutory.[8] Trial procedures, including the rules on the admissibility of evidence, are largely based on common law. Procedure is frequently caricatured as clerks' bureaucracy but the rules reflect key ethical principles and are underpinned by a concept of fair treatment, now reinforced by the provisions of Article 6 of the European Convention, which guarantees the right to a fair trial.

- **law enforcement agencies**—the police service is the agency primarily responsible for the investigation of crime but there are many others such as Customs and Excise, trading standards departments or environmental protection. Although these are responsible for investigation of complaints, the public usually initiates such action.

---

[4] Ashworth A., *The Principles of Criminal Law* (3rd ed., 1999) Chap. 2.
[5] *DPP v. Withers* [1975] A.C. 842.
[6] *R.* [1991] 4 All E. R. 481.
[7] For example, *A v. UK* (1999) 27 E.H.R.R. 611 will affect the defence of reasonable chastisement.
[8] Police powers are basically laid down in the Police and Criminal Evidence Act 1984, although this is been added to and amended.

- **prosecution of offenders**—the preparation of a case for trial and the presentation of that case at magistrates' and Crown Courts is predominantly undertaken by the Crown Prosecution Service (CPS)—agencies such as Customs and Excise may be responsible for mounting their own prosecutions.

- **legal representation of offenders**—the Legal Services Commission is responsible for the public funding of defence work in April 2000.[9] The Commission established the Criminal Defence Service—this will introduce a mixed system by which criminal defence will be organised through, on one hand, contracted private practitioners and on the other, public salaried employees.

- **trial and sentencing of the accused**—magistrates' and Crown Courts are responsible for making the initial decision of guilty or not guilty as well as for imposing penalties—these ranging from the financial to community-based sanctions to imprisonment. The appellate courts of the Court of Appeal and the House of Lords are responsible for reviewing that the law has been properly applied and that the sentence is appropriate.

- **a correctional system**—these are the processes for enforcing sentences laid down by the court. These range from fine-enforcement procedures administered by the magistrates' court to the probation services to the prisons.

- **strategy and policy formulation**—this is undertaken by a range of government departments responsible for differing parts of the criminal justice system. The Home Office (police and prisons), the Lord Chancellor's Department (the court service), the Attorney General (the prosecution system) all play a role as do executive agencies such as the Youth Justice Board and the Audit Commission.

These will all be explored in more detail later but the process is set out in simple terms in Table 1.1. The criminal justice system is usually mobilised by a member of the public, who is a victim or a witness, who sees the event as a crime and who reports it to the police. The police must agree that an offence has taken place and may choose to record the incident as a crime. They may decide to investigate but finite resources have meant that increasingly an investigation may be limited to the telephone where the nature and circumstances of the incident warrant it. The police may arrest a suspect and if they are satisfied that he or she has committed the offence, they have various options. They may decide to take no further action, to issue a formal caution about future conduct with the threat that next time there will be a prosecution, or to charge or summons the individual. The police will now hand the prosecution of the case to the CPS who have the responsibility for the case for all court proceedings. They also have options as they may decide to discontinue the proceedings because of lack of evidence or on public policy grounds.

If not discontinued, the case will proceed to an initial hearing in the magistrates' court. All cases are brought before the magistrates' court with the exception that the most serious offences, triable only on indictment in the Crown Court, will be transferred directly to that court. In the magistrates' court, the outcome depends on the nature of the crime charged:

---

[9] Access to Justice Act 1999; www.legalservices.gov.uk/.

- if it is a summary offence, the case will be dealt with at this point and the accused will be found guilty or acquitted. If the former, the court proceed to sentence;

- if it is an offence that can be tried in either the magistrates' court or the Crown Court, the magistrates can

  - elect to try the case themselves with the consent of the defendant
  - decline jurisdiction (or the defendant may opt for jury trial), in which case there is a brief preliminary hearing and the case is committed for trial at the Crown Court

The most serious (indictable) offences are tried in Crown Court where, if the defendant pleads not guilty, the case is heard before a judge and jury. The Crown Court judge will also hear appeals against conviction from the magistrates' court as well as sentencing offenders, convicted by the magistrates who have decided that their sentencing powers are not sufficient. If convicted, defendants can appeal to the Court of Appeal against conviction and sentence. If their case raises issues of law of public importance, they are able to appeal further to the House of Lords. After these avenues of appeal have been exhausted, a defendant may still apply to the Criminal Cases Review Commission or the European Court of Human Rights.

This network of criminal justice agencies is fully occupied. In recent years, the police have recorded over 5 million notifiable[10] offences annually. This represents over 9,900 offences for every 100,000 people, although this figure has been declining since 1992.[11] The police caution over 250,000 people for all offences, excluding motoring offences.[12] Approximately 1.3 million persons were sentenced at magistrates' courts and over 70,000 in Crown Courts. Approximately 105,000 offenders were sentenced to immediate custody by the courts. In 1993 that figure was 58,400—the courts are making more use of custodial sentences for men and women than ever before. Not only are more people being sent to prison, the average length of sentence handed down has increased—in magistrates' courts it approaches three months and in Crown Courts twenty-four months. This has meant that the prison population in England and Wales at the end of June 2002 was over 71,000, the highest it has ever been.

The statistics of officially recorded crime tell us that the police, courts and prisons are fully occupied. Statistics are produced to tell us what the producer wishes us to know and criminal statistics are notoriously unreliable. But they do tell us about the behaviour of state agencies who arrest, prosecute and imprison more people than ever before. It appears to be an ever-widening net. Throughout the twentieth century recorded offences rose inexorably at an average of 5.1 per cent per year.

---

[10] This includes most indictable offences and offences triable either way as well as certain summary offences.
[11] The most up-to-date figures can be found in: Simmons J., *et al.*, *Crime in England and Wales 2001–2002* (Home Office, 2002).
[12] Figures for these and the following statistics are to be found in *Home Office, Statistical Bulletin 19/00 Cautions, Court Proceedings and Sentencing, England and Wales 1999.*

Table 1.1 Flow through the criminal justice system

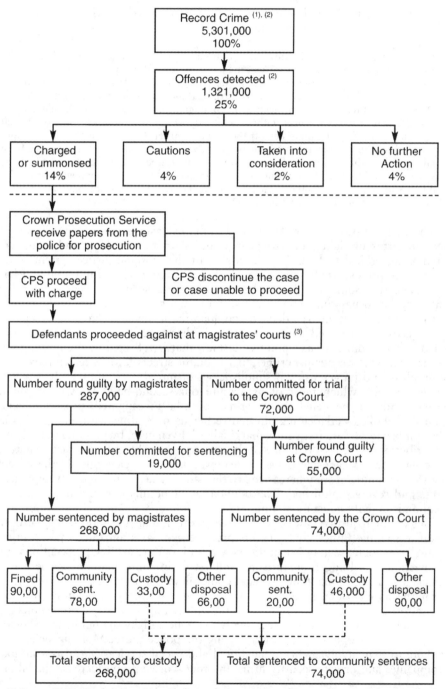

(1) Covers all indictable, including triable either way, offences plus a few closely associated summary offences.
(2) In the financial year 1999/00.

1.2 DIFFERENT PERSPECTIVES ON CRIMINAL JUSTICE

Marx, slightly tongue-in-cheek, suggested that crime and the criminal contribute in many ways to a community:

'The criminal produces an impression now moral, now tragic, and renders a "service' by
arousing the moral and aesthetic sentiments of the public. He produces not only textbooks on criminal law, the criminal law itself, and thus legislators but also art, literature, novels and the tragic drama ... The criminal interrupts the monotony and security
of bourgeois life. Thus he protects it from stagnation and brings forth that restless
tension, that mobility of spirit without which the stimulus of competition would itself
become blunted. ... Crime takes off the labour market a portion of the excess population, diminishes competition among workers, and to a certain extent stops wages from
falling below the minimum while the war against crime absorbs another part of the
same population. ... The influence of the criminal upon the development of the pro-
ductive forces can be shown in detail. Would the locksmith's trade have attained its
present perfection if there had been no thieves? ...[13]'

There are serious points to be gleaned from this passage—crime is traditionally
seen in terms of right and wrong, in terms of moral absolutes and as underpinning an ethical system. Any discussion of the criminal justice system starts
with assumptions that 'crime is crime', that it is immoral and intolerable behaviour and that something has to be done. Crime is seen as a clearly separable
category of behaviour which, allied with statistical analysis, leads to the
assumption that 'crime' is a defined and quantifiable given, behaviour which can
be objectively measured. Furthermore, once discovered, it can only be approached in a one-dimensional, punitive fashion that is reflected in the language of
confrontation ('war against crime', 'battle on the streets'), too often employed by
journalists and judges using a simplistic set of moral prescriptions. It is a language through which most of us acquire our second-hand knowledge about
crime, leads to the belief that a crime must be investigated, prosecuted and
punished. Policies advocating alternative means of dealing with disruptive and
deviant behaviour are frequently marginalised. Even here, by pointing out crime's
contribution to the economic life of the country, Marx hints at the relative nature
of crime—two decades ago, insider dealing was seen as clever use of the system
by sharp manipulators whereas today the same behaviour is morally reprehen-
sible and severely punished. The boundaries of permissible and impermissible
economic activity constantly shift.

But criminal justice can be seen in ways other than the moral. It is also an
industry: Home Office civil servants produce new laws and thereby new criminals;[14] any increase in police numbers will lead to more arrests, prosecutions and
convictions; building more prisons will result in more prisoners. There is a
chicken and egg problem here—what comes first, the increase in reported crime
or in the activity of criminal justice agencies? In the twenty-first century, we deal
more formally with behaviour, which previously might have been the subject of
informal resolution. Agencies, especially the police, make the public more aware
of crime and people respond by involving the police more. More agencies contribute to that involvement—educational and social services but also insurance
companies and private security firms. In other words, if you increase the labour

---

[13] Marx, K., *Theories of Surplus Value* (1969) Vol. 1 pp. 387–388.
[14] There have been some 85 statutes dealing with crime and justice since the 1980s.

Table 1.2 Expenditure on the criminal justice system

Agency	1987–88	1999–2000
Police	£3,512m	£7.5b
Magistrates' court	£213m	£0.3b
Crown Court	not available	£0.2b
Legal aid	not available	£0.9b[15]
CPS and Serious Fraud Office	£121m	£0.3b
Prison	£775m	£1.9b
Probation	£225m	£0.5b
Criminal Injuries Compensation	not available	£0.2b

force within the criminal justice industry, they will ensure that they are fully occupied.

Crime and criminal justice is big business: it has been estimated that the value of property taken in 1999 in offences of residential burglary was £1.2b, in vehicle theft £1.75b and through fraud and forgery, £10.3b.[16] But the same study showed that the costs of crime went far beyond the property involved—the authors look at the costs incurred in the anticipation of crime in security and insurance arrangements, at the emotional and physical costs to the victims as well as the cost of the criminal justice system's response to crime. The costs of violent crime are enormous—there are perhaps 1,100 homicides in the country each year—the total cost of each is considered to be £1.1m, largely because of the emotional and physical impact on the victims (some £700,000) and the lost output (£370,000). Overall Brand and Price conclude that the social and economic costs of crime are £59.9b (at 1999 prices). 28 per cent of that total is the result of violent crime, 23 per cent is the result of fraud and forgery and 15 per cent relates to crime within the commercial and public sector. Burglary accounts for just 4 per cent of the total costs.

Large numbers of professionals are involved in the criminal justice system—there are over 120,000 police personnel, several thousand lawyers, judges and other court employees, there are social services and probation officers, prison officers and ancillary staff, the insurance industry, security systems and private security firms, crime journalists, civil servants, dozens of different victim and offender charities and policy pressure groups, (let alone the academic criminologists). State expenditure in the late 1980s was approximately £5b per annum. In 1999–2000 the criminal justice system cost over £12b to run.

Criminal justice is also a political and cultural process. Perhaps with the

---

[15] This is a global figure, including representation in magistrates and Crown courts as well as advice in police stations.

[16] Brand S. and Price R., *The Social and Economic Costs of Crime (2000)* (Home Office Research Study 217).

decline of organised religion, we need a place for society to demonstrate such moral certainties and ethical boundaries. But we should not forget that deviant behaviour has played its part in most people's biographies. Almost everyone has committed offences for which they could be imprisoned but most of us by luck or accident have avoided involvement in the criminal justice system. There is an infinite variety of motives and meanings that we attach to that behaviour and we justify and explain our actions to ourselves, rarely labelling ourselves as 'criminals'. Individually and socially we approach such conduct through a range of interpretative and therapeutic mechanisms. The court and penal system is the crudest of all of these and this is reserved, sometimes for those who pose a high risk of danger to the community but more often for those who are persistent, inadequate, disturbed or addicted nuisances. Should we punish such people or do we need different policies and responses? Dealing with the illiterate, the alcoholic, the drug addict or the mentally disturbed through a penal system is of dubious morality. This argument will continue as will the search for those ethical principles, which should underpin reforms within the system. But it is unlikely, to say the very least, that the criminal justice system will be fundamentally overhauled.

As Marx states, criminal justice demonstrates who possesses social and economic power. Criminal law and criminal justice have important symbolic functions as well as instrumental ones—while their goal of protecting individuals from violence and exploitation is obvious (although their efficacy is far from unquestionable), the part played in regulating the economy[17] or in establishing ethical frontiers is less clear. Furthermore the criminal justice system has an important symbolic role in regulating our political life. Any country that lacks a written constitution requires constitutional arrangements, the relationships between citizen and state, to be visibly demonstrated. The key adjectives 'liberal' and 'democratic' in relation to the state only have meaning if the overwhelming power of the state in dealing with individuals is shown to be restricted by the rule of law: that police investigations are limited in their legal powers of detention and interrogation and in their use of force; that convicted prisoners can rely on proportionality of punishment and on humane treatment. State and citizen are both bound by law which itself rests on ethical notions which might be summarised as 'fair dealing' and the police station and court are important sites to demonstrate this.

Another favourite media parlour game is the use of the criminal justice statistics as a moral barometer of the state of the nation, pointing to the large increase in recorded crime in the second half of the twentieth century. The overwhelming bulk of this increase was acquisitive crime since the spiralling prosperity of the past 40 years has resulted in a huge amount of high value, easily moveable, personal possessions in cars, shops and houses. In 2000, 83 per cent of offences were against property and 14 per cent were crimes of violence.[18] Interpersonal violence has increased by 6.4 per cent per year since 1947, and we have some of the highest victimisation rates in the world for contact crime.[19] Paradoxically we also have one of the lowest homicide rates in Western Europe—

---

[17] Hall J., *Theft, Law and Society* (2nd ed., 1952) explores this idea in relation to the history of property offences.
[18] *Op. cit.* fn. 11.
[19] Home Office, *The 1996 International Crime Victimisation Survey* (Home Office Research Findings No. 57).

London as 2.15 homicides per 100,000 population whereas Washington DC has 59.90.[20]

This game extends to police work: in 2000, 24 per cent of recorded offences were cleared up by primary means, a clear up rate that has declined from 45 per cent in 1974, although that figure included clear ups by secondary means (normally by interviews of convicted prisoners). This rate varies according to the nature of the offence—offences of violence are more likely to be cleared up than crimes involving criminal damage. It also varies according to the area of the country—the rate at which offences are cleared up in London is much lower than, say, in Dyfed-Powys. The actual number of offences being cleared up rose to approximately 1.5m in 2000, with each police officer clearing up about 12 offences, a rise from 9.4 offences cleared up per officer in 1983.

Have we become less honest and more violent? Are the police less effective? We might argue complacently that the recorded figures merely reflect the increase in opportunities for crime. Alternatively we might see a shift in moral standards as the individualism and materialism of the free market have changed aspirations and as structural unemployment has opened up a gulf between cultural goals and realistic opportunities of achieving those goals. Have we become more violent? In 1870s London there were 200+ offences against the person per 100,000 of the population.[21] In 2000, there were 1384.[22] Given the unreliability of the Victorian data, this is a modest rise. Although there is considerable fear of violence and well-merited concern about sexual and physical abuse of women and children and racially motivated assaults,[23] there is insufficient evidence to suggest that we are a less orderly or more violent society than previously.[24]

It is never justified to use statistics to evaluate our moral state. All the figures do is to tell us about the activities of the police and the courts—and our efficiency in collecting statistics! Our late capitalist society may (or may not) have produced more crime than other social forms but it certainly has produced an explosion in the number, size and functions of criminal justice agencies—the last five years have seen the emergence of a National Crime Squad (NCS) as well as a National Criminal Intelligence Service (NCIS). This raises further questions. If you recruit more police officers, does this produce more crime? If you build more prisons, do you create more prisoners?[25]

1.3 A SYSTEM GOING WRONG

By the middle of the last century, the common law criminal justice system possessed an enviable reputation for efficiency, incorruptibility and justice. Its twin pillars were the police constable and the jury. But whether it ever deserved its reputation is moot: miscarriages of justice are not new and throughout its history, the criminal justice system has seen its fair share of disasters. Adolf Beck at least survived his imprisonment for fraud in 1895, having been wrongly identified

---

[20] Home Office, *Statistical Bulletin 04/00. International Comparisons of Criminal Justice Statistics 1998.*
[21] Gurr T., Grabosky P. and Hula R., *The Politics of Crime and Conflict* (1977) p. 128.
[22] This figure is considerably increased as a result of the new counting rules introduced in 1998.
[23] Hale C., *Fear of Crime* (Metropolitan Police Working Party on Fear of Crime 1994).
[24] Pearson G., *Hooligan* (1983).
[25] Michael Zander has pointed out that in the 1970s those American states that built most prisons increased their prison population significantly whereas those that built least decreased theirs—*New Society*, December 13, 1979.

by several victims. On release he was imprisoned a further time, again through misidentification. Beck died, a broken man, in 1909. He had been convicted on two separate occasions for crimes he did not commit, and spent years in gaol for those crimes. One result of the Beck trials and the subsequent inquiry was the establishment, in 1907, of the Court of Criminal Appeal but this did not save Timothy Evans, who was executed in 1950 for murders committed by John Christie,[26] Derek Bentley who was hanged in 1953 when his accomplice, the killer and principal, was not[27] and in 1962 James Hanratty who was hanged for the A6 killing of Michael Gregsten.[28]

These cases were often portrayed as discrete events, their very rarity demonstrating the overall reliability of the system. But in the past twenty years, following the release of the Guildford Four in October 1989, the Court of Appeal has quashed convictions in a number of highly publicised cases as the trickle of wrongful convictions became a flood with convictions quashed in cases such as the Birmingham Six,[29] the Guildford Four,[30] Stefan Kiszko in 1992,[31] Winston Silcott in 1991 for the killing of PC Blakelock at, Broadwater Farm, Judith Ward,[32] the Cardiff Three,[33] Bob Maynard and Reg Dudley,[34] let alone those attributable to the activities of the West Midlands Serious Crime Squad.[35] Civil liberty organisations and TV programmes such as the BBC's *Rough Justice* have identified dozens of further cases where there is cause for doubting the propriety of the convictions. Inevitably the public have become aware that there are serious flaws in the criminal justice system.[36]

'Leaving aside issues of evidence and proof, one possible definition of "miscarriage" in the context of criminal justice will now be suggested, and it is one which reflects an individualistic rights-based approach to miscarriages of justice. A miscarriage occurs as follows: whenever suspects or defendants or convicts are treated by the State in breach of their rights, whether because of, first, deficient processes or, second, the laws which are applied to them or, third, because there is no factual justification for the applied treatment or punishment; fourth, whenever suspects or defendants or convicts are treated adversely by the State to a disproportionate extent in comparison with the need to protect the rights of others; or, fifth, whenever the rights of others are not effectively or proportionately protected or vindicated by State action against wrongdoers or, sixth, by State law itself...

These six categories, which revolve around themes of breach of rights of suspects/ defendants, the disproportionate treatment of suspects/defendants or the non-vindication of the rights of victims, might be termed direct miscarriages. In addition, it may be possible to derive from their infliction a seventh, indirect miscarriage which affects the community as a whole. A conviction arising from deceit or illegalities is corrosive of the

---

[26] Kennedy L., *Ten Rillington Place* (1961).

[27] Bentley I. With Dening P., *Let Him Have Justice* (1995).

[28] Foot P., *Who Killed Hanratty?* (1971); Woffinden B., *Hanratty: The Final Verdict* (1997)—but the Court of Appeal accepted that DNA evidence linked Hanratty to the crime—*The Guardian* May 11, 2002.

[29] Mullin C., *Error of Judgment* (1986).

[30] Kee R., *Trial and Error* (1986).

[31] Rose J., *Innocents* (1998).

[32] (1993) 96 Cr. App. R. 1: Ward J., *Ambushed—My Story* (1993).

[33] *R.v. Paris* (1992) 97 Cr. App. Rep 99

[34] *The Guardian* July 17, 2002.

[35] Kaye T. *Unsafe and Unsatisfactory* (1991).

[36] See *www.innocent.org.uk/*. We are not alone—Langlois D., *Les Dossiers Noirs de la Justice Francaise* (editions de Seuil 1974); Begue B., *La Mauvaise Reputation* (Politics, October 10, 1991).

State's claims to legitimacy on the basis of its criminal justice system's values such as respect for individual rights. In this way, as well as the undesirable fate of the individual, the "moral integrity of the criminal process" suffers harm. Moreover, there may be practical detriment in terms of diminished confidence in the forces of law and order leading to fewer active citizens aiding the police and fewer jurors willing to convict even the blatantly "guilty".'[37]

Analysis of such miscarriages has revealed no single cause but shows that different elements of the system itself have at times been at fault: poor investigative procedures or oppressive interrogation by the police; failure to disclose evidence by the prosecution; the trial court's failure to assess properly the weight of evidence; the unwillingness of the Appeal Court and the Home Office to admit that things had gone wrong. In aggregate these illustrate a culture unwilling to see its function as the uncovering of the truth and more concerned with results—arrests and convictions; a culture moreover that refused to deal with defendants with openness and fairness and that regarded recognition of such injustices as undermining the criminal process system. That culture has shown some signs of change—the key recommendation of the Royal Commission on Criminal Justice[38] that reported in 1993 was the introduction of an independent body to investigate miscarriage cases to replace the woefully inadequate Court of Appeal. This recommendation was supported by Sir John May's report into the Guildford Four.[39] In 1995, the Criminal Cases Review Commission was established[40] with the power to investigate alleged miscarriages and to refer the case to the Court of Appeal.

During the 1990s, awareness of the flaws of the investigation, prosecution and appeal system in dealing with defendants fairly were paralleled by recognition that prisons were also failing to deal with inmates humanely. In the early 1990s there were many disturbances, the most serious being at Strangeways Prison in Manchester; this started on April 1, 1990 and continued until April 25 with loss of life, injuries and enormous property damage. It led directly to the Woolf Report[41] with its plethora of proposals and recommendations for the improvement of the physical conditions, the regimes and the management of the prison system, proposals which have been consistently reinforced by the reports of Her Majesty's Chief Inspector of Prisons.[42] These reports have led to important changes in the prison service, not least in the disciplinary system.

A wholly different reason for the continuing public scrutiny of criminal justice has been the failure to protect the rights of victims through the system's perceived ineffectiveness in dealing with crime. That is reflected in a general concern about the level of crime: recorded crime rose consistently from the 1950s until the early 1990s. Despite significant decreases in acquisitive crime since 1993, fear of crime

---

[37] Walker C. and Starmer K (eds.), *Miscarriages of Justice* (1999) Chap. 2.

[38] Royal Commission on Criminal Justice: *Report*, Cm. 2263 (1993).

[39] Sir John May has produced two reports into the Guildford bombings, the first into the ancillary Maguire convictions and the second (in July 1994) into the Guildford Four convictions. See Chris Mullin's comments in *The Guardian* July 1, 1994, p. 24.

[40] Part II, Criminal Appeal Act 1995; *www.ccrc.gov.uk/*. By October 2001, there had been over 4400 applications, 148 cases had been referred to the Court of Appeal. 73 of those had been heard by the Court which had quashed the conviction in 55 cases and upheld it in 18.

[41] *Report of an Inquiry into Prison Disturbances April 1990*, Cm. 1456 (HMSO 1991).

[42] Both reports on individual establishments and thematic reports can be accessed through *www.homeoffice.gov.uk/hmipris/hmipris.htm*.

still affects people's lives. This varies[43] according to personal experience, where people are, the time of day or night and who else is around. Young people are actually more fearful of crime than has been recognised in the past—of other groups of young people, especially on public transport. While young women frequently experience sexual harassment, youths are most fearful of physical assault from particular sub-groups of other young men. But young women and men still go out at night and use public transport. Older people are less fearful of crime than was previously thought although they are afraid of property crime and home invasions. Older people are frequently more concerned for young people than for themselves. Parents have stronger fears for their children than for themselves. Most people have a general fear about 'unpredictable strangers', especially in public places at night. But these studies do not reflect the low level of incivilities and incidents of harassment, which over time, contribute to a person's sense of vulnerability and anxiety. People develop individual strategies for dealing with fear and risk. For example, they secure their homes and in public they remain constantly aware, monitoring their environment and the people in it. The theme of 'redressing the balance' between defendants and victims is taken up in the White Paper 'Justice for All' in 2002:[44]

Police community support officers have been introduced in several forces in 2002 as a result of Part IV of the Police Reform Act 2002 and police numbers reached record levels in September 2002. As well as a general concern about the level of crime, individuals and pressure groups have attacked specific aspects of the system such as:

- police enforcement policies, usually for failure to protect specific categories of victim, for example, domestic violence, sexual assaults[45] or racial attacks.[46] There is also criticism of over-policing in industrial disputes or in inner city areas.

- the CPS for decisions to discontinue certain prosecutions[47] and, less publicly, for the level of acquittals in contested cases in Crown Court.

- the courts when sentencing has been regarded as too lenient[48] or for occasions when confessions have been excluded from evidence and the defendant has been acquitted.

- the poor treatment that victims receive at all stages of the process which has led to the growth of victim support groups.[49] These have highlighted such matters as the initial interview by the police (especially of sexual assault victims); the failure by the CPS to keep the victim in touch with the course

[43] Hale C. (1994), *op. cit.*; Mirrlees-Black C. *et al.*, 'Concern About Crime: Findings from the 1998 British Crime Survey' (Home Office, Research Findings No. 83).
[44] Cm. 5563.
[45] Jessica Harris and Sharon Grace, 'A question of evidence?Investigating and prosecuting rape in the 1990s' (Home Office, Research Study No. 196).
[46] *Report of the Stephen Lawrence Inquiry* (1999) (The MacPherson Report, Cm. 4262).
[47] Butler G., *Inquiry into Crown Prosecution Service Decision-Making ... Relation to Deaths in Custody and Related Matters* (1999) S. 7.
[48] In December 2001, Roy Whiting, was jailed for life for the murder of a young girl. It emerged that he had committed a similar offence in 1995 although without killing the victim. He had been released after 30 months of a 4 year sentence. The 1995 trial judge defended his sentence in the media.
[49] *www.victimsupport.com*; Shapland J. *et al.*, *Victims in the Criminal Justice System* (Gower, 1985); Morgan J. and Zedner; *Child Victims* (Oxford, 1992).

of proceedings; the witness's treatment while testifying especially where cross-examination involves allegations of lying; the lack of legal advice and representation leading to lack of awareness of compensation orders or the criminal injuries compensation scheme; the lack of any requirements for the court to take into account 'victim-impact' statements in sentencing.[50]

These failures of the criminal justice system have highlighted not only the need for protection for the accused but also the needs of the community and of individual victims. Public and political debate tends to polarise between such divergent positions, with the liberal wing advocating the protection (and increase) of the rights of defendants and more conservative thinkers advocating policies espousing greater police powers and higher tariff punishments in the belief that this will reduce crime levels in the interests of the community and the victim.

How can these opposing positions be reconciled? The police,[51] prosecution service,[52] courts,[53] sentencing[54] and prisons[55] have all been the object of government reports, inquiries and unceasing legislation, but scrutiny and analysis of the process as a whole has been non-existent.[56] Although there have been two recent Royal Commissions,[57] the first reporting in 1981 and the second in 1993, neither considered the manner in which we structure criminal justice: yet the critical flaw is the lack of overall structure. While individual agencies such as the police or the CPS may have clear objectives and principles and are accountable in various ways, most of these agencies operate autonomously. The extraordinary facet of criminal justice is that there is no overarching ministry of justice with responsibility to Parliament for the whole structure. Different ministers of the Crown, such as the Lord Chancellor (for the magistracy), the Home Secretary (for the police, prisons and probation service) and the Attorney General (for the Crown Prosecution Service) assume responsibilities for different parts of the system. Certain agencies, especially the police and the courts, avoid even this direct constitutional accountability. Such a structure invariably affects the extent of mutual co-operation and shared coherence of policy objectives.

Comparison with other public services, such as education or health, is illuminating—they are characterised by unifying purposes and principles, a clear organisational structure, identifiable lines of management and recognised and effective means of accountability, normally ending with ministerial responsibility to Parliament. Although such a description may be seen as a rose-tinted view of

---

[50] See 'Speaking Up for Justice' *A Report of the Interdepartmental Working Group on the treatment of Vulnerable or Intimidated Witnesses in the Criminal Justice System* (1998); many of the recommendations were legislated for in the Youth Justice and Criminal Evidence Act 1999.

[51] *Inquiry Into Police Responsibilities and Rewards*, Cm. 2280 (Sheehy Report (1993)); White Paper. *Police Reform*, Cm. 2281 (1993); 'Policing a New Century: A Blueprint for Reform.' Cm. 5326 (2001).

[52] *Review of the Crown Prosecution Service*, Cm. 3972 (The Glidewell Report, 1998).

[53] *Review of the Criminal Courts* (The Auld Report, 2001).

[54] *Making Punishments Work: The Report of a Review of the Sentencing Framework* (The Halliday Report, 2001).

[55] *Report of the Inquiry into the United Kingdom Prison Services*, Cmnd. 7673 (The May Report, 1979); *Report of an Inquiry into Prison Disturbances. April 1990*, Cm. 1456 (The Woolf Report, 1991).

[56] But see 'Criminal Justice: The Way Ahead', Cm. 5074 (2001).

[57] Royal Commission on Criminal Procedure, Cmnd. 8092 (HMSO 1981). Royal Commission on Criminal Justice, *op. cit.*

our education or health systems, it is basically accurate. It is not possible to identify any of these characteristics within the English criminal process, the structure of which is simply a historical accident.

In criminal justice, the possibilities for a unified approach are more limited than those in other public services. In education for instance, although certain aspects may be controversial (*e.g.*, the details of the national curriculum), there is a broad consensus about the overall aims of the teaching profession and this is also reflected in other public sector agencies such as welfare or health. Schools and hospitals may have serious difficulties but there is a coherent structure with consistent principles, objectives and mechanisms of accountability. From 1997 the Labour administration has sought to co-ordinate the work of many of the criminal justice agencies—under the Crime and Disorder Act 1998, issues of crime and disorder were for the first time made the statutory responsibility of local authorities who were expected to conduct a 'crime audit' to identify local community safety issues and develop initiatives to resolve them. But there is still an absence of co-ordination in the formal criminal justice system. This was recognised by the government in 2001 '*Criminal Justice: The Way Ahead*'[58] which talked of the need to reform the system to work as a '... *joined-up system, with all those involved adopting a common set of values to meet a common set of goals in order to reduce crime, to deliver justice and to enhance public confidence..*' Recommendations towards this goal have been made in the White Paper '*Justice for All*' in 2002.[59] This does not discuss the need for developing a unified strategy at ministerial level or the creation of a single ministry of justice.

It may be that criminal justice is unlike other public sector services—the demands we make of our criminal justice agencies are too varied to permit this. At present, although individual agencies have objectives and performance indicators, the values and principles underlying and affecting the work of the different agencies are often irreconcilable—for example, the police associate themselves with 'uncovering the truth' and 'putting villains away' so that identification with victims can weigh more heavily than the means by which that is achieved; the lawyers and the court assume the legal values of 'due process' which are inevitably more technical and whose abstract rationales rarely appeal to the everyday concrete experience of the police; probation officers and social workers, especially in the juvenile sphere, are most concerned with the development of the individual, 'the best interests of the child or the client', often seeing the police and court experience as an irrelevance to the substantive objective of the reform of the defendant.

1.4 A BRIEF HISTORY

The disarray of the system is to a certain extent due to its historical development. Criminal justice is about state interference with people's behaviour. The concept of crime is used to justify our collective interference with and control of the actions of other people, seeking that justification in such ideas as preventing harm or exploitation as well as to the objectives of deterring or reforming 'criminals'. But where does this concept emerge from? There is a great temptation to read our history from earlier and simpler societies to modern times in terms of a straightforward progression—as society becomes less 'barbaric', more 'civilised',

---

[58] *op. cit.*
[59] Cm. 5563, Chap. 9.

we act collectively to protect the individual members from harm and to preserve the overall interests of the group. The vulnerability of individuals leads us to act co-operatively in self-defence and to develop shared norms of behaviour that reinforce social cohesion. While these are important factors, suggesting a 'natural evolution' for criminal justice, the system's history shows a more complex relationship between criminal justice, social order and the state.

1.4.1 *Remote Origins—Reparation to Retribution*

In Anglo-Saxon England, the existence of normative codes did not inevitably involve the infliction of state punishment. State involvement in investigation or in the infliction of punishment was rare. Social structure was centred on the kinship group, as land settlement and the development of agriculture had led to significant autonomy for the family. The role of the king was very limited. But this was not some rural idyll—England in the 10th and 11th centuries was certainly a place where people were easily provoked to anger and violence was a common feature of life.[60] Legal sanctions could be equally bloody—outlawry, slavery or even summary execution for the thief caught in the act. Underpinning all these was the system of private, not state, retaliation known as the 'feud' by which a family would wage war upon another in redress of grievances.

For the Anglo-Saxons, wrongs were wrongs and were not to be differentiated into whether they were litigated in the magistrates' court or the county court. In other words, there was little distinction between modern categories of crime and tort. Additionally, wrongs were at base private matters between the individuals or families involved and could always be paid for—in livestock, armour, money or, if necessary, in blood through the feud.[61] Each person had a set of rights according to status and these were protected by money penalties (*wer, bot, wite*). There was furthermore collective responsibility of the kin group for the wrongs of its individual members, with the ability to provide collective resources for compensation. Sophisticated ideas of individual responsibility and state punishment were for the future.

Public involvement through the king was minimal, the kingdom was self-governing, and government was local government. Routine disciplining of the population was not the king's affair—he intervened only when his interest (usually matters concerning his purse or his authority) was aroused. The legislation (decrees) of the Anglo-Saxon kings bears this out;[62] none assert any overriding public interest in the wrongs themselves. The king may be concerned about the destructive effects of the feud on social order—when conducted between powerful kin groups, feuding could threaten the political consensus and the fragile basis of kingship, so the laws sought to restrict the right to self-help and insisted that compensation must be demanded and refused before resort to the feud. Yet the general legal framework for maiming or homicide was 'How much?' and the legislation laid down detailed tariffs of payment for particular

---

[60] Gurr T., 'Historical Trends in Violent Crime' in *Crime and Justice: An Annual Review of Research*, Vol. III, pp. 295–353 (1981).
[61] Goebel J., *Felony and Misdemeanour* (1976) pp.15–16.
[62] Aethelbert in early 7th century Kent; Ine in 7th century Wessex; Alfred in 9th century Wessex; Cnut in 11th century England—described in Plucknett T., *Edward I and the Criminal Law* (1960) Chaps 1 and 2.

wrongs, not merely to the victim but to the kin, the lord, the owner of the land where the act took place as well as the king.

Such a system, based on compensation, seems to contradict theorists such as Durkheim who suggest that penal law moves from the repressive to the restitutive.[63] In fact, the movement from the eighth century to the eighteenth century suggests an opposite movement, away from the private and compensatory towards a public and ever more brutal form of criminal law. The initial change is prompted in the 11th and 12th centuries by the imposition of feudal political and economic structures and by the changing face of kingship that accompanies these. The role of the Anglo-Saxon king was quite limited, a leader in time of war but with little machinery of government or power. He was *primus inter pares* and possession of royal blood was only one factor in his ascendancy to the throne, to be placed alongside others such as nomination by the late king and acceptance by the aristocracy.[64] This gradually changes as the Anglo-Norman kings can be seen more as territorial leaders through the imposition of the system of feudal land tenure. The concept of kingship evolved with the strengthening of the system of primogeniture and an increasing sense of the king's divinity—the coronation ceremony, first emerging in the ninth century, cast God's protection upon his anointed.[65]

Yet the strengthening of the monarchy, increasing stability and centralisation, initially made little difference to the systems of social control, which remained local (either through community courts or franchised ones in the hands of the major landholders) and private (the compensatory principle still applied). For William I and also in the *Leges Henrici Primi*, passed by Henry I on his accession, the old restitutive principles still applied in full force. Under the Anglo-Norman dynasty, the community paying the 'murdrum fine' could excuse even the killing of a Norman soldier. This continues until the reign of Henry II (1154–1189) when the first legal 'textbook', known by the name of its author as Glanvil, no longer uses the language of restitution of *wer, wite* or *bot* but talks the language of 'felony'.[66]

It is at this point that an embryonic criminal justice system emerges, with its key components of itinerant royal justices and juries of presentment.[67] These developments do not come about in response to a 'crime' problem or to protect the individual rights of the victim but evolved as a result of the political and social conditions of the time, in particular the changing form of the machinery of state. At the point of Henry II's accession, the 'state' in England is weak—an economy based on feudalism is invariably decentralised and destabilising unless there is some form of strong central control. Under feudalism, the landowning 'lords' were able to accumulate the surplus product from the land with little to hinder them. There was vast scope for conflict as to rights over land and over such appropriation. In the twelfth century, the 'anarchy' of Stephen's reign saw a struggle between Matilda and Stephen over the succession, with private baronial

---

[63] Durkheim E., *The Division of Labour in Society* (1984); Maine H., *Ancient Law* (1915); Sheleff L., 'From Restitutive to Repressive Law' *Archiv. Europ. Sociol.* [??014] Vol. XVI, p. 16 (1975).
[64] Loyn H.R., *The Governance of Anglo-Saxon England* (1984).
[65] Barlow F. 'The Holy Crown' in Barlow F.(ed.), *The Norman Conquest and Beyond* (1983) p. 3.
[66] The essence of felony was personal, namely the breach of the homage vow between lord and man which was the core of the feudal relationship. It was not the substance of the act but the breach of loyalty that mattered.
[67] Jeffery C.R., 'Crime in Early English Society' in 47 *Journal of Criminology, Criminal Law and Police Science*, p. 647 (1957).

wars and massacres of the peasantry: the legitimacy and the power of central authority was at a low ebb.

Henry II was faced with the aftermath of this civil war. In addition not only was he the Duke of Normandy but marriage and succession in Aquitaine and Maine meant that his realm stretched from Scotland to the Pyrenees. This compelled the building of an administrative structure that relied upon delegation to local officials (sheriffs) but also reliable channels of communication and decision-making (itinerant justices and an extension of the use of juries). The criminal justice system emerges, it is suggested, as a by-product of measures introduced by a king who saw the need to develop stable and more centralised structures to maintain his own authority and the overall political and economic system. In the process he created '... a royal state unrivalled in its authority and efficacy throughout Western Europe'.[68]

Such centralism was shown in Henry's pragmatic response to rights over land since unlawful entries and evictions during previous decades had caused chaos. In 1164 he arrogated jurisdiction over land possession through a set of emergency courts known as the 'possessory assizes', which superseded the delay and technicalities of the old procedure.[69] He also expanded the jurisdiction of the royal courts in Westminster, and thus began the process of downgrading the communal courts of the county and the hundred as well as the seigniorial courts belonging to the lord of the manor. Furthermore he attacked the jurisdiction of the Church through the Assize of Clarendon in 1166. Another initiative was the institution of a system of itinerant royal justices travelling throughout the realm on 'eyre'. These justices could call together juries of landholders in any locality who would 'present' to the justices any information that they had about royal interests. Now this included any felonies that had been committed, since the king had a pecuniary interest in the conviction of felons as all the felon's property was regarded as forfeit to the Crown. Thus for the first time the king is taking the initiative in gathering information about and prosecuting wrongs.

These changes signal the end of the compensatory system since the king also stiffened punishments and the right to inflict punishment slowly became to be monopolised by the Crown. The old concept of felony or breach of homage was 'botleas', un-atonable except through physical punishment, mutilation or death. But it had been a private affair between lord and man—whereas through the twelfth and thirteenth centuries, the pleadings of '*vi et armis*' and '*contra pacem regis*' gave it a different flavour as a matter between king and subject. Composition between victim and wrongdoer thus became more difficult: victims of theft who entered into agreements with the thief could be prosecuted themselves. Change was slow—through the thirteenth and fourteenth centuries, agreement on the amount of compensation to be paid would mean that private prosecutions for homicide or rape (known as appeals of felony) would be discontinued.[70] But hangings were the province of the king and a symbol of royal authority—local lords were fined for infringing the royal rights. There is little evidence of excessive executions or other physical punishments. Barbarous punishments are the hallmark of the sixteenth century and beyond.[71]

---

[68] Anderson P., *Lineages of the Absolutist State* (1979), p. 113.
[69] Simpson A.W.B., *A History of Land Law* (2nd ed. 1986).
[70] Given J., *Society and Homicide* (1977), p. 100.
[71] This is borne out by Chambliss' study of the Vagrancy Acts in the 14th century which, though penal in form, were operated leniently compared to their enforcement two centuries later—Chambliss W. 'The Law of Vagrancy' in Chambliss W. (ed.), *Crime and the Legal Process* (1969), p. 51.

Angevin reforms were directed as much at the nobility as at the lower classes. Henry had no interest in the peasantry although there was an immediate interest in the doings of the aristocracy and a desire for 'legitimate' techniques to control them. Although there is little evidence of criminal prosecutions of the nobility *per se*, 'justice' was an important symbolic representation of the king's power and authority (especially when embodied in a hanging). The nobles who exercised jurisdiction, did so as delegates, no longer possessing power as of right but as subordinates to the monarch.[72]

Despite the reforms, the vast majority of cases would be before local and seigniorial courts.[73] Social discipline must still have rested firmly in the manor,

> ...the manorial system arises at the end of the Old English period mainly in consequence of the subjection of a labouring population of free descent to a military and capitalistic class.[74]

Even in front of royal justices, local juries made up their minds on their own knowledge of the facts—with 40–50 cases in front of the court each day. Medieval justice was still local and, although rubber-stamped by the royal imprimatur, it was far from the system of routine state control to which the population in the twenty-first century is so accustomed.

1.4.2 *From Savagery to Cells*

Henry's reforms produced a genuine, but embryonic, criminal justice system, although the consolidation of feudalism through centralised royal power was far from over. Other monarchs sought to develop the system, especially Edward I in the last quarter of the thirteenth century.[75] But it was the Tudors who significantly expanded the criminal justice system, which went hand-in-hand with this new authoritarianism of the absolutist feudal state.[76] This expansion was in two directions, against the aristocracy on the one hand and against the new poor on the other. In the early sixteenth century, the Crown was in direct conflict with the nobility over such issues as the maintenance of private armies. The ordinary mechanisms of criminal law were failing to control such subjects and Henry VII and Henry VIII developed new courts such as the Star Chamber, outside the common law system as well as special courts for other purposes: the High Commission, the Councils of the North and of the Marches.[77]

The focus of attention now swings away from the aristocracy towards the large pool of surplus labour created through economic policies such as the enclosure movement and the dissolution of the monasteries. The penal law became increasingly repressive, with severe punishments, with greater powers given to justices of the peace as well as the development of the Poor Law and new laws against the able bodied poor. No longer tied to particular localities and with the increasing size of the towns, this army of unemployed began to pose a public

---

[72] Sutherland D.W., *Quo Warranto Proceedings* (1963).
[73] Although justices of the peace were known from 1195, their duties only expanded in the 14th century—Moir E., *The Justice of the Peace* (1969).
[74] Vinogradoff P., *The Growth of the Manor* (1911), p. 235.
[75] Plucknett T., *op. cit.*
[76] Anderson P., *op. cit.*
[77] This is a process that might be compared to the creation of the Diplock Courts in Northern Ireland in the 1970s—Diplock Commission: *Report* (1972) Cmnd. 5185.

order problem. Consequently the criminal law took on a modern tinge as the mechanism for class domination of a social and economic underclass.

In 1554, in Mary's reign, came legislation that enabled justices of the peace to play a more active role in investigating and prosecuting offences.[78] When these statutes are linked to the stiffening of the Vagrancy Acts in 1571 and the consolidation of the Poor Law in 1597, we can see the beginnings of the more active use of the machinery of justice as social control.

This is certainly the impression gained by considering the eighteenth century criminal justice system—gone is the link with the personal authority of the monarch. There has been a major transformation in the nature of the State and in the powers of Parliament, while at the same time the economic base is in transition with the growth of trade, the development of industrial and agricultural capitalism. There are demographic changes as more and more people are forced off the land through enclosures. The old patterns of social authority are breaking down— no longer does the land-tie relationship permeate all levels of society and the traditional authority structures of rural England can no longer be depended upon.

There are changes in property relationships and in property itself—the old rights of common are disappearing as property becomes private.[79] Equally the reciprocity of social relationships diminishes. For John Locke at the end of the seventeenth century, the chief ends of government were the maintenance of civil peace, and the security of person and of property. 'Such a theory, diluted by self-interest and prejudice, might provide the propertied classes with a sanction for the most bloody code penalising offenders against property.'[80] The 'new property' is protected through the criminal law with a mass of legislation, all ultimately dependent upon the death penalty. By the turn of the eighteenth century there were well over 200 offences punishable by death.

In the eighteenth century, the criminal justice system became representative of the interests of the dominant propertied classes. The old feudal relationships of subordination and deference, ideas of personal loyalty, local ties and custom and a sense of social place had been fatally weakened by social and economic change as gradually the factory, wage labour and the contract of employment were to take over in place of the reciprocal and all-pervasive nature of rural life. During this period of transition, Douglas Hay has argued that the propertied classes mobilised and enforced the criminal law, through which they sought to maintain and reinforce the new property interests while masking the reality of the social world through the majesty of the law and through the process of pardons and mercy.[81]

As the pace of this change quickened in the early nineteenth century, the government recognised that the law needed to intervene between the capitalist and labour—the subjective and discretionary justice of earlier eras would aggravate the more overt tension between the classes. Law (and criminal law) needed to be presented as a neutral force in this conflict. In the nineteenth century criminal justice took the shape that we recognise today. The laws themselves were reformed—larceny, for example, had become very complex as new forms of property and of theft had emerged in the eighteenth century[82] but it had also become quite personal with statutes protecting the property of specific compa-

---

[78] Langbein, J., *Prosecuting Crime in the Renaissance* (1974).
[79] Thompson E. P., *Whigs and Hunters* (1975).
[80] Thompson E.P., *The Making of the English Working Class* (1968) p. 87.
[81] Hay D., 'Property, Authority and the Criminal Law' in Hay D. (ed). *Albion's Fatal Tree* (1975).
[82] Hall J., *Theft, Law and Society* (2nd ed., 1952).

nies: these were repealed when the law was generalised in 1816. Theoretically the law protected everyone, property owners and the dispossessed alike.

Victorian social policy, linked with political reforms, was more rationalist in many areas such as public hygiene, schools and welfare. This utilitarian approach also showed itself in criminal justice, although with a more ideological impact as it underpinned the 'rule of law', which was so important in the incorporation of all classes into the parliamentary, democratic state. The most visible sign of the 'rule of law' was the 'New Police', starting in 1829 with the creation of the Metropolitan force but with forces all across the country by 1856. The police were the embodiment of the values of the rule of law—neutrality, equality, universality. But reform affected all areas: the repeal of many of the capital punishment statutes in the early 19th century removed much of the brutality of the old law, reflecting the utilitarian principle that punishment had to be proportionate to the offence; the new penitentiaries that were completed in the 1840s were designed for the reform of the offender through work, the Bible and solitary confinement in individual cells;[83] more formal trial procedures and rules of evidence also took root at this time.

One obvious finding from this brief survey is that the criminal justice system has never been planned as a 'system' and to refer to it as one is simply a convenience. A second conclusion is that its origins are not to be found in the objectives of crime reduction or of protecting victims but in the political exigencies of medieval England. This focus must not be lost since criminal justice has to be understood, at least in part, as a means of maintaining and reinforcing state authority and its evolution has as much to do with politics and economics as law or morals. The form that the criminal justice system takes necessarily changes as the form of the state changes. In protecting the state, the criminal justice system necessarily protects the interests of those individuals and classes that dominate and form the state—the personal monarch, landholders, industry and finance capital.

1.5 SOURCES OF CRIMINAL LAW AND KEY CHARACTERISTICS

Once a complaint from the public has been received, the critical issue for the police is whether this amounts to a crime? The whole idea of the criminal law rests on the idea of criminal offences—people cannot be arrested, charged, prosecuted or punished without legal authority. What gives this legal authority and defines an offence? This is straightforward—an offence must either be created by statute or by the operation of the doctrine of precedent in case law. Although the majority of offences are statutory, a number of significant ones are still common law offences, including murder and manslaughter. The core definitions of such crimes are still to be found in decided cases itself although sometimes these common law crimes have been affected by statutory amendment—for example, the Homicide Act 1957 introduced various defences to murder. The Act of Parliament or the appellate decision will give us the basic elements of an offence, which the prosecution must prove to obtain a conviction. Without such specific legal authority, the police cannot proceed.

This is the basic principle of legality for criminal lawyers—the Latin tag is

---

[83] Ignatieff M., *A Just Measure of Pain* (1978).

nulla poena sine lege. This principle is to fetter the power of public officials—if certain formal steps to create law must be followed, officials cannot exercise arbitrary powers. Such arbitrary powers are the hallmarks of totalitarian societies where immense control is placed in the hands of state officials over what constitutes crime as well as over the manner of enforcement.[84]

Ashworth[85] stresses that there are central characteristics of this principle, in particular the principles of non-retroactivity, maximum certainty and strict construction:

1. Article 7 of the European Convention, which states that nobody shall be found guilty of a crime, which was not an offence under national law at the time when it was committed. Statutes were unlikely to be expressed retrospectively and Article 7 now reinforces this. This has been more of a problem for the English common law, because of its reliance on judicial interpretation and law-making, necessarily involves amendments to the law which infringe the principle of legality.[86] It is shown at its worst in *Shaw*[87] where the accused published a reference book to London prostitutes, only to be convicted of a conspiracy to corrupt public morals. In *Shaw* Lord Simonds said:

   '...I entertain no doubt that there remains in the courts of law a residual power to enforce the supreme and fundamental purpose of the law, to conserve not only the safety and order but also the moral welfare of the State and that it is their duty to guard it against attacks which may be the more insidious because they are novel and unprepared for.'

   Although the courts now disclaim their lawmaking role, this re-emerged as recently as 1992 in *R. v. R.*[88] where the defendant was convicted of raping his wife. The House of Lords upheld the conviction despite the centuries-old rule that the marriage vow implied consent to sex and thus a husband was not capable of raping a wife. This can be seen as creating a new offence or at the very least as denying the defendant the benefit of a defence that had existed for centuries.

2. The idea of certainty itself reflects the principle of non-retroactivity but it also means that penal laws should be accessible and specific, with only the minimum necessary scope for discretion. General terms such as 'reasonableness' and 'dishonesty' are difficult to avoid. There are certain offences, such as conspiracy to defraud,[89] which are so inherently vague that the outer limits are barely discernible.

3. There is a principle of statutory interpretation that requires penal statutes to be interpreted narrowly and in favour of the liberty of the defendant.[90] This principle is rarely mentioned, let alone invoked by the appeal courts. One example would be the extension of the law of theft by the House of

---

[84] An example would be the Nazi legislation that proscribed 'anything which is deserving of punishment according to the fundamental idea of a penal law AND the sound perception of the people'.
[85] Ashworth A., *op. cit.*, Chaps 2 and 3.
[86] Smith A.T.H., 'Judicial Lawmaking in the Criminal Law', (1984) 100 L.Q.R. 46.
[87] (1962) A.C. 220.
[88] (1992) 1 A.C. 599; Giles M., 'Judicial Law-Making' (1992) Crim L.R. 407.
[89] *Scott v. MPC* (1975) A.C. 819.
[90] Jeffries J.C., 'Legality, Vagueness and the Construction of Penal Statutes' (1985) 71 *Virginia L.R.* 189.

Lords in *Gomez*,[91] an obvious case of obtaining property by deception contrary to section 15 of the Theft Act 1968 but which had been charged and prosecuted as theft. Their Lordships chose the broader of the possible interpretations of the term 'appropriation' under section 3 of that Act, reducing the offence to one where the key element of the offence is the 'dishonesty' of the accused and obliterating any sensible distinction between theft and deception. Although the accused was patently dishonest in this case and to that extent deserved to be convicted, there is a further principle that offences should be properly demarcated and labelled and that people are entitled to rely on this.

A criminal offence can be created in conformity to such principles but substantively it might still be argued that the substance of the offence, the conduct it proscribes, should not be the business of the criminal law. A crime involves conduct prosecuted by the state, which results in a court punishing the individual. This requires a vast network of criminal justice agencies, following complex procedures at no little cost to the public: the involvement of the state suggests that there has to be a definable public interest as criminal justice should not be a way of pursuing purely private affairs. But even where there is a discernible public interest, penal approaches should be kept to a minimum if that interest can be protected by other means.

1.6 CRIMINALISING BEHAVIOUR

What conduct should be treated as a crime? This is the next key question—are the core substantive and procedural values of criminal justice absolute and universal or are they shaped by economic and social determinants? Having looked at the evolution of the system, it is tempting to agree with Marxist scholars who would accept the latter focus, emphasising that the 'values' behind criminal law are relative. There are few, if any, offences on our statute book that have not been tolerated at another time or in another society. Marxists would also argue that our entrenchment of certain values in the law is ideological in the sense that in the guise of criminal offences, these values disguise and legitimate class interests. As we shall see, the modern criminal law certainly is open to the charge that its definitions only proscribe particular categories of dishonesty, violence and exploitation while permitting others.

But criminal justice is not simply a system of disguising the interests of power. It is inevitably linked with moral discourse—codes of conduct and the manner in which we deal with those who break the rules reflect important values about cultural identity and constitutional relationships.[92] The criminal justice system is one place where moral codes and notions of 'due process' are made concrete by definition and enforcement. This is not just a legal exercise but also a cultural one—the way in which we deal with dishonesty, violence and exploitation and with the perpetrators of such acts expresses certain ideas about how we should relate to each other and certain values which provide us with reasons for social cohesion and identity.

---

[91] [1993] 1 All E.R. I—another example would be '*Charles*' (1976) 63 Cr. App. R. 252—for discussion, see Smith A.T.H., *op. cit.*
[92] Dostoevsky is reported to have said that if you wanted to know about a society, you should look at the state of its prisons.

As soon as we mention 'values', issues become subjective and complex. Moral values are debated and negotiated within each society, shaped by the history and the present. Penal sanctions are justified by social beliefs that certain conduct is wrong. This implies that there are no universal standards of right and wrong, that these are relative to each society and that we are not able to criticise another society's standards. But seeing penal law in terms of cultural relativism has serious limits—the fatwah pronounced by Iranian Islamic courts on the novelist, Salman Rushdie, may be understandable as a reaction from a deeply religious culture but such understanding should not debar us from criticism of such decisions: expression of ideas should never be a criminal offence; conviction should only take place after trial with proper opportunities for representation, for confronting witnesses and for producing counter evidence; and punishment must always be proportional and the minimum necessary for the offence.

The Rushdie example immediately illustrates the problem about the substance of penal laws—what behaviour is so serious that fundamental freedoms such as the right to liberty be curtailed? What behaviour is so serious that collective intervention is required? This book adopts a liberal position, that the boundaries of the criminal law should be as narrow as possible. State intervention should only occur where the conduct involves a positive harm to another person and where there is an identifiable public interest in imposing penal sanctions. Modern criminal law does not reflect these principles as is readily apparent to those who have checked awesome breadth of the index of a criminal law textbook. That breadth encompasses not only physical violence and property offences but also a plethora of public order offences, moral offences where it is often difficult to discern a 'victim' in the traditional sense (possession of drugs, prostitution, kerb-crawling or the behaviour of consenting sado-masochists in *Brown*[93]), offences which are created for the protection of the state and a vast array of regulatory crimes, from traffic to factories to pubs (the regulation of public enterprises of all kinds). This entire area of some 7,000 offences is defined as 'crime'.

1.6.1 *The Case of Heroin*

The difficulty of identifying the proper boundaries of penal law can be seen with the misuse of drugs. Cannabis users are (sometimes) imprisoned whereas smokers are (frequently) hospitalised. This contrast arouses controversy and there has been greater tolerance of cannabis use in recent years—in 2002, it has been reclassified from a Class B drug to a Class C, putting it on the same level as steroids and anti-depressants and as such cannabis possession has become a non-arrestable offence; some police forces have already experimented with merely cautioning people for cannabis possession.[94]

On the other hand, very few argue for the decriminalisation of narcotics such as heroin. It should be recognised that until the 1960s, Britain had an enlightened attitude towards narcotic addicts who were treated by ordinary doctors who were able to prescribe heroin for their patients. As a result the addict got a pure drug, clean needles, at low cost, proper advice and assistance. The cost of this was over-prescribing by some doctors that led to a 'grey' market in the drug—this was sale by patient/addicts. It was a medical/therapeutic model of dealing with a

[93] [1993] 2 All E.R. 75.
[94] *The Guardian*, March 21, 2002.

social problem, which did not involve the criminal justice system.

But the various moral panics about the hedonistic use of drugs by young people in the 1960s led eventually to the Misuse of Drugs Act 1971, introducing a more punitive approach. Treatment and prescribing were taken away from GPs and treatment centres were established, often using methadone as a substitute for heroin. Addicts avoided these centres and consequently a black market in narcotics was established. As a result the cost soared, the product was adulterated, the addicts used poorly sterilised needles, stole to finance the habit and failed to eat. Deaths occurred from overdoses (since addicts no longer knew the purity of the drug), from malnutrition, from blood poisoning and diseases such as hepatitis B and, more recently, AIDS which are contracted through sharing of dirty syringes. There has been a steady increase in the number of drug related deaths reported in England, from 2,041 in 1990 to 2,922 in 1998.[95]

In 2000/01 there were 113,500 drug offences recorded by the police—92,700 were possession offences, mainly of cannabis and 19,800 for dealing.[96] Although only 1 per cent of the general population report having used heroin, a survey of the drug use of remand and sentenced prisoners in 1997[97] showed that over 80 per cent of male prisoners reported any lifetime illicit drug use prior to imprisonment, compared to around 70 per cent for female prisoners. In terms of more recent drug use, between 10–20 per cent of all prisoners reported having used heroin, and 5–8 per cent of sentenced prisoners reported using crack, during their current stay in prison.[98] There is a clear link between drugs and crime and the expense for the addict of supporting the habit has also led to a vast increase in drug-related property offences.

These bald facts lend weight to the argument that the consequences of dealing with the problem of drug abuse through the penal model are worse than the problem of over-prescription created by the medical model. It is difficult to distinguish the addictive nature, the health-threatening qualities and the distressing social consequences of heroin abuse from alcoholism or smoking. But public opinion would certainly find intravenous narcotic use both repellent and 'wrong' in the sense that people should not act in that way.[99] Furthermore they may argue that tolerance of narcotic use creates the climate of acceptance that may encourage young people to experiment—although the drug user is not a direct 'victim' as he makes a free choice but by tolerating that choice, we create the possibility of indirectly causing harm to others. Hence the example of heroin poses no difficulty for a traditional model of criminal justice that sees the law as representing the moral judgments of the majority of the community. This model considers that 'immorality' is a necessary condition of any act to be criminalised—only conduct generally and without significant dissent considered 'immoral' should be penalised.[100]

One problem is discovering whether something is immoral—it can be based either on some absolute idea of good and evil to be found in an acknowledged and authoritative text such as the Bible or Quran. Alternatively some commen-

[95] U.K. Drug Situation 2000 (available at www.drugscope.org.uk).
[96] Criminal Statistics 2000, op. cit. Chap. 2.
[97] Singleton, N., Meltzer, H. and Gatward, R. (no year given), Psychiatric morbidity among prisoners. (London: ONS and Department of Health.)
[98] U.K. Drug Situation 2000. op. cit.
[99] It is interesting to consider how 'knowledge' of this kind is constructed through social processes—Berger P. and Luckman R., Social Construction of Reality (1971).
[100] Packer H., The Limits of the Criminal Sanction (1968) p. 262.

tators give it a more secular and democratic meaning characteristic of the 'immoral' emerge through demonstration, referendum or through the editorials of national newspapers. Even assuming that this difficulty can be overcome and while it can be argued that the criminal justice system gains its legitimacy from the fact of an action's 'immorality', is this ever sufficient?

The example of the imposition of the fatwah on Salman Rushdie illustrates that both religious text and popular feeling in Islamic countries would treat the publication of the Satanic Verses as immoral and thus justify the sentence. As we have seen, heroin use in this country fulfils the latter condition—the majority certainly regard it as an evil. But is this enough? In other words, is immorality not just a necessary condition but also a sufficient one? Most commentators would argue that behaviour must not only be immoral but must have some other quality before it can be criminalised—classic liberal commentators such as Mill[101] in the 19th century or Hart[102] would argue that immorality *per se* is necessary but not sufficient and that we must be able to identify an objective harm to others before we treat another person's behaviour as criminal. Against that position, Devlin[103] argues that public morality is a vital ingredient for society, the cement between the bricks, and that the state has the right to safeguard its existence. Devlin uses that position to argue, for example, that the practice of homosexuality is injurious to society, which thus has the right to limit or eradicate it.

1.6.2 *Immorality, Crime and the Sado-Masochist*

A second illustration of the difficulty of identifying the proper boundaries of penal law can be taken from the area of sexual behaviour. In *Brown*[104] the House of Lords were considering whether a criminal assault occurs where the 'victim' has consented to that assault which has caused actual, but not necessarily serious, bodily harm. The context was the practices of a group of homosexual sadomasochists. In legal terms, there were two issues—the first of these was the question of whether a person could consent to any level of physical injury at all? There was authority going back to Fitzjames Stephen[105] in the nineteenth century to suggest that the line should be drawn so that, while you could not consent to being maimed or killed, you could consent to lesser forms of harm. The rationale suggested was that the able-bodied male had to be prepared to serve king and country, a discernible public interest. The implication was that the victim's consent to any lesser form of assault would provide a defence to any criminal charge.

More recently the Court of Appeal has limited the extent to which consent can be a defence.[106] This involved a brawl outside a pub and the defendants argued that they had agreed to fight and thus there could be no assault. The court held that it was not in the public interest for people to cause each other actual bodily harm. They could have limited the scope of their judgment by treating the context as relevant since such brawls can easily lead to public disorder. The court rejected this approach and held that consent was irrelevant regardless of whether

---

[101] Mill J.S., *On Liberty* (2nd ed., 1859).
[102] Hart H.L.A., *Law, Liberty and Morality* (1963).
[103] Devlin P., *The Enforcement of Morals* (1965).
[104] *op. cit.*
[105] Stephen J.F., *A General View of the Criminal Law* (2nd ed., 1890).
[106] *Attorney-General's Reference No. 1 of 1980* (1981) Q.B. 715 following prize-fighting cases such as *Coney* (1882) 8 Q.B.D. 534.

the incident was in public or in private. The House of Lords in *Brown* followed this decision. The House agreed that, while people could injure themselves and commit no offence, they could not consent to an injury by another causing any visible physical harm. The only exceptions to this (the second issue) was where the assault had social utility such as competitive sports or surgery, including cosmetic surgery, and also, bizarrely, tattooing.

Liberal commentators would argue that a core idea of liberal society must be ownership of your own body, expressed in the 'right to physical integrity' that nobody else has a right to interfere with your body. If you choose to have your ears pierced, your torso tattooed, circumcision or even suicide, this is a voluntary choice that must be respected if individuals are to be treated as autonomous rational beings with self-determination. Limits on that right in the name of 'public interest' become very difficult to justify—if my right hand offends me and I chop it off, I cannot be prosecuted for causing myself GBH. If I hire a surgeon to do the chopping, how can he be blamed? Indeed there is an extremely rare form of body dysmorphic disorder known as apotemnophilia. Those suffering from the disease have an obsessive belief that their body is 'incomplete' with four limbs and will only be complete after amputation. Does a surgeon who amputated the healthy limbs from such patients commit a criminal offence?[107]

Treating the sexual preferences of others as crimes requires justification. The House of Lords sought that justification in paternalism—that the state was entitled to intervene to prevent people from engaging in practices which the majority would regard as self-harm. In *Brown*, Lord Templeman discusses drug abuse and states, '... the criminal law restrains a practice which is regarded as dangerous and injurious to individuals ...'[108] and later refers to the dangers of the participants contracting HIV and AIDS. The need to protect the young is also mentioned as the appellants '... were responsible in part for the corruption of a youth "K" ... It is some comfort at least to be told ... that "K" has now it seems settled into a normal heterosexual relationship.'[109] This latter comment shows a Devlinesque moralism. If such practices were allowed and extended, this would be 'harmful to society generally' which Lord Templeman later expands on, 'Society is entitled and bound to protect itself against a cult of violence. Pleasure derived from the infliction of pain is an evil thing. Cruelty is uncivilised.'[110] Such words can be compared with those of Lord Simonds in *Shaw* when he talked of, '*the supreme and fundamental purpose of the law, to conserve not only the safety and order but also the moral welfare of the State*' as he sought to justify the creation of an offence not previously known to law. But his words can equally be applied here to the restriction of the defence of consent. The 'moral welfare' of the state is being pursued by penalising homosexual behaviour, the expression of which is barely tolerated and then only within the narrow ambit of the 1967 legislation.[111]

---

[107] See the case of Robert Smith who operated on two men in Falkirk—*The Guardian*, February 1, 2000.

[108] *supra* at 82f.

[109] *supra* at 83a–b.

[110] *supra* at 84g.

[111] The Court of Appeal has recently applied Brown to sado-masochism in heterosexual cases—*Emmett*, *The Independent* (C.S.), July 19, 1999. See *Laskey v. UIL* (1997) 24 EHRR 39.

1.6.3 *Legislating Morals*

The examples of drugs and sexual behaviour demonstrate the difficulty of formulating a clear principle, which would justify the state in treating individual's conduct as criminal. There are several competing models. The first of these would be based unapologetically on the idea that a society is justified in controlling personal morality. For Devlin,[112] the legal and moral codes are closely related—laws possess a symbolic importance in reaffirming certain cherished values in society. Furthermore he argues that the maintenance of such values is necessary to preserve society from disintegration. Personal moral behaviour and moral codes are the cement of a social order—the importance of the economic, reproductive, socialisation and protective functions of the family is affirmed by motivating people to form families, adhere to them and accept their discipline. Prostitution, adultery and homosexuality are discouraged as posing a threat to the stability of family relationships whilst providing attachments that compete for the 'man's' loyalty, affection and resources.

Devlin's theory raises interesting thoughts about the nature or existence of the 'weak forces' that underpin social order. To what extent are shared beliefs or values crucial to a viable society? How far are we justified in defending those values? Historically recusancy, the failure to attend church, was a crime and societies would certainly regard adherence to a shared religious faith as critical and punishment of non-believers as justified. People died for the idea of freedom of belief and of expression and yet nowadays religious belief remains an important and central element of many communities. Such communities would justify using the law to enforce conformity. In contrast, Western thought[113] now emphasises diversity and tolerance and yet still punishes those who use conscious-altering drugs or engage in certain deviant sexual practices—are such activities so important and central that we should use the criminal justice system to outlaw them?

Those who argue for a close relationship between morality and criminal law also need to demonstrate the nature of the 'injury' that society allegedly suffers. In *Knuller*,[114] the House of Lords were faced with an appeal against a conviction for 'conspiracy to outrage public decency'. The court upheld the existence of such an offence when it was 'destructive of the very fabric of society'. The case involved publishing adverts from homosexuals seeking like-minded partners and it is difficult to understand the factual basis for upholding the convictions. Hart has pointed out that empirically this traditional model suffers from the difficulty that no society can be demonstrated to have collapsed as a result, for example, of liberalising its sexual codes—since *Knuller* was decided, millions of such advertisements must have appeared in mainstream publications without English society collapsing.

Devlin talks of 'deep disgust' when referring to homosexuals and this was an attitude mirrored by the House of Lords in *Brown*. This is more an emotive reaction based on ignorance, fear and superstition rather than rational judgment, which would demand clear identification of the social threat. Moralists wish to control the behaviour of other people, regardless of whether it affects them. Ultimately it is a position that lacks limiting conditions—it is only too easy to

---

[112] Devlin P., *The Enforcement of Morals* (1965).
[113] Art. 10 European Convention on Human Rights.
[114] [1973] A.C. 435.

discover 'harms' from which society must protect itself, as opposed to protecting the individual. Again it is useful to consider *Brown* in this context—in essence this was a private affair and if there is consent to the practices, where lies the 'harm' if the 'victim' refuses to define himself as a victim? Lord Templeman circumvented this when he adverted to Article 8 of the European Convention on Human Rights which talks of '... the right to respect for his private and family life.' and suggested that these activities were not exercises of such rights. In other words, the guarantees of the Convention only protect certain choices. But can there be a public interest in criminalising people's voluntary actions in relation to their own bodies?

In hunting for some principle to underpin the criminal law, there is a second model, which fits in more comfortably with a diverse and multicultural society. It owes more to the liberal tradition of Mill and Hart than to Devlin's moralism or to its diluted version in the paternalism of *Brown*. This tradition points instead to the idea of 'harm to others'. Society is only entitled to intervene and to punish to prevent objective harm to others, if only for the reason that without such collective protection, individuals would not be motivated to remain in society. This tradition argues that we are not entitled to use social power to impose a set of moral standards where breach of the standards causes no injury to another nor should we use our collective might to dictate a person's behaviour because it is felt that it is not in someone's best interests to act in a particular manner. This 'harm principle' rests on the idea of autonomous choices and this requires that a person have the capacity to make those choices. The requirement of capacity to make valid choices permits us to intervene to protect children or the mentally handicapped: it can be argued that young people should be limited in their opportunities to drink, engage in sex or bet until they are of an age when they can appreciate the consequences of such behaviour.

The criterion of 'objective harm' limits the scope of criminal law but still has inherent problems. The feminist would argue that the publisher of pornography degrades women as a class and renders them more likely to become victims of sexual attack. The moralist would say that such publications 'deprave and corrupt' their readers.[115] Is there sufficient 'harm' to justify criminal sanctions here or does the liberal, having identified harm to others as justification for intervention, limit that by specifying that there must be a direct damage rather than indirect harm? The word 'harm' is wide and not inherently self-limiting, for example, to physical or property damage. In *Ireland*[116] the appellate court accepted that the psychological damage caused by hoax telephone calls constituted 'actual bodily harm' for the purposes of section 47 of the Offences Against the Person Act 1861. The court still requires evidence of recognised psychological illness before conviction. The liberal might well go further and argue that deliberately causing emotional trauma or offending 'sensibilities' through pornography or blasphemy should be criminal harms. Certainly the idea of 'indirect' harms has been used to justify penal sanctions for a failure to wear crash helmets or seat belts since young children 'model' themselves on adult behaviour and are thus being put at greater risk.

The liberal model is attacked for being too narrow. The harm principle often concentrates on the idea of harm at the expense of that elusive element of public interest. When we consider crimes by corporations, who suffers directly when a

---

[115] Obscene Publications Act 1959, s. 1.
[116] [1998] A.C. 147.

board of directors act illegally to block the takeover of their company by another organisation? Yet the community response is often a desire to see the prosecution of senior management and the labelling of their actions as criminal. If we allege that there is a stronger public interest in such cases (that large corporations must be effectively regulated) and that as a result, there is less need to show direct harm, are we falling back into the logic of legal moralism? This criterion of 'public interest' is addressed by Lacey[117] with her principle of 'welfare'. In this approach, criminal justice is the imposition of standards of behaviour on individuals and those must reflect the values, needs and interests which a society decrees as fundamental to its proper functioning. It is this principle and not individual autonomy that Lacey sees as the predominant criterion in criminalising conduct. It is a principle that skirts with moralism, especially where morality and welfare are both identified by the will of the majority. But Lacey sees welfare as bring in creative tension with 'autonomy'. Community goals must be given due weight but as Ashworth puts it, '... the value of autonomy as a restraint upon collective and state action should not be overlooked'.[118]

1.6.4 *Politics and Legislating Morality*

The core of a criminal justice system is the criminal law, which identifies the behaviour defined as crime. Not only do we lack a Code of Penal Law but also as the previous discussion has shown, there is no consensus over what principles should govern the proper boundaries. The continuous tinkering with the criminal law by Parliament often reveals political expediency to be at the root of the process. There is a steady and insidious expansion, creating new offences without attention to underlying principles as to what should constitute a crime and when social issues such as drug use, abortion, homelessness and squatting, raves and travellers are approached through the medium of the penal law, it might be argued that penal law has expanded beyond its proper boundaries.[119]

There is a fundamental problem about the nature of politics in a democracy. Drawing the line between the acceptable and the unacceptable is difficult, especially where there is wide diversity of moral and cultural beliefs and attitudes. But the legislature eschews any scientific or principled approach and political considerations dominate, often concealed under the rhetoric of the overall public interest but lying behind this are real issues about economic and social interests and social authority, let alone votes.

Where the laws seem unrelated to the economic, the campaigns to get such legislation on the books can, in Howard Becker's terms, be seen as a 'moral enterprise' with the campaigner as a 'moral entrepreneur'.

'Rules are not made automatically. Even though a practice may be harmful in an objective sense to the group in which it occurs, the harm needs to be discovered and pointed out. People must be made to feel that something ought to be done about it. Someone must call the public's attention to these matters, supply the push necessary to get things done and direct such energies as are aroused in the proper direction to get a rule created.[120,]

[117] Lacey N., *State Punishment* (1988).
[118] Ashworth, *op. cit.* p. 31.
[119] Criminal Justice and Public Order Act 1994 Part V.
[120] Becker H., *Outsiders* (1963).

Such campaigns are often symbolic crusades on a broader level—Gusfield[121] suggests that for those who affirm a strong moral position, the power to legislate documents their status in society. In his study of the prohibition laws in the U.S., he suggests that drinking was a focus of conflicts between Protestant and Catholic, rural and urban, native and immigrant, middle class and lower class in American society. Legal affirmation was thus important for what it symbolised— even if the law was broken, it was clear whose law it was.[122] It is not enough in talking about crime to state simply that it deals with immoral or evil behaviour. Even the most fundamental crimes such as violence or homicide are tolerated in certain situations. But the vast bulk of offences become crimes for very different reasons—it becomes important to recognise who is doing the defining and for what reasons.

1.7 DEFINING THROUGH ENFORCEMENT

If we were asked the questions 'when is physical violence a crime?' or 'are any types of physical violence tolerated?', the lawyer would point to the common law of battery which criminalizes any form of physical contact without consent. She might go on to point out the relevant sections of the Offences Against the Person Act 1861, which lay down heavy sentences for aggravated assaults. In theory, the boundaries of crime are delineated by the text of penal statutes and in the area of violence there is little tolerance. Yet the practical borders are very different— there are many situations where people are killed or seriously injured and yet the state does not routinely prosecute. A truer picture of these are measured by the day-to-day enforcement through the police and the courts, which can produce a different image as to what is socially acceptable or unacceptable and can distort social perception of what is seen as 'real' crime.

The laws on physical violence present a clearly delineated hierarchy of offences, ranging from murder, manslaughter, through serious physical harm (grievous bodily harm), unlawful wounding to lesser physical harm (actual bodily harm) and common assault. The parameters of the law are drawn in a precise and objective fashion, carefully scaling the offences to the degree of injury caused.[123] Is this all that we need to know about the violence which society finds acceptable or unacceptable?

To concentrate on simply the text of the law would inevitably be misleading— in practice, the enforcement by police, prosecutors and courts defines the limits. The courts will not define boxing, even in an unlicensed bout, as assault and battery. Change the context so that the fight takes place outside a public house and the courts will convict.[124] Change the victim to a wife and the police become unwilling to investigate, let alone prosecute, what is still termed a 'domestic' and unworthy of overlong police intervention.[125] By intervening or not intervening, the police practice reflects public perceptions of 'real' crime but at the same time it also affects those perceptions, reinforcing the image that a man hitting his wife

---

[121] Gusfield J.R., *Symbolic Crusade* (1966).

[122] Generally see Schur E.M., *The Politics of Deviance Chap. 3* (1980).

[123] There is a little poetic licence in this statement as lawyers rely on an ancient and outmoded statute, the Offences Against the Person Act 1861, which has very little precision.

[124] *Attorney General's Reference No. 6 of 1980* (1981) Q.B. 715.

[125] Mirrlees-Black C., *Domestic Violence: Findings from the British Crime Survey* (Home Office Research Study No. 191) (1999); Grace C., *Policing Domestic Violence in the 1990s Survey* (Home Office Research Study No. 139) (1995).

is in some way acceptable.

Underlying the enforcement of these laws against violence is a complex moral debate, resting upon the ethical basis that we all possess a 'right to physical integrity' and requiring elucidation as to when that can be infringed. This discussion surfaces in many forms—the doctor with the terminally ill patient or the severely deformed new born baby, the soldier on checkpoint duty in Northern Ireland shooting an unarmed joy rider believing him to be a terrorist, the police officer using excessive force to restrain a suspect. All of these might frame a dramatic individual instance of what is acceptable violence. The law presents us with different coded messages—the doctor still does not have a clear-cut defence to murder even when the motive is to relieve unbearable suffering;[126] whereas the soldier is regarded as justified, even though not fired at, if he believed mistakenly that he was acting in self-defence.[127] Both felt compelled to act as they did but the law regards only one as 'justifiable force'.

There is a still wider frame of reference. One function of the criminal justice system is to protect us from physical injuries and yet the major causes of death and disablement are rarely prosecuted. Reiman[128] and Box[129] give the illustrations of the tobacco industry[130] and factories and workplaces:[131] many thousands of avoidable deaths and injuries are either regarded as accidents (traffic),[132] as not criminal (lung cancer through smoking)[133] or not real crime (occupational deaths).[134]

In its enforcement if not in theory, the criminal law acts as a 'distorting mirror', portraying criminal violence as individual acts of brutality usually by a stranger. We accept almost nonchalantly the corporate violence of the factory or of retailing dangerous substances. Equally we accept the violence of the school or the family as outside the criminal justice system. The 'right to physical integrity' for women and children is a fragile one since the home can be a very dangerous place. In 2000/01 there were 846 deaths initially recorded as homicide.[135] Of these, 417 (51 per cent), the murder suspect was part of the family or a friend.[136] Similarly approaching 20 per cent of non-fatal assaults are significantly domestic in character.[137] This violence is widely spread through all sectors of the community and the BCS figures are probably an under-estimate because both men and women often do not disclose incidents in face-to-face interviews. In self-completion modules, rates of domestic violence are three times higher for women and ten times higher for men. Even if reported, it can go unrecorded by the

---

[126] See the discussions in the case of the patient in a 'persistent vegetative state'—*Airedale NHS Trust v. Bland* [1993] 1 All E.R. 821.

[127] *Attorney General for N. Ireland's Reference* (1977) A.C. 105.

[128] Reiman J., *The Rich Get Richer and the Poor Get Prison* (1984).

[129] Box S., *Power, Crime and Mystification* (1983).

[130] Deaths attributable to smoking are in the order of 100,000 a year.

[131] Bergman D., *Deaths at Work: Accidents or Corporate Crime* (1991)—there are a significant number of avoidable deaths through breaches of the health and safety regulations in the workplace, www.corporateaccountability.org.

[132] Causing death by dangerous driving is still less likely to attract a prison sentence than burglary.

[133] An innovative prosecutor might see it as grievous bodily harm, administering a noxious substance or even a conspiracy to corrupt public health!

[134] Often dealt with, if at all, by prosecutions for infringements of the Health and Safety Regulations.

[135] *Criminal Statistics 2000*, Cm. 5312, Table 4.4.

[136] This year's figures were skewed because of a single incident in which 56 immigrants were killed. Normally the percentage where the victim and suspect are acquainted runs at over 60%.

[137] *2001 British Crime Survey* (Home Office Statistical Bulletin 18/01 p. 28); Mirrlees-Black C., *op. cit.*, Grace C., *op.cit.*

police; even if recorded, is often not prosecuted. It is still not perceived as 'real' crime and thereby conceals an underlying reality of male aggression towards women. In its enforcement, if not in its definition, the criminal law incorporates a gender bias. Rather than being the neutral factor suggested by the simple text of the law, the enforcement process changes our definitions, in this case providing one, which underpins patriarchal social relations.

The employee, the consumer, the wife, women and ethnic minorities generally are subjected to a range of physical threats against which the criminal law offers either no protection or very partial safeguards.

1.8 CRIMINAL JUSTICE AND CONSTITUTIONALISM

Public expression of concern about crime rates and miscarriages of justice often shows how the criminal justice system operates as the barometer of the moral economy, providing a pivot around which we discuss moral issues: there is an expository or denunciatory aspect, as the system lays down the limits of acceptable and unacceptable behaviour. But alongside this moral discourse, the system has a constitutional significance: its operations provide the acid test of fairness within society and of the relationship between individuals and the state. This is crucial where a state has no constitutional document to lay down the principles on which the society is constituted, the rights of citizenship and the limits of state power. In the absence of a written constitution, these rights and principles need to be represented by other means. 'Injustice', it appears, has a symbolic status of its own:

> The importance of a fair trial is advanced as much by its failure as by its success. Any violation of the symbol of a ceremonial trial arouses people who would be left unmoved by ordinary non-ceremonial injustice. Harmless anarchists may be shot by the police. Liberals will be sorry and forget. But let them be treated unfairly by the court and before dissatisfaction has died away, the prejudice and phobia which created the atmosphere of the trial will receive a public analysis and examination which otherwise it would not get.[138]

As long ago as 1962, Arnold was suggesting that the trial has great symbolic force, not merely representing the rule of law, but metaphorically embodying moral and rational government. It is a thesis that can be applied to the criminal justice system as a whole. Liberal democracy has at its root the categorical opposition of the individual against the state. The system of justice incorporates many of the ideas and values that we hold about that opposition, especially in regard to the rights of the individual opposed to the state and the balance between authoritarian and libertarian forms of government. Criminal justice is an area where this balance is constantly and dramatically demonstrated and where the rights of the individual should be seen at their most inviolable. The investigation, prosecution and punishment of crime are points at which there is not merely intervention by state agencies—such intervention can also be seen with other public services such as health or education—but that intervention has an intensely coercive quality. The enforceable detention of an individual by the state has constitutional significance as it lays down the borderline between state power and the liberty of the citizen. This is done in a formal and dramatised

---

[138] Arnold T., *Symbols of Government* (1962) Chap. VI.

fashion, whether in the police station or in the trial.

The process is not merely concerned with fairness between the parties—it is the embodiment of the idea of the 'rule of law' itself in that law is a body of doctrine that not only controls the individual but also the state. The niceties of due process highlight that separation of the law from the social and political world. Hay makes this point in regard to the eighteenth century:

> 'The punctilious attention to forms, the dispassionate and legalistic exchanges between counsel and judge, argued that those using and administering the law submitted to its rules. . . . It became a power with its own claims, higher than those of prosecutor, lawyer or even the judge himself. To these too, of course, the law was The Law. The fact that they (the judges/lawyers) reified it . . . heightened the illusion. Its very inefficiency, its absurd formalism, was part of its strength as an ideology.[139]'

Any discussion of the development or the boundaries of the criminal justice system quickly moves from the straightforward idea that the purpose of a criminal justice system is to establish legal and moral frontiers for society and to patrol those frontiers. It is difficult enough to state with certainty where those boundaries lie let alone when they are crossed. But these key questions, about what (and who) is criminal, deviant or delinquent, are not simple. The history of crime and justice demonstrates that the power to define crime parallels economic and social power within a society—we are all against violence and support prosecution of those who harm others. But, as has been argued, deaths in the workplace or the hospital, corporate killings or violence by the police or military almost invariably goes unpunished.

We might argue that the functions of the criminal justice system go further— the mechanisms possess a metaphorical quality. By this is meant that law enforcement, courts, trials and the technical rules of evidence and procedure are a concrete demonstration of principles underlying constitutional relationships. In the absence of a written constitution, the processes of criminal justice reveal the nexus between the citizen and the state and give concrete meaning to the idea of the 'rule of law'. There are other manifestations of this relationship such as parliamentary democracy or constitutional monarchy but crime and justice, in narrative terms, are much more effective. Crimes and trials are everyday occurrences, relatively simple to understand but which show the physical and legal power of the state to deal with citizens constrained by principles that demand that there is 'due process' of law. Individuals should be dealt with by the state in a necessary, proportionate and fair fashion and in a manner guaranteed by law. To ignore such rights and to allow the state to operate in a unregulated fashion is to put the stability of social structures at considerable risk. The passage of the Human Rights Act 1998 has reinforced this model of the criminal process as all public authorities must implement the requirements of Article 6 of the European Convention, the right to a fair trial.

The argument that the criminal justice system should give priority to such 'due process' requirements invariably is in tension with the requirements of 'crime control'. This latter approach would configure the system around the instrumental purposes of the system, in particular the reduction of crime.

'The failure of law enforcement to bring criminal conduct under tight control is viewed

---

[139] Hay D., *op. cit.*

as leading to the breakdown of public order and thence to the disappearance of an important condition of human freedom. If laws go unenforced, which is to say, if it is perceived that there is a high percentage of failure to apprehend and convict in the criminal process, a general disregard for legal controls tends to develop.[140,]

Failure to control crime also carries a risk to social order. People are entitled to security in their lives and protection from those harms from which individuals find it difficult to protect themselves. Failure to provide this may well bring the law into disrepute. Yet so does the imprisonment of the innocence. 'Crime control' and 'due process' should not be alternative models of the criminal process. The problem is to provide that there is effective machinery of enforcement to meet the legitimate concerns of the public while at the same time ensuring that there is no derogation from principles of fairness?

---

[140] Packer H.L., 'Two Models of the Criminal Process' 113 *University of Pennsylvania Law Review* (1964) p. 1 at p. 9.

CHAPTER TWO

The Police—Organisation and Accountability

2.1 THE POLICE AND CRIMINAL JUSTICE

In comparison to other countries, the police in the U.K. play a dominant role within the criminal justice system. They possess an enviable autonomy in their relationship with both national and local government and with the judiciary as well as considerable respect from the public.[1] They present a unified front through organisations such as the Association of Chief Police Officers (ACPO) and the Police Federation and are adept at putting across a police viewpoint on all criminal justice issues, whether to the media or to government reform commissions. This can be contrasted with the lack of independence, of political influence or indeed of public recognition of other criminal justice agencies.

One factor that has contributed to this centrality is that there has never been a unified approach to the management of the criminal justice system in modern times. There are a number of public sector agencies with responsibilities such as the police, the prosecution service, the courts, the probation service, youth justice

---

[1] Skogan W., *Contacts Between the Police and Public* (Home Office Research Study 134)(1994).

board and the prison service. There are also a number of voluntary agencies working in such areas as victim support or the rehabilitation of offenders. The different agencies operated autonomously. There was and is no ministry of justice with overall responsibility to Parliament for the system. The Home Office assumes responsibility for the police, the prisons and the probation service, the Attorney General for the prosecution service and the Lord Chancellor for the magistracy. It is not a recipe for shared principles and policy objectives nor for co-operation.[2] The problem is addressed in the White Paper 'Justice for All'.

With different agencies and different ministers responsible for different aspects of criminal justice, the twentieth century saw a power vacuum in the criminal justice system and in this context the police have developed a central role:

- police officers perform the key roles as the gatekeepers of the criminal justice system, deciding where to use their resources, who to arrest, caution or prosecute.

- there is no job specification for the police defined by law so they were able to become involved not just in investigating but also in prosecuting offences. Until 1985, they cast their net widely over the criminal process. Indeed with schemes such as 'caution plus', it may be said that they investigate, prosecute, sentence and carry out that sentence.

- the police have never been subject to judicial control.

- the police have always been better resourced than other agencies.

Since the Police Act 1964, Chief Constables have exerted a powerful influence over criminal justice strategy. One might argue over the consequences of this. Has it contributed to the predominant public view of the police as crime fighters? By this is meant that narrow philosophy of policing which stresses crime control and evaluates the quality of policing in terms of response to crime reports, arrests, convictions and overall crime rates. Yet while publicly emphasising their crime fighting role, the police have always operated to a wider remit, maintaining order, providing services and assistance to the public, visiting schools, working in crime prevention (as well as acting as watchdog over political and industrial unrest!). Whatever the public rhetoric, the reality of day-to-day policing requires a broader philosophy, which embraces partnerships with local communities, working jointly with other public sector agencies and giving greater emphasis to crime prevention.

This reality was recognised when a statutory scheme for developing local criminal justice policy was introduced in the Crime and Disorder Act 1998.[3] For the first time, local authorities were given a statutory role alongside the police and other agencies in creating a community safety plan for their localities. They were given the job of preparing a crime and disorder audit and subsequently of producing a community safety plan in co-operation with the police, probation service, health authorities and other agencies. Local authorities are also required to consider the crime and disorder implications of any of their actions.[4] This duty

---

[2] Audit Commission, *Route to Justice* (2002).
[3] ss. 5 and 6. The strategy is based on *Safer Communities: the Local Delivery of Crime Prevention through the Partnership Approach* (Home Office, 1991) and the consultation paper *Getting to Grips with Crime: a New Framework for Local Action* (Home Office, 1998).
[4] s.17.

will add a '*powerful dynamic in promoting the expansion of community safety*.'[5]
The local partnerships which emerge may well become more equal and less
police-driven as other agencies treat crime and disorder as one indicator among
many of social problems and seek to address these through other strategies, be
they education, health, consumer protection or planning rather than the narrow
focus of crime, responsibility and punishment.

2.2 POLICE STRUCTURE AND FUNCTIONS

How are police forces organised? Under the Police Act 1996, England and Wales
is divided into police areas, each with a police authority. The authority is obliged
by section 6 to maintain an efficient and effective police force for that area. In
England and Wales there are currently 43[6] separate forces—2 of these are in
London (the Metropolitan and the City forces[7]), others are based on either major
conurbations (Merseyside, Greater Manchester, West Midlands), single counties
(Kent, Cheshire, Gwent) or on groups of counties (Thames Valley, Dyfedd-
Powys, Devon and Cornwall).

These forces vary in size—the largest is the Metropolitan police with over
26,000 officers[8] whereas the Dyfed-Powys force covers the largest area of any
police force—an area over half of Wales—and has only 1,000 officers. In 2000,
the total force comprised 124,335 officers[9] with another 44,646 civilians. The
total strength has declined over the past five years but the Home Office intends to
increase strength by 5000 by 2003.[10] In the twenty-first century the proportion of
police officers to the population is about 1:400 whereas in the nineteenth century,
that ratio was not permitted to exceed 1:1000.

Table 2.1 Police Personnel 1960–2000, England and Wales

Year	Total Police Strength*
1960	72,252
1970	94,312
1980	117,423
1990	127,090
2000	124,335

* *This figure includes Home Office approved supernumeraries and secondments*

[5] Crawford, A. *Crime Prevention and Community Safety* (1998) p. 59.
[6] For a list, see Sched. 1, Police Act 1996. The government has power under s. 32 to amalgamate
existing forces—see also White Paper: *Police Reform* (1993), Cm. 2281 Chap. 10.
[7] The legal basis of the Metropolitan and City forces is different to that of provincial forces. The
Metropolitan force is set up under Metropolitan Police Act 1829 and the City of London force under
Metropolitan Police Act 1839.
[8] Difficulties in recruitment have seen numbers dropping from 28,135 in March 1994 to 26,707 in
March 1998.
[9] Of that figure, 1,730 were from ethnic minorities compared with 1105 in 1987. Approximately
16% of the force are women and 2% are from ethnic minorities.
[10] These figures do not include special constables, cadets or traffic wardens.

In September 2002, police numbers reached a record 129,603 police officers in England and Wales.[11] The 'police family' has, in the past, been supplemented by special constables, traffic wardens and neighbourhood wardens but the Police Reform Act 2002 has led to the recruitment of Community Support Officers. In uniform, the CSOs are not constables and represent part of the government policy to increase the visibility of officers on the beat and provide reassurance. They will have limited powers, including that of detaining suspects until an officer arrives.[12]

Excluding capital charges, the total gross expenditure of police authorities in England and Wales was £7.8 billion in 1999–2000. The income for this derives from three main sources: the police grant from the Home Office, revenue support or non-domestic rates from the Department of the Environment and from the council tax from local government. For the purposes of collecting council tax, the police authority is a precepting authority.[13] Although the authority will set a budget each year, the total amount to be spent is determined by the Home Secretary.[14]

What are the basic functions of the police? Law has never laid these down—police powers of arrest and detention are strictly and legally defined[15] but this does not extend to defining the boundaries of police activity. In a sense, this is a position that reflects the traditional image of the constable as simply a private citizen in uniform who may do anything which is not prohibited by law. Should a police force have issued a list of kerb-crawlers to local media in order to 'name and shame? Should they have introduced CCTV surveillance of city centres? Should they have run 'caution plus' schemes for juvenile offenders? These examples are all indirect means of detecting and preventing crime but should they have been undertaken without specific legal authority or consultation and agreement with the local democratic process? Such questions raise a nice question of what police activities would be seen as *ultra vires* and outside their constitutional remit.

If not defining the proper remit of policing, the Report of the Royal Commission on the Police in 1962[16] at least described it. It saw the police providing a broad range of services to the public and to government. The police possessed:

i) a duty to maintain law and order and to protect persons and property.

ii) a duty to prevent crime.

iii) a responsibility for the detection of criminals and, in the course of interrogating suspected persons, they have a part to play in the early stages of the judicial process.

iv) some responsibility for the decision whether or not to prosecute persons suspected of criminal offences.

v) the duty of controlling road traffic.

vi) duties on behalf of Government departments.

---

[11] Home Office Press Release Sep 24 2002, Ref: 258/2002.
[12] Police Reform Act 2002 Sch. 4 Part 1.
[13] Police and Magistrates' Courts Act 1994, s. 27.
[14] Police Act 1996, s. 46.
[15] By the Police and Criminal Evidence Act 1984.
[16] Royal Commission on the Police: Final Report. Cmnd. 1728, p. 22 (1962).

vii) a duty to befriend anyone who needs their help.

The Report reflected a force that provides a 24 hour emergency service for the community, not only in the area of crime and public order but also in response to a wide range of requests. This is still true—about 60 per cent of calls to a police station are not related to crime but to personal difficulties and problems such as noise, disputes between neighbours, missing persons or lost property.[17] The force operates as a focus for and provides information about many other assistance agencies—the homeless, women's refuges or drug and detoxification centres.

During the Thatcher administration, that broader approach was under attack with increasing emphasis on crime detection and the maintenance of public order. One factor accelerating this is the increasing use of performance indicators.[18] Such indicators can provide desirable and objective measurement of a force's effectiveness but they also mean that resources are channelled towards the activity being measured. The indicators favoured by politicians and by the press are invariably crime-related—the most basic being the number of offences in relation to population and the clear up-rate.[19] In 1994 the Home Secretary was empowered by statute to set objectives and performance targets for the police.[20] The first key objectives[21] had come earlier in 1993 which emphasised the number of detections for violent crimes and burglaries, the targeting of crimes which are particular local problems in partnership with the public and other local agencies, high visibility policing to reassure the public and prompt response to emergency calls. Emphasising such factors did not provide an incentive to police managers to use resources on schools liaison, community work or even on general crime prevention, none of which will have a direct, short term effect on crime figures.

In contrast, the Labour administration has adopted a different tack. The ministerial priorities for 1999/2000 were:

1. to deal speedily and effectively with young offenders and to work with other agencies to reduce offending and re-offending.

2. to identify and reduce local problems of crime and disorder in partnership with local authorities, other local agencies and the public.

3. to target and reduce drug-related crime in partnership with other local agencies, via the local Drug Action Teams, in with the Government's strategy 'Tackling Drugs to Build a Better Britain'.

The government has also published aims and objectives for the police. Currently there are 3 aims:

---

[17] This figure (that 60% of total police effort is not related to crime) was suggested by (*inter alia*) Chatterton M: 'Police in Social Control' in King M.(ed.), *Control Without Custody* (Cropwood Papers 7, Cambridge Institute of Criminology, 1976). It has recently been confirmed by Audit Commission, *Helping With Enquiries* (Police Paper 12 1993), and PA Consulting Group: Diary of a Police Officer (2001) (Police Research Series Paper 149).

[18] Weatheritt M., 'Measuring Police Performance' in Reiner R. and Spencer S. (eds): *Accountable Policing* (1993), p. 24.

[19] Although those used by the Audit Commission, HM Inspectors of Constabulary and the Association of Chief Police Officers are much broader and subtler—see Weatheritt (1993): *op. cit.* Appendix p. 45.

[20] Police and Magistrates' Courts Act. s. 15, now s. 37 and 38 Police Act 1996.

[21] In a letter to Chief Constables dated December 3, 1993.

1. to promote safety and reduce disorder

2. to reduce crime and fear of crime

3. to contribute to delivering justice in a way which secures and maintains public confidence in the rule of law

They have also specified 12 objectives including reducing anti-social behaviour, reconciling conflicting rights and freedoms of the public, reducing criminality and the contribution to reducing the causes of criminality, dealing with suspects fairly, helping to meet the needs of victims and dealing transparently with police wrongdoing. Again these must be seen to fit in with the overall crime and community safety strategy introduced by the Crime and Disorder Act 1998. Complementing that will be an annual national policing plan from the Home Secretary under section 1 of the Police Reform Act 2002.

2.3 CONSTABLES AND CHIEF CONSTABLES

Who and what are police officers? Historically a constable was the holder of an unpaid and independent Crown office, recognised by the common law.[22] Nowadays in order to be a member of a police force, an officer must be attested as a constable by making a declaration in front of a justice of the peace.[23] A police authority also employs them albeit under conditions of service, which are laid down by the Home Secretary.[24]

In theory, a constable's position as an individual reflects the autonomy of the police as an organisation.[25] Officers exercise their authority and their powers independently by virtue of the common law,[26] as amended by statute.[27] Constables were historically subordinate to local magistrates—and these origins can still be seen in the fact that Commissioners in London are themselves sworn in as justices—but it would be a brave magistrate nowadays who would enter a police station and instruct the officers what to do. Neither the Police Authority nor the Home Secretary can instruct a constable on what to police or how to do it. High Court judges have restricted their scope to intervene.[28]

That independence is not reflected internally where the Chief Constables have the 'direction and control'[29] of their force and can direct their officers to undertake the tasks and activities that they consider appropriate. To fail to obey such instructions would be a disciplinary offence. As such the modern reality is that there is little independence for the constable and the 'contemporary police

---

[22] Walker N., *Policing in a Changing Constitutional Order* (2002); Lustgarten L., *The Governance of Police* (1986) Chap. 2; Jefferson T. and Grimshaw R., *Controlling the Constable* (1984).

[23] Police Act 1996, s. 29 and Sched. 4. Members of the Metropolitan and City of London forces are sworn in before the commissioner or assistant commissioner who are J.P.s in their own right by virtue of the Metropolitan Police Acts 1829 and 1856.

[24] Police Act 1996, s. 50.

[25] Police authorities are not responsible at common law for the acts of constables (*Fisher v. Oldham Corporation* (1930) 2 K.B. 364) although Chief Constables are treated as joint tortfeasors by statute (s. 88, Police Act 1996).

[26] Although such common law powers differed little from those of the private citizen—Lustgarten, *op. cit.* p. 26, fn. 5.

[27] Their powers are significantly codified in the Police and Criminal Evidence Act 1984.

[28] *R. v. Metropolitan Police Commissioner, ex parte Blackburn* (1968) 2 Q.B. 118.

[29] Police Act 1996, s. 10.

officer is less a descendant of the nineteenth century constable than a distant cousin several times removed.[30]

Once on patrol it is a different matter. An officer operates independently of direct control (except through the radio), exercises a discretion on whether to stop, search and question. Such policing is of low visibility and almost impossible to supervise.[31] But above street level, there is a tight and hierarchical chain of command, culminating in the Chief Constable. The officer's autonomy disappears and there is a military quality to policing which is seen at its extreme in the control of public disorder, when the officer works as part of a squad, directly responding to an officer's commands and where individual discretion is non-existent.

The ranks include constable, sergeant, inspector, chief inspector, superintendent, chief superintendent, assistant chief constable, deputy chief constable and chief constable[32]—there was an attempt to streamline the management structure through the Sheehy Report[33] with the removal of the ranks of chief superintendent and deputy chief constable but these ranks have now been reinstated. The old model of management involved police stations in most towns and often villages. Above them came two intermediate tiers (sub-divisions and divisions) with final control at force headquarters. Over the past few years, most forces have swept away this intermediate management. A force will be divided into policing areas (sometimes known as Base Command Units (BCUs)) under the direction of a superintendent.[34] The area is designed to be large enough to meet normal policing needs but small enough to maintain effective management control and sensitive to local community interests, an important consideration in formulating community safety plans with the local authority.[35] The superintendent will have responsibility for a devolved budget and to be immediately accountable to headquarters.

> Introducing the (B)CU reduces the need for police hierarchies by flattening police management structures. Smaller police units will maximise service delivery and, by cutting overheads, offer a more cost effective service. (B)CUs may also release resources from a traditionally centralised service and are expected, if properly resourced and made coherent in terms of service responsibility, to form the basis of a regionalised system of policing. This would offer the opportunity of reducing the overhead costs of numerous headquarters, staffs and bureaucracies. With devolved budgeting and performance measurement, a reduced number of small police headquarters could be made responsible for general policing policy and inspection supporting a large number of (B)CUs.[36]

Headquarters will form and implement force policy as well as providing specialist services beyond the resources of any area. A typical city force HQ, such as

---

[30] Lustgarten: *op. cit.* p. 29.
[31] Maguire M. and Norris C., *The Conduct and Supervision of Criminal Investigations*, Royal Commission on Criminal Justice Research Study No. 5 (1992).
[32] Police Act 1996, ss. 12 and 13—these differ in the Metropolitan force.
[33] *Inquiry into Police Responsibilities and Rewards* (1993, Cm. 2280).
[34] The BCU concept was advanced in Audit Commission: *Reviewing the Organisation of Provincial Police Forces* (Police Paper No. 9 1991); Her Majesty's Inspectorate of Constabulary (1992, *op. cit.* p. 18–19. To understand the diversity, browse police force webpages—a list is provided at www.policelaw.co.uk/.
[35] Crime and Disorder Act 1998, s. 6.
[36] Loveday B., '*Local Accountability of Police: Future Prospects*' in Reiner R. and Spencer S. (eds) (1993): *op. cit.* p. 55 at p. 63.

Manchester, has departments for corporate development and performance review which ensures quality of service and best value as well as internal inspection; community and internal affairs which deals with press relations but also handles disciplinary matters; personnel and training; crime operations which houses Special Branch and also deals with serious crime which cuts across force boundaries; administration and technical services looks after financial management, competitive tendering, procurement, estate management and transport; uniform operations which includes an air support unit, a mounted unit for crowd control, an underwater search unit, an obscene publications unit as well as a tactical support section a firearms unit; operational support has a legal section responsible for, *inter alia*, defending the Chief Constable in lawsuits, an area operations rooms which provide a computerised command and control system and a prosecutions section which deals with fixed penalty fines.

The Chief Constable[37] is the director of these services.[38] His position is quite different in kind from that of the other directors of public services such as health, welfare or education. Such directors would normally be answerable, in terms of planning and performance, initially to local authorities themselves, then to regional and national levels of management and through secretaries of state to Parliament. Contrary to this, the Chief Constable's operational control is to a large extent autonomous and does not accord to the normal principles of local democratic scrutiny or parliamentary accountability. This is extraordinary considering that a chief officer controls a large force of trained, militarily organised and armed personnel with broad legal powers. The capacity to intervene in the life of civil society is considerable and can encompass involvement in industrial disputes, scrutiny of political groups, monitoring of animal rights protesters or the surveillance and investigation of organised crime.

The statutory and constitutional position of the Chief Constable is laid down by section 10 of the Police Act 1996 where he[39] is given 'direction and control' of the police force while having regard to the local policing plan. He has the power of appointment, conditions of employment,[40] discipline and dismissal of all the constables and civilian personnel within the force. He is responsible for the operational deployment of the force and its financial management. That power is constrained as the Chief Constable is part of a tripartite system of control with the Home Secretary and the Police Authority being the other parts. But the Chief Constable is not subject to direct control by either of these. He can only be dismissed by the authority in the 'interests of efficiency or effectiveness' and only then with Home Office approval.[41]

Despite inquiries and reports,[42] the constitutional position of the police will remain anomalous in comparison to the provision of other public services. Why

---

[37] In the Metropolitan and City forces, the chief officers are known as Commissioners.

[38] For a study of modern chief constables, see Reiner R., *Chief Constables* (1991).

[39] There are now three women Chiefs—Pauline Clare in Lancashire (the first in 1995), Elizabeth Neville in Wiltshire and Jane Stichbury in Dorset. There remains discrimination against women (*Halford v. Sharples* (1992) 3 All E.R. 624) as well as unacceptable sexual harassment—see Her Majesty's Inspectorate of Constabulary, Annual Report 1998/99 (HCP 1998/99 804) which documents that in 1998/99, there were still a number of very high profile industrial tribunals relating to equal opportunities.

[40] Subject to regulations made by the Home Secretary under s. 50 of the Police Act 1996.

[41] Lustgarten: *op. cit.* pp. 75–77 but now see the procedure under s. 11 of the Police Act 1996.

[42] Audit Commission: *Police Papers* (Nos. 1–12); *Inquiry into Police Responsibilities and Rewards* (the Sheehy Report) (Cm. 2280); *Police Reform* (White Paper Cm. 2281).

do we derogate from the normal constitutional mechanisms when it comes to the police? The answer to that question lies partly in the force's history.

2.4 THE DEVELOPMENT OF THE POLICE[43]

Although the office of constable has a long history going back to Anglo-Norman times,[44] it was low status and until the nineteenth century, law enforcement such as it was remained the province of the middle and upper classes. In the countryside, the Justices of the Peace Act 1361 led to three or four justices being appointed for each county to *'restrain offenders and rioters and to arrest and chastise them according to the law.'* Generally how the law was used, against whom and when it was enforced were not matters for state initiative but for the aggrieved private citizen. This operated well within a status-based, homogeneous, essentially rural society but the transition from a feudal to a capitalist economy in the eighteenth century brought changing forms of economic organisation and wealth. The criminal justice system evolved to protect these directly through new statutory and common law offences[45] and indirectly it brought about changes of attitude towards the idea of 'property'.[46] But in terms of procedures, institutions and enforcement, the eighteenth century showed little in the way of development in the criminal justice system. One exception was Henry Fielding who, as chief magistrate for Bow Street, formed the first paid 'police' force. These Bow Street Runners were thief takers and later an armed patrol on the roads into the capital. Yet the patterns of social control were still largely centred in civil society and regulation of behaviour was frequently a personal matter, involving the propertied classes in their roles as squire or master as well as magistrate, member of the militia and sheriff. In the counties, the land-tie touched all points of existence, encompassing the worker not merely during working hours but also involving family relationships, the church, leisure and politics. The use of the criminal law, where needed, reinforced the bonds of authority and deference, bonds which themselves rested on property relationships.

The nineteenth century saw the disappearance of the local, personal and voluntary basis of law enforcement with the creation of an organised and disciplined force with responsibilities for public safety and the prevention of crime. The idea of a patrolling force with the objective of preventing crime had been taking root during the latter half of the eighteenth century in the writings and actions of men such as the Fielding brothers and Colquhoun—the latter responsible for the Dock Police, a force put on a statutory footing in 1800, the purpose of which was to prevent pilfering from the property of the West Indian sugar merchants. These practical experiments fitted in well with the utilitarian social philosophy of the time, in the writings of Bentham and the reformist ideas of the Italian, Beccaria. His ideas, expounded in 1764 in his *Essay on Crime and Punishment*, swept across Europe and influenced criminal justice reform in many countries. He argued for clear and well-publicised laws, proper procedures at

---

[43] The standard history of the police is Critchley, T. *A History of the Police in England and Wales* (1978). A more critical account might be found in Reiner, R., *The Politics of the Police* (3rd ed., 2002) or Emsley C. *The English Police* (2nd ed., 1996).

[44] Lustgarten, *op. cit.* Chap. 2; Jefferson and Grimshaw, *op. cit.* Chap. 2.

[45] Hall J., *Theft, Law and Society* (2nd ed., 1952).

[46] See Thompson, E.P., *Whigs and Hunters* (1975); Hay, D., 'Property, Authority and the Criminal Law' in Hay, D. (ed.), *Albion's Fatal Tree* (1975).

trial, proportional punishment and a humane prison system and alongside such reforms was highlighted the need for a police force with the aim of preventing and detecting crime.

What is surprising is that reform along these lines was delayed for so long—various Parliamentary committees studied proposals during the period 1770–1822 but they all opposed the creation of a police force. As the 1822 committee put it,

> '... it is difficult to reconcile an effective police force with that perfect freedom of action and exemption from interference which are the great privileges and blessings of society in this country.'

This constitutionalist and libertarian opposition remained strong, particularly among the Whigs but in 1829, Parliamentary opposition collapsed and the political acumen[47] of Peel steered the Metropolitan Police Act through Parliament with relatively little trouble.[48] The new police even survived the election of a Whig administration in 1832.

The social and economic reasons for the creation of a police force are apparent. The old techniques of social control were no longer appropriate in the new industrial towns where the propertied classes were less eager to turn out as militiamen and saw it as the government's job to protect them and their property. The contract of employment in the factory or mill counted for much less than the reciprocity of social obligations implied in the land-tie. Social control problems were exacerbated by major shifts of population from the country into the town where the early decades of the nineteenth century saw acute unemployment and poverty. While the growth of a large and flexible pool of cheap labour was of great utility for industrial capital, such a population would scarcely remain docile. Crime and disorder arising from poverty was an obvious consequence and there was also the increasing capacity of the working class to mobilise politically. Peterloo, Captain Swing, the Chartists were all clear threats to the 'social harmony' of the market place necessary for the new mode of production and for capitalist accumulation. Class conflict was much nearer the surface of everyday life.[49] State intervention in the form of police forces was a reaction to the problems of urban order but they could not be seen simply as government 'troops': police were to be seen as independent and neutral, thereby legitimating not only themselves but also the law itself. The removal of the law and the state from close identification with the capitalist class was a necessary step for the establishment of capitalist hegemony.

Outside London, the extension of the franchise in 1832 and the subsequent democratisation of the boroughs led to the Municipal Corporations Act 1835 which required 178 boroughs to form Watch Committees for the creation of police forces. Few boroughs actually did so. In 1839, the County Police Act permitted (but did not require) the formation of forces in rural areas, a move hastened by the spread of the Chartist movement. Consolidation and compulsion arrived in 1856 when Palmerston forced through the County and Borough Police

---

[47] *e.g.*, Peel had to exclude the City of London from the provisions of the Act in order to secure its passage. The City had had its own watchmen since 1663—its own police force was created in 1839.

[48] See Lyman, J., 'The Metropolitan Police Act 1829' in *Journal of Criminology, Criminal Law and Police Science* (1964) 55, p. 141.

[49] This can best be seen by reading realist novels of this period such as those by Elizabeth Gaskell, *North and South* and *Mary Barton*, both of which deal with factory life in Manchester in the 1840s.

Act, which required all areas to form a police force, and by 1857 there were some 239 forces operating in England and Wales. Apart from the Metropolitan police, which was directly accountable to the Home Office, all other forces were free of national government interference—it was the 'local state', which supervised the police. Indeed it was this element of local control that helped to reconcile the middle classes to this new phenomenon. Each force was controlled either by the Watch Committees in the towns or (after 1888) by the Joint Standing Committees in the counties.

In Victorian England, the middle classes accepted the police, not only because they controlled them through the watch committees but also because they provided useful services. Moreover it was an age that was embracing the ideology of the rule of law and the new police could be seen as a legitimate mechanism for upholding the law. Consent to policing was consent to the rule of law. This was contingent upon police practices and the police could never depend on the fact of consent. On the street and in working class areas that consent was constantly negotiated and renegotiated.[50] This carries on nowadays and can be shown in inner city disorders where for some communities with their 'accumulation of anxieties and frustrations', the police were seen as representing an establishment, which was 'insensitive to their plight'.[51]

Table 2.2 Commissions and Legislation affecting the police

Year	Report/Statute
1829	Metropolitan Police Act (creates London police force)
1835	Municipal Corporations Act (178 new boroughs required to form watch committees)
1836–39	Commission on the Rural Police
1839	Metropolitan Police Act (provides for wide-ranging police powers)
1839	County Police Act ('permits' formation of forces in rural areas)
1856	County and Borough Police Act (Palmerston's compromise—all local authorities required to create police forces)
1888	Local Government Act (gets rid of domination of JPs in shires—creates 'joint standing committees' similar to boroughs' 'watch committees; Exchequer bearing half the cost of policing)
1919	Desborough Committee Report; Police Act (prohibits police from joining a union; established Police Federation; more central guidance from Home Office)
1962	Royal Commission Report
1964	Police Act (establishes tripartite structure for policing)

[50] Storch R., 'A Plague of Blue Locusts' *International Review of Social History 20*, p. 61; Storch R. 'The Policeman as Domestic Missionary', *Journal of Social History* (1976), p. 481.
[51] Lord Scarman, *The Brixton Disorders* April 10–12, 1981, Cmnd. 8427 (1981) para. 2.36; MacPherson Report (Home Office 1999).

1994	Police and Magistrates' Courts Act establishes police authorities and updates police management. Consolidated in the Police Act 1996
1997	Police Act establishes National Criminal Intelligence Service and the National Crime Squad
2002	Police Reform Act broadens Home Secretary's powers in relation to local forces and creates new complaints machinery

The mere formation of a police force does not lead to public acceptance of them as holding legitimate authority. This has always depended on the police exhibiting various characteristics that can be seen as positive attributes or conversely as self-imposed constraints on the physical power of the state:

a) the police present themselves as independent of the state—this is linked to a convention that the government of the day does not identify itself with particular policing policies.[52] The social engineering policies of New Labour open them to the charge of 'meddling in operational policing'.[53]

b) the forces are organised on a local and decentralised model—the structure emphasises that policing arises out of the community rather than being imposed from above. There is a strong belief in local policing, shown, for example, by the continuous demands for more officers patrolling the beat. Local government has always fought to retain some say in local policing—in 1854 Palmerston had to concede defeat to deputations from the boroughs over his proposals for a more centralised force. In 1993 Michael Howard had to do the same when he proposed changes to the membership of police authorities, which would have led the chairman being chosen from 'independent' members chosen by the Home Secretary. The scheme was vigorously opposed and defeated, allowing for a majority on an authority of elected councillors.[54]

c) the police are presented as accountable to law so that police actions and decisions are reviewable by the courts.

d) the police are regarded as governed by principles of fairness, in particular being non-partisan in regard to class, gender or race.

e) the police are restricted in their capacity to interfere in everyday life because of the limits on the legal, economic and technical resources available to them.

f) the police are constrained by a doctrine of minimum force—the police are not generally armed and can only use 'reasonable force' when effecting an arrest.[55] Such a principle places the constable on the same level as the citizen.

---

[52] The significance may be seen in the police's continued resentment at the charge of being 'Maggie's boot boys' during the miners' strike of 1984–85.
[53] *Police Review*, July 12, 2002, p. 18.
[54] Such changes were suggested in the debates on Police and Magistrates' Courts Bill in 1994 and provoked opposition from two former Home Secretaries, the Conservative, Lord Whitelaw, and the Labour, Lord Callaghan.
[55] Criminal Law Act 1967, s. 3.

g) the police provide services which goes beyond the area of crime, whether in emergencies or in daily life, in helping and advising people with difficulties.

Many of these characteristics would need further description and substantial qualification in modern Britain and are discussed more fully later. But they were characteristics that led to the acceptance of the police in the nineteenth and early twentieth centuries.

Until 1908, constables worked seven days a week and their wages were similar to those of an unskilled labourer. Movements towards a police union in the nineteenth century had been unsuccessful. During the First World War, the cost of living rose, rest days were abolished and beat sizes increased. There was considerable discontent and demands for a union to negotiate on behalf of policemen—in August 1918 there was even a police strike in London. The resultant Desborough Report led to an immediate increase in pay and a recommendation that a police federation be formed which would eschew the right to strike but was designed to have a *'veneer of consultation and to impede industrial militancy'*.[56] In August 1919 a strike in support of the union was geographically more widespread but less well supported—it was a disaster for the embryonic union and the men who supported it. The Desborough reforms were incorporated into the Police Act 1919, uniform pay and conditions were introduced, the central government became responsible for half of the total cost of local policing but crucially the right to strike was taken away and the Police Federation became the representative body.

Amalgamations reduced the number of forces to 125 by 1960 but the local watch committees or joint standing committees still heavily influenced these forces. The 1950s saw criticisms about the relationship between the police and local government: there were several scandals, not least in Nottingham where the Watch Committee sought to inquire into police investigations into local government corruption.[57] This concern led to the Royal Commission[58] and the Police Act 1964. Although the Commission's Report rejected the idea of a national force and endorsed local independence, the 1964 legislation broke with the idea of the small, decentralised force. The result of subsequent rapid amalgamations was the creation of just 43 forces. The Act also introduced the tripartite system of control by which the management of police forces was shared between the Chief Constable, national government in the shape of the Home Secretary and local government represented by the Local Police Authority—the latter had a membership of JPs and councillors and was a sub-committee of the county council.

This remained the structure until 1994 when the Police and Magistrates' Courts Act introduced the modern police authority—a body corporate with independent members appointed by the Home Secretary as well as JPs and elected councillors. The links with the county authority became more tenuous. There was a genuflection towards more local involvement in the statutory duty to develop local policing objectives and plans but the Act significantly strengthened the hand of the Home Secretary who was, for example, empowered to set

---

[56] Emsley C., (1996) *op. cit.*, p. 136.
[57] *ibid.*, p. 172.
[58] For the background to the setting up of the Royal Commission, see Critchley (1979): *op. cit.* p. 270 ff.

objectives and performance targets for the police[59] and to give directions to police authorities in the event of adverse reports by the inspectorate.[60] The legislation was consolidated in the Police Act 1996 which drew together the 1964 and 1994 provisions as well the complaints and discipline provisions of the Police and Criminal Evidence Act 1984.

The Police Reform Act 2002 introduces more change, generally increasing the Home Secretary's powers over local police forces. He will now introduce an Annual National Policing Plan setting out the Government's strategic priorities for policing over the coming year and require police authorities to produce a three year strategy plan consistent with the national policing plan. He will have powers to require a police force to take remedial action (to be set out in an action plan submitted by the Police Authority to the Home Secretary) where that force is judged by HMIC to be inefficient or ineffective. There will be statutory codes of practice for chief constables. The Act also creates independent arrangements for the investigation of complaints against the police and the Independent Police Complaints Commission.

Over the past 20 years, many changes have affected the police, discussed in the next section. But one theme has been 'efficiency and effectiveness' in the police as successive governments have attempted to reduce public sector spending. For many years, this scarcely affected the police whose pay rose 41 per cent in real terms between 1979 and 1989. But the police were not to be immune from the commercial management techniques and the value-for-money assessments that affected the public sector in the 1980s. The first shot in this battle was Circular 114/1983[61] which led to considerable civilianisation of police posts so that officers could be returned to active duty. In the early 1990s the rent allowance was drastically changed; the Sheehy Report[62] proposed changes in rank structure, pay and conditions, although many of those recommendations were subsequently shelved; there have been national policing objectives and performance indicators. From April 2000, police authorities and forces themselves are expected to implement 'best value':

> a best value authority must make arrangements to secure continuous improvement in the way in which its functions are exercised, having regard to a combination of economy, efficiency and effectiveness.[63]

Another, less overt, theme is the continuing public acceptance of the police as possessing legitimate authority to patrol and intervene in everyday life. Senior police management frequently voice the opinion that communities are policed 'by consent' and the image of the avuncular British bobby still survives. 81 per cent of people believe that the police do a very or fairly good job.[64] This is higher than public confidence in any other public sector and yet that finding comes after three decades when the police have faced crisis after crisis which should have dented that public confidence. Through the last 30 years there have been many major

---

[59] Now Police Act 1996, ss. 37 and 38.
[60] *ibid*, s. 40.
[61] 'Manpower, Effectiveness and Efficiency in the Police Service' (Home Office).
[62] *op. cit.*
[63] Local Government Act 1999, s. 3.
[64] Yeo H. and Budd T., 'Policing and the Public: Findings from the 1998 British Crime Survey' (Home Office, Research and Statistics Directorate, Research Findings No. 113)—this has remained steady throughout the 1990s although it is lower than the early 1980s.

industrial disputes; inner city disturbances; disasters at football grounds; deteriorating relationships with ethnic communities and official statements that forces were institutionally racist; public protests against the council tax, the building of motorways and the export of live animals; miscarriages of justice as a result of police malpractice; public concern about deaths in custody. Most illustrate what Emsley has called the 'dark side' of police culture.[65] Despite this, there is a residual confidence in the police, which is perhaps surprising. Does it reflect a belief that those principles seen in the police by the Victorians still continue? In the absence of any written constitution, the police officer in a patrol car can still provide an everyday, physical and visible representation of constitutional values, in particular the relationship between citizen and state. Liberal society perceives itself as an aggregation of individuals with certain interests in common (mutual defence, regulation of economic and social relationships, provision of basic services) but with a belief that the collective state should interfere with the life of the individual as little as possible. Of course, state agencies intervene constantly into the life of an individual—education, health, welfare and tax. But all these agencies possess clear limits to their powers and rights of intervention and they are restrained[66] by their own specific purposes.

The constitutional significance of the police is, not least, that they may exercise the state's monopoly of physical force in civil society[67] and by its very nature police work can invade many aspects of individual lives, up to and including arrest of the person. We are inevitably more sensitive about the police than we are about the teacher or tax-collector. In their actions, police officers represent the state and thus should possess essential characteristics, which we perceive as representing good government. Any breach of those principles or constraints reflects not simply on the police but also upon the government. But it goes further than that—the police are more than another public service. They are commonly referred to as 'the law' and as such are separate from and independent of the government. Not only is the citizen subject to the rule of law, so are state officials, the state itself and the police.

So the police are the litmus paper of the nature of the state—changing from the liberal to more authoritarian or vice versa. They are also a symbol of government.[68] At its most basic, the characteristics reside in the physical image of the officer which is peculiarly evocative: the anachronistic uniform and the bike reflect the timelessness and continuity in the 'rule of law' itself and indirectly the stability and natural quality of our social order. But they also physically represent the existence of law and when the public declare their confidence in the police, they are stating their confidence in the rule of law. Fictional representations of the police have moved from the 1960s' dewy-eyed romanticism of *Dixon of Dock Green* via the 1970s' violence (but always in the right cause) of John Thaw in *The Sweeny* to the 1990s' 'warts and all' realism of *Cops*.[69] But do any of these reflect the fundamental alterations in policing over the last 20 years?

---

[65] *op. cit.*, 217.

[66] Although draconian powers can lurk in specialist legislation such as the search and seizure powers in the Customs and Excise Management Act 1979 or powers of entry for consumer protection officers.

[67] Perhaps more important in this country than in other jurisdictions such as the U.S. which recognises the citizen's right to bear arms.

[68] Arnold T., *Symbols of Government* (1962).

[69] Reiner R. '*Romantic Realism*' in Leishman F(ed.) *Core Issues in Policing* (2nd ed., 2000), p. 52.

2.5 NATIONAL OR LOCAL CONTROL?

British policing has always been part of the local state—in the boroughs, the chief officer was expected to act on the instructions of the watch committee; in the counties the justices of the peace ran their forces until 1888, after which there were 'joint standing committees' with representatives of JPs as well as elected county councillors. Moves towards greater centralisation were always resisted. Chief officers were very different animals from their modern counterparts.[70] It was a position that continued until the 1950s. But there was an emerging doctrine that constables were not the servants of the local authority. This was fuelled by the decision in *Fisher v. Oldham Corporation*.[71] It was a doctrine that suited chief officers and the Home Office, if not local authorities. In the 1950s the issue of the relationship between the police and local government was brought to a head by a series of scandals involving chief constables. In particular there was a confrontation between the chief officer and his watch committee in Nottingham where the committee sought to intervene in police investigations into local government corruption.

These concerns led to a Royal Commission.[72] The key issue was control of the police. The Report rejected the idea of a national force and endorsed local independence—although one member, Professor Goodhart, wrote a strong note of dissent,[73] pointing out that if local connection was unnecessary to preserve individual rights and if the local authority was not to have power to control the police, the logic was to create a national force. The majority recommended a tripartite system of control, which was implemented in the Police Act 1964. The Commission accepted the doctrine of constabulary independence and the subsequent legislation meant that the police authority no longer had primary responsibility for the policing of its area. The Chief Constable had 'direction and control' of the force; the authority had to 'maintain an adequate and efficient' force; the Home Secretary had supervisory but limited powers.

One of the Home Secretary's powers was that of amalgamation and the exercise of this power soon disposed of the pattern of small, decentralised forces. There were still 120 in existence in 1960 but by 1972, 43 forces were left. Although the provincial forces are still 'local', responsible to a police authority, the latter half of the century has seen a weakening of local ties, coupled with the strengthening of the roles of Chief Constable and of the Home Office. But there has been no new proposal to move towards a national force.

A national police may have been rejected but not greater centralisation. This again suited senior police management and the Home Office well, leaving the former with the benefits of operational autonomy without the interference from local councils; the latter substantially increased its 'influence'. That influence came from providing various national facilities, overseeing the inspection of forces and laying down guidelines for operational and financial management, let alone providing significant amount of police funding. The influence has been extended by Police Act 1996, which enables the Home Secretary to set national

---

[70] Emsley *op. cit.* p. 84.

[71] (1930) 2 K.B. 364—for a critique of this decision, see Walker N. *Policing in a Changing Constitutional Order* (2000) Chap. 2.

[72] The chairman was Henry Willink Q.C. For the background to the setting up of the Royal Commission, see Critchley (1979): *op. cit.* p. 270 ff.

[73] Royal Commission on the Police, *op. cit.* paras 157–79; Lustgarten, *op. cit.*, p. 51.

objectives for policing, to require performance targets to be set for measuring the achievement of those targets, to issue Codes of Practice for the performance of police authority's functions, to require reports from the authority on any matter concerning the policing of that area and to give directions to authorities following any adverse report by the inspectorate.[74] The Police Reform Act 2002 has further extended that influence.

Centralisation was also enhanced by co-operation and co-ordination between individual forces. Mutual assistance between forces was first given statutory recognition in 1890.[75] The power of a Chief Constable to provide assistance to other forces is now governed by section 24 of the Police Act 1996:

> *The chief officer of police of any police force may, on the application of the chief officer of police of any other police force, provide constables or other assistance.*

In 1972 the National Reporting Centre,[76] based in New Scotland Yard, was set up to organise the provision of mutual aid, co-ordinating the movement of constables between forces in times of emergency. It has been activated on occasions such as the prison officers' dispute of 1980–81, the inner city disturbances in 1981, the papal visit in 1982 and, most controversially, the miners' strike in 1984–85.[77] During that latter dispute, there was, at least, the appearance of co-ordination between government, Coal Board and police. It was a time that revealed how easily the police could be organised on a national basis and put under political control.[78] Although such mutual aid has the appearance of voluntary collaboration, the Home Secretary has powers to require that such assistance be given.[79]

Such mutual aid can be temporary, providing extra officers for public order duties, or permanent when personnel are seconded to regional or national specialist squads. The oldest of such squads, dating from 1965, were the regional crime squads (RCS). RCS responsibilities were to identify and arrest those responsible for serious offences that transcend force boundaries, to cooperate with regional criminal intelligence officers in generating intelligence and to assist in the investigation of serious crime, usually for a limited period.[80] Detectives from adjacent forces staff the squads. There were perhaps 1,200 officers seconded to RCS at any time. During 1995–96, the squads made 3,180 arrests, seized drugs with a street value of £252m and recovered property worth £33m.[81] Maguire and Norris[82] made the salient points that the operations of the RCS cross the normal boundaries of accountability—there was a Management Committee of Chief Constables to oversee operational activity and a committee of Police

---

[74] Police Act 1996, ss. 37–40.
[75] Police Act 1890, s. 25.
[76] Later renamed the mutual aid centre.
[77] Kettle M., '*The National Reporting Centre*' in Fine B. and Millar R. (eds), *Policing the Miners' Strike* (1985) Lustgarten, *op. cit.* p. 109; Reiner R. (1991), *op. cit.* p. 186; Uglow S., *Policing Liberal Society* (1988) p. 43.
[78] Walker N. *op. cit.* chap. 3.
[79] Police Act 1996, s. 24(2) and s. 23(5)—for a discussion of the legal basis of mutual aid, see Lustgarten, *op. cit.*, Chap. 8.
[80] The current terms of reference are set out in Home Office Circular No. 28/1987. For a discussion of RCS work, see Maguire M. and Norris C. (1992), *op. cit.*, p. 73.
[81] Timothy Kirkhope, Parliamentary Debates (HC) Standing Committee F on the Police Bill (March 4th, 1997) col. 120.
[82] *op. cit.*

Authority representatives to provide resources.[83] The squads had no independent statutory basis, having simply been established under collaborative agreements under the predecessor of section 23 of the Police Act 1996. Although forces could withdraw from such agreements, the Secretary of State can, by section 23(5), direct that a force enter into an agreement.

Part II of the Police Act 1997 set up a National Crime Squad (NCS) not merely to co-ordinate the work of the RCS but to absorb those squads into a national, although regionalised, structure, under the direction and control of a Director General. NCS will also have a Service Authority responsible for it in a similar fashion to police authorities under the Police Act of 1996. Section 48 of the Act defines the function of NCS as the prevention and detection of serious crime that is of relevance to more than one police area in England and Wales. NCS was established in its own right as an independent agency, able to employ its own staff direct and have greater operational freedom. However, NCS is not a police force, in the sense the term is used by section 2 of the Police Act 1996 and where legislation uses this term, it cannot be taken to include NCS.[84]

The 1997 legislation also set up on a statutory basis the National Crime Intelligence Service (NCIS), established on a non-statutory basis in 1992, to develop along the lines of the FBI.[85] It is an independent agency, accountable to a new service authority. NCIS is able to employ its own staff direct. As with NCS, NCIS is not a police force, in the sense the term is used by section 2 of the Police Act 1996. The need for a national intelligence unit grew from the recognition of the increasing sophistication of major criminals, of the extent of national and international co-operation between such people, and especially of their ability to exploit global financial systems to launder proceeds of crime. NCIS brought together police and Customs and Excise in order to collect, develop and analyse information up to the point at which intelligence packages could be passed on to the police or Customs for enforcement.[86]

NCIS, with staff drawn from 22 partner agencies, was one of the first services to be set up in Europe with a basic objective of helping law enforcement and other agencies, by processing and disseminating information, giving guidance and direction, and analysing major criminal activity.[87] A Director General heads it. In addition to the role at NCIS, the Director General acts as the co-ordinator for the activities of the Security Service when they act in support of the police—under the Security Service Act 1996, the security services may now function to prevent and detect serious crime. NCIS is also the international link for the police. The International division house the U.K. Europol Unit as well as the National Central Bureau of Interpol. It also manages a network of European Drugs Liaison officers and is linked up with the world-wide DLO network managed by Customs and Excise.

NCIS has taken on responsibilities over a range of crimes especially in relation to organised crime, whether regionally (Turkey and West Africa) or with respect to particular activities such as vehicle crime. There are units dealing with illegal immigration, football hooliganism, money laundering and paedophiles. It pro-

---

[83] Squads are also subject to HMI inspection.
[84] Uglow S. with Telford V., *The Police Act* (1997), chap. 2
[85] Her Majesty's Inspectorate of Constabulary (1992), *op. cit.*, p. 30.
[86] Information (including the annual reports) on NCIS can be found at *www.ncis.co.uk/*.
[87] The work of NCIS is described in the Director General's evidence to the House of Commons Home Affairs Committee in their inquiries into organised crime—HCP 1994–95/18–II 63ff.

vides intelligence on organised crime trends, threats and activity.[88] The Drugs Unit provides strategic intelligence on drugs, including reports on developing trends and on illicit laboratories.[89] The Economic Crime Unit (ECU) deals with financial disclosures and money laundering, gaming and lotteries and white-collar crime. The ECU has a financial intelligence and money-laundering sec-tion—U.K. legislation[90] requires the reporting of all suspicious financial trans-actions to NCIS, ensuring that financial regulators report under the money laundering regulations. It is estimated that the overall figure in the U.K. alone for the laundering of drug money is £2.5b and that worldwide it exceeds £500b.

NCIS and NCS are statutory bodies, which reflect a growing centralisation within the police. Collaboration and close identification with government has also come about with the strengthening role of the Association of Chief Police Officers (ACPO), who have been described as a 'focal part of the policy-making scene' and the 'vertebrae of more centrally co-ordinated policing'[91] and who are an influential lobby group on all matters of criminal justice policy.[92] Oper-ationally they have developed their own operational manuals on topics such as public order tactics or covert law enforcement techniques. These centralising tendencies reinforce the chief officer-Home Office axis at the expense of local input into policing, and this was strengthened in the 1980s by the close ideolo-gical affiliation between the police and the 'law and order' policies of the Thatcher administration. More recently that affiliation has been echoed in the managerialist approaches of senior police and of New Labour.

Despite this, local forces are anxious to maintain their own identity and their independence from both local and national government. The Home Office reci-procates this ambition—the 1993 White Paper[93] foresaw reductions in the number of forces[94] but nowhere suggests the creation of a national force. The local element was strengthened by the Police Act 1996 with its provisions for authorities to publish local policing plans, identifying policing priorities as well as granting greater autonomy from local authorities.[95] But alongside enhanced powers, the authority's local democratic identity was decreased by the appoint-ment (by the Home Secretary) of independent members, although not of the chairman. Further local input into policing came with the Crime and Disorder Act 1998 that placed a duty on local authorities to carry out crime audits and draw up community safety plans for their areas.

These reforms raise interesting questions about the shape of policing over the next decade. The new legislation not only places a duty on the local authority but also the superintendent in charge of that policing area. This delegation, allied with the financial and management responsibilities that have been devolved, means that everyday operational policing is being decentralised to the level of BCUs. One future scenario may be that regional forces will take over from local forces, just as capable as meeting the needs of the BCU and probably more efficiently. This

---

[88] For example, Threat Assessment on Serious and Organised Crime (NCIS 2000).
[89] For example, in 1998 Operation Pirate targeted amphetamine production in the north of England.
[90] See Money Laundering Regulations 1993 under the Criminal Justice Act 1993.
[91] Reiner R. (1991), *op. cit.* p. 367—see Appendix C on the history and structure of ACPO.
[92] An example is the restrictions on the right to silence incorporated in ss. 34–37 of the Criminal Justice and Public Order Act 1994.
[93] *Police Reform, op. cit.*
[94] *ibid.* Chap. 10; provisions for simplifying current arrangements for force amalgamations are contained in s. 32 of the Police Act 1996.
[95] *ibid.* Chap. 4 and s. 3 of the Police Act 1996.

would mean fewer but more powerful Chief Constables? Furthermore NCS and NCIS meanwhile develop to take over intelligence and operational work with regard to most serious and organised crime. The Home Office increasingly lays down a general strategy, which all forces are expected to follow.

2.6 POLICING STRATEGIES

For the public the predominant strategy of policing that they wish to see is the individual officer patrolling the beat. The most frequently articulated demand remains a desire to see more police on the beat. The traditional idea was that the front line was the foot patrol. But although the patrolling officer gave the public confidence, it was ineffective in preventing or detecting crime.[96] Reliance on foot patrol declined with the introduction of unit beat policing in the 1960s. When Lancashire police decided that foot patrols in the new town of Kirby had become impractical, they reorganised eleven foot beats in the town into five mobile beats patrolled by officers in cars, each supplied with personal radios to keep in touch with the station. The system was soon adopted elsewhere[97] but also evolved, using a foot patrol officer with responsibility for his area, a car covering two such beats and a station collator analysing the information collected by the patrols. Cars rather than home beat officers became used for general patrolling, although behind the wheel of a car officers were increasingly at a remove from the community. Such foot patrolling as survived, despite its importance to the public, was low status, undertaken by the younger, less experienced or less successful officers. Promotions and commendations tend not to go to beat officers[98] and the status of the ordinary constable has been reduced as 'real' policework is left to the specialist. Patrolling was never seen as a specialist function and there is little training for beat work. It is still the beat that will be denuded of manpower in order to fill gaps in other sections. The ambitious officer looks for career opportunities elsewhere,[99] to be found in specialist squads.

2.6.1 Reactivity, Fire Brigading and Specialisation

By the 1970s, policing had become increasingly reactive, responding to crime reports, usually as a result of phone calls from the public, and little attention or priority was given to crime prevention. Driven by the steep rise in reported and recorded crime, the police emphasised enforcement with consequent attention to response times and clear-up rates. This was referred to as fire brigade policing with a crime-oriented approach and a concern with the quantitative rather than the qualitative aspects of policing.[100] A modern example of this enforcement approach can be seen in zero-tolerance policing.[101]

Concern with enforcement can lead to the development of specialised squads. This development fits well with police culture, which has always stressed 'crimebusting'. Specialisation dates back to 1842 when Mayne persuaded the

[96] Morris P. and Heal K., *Crime Control and the Police* (Home Office Research Study 67) (1981).
[97] The system was recommended by the Home Office: *Police Manpower, Equipment and Efficiency* (1967); Holdaway S., *Inside the British Police* (1983) pp. 134–138; 159–163.
[98] Jones M. and Winkler J., 'Policing in a Riotous City' 9 *Jour. Law and Soc.* 103 at 110–111 (1982).
[99] Jones M., *Organisational Aspects of Police Behaviour* (1980).
[100] Johnston L., *Policing Britain* (2000) 45.
[101] discussed below.

Home Secretary to appoint officers for detective work, the origins of the Criminal Investigation Department (CID). CID itself was significantly reorganised by Howard Vincent in 1878 after a series of scandals.[102] In the 1880s the Special Irish Branch[103] was organised to deal with the Fenian campaigns and later came the most famous squad of all, the Sweeney—aka the Met's Flying Squad.

Nowadays all forces will run a series of specialist and usually centralised squads dealing with such matters as drugs, fraud, robberies, public order, child protection as well as support units—dogs, air, firearms or public order. There are obvious managerial justifications for such squads since they allow for the development of special knowledge and skills and the co-ordination of effort over a broad geographical area.

But such policies have costs especially where such activities impinge directly on BCU territory. Firstly, in public order work, local communities will experience specialist squads as more coercive and the local officer's expertise can be over-ridden and work at building up community confidence in the police can be destroyed, especially with inner city and ethnic communities.[104] Secondly the internal objectives of a squad will invariably be narrow: drugs or robbery squads will measure their performance in terms of offences cleared up and convictions obtained, a crime-centred approach which may be appropriate but when it involves aggressive searches in sensitive communities, may undo much trust-building liaison work.

There are more general dangers—concentration on detection rates can encourage officers into unethical conduct. The methods alleged against the West Midlands Serious Crimes squad included fabricated confessions, flawed identi-fication procedures, inconsistent timings and accusations of attempted bribes by the accused's solicitors.[105] Squads such as that in the West Midlands can even threaten central management by operating quasi-autonomously.[106] That auton-omy can also mean lack of proper supervision and many corruption scandals[107] have involved specialist squads. Recently improved management has apparently lessened these risks.

2.6.2 *Proactivity and Intelligence-led Policing*

Major changes in police strategy were taking place during the 1990s. These grew out of recognition within the police that the traditional models of policing were no longer effective. Police tactics had always been essentially reactive. By this it is meant that the police did not actively hunt out crime: the normal pattern of investigation would be that an offence was reported by a member of the public to the police who (resources permitting) investigated the incident and, if successful, took some form of action (caution or prosecution) against the perpetrator. Under this reactive model, the police were receivers of crime reports, recorders and resolvers of crime. But as a broad strategy, this failed to contain recorded crime,

---

[102] Emsley, *op. cit.*, 72–73.
[103] The 'Irish' was later dropped as it became known as Special branch.
[104] e.g., Operation Swamp in Brixton in 1981—Lord Scarman, *Report of Inquiry into the Red Lion Square Disorders.* Cmnd. 5919 (HMSO 1974).
[105] Kaye T., *Unsafe and Unsatisfactory* (1991) Appendix B.
[106] West Midlands Chief Constable, Geoffrey Dear, saw that the squad was beyond normal man-agement control when he disbanded it in August 1989.
[107] The preponderance of these in modern times have been in the Metropolitan force in the 1970s—Cox B., Shirley J. and Short M., *The Fall of Scotland Yard* (1977).

which has increased steadily since the war. This increase in the volume of crime was highlighted by critics of reactive policing as an argument for change—although it may be argued that any such increase is not a true measure of police performance and effectiveness but only of demand for its services.[108] Crime is discovered by the public who report offences and the police workload is thus dictated by public demand. That demand can be seen in Kent where for each day in 2001 the force received 12,400 phone calls, attended 1114 incidents, recorded 362 crimes and made 149 arrests. There has been a 74 per cent increase since 1982. Yet the police are clearing up more offences per officer than ever before.

By the early 1990s, the government was imposing both cash limits and specifying key performance indicators on police forces. Senior management realised the need for officers to be deployed in as effective a manner as possible. As a result, an increasing number of forces experimented with 'proactive' models of policing: by 'proactive' was meant:

- the identification of particular categories of offences or offenders which were identified as problematic in a particular area and,

- the use of strategic initiatives against these.[109]

Such proactivity was intelligence-led as it involved the gathering of information, the analysis of that information and of crime patterns associated with it. The purpose was the targeting of specific, 'criminally-active', individuals to monitor their activities. Such operations were undertaken to obtain evidence for a successful prosecution and might be contrasted with the 'accidental' convictions of such people for offences that happen to come to police attention. Some specialist squads, for example, dealing with drugs or robberies, had adopted such an approach for many years but this had very little part of play in the everyday work of a police area where the police still relied on the public to report crime to them.

Previously commentators[110] suggested that an analysis of police detection methods called into question the effectiveness of patrolling systems and of criminal investigation strategies. Changes in organisation or increasing the resources available to the police are unlikely to do more than marginally affect clearance rates. In other words, the police could do little about crime. But such conclusions were based on studies of marginal refinements to the traditional reactive style of police work and did not apply to the more radical approach involved in intelligence-led police work. The arguments that prevailed were:

- a strategic approach to tackling crime was required—although reactive policing is an inevitable part of police work, it is short-term and prevents developing priorities.

- a broader, multi-agency, philosophy of policing, which sets out to prevent and disrupt criminal activity, was preferable to a narrow view of police work in terms of detection and prosecution.

---

[108] Audit Commission: *Helping With Enquiries: Tackling Crime Effectively* (Police Paper 12, 1993) p. 31.
[109] e.g. Operation Bumblebee against burglary in the Metropolitan police force area. See Amey P., Hale C. and Uglow S., *Development and Evaluation of a Crime Management Model* (Home Office, Police Research Series 18, 1996).
[110] Morris P. and Heal K., *Crime Control and the Police* (Home Office Research Study No. 67) (1981).

- reactive policing is 'victim friendly' and resource-intensive—the emphasis is detection of the particular offence. While the number of crime reports remains low and resources remain high, this is effective but as demand increases and resources fail to keep pace, time devoted to any case falls. Inevitably there are fewer detected cases and victim-satisfaction is reduced. If the police try to react to all crime reports, this involves wasteful use of resources.[111]

As crime reports become more numerous, the weaknesses of reactivity emerge—instead of dealing with all crimes, only some crimes can be allocated time. These would include the obviously serious (HOLMES inquiries[112]) and perhaps the easily-resolved but elsewhere there are no means of identifying which categories of offence should be given priority because there are no links with the community, no internal procedures, no crime management system and no systematic storage or analysis of intelligence.

The large increases in the volume of recorded crime in the early 1990s allied to public dissatisfaction led to local experiments in setting policing priorities and allocating resources. The strategy adopted was that of giving greater emphasis to proactive, intelligence-based approaches. For local forces, in outline this involved:

- a crime management system—only certain offences would receive visits from investigating officers. Other crime reports would be subject to telephone investigation or simply recorded.

- local management would set intelligence targets for an area—normally particular individuals who were considered to be criminally active or perhaps specific offences which were prevalent.

- units within areas would develop intelligence packages for action.

- specialist squads would be established to pursue these. All officers would be encouraged to contribute to developing intelligence.

This is a strategic approach to crime and requires an integrated package of measures, often on a multi-agency level. It relies heavily on the cultivation of informants, surveillance and undercover work by officers generally, which creates issues of accountability and the risk of corruption.[113] There is now a *Code of Practice on Covert Law Enforcement Techniques*, issued by ACPO. There is now a National Intelligence Model,[114] which has been developed by NCIS and which forces around the country are expected to adopt.

2.6.3 *Community Policing and POP*

In the 1970s the antithesis to reactive policing was being introduced in Devon and Cornwall as 'community policing'[115] by Chief Constable John Alderson. It was a concept that gave greater priority to crime prevention and community

---

[111] Audit Commission: *op. cit.*, Exhibit 15 'Response to Burglary' at p. 22.
[112] An acronym for Home Office Large Major Enquiry System.
[113] Johnston, *op. cit.*, 56ff.
[114] *www.ncis.gov.uk/nim.asp*.
[115] Alderson J., *Policing Freedom* (1979).

safety and to a multi-agency approach to issues. Such programmes will usually include community constables, community liaison officers, schools liaison, youth programmes, consultative committees, crime prevention initiatives, neighbourhood watch and some increase in foot patrol.[116] Many of these elements may be seen within the current crime and disorder strategy of the Labour government with its emphasis on crime prevention, expanding local authorities' responsibility for community safety, work with communities as well as fostering multi-agency approaches to social problems.

Such a strategy assumes that response to crime should not be a matter only for the state and the police and that within communities there is a capacity for self-regulation through informal networks and techniques. Yet community policing remains police-led and there remains the dangers attached to the deeper penetration of civil society by the state, let alone the emergence of 'local police states'. Johnston has pointed to[117] the dangers of treating communities, nostalgically, as embodiments of collective sentiments. Instead there is a diversity of modern communities, not simply geographically situated but communities that are tied together by moral choices, life style, ethnicity, sexual orientation, or even contractually. Diverse communities require diverse policing, increasingly based on accurate assessment of risk.

Problem-oriented policing (POP) is a development of the ideas that inform community policing.[118] As officers are routinely deployed to deal with the same problem in the same area, there is recognition that it would be more effective to tackle the roots of the underlying problem and, if not to eliminate it, to minimise its effects. Originally referred to as situational crime prevention, POP deploys dedicated officers to specific areas to devise proactive responses to problems. POP encourages officers to spot problems using their knowledge but other data, to analyse the characteristics and causes, to work with the community to devise a solution and also to evaluate the response to see if it worked and whether lessons can be learned. It builds upon the experience of the patrolling officer to understand local problems and to devise solutions. This necessarily involves the active involvement of the community and other agencies.

POP is clearly a move away from reactive policing and, in recognising that resources must be targeted towards identified problems, embraces much of proactive thinking.[119] An interesting example illustrating some of these ideas was the West Midlands whose 21 BCUs have developed a sector policing model, with uniformed constables taking personal responsibility for local areas known as 'microbeats'. This allowed them to work closely with communities, local authorities and other agencies to tackle local problems. It crucially differs from intelligence-led policing as it adopts a bottom-up approach with patrolling officers identifying problems and producing solutions. This is unlike the top-down system of many crime-management models where both issues and strategies are dictated by middle managers.

---

[116] Bennett T., 'Some Recent Developments in Community Policing' in Stephens M and Becker S. (eds) *Police Force, Police Service* (1994) 107–129.

[117] *op. cit.*, 53–56.

[118] see www.lancashire.police.uk/pop.html—other forces to embrace POP include Surrey and Thames Valley.

[119] Leigh A., Read T. and Tilley N., *Problem-Oriented Policing: Brit Pop* (Home Office Crime Detection and Prevention Series 75, 1996).

2.6.4 *Zero-tolerance Policing*

Zero-tolerance policing (ZTP) was very much an import from experiments in New York—an approach that encourages officers not to tolerate even the most minor offence. The belief is that, by re-establishing control on the streets of minor matters, the 'spiral of community decline'[120] can be arrested and the police will be better placed to make inroads into major offences. The thesis goes that visible signs of decay such as litter, broken windows, graffiti, abandoned housing signals public disinterest. Fear of crime is greatest in these neighbourhoods, which prompts 'respectable' community members to leave. This undermines the community's ability to maintain order and decline follows. Reasoning that it is easier to prevent a neighbourhood's slide into crime than trying to rescue it, the theory demands that even minor misdemeanours must be pursued with the same vigour as serious crimes.

Cleveland police were the first to adopt the strategy in 1996. Such an approach appears to stress enforcement of the criminal law and is very reactive. For the public, it is popular as the police are seen to be dealing with 'quality of life' issues. But for police managers, ZTP may also be part of a proactive strategy so that it may be linked with information-gathering activities and intelligence-led policing. It can also sit alongside POP so that the ZTP represents metaphorically a clearing of the undergrowth within an area to enable the police identify the true problems and ultimately to re-impose their authority.

Figures from New York suggest that ZTP is effective in reducing crime but there may be other reasons for this—crime has also fallen in areas without zero tolerance policing. There are negative consequences of aggressive policing with accusations of heavy-handedness by police. The long-term effects are unknown. It works well in densely populated areas with high policing levels and large amounts of petty crime. But where the population is dispersed or the crime rate is low, it may have little effect. Furthermore, in areas of high racial tension, the policy might leave locals feeling victimised, as ZTP is a strategy in which the law is enforced on behalf of some community interests against others.

2.7 THE POLICE USE OF FORCE

The constable's unarmed status was part of Peel's campaign to separate his police from the military, representing the prohibition on the arbitrary use of force by the state. Historically weapons such as truncheons and sabres for mounted police were issued even for Peel's police. In 1884, the Metropolitan Police, after the murders of two constables, were given permission from the Commissioner, to carry revolvers during uniformed night patrols. These were called 'Comforters' and each officer would make up their own mind if they wished to carry them. This remained the case until 1936 when the revolvers were taken off the constables and kept locked in a cupboard back at the station. In London and elsewhere, the police themselves had a stock of firearms,[121] although often it would be the army who were called in to control crowds.[122] Police stations would only

---

[120] Johnston *op. cit.*, 63.
[121] Lee Enfields were used in the siege of Sydney Street in 1911.
[122] In the miners' strikes of 1910 and 1911, there were fatal shootings by soldiers at Tonypandy and Llanelli. In 1980 the SAS were used to end the Iranian Embassy Siege.

have a limited stock of weapons, issued rarely. Even the most minor assault alleged against a police officer might provoke parliamentary attention.[123]

Over the last thirty years, that position has changed and there have been a number of incidents which have suggested that the police had redefined the threshold of 'minimum force': in 1973, the Special Patrol Group shot dead two Pakistani youths holding hostages with artificial firearms in India House; in April 1979 the same unit was responsible for the death of Blair Peach in Southall;[124] 1983 saw the shooting of Stephen Waldorf in London, mistaken for an armed and dangerous criminal while five year old John Shorthouse was shot by officers on a 'routine' house search in the West Midlands; in 1985, there was the accidental shooting of Cherry Groce in Brixton and in the same year Mrs Cynthia Jarrett died of a heart attack during a police search of her home at Broadwater Farm, both factors in subsequent riots in North London. In 1999, Harry Stanley, a 46-year-old Scottish painter and decorator and father of three, collected a table leg from one of his brothers who had fixed it after it had been damaged earlier in the year. The police were telephoned by a man who said that a man with an Irish accent was leaving the pub with a sawn-off shotgun in a plastic bag. Within a few minutes an armed response unit from the Metropolitan Police service specialist firearms unit SO 19 had shot him dead. Nobody was prosecuted or disciplined. Figures from *Inquest*[125] suggest that between 1990–2001, 27 people died as a result of being shot by the police, under 5 per cent of all deaths in police custody.

In the late 1980s, there was a change of policy, away from increasing the numbers of officers who were 'authorised shots' and away from the increasing regularity with which ordinary divisional officers were issued with firearms. The Home Office encouraged forces to set up specialist tactical firearm units such as D11, the Blue Berets of the Metropolitan force,[126] although other units such as those on royal and diplomatic protection duty and tactical support units are still routinely armed.[127] The Met's Force Firearms Unit is now known as SO19— since 1991, there have been 'armed response units' and with 3 uniformed officers who have been selected and trained to stabilise and control armed incidents, stop and search suspects, their vehicles and to search premises for armed suspects. All these officers are personally armed with Glock 17 self-loading pistols and two of the officers have access to 'Heckler and Koch' MP5 carbines. In 1999, they were deployed 1,440 times on incidents involving firearms.

A provincial force such as Surrey has 70 officers who are trained in the use of firearms. Some carry out protection and containment duties. The others are members of the Tactical Firearms Unit who have received more specialised training and are used in serious and lengthy incidents. The Force can respond to incidents involving firearms 24 hours a day by having trained officers on-call for Armed Response Vehicle (ARV) duties.

Police in Britain still use firearms rarely in comparison with any other country.

---

[123] Critchley: *op. cit.*, pp. 273–274; Waddington P.A.J. *The Strong Arm of the Law, Armed and Public Order Policing*, (1991).

[124] Dummett M., *Southall April 23, 1979* (1980).

[125] An organisation that monitors deaths in police and prison custody—www.gn.apc.org/inquest/. See Table 2.3.

[126] Judging from TV documentaries (*Police*, BBC 1982; *Scotland Yard*,—Carlton 1993), the tactics for such units involve saturation of an area regardless of the level of risk. Only when all risk has gone are weapons holstered!

[127] Many forces that have responsibilities for patrolling motorways are likely to have an armed patrol vehicle operating at all times.

Table 2.3 Deaths in Police Custody 1990–date (England & Wales)[128]

Force	Type	1990	1991	1992	1993	1994	1995	1996	1997	1998	1999	2000	2001	Total
Metropolitan Police	Custody	19	24	15	18	16	9	20	15	13	13	5	9	179
	Pursuit	N/A	N/A	N/A	N/A	N/A	1	0	1	3	0	2	1	8
	RTA	1	N/A	N/A	N/A	N/A	N/A	1	3	1	0	0	1	7
	Shooting	0	0	1	2	0	1	1	0	0	1	1	2	9
Other Forces	Custody	40	36	32	18	36	36	33	43	52	31	30	25	412
	Pursuit	N/A	N/A	N/A	N/A	1	1	9	16	7	7	22	24	87
	RTA	0	1	1	0	0	0	4	5	5	5	4	8	33
	Shooting	2	3	2	1	1	1	1	0	2	2	1	2	18
All Forces	Custody	59	60	47	36	52	48	53	58	65	44	35	34	591
	Shooting	2	3	3	3	1	2	2	0	2	3	2	4	27

128 Source: INQUEST monitoring—figures last updated February 26, 2002 (www.gn.apc.org/inquest/).

Although police firearms were deployed in 11,842 operations during 1997–98, the number of incidents where they were fired was only five. In 1998–99 weapons were fired in nine incidents. Any police shooting receives close media attention and the police continue to experiment with interventions that are non-lethal and which represent a middle way between batons and firearms such as CS gas, pepper sprays or tranquilliser guns. For example, the *Taser*[128] looks similar to a pistol. It fires two probes simultaneously that trail electric cable back to the taser. These can be fired from a distance of 21 ft, and when the probes make contact with the target they transmit 50,000-volt electrical pulses along the wires and into the body of the target. This causes an uncontrollable contraction of the muscle tissue, thereby knocking the target to the floor. Police in Northamptonshire have already begun researching the weapon.[129]

There are circumstances where the police need credible means of countering threats. The use of weapons presents them with a problem of balancing human considerations as well as judicial and societal requirements. No matter what the incident is, an officer is expected to protect innocent people, himself or herself, and to cause no more harm than is justifiable and unavoidable. Denying legitimate use, as well as allowing uncontrolled use, may lead to unnecessary injuries and deaths. Technology is offering interesting possibilities but new weapons often *appear to be* rather than *are* safe. Their very availability can lower the threshold at which officers are willing to use force, change the strategic thinking of police management and alter the basis of the police's relationship with the community.

2.7.1 *The Defence of Necessary Force*

'Minimum force' is no longer interpreted as the last resort, defensive response. Instead the interpretation is in accord with the concept of self-defence in the criminal law, which accepts that people are justified in reacting if they believe that they are in imminent danger and that their response is reasonably proportional to that danger. Armed police need not wait to be attacked before responding nor do they have to have objectively reasonable grounds that they are in imminent danger, although they must have an 'honest belief' that this is the case. At common law, the officer would be protected from prosecution because of the defence of self-defence but there is also a statutory defence under section 3 of the Criminal Law Act 1967: '... *a person may use such force as is reasonable in the circumstances in the prevention of crime*...' This would operate either where an officer was under attack or where he or she was effecting an arrest. The force used must be necessary and the response proportional. The key point in domestic law is that it is the officer's belief as to the imminence of the attack that is central—if officers make a mistake and believe that they are under attack when they are not, the defence of self-defence is still available,[131] whether there are reasonable and objective grounds for that belief or not.

How does this fit with the European Convention, especially Article 2 which protects the right to life? This provision foresees that there will be deprivation of life under certain circumstances but the state should only use lethal force only where it is absolutely necessary, and strictly proportionate. Such force can only

---

[128] www.airtaser.com.
[129] See Bradford Non-Lethal Weapons Project Report No. 3, www.brad.ac.uk/acad/nlw/index.html.
[131] *Gladstone Williams* (1984). 78 Crim. App. Rep. 276.

be used in one of three situations, namely in defence of any person from unlawful violence, in order to effect a lawful arrest or to prevent the escape of a person lawfully detained or in an action lawfully taken for the purpose of quelling a riot or insurrection

In *McCann v. UK*[132] three suspected IRA terrorists were shot dead in Gibraltar by security forces. By a majority of 10–9, the Court held that the U.K. had violated their right to life. In *Andronicou v. Cyprus*[133] security forces stormed a flat where there had been a domestic assault and where a man with a shotgun was holding a young woman. Both were killed. In this case, by a majority of 5–4, the Court held that Article 2 was not violated. In both cases, however, the Court agreed,

> 'that the use of force by agents of the State in pursuit of one of the aims delineated in paragraph 2 of Article 2 of the Convention may be justified under this provision where it is based on an honest belief which is perceived, for good reasons, to be valid at the time but which subsequently turns out to be mistaken. To hold otherwise would be to impose an unrealistic burden on the State and its law-enforcement personnel in the execution of their duty, perhaps to the detriment of their lives and those of others'[134]

The Court talks of the soldiers' 'honest belief ... for good reasons'. This raises questions about the boundaries of self-defence as it suggests an objective test of the necessity criterion and runs counter to the principle stated in *Gladstone Williams*.[135] If U.K. courts follow the Strasbourg principle, that latter decision will need to be reconsidered in relation to ordinary criminal cases where the defence is raised. In addition, when the police use force to make arrests, that force must be absolutely necessary and strictly proportionate to the threat faced, judged by what an objective observer would have seen as necessary and proportionate in such circumstances. But the Court's main thrust was towards the State's planning, organisation and control of such operations,

> 'The Court's sole concern must be to evaluate whether in the circumstances the planning and control of the rescue operation including the decision to deploy the (security force) officers showed that the authorities had taken appropriate care to ensure that any risk to the lives of the couple had been minimised and that they were not negligent in their choice of action.'[136]

In *Andronicou* the Court held, possibly bizarrely on the facts of the case, that sufficient care had been taken and the risk minimised. In *McCann*, they came to the opposite conclusion.

> 'Although detailed investigation at the inquest into the training received by the soldiers was prevented by the public interest certificates which had been issued, it is not clear whether they had been trained or instructed to assess whether the use of firearms to wound their targets may have been warranted by the specific circumstances that confronted them at the moment of arrest. Their reflex action in this vital respect lacks the degree of caution in the use of firearms to be expected from law enforcement personnel in a democratic society, even when dealing with dangerous terrorist suspects, and stands

---

[132] *Application No. 18984/91*, 21 E.H.R.R. 97 (1996).
[133] *Application No. 25052/94*, 25 E.H.R.R. 491, [1998] Crim. L.R. 823 (1998).
[134] McCann at para. 200; quoted with approval in Andronicou at para. 192.
[135] *supra*.
[136] Andronicou at para. 181.

in marked contrast to the standard of care reflected in the instructions in the use of firearms by the police which had been drawn to their attention and which emphasised the legal responsibilities of the individual officer in the light of conditions prevailing at the moment of engagement.'[137]

This ruling contains implications for senior police management who provide guidelines for the use of force or who are responsible for training officers to deal with, for example, hostage situations or who are in charge of the policing of such incidents. For the officers immediately concerned there would be no violation of Article 2 where fatal force is used, as long as the officers were acting on a belief in circumstances that they reasonably believed to exist—information passed to them by control rooms would come within that category. Senior management may face homicide prosecutions where the training, planning and control is deficient and there was not appropriate care to ensure that any risk to the lives had been minimised.

In particular this applies to public order situations—again Article 2 specifically refers to the justifiability of using force in a riot or insurrection. The same principles would apply—the individual officer who acts on reasonable, albeit mistaken, beliefs would have a defence to subsequent charges. But senior management would need to show that the correct procedures had been in place for training officers in crowd control techniques, for planning and controlling the particular operation and for minimising the risk to life.

2.8 PUBLIC ORDER

The use of force is also a central problem in policing crowds and public order situations. The management of demonstrations, processions or industrial action is one of the more perennial, visible but intractable problems facing the police and the government. The mishandling of public protests can have political repercussions for an administration but can also affect the police's relationship with the community. Police forces have traditionally viewed public demonstrations as unnecessary and 'quasi-unlawful', regarding the constitutional institutions as sufficient mechanisms for the expression of dissent. Protest marches and meetings would be broken up, arrests would be made and prosecutions would follow. Police forces are now more likely to talk of the need to control such events '*in an even-handed manner and seek to defuse situations likely to deteriorate into violence, ensuring public safety and minimising disruption to the public.*' This change of attitude may have been triggered in the 1990s by the middle classes taking to the streets to protest about environmental issues, animal rights or the freedom to hunt with dogs. It was certainly reinforced by the passage of the Human Rights Act 1998 so that public authorities such as police forces were obliged to act to protect European Convention rights such as the Article 10 right to expression and the Article 11 right to freedom of assembly. This is illustrated in *Steel v. U.K.*[138] where the police arrested people handing out leaflets and holding banners at a 'Fighter Helicopter' conference in London, detaining them and later releasing them without charge. This would have passed without notice in domestic courts since officers had the power to arrest when they apprehended a breach of the peace but the European Court held that the officers,

---

[137] McCann at para. 212.
[138] *Application No. 24838/94*, 28 E.H.R.R. 603(1998), [1998] Crim. L.R. 893 (1998).

in forming their beliefs about a potential breach of the peace, should have given due weight to the applicants' rights to freedom of expression under Article 10 and of peaceful assembly under Article 11. Any interference with a person's rights must be a necessary and proportionate response to the apprehension of disorder or suspicion of crime.

Such a balancing act has to be a function of senior police management—it can scarcely be delegated to a constable to make *ad hoc* decisions. Where the protest is organised,[139] senior officers must recognise the legitimacy of collective freedom of expression and emphasise working in partnership with the community and event organisers to ensure that they pass off peacefully and minimise the opportunities for confrontation. This is echoed by the HMIC whose thematic report on the issues[140] lays down a three stage process of, first, assessing the risk by considering indicators of tension such as hostility on routine work, incidents within the community and by using intelligence; second, of minimising and managing the event by early pre-emptive action in partnership with other parties—decisions can be taken as to the size and nature of the police presence as to whether the event requires a few uniformed officers or full public order kit with others held in reserve; and third, of responding to disorder when the first two are insufficient. The police must ensure that the protestors can make their point, that participants and bystanders are safe and that disruption to other people is minimised.

Senior management and politicians seek to portray the police as neutral in these situations—this is not difficult where a town's population turns out to protest at the closure of the local hospital and is marshalled by officers sympathetic to their cause. That homogeneity of interests is not always present. The law itself is not neutral in social conflict and the police are present to enforce that law. It is harder to convince protestors or even crowds that the police are acting neutrally—several years ago, there was the Pavarotti concert in Hyde Park with quarter of a million people. If the same people had been in the same place at the same time with techno music at the same volume, it would have been an illegal rave under the Criminal Justice and Public Order Act 1994 since it contained music 'wholly or predominantly characterised by a succession of repetitive beats'. Quite possibly police would have broken it up. The law embodies certain 'values', which the police must enforce. In this case the 'value' is just snobbery; opera is *real* music, techno isn't. The distinction is as ludicrous as if the Home Secretary had sent the police in to break up Beatles gigs in the 60s.[141] These issues become more fraught, if not more complex, where the crowd itself is polarised between, for example, the British National Party and anti-fascist demonstrators. The police cannot choose not to enforce the law: this has been dramatically illustrated by the Orange Order parades in Northern Ireland in recent years, especially the problems at Drumcree.[142]

Sometimes the law itself is not neutral. But the legal powers under which a march may be banned or its timing or route altered are without exception open-textured—for example, what constitutes 'reasonable' apprehension of disorder? Discretionary powers such as this will inevitably attract accusations of bias on

---

[139] As opposed to spontaneous and often violent disorder such as the race riots in northern cities in summer 2001.

[140] HMIC Thematic Report. *Keeping the Peace* (1999).

[141] I am in debt to 'Merrick' at home.freeuk.com/rooted/policing.html.

[142] See the report of the Independent Commission on *Policing in Northern Ireland* (1999) especially Chap. 9—www.belfast.org.uk/report.htm.

the part of the police. The House of Lords has recently identified the balancing act, which the police need to adopt in exercising this discretion: animal rights protestors sought to prevent the export of live animals from the Sussex port of Shoreham. It took a large number of police officers to ensure that the company, International Trader's Ferry Ltd, could continue to operate. The Chief Constable sought to restrict police protection to two days a week and for no more than ten lorries. ITF challenged this and the Lords held that neither the right to trade lawfully nor the right to protest lawfully was absolute—the police had to balance one against the other and in doing this, the Chief Constable was entitled to exercise a margin of discretion. The police could also take into account the resources available, and the other demands on police time.[143]

Demonstrations and protests may centre on national or international issues, and governments can bring pressure on police operational decisions—the National Reporting Centre,[144] based in New Scotland Yard, was set up to organise the provision of mutual aid, coordinating the movement of constables between forces in times of emergency. Its most controversial role was during the miners' strike in 1984–85[145] when it was revealed how easily the police could be organised on a national basis and put under political control.[146]

'The NUM, supported by the Labour Party, accused the police of intervening in the strike on the orders of the Thatcher government, and indeed there is evidence that the Premier, Home Secretary Leon Brittan, and other ministers in the cabinet committee that was coordinating the government's response, were directly involved in giving instructions to chief police officers. Paradoxically, throughout the strike, Sir Ian Mac-Gregor, the American chairman of the National Coal Board, was complaining to Thatcher that the strike was 'between men who want to work and a bunch of thugs, yet the police seem to want to keep out of it'. He claimed that it was after he had spoken to Thatcher that the police were ordered to activate the National Reporting Centre, and revealed what many senior officers of the time had always suspected; that it was Government policy not to use its own Industrial Relations Act to seek civil remedies against the NUM, but to rely on the police to enforce the criminal law.'[147]

Public protest frequently brings demonstrators into confrontation with the state. In other jurisdictions, decisions about the conditions under which marches and assemblies can take place are removed from the police and the government— the Parades Commission in Northern Ireland is an example.[148] In this country, those powers are vested in the police, particularly under the Public Order Act 1986,

- section 11 imposes a duty upon organisers of marches to inform the police.

- section 12 allows the police to impose conditions (*e.g.*, to change the timings or the route) where the event involves serious disruption to community life.

- section 13 allows the police to issue banning orders.

[143] R. v. Chief Constable of Sussex, ex parte International Trader's Ferry Ltd [1999] 1 All E. R. 129.
[144] Later renamed the mutual aid co-ordination centre.
[145] Kettle M., 'The National Reporting Centre' in Fine B. and Millar R. (eds), *Policing the Miners' Strike* (Lawrence and Wishart, 1985) Lustgarten, *op. cit.*, p. 109; Reiner R., (1991): *op. cit.*, p. 186; Uglow S., *Policing Liberal Society* (1988) p. 43.
[146] Walker N., *op. cit.*, Chap. 3.
[147] Judge T., Orgreave 1984. *Police Magazine*, March 2002.
[148] www.paradescommission.org/.

These are supplemented by other powers, especially under the Criminal Justice and Public Order Act 1994—section 60 empowers a superintendent, believing that serious violence is likely in an area, to authorise officers to stop and search regardless of whether there are reasonable grounds for that search in any individual case; section 65 permits an officer to stop anyone on their way to a 'rave' and direct them not to proceed; section 71 gives similar powers in relation to trespassory assemblies.

The police necessarily occupy an ambivalent and difficult position when making decisions regarding public order. Less problematic have been the changes in equipment, organisation, training and tactics employed by the police since the1980s. For some commentators, these changes symbolise a growing authoritarianism in the state. Others would argue that these represent a growing realism when the police were likely to be faced not just with projectiles but firearms and petrol bombs. The paramilitary appearance of a modern PSU (Police Support Unit) can be contrasted with the decades after the end of the First World War, when the police first took over responsibility for public order from the military.[149] That led to a marked decline in violent confrontation.[150] Unlike the soldier, constables were trained to operate independently and to enforce the law on their own responsibility. The unarmed constable required a flexible approach, working to defuse situations rather than relying on defensive equipment or firepower. Crowds responded in kind: *'[disputes] were characterised by order rather than disorder. On the whole, strikers refrained from rioting, destroying property and even ... violent picketing'*[151] A certain constitutionalism evolved in which violence was rare, police intervention minimal and although the legal basis of marching and assembly was obscure, the right to do so within a political consensus seemed well established.

That consensus disappeared in the early 1970s when there was a re-assessment of public order strategy following the mass picketing that led to the closure of a coking works at Saltley in 1972 by striking miners. There was a radical overhaul of the training and equipping of officers to deal with the numerous industrial disputes, which took place over the next two decades. Nowadays all forces have a proportion of officers trained in crowd control techniques—the West Midlands training course specifies that in any operational command unit, all uniformed inspectors, 50 per cent of the sergeants and between 63 and 105 constables should have received such training. The training encompasses foot manoeuvres and shield tactics, deployment from vehicles, closed space tactics and how to deal with petrol bombs.[152] The officers themselves are trained to act in concert on command, either defensively with long shields or offensively with round shields, baton rounds and water cannon. They operate in squads in a military fashion, a far cry from the notion of the 'independent office holder' or the 'citizen in uniform'. Although such officers will be on normal duties, PSUs can be mobilised rapidly to deal with disorder either within their own force boundaries or for adjacent forces. This latter function is under the mutual aid provisions of the Police Act 1996.[153] Thus there is a capacity to mobilise large numbers of officers

---

[149] The army were still used to quash strikes by miners in South Wales in 1911.

[150] This is charted in industrial disputes by Geary R., *Policing Industrial Disputes* (1985).

[151] Geary, *op. cit.*, p. 66.

[152] The Met have entered into a PFI agreement in 2001 for a state of the art firearms and public order training complex at Gravesend in Kent—the cost will be £55m.

[153] s. 24.

to confront strikers or demonstrators[154] and to prevent a demonstration from taking a particular route or workers from closing a particular plant.

ACPO have also developed a Guide for Public Order Policing.[155] They prescribe a public order command structure for large-scale public disorder, for example where there is serious rioting over a period. Police managers are designated either bronze (leading the front line teams), or silver (co-ordinating the tactical response and required to deliver the overall strategy) or gold (sets the overall strategy and is in overall command). Some forces operate with fully equipped control rooms with communications, briefing facilities and mapping and plotting aides. Other forces, with fewer incidents to deal, make do with less sophisticated facilities.

Other countries have adopted a third force approach—a group between the ordinary police and the army. In France this is the Compagnies Républicaines de Sécurité[156] or CRS, a permanent force employing 14,000 people. Along with public order, they are also involved in port and airport security as well as diplomatic protection. The Dutch, on the other hand, retreated in the 1980s to a decentralised approach. Similarly the British police have no such large mobile reserve. Forces do supplement the PSU strategy by relatively small, specialist, public order squads, able to be moved quickly to the scene of any disturbance. The first of these, set up in 1965, was the Metropolitan Force's Special Patrol Group, replaced and renamed in 1987 as the Territorial Support Group. The history of such units has not been uncontroversial[157]—the Scarman Report[158] is a detailed account of the SPG operations against street robberies in Lambeth especially in 1981. Codenamed SWAMP '81, the aggressive and confrontational policing used arbitrary roadblocks, stopping and searching of pedestrians and mass detention—there were 943 stops, 118 arrests and 75 charges, only one of which was for robbery. It left police-community relations in a shambles and had little if any effect on crime figures.

Despite this history, these units exist in the majority of forces and are on permanent standby with their Transit vans containing weaponry and riot gear. In the West Midlands, the unit is known as the Operational Support Unit (OSU) whose main role is to provide a reserve of officers to respond quickly at times of public disorder. The unit also has specialist training in searching crime scenes— for example, fingertip searches; house-to-house enquiries relating to serious incidents; searching for drugs; helping at pre-planned events.

2.9 HIGH TECHNOLOGY AND POLICE WORK[159]

The impact of a range of technologies in police work is less visible than policing

---

[154] At Orgreave on May 29, 1984 there were 1,700 officers from 13 different forces confronting 1,500 pickets. For the May Day demonstrations in 2002, there were some 5,000 officers on the streets of London or held in reserve.

[155] This is still mainly confidential—the HMIC Thematic Report (1999) considered that the tactics did not take account of newer forms of protest adopted by groups such as environmental protestors.

[156] www.interieur.gouv.fr/rubriques/c/c3_police_nationale/c33_organisation/Service_central_des_compagnies _republicaines_de_securite.

[157] Dummett M. (1980), *op. cit.*, Lord Scarman: *Report of Inquiry into the Red Lion Square Disorders*, Cmnd. 5919 (1974); generally Brake and Hale (1992): *op. cit.*, p. 46ff.

[158] Scarman (1981), *op. cit.*

[159] Manwaring-White S., *The Policing Revolution* (1983) Chap. 4; Bunyan T, (1977) *op cit.*, Uglow S., op. cit. (1988) Chap. 6.

the streets but equally important. The means of gathering information has expanded: telephone calls can be easily monitored; video cameras are commonplace in many public areas;[160] on major roads where number plates can be scanned and recorded.[161] Storage and retrieval of information through computerisation has changed the police job with the policeman on the beat having access to a range of local and national police databases. Pro-active and intelligence-led policing means an increase in the use of informants and of intelligence and this requires the establishment and manipulation of sophisticated databases, of software for crime pattern analysis, linked to geographic information systems.

The managerial needs for new technology are undoubted, in areas of communications, management of information, activity analysis and resource management. As the police strategy moves to a more proactive approach, information technology plays a critical role. The Home Office have been providing centralised information technology services for police for many years. Under section 57 of the Police Act 1996[162] the Secretary of State has power to provide or maintain such organisations, facilities and services that he or she considers necessary or expedient for promoting the efficiency and effectiveness of the police. But there have been problems for many years in IT provision—the autonomy of chief constables has meant that local forces have undertaken their own IT development. The lack of a national strategy has resulted in the incompatibility of police forces' hardware, let alone software, and the duplication of IT initiatives. With compelling economic and operational reasons for central provision of IT, the police information technology organisation (PITO) was set up on a statutory basis under the Police Act 1997.[163] Its management consists of a governing body with representatives of ACPO and police authorities. Some of its projects include:

- Airwave is set to be the first digital national radio communication service designed for police forces. It will give guaranteed coverage, better voice quality as speech is digitally coded to minimise the effect of background noise on speech quality. The handsets will link directly to the regular telephone system and there can be encryption for all transmissions. Analogue transmissions, on the other hand, have always been vulnerable to interception.

- the creation of a national automated fingerprint identification system (NAFIS): this allows forces access to a collection of over five million records and provides a computerised matching service. Delivery to forces in England and Wales was completed in 2001.

- the case of the Yorkshire Ripper showed that the ability to review crime patterns across regions was hindered by the sheer numbers of documents stored locally on manual systems. The Home Office Large Major Enquiry System (HOLMES) was conceived and has now been superseded by HOLMES 2 which enables nation-wide database comparison and incident linking. It features an integrated suite of applications used for the investi-

---

[160] And can play a major role in detection—the two young boys convicted in 1994 of murdering James Bulger were caught on video in the shopping centre. Newburn T. and Hayman S., *Policing, Surveillance and Social Control* (2001).
[161] The surveillance powers of the police are discussed in Chap. 4
[162] Previously s. 41 of the Police Act 1964.
[163] Uglow S., *The Police Act 1997* (1997) Chap. 5; www.pito.org.uk.

gation of major and serious linked crime and casualty bureau handling arising from major disasters.[164]

- the National Strategy for Police Information Systems (NSPIS), was launched in 1994 and focused on the production of standard software for national use such as the following:

Vehicle Procedures Fixed Penalty Office (VP/FPO) software for tracking fixed penalty notices issued by the police and the collection of payments and enforcement of notices by the Magistrates' Courts. The combined system, which supports the use of conditional offers, has been delivered to 38 forces.

National Legal Database is software to supply appropriate charge wording, advice on stated cases, local regulations and bylaws. It can link to both Case Preparation and Custody software.

Case Preparation software is designed to process cases from initiation to disposal. It allows the tracking of a case over its lifetime, production of all the documents needed by the police, CPS and courts and provides support to victims and witnesses. It is designed to interface with Custody and the Police National Computer (PNC)).

Custody software is designed to assist the Custody Officer in dealing with offenders so that all statutory requirements are met and there is effective administration and recording of information. It is designed to interface with Custody and the Police National Computer (PNC).

Command and Control is designed to support real time resource management, incident management and support for special operations.

Crime and Incident Recording allows the recording of crimes and provides crime pattern analysis and facilities. It also handles records of property which has been the subject of crime.

National Management Information System (NMIS) provides an integrated package of tools for delivery of management information at all organisational levels.

One essential aspect of PITO's work has been the development of the Police National Computer, which has been operated by the Home Office at Hendon Data Centre since 1974. It provides officers with access to some 55 million records covering registered vehicles, criminal names, wanted and missing persons and stolen firearms, among others. Planning for the next generation of the PNC is underway. Another major database will be that for DNA—by section 82(2) of the Criminal Justice and Police Act 2001, the police will be permitted to retain the DNA (and fingerprints) of suspects taken in the course of an investigation even if the individual is not subsequently prosecuted or is acquitted. This information can be used for the investigation of an offence and the conduct of a prosecution. Although the fingerprint and DNA databases are registered with the Data Protection Registrar and information stored on them is covered by data protection legislation, the retention of data on people who have not been convicted of any offence seems a disproportionate infringement of the individual's right to privacy and a small step on the way to the compilation of a mass DNA

---

[164] A demonstration can be seen at www.holmes2.org/.

database. Further, section 82(4) allows for the retention of volunteer DNA samples and fingerprints given for elimination purposes. These cannot be used in connection with the investigation of another offence unless there is written consent—in that case, the samples can be used for the investigation of an offence and the conduct of a prosecution. Once given, that consent cannot be withdrawn.

Technology raises difficult ethical questions for policing—their legitimacy relies on police operating in the public sphere and not intruding into the private. Article 8 of the European Convention places an obligation on the state to respect private and family life. Such a principle is axiomatic for the liberal democrat who sees all citizens as entitled to privacy—that is, that there is a domain of thoughts, beliefs and behaviour which should remain unregulated by the state. Many jurisdictions possess constitutions specifically protecting rights to privacy. But it remains difficult to identify the criteria that mark a boundary between the public and the private. State intervention is everywhere and the language of privacy provides no obvious boundaries. This leads some theorists to conclude that the concept of privacy is simply ideological, an abstract concept which masks a concrete reality, thereby precluding certain forms of intervention and reinforcing inequalities of power. In this way O'Donovan sees privacy as masking male dominance within the family.[165] But notions of privacy are part of our everyday language, which takes for granted personal, internal worlds, and our relationships with others rest on the recognition of those and of our own private identity. To erode the domain of the private is to legitimate and encourage state intervention with all the consequent dangers and to that end liberal theory would restrict the state's power to gather information about individuals.

Such large databases holding information on people's private lives pose problems, especially when forces adopt proactive strategies to police communities. There are few legal limits on police work in this sphere and difficulties arise: firstly, there is the question of evaluation of the intelligence since not only must the information received be reliable, the quality of analysis must be high before it is of value otherwise individuals will be the object of unjustified surveillance; secondly, there are ethical issues since if an individual is 'targeted', there should be a proper level of evidence against him or her, such as reasonable suspicion of involvement in organised or persistent or serious criminal activity, already in existence; thirdly concerns arise about the sheer capacity to gather, store and retrieve large quantities of data on every individual in the country, regardless of whether they have committed offences or not. This is already the case in Northern Ireland. In 1994, there was a plan to mount a joint operation to monitor the movements of all 'New Age' travellers by tracking their vehicle movements and thus maintain a database enabling them to intervene more easily in the event of trespasses at Stonehenge or the holding of music festivals. Such an operation would have been impossible without new technology and contains disturbing implications for all dissident groups, whether environmentalists, anti-nuclear protestors, animal rights activists, hunt saboteurs, trade unionists, left or right wing splinter groups and whether they operate within the normal channels of political and industrial protest or not. Such concerns raise questions as to the effectiveness of our techniques for making the police accountable.

---

[165] O'Donovan K., *Sexual Divisions in Law* (1985) p. 181.

2.10 ACCOUNTABILITY

Those who provide education, health, transport, policing or other public sector services have become accustomed to a less deferential attitude in recent yeaars. No longer do communities accept what they are given—they wish to be involved in the formulation of policy, to protest against decisions that adversely affect them, to be given full and frank explanations when things have gone wrong. Such mechanisms can be prospective in seeking to influence policy or retrospective in ensuring that a public service accounts for its decisions and actions. Certain basic issues need addressing:[166]

1. what type of decisions do the police make? Different types may require different mechanisms of accountability. Where the decision involves issues of general policy, such as a community safety policy, guidelines for hot pursuit or whether to buy British cars for the force, a democratic forum may be required. At the other end of the spectrum, individual officers make decisions, often at street level, about individual cases. These often require, at least initially, an investigative process

2. to whom should the police be accountable? In many cases an officer is responsible to some other part of the legal process, whether a superior officer, the Crown Prosecution Service or the courts. In others, it might be an external body such the Independent Police Complaints Commission, the Police Authority or a community forum.

3. what remedies may be sought? These may encompass an apology at one level or a change of policy at another. A person adversely affected by a police decision may seek disciplinary action against an officer by the force, exclusion of evidence by a court or compensation through damages.

4. what sort of accountability should we look for? Marshall developed a distinction between 'subordinate and obedient' and 'explanatory and co-operative'.[167] Historically the Watch Committees controlled the police but the reforms of the 1960s abolished these and set up Local Police Authorities (LPAs). In the 1980s active Labour local authorities sought a greater say in the policing of their communities but with little success.[168] The Local Government Act 1985 abolished these metropolitan authorities and replaced them by less radical joint boards. Marshall suggests that the 'explanatory and co-operative' style underlay the Police Act 1964, not just with LPAs but also with the Home Office. Despite the latter's considerable financial influence, policy is formulated only after significant consultation with ACPO.

The police authorities were reformed again in the 1990s.[169] Reiner has suggested that a third mode, 'calculative and contractual' will be the result of these government policies, as the authority looks for the 'best value' in the provision of policing services for the local area. Police forces are

---

[166] Reiner R., 'Police Accountability' in Reiner R. and Spencer S. (eds) (1993): *op.cit.*, p. 1 at p. 6.
[167] Marshall G., *Police and Government* (1965) p. 61.
[168] Simey M., 'Police Authorities and Accountability: The Merseyside Experience' in Cowell D. *et al.* (eds), *Policing the Riots* (1982).
[169] These were first brought in by the Police and Magistrates Courts Act 1994.

increasingly faced with key objectives and performance indicators. It is a debate that leads to issues surrounding the identification of 'core' policing tasks and the possible privatisation of ancillary jobs.[170] In this scenario, while formal constabulary independence is preserved, the police become more responsive and sensitive to local policing concerns. These reforms (and those contained in the Police Reform Act 2002) give the Home Secretary unprecedented influence over local police decision-making.[171]

Public sector services, such as education, health and social services are scrutinised by politicians, national and local, and the media. There are complaints procedures, legal remedies as well as the responsible authorities. The police are no exception—officers may feel that their failings are dissected in detail where similar failings by other professions go unremarked. Certainly that scrutiny can take many forms:

2.10.1 *Media and Public Attention*

There is a long tradition of reports of crimes and their detection, especially the accounts of hangings and murders featured in eighteenth century broadsheets. Most of us will still glean our knowledge of the police and the criminal justice system at second hand through newspapers or TV. The quantity of coverage is extraordinary and 25 per cent of newspaper copy is about crime.[172] Television coverage is also extensive in both documentary and fictional formats.[173] The bulk of such coverage is supportive of the police, presenting them as necessary and in the main effective. This is especially so in those programmes which reconstruct offences such as *Crimewatch*. These help to maintain and reinforce a perception of a force battling with a 'law-and-order' problem. The caricature of the good bobby was *Dixon of Dock Green*—honest, trustworthy, brave, hard working, punctual, reliable and helpful, Dixon was a 'community copper'. Representations of the police have moved on from this legitimising myth to present the police as flawed, fallible people undertaking a difficult job. Certainly this evolution can be seen from *Dixon* to *Z Cars* and *The Sweeny* to the confrontation of sexism, racism and homophobia in the force in *Prime Suspect*.[174] Crime fiction offers a vicarious experience of the deviant and abnormal, a 'fictional playing out of the parameters of socially acceptable behaviour'. Alongside this fascination for transgression on one side, the actions of the police permit an exploration of the limits of order on the other as well as confronting issues of justice, legality, morality and individual rights.

There are, more occasionally, critical investigations by newspaper, radio or TV programmes such as *World In Action's* investigation into the Birmingham Six or the BBC's *Rough Justice* series. The massive attention devoted to cases of miscarriages of justice has meant that the public have a more sophisticated, less deferential attitude towards the police and the media contribute to criticism not only of particular police actions but also of broader policing policies. The public

---

[170] Home Office, 'Review of Police Core and Ancillary Tasks' (1995).
[171] Reiner R., (1993): *op. cit.* at pp. 19–20.
[172] Chibnall S., *Law and Order News* (Tavistock, 1977).
[173] Reiner (2000), *op. cit.*, Chap. 5 gives a detailed analysis of media presentations of the police.
[174] ITV's *The Bill* has consistently and effectively covered difficult issues, providing a realistic view of policing to a prime time audience.

are increasingly directly asked their opinion about ministerial and force objectives—for example, fear of crime or satisfaction with foot or car patrolling. Public satisfaction with police performance in a range of matters features among the key performance indicators.[175] That in itself ensures that the police pay attention to media coverage, both national and local.

2.10.2 *Accountability through the Courts*

The police argue that they are first and foremost accountable to the law and the courts. As will be seen, their powers and decisions are often low visibility and are characterised as much by discretion as by rules. Discretion, such as the decision based on 'reasonable suspicion' to stop and search a person under section 1 of PACE, is often not justiciable. But the police may face three broad categories of court action:

2.10.2.1 CRIMINAL AND CIVIL ACTION AGAINST THE POLICE

Individuals do have redress through the criminal and civil courts. Police officers may commit criminal offences in the course of an investigation such as assault or perversion of the course of justice. 'Law enforcement' cannot as yet be argued as a defence were an officer to be charged and prosecuted, although Law Commission thinking has moved in that direction.[176]

Alternatively there can be civil actions[177] for compensation, for assault or wrongful detention against officers. In addition there may be actions for trespass to land or goods or, possibly, breach of confidence. Many solicitors often prefer civil remedies. They advise their clients to ignore the formal police complaints machinery and proceed against the Chief Constable under section 88 of the Police Act 1996. This section ensures that the general principles of vicarious liability, (*i.e.*, that an employer is responsible for damage caused by the torts of his employees acting in the course of employment) apply to the police. Such liability is a form of strict liability because it arises from the employer-employee relationship, without reference to any fault of the employer. In all cases of vicarious liability the employer is liable in addition to the employee, who remains legally responsible for his or her tort. The essential requirements for vicarious liability are the existence of a tort, committed by a police officer who was acting in the course of his or her employment.

This is straightforward where the plaintiff has suffered an injury or damage as a direct result of the acts or omissions of a police officer.[178] But where damage has been caused by a third party, civil actions against the police force have failed on the grounds that a legal duty cannot arise in the absence of a special relationship between the police and the injured party. It must be noted that even if a special relationship be established in an extremely exceptional case, the appellate

---

[175] Weatheritt M. (1993), *op. cit.*, Skogan (1994), *Contacts Between the Police and Public* (Home Office Research Study 134); police performance in these matters is documented in *Chief Constables' Annual Reports*.

[176] Law Commission, *Assisting and Encouraging Crime* (Consultation Paper No. 131) (1993) at pp. 120–122.

[177] Clayton R. and Tomlinson H., *Civil Actions against the Police* (2nd ed. 1992); Walker N., *Policing in a Changing Constitutional Order* (2000) p. 132 ff.

[178] *Knightley v. Johns* [1982] 1 All E.R. 851; *Rigby and another v. Chief Constable of Northampshire* [1985] 2 All E.R. 985.

courts may refuse to impose a legal duty on grounds of public policy considerations, if to do so would be unjust and unreasonable.[179] Such a special relationship probably exists where it is assumed by the police. This can be the case with informants, a particular concern for bodies such as NCIS—in *Swinney v. Chief Constable of Northumbria*,[180] the plaintiff passed on information about someone implicated in the killing of a police officer. She was very insistent that the information should not be traced to her and yet the police left a document naming her in an unattended police car from which it was stolen. She was then threatened. The claim was initially struck out as disclosing no cause of action but was reinstated and the Court of Appeal dismissed the police appeal, holding that it was at least arguable that a special relationship existed.

The European Court of Human Rights in *Osman v. UK*[181] considered whether the exclusion of a remedy in such cases of police negligence was in breach of the Convention. This case concerned a schoolteacher who developed an obsession with a 15-year-old schoolboy. The teacher harassed the boy and his family and this was reported to the police. The police took no effective action and the man eventually broke into the family home, shot and severely injured the boy and shot and killed the father. The mother brought an action alleging negligence—the police had been aware of the teacher's activities but failed to apprehend him, search his home or interview him. The common law courts held that, although the police were under a duty to prevent crime, that did not carry with it a duty to individuals for the damage caused to them by offenders whom the police had negligently failed to apprehend. It was against public policy to impose such a duty as it would not promote the observance of a higher standard of care by the police and would result in the diversion of resources from the investigation and detection of crime. But the European Court held that a blanket immunity for the police from such actions was a breach of Article 6(1), the right to a fair trial, and amounted to an unjustifiable restriction on the applicant's right to have the merit of the claim determined. It constituted a disproportionate restriction on the applicants' right of access to a court.[182]

2.10.2.2 EXCLUSION OF EVIDENCE

Police decisions and actions come under intense critical scrutiny by defence lawyers at any criminal trial. The court has various strategies that it can adopt to, in effect, discipline the police for improper conduct in obtaining evidence. Such conduct might have amounted to breaches of the criminal or civil law, to infractions of the PACE Codes of Practice or to a failure to observe the human rights of the defendant.

- A court can stay proceedings on the grounds that the police conduct was an abuse of process. In *Loosely*[183] undercover police officers supplied the defendant with cheap cigarettes and asked him to supply them with heroin,

---

[179] *Hill v. Chief Constable of West Yorkshire* [1988] 2 All E.R. 238; *Clough v. Bussan* [1990] 1 All E.R. 431. *Alexandrou v. Oxford*, [1993] 4 All E.R. 328; *Osman v. Ferguson* [1993] 4 All E.R. 344; *Hughes v. National Union of Mineworkers and others* [1991] 4 All E.R. 278.
[180] [1996] 3 All E.R. 449.
[181] 29 E.H.R.R. 245, [1999] Crim. L.R. 82, (1999) 1 F.L.R. 193.
[182] The limits of this can be seen in *Ivison v. UK* (2002) (Admissibility Decision) Application No. 00039030/97.
[183] Loosely, *A-G's Reference, No. 3 of 2000* [2001] 1 W.L.R. 2060.

on the promise that he would be provided with further cheap cigarettes for so doing. The accused duly obtained the heroin. The judge stayed the trial on the grounds that the entrapment constituted abuse of process. The House of Lords upheld this decision—police conduct that brought about state-created crime was unacceptable and improper, and to prosecute in such circumstances would be an affront to the public conscience.

● The alternative to a stay of proceedings would be the exclusion of the evidence that had been obtained by improper means. If the evidence constitutes a confession (an incriminating statement by the accused) the criteria for its admission as evidence is laid down by section 76 of PACE. However the court has a wider power to exclude improperly obtained evidence (and often to ensure the acquittal of the accused). This is under section 78 of PACE which states that the trial judge shall not admit evidence if the admission of the evidence would be to have an adverse effect on the fairness of the proceedings. This mirrors the 'right to a fair trial' principle embodied in Article 6. This has had far-reaching consequences in relation to the right to legal advice as well as to police techniques of investigation such as entrapment or surveillance.

The implementation of these principles is discussed in greater depth in the following chapters on police powers of investigation but it is instructive to compare the approach of the U.S. Supreme Court with common law. The American court has on several occasions excluded evidence that has been illegally obtained acting under the Fourth Amendment to the Constitution, which forbids unreasonable searches and seizures. The key case is *Mapp v. Ohio*[184] where police officers broke into a boarding house, in search of both gambling paraphernalia and a fugitive. They had no warrant and it was clear that a warrantless search was not authorised. The evidence obtained was excluded. The Court gave three important reasons. The first is that exclusion removes the incentive for police to conduct illegal searches. The second is 'the imperative of judicial integrity', the notion being that it is dishonest and hypocritical for courts to admit illegally obtained evidence. The third ground is that exclusion of illegally obtained evidence is in some moral sense the defendant's entitlement, that it does no more than right the wrong the police have done. U.S. courts now automatically supress evidence obtained as a result of an unlawful search.

In the U.S. the Supreme Court has actively policed the police through these methods. In the U.K., the abuse of process doctrine and the exclusionary power under section 78 are both discretionary and not automatic. The judge must address the issue of whether the admission of the evidence affects the fairness of the proceedings. If he or she decides that it does not, the appellate courts tend not to intervene. Thus in *Khan*[185] the police committed trespass to bug the defendant's house. The House of Lords held that prima facie all relevant evidence was admissible even if obtained illegally. The minor damage to the building and the intrusion on privacy were not sufficient reasons to exclude this evidence and its prejudicial effect did not exceed its probative value. The trial judge was correct in holding that this was not a case in which he should refuse to admit the evidence under section 78. The divergence between the English and American courts

---

[184] 367 U.S. 643 (1961).
[185] [1997] A.C. 558—the approach was upheld by the European Court of Human Rights.

shows the differing public interests involved: on the one hand, the priority for the English courts is that proper determination of cases requires that all relevant and reliable evidence is before the courts whereas for the Americans, it is the integrity of the judicial process—the due process of law doctrine states that the proper administration of justice requires respect for the rights of the accused—with the corollary that state officials must be deterred from committing illegal acts.

2.10.2.3 JUDICIAL REVIEW OF POLICE ACTION

An important means of redress for people who are adversely affected by a general policy or a particular decision of a public agency is to have that policy reviewed by the Divisional Court of Queen's Bench under its power of judicial review. Finally by the orders of mandamus, prohibition and certiorari, the court can order an inferior court or public body to take action where it has failed to do so, desist from action or quash a particular decision. By the writ of habeas corpus, the court can review the conditions under which anyone is held in detention. Finally by seeking a declaration, a litigant can obtain a authoritative ruling on the law.

The divisional court has been reluctant to interfere in police decisions. In *Blackburn No. 1*[186] the applicant was seeking an order to compel the police to enforce the law against illegal gaming in London. The Divisional Court, while accepting that the Commissioner was ultimately answerable to the law, stated a doctrine of constabulary independence from democratic control, which went well beyond precedent:

> No minister of the Crown can tell [the Commissioner] that he must, or must not, keep observation on this place or that; or that he must, or must not, prosecute this man or that one. Nor can any police authority tell him so. The responsibility for law enforcement lies on him. He is answerable to the law and to the law alone.[187]

The court's conclusion was that the Commissioner exercised discretion as to operational matters and so long as he stayed within the broad parameters of that discretion, the court would not interfere. Those parameters would include a decision not to prosecute for attempted suicide or for sex with girls under 16 but apparently a decision not to prosecute for thefts under a certain value would not be. As Lustgarten says, 'Why?'

Mr Blackburn was not yet beaten. In *Blackburn No.3,*[188] he sought an order to ensure that the Metropolitan Police enforced the Obscene Publication Acts. Again the court decided that it would not normally interfere in the exercise of a chief officer's discretion. This approach can also be seen in *ex parte* CEGB[189] where the applicant sought mandamus against the Chief Constable who had refused to order his officers to clear a site of demonstrators protesting peacefully and with the landowner's consent in order to prevent a survey of the land for a planned nuclear power station. The court stated what the police powers were in such a situation and clearly felt that they should be exercised but refused to order the Chief Constable to exercise them. It is also a clear expression not only of the

---

[186] R. v. *Metropolitan Police Commissioner, ex parte Blackburn* (1968) 2 Q.B. 118.
[187] *per* Lord Denning at p. 136. For a compelling and destructive analysis of errors of law and logic contained in this judgment, see Lustgarten, *op. cit.*, pp. 64–65; Walker N., (2000) *op. cit.*, pp.77–78.
[188] (1973) Q.B. 241.
[189] R. v. *Chief Constable of Devon and Cornwall, ex parte Central Electricity Generating Board* (1981) 3 W.L.R. 961.

chief officers' discretion but also of the individual constable—he or she can be ordered to a particular site but could not be told to 'Arrest that man!'. That discretion to arrest is granted by statute and cannot be taken away by superior officers.

But the court will review the substance of the policy complained of—in *ex parte Levey*[190], after riots in Toxteth, the Chief Constable had instructed officers not to enter that area of Liverpool in police vehicles. The applicant had property stolen and a police car was pursuing the thieves. The police vehicle stopped at the border and abandoned the pursuit. Although resolved on different issues, Watkins L.J. concluded that the policy was in line with Scarman recommendations on inner city policing and decided that the Chief Constable of Merseyside was justified in issuing the instructions.

The House of Lords has recently reassessed the extent to which the courts will intervene in the decision-making of chief constables. In the *International Trader's Ferry* case[191] there was a suggestion that the courts might take a more robust approach to judicial review of police action. The police must show that the balancing act between the right to trade lawfully and the right to protest lawfully was proportionate and that a fundamental freedom should not be restricted any more than is necessary. Although the Chief Constable was entitled to exercise a margin of discretion, it is one that is susceptible to review by the courts.

2.10.3 *Relations with the Crown Prosecution Service*

After investigation, the initial decision whether to charge a suspect lies with the police. In essence, they have three options: the police could decide to take no further action, to issue a caution[192] or to charge with a view to prosecution. This is changing: the Auld Report recommended that the CPS be given greater legal powers, in particular the power to determine the initial charge.[193]

There is no scrutiny of police decisions not to prosecute. Research suggests that no further action was taken in about 26 per cent of cases of arrested adults[194]— an internal inspection of a southeast force in 2001 showed that 27 per cent of people arrested are eventually released without charge. Although some arrests can quite legitimately result in a 'refused charge', this figure raises issues about the effectiveness of training, the impact of performance culture and the lack of internal supervision and of external review.

There will be a review where the decision is to prosecute.[195] In this case the file will be sent to the CPS who will review that decision. When the CPS was set up in 1985, they were given the power to discontinue prosecutions[196] without further reference to the police. It is also possible that on the day of the trial, the prosecution will offer no evidence and the defendant will be discharged. The difference is that if there is a formal and early discontinuance, further proceedings against the suspect remain possible but if no evidence is offered, the court will

---

[190] *R. v. Oxford, ex parte Levey* (1987) 151 L.G. Rev. 371.
[191] *R. v. Chief Constable of Sussex, ex parte International Trader's Ferry Ltd* [1999] 1 All E.R. 129.
[192] A reprimand or final warning in the case of juveniles.
[193] Lord Justice Auld, *A Review of the Criminal Courts of England and Wales* Chap. 8 (2001) Chap. 10 para. 12.
[194] McConville M., Sanders A. and Leng R., *The Case for the Prosecution* (1991) p. 104.
[195] Such a decision might also be the subject of judicial review—*R. v. Chief Constable of Kent, ex parte L.* [1993] 1 All E.R. 756.
[196] Prosecution of Offences Act 1985, s. 21.

usually enter a formal verdict of not guilty with no possibility of future action. In 2000–2001, the CPS discontinued 13 per cent of magistrates' court cases and did not proceed with 12.3 per cent of Crown Court cases.[197] The Code for Crown Prosecutors sets out the formal evidential and public interest criteria on which continuance or discontinuance may be based—in practice the important factors are where there is a police failure to fill gaps in evidence, where witnesses fail to turn up or where review reveals shortcomings in the prosecution case.[198]

It is a moot question whether the CPS are an effective check on police decisions. The sceptical view is that they are a body that lacks either effective powers or collective confidence. As a result, the discontinuance of cases has little impact on the police who might or might not review their investigative and interrogation procedures to prevent the difficulties re-occurring. This is illustrated by patterns of prosecution and cautioning rates—the creation of the CPS was expected to lead to consistent application of national guidelines in relation to these yet they still vary across forces.[199] Sanders has argued[200] that the CPS are ill placed to judge the propriety of individual prosecutions and whether they are in the public interest. Indeed the CPS seem too willing to defer to the police on matters of policy.[201] Apart from discontinuance, the CPS possess no effective sanctions, either for breaches of the Codes or for ill-considered prosecutions.

An alternative view is that the CPS will not be content to be the subordinate partner in the criminal justice system, occupying an obscure space between the police and the courts. The 1985 legislation does not define the relationship with the police but the power to discontinue prosecutions is significant. A more active CPS, requiring further and better investigation or demanding equal status with the police in laying down policy guidelines for prosecutions, is a viable scenario. It is a role that prosecutors have adopted in other European jurisdictions.[202] In the 1990s, the Royal Commission on Criminal Justice had the opportunity to define and clarify the relationship between the CPS and the police but their Report merely suggests that the police should seek CPS advice in a greater number of cases in accordance with guidelines to be agreed between the two services.[203]

But the attrition rate—the level of 'refused charge', of CPS discontinuance, of the prosecution offering no evidence in court or the judge directing a 'not guilty' plea after finding that there was 'no case to answer'—has led to pressure for change from the Home Office. In 1998 the Glidewell Report[204] proposed a move to a single administrative unit, co-locating police and CPS staff, in order to maximise efficiency and eliminate duplications within the prosecution process. Such criminal justice units (CJUs) have been set up with the aims of improving communication between police and CPS; minimising transport of files; savings costs by reduction of duplication and having a single file system; improving file

---

[197] CPS. Annual Report 2000–2001 p. 26 ff.
[198] *The Code for Crown Prosecutors* (4th ed., 2000)—it is also published on the CPS website—www.cps.gov.uk. For further discussion of the discretion to prosecute, see chap. 5.
[199] Nationally 32% of offenders are cautioned but this goes up to 45% in Surrey and down to 15% in South Yorkshire—*Criminal Statistics 2000*, Cm. 5312 Tables 5.1–5.3 p. 109ff.
[200] Sanders A. 'Controlling the Discretion of the Individual Officer' in Reiner R. and Spencer S. (eds) (1993), *op. cit.* p. 96ff.
[201] McConville M. *et al.* (1991), *op. cit.* p. 142.
[202] See Downes D., *Contrasts in Tolerance* (1988) p. 13 for contrast with Dutch prosecutors. *Infra* para. 4.2.
[203] Royal Commission on Criminal Justice; *op. cit.*, para. 5.18.
[204] Sir Iain Glidewell, *The Review of the Crown Prosecution Service* (1998) Cm. 3972.

quality and timeliness for both organisations; improving witness warning, witness care and victim support and with a clearly defined single-focus location for the courts and other agencies.

Further the Auld Report recommended that the Crown Prosecution Service should take over from the police responsibility for charging defendants at the outset of prosecutions.[205] As well as being wasteful, the Auld review noted that if a charge has to be downgraded or amended at a later date it raises expectations for victims and witnesses who can be upset by the changes. Pilot schemes[206] were launched in 2002 where the CPS determine the charge against defendants in all but minor or routine cases. There are cases where the police will need to continue to charge but these will be in the form of a holding charge. They will either be affirmed or not after a review by the CPS. The objective is a reduction of the number of charges being altered, and a reduction in the time between arrest and sentencing. The pilot schemes have been hailed as a success. It is likely that plans to shift responsibility for the charging of suspects from the police to crown prosecution service lawyers will be implemented nationally.[207] Such a development is another example of increasingly close co-ordination and co-operation between the police and the CPS.

2.10.4 *Police Authorities*[208]

The central plank of police accountability remains the so-called tripartite structure, the three-cornered relationship between the Chief Constable, the Home Office and the Police Authority. It obtained its legislative imprimatur under the 1964 Police Act, which increased the say of local government in the management of policing services. That Act abolished the Watch Committees and the Joint Standing Committees and in their place created 'local police authorities' for every force (except London). The membership of these authorities consisted of two-thirds local councillors and one-third magistrates[209]—they were a sub-committee of the county or metropolitan council although that body had little power to interfere. These authorities were reformed again by the Police Act 1996.[210] There are now autonomous authorities for each police force, each normally with 17 members–9 members from the relevant councils, 3 local magistrates and 5 independent members appointed by the Home Secretary. However, at present there remain differing forms of police authority:

1. in London, an independent police authority was set up in 2000. Previously there had been no local input and the Commissioner of the Metropolitan force was directly responsible under the Metropolitan Police Act 1829 to the Home Secretary. The new authority has twenty-three members, twelve

---

[205] Lord Justice Auld, *A Review of the Criminal Courts of England and Wales*, pp. 408–413 (2001).
[206] In Bath, Halifax, Essex, Medway and Wrexham.
[207] *The Guardian* June 4, 2002.
[208] Lustgarten, *op. cit.*, Chap. 6; Reiner R. (2000), *op. cit.*, Chap. 6; Walker N., op. cit., Chap. 4; Jones T. and Newburn T., *Policing After the Act* (1998). See also the Association of Police Authorities website at www.apa.police.uk.
[209] The presence of magistrates is described by Lustgarten (p. 80) as an 'indefensible anachronism'. Critics of the legislation in 1888 (which set up joint standing committees with half the members being magistrates) and in 1964 suggest that the main motive for the inclusion of J.P.s was the distrust of elected members.
[210] This Act consolidates the changes first introduced by the Police and Magistrates Courts Act 1994.

drawn from the new Greater London assembly, four magistrates and seven independent members.[211] The City of London police have the Common Council of the City of London as their police authority.

2. the standard model is to be found in the provinces where the force is based on a single county or a group of counties (such as Devon and Cornwall or Thames Valley). The authority is no longer a committee of the council but an independent legal entity, a body corporate.[212] The body corporate status means that the authority is a legal entity that is able to employ staff, purchase property and enter into contracts. Although they must make a member of the authority available to be questioned by the full council,[213] that body has no power to interfere with authority decisions, except on financial matters. Where one police authority serves a group of counties, that political accountability is reduced still further.

3. in 1985, many metropolitan councils (as in London or Manchester) were abolished and district councils set up in their place.[214] Under the Police Act 1996 the authority for such areas is a joint board[215] comprised of nominees of the metropolitan districts.[216]

4. the Police Act 1997 set up two national police bodies, the National Criminal Intelligence Service (NCIS), as well as the National Crime Squad (NCS).[217] Their governance is modelled on that of the local police forces. Under the Act, bodies corporate are set up as the Service Authorities for NCS and NCIS. This is the same status as that enjoyed by other police authorities. These authorities are freestanding bodies outside the Home Office. The membership is limited to 19, made up of independent, police authority and police service members with one Home Office representative. Because of its national remit, the authorities also have representatives of the Secretaries of State for Scotland and Northern Ireland, representatives of the police authorities and police forces of those countries and a representative of Customs and Excise. Concerns were voiced about the lack of independence[218] and the absence of community representation.[219] NCIS and NCS are intended to act in support of local police forces and are funded by a levy on police authorities and hence, indirectly, on the local authority itself.[220]

To what extent have police authorities been an effective means of accountability for the police? Their express powers, since they were first constituted in

[211] The authority was set up under the Greater London Local Authority Act 1999—www.mpa.gov.uk/.

[212] Police Act 1996, s. 3.

[213] *ibid.*, s. 20.

[214] These metropolitan authorities were all Labour-controlled and the LPAs were active and critical of the police—Simey M., *op. cit.*

[215] Loveday B., 'The New Police Authorities' in [1] *Policing and Society* (1991) 3.

[216] Scheds 1 and 2 of the Police Act 1996.

[217] Set up under Pts I and II of the Police Act 1997 as amended by Pt 5, Criminal Justice and Police Act 2001.

[218] All independent members of police authorities were checked by the government whips' office—Lord Harris of Greenwich—Hansard (HL) Vol. 576 No. 20 col. 130.

[219] Baroness Hilton of Eggardon—*Hansard* (HL) Vol. 575 No. 11 col. 831; Alan Beith, *Parliamentary Debates (HC) Standing Committee F on the Police Bill* (February 27, 1997) col. 33.

[220] Uglow S., *The Police Act 1997* (1997) Chaps 1 and 2.

1964, have proved quite limited—the Chief Constable exercises 'direction and control' of the force[221] whereas the police authority must secure the maintenance of an 'efficient and effective' force. These terms remain undefined but it is accepted that responsibility for delivering policing services rests with the chief constable who has operational independence. The police authority's key responsibility is to monitor how well those services are being delivered on behalf of the local community. The authority also sets and monitors the budget. The authority's capacity to do this has been enhanced since 1994 when the police authority were made responsible for preparation of an annual policing plan, setting out local priorities and targets[222]—and under the Police Reform Act 2002, they will also be responsible for producing a three year plan setting out the strategic direction for the force. The plan will be informed by:

- national objectives set by the Home Secretary.[223]

- performance targets set by the Home Secretary.[224]

- objectives set by the authority itself.[225]

Since April 2000 police authorities have in addition been required to deliver continuous improvement by conducting best value reviews of all aspects of policing performance and activity.[226] All these processes improve the transparency of local policing but not necessarily the effectiveness of the authority's monitoring function. Authorities are sensitive about encroaching on the operational independence of the Chief Constable and the joint annual reports of police force and police authority tend to be upbeat and bland, with little evidence of any critical appraisal of performance—at least publicly.

The police authority is financially responsible for local policing.[227] Excluding capital charges, the total gross expenditure of police authorities in England and Wales was approximately £7.8 billion in 1999–2000, 85 per cent of which went on pay. The authority is treated as if it were a local authority for the purposes of funding. In any given year the government sets the total amount of spending on the police that it is prepared to support—this is the Total Standard Spending or TSS. This is allocated to individual forces by the process known as the Standard Spending Assessment or SSA, which utilises a complex police funding formula. The outcome of this process is the actual share of the funding that each police authority will receive. That amount will come from four main sources:

- the Home Office provides approximately 50 per cent as the specific police grant

- the Department for the Environment, Transport and the Regions provide approximately 20 per cent through the rate support grant.

- the DETR also provide approximately 15 per cent through the distribution

---

[221] Police Act 1996 s. 10.
[222] *ibid.*, s. 8.
[223] *ibid.*, s. 37. These will be set out in the annual national Policing Plan under s. 1 Police Reform Act 2002.
[224] *ibid.*, s. 38.
[225] *ibid.*, s. 7.
[226] under the Local Government Act 1999.
[227] Association of Police Authorities, *Pounding the Beat* (1999).

of the non-domestic rate. This is based on the rateable value of non-residential property. Although this is collected locally, it is paid over to the government who share it out between all authorities.

- the local authority provide the remainder from the council tax—the police authority is a precepting body for this purpose.

The SSA need not be the ceiling for police expenditure for any authority—the authority might use its reserves, might obtain sponsorship or might persuade the local authority to boost its council tax (subject to the capping powers of the government) to increase police spending.

Approximately 85 per cent of police spending is met from central government sources. Lustgarten has pointed out that it is probable that this stimulated a permissive attitude towards policing costs in the 1970s and 1980s.[228] Now section 46 of the Police Act 1996 allows the Home Secretary to determine the overall amount of grant and the amount to go to each authority. This must be decided in consultation with the Treasury. Under subsection (4) the Secretary of State is entitled to apply rules or formulae at his or her discretion. These rules may be different for different authorities or different classes of authority (subsection (5)), thereby allowing the Secretary of State to adopt different considerations, for example, for metropolitan forces as opposed to shire forces.

The extent to which a police authority can make significant decisions on finance is very limited—police pay and pensions comprise some 85 per cent of expenditure and these do not require police authority approval.[229] Of the residue, police authorities retain control at a strategic level but all have delegated the day-to-day management of the budget to the Chief Constable. It is possible that an authority might specify maxima for certain categories of expenditure or indeed require the Chief Constable to seek approval before any expenditure over a particular amount, but to impose such financial constraints impinges on operational policy. In the past, certain police authorities have adopted this latter approach as a tactic to enable them to debate the merits of certain expenditures— whether to purchase contentious equipment such as plastic bullets or CS gas would be an example. Such tactics have demonstrated how little real power police authorities have. In *ex parte Northumbria Police Authority*[230] the courts held that in exercise of prerogative powers, the Home Secretary can supply equipment to a force without the consent of the police authority. Section 41 of the Police Act 1964 was held to authorise the Secretary of State to supply equipment (in this case CS gas and plastic baton rounds) from a central store if he considered it necessary or expedient for promoting the efficiency of the police and his right to do so was not restricted to an emergency nor did he need the consent of the police authority.[231] The powers given to the Home Secretary by section 41 have been more broadly drawn in the legislation which replaced it, namely section 57 of the Police Act 1996 which gives the Secretary of State this power explicitly.

The *Northumbria* case demonstrates the practical limits of police authorities'

---

[228] Lustgarten: *op. cit.*, p. 116.
[229] Police Act 1996 s. 50 empowers the Secretary of State to make regulations regarding pay and allowances.
[230] *R. v. Secretary of State for the Home Department, ex parte Northumbria Police Authority* [1987] 2 All E.R. 282.
[231] Walker, *op. cit.* p. 14 ff.

control. They are very much the junior partner in the tripartite structure. Until the 1970s, the authorities were quiescent about their function. The urban unrest in the early 1980s and the increasingly militaristic response led several metropolitan authorities to challenge their Chief Constables[232] but the limits of any control, operational or financial, were shown during the miners' strike of 1984/85.[233] The strategy chosen to police the dispute was to confront picket lines with equal or superior numbers of police, utilising the 'mutual aid' provisions in the Police Act 1964. 'Receiving' authorities found themselves faced with bills for overtime payments for officers from other forces. 'Providing' authorities found that they initially had to foot the bill after their own forces had been decimated to provide assistance in other parts of the country. The police authorities in mining districts found that they were unable to prevent their Chief Constables from spending above the agreed budgetary ceiling. For many councils, this was a particular problem because it also meant that local authorities exceeded 'rate-capping' levels imposed by central government and thereby attracted additional penalties. South Yorkshire's refusal to pay for billeting the officers involved in policing at the Orgreave coking plant was met with the threat of court action by the Attorney General—in the event further financial assistance from central government was forthcoming and the issue was never litigated. Another tactic of cutting expenditure in other areas of the police budget brought further threats of court action from the Home Office when South Yorkshire announced the abolition of its mounted police squad. What the legal basis of such an action might have been was never revealed.[234] It was a period that raised but did not resolve legal and constitutional issues over the tripartite structure.

Police authorities have the power to appoint senior officers.[235] Any such appointment is subject to the approval of the Home Secretary and so in practice the authority works from an authorised short list drawn up by the Home Office. Authorities may call on such senior officers to retire in 'the interests of efficiency or effectiveness'[236] and usually such senior officers retire 'voluntarily' before they are forced to retire. The police authority still requires the approval of the Home Secretary. The early departure of chief constables is likely to be controversial—in 1998, Sussex police shot James Ashley in his flat when he was unarmed and naked. The Chief Constable, Paul Whitehouse, defended the action, suggesting that he was armed and wanted for attempted murder. Two inquiries were mounted—one by Kent police concluded that the operation was catastrophically flawed in every phase, that the force was riven with incompetence and that there was evidence of 'corporate failures' that made the actions of individual officers difficult to criticise. A subsequent inquiry into Whitehouse's conduct by the chief constable of Hampshire accused him of making statements that were 'unsustainable in any rational sense ... and plainly perverse.' After the Sussex police authority had decided not to call on their chief constable to retire, the Home Secretary wrote to them urging them to reconsider and Whitehouse stepped down in June 2001.[237]

The police authority is entitled to a report each year from its Chief Con-

---

[232] Simey M., 'Police Authorities and Accountability: The Merseyside Experience' in Cowell D. *et al.* (eds), *Policing the Riots* (1982).
[233] Spencer S., *Police Authorities During the Miners' Strike* (1986); Lustgarten, *op. cit.*, pp. 118–125.
[234] Spencer, *op. cit.*, p. 40–41.
[235] Namely chief constables and assistant chief constables—Police Act 1996 ss. 11 and 12.
[236] *ibid.* s. 11(2) and s. 12(3).
[237] *The Guardian* June 27, 2001.

stable.[238] The authority can also require reports on other matters concerning policing the local area but the Chief Constable can refuse to produce such a report, if he and the Home Office thinks fit.[239] Although the Chief Constable must have 'regard to the local policing plan issued by the police authority',[240] ultimately the authority is unable to force the police to do anything that Police Senior Management is unwilling to do.

It was envisaged that the new style police authorities introduced in 1994 would be more powerful than the old, not only producing local policing plans and objectives but acting independently of local government, able to employ hand to contract for goods and services. Each year it must issue a report, an account of its stewardship, which assesses the extent to which the local policing plan has been carried out. These obligations allied to 'best value' procedures mean that the modern authority must work closely with and monitor in detail their local police. While the authority is clearly independent of local government, it is less apparent that it is independent of the police—the authority's offices are often found within police HQ and their websites are integrated with that of their force. While the new legislation has brought about greater transparency, there is still too little critical scrutiny nor has there been any change in the relationship between the Chief Constable and the police authorities.

2.10.5 *The Home Office*

In 1928, Sir Edward Troup[241] wrote:

> The central government should have complete control of the police in the seat of government. It would be intolerable that the legislature or executive should be at the mercy of a police force controlled by a municipal authority, which might come into violent conflict with the national authority.[242]

Such sentiments have not changed. The decline in local influence has been matched by an accompanying shift of power to senior police officers and the Home Office. For 170 years, the Home Secretary had a dual role: firstly there was direct responsibility as the police authority for the Metropolitan force. This was justified by reference to the width of their national functions including royal and diplomatic protection as well as security work, the policing of national demonstrations and a range of services, both records and forensic, that are provided to other forces. Londoners, who contribute large sums to the policing of the capital, had no democratic input into how those services are provided. This was rectified in 2000 when an independent Metropolitan police authority was set up.

The Home Secretary has significant but indirect functions under the Police Act 1996. Under section 36 it is his duty to promote police efficiency and effectiveness. If a force is failing to do its job, there is no residual control to take over the financial or operational management of a force.[243] But under section 40,[244]

---

[238] Police Act 1996, s. 22(1).
[239] *ibid.* s. 22(5).
[240] *ibid.* s. 10(2).
[241] Until 1928, for 14 years the Permanent Under-Secretary in the Police Department.
[242] Troup E., 'Police Administration, Local and National' (1928) 1 *Police Journal.* 5 at p. 9 (quoted in Lustgarten *op. cit.*, p. 95).
[243] This is unlike other public services such as education.
[244] As amended by the Police Reform Act 2002, s. 3.

where there has been an adverse report on the policing of an area by an inspector of constabulary acting under section 54, the Secretary of State can direct the police authority to take such measures as he or she specifies, although such measures must be those that will improve the efficiency or effectiveness of the force. A further radical power was introduced by section 4 of the Police Reform Act 2002 which allows the government to direct a chief officer to take remedial action if he is satisfied that the whole or any part of the force is inefficient or ineffective, either generally or in specific respects.

Section 36 was amended by section 1 of the Police Reform Act, which places a duty on the Home Secretary to prepare a National Policing Plan, which will be laid before Parliament. The plan will set out strategic priorities for the police service for the coming 3-year period. The Plan will include the Home Secretary's objectives for police authorities and identify proposals for making regulations and for issuing codes of practice and guidance.

Perhaps the most powerful sanction that the Home Secretary has is the power to withhold the central government grant from forces deemed to be 'inefficient' by HM Inspectorate of Constabulary.[245] A recent example, during the early 1990's, was the HMI refusal to grant successive certificates of efficiency to Derbyshire force—these shortcomings which were the result of persistent and severe shortfalls in funding. The 1994 Inspection revealed betrayed some frustration at the County Council's refusal to fund the Force at the minimum levels required by the police authority, stating that '*HM Inspector has reported on this situation in four previous reports … it must be clear to any objective observer that the situation should have been addressed already and should not be allowed to continue*'.[246]

The Home Secretary can inform himself by various means including the HMIC (below): under section 44 of the Police Act 1996, the chief constable of a force must submit two different sorts of report to the Secretary of State—the first. of these is the routine annual report submitted to the police authority, a copy of which must also be sent to the Secretary of State; secondly the Secretary of State has the power to require reports from a chief constable on a matter concerned with the policing of an area. The chief constable must comply with such a request. The police authority must also provide such a report if required to do so.[247] By section 49 of the Police Act 1996 the Home Secretary is able to institute an inquiry into policing matters. Dramatic examples from the past are the Scarman Report into the Brixton disturbances or the investigation into the brick-planting techniques of Detective Sergeant Challenor in London in the 1960s.[248]

Police authorities finally make the decisions on the appointment of senior officers. But a short list of candidates is provided by the Home Office for the authority because, as has been mentioned, section 11 of the 1996 Act requires the Home Secretary's approval before a Chief Constable (or Assistant Chief Constable) is appointed or dismissed by the authority. Under section 42 the Home Secretary can also require the authority to dismiss its Chief Constable. Under Part 3 of the Police Reform Act, the authority now has the power to suspend senior officers.

---

[245] Both the power to withhold the grant and the HMI itself were set up by the 1856 County and Borough Police Act.
[246] HMIC Inspection, Derbyshire Constabulary 1994, p. 2–3.
[247] Police Act, 1996, s. 43.
[248] Report of Inquiry by A.E. James Q.C. Cmnd. 2735 (1965).

The Home Office also provides a range of forensic science services[249] and computing services—the police information technology organisation (PITO) was set up on a statutory basis under the Police Act 1997.[250] The Home Office also oversees training, both for probationers[251] and for higher command.[252] Furthermore the Secretary of State has wide ranging power to make regulations concerning the 'government, administration and condition of service of police forces',[253] which includes pay and conditions of service as well as discipline. By these means he is able to impose conformity and limit local autonomy.

Involvement at an operational level is limited but section 24(2) of the Police Act 1996 allows the Home Secretary to order a Chief Constable to provide mutual aid. Furthermore, as has been discussed, the Home Secretary can supply equipment to a force without the consent of the police authority—in *ex parte Northumbria Police Authority*[254] the courts held that in exercise of prerogative powers, the Secretary of State could supply CS gas and plastic baton rounds from a central store if he considered it necessary or expedient for promoting the efficiency of the police. This power is now more explicit under section 57 of the Police Act 1996. Furthermore section 6 of the 2002 Act enables the Home Secretary to require forces to use only specified equipment.

The tripartite structure has in fact only two full partners and the extent of democratic involvement in policing policy is very limited. At the national level, the Home Secretary is not responsible to Parliament for the police, despite his remarkably wide powers and influence—he is entitled to refuse to answer parliamentary questions that are on 'operational' issues. At the local level, the reforms promulgated in 1994, although designed to give more power to police authorities, were also intended as a further centralising measure by replacing some of the elected councillors with Home Office appointees. There seems little prospect of genuine local democratic accountability with police authorities having the power to discuss and decide operational priorities, to exercise proper financial controls, to create and supervise a local complaints machinery and to establish links with the HMI.

2.10.5.1 HER MAJESTY'S INSPECTORATE OF CONSTABULARY AND THE AUDIT COMMISSION

The Home Secretary's eyes and ears are Her Majesty's Inspectorate of Constabulary, which has the statutory duty to inspect and report to the Secretary of State on the efficiency and effectiveness of all the police forces and police authorities.[255] There is a Chief Inspector of Constabulary and five Inspectors, each with a small team of staff officers and support staff, based in four regional

---

[249] HMIC, *Under The Microscope: A Thematic Inspection Report on Scientific and Technical Support* (2000).
[250] Uglow S., *The Police Act 1997* (1997) Chap. 5; www.pito.org.uk; supra at 2.9.
[251] Audit Commission: *The Management of Police Training* (Police Paper No. 4, 1989), which led to such training has become concentrated in regional centres following a national curriculum; see also HMIC: *Training Matters: A thematic inspection of probationer police training in England and Wales* (2002).
[252] All those of ACPO rank will have passed through the Senior Command Course at the Police Staff College at Bramshill.
[253] Police Act 1996, s. 50.
[254] *R. v. Secretary of State for the Home Department, ex parte Northumbria Police Authority* [1987] 2 All E.R. 282.
[255] Police Act 1996, s. 54; Home Office Circular 67/94, '*Role of HM Inspectorate of Constabulary*'.

offices. The Chief Inspector co-ordinates their work and advises the Home Secretary on police matters. Until recently the Inspectors would all have served at ACPO rank, but now there are non-police Inspectors, for police training, for Community and Race Relations and for Best Value.

Inspectors conduct formal inspections of the forces in their regions and produce reports, which have been published since 1990.[256] They also visit for other reasons, including furthering the professional relationship with Chief Constables and police authorities. Inspectors also inspect various police forces outside of England, Wales and Northern Ireland, by invitation, reporting to their representative authorities.[257] The scope of inspection regimes has developed as HMIC has attempted to meet such increasingly specific demands.[258] In the early 1990's, forces could expect in alternate years to undergo either a 'primary' (full) inspection, or an intermediate inspection, which would focus in greater depth upon particular issues identified by HMIC and the Home Office. Additionally, the Inspectorate undertook occasional 'thematic' inspections, examining a single issue across a sample of forces in order to identify and disseminate best practice. More recently the work of HMIC had been refocused towards the fulfilment of governmental requirements with the purpose of examining 'the development, implementation and delivery of force strategy, on the formulation of local policing plans and on force performance, particularly in relation to the Home Secretary's key objectives'.[259]

There are currently four sorts of review:

- Best value reviews—the Local Government Act 1999 placed a statutory duty on police authorities to secure continuous improvement in the delivery of police services, having regard to a combination of economy, efficiency and effectiveness. The Act also amended the Police Act 1996 to introduce a responsibility for HMIC to inspect police authorities for the purposes of Best Value

- BCU inspections—the HMIC undertook, from April 2001, a rolling programme of inspections of all BCUs in England and Wales over a five-year period. This was designed to examine in more detail the complexity of policing at local level and to identify the reasons why performance varies so markedly in apparently similar BCUs

- Force inspections—the Inspectorate no longer routinely inspects every police force at set intervals but has continued to carry out inspections of selected police forces. It has moved to a risk based assessment process designed to target inspections. Using a variety of indicators, the model generates tables of performance in which police forces are ranked against each other, in order to identify best-performing forces and encourage the remainder to match their achievements. On the basis of the model and depending upon the severity of apparent problems, HMIC may decide upon one of three levels of Inspection. The first is essentially paper-based, the second is a formal inspection covering a limited range of activities, and the third is a comprehensive inspection. The latter will take place in every force

---

[256] *ibid.*, s. 55.
[257] www.homeoffice.gov.uk/hmic/.
[258] I am indebted to the work of Rob Heaton for much of the following.
[259] HM Chief Inspector of Constabulary, Report 1994–95, p. 10.

every three years, regardless of performance indicators. It has continued to scrutinise the efficiency plans of all forces

- Thematic inspections—HMIC has also maintained a programme of thematic inspections of specific aspects of police performance. For example, '*Winning the Race—Embracing Diversity*' examined the problems that forces encounter with community race relations. Recently they have also carried out joint inspections with other agencies.[260] The report '*Calling Time on Crime*'[261] advocated an integrated crime reduction model including intelligence-led policing, problem solving and partnership approaches. 'Models of success' checklists were provided, against which the success of forces in setting up appropriate crime reduction structures were to be judged.

The form and content of the inspections has never been defined, although the HMI provides guidance in the shape of policy statements and 30 questions in relation to seven key areas: personnel and organisation; technology; operational performance; quality of service; community relations; complaints and discipline; counter-terrorism and war planning. Each of the five inspectors is attached to a particular region, not only inspecting the forces but also acting as convenor and chairman of regional conferences and promoting co-operation. Local forces are inevitably influenced by the HMI, a crucial conduit between them and central government, by which the policy concerns of the Home Office are communicated as well as being the means by which the Home Office gains information on how those policy priorities are being implemented in the field.[262]

That process of communication and influence is also carried on through the Home Office's series of 'advisory circulars' that it issues to forces on management, financial and operational issues. There were 50 in 2001. These are frequently the product of consultation between the Home Office and ACPO and police authorities are not normally consulted even when the advice might impinge directly on the their financial responsibilities. The authorities do not have a right to see them nor Parliament to discuss them but a selection of the circulars is now available on the Home Office website.[263] Such circulars might signal important changes in criminal justice policy—for example, Circular 18/94 marked a restriction on the police use of informal cautions. Crucially Circular 114/83 applied the government's financial management initiative to the police. Since that time, through HMI inspections, there has been a steady tightening of financial and managerial accountability. Weatheritt sees this circular as marking the beginning of the police identifying policing problems, setting themselves objectives, deploying resources to meet those objectives and reviewing performance, developing a much more 'performance conscious culture' within forces.[264]

The growth of this culture has been accentuated by the entry of the Audit Commission onto the policing scene—created by the Local Government Finance Act 1982, the auditors have a brief to satisfy themselves that the resources are

---

[260] HMIC and CPS Inspectorate: *Investigation and Prosecution of Cases Involving Allegations of Rape* (2002).
[261] HMIC (2000), 'Calling Time on Crime'.
[262] Weatheritt, *op. cit.* p. 29.
[263] www.homeoffice.gov.uk/circulars/.
[264] Weatheritt, *op. cit.*, p. 25 ff.

being used economically, efficiently and effectively. The powers of the Audit Commission and its influence upon the work of public services grew, as it was seen by successive governments as a key weapon in the battle to improve both effectiveness and the elusive goal of public satisfaction. The remit of the Commission was reinforced and consolidated by the 1992 Local Government Act, the 1998 Audit Commission Act and the 1999 Local Government Act. The last of these, in establishing the Government's 'Best Value' regime of continuous improvement of public services, gave the Audit Commission a key role in target-setting, stating that the Secretary of State, in specifying performance indicators and performance standards, *'shall have regard to any recommendations made to him by the Audit Commission'*.[265] The Home Secretary has the power to set national objectives and key performance indicators under sections 37 and 38 of the Police Act 1996.

Since 1988, the Commission has published a series of studies on the police, developing performance indicators, which are not simply financial but seek to identify the quality of service being provided by the police.[266] *'Helping with Enquiries'*[267] was the first report to examine core aspects of policing. Other publications have covered the subjects of patrol work[268] and BCUs.[269] Recent years have seen increasing collaboration between Her Majesty's Inspectors and the Audit Commission, a process given impetus by *'Helping with Enquiries'*. HMIC reviewed the intelligence function and endorsed the intelligence-led policing style.[270] In 2002 it published a substantial report on improving the criminal justice system.[271]

2.10.6 COMMUNITY LIAISON

Since the passage of section 106 of PACE, the police authority has been responsible for making arrangements to obtain the views of local people living in the area about matters concerning local policing and for obtaining their co-operation with the police in preventing crime. This was a recommendation of the Scarman Report.[272] If the arrangements are inadequate, the Home Secretary retains the power to require a report from the authority. While consultative arrangements may provide a forum for local people to express their genuine feelings on crime and policing, Lustgarten points out[273] that there is a fundamental problem for democratic theory in interposing a non-elected body between the police and elected representatives.

The development of consultative committees in the ten years since PACE seems unconvincing and they often operate as little more than talking shops dominated

---

[265] Local Government Act 1999, s. 4(5).
[266] Weatheritt: *op. cit.*, p. 32.
[267] Audit Commission (1993), *'Helping With Enquiries: Tackling Crime Effectively'*, Police Paper No. 12.
[268] Audit Commission (1996), *'Tackling Patrol Effectively—Management Handbook'*.
[269] Audit Commission (2001), *'Best Foot Forward: Headquarters' Support for Police Basic Command Units'*.
[270] HMIC (1997), *'Policing With Intelligence—Criminal Intelligence—A Thematic Inspection on Good Practice'*.
[271] Audit Commission (2002), *'Route to Justice'*.
[272] Scarman (1981): *op. cit.*, paras 5.55–5.66.
[273] Lustgarten, *op. cit.*, p. 89 ff.

by a police agenda.[274] However as changes in police organisation place more emphasis on the base command unit as the fundamental element of policing, such consultative bodies will provide a more natural link with BCUs and a forum for the articulation of views on policing objectives and police performance in a locality. This process will benefit from the creation of community safety partnerships under the Crime and Disorder Act 1998.

2.10.6.1 INDEPENDENT CUSTODY VISITORS

Independent custody visitors are members of the local community who visit police stations unannounced to check on the welfare of people in police custody.[275] They come from a variety of backgrounds and sections of the community. They must be over 18 and have no direct involvement in the criminal justice system, for example, serving police officers or special constables. Appointment is by a committee of the police authority and representatives of the Chief Constable. The aim is to increase public confidence in the fair and proper treatment of detainees by the police by having independent people able to see all detainees in police custody without notice and to check on the operation in practice of statutory and other rules governing their welfare. Visitors can raise welfare issues such as requests for a meal, a blanket or exercise, requests to speak to a solicitor for relatives to be informed of their detention, all of which may be resolved with the Custody Officer at the time of their visit. Visitors are allowed access to cells, detention rooms, charging areas, washing facilities, kitchen and food preparation areas and medical rooms. All detainees in police custody may be visited, including remand and convicted detainees, both adults and juveniles. This system was put on a statutory footing by section 51 of the Police Reform act 2002.

2.10.6.2 COMMUNITY SAFETY PARTNERSHIPS

Separate and distinct from police authorities are the community safety partnerships, which were set up as a result of the Crime and Disorder Act 1998. These represent another technique by which local people are able to monitor and influence policing in their area. The legislation required the 'responsible authorities' (the local authority and the corresponding Police Force), to co-operate and collaborate with a range of organisations to develop a local strategy to tackle the problems of crime and disorder. The partnership has to carry out a crime audit, which in many cases was the first analysis of local crime and problems for many areas. An effective audit determines the key priorities for both immediate and long-term action. Each community safety partnership must produce a three-year strategy for its local area. This is a public document that states the partnership's priorities and the specific action it intends to take, in response to identified local problems. Each strategy should comprise a balance of short and long-term activity that addresses both the immediate problems and their underlying causes. The first strategies were published by April 1, 1999, and by 2001, 376 partnerships were implementing them.[276]

---

[274] Morgan R., 'Policing by Consent—Legitimating the Doctrine' in Morgan R. and Smith D. (eds), *Coming to Terms with Policing* (1989).
[275] www.icva.org.uk.
[276] www.audit-commission.gov.uk/comsafe/.

2.10.7 POLICE COMPLAINTS

The most straightforward system of accountability will always be the individual complaints about a person's behaviour to their superiors. Anyone aggrieved by the behaviour of a police officer would anticipate a simple mechanism for complaining and would expect an explanation, apology and perhaps some form of reprimand or disciplinary action. The machinery for investigation of complaints against the police was first established by section 49 of the Police Act 1964. The basic objection to that machinery was that it left the investigation and adjudication of the complaint to other police officers, often serving in the same force. Originally the only independent element was the Director of Public Prosecutions who had to decide whether or not an allegation of crime against an officer should be prosecuted. Limited reform came about through the Police Act 1976 which introduced the Police Complaints Board (PCB), an independent body which looked at all reports of investigations into complaints except those involving possible criminal charges which still went to the DPP. The Board had neither the power nor the staff to carry out its own inquiries but they could request further information and advise that disciplinary action be taken.

The system did not inspire great police or public confidence. Police resentment at the PCB died away as it became apparent that the Board almost invariably supported police disciplinary decisions. The DPP's office also gave the police little cause for concern, recommending prosecutions in only 2 per cent of the cases referred to them. Furthermore a 1981 survey[277] revealed that many respondents believed that they had been the victims of illegal police behaviour but had not made a complaint. Unpublished Home Office research at that time suggested that those entrusted with investigating complaints of assault were too often concerned with the criminal guilt or untrustworthiness of the complainant.

There was further demand for an increased independent element and criticism of the requirement that all complaints had to be recorded and an investigating officer appointed. This led to a host of trivial matters being dealt with formally. In 1984 there was further reform under PACE whereby, although all complaints are recorded, an investigating officer is not appointed if it is possible to resolve the matter informally by way of explanation or apology. If it is pursued formally an officer will be appointed, normally from the same force but from other forces if the complaint is serious, is a matter of public concern or if it relates to an officer of the rank of superintendent or above. The Police Complaints Authority (PCA), successor in title to the PCB, supervises investigations.[278] The powers of the PCA include approval of the investigating officer and the appointment of a supervisor from with the PCA itself. All complaints within certain categories (including death and assault) will be referred to the Authority but it also has the power to deal with other categories of complaint and indeed with matters that are not subject to complaint at all. The ambit of the Authority still excludes[279] matters of operational policy.

At the time of writing, we are in a period of transition. The legislative structure is now contained in the Police Act 1996, which in the main retains the 1984

---

[277] Tuck M. and Southgate P., *Ethnic Minorities, Crime and Policing* (Home Office Research Study No. 70) 1981.
[278] www.pca.gov.uk/.
[279] PACE s. 84(5).

system. The effectiveness of the PCA still attracted criticism.[280] Very few complaints succeed and the level of withdrawal is still high. The PCA only supervises in the most serious of cases and is in the position of evaluating the police's work on the basis of the police's own paperwork. The Authority still only publishes annual reports and not detailed reports on individual incidents. In a number of high profile cases of deaths in police custody, such as those of Harry Stanley, Shiji Lapite and Roger Sylvester, the investigation, and subsequent proceedings were widely criticised, not least for their lack of independence.[281] It is hard to disagree with Sanders,

> ... it is not that investigators wish to exonerate officers who 'overstep the mark' but that policing norms create 'codes of silence' which are almost impossible to penetrate and that 'the mark' is not a clear or unchanging line. It depends more on police culture and informal working rules than it does on law or official policy. Thus the complaints system will be unreformable until police culture and working rules are fundamentally changed which is not at all likely...[282]

Further information is imminent as a direct result of the MacPherson Report[283]. The Police Reform Act 2002 set up the Independent Police Complaints Commission (IPCC). The government's objectives are increased public confidence in the police and in the complaints system, increased accessibility, openness and independence, quicker resolution of complaints, improved communications with complainants and improved collection, collation and reporting of data. The new system[284] will broaden the definition of a complaint—although any complaint about the direction and control of a force by its chief officer is specifically excluded from the work of the IPCC. It will also widen the definition of a complainant to include witnesses as well as those adversely affected by the conduct. All ranks will be treated in the same fashion, unlike the previous system, which provided privileged treatment for senior officers.

Although the responsibility for recording complaints remains with the police and the police authority, the legislation aims to widen the gateways providing access to the complaints procedure—it will be possible, for example, to complain at a Citizen's Advice Bureau. Certain complaints must be referred to the commission, including complaints concerning death or serious injury, but not other categories, such as those involving corruption by a police officer or those including an allegation of racial discrimination by a police officer. Under the PCA, about a third of all complaints were resolved locally, a quick resolution in less serious cases. Under the IPCC, this is retained and more widely applied but the authority will be required to apply to the Commission for dispensation to deal with such cases by local resolution. The intention is to create a climate of conciliation in which the officer will have the opportunity to explain his behaviour and apologise to the complainant.

The key to the success of this reform will be the perception that serious complaints will be independently investigated. Under the legislation, the Com-

---

[280] Maguire M. and Corbett C., *A Study of the Police Complaints System* (1991).
[281] Harrison J. and Cunneen M., *An Independent Police Complaints Commission* (2000).
[282] Sanders (1993): *op. cit.*, p. 102.
[283] *Report of the Inquiry into the Matters Arising from the Death of Stephen Lawrence* (Home Office, 1999) Recommendation 58.
[284] A discussion document on the new system can be found at www.homeoffice.gov.uk/pcrg/policec.htm.

mission will have four options:

- a police investigation on behalf of the appropriate authority and where the complaint is not suitable for local resolution;

- a police investigation supervised by the Commission—this replicates the provisions in the 1996 Act.

- a police investigation managed by the Commission. This is a new concept to be used in more serious cases. It is intended that the greater degree of independence will come from the strategy and direction provided in an investigation by the Commission and the managerial control it will exercise on a day-to-day basis. The Commission will be responsible for the investigation but the investigation itself will be carried out by the appointed investigating officer.

- an investigation by the Commission independent of the police. The Commission will designate a person from its own staff (which will include police officers seconded to the IPCC) to take charge of the investigation so that it is clear who has responsibility for managing the day to day running of the investigation and for producing the report at the end. In an investigation by the Commission, its investigators will have all the powers and privileges that would be available to the police in such an investigation.

Liberty have argued[285] that if only a small number of high profile and serious complaints are independently investigated, this will do little to restore the confidence of complainants in the system as a whole and may be viewed as a superficial exercise. Whether the IPCC turns out to be a viable mechanism for police accountability remains to be seen.

---

[285] Harrison J. and Cunneen M., *op. cit.*

CHAPTER THREE

The Investigation of Crime(1): Basic Powers

3.1 CRIMEFIGHTERS?

Public expectations of the police are many and various—to provide information, to maintain an order in public spaces, to work with the homeless, the substance abusers or the rootless young, to mediate in disputes, to deal both practically and emotionally with death and disaster in the community and last but not least to enforce a complex set of rules and procedures governing the criminal law. The police represent a 24-hour a day resource for any and every kind of problem. Perhaps simplistically, the force maintains order and resolves disorder. Order is maintained by the patrolling of the streets, dealing with the homeless, with rowdy groups, organising traffic or demonstrations, preventing vandalism. It is sometimes referred to as 'quality of life' policing but whose? It is an order that reflects, by and large, the interests of an older, employed, propertied, quiescent majority in a routine existence. Whereas order maintenance is discretionary and normally low profile, resolution of disorder is inevitably more controversial. The freedom of individuals to act as they see fit will come into conflict with the constraints of the criminal law.

Order maintenance or service to the community are not the standards that we use to judge the effectiveness of the police. Instead in the media and in the utterances of politicians, the police are portrayed predominantly as crime fighters, protecting the public against physical violence, burglaries, vandalism and thefts of all kinds. The police share this perception and see other activities as not proper 'police' work.[1] This image of proper policing exists not only in the 'canteen' culture[2] of constables but also underpins the arguments of senior officers for enhanced resources (whether personnel, legal powers or equipment) who quote rising crime figures and draw on the military[3] imagery of the 'war against crime'. It was also the focus of the government in the early 1990s that regarded clear-up rates as the key performance indicator.[4]

Crime fighting was and remains a narrow philosophy of policing but it affects the attitude that the ambitious junior officer takes towards the job. It is still dominant although the decline in recorded crime in the last decade has enabled the Labour administration that took office in 1997 to adopt a different strategy, not merely 'tough on crime' but 'tough on the causes of crime'. A policy based on such sound bites is easily caricatured but it has the merit of recognising some of the complexities of the issues, beyond the black-and-white simplicity of a criminal class at war with the rest of society. We experience 'crime' as a phenomenon, both individually and collectively, as victims but also as perpetrators, personally or vicariously through friends or family members. We know that more and severer punishments have little effect and the current policy at least emphasises a 'what works', evidence-led approach to reducing crime rather than merely arresting criminals. This prioritises prevention of crime and the results can be seen in some of the radical changes in the youth justice system as well as in encouraging creative thinking by the police, local authorities and other public and private sector agencies so that they work together to develop community safety partnerships.[5]

3.2 MEASURING CRIME

Our topic in this chapter is the police role in the investigation and prosecution of crime. The first questions must relate to the amount and nature of the crime problem. In the nineteenth century, crime was measured by the use of statistics from the courts and the prisons but such figures merely reflected the activities of those institutions and did not measure the amount of crime on the streets. Nowadays the police are under a statutory obligation[6] to transmit information to the Home Secretary about offences and these notifiable offences are the source of the Criminal Statistics published by the Home Office. Even these, for the reasons discussed below, are of limited value and understate the level of crime. An alternative approach, which gives a truer picture, is to conduct victim surveys— the British Crime Survey[7] (BCS) surveys households as opposed to the use of official statistics and consequently gives a more accurate and complete picture of crime trends. The survey moved to an annual cycle from 2001, with 33,000 interviews of people aged 16 or over now taking place per year. The major

---

[1] Punch M., 'The Secret Social Service' in Holdaway S. (ed.), *The British Police* (1979)).
[2] Reiner R., *The Politics of the Police* (3rd ed. 2000) Chap. 3.
[3] Such language is often employed but has little to commend it, not least because it leads to confrontation, stereotyping and depersonalising of those involved.
[4] White Paper, *Police Reform* (1993) Cm. 2281 Chap. 7 esp. para. 7.7.
[5] Home Office, *The Government's Crime Reduction Strategy* (1999), www.crimereduction.gov.uk/.
[6] Police Act 1996, s. 45.
[7] 2002 sees the tenth such survey since 1983.

omissions are that it does not measure victimless crimes, sexual offences or crimes against under–16s.

Recorded crime increased steadily since the war although the rate of increase slowed down in the late 1970s and again in the late 1980s. The official figures peaked in 1992 and have been declining since. In interpreting the data, there is an important caveat—a major change in the counting rules in 1998 increased the amount of crime recorded.[8] This makes comparisons difficult but the last five years has seen a significant reduction in crime.[9] Possible reasons that account for these trends are increased levels of home and vehicle security as well as local policing and crime reduction initiatives.[10] Another factor may be the state of the economy, with low levels of unemployment and relatively high levels of disposable income. The BCS suggest that it is possible that the nature of crime is changing, and that crimes of the future will less concern the familiar household crimes—such as burglary or vehicle theft—but rather new types of crime involving fraud, or the Internet, or personal crimes such as stalking and sexual abuse.

The picture of declining property crime is reflected in many other countries—if we look at police-recorded domestic burglary between 1995 and 1999 there was an average 14 per cent fall across all European Union countries, with the greatest decrease in England and Wales (31 per cent) followed by Germany (29 per cent), Austria (26 per cent), the Netherlands (22 per cent) and France (20 per cent). Between 1995 and 1999 domestic burglary in the U.S. fell by 19 per cent.[11]

Crime is not spread evenly across the UK—as would be expected the highest crime rates are in metropolitan areas with Greater Manchester having the highest rate in the year 2000 with 14,100 recorded offences per 100,000 inhabitants. In contrast, Dyfed-Powys had a rate of 4,800. Other rural counties also had low rates.

Table 3.1 Recorded Crime 1950–2000[12]

Year	Number of Offences	Offences per 100,00 population	BCS incidents of crime[13]
1950	479,400*	1,094	Not available
1960	800,300*	1,742	Not available
1970	1,568,400*	3,221	Not available
1980	2,688,200	5,459	11,046,000 *(1981)*
1990	4,543,600	8,986	Not available
1992	5,591,700	10,943	18,559,000 *(1993)*

[8] For details, see *Criminal Statistics 2000* Cm. 5312 App. 2 p. 244.

[9] *2001 British Crime Survey* (Home Office Statistical Bulletin 18/01 Table A2.1, p. 45) showed a decrease of 12% from 1999–2000 whereas *Criminal Statistics 2000* (*op. cit.*, Chap. 2.) showed a decrease of 2.5%. There are indications that this decade of decreasing figures is coming to an end.

[10] Kershaw C. et al., *2000 British Crime Survey* (Home Office Statistical Bulletin 18/00) discusses these reasons.

[11] Barclay G., et al., *International comparisons of criminal justice statistics 1999* (Home Office Statistical Bulletin 6/01).

[12] *Criminal Statistics 2000, op. cit.*, Table 2.2 p. 40.

[13] *2001 British Crime Survey, loc. cit.*

| 1995 | 5,100,200 | 9,880 | 19,161,000 |
| 2000/01 | 5,170,800 | 9, 814 (8,600)[14] | 12,899,000 |

* *These exclude offences of criminal damage where the value is less than £20*

As Table 3.1 shows, the official statistics give only a partial picture of the amount of crime—as will be discussed later, the BCS suggests that perhaps less than a quarter of all crime is recorded. Interpreting trends in criminal behaviour from such global figures is fraught with risks. Analysing the data according the type of offence can derive more information but the problems remain, not least because the official statistics are in effect directly measuring certain decisions made by the public and the police. Only indirectly are we able to derive data about crime. However Table 3.2 shows that, in terms of quantity, the crime problem, as reported to and recorded by the police, is about property offences, especially shoplifting, auto theft and burglary. Perhaps there is an analogy with the civil legal process and civil courts, which are sometimes characterised as a debt collection agency. A visiting Martian might well view the protection and maintenance of an existing structure of property rights as a major function of the police and the criminal courts.

Table 3.2 Recorded Crime by Offence Categories 1983–2000[15]

Type of Offence	1983	1990	1995	2000	Average Annual % Increase 1990–2000
Serious Violence	6,700	14,700	19,200	31,700	+7.8
Less Serious Violence	111,300	170,000	193,400	569,200[16]	+3.7
Rape[17]	1,300	3,400	5,100	8,600	+9.4
Indecent Assault on female	10,800	15,800	16,900	20,300	+2.6
Other sex crimes	8,200	9,900	8,300	8,400	−3.0
Robbery	22,100	36,200	68,100	95,200[18]	+9.7
Burglary	808,300	1,006,800	1,239,500	836,000	−3.1
Theft of or from vehicle	749,900	1,267,300	1,321,500	968,400	−3.2

[14] New counting rules were implemented in April 1998—the figure in brackets represent the figure under the old rules.
[15] *Criminal Statistics 2000, op. cit.*, Table 2.1, p. 38 and Table 2.15, p. 52.
[16] This is accounted for by the new counting rules and the inclusion of common assault, assault on a PC and harassment offences which were not included in the 1995 figures.
[17] Criminal Justice and Public Order Act 1994, s. 142, expanded the offence of rape to include rape of a male. Male victims of forced buggery are now classified as rape. There were 654 such offences recorded in 2000.
[18] This rise is mainly in robbery of personal property, *Criminal Statistics 2000, op. cit.*, Table 2.16, p. 53.

Other theft or handling	956,000	1,107,100	1,130,600	1,177,000	+0.7
Fraud and forgery	121,800	147,900	133,000	319,300	+2.5
Arson	17,100	26,500	30,000	52,800	+5.0
Other criminal damage[19]	426,200	707,000	884,000	907,300	+1.8
Drug Offences	5,000	10,000	21,300	113,500	+5.6
Other notifiable offences	8,800	21,100	26,100	63,200	−0.8
TOTAL	3,247,400	4,543,600	5,100,200	5,170,800	−0.4

3.3 UNREPORTED CRIME AND UNRELIABLE STATISTICS

These official statistics reveal an underlying pattern of crime, consisting predominantly of property offences. Analysis occasionally suggests that there are certain trends, perhaps to a more violent society.[20] The media, professional groups of all varieties and politicians seize on these statistics, derive conclusions about the moral economy of our society and formulate policy, whether through legislation, additional police resources or changes in sentencing practice. But there are important qualifications that must be made before such statistics are used in this way: the majority of crime is discovered by the public who report it to the police and thus the statistics only measure the decision-making of those members of the public who choose to report offences. Furthermore the statistics reflect the behaviour of the police—not only in whether an officer chooses to formally record the complaint but also in his or her choice of offence category. For example, if a bag is snatched from a person, it might be recorded as theft from the person but if the victim hangs onto her property, even for a moment, it might well be regarded as robbery. At most, the official statistics give us what is no more than an indicative measure of crime.

Table 3.3 BCS Incidents of Crime by Offence Categories 1983–2000[21]

Type of Offence	1981	1993	1995	2000	% change 1983– 2000
Common assault	1,403,000	2,550,000	2,820,000	1,890,000	+35.0
Wounding	508,000	762,000	862,000	417,000	−18.0
Robbery	164,000	237,000	314,000	276,000	+68.0
ALL BCS VIOLENCE	2,160,000	3,635,000	4,071,000	2,618,000	+21.0

[19] Excluding criminal damage under £20.
[20] Muncie J. *et al.*, *focus on the use and abuse of criminal statistics* (NACRO 'Safer Society' Winter 2001 p. 14ff).
[21] *2001 British Crime Survey, loc. cit.*

Vandalism	2,715,000	3,403,000	3,419,000	2,608,000	−4.0
Burglary	750,000	1,775,000	1,755,000	1,063,000	+42
Theft of or from vehicle	1,752,000	4,344,000	4,318,000	2,619,000	+50
Bicycle theft	216,000	602,000	660,000	377,000	+74
Other household theft	1,518,000	2,366,000	2,267,000	1,616,000	+6.0
Theft from the person	434,000	601,000	670,000	629,000	+45.0
Other thefts of personal property	1,586,000	1,921,000	2,074,000	1,404,000	−11.0
ALL BCS CRIME	11,046,000	18,559,000	19,161,000	12,899,000	+17.0

The media and politicians prefer the 'official' statistics to the BCS. That survey asks a random sample of victims and its data gives a more complete picture of the risks confronting households. But the survey is still reliant on the victims' interpretation of the event. This raises the question as to whether it is possible to know the 'real' crime rate. This is probably impossible for various reasons:

- we cannot measure all crime—the very breadth of the criminal law and number of offences from the bureaucratic to the trivial to the serious prevents this.

- we only have an authoritative, legal interpretation of whether an act is criminal in probably less than 1 per cent of all potential crimes i.e. there cases decided by a court. Any statistics on a 'real' crime rate will always depend on subjective interpretation as to whether the conduct is a crime or anti-social or simply behaviour the person does not approve of.

- large areas of potentially criminal behaviour do not come under regular official scrutiny—examples would be physical and sexual abuse in the home, unacceptable risk-taking in the workplace or financial fraud in large corporations.

- only a relatively small proportion of incidents that could be labeled as criminal are ever reported to the police

- only a proportion of the incidents reported to the police will be officially recorded as an offence.

Why chase the chimera that is an 'absolute' figure of crime? Although it is an illusion, it may also be a useful device. To suggest that there is an absolute level of crime that is measurable suggests that there is a 'dark figure' of crime hidden from the official statistics. This figure contains offences that, firstly, neither the public nor the police know about or, secondly, do not regard as crime or, thirdly, choose not to report or record. It is this figure that makes drawing conclusions from the criminal statistics so difficult, particularly when faced with increases in recorded crime. Obviously there are some categories of offence where there is a high rate of reporting—car theft is one—and conclusions can be drawn confidently from any increase recorded in the statistics. But there are few crimes that are invariably reported and thus increases are as likely to reflect changes in reporting or recording behaviour as any increase in the actual amount of the crime. At this stage this dark figure is a helpful device as we analyse how and by whom the mechanisms of the criminal justice system are being mobilized. When do individuals or companies call the police and when do they not? What areas of crime do the police focus on? To what extent does the state or powerful individuals or groups influence them?

There are many reasons why people do not report an incident:[22]

1. although the incident is technically a crime, the individual might not share that perception. Students will not report cannabis smoking and employees might not report thefts from the workplace that are seen as 'perks' of the job.

2. the incident might be regarded as too trivial or indeed too common—how many of us ever report road traffic offences? In 2000, victims told the BCS that the incident was too trivial in 72 per cent of unreported crimes—these were mainly property offences. The trivial nature of the incident was the reason for not reporting in just 42 per cent of violent offences.

3. the police might be viewed as ineffective—the victim, aware of the low clear-up rate, might not report a domestic burglary unless there was a positive reason such as a potential insurance claim.

4. the matter might be regarded as a private affair and not the business of the police. Close-knit groups (families, workplaces, schools, small communities) often choose to deal with the incident themselves? In 2000, victims told the BCS that the incident was a private matter in 22 per cent of unreported crimes. However with violent offences, the private nature of the incident was the reason for not reporting in 49 per cent of cases.[23]

5. groups might be united by race, age or class in their hostility to the police.

6. people might be discouraged from reporting offences where they are aware that being a witness entails a considerable degree of personal inconvenience.

7. with some crimes such as blackmail, the sheer embarrassment for the victim might ensure the crime is never reported. Companies providing financial services might wish to conceal the fact that they have dishonest employees in order to maintain a public image of probity.

Less research has been done on the positive reasons why we report an incident. Is there a sense of civic duty and does that lie behind the proliferation of neighbourhood watch schemes? Do we seek to avoid inconvenience or being involved? Or are we more utilitarian, looking for personal benefit? The police may be seen as protection for yourself from, say, the assault occurring again. With property offences, the report may lead to recovery of stolen property (especially with cars) or at least be a preliminary step to making an insurance claim. The rise in home ownership and in contents insurance cover thus leads to more reported offences.

The BCS has revealed that the overall rate of reporting of offences varies—in

---

[22] Mayhew P. et al., *The 1992 British Crime Survey* (Home Office Research Study No. 132) (1993) Chap. 3; *2001 British Crime Survey, op. cit.*, Table A2.5, p. 49.

[23] *2001 British Crime Survey, loc. cit.*

1981 36 per cent of offences notified to the BCS were reported to the police. This rose to 50 per cent in 1991 but by 2000 had fallen to 45 per cent. The majority of incidents, perceived as crime by the respondents to the survey, were not reported to the police. Reporting varies considerably according to offence—90 per cent of vehicles thefts and 84 per cent of burglaries involving loss were reported in 2000. In contrast 30 per cent of cases of damage to a vehicle or theft of a bicycle were reported.[24]

Many of these unreported incidents are less serious but it would be an error to assume that unreported crime is merely a mass of trivial incidents not worth the effort to report, record or investigate—the 'dark figure' contains many serious offences and the BCS found that merely 46 per cent of robberies were reported. Similarly it is an error to assume that official statistics only record serious crime. Firstly those offences that are reported and prosecuted can themselves be trivial: several years ago a child was tried at the Old Bailey for theft of an iced bun! This point is illustrated by the fact that 25 per cent of the burglaries recorded in the Criminal Statistics involve no loss of property at all.[25] Approximately 15 per cent of recorded criminal damage cases involve damage of less than £20. Secondly, while the official crime figures inevitably contain much minor crime, it is clear that these figures ignore much serious crime, especially in the areas of violence against women (particularly domestic violence and sexual assault) and white-collar crime. Racial assaults have been another such area but there are now crimes of racially aggravated assault, harassment and criminal damage and these are now detailed in the official data—there were over 20,000 such cases recorded in 2000. But the under-reporting and under-recording of such crimes that official statistics present a skewed picture of the real threats to property and person that we face.[26]

Just because the public choose to report an 'offence', does not mean that the police will record it as such. One of the primary measures of police efficiency is the percentage of offences that are resolved—the clear-up rate, discussed later. Almost invariably, the more offences that are reported and recorded, the lower will be the clear up rate. Officers have a personal stake in their station's efficiency and, confronted with a report of an alleged offence, may choose not to record it as such. This point can be illustrated by looking at the residential burglary figures and by comparing the results of the BCS with the Criminal Statistics.

Table 3.4 BCS and Criminal Statistics: Incidents of Burglary 2000[27]

	Police (000s)	BCS (000s)	%BCS reported	% reported recorded	% recorded of all BCS
All domestic burglary	409	1,063	66	59	38
Attempts and no loss	106	660	55	30	16
With loss	303	403	84	90	75

[24] *2001 British Crime Survey*, op. cit., Fig. 2.2, p. 9 and Table A2.4, p. 48.
[25] However the harm suffered by victims in the invasion of their home is not necessarily measurable in terms of property loss—Morgan J. and Zedner L., *Child Victims* (1992), pp. 54–55.
[26] Box S., *Power, Crime and Mystification* (1983).
[27] *2001 British Crime Survey*, op. cit., Table 2.1, p. 8.

The BCS estimated that there were 1,063,000 burglaries in 2000 and that the public reported some 700,00 (66 per cent). But, in stark contrast, the Criminal Statistics recorded only 409,000 (38 per cent). How can this be? There are several explanations. Firstly the police might re-define the event: the victim would not know how the law distinguishes a theft from a burglary from a robbery so the police might re-classify so that if money is taken by a trespasser from a gas meter, it might be seen by the victim as a burglary but the police are likely to record it as theft from a dwelling. Secondly, the police might decide that there is insufficient evidence that a crime has taken place at all—the incident can be no-crimed and not recorded. Less legitimately, if the offence is minor and there is no hope that the offender will be caught, the officer might just decide to lose the report in the wastepaper bin, a practice that aids the clear-up rate and is known as 'cuffing'. As can be seen in Table 3.4, large numbers of reports of attempted burglaries and burglaries not involving loss are never formally recorded.

The BCS concluded that only 56 per cent of reported 'crime' was actually recorded by the police as crime in 2000,[28] down from an estimated 60 per cent in 1992. Thefts of cars and burglaries with loss are most likely to be recorded whereas common assault and theft from the person is least likely. Many forces have introduced centralised crime desks, manned by civilians, as the initial stage for any crime report. Such staff may well be less concerned about clear-up rates and the impact of this innovation may be that more offences are recorded. Furthermore police forces are adopting a National Crime Recording Standard and this is likely to result in a continuation of the trend towards increased recording.[29]

A further problem in using the official statistics is that of assessing trends in crime. This is illustrated by using BSC data since 1981. Although difficult, it is possible to compare some of the offences measured in the official statistics and in the BCS. If the figures for 1981 are indexed at 100, between 1981 and 2000 the number of *recorded crimes* rose by 52 per cent, whereas the *total number* of comparable BCS crimes, whether reported or not, rose less, by 22 per cent. The estimated number of comparable BCS crimes that had been *reported* to the police rose by 58 per cent. This suggests that the greater rise in the official statistics can be accounted for by a greater willingness to report crime than a rise in crime *per se*. Since 1997, the fall in crime has been more marked in the BCS figures than in the official statistics—this is consistent with more offences being reported to the police and more such reports being formally recorded by the police.

The willingness of people to report offences has risen since the start of the BCS—in 1981, 36 per cent of crimes were reported to the police; in 2000, 47 per cent were reported. The highest rates of reporting are for vehicle theft and burglary involving loss and the spread of insurance is certainly a factor. But the BCS also shows that victims are regarding crime, especially violence, more seriously, which suggests less tolerance and a greater likelihood that an incident will be reported.

3.4 THE PATTERN OF CRIME

Despite the fluctuations in the volume of crime, there remains a steady underlying pattern in which property offences are predominant: in 2000/01, the police

[28] *2001 British Crime Survey, op. cit.*, Fig. 2.4 p. 12.
[29] Simmons J., *Review of Crime Statistics* (Home Office, 2000).

recorded some 5.2m offences and 82 per cent of these were against property, namely burglary, theft, criminal damage and fraud. The figures for theft of and from cars and shoplifting reflect the increased opportunities for crime with 27m vehicles on road, often with high value accessories; easily transportable electrical items in the home which can quickly converted into cash; the open shelves and marketing strategies of large retailers. The 1992 BCS found that one in five car owners were victims of crime in 1991, nearly 5.5m offences, although most were not reported to the police.[30] Despite this huge amount of recorded property crime, the figures still exclude a large amount of employee-related theft and white-collar crime generally.[31]

3.4.1 *Vehicle crime*

Vehicle crime is the largest single category of *recorded* crime. There are about 27.5 million vehicles registered with the Driver and Vehicle Licensing Agency (DVLA), of which cars are the largest single category. Cars account for about 72 per cent of total vehicles but a disproportionately high rate of 81 per cent of vehicle theft. It is estimated that about 360,000 vehicles stolen in 2001 and 180,000 of those were not recovered.[32] Theft from vehicles is very significant—the BCS estimates that there were 2.3m thefts from private vehicles in 2000. Over 10 per cent of households suffer annually from vehicle crime and, quite realistically, consider that it is likely that they will become the victim of such an offence within a year. The most likely location for the offence is in the street by one's home (36% of cases). The main items stolen from vehicles are external fittings (36% of cases), personal goods left in the car (29%) or the radio or stereo (27%). Thefts involving car radios/stereos are most likely to be reported.

3.4.2 *Shoplifting*

There were 293,000 recorded offences of shoplifting in 2001—obviously this nowhere corresponds to the real total as it is only when an offender is caught that the offence is reported or recorded. The British Retail Consortium's annual Retail Crime Survey[33] suggests that retailers apprehend nearly three times that total. Perhaps this is one of the most widespread of all offences—shoplifters come in many shapes and sizes: often they are non-professional such as opportunist thieves, influenced by opportunities such as easily accessible display areas; juveniles influenced by peer pressure and part of a 'group syndrome' where young people only steal when they are together—they tend to steal such items as electronic games, CDs and fashion goods; the mentally disturbed, a small group who have a mental disorder which compels them to steal, often goods which are of no value to the thief (such as single shoes), and when caught, they are often found to have large quantities of such goods hoarded at home; drug abusers steal to support a drugs habit, which can cost addicts hundreds of pounds a week and often see shop theft as the easiest way to raise money. Professional thieves on the

---

[30] Light R. *et al.*, *Car Theft: The Offender's Perspective* ((Home Office Research Study 130; HMSO 1993); NACRO, Car Crime (Briefing Paper 65 1994).

[31] Henry S., *Informal Economy* (1978); Ditton J., *Part-Time Crime* (1977).

[32] www.crimereduction.gov.uk/vc_index.htm.

[33] This survey captured information from over 17,000 retail outlets, with 891,000 employees with a turnover of £100 billion (45% of U.K. turnover).

other hand target high value goods, and often work in teams passing the goods through several pairs of hands before they are eventually taken away. Some gangs also employ 'minders' to protect them. One technique is steaming where a large gang will enter a shop and intimidate, threaten or distract staff in order to steal large quantities of goods before running off. But despite the attention given to shoplifters, it must be remembered that staff themselves are responsible for a large proportion of retail theft and indeed sometimes help thieves to steal, either actively, or by turning a blind eye to what is going on.

The 8th British Retail Consortium's Retail Crime Survey estimated that total losses from retail crime in 2000 were £1.41 billion. The cost of customer theft was £746 million and of staff theft £426 million with burglary and robbery making up the difference. The total cost of crime to the retail industry must include the spending on crime prevention which was £626 million so that the total cost of crime and crime prevention amounted to £2.044 billion in 2000, equating to a cost of £85 per household or 0.91 per cent of retail turnover, approximately half the level recorded in the first retail crime survey of 1994.

3.4.3 *Burglary*

Burglary, of all offences, is the offence about which people are most anxious. Media reporting of increases in the level of crime have fed these anxieties.[34] The fear is that there is a high risk of being burgled (nearly a quarter believe it likely that they will be burgled in the next year but only 3.4 per cent of homes were burgled in 2000) or of confrontation with the burglar and damage (but there are very few aggravated burglaries.) Recently levels of anxiety have decreased[35] reflecting the reduction in the number of burglaries from 1.4m in 1993 to 836,000 in 2000. The risk of burglary is not evenly distributed—those at higher risk include younger householders, especially single parents, on low income, living in inner city, and in public sector housing.

In 2000 there were 403,000 domestic burglaries and 433,000 commercial burglaries. 32,800 people were either convicted or cautioned for the offence. For burglaries with loss, the average gross value of property stolen was £1,273. This average masks considerable variation. In 27 per cent of burglaries with loss less than £100 worth of property was stolen, while in 32 per cent the loss amounted to a £1,000 or more. But the overall cost is greater—the most up-to-date estimate of the average cost of domestic burglary has been calculated as £2,300.[36] The crime is normally committed by a young male—of that 32,800, 17,100 were under 21 and 11,200 were under 17,[37] who spends little time in the house, takes property of little value, commits little damage and less violence.

3.4.4 *Homicide*

England and Wales are relatively peaceful societies—846 offences were initially classified as homicide in 2000, a rise from 620 in 1980.[38] This may be compared

[34] Maxfield M., *Fear of Crime* (Home Office Research Study No. 78) (1984).

[35] *2001 British Crime Survey, op. cit.*, Fig. 5.5 p. 38.

[36] Brand S. and Price R., *The economic and social costs of crime* (Home Office Research Study 217 (2000)).

[37] *Criminal Statistics 2000, op. cit.*, Table 5.10 at p. 121.

[38] *ibid.*, Tables 4.1. p. 78.

with the USA where in 1998 there were 12,102 homicides committed with guns.[39] England has 1.4 homicides per 100,000 of the population whereas in the U.S. the rate is 7.3, in Russia 19.9 and in South Africa 58.9. The safest city in the world is Canberra with a rate of 0.64 whereas London has a rate of 2.17, Pretoria 41.13 and Washington DC 64.08.[40]

The figures in 2000 were higher as a result of the deaths of 56 Chinese who were collectively suffocated in a lorry en route to the U.K.—there has however been a gradual rise in numbers from 7.0 per million in 1970 to 13.2 in 1999. Both the killer and the victim will be predominantly male. But it is the child under 1 year old who remains most at risk—with 50 deaths per million, she or he is about four times more likely than average to be killed. Stranger killings are still the exception—the victim and the killer will be blood relatives, spouses, lovers or other acquaintances in over 60 per cent of cases. The cause of the killing is usually a quarrel, revenge or loss of temper with only 7 per cent being in furtherance of gain.

3.4.5 *Violence*

Recorded assaults have continued to increase throughout the past decade—this is in contrast to BCS figures which suggest that violence has decreased by a third since 1995, at an average of 6 per cent a year. Perhaps this reflects a higher reporting and recording rate—the BCS found that the public regards all forms of violence more seriously than previously and is more likely to report incidents to the police. Despite increasing public intolerance of violent behaviour, assaults still go unreported more frequently than property offences and the true level of violent offences is much higher than that given in the official statistics. The BCS[41] suggests that there were over 2,600,000 offences of violence in 2000, representing 20 per cent of all crime—the official statistics suggest that violence represents about 14 per cent of all offences. Table 3.5 shows the breakdown of the categories of incidents of violence recorded by the BCS:

Table 3.5 British Crime Survey 2000: Incidents of Violence

	Number	*Percentage*
Domestic Violence[42]	499,000	19%
Acquaintance Violence	770,000	29%
Stranger Violence	992,000	38%
Robberies/muggings	312,000	12%
Other	45,000	2%
TOTAL	2,618,000	100%

[39] www.gun-control-network.org/.

[40] Richards P., *Homicide Statistics* (House of Commons Research Paper 99/56).

[41] *See 2001 British Crime Survey, op. cit.*, p. 28 ff. for discussion of violent offences.

[42] This is an under-estimate as both men and women often do not disclose incidents in face-to-face interviews. In self-completion modules, rates of domestic violence are three times higher for women and ten times higher for men.

The random assault by a stranger in a public place is the media's favourite image but the real risks are elsewhere. Violence is frequently work-based, home-based or in and around pubs/clubs. In recent years, domestic and acquaintance violence has decreased significantly. About 4 per cent of the population experience violence in any year but that risk varies considerably. It rises if you are young, unemployed and single and for the young (16–24) male, nearly 20 per cent of whom will experience some form of assault.

Firearms were used in 17,589 offences in 2000[43] although many of these are trivial incidents. 60 per cent of cases involved air weapons, typically used for criminal damage. The proportion of offences in which firearms are used remains small, 0.3 per cent in 2000 and this has varied little over the past ten years. Shots are fired in less than a quarter of cases involving firearms other than air weapons. But the number of such offences recorded by the police has risen for the past five years. The weapons are mainly handguns and they are used mainly in offences against the person or armed robberies. There were 1957 such robberies in 1982 and 3965 in 2000. The armed robbery is most likely to occur in a shop or on public highway. In 2000, there were only 222 robberies in banks or building societies, a considerable decline on the 1395 offences recorded in 1991. This reflects heightened security in such premises—robberies of garages and post offices have also declined.

3.4.6 *Sexual Assault*

The figures for rape and sexual assault are very difficult to interpret. Probably less than one in five rapes are reported and with such a large number of unreported offences, any increase in recorded crime is as likely to reflect a greater willingness on the part of women to go to the police as an increase in male sexual violence. Although there has been a significant rise in recorded assault over the past ten years, the vast majority of sexual attacks still go unreported, not least because the victim often finds herself victimised again. This can be through the loss of social reputation based on the 'myths' of rape that 'nice girls don't get raped' or that the rape must have been 'victim-precipitated' because of the victim's dress or being in the wrong place at the wrong time. Equally significantly the victim is unwilling to go through the ordeal of police investigative procedures although these have improved with the recognition of rape trauma syndrome, which has led to special investigation units for sexual assault. However women still choose not to report the crime rather than put themselves in the ambivalent positions of rape victims. This is reinforced by the perception that courts will not protect the rape victim in the witness box during cross-examination: this is despite the fact that the legal position has been improved recently by the abolition of the requirement for a corroboration warning[44] and by a strengthening of the rules regarding questioning on the victim's prior sexual experience.[45] But the risks of reporting a rape and of testifying are well known and this contributes to a pattern of reporting which presents the stereotypical rape as an assault by a stranger in a public place whereas it is more likely to be committed by a person known to the victim, often in the victim's home or workplace.[46] Although more mundane, this scenario

---

[43] *Criminal Statistics 2000, op. cit.*, Chap. 3.
[44] Criminal Justice and Public Order Act 1994, s.32.
[45] Youth Justice and Criminal Evidence Act 1999, s.41.
[46] Temkin J., *Rape and Legal Process* (1987); Box S. *op. cit.*, Chap. 4.

indicates that men present a more general threat of sexual assault to women than is suggested by the 'official' picture of assault by the psychopathic stranger.

Table 3.6 Recorded sexual offences 2000:

	1990	*1995*	*2000*
Rape	3,400	5,100	8,600
Indecent assault on a female	15,800	16,900	20,300
Other sexual offence	9,900	8,300	8,400
TOTAL	29,000	30,300	37,300

Rape is an offence that can only be committed by a male either on a woman or another man. In 2000 7.5 per cent of recorded rapes were committed on a male. Of all offences of violence against the person, rape has the lowest clear-up rate—less than 50 per cent in 2000, although historically it has been much higher. Generally there is a high attrition rate so that successful prosecutions are relatively rare—fewer than 10 per cent of recorded offences of rape lead to a conviction.[47] Not only is there a low clear-up rate by the police, only 31 per cent of defendants accused of sexual offences pleaded guilty in 2000. Of the 69 per cent who pleaded not guilty, two thirds were acquitted.[48]

3.4.7 Drugs

Drugs have been a major problem for law-enforcement agencies since the 1960s, with considerable resources devoted to preventing importation and dealing in proscribed drugs. The criminalisation of drugs has produced many unwanted side effects, providing fertile ground for organised crime. The cost of drugs has led to many addicts financing their habit by property crime especially burglaries, auto-theft and shoplifting. There is a serious public health risk. Such factors have led senior police officers and right wing thinkers[49] to argue that decriminalisation and regulation, as is the position with alcohol and gambling, is a more sensible policy. More humanely, legalisation could only have beneficial effects for drug-users themselves. The government policy towards cannabis has begun to change—it is to be reclassified as a Class C drug and furthermore there has been a well-publicised and successful experiment in Lambeth in 2001 involved the police simply issuing a verbal warning for possession of cannabis. The benefits were seen as saving of police time and an increase in arrests for dealing, both for cannabis and for Class A drugs.

[47] Harris J. and Grace S., *A Question of Evidence? Investigating and Prosecuting Rape in the 1990s* (Home Office Research Study No. 196 (1999)).
[48] *Criminal Statistics 2000, op. cit.* Table 6C, p. 141.
[49] Stevenson R., *Winning the War on Drugs: To Legalise or Not?* (Institute of Economic Affairs 1994).

Table 3.7 Recorded drug offences 2000:

	1990	*1995*	*2000*
Trafficking in controlled drugs	9,998	21,272	19,820
Possession of controlled drugs	Not collected	Not collected	92,716
Other drug offence	Not collected	Not collected	922
TOTAL	9,998	21,272	108,183

The typical offender is male, in his mid–20s and charged with possession of cannabis.[50] The proportion of offenders cautioned was 32 per cent in 1989, but increased substantially for the next seven years to peak at 52 per cent in 1995.[51] In 2000, some 41,000 offenders were cautioned and 45,000 sentenced by the court. The current cautioning rate varies between police forces in England and Wales. First-time offenders and offenders charged with possession of Class B and C drugs were more likely to receive cautions than other drug offenders.

The courts sentenced 36,000 offenders (80 per cent) to a community sentence, fine or discharge. A new disposition, the Drug Testing and Treatment Order (DTTO), was introduced by the Crime and Disorder Act 1998. They are targeted at dependent drug mis-users with a view to reducing the amount of crime committed to fund a drug habit. When a court makes a DTTO (with the offender's consent) it specifies that: (a) the offender undergoes treatment as part of, or in association with, a community sentence; (b) the offender undergoes regular drug testing; and (c) the court regularly reviews the offender's progress.[52] The evaluation of the DTTOs suggested that the order reduced the average amount spent on drugs and that there were commensurate reductions in acquisitive crime. The link between drugs and offending has been the subject of considerable research—in one study[53] 69 per cent of arrested persons tested positive for drug use (excluding alcohol) including 29 per cent testing positive for opiates and 20 per cent for cocaine. This latter group reported that they spent over £16,000 a year on drugs and that almost £13,000 of that was obtained illegally through shoplifting, burglary and robbery. There are clearly strong correlations between drug use and crime.

3.5 CRIMEFIGHTING—THE SUCCESS RATE

This chapter is now concerned with how the police investigate crime reports. Until the mid–1990s, police tactics have been essentially reactive: by that it is meant that an offence is reported by a member of the public to the police who (resources permitting) investigate the incident and, if successful, take some form

[50] Ramsay M. *et al.*, *Drug misuse declared in 2000: results from the British Crime Survey* (Home Office Research Study No. 224 (2001)).
[51] Corkery J., *Drug Seizure and Offender Statistics* (Home Office Statistical Bulletin 5/01).
[52] Turnbull J., *Drug Treatment and Testing Orders—Interim Evaluation* (Home Office Research Findings No. 106(1999)), Turnbull J. *et al*, *Drug Treatment and Testing Orders—Final evaluation report* (Home Office Research Study No. 212(2000)).
[53] Bennett T., *Drugs and Crime: the results of the second developmental stage of the NEW-ADAM programme* (Home Office Research Study No. 205 (2000)).

of action against the perpetrator. The police react to the demands made on them by the public. As a broad strategy, this has not succeeded in containing recorded crime that has increased steadily since the war. The alternative approach is proactive policing: by 'proactive' is meant that the police take the initiative in crime-reduction—for example intelligence-led policing utilises the gathering of intelligence, the analysis of that information and of crime patterns with the purpose of targeting of specific, 'criminally-active', individuals to monitor their activities and to obtain evidence for a successful prosecution rather than 'acci-dental' convictions of such people for offences which happen to come to police attention. Proactivity also implies strategic initiatives against particular cate-gories of offences that are identified as problematic in a particular area.[54] Some specialist squads, for example, dealing with drugs or robberies, have adopted such an approach for many years and NCIS has now developed a National Intelligence Model, which will be implemented by all forces.

But the police still rely on the public to report crime to them. The beat officer whether on foot or in a car is unlikely to stumble across a crime in progress—it has been suggested that an officer would walk a beat for 14 years before inter-cepting a street robbery in progress.[55] Under this reactive style of policing, the police are receivers, recorders and resolvers of crime. How effective are they at this latter task? The most immediate measures are the overall crime rate and the clear-up rate. It has been said that the increase in the volume of crime is not a measure of police performance nor is it a criticism of reactive policing. The rise in reported and recorded crime merely measures the rise in the demand for policing services.[56] The public uncover crime and report offences. As the police react to such reports, the police workload is thus dictated by public demand. That demand for police services has increased to such an extent that in 2000 there were now 590 crimes recorded every hour by the police in England and Wales, an increase of some 13 per cent since 1990.

The public dictate not only the amount of crime that comes to the attention of the police but also the type. The 'dark figure of unreported crime includes much serious crime, especially in the areas of violence against women, racial assaults and white-collar crime. Demand policing is not an adequate mechanism to cope with such problems. It may be argued that reactive policing encourages:

a) public demand for police services since reactive policing increases reporting and recording. The public have become more willing to report offences. One proposal is to give the police 'ownership' of the volume of crime in order to encourage them to adopt more proactive and pre-ventative strategies, dampening that demand.

b) reactive policing also discourages the police and the public from adopting longer term, strategic views which would involve defining 'seriousness' in crime and identifying community and police priorities.

Reactive policing has not stemmed the rise in recorded crime but is it successful in the investigation and detection of crime? The yardstick is the clear-up rate but

[54] An early example in 1993 would be Operation Bumblebee which was mounted against burglary in the Metropolitan police force area: www.met.police.uk/bumblebee/index.htm.
[55] This was the conclusion in the U.S. of President's Commission on Law Enforcement and the Administration of Justice (1967).
[56] Audit Commission, *Helping With Enquiries* (Police Paper 12, 1993), p. 31.

there must be caution in using this as a headline measure, not least because 'detected' crime includes not merely those offences ending in caution or conviction but also those regarded as cleared-up by other means such as being 'taken into consideration' or admitted to by a prison inmate.

In national terms, the clear-up rate is running at 24 per cent in 2000 having declined from 45 per cent in 1974. This is the lowest it has ever been, although the rate has been under 30 per cent throughout the 1990s:

Table 3.8 Offences Cleared Up 1990 and 2000[57]

Offence group	1990 (%)	2000 (%)
Violence	141,700 (77%)	370,000 (62%)
Sexual offences	22,000 (76%)	19,700 (53%)
Robbery	9,600 (26%)	17,000 (18%)
Burglary	255,900 (25%)	101,100 (12%)
Theft and handling	709,800 (30%)	373,600 (17%)
Fraud and forgery	89,800 (61%)	92,200 (29%)
Criminal damage	120,500 (22%)	136,600 (14%)
Drugs	Na	108,200 (95%)
Other notifiable	30,000 (96%)	45,800 (73%)
TOTAL	1,379,400 (32%)	1,264,100 (24%)

This decline does not necessarily indicate a reduction in police efficiency. A crude measure of workload is the number of recorded crimes per officer—in the early 1980s, this was approximately 26 and the rise in recorded crime has meant that this has risen to 41 in the year 2000. Clear—ups per officer have also risen over this period. Recently the absolute numbers of crimes solved as well as the number of crimes solved per officer has shown a small decrease but it must be remembered that the Home Office criteria under which detections can be recorded as cleared up were tightened up in 1999, which meant a reduction in the absolute numbers regarded as cleared up as well as the overall rate.[58]

Clear-up rates do provide a measure of comparative efficiency: the Metropolitan Force resolves just 15 per cent of recorded offences whereas West Midlands, another metropolitan force, achieves 28 per cent. The most successful forces are Welsh—Dyfed-Powys has a clear-up rate of 63 per cent and Gwent 57 per cent. The former is a rural widespread force with a philosophy to investigate all reports of crime taking a positive approach with the aim of early detection—a reactive yet highly successful approach.

As a headline measure of police efficiency, the clear-up rate is very limited, failing to describe the extent of police involvement (that is, relative ease or

---

[57] *Criminal Statistics 2000, op. cit.*, Table 2.8, p. 45.
[58] *ibid.* Appendix 2.

difficulty of detection) or to distinguish between the seriousness of offences (for example, the detected assault could have been life-threatening whereas the undetected offence relatively minor):

1. the overall rate tells us little—detection rates vary dramatically from offence to offence. In the areas of sex and violence, where the offender is often known to the victim, the rate is traditionally high. On the other hand vehicle crime and burglary have very low success rates: even Dyfed Powys struggles to clear up one third of its burglaries and car crime whereas the Met clear up only one in ten burglaries and 5 per cent of its vehicle crime. The clear-up rate in murder is high—suspects are identified in 85 per cent of cases[59] as it is in shoplifting while fewer than 8 per cent of arson offences will be solved.[60]

2. even on a narrow, single offence, basis, these figures are scarcely an adequate measure of police effectiveness. Certainly the high clear-up rate for homicides reflects the effort and resources put into such investigations but for all offences of violence, the assailant is likely to be known to the victim. Identify the family and close friends of the victim and you have a small group, which in all probability contains the attacker. The same is true of offences of violence generally. Ease of detection also exists with shoplifting, which is rarely reported unless there is an immediate suspect. High clear-up rates are more to do with the factors surrounding particular offences than with good police work. Arguably sensible use of police resources, effective strategies or intelligent analysis of information will never affect crime rates or clear up rates more than marginally.

3. clear-up rates owe much to the public. Not only do the public report crimes to the police, they are also mainly responsible for solving them. Clarke and Hough[61] have suggested that there are four categories of action which equally contribute to the clear-up rate—

   i. where the offender is clearly identified by a witness or detained at the scene either by a member of the public or as a result of police observation.

   ii. where the offence is cleared up by being 'taken into consideration' at a subsequent court hearing. In other words, a suspect arrested for another offence admits this offence for the purpose of wiping the slate clean, at the risk of some additional punishment. Although offenders will be unlikely to ask for violent or sexual offences to be taken into consideration, nearly 40 per cent of burglaries are dealt with in this fashion. The Oxford Penal Research Unit discovered a Sheffield defendant who asked for over 1000 other offences to be TIC'd.[62]

   iii. where the case is resolved as a result of information from the public, usually identifying the offender.

[59] *Criminal Statistics 2000, op. cit.*, Table 4.4, p. 83.
[60] *ibid.* Table 2.20, p. 55.
[61] Clarke R. and Hough J., *The Effectiveness of Policing* (1980); McConville M. *et al*, *The Case for the Prosecution* (1991) Table 1, p.19.
[62] The Home Office and police now distinguish between 'primary' and 'secondary' clear up rates—the former being seen as a more reliable performance indicator while the latter includes TICs and offences admitted to by prison inmates.

iv. where the police undertake their own investigations through informants, plants, vigilance, special inquiries.

4. the focus on the 'clear-up rate' in the media encourages a narrow conception of police work as crime-fighting. The press concentrate on offences after they have occurred rather than on more proactive police responses—the front page will be the murder or the statistics (often with a graph with a restricted scale) of a rise in robberies. On page 15 of the local paper we might find the story on liaison work in the schools and community or the increased resources and status for crime prevention units. The by-product of this is increased public anxiety and fear of crime.

Can police patrolling systems and criminal investigation strategies be made more effective? Pauline Morris[63] suggested that an analysis of police detection methods such as that of Clarke and Hough calls this into question. Changing the organisation or increasing the resources available are unlikely to do more than marginally affect detection and clearance rates. However Morris was considering the impact of some marginal refinements to the traditional reactive style of police work. The new styles of policing whether intelligence-led policing, problem-oriented policing or geographic policing are more radical and more proactive. They also emphasise not simply detection but also preventative police work.

These arguments were rehearsed in the previous chapter but with reactive policing the stress is on detection of a particular incident. This approach is 'victim friendly' so long as demand remains low and resources remain high. As reported crime and demand increase, resources fail to keep pace, time devoted to any case falls, the proportion of recorded crime detected falls and victim-satisfaction is reduced. The weaknesses of reactivity emerge—instead of dealing with all crimes, only some crimes can be allocated time. These would include the obviously serious (HOLMES inquiries[64]) and perhaps the easily-resolved but elsewhere there are no means of identifying which offences should be investigated because there are no links with the community, no internal procedures or crime management system and no systematic storage or analysis of intelligence. As police try to react to all crime reports, this involves wasteful use of resources.[65]

Stressing investigation and detection as the primary concerns of a crime strategy means that reactive policing has encouraged the police into eschewing responsibility for the volume of crime and into failing to set priorities or allocate resources rationally. Overwhelmed by the sheer volume, it also contributes to police criticisms of, and alienation from, other criminal justice agencies. A reminder of first principles is in order: '*The principal object to be attained is the prevention of crime. To this great end, every effort of the police is to be directed.*' In 1829, the first Commissioners of the Metropolitan Police, Rowan and Mayne identified prevention as the core objective of the police. From this, two strategies suggest themselves: putting greater resources into crime prevention; secondly, giving greater emphasis to proactive intelligence-based approaches. Proactive policing allows a force to adopt a strategic approach to tackling crime, either in terms of volume or in terms of priorities. This requires an integrated package of

---

[63] Morris P. and Heal K., *Crime Control and the Police* (Home Office Research Study No. 67) (1981).

[64] An acronym for Home Office Large Major Enquiry System.

[65] Audit Commission, *op. cit.* Exhibit 15 'Response to Burglary', p. 22: but see earlier comments on the success of Dyfed-Powys force in maintaining this approach.

measures, both on a local and national level. For example, the targeting of drugs importers and major suppliers could be linked to initiatives within schools as well as to the phased decriminalisation of drugs. Although there will always be opportunist and casual crime for the police to react to, a proactive policing strategy as a part of an integrated approach to tackling crime has several positive attributes as it can lead to, first, community input into priorities for prevention and prosecution; second, the building up of reliable information about problems, the careful analysis and constructive response to them, must be in the long term interests of policing and the community; third, constructive responses to crime which are not necessarily arrest and prosecution. The penal approach is an expensive option and one that is encouraged by the reactive approach. Proactivity should involve partnership work with a range of local agencies—education, health, social services, planning and other council departments, victim support groups, probation and prisons.

3.6 POLICE POWERS OF INVESTIGATION—SOME HISTORY

The police constable is an officer whose,

> '...authority is original, not delegated, and is exercised at his own discretion by virtue of his office; he is a ministerial officer exercising statutory rights independently of contract...'[66]

This ideal of the autonomous constable does not stand up to scrutiny today—the nature of modern policing has made the constable's job more akin to a squaddie, acting under orders. But the basic powers of a police officer still flow from the status of constable,[67] not from his or her contract of employment or from any para-military aspects of the job. The constable is the holder of an office under the Crown, recognised by the common law, as a person lawfully invested with powers to keep the peace. Prior to 1964, the constable was under a statutory duty to obey the orders of J.Ps and Watch Committees,[68] although the local authority was not liable for his tortious acts.[69]

At common law, the original powers of a constable to keep the peace and to intervene, detain and arrest without judicial supervision were essentially those of a private citizen. There were no special powers for the constable and no special immunities. Nor indeed were there special powers for the State and even ministers could not authorise arrests or searches unless the legal grounds for such action existed. State necessity did not suffice.[70] A private citizen still possesses several of the basic powers of the constable but modern additions to police powers can only be exercised by a constable or even a constable in uniform. The essential powers are contained within the Police and Criminal Evidence Act 1984 (PACE) but firstly we will examine the common law nature and history of those powers.

---

[66] *Attorney-General for NSW v. Perpetual Trustee Company* (1955) A.C. 477 at 489.
[67] The basic powers are the same regardless of rank—certain authorisations must be made by senior officers, e.g. Police and Criminal Evidence Act 1984, s. 42, gives superintendents the power to extend periods of detention. Police ranks do not exist at common law but are created by statutory regulations—Critchley T., *A History of the Police* (1978) p. 125 fn.
[68] With county forces, the power lay with the Joint Standing Committees.
[69] *Fisher v. Oldham Corporation* (1930) 2 K.B. 364—nowadays the Chief Constables are liable for the torts of his officers under s. 88 Police Act 1996.
[70] *Entick v. Carrington* (1765) 19 State Tr. 1029.

3.6.1 *Arrest*

At common law,[71] a person is under no duty to assist the police by answering questions, providing information[72] or allowing a search of person, property or premises. Unless a person was willing to assist voluntarily, the constable would have to use powers of arrest if he wished to detain that person. A lawful arrest could only be made when the officer possessed 'reasonable suspicion' that a felony had been, was being or was about to be committed, when the officer (normally) physically touched the person to be arrested and when words indicating an arrest were spoken. The constable must also inform the accused of the grounds for arrest and a failure to do this or the giving of the wrong reason could make the arrest unlawful.[73] Arrest was for breach of the peace or for a felony and the constable was unable to arrest for misdemeanours unless they involved a breach of the peace which took place in the constable's own view. The officer could not arrest for assault or obtaining by false pretences but could arrest for theft of sixpence or 2½p.

On lawful arrest a person's freedom of movement is curtailed. The original purpose of arrest was to bring the offender before the courts. It was not to detain for the purposes of interrogation, which was not the constable's function. The common law has never recognised the power of 'detention for police questioning'. At common law, arrest was thus quite a late stage in the investigative process. As late as 1929 the Royal Commission on Police Powers could state that a constable should not question a prisoner after arrest but should take him to a police station for formal charging.[74] Despite this, arrest soon became the mechanism by which the police were enabled to detain people while further investigation and interrogation took place. This practice was approved by the House of Lords in *Mohammed-Holgate v. Duke*[75] when it was held that an officer was not acting unreasonably when arresting someone against whom there existed reasonable grounds for suspicion because it was more likely that the suspect would confess in the police station than elsewhere.

These limited powers of arrest were extended by statute, sometimes extravagantly: for example, section 6 of the Vagrancy Act 1824 enabled the arrest of a suspected person in a public place while a similar wide power in section 64 of the Metropolitan Police Act 1839 gave a wide power of arrest but created no offence. By the 1970s there were some 70 statutes detailing powers of arrest. The general power of arrest was codified by section 2 of the Criminal Law Act 1967. This statute also abolished the old categories of felonies and misdemeanours and created a broad category of 'arrestable offence'. A lawful arrest without a warrant required that the police had to have reasonable suspicion that the suspect had committed an arrestable offence (basically one which carried a maximum sentence of five years imprisonment or more) or that the statute creating the offence gave a power of arrest. Sections 24–25 PACE have now replaced this.

---

[71] For the development of police powers, Leigh L., *Police Powers* (2nd ed., 1985) Chap. 2.
[72] Nowadays there are statutory obligations to provide information in relation to road traffic offences, terrorism and serious fraud.
[73] *Christie v. Leachinsky* (1947) A.C. 573.
[74] Royal Commission on Police Powers and Procedures: Report (1929) Cmd. 3297 para. 137.
[75] [1984] A.C. 437.

3.6.2 *Search of Persons and Premises*

At common law, a constable's power to search was very limited. A search of the person could only take place on arrest. There was no general power for a constable to detain a person temporarily for the purpose of a search, although again there were some statutory exceptions. Under section 66 of the Metropolitan Police Act 1839, a constable could stop and search a person believed to be in possession of stolen property and there are similar powers under the Misuse of Drugs Act 1971.[76] The power to enter and search premises was also restricted.[77] If a constable made an arrest, the premises immediately under control of the suspect could be searched. In almost all other cases, a magistrates' warrant made under the relevant statute[78] was required although some statutes permitted entry and search on the authority of senior police officers.[79] Even then, the police could only search for the property specified in the warrant. A warrant to search for stolen goods could not justify a general rummage through interesting documents in the filing cabinets. These statutory powers regarding the issue and execution of warrants must now be exercised in accordance with sections 15–23 of PACE.

3.6.3 *Detention and Interrogation*

The supervisory role of JPs over the issuing of warrants is a relic of a period when JPs played a much wider role in the administration of criminal justice than their predominantly judicial role today. In the eighteenth and nineteenth centuries, magistrates interrogated suspects and made decisions as to whether to discharge, release on bail or remand to prison. The Summary Jurisdiction Act 1848 restricted their role in the supervision of investigation. This change may have been responsible for the considerable uncertainty, not to say hostility, with which nineteenth century judges regarded police powers to detain and to question suspects. Generally arrest signalled the end of police interrogation. The courts sought to limit the police powers of interrogation and insisted that a suspect should be taken before a magistrate with all speed, normally within 24 hours. Judges took divergent attitudes towards statements made to the police while in police custody, some happy to admit such statements as evidence while others excluded them.

Eventually it was the Judges of the King's Bench Division themselves who took the initiative to resolve this uncertainty by issuing the *Judges' Rules* in 1912 to regulate police procedure over the treatment of detained persons. Although these Rules had neither the authority of common law nor of statute and thus in legal theory possessed no legal force, they remained as influential guidelines until 1984 and a basis for the courts to decide on whether to admit incriminating statements into evidence. Originally they prohibited police questioning after arrest, still reflecting the nineteenth century distrust of the 'new' policing arrangements. It

---

[76] There is a list in Annex A to the PACE Code of Practice A which details 18 statutes with stop and search powers—the oldest is s. 6 of the Public Stores Act 1875 allowing a constable to search for stolen HM stores.

[77] Leigh, *op. cit.* p. 199–201.

[78] For a list, see Leigh, op. cit., Appendix p. 288 ff.

[79] *e.g.* Licensing Act 1964, s. 45 (to inspect premises); Official Secrets Act 1911, s. 9 (on suspicion that an offence is about to be committed) and Prevention of Terrorism Act 1984, Sched. 3, Pt III, para. 4 (to search for evidence justifying an exclusion order).

was not until the revision of the Rules in 1964 that the police power to question while the suspect was in custody was recognised. Although the Rules are quoted in the American landmark case of *Miranda v. Arizona*[80] as support for the introduction of proper cautioning of suspects in the U.S., by the 1960s, the judicial attitude in the U.K. towards breaches of the Rules had become very permissive—rarely did police misconduct lead to the exclusion of the evidence.[81] By the 1970s, although police powers appeared quite restricted as a matter of law, in practice they were wide: the power to stop, search and question on the streets was exercised *de facto*; premises were often searched without the 'technicality' of a warrant; people 'assisted the police with their enquiries' at police stations (although the courts did not recognise the legal concept of 'detention for questioning'); suspects were held for extended periods without access to legal advice. The Judges Rules provided no barrier to miscarriages of justice and many of the most notorious cases date from this period.[82]

3.7 POLICE POWERS OF INVESTIGATION—REFORM AND PACE

There is now a single statute, namely the Police and Criminal Evidence Act 1984, which codifies pre-trial procedures including the powers of the police to stop people, search them, arrest them, hold them in police custody and interrogate them.[83] It also lays down the suspects' rights and privileges. The statute's history was tortuous.[84] The need for reform had been recognised for many years but the spark came in Catford, South London in April 1977 where Confait, a homosexual, was found strangled with electric flex in a burning house. Three boys (14, 15 and 18 and in one case, educationally subnormal) were arrested, interrogated and, as a result of their confessions, charged with murder. Three years later, they were all released after the Fisher Report concluded that they had nothing to do with the killing.[85]

The Labour government set up the Royal Commission on Criminal Procedure (RCCP) to examine police procedures. The establishment of the Commission was claimed as a victory for civil liberty groups but it rapidly became apparent that the most coherent evidence and proposals were coming from the police and Home Office. The Police Federation and ACPO were able to alter the Commission's focus, away from the abuses of police powers and onto the artificial restrictions on those powers that were alleged to hamper the police's fight against the rising crime rates.[86] It was an argument that was to find favour with the new Conservative administration.

---

[80] 384 U.S. 436 (1966).
[81] See *Jeffrey v. Black* (1978) Q.B. 490 where evidence resulting from an illegal search was admitted. If the misconduct was in the police station, a different attitude prevailed—[1960] Crim L.R. 298–356; [1964] Crim L.R. 182.
[82] Stefan Kiszko, Judith Ward, the Maguires, the Guildford Four and the Birmingham Six were all 1970s investigations.
[83] But not covert police powers which are regulated by the Regulation of Investigatory Powers Act 2000.
[84] de Gama K., 'Police Process and Public Prosecutions: Winning by appearing to Lose' 16 *Int. Jour. Soc. Law* (1988) 339.
[85] Fisher Sir H., *The Confait Case: Report* HCP 1977/78 90.
[86] There is little evidence that changes in police powers affects crime rates in any way.

The recommendations in the Commission's Report[87] were presented as balancing the 'interests of the community' (sufficient police powers to tackle the crime problem) with the 'liberties of the individual' (providing safeguards for suspects in the police station). The left-wing libertarian commentators[88] criticised the Report and the subsequent Act as unjustifiably extending police powers, especially in the areas of stop and search, arrest and detention at the police station. These criticisms were answered in various ways:

a) the old rules were never adhered to as people were stopped and searched on the street or detained at the station for excessive periods. This could not be eradicated and thus it was better to legalise the old (mal) practices and to regulate their exercise, mainly by adherence to the Codes of Practice.[89] Although this argument has its merits in relation to low-visibility, street searches, it does not justify the extension of powers of detention in a police station, where abuses were very visible and easily controllable.

b) the new powers would affect very few people. It is true that few people are detained for longer than two or three hours but it is strange to see central values of criminal justice, in relation to powers of detention, disposed of by a statistical rather than an ethical argument. More significantly stop and search powers have affected many hundred thousand people a year and have been a major factor in the breakdown of relationships between the police and inner city communities, especially ethnic minority communities.

c) there were new controls especially the custody officer and documentation procedures, tape-recording of interviews, access to legal advice, a duty solicitor scheme, an independent prosecution service and a revamped Police Complaints Authority. But the imperative for such controls came about because of the abuse of the old powers and such safeguards were not in themselves justification for new powers. Since the implementation of PACE, the police have fought a campaign to reduce the effectiveness of these new protections, especially on the issue of the right to silence but also on the more mundane issue of excessive bureaucracy.

3.8 POLICE POWERS OF INVESTIGATION—PACE AND BEYOND[90]

Prior to PACE, there were no obvious gaps in police powers, the filling of which would significantly affect crime rates. The clarification and codification of those powers was undoubtedly long overdue as were the safeguards for the provision of legal advice, the monitoring of interviews and the proper recording of the exercise of police powers and the period in custody but the fight for the extension

[87] Royal Commission on Criminal Procedure: Report (1981) Cmnd. 8092.
[88] Opposition was widespread especially amongst groups such as the GLC's Police Committee—Christian L., *Policing By Coercion* (1983).
[89] There will be six (including visual recording of police interviews) statutory Codes promulgated under s. 66 PACE. They do not bind the courts nor do breaches automatically lead to disciplinary action for the officer involved. However, as will be seen, used in combination with s. 78, the courts have treated braches of the code as justification to exclude evidence.
[90] In 2002 the Home Office mounted a fundamental review of PACE and its associated Codes of Practice.

of those powers was more symbolic than instrumental, charting the status and authority of the police rather than any demonstrable affect on the incidence of crime. The one exception to that is perhaps the power to stop and search.

3.8.1 *Stop and Search*

Prior to 1984, over most of the country,[91] the police had no power to stop pedestrians in order to question them or to search them. Indeed if they sought to do so, they might easily find themselves sued for assault.[92] The police argued that this power was important for crime detection since possession of prohibited articles could only be detected by such a measure.[93] Despite studies which suggested that existing stop and search powers were already being used arbitrarily and with limited success,[94] section 1 of PACE provided a general power that the police could, on reasonable suspicion that any person or vehicle was carrying stolen goods or other prohibited items, stop that person or vehicle and conduct a limited search, such as checking pockets or looking in bags. There are also such powers under other statutes such as the Sporting Events Act 1985.[95]

Searches must be recorded[96] and be available to a suspect on request unless they are 'voluntary'. Forces publish statistics for such searches in their annual reports. Forces vary considerably in their use of section 1 powers—in Bedfordshire in 2000, there were 517 stops per 100,000 whereas in Cleveland the figure was 6,529. Nationally in 2000/01, there were 714,100[97] stops and searches.[98] This was 16 per cent fewer than in 1999/00 and followed a fall of 21 per cent between 1998/9 and 1999/00, which was the first time the number stopped and searched, had fallen. The Metropolitan Police area showed a fall of 6 per cent in the number of stops and searches. These falls followed the publication of the MacPherson Report[99] and its castigation of the Metropolitan force for its racism. Since then there has been considerable research into the impact of these powers.[100] This research found overall that searches are most effective when they are used in a targeted, intelligence-led way, focused on more serious crimes and more prolific offenders.

41 per cent of stops and searches were to look for stolen property, 33 per cent were to look for drugs and 12 per cent of stop/searches were to look for articles which could be used in burglary or theft ('going equipped'). 95,400 people were

---

[91] For Londoners, there was such a power under s. 66 of the Metropolitan Police Act 1839.

[92] Where the person resisted, was arrested and charged with assault on a constable, frequently the court had to decide whether that officer was acting outside the execution of his or her duty—*Collins v. Wilcock* (1984) 3 All E.R. 374.

[93] The effectiveness of such measures was demonstrated in Willis C., *The Use, Effectiveness and Impact of Police Stop and Search Powers* (1983) Home Office Research and Planning Unit Paper No. 15.

[94] Smith D. and Gray J., *Police and People in London* (1983) Chap. XI.

[95] PACE s.7—for a full list, see Code of Practice A Annexe.

[96] *ibid.*, ss. 3 and 5.

[97] 686,100 persons and 28,000 vehicles.

[98] Ayres M., *et al. Arrests for Notifiable Offences and the Operation of Certain Police Powers under PACE* (Home Office Statistical Bulletin 19/01 (2001)).

[99] *Report of the Inquiry into the Matters Arising from the Death of Stephen Lawrence* (Home Office, 1999).

[100] Miller J. et al., *The Impact of Stop and Searches on Crime and the Community* (Home Office Police Research Series Paper 127 (2000 Quinton P. et al., *Police Stops, Decision-making and Practice* (Home Office Police Research Series Paper 130 (2000)); Bland N. et al., *Managing the Use and Impact of Searches* (Home Office Police Research Series Paper 132 (2000)).

arrested following a stop and search—13 per cent of all the stops.[101] Research suggests that policing practice before and after PACE has changed little,[102] and that there is little supervision of the individual officer's discretion either by superiors or by the courts.[103]

The 2000 BCS contains estimates of stops and searches—their estimate was 1,102,000 compared with the police count of 825,356. This implies that the police record such stops in 74 per cent of cases. However this figure must be treated with caution. The survey also found that the police approached 25 per cent of the adult population in 1999—most commonly these involved vehicle stops. The most usual individual to be stopped would be the young male between 16–29—older men and women were less likely to be stopped. Recent research shows that, of those stopped and searched, disproportionately, 8 per cent will be black suspects and 4 per cent Asian suspects—while 16 whites per 1000 will be stopped and searched, 81 blacks will be stopped under section 1.[104]

The MacPherson Report has brought the human rights aspects of such powers into sharp relief.[105] This inquiry emphasised minority ethnic communities' lack of trust and confidence in the police, particularly because of their long-standing concerns about the use by the police of stops and searches. '*No one shall be deprived of his liberty save in the following cases* …'—once the State is seen as depriving a person of his or her liberty, that has to be justified by one of the paragraphs in Article 5(1)(a)-(f). Does short-term detention such as stop and search require justification under the Convention? The decision by the Strasbourg Court in *McVeigh v. UK*[106] suggested that the State was entitled, under the Prevention of Terrorism Act 1976, to stop all persons entering the country to submit to examination at the point of entry to determine whether they had been involved in terrorism. This provides a principle that justifies the State in its use of stop and search powers, breath tests and roadblocks. It probably would justify identity checks, were such to be introduced. But a section 1 stop is only lawful if it is based on reasonable suspicion that the person may be in possession of prohibited articles. This concept is the key element in the exercise of these powers.[107] The Code,[108] outlining how these powers should be exercised, does not define it positively but does seek to prevent officers from exercising their powers on the basis of ethnicity, age or clothing. An officer should be able to identify an objective basis for the stop, which should not include a refusal to answer questions but would include attempting to run away. Research findings, which are supported by the low incidence of arrests following stops, question whether individual officers who carry out stops do in fact have 'reasonable suspicion'. Sanders and Young suggest that the vagueness of this test rules out the

---

[101] Researchers suggest that PACE has not really affected previous informal police practice—Skogan W., *The Police and Public in England and Wales* (1990) Home Office Research Study No. 117.

[102] Smith and Gray, *op. cit.*, McConville M., Sanders A. and Leng R., *The Case for the Prosecution* (1992).

[103] Sanders (1993), op. cit., p. 87, suggests that to impose more controls in an area of low visibility policing would have negative effects.

[104] *Statistics on Race and the Criminal Justice System* (Home Office, 2000) p. 10 Table 3.2; *cf.* Brown D., *PACE 10 Years On: a Review of the Research* (Home Office Research Study 150).

[105] *Report of the Inquiry into the Matters Arising from the Death of Stephen Lawrence* (Home Office, 1999).

[106] *Application No. 8022/77, 5 E.H.R.R. 71, 25 D.R. 15* (1981).

[107] Sanders A. and Young R., *Criminal Justice* (2nd ed., 2000) p. 84ff for a helpful discussion.

[108] Code of Practice A—for the exercise by police officers of statutory powers of stop and search. A revised code was published for consultation in March 2002.

possibility of strict adherence to the formal criteria and permits unjustified invasions of personal liberty and privacy.[109]

The decision to stop is often based not on legally relevant criteria but on the officer's own informal norms, the three most important of which are firstly previous convictions known to the officer, secondly the maintenance of order and of police authority and finally general suspiciousness, being in the wrong place at the wrong time.[110] Officers rely on instinct and this can lead to class and race bias[111] in making stops and in turn, that can lead to a group's perception that officers harass them. This reluctance of the English courts to inquire into the basis of the police beliefs may well have to change and future courts may require that officers should act with increasing care, that 'suspicion' is founded on objective grounds that will satisfy the court.

A thought-provoking parallel is to be found in *McLeod v. UK*[112] where the European Court found that the officers' acts in entering a private house, ostensibly to prevent a breach of the peace as a estranged husband sought to remove personal property, were a disproportionate response to this aim since they had not checked the court order to ensure that the husband was entitled to enter and remove the property and since the fact that the wife was away meant that there was little risk of any disorder occurring. The principle behind *McLeod* is that, in forming their beliefs and in exercising their powers of entry, the police must balance the necessity for their actions against the interests they are violating—in this case the wife's right to respect for the privacy of her home. This can also be seen in *Steel v. UK*[113] where the police arrested certain demonstrators, detaining them and later releasing them without charge. The Court held that the officers, in forming their beliefs about their apprehension of a breach of the peace, should have given due weight to the applicants' rights to freedom of expression under Article 10 and of peaceful assembly under Article 11. It suggests that any interference with a person's rights must be a necessary and proportionate response to the apprehension of disorder or suspicion of crime.

If we apply this reasoning to the police officer's decision to stop and search a suspect, it suggests that a constable must balance the strength of his or her suspicions against the person's rights, in particular the right to freedom of movement and to liberty but also, especially in the light of the MacPherson Report, the right not to be discriminated against under Article 14. Furthermore, were the issue to arise in court, the judge not only would have to consider whether the officer had well-founded reasonable suspicion but also would have to address the balance between the importance of the obligation to enforce the law and the right to liberty. It may be possible to challenge under the Race Relations (Amendment) Act 2000 on the basis of direct discrimination or victimisation.

The Criminal Justice and Public Order Act 1994 introduced new powers to stop and search persons and vehicles—section 60 enabled such searches to be made generally where there is an anticipation of violence; section 65 permits an officer to stop anyone on their way to a 'rave' and direct them not to proceed; section 71 gives similar powers in relation to trespassory assemblies [these may

---

[109] Sanders and Young, loc. cit; *Lodwick v. Sanders* [1985] 1 All E.R. 577.
[110] Sanders A., 'Controlling the Discretion of the Individual Officer' in Reiner R. and Spencer S. (eds), *Accountable Policing* (I.P.P.R. 1993) p. 83.
[111] Smith D. and Gray J., *op. cit.*
[112] *Application No. 24755/94*, 27 E.H.R.R. 493, [1999] Crim. L.R. 155 (1998).
[113] *Application No. 24838/94*, 28 E.H.R.R. 603, [1998] Crim., L.R. 893 (1998).

include the gathering of the Druids at Stonehenge on Mid-year's day or those seeking to sabotage a hunt meeting and is a draconian power that can be exercised within five miles of the assembly]; section 81 enables stops and searches to be made to prevent terrorism.[114]

The most used of these new powers is under section 60 which empowers a superintendent or above, believing that serious violence is likely in an area, to authorise officers to stop and search regardless of whether the officer has reasonable grounds for that search in any individual case. Such searches are relatively frequent—approximately 6,000 such searches are made each year, although the West Midlands Operation Safer Streets added 4,000 to that total in 2000. Over the past five years, 3 per cent of those searched are found to be carrying an offensive weapon and the search results in an arrest in fewer than 6 per cent of cases.

3.8.2 *Road Checks*

Prior to 1984, this was an area of uncertainty: although the 1972 Road Traffic Act[115] gave a constable power to require a vehicle to stop, there was considerable doubt as to whether this could be exercised for purposes other than those under the Road Traffic Act itself; there may also have been a general common law power to detain vehicles, deriving from a constable's general duty to prevent crime.[116] Such doubts were resolved by section 1 of PACE which entitled a constable in uniform to stop and search vehicles and section 4 which gives the police, for the first time, statutory powers to conduct road blocks.

An officer of superintendent rank or above may authorise a road block if there are reasonable grounds to believe that it will lead to:

i) the apprehension of a person who has committed a serious arrestable offence—a bank robbery might justify setting up checks on all exits from the area

or

ii) the apprehension of someone who is about to commit such an offence—targeting drug dealers in an area could lead to wide-scale checks especially since vehicles may be stopped using 'any criterion' (section 4(2))

or

iii) the tracing witnesses to such an offence—a murder might be followed by a road check at the same time and place a week later

or

iv) the detention of someone unlawfully at large.

---

[114] Now in Terrorism Act 2000, s. 44.
[115] Now Road Traffic Act 1988, s. 163.
[116] *Steel v. Goacher* (1983) R.T.R. 98.

Table 3.9 Road Blocks by Reason and Result 1986–2000

Year	No. checks	Reason for roadblock			Arrest			Vehicles stopped	Roads obstructed
		Committed SAR*	Intent to commit SAR	Witness to SAR	Unlaw-fully at large	Linked to reason for check	Not linked to reason for check		
1986	377	195	24	148	26	34	30	na	na
1990	298	167	15	97	22	18	33	38,700	830
1993	3,560	142	3,377	71	19	50	902	48,800	7,320
2000/01	181	72	22	84	3	3	34	17,900	162

* serious arrestable offence

Between 1990 and 2000 the police mounted about 200 roadblocks a year—with the exception of 1993–94 when several thousand were mounted in the City of London as a response to terrorist activity. As is shown in Table 3.9, in normal years there are relatively few road checks. Over the past five years, the reason for the roadblock in 40 per cent of cases is to search for a person who has committed a serious offence or, in 20 per cent of cases is to search for a person who is intending to commit such an offence. The remaining 40 per cent is to search for witnesses. The five-year average shows that these checks stopped 23,000 vehicles, blocked 336 roads and produced 47 arrests, 34 of which were unconnected with the reasons for setting up the roadblock.[117] There was one arrest for every 489 vehicles stopped.

3.8.3 Searching Suspects

Under PACE an officer can physically search a suspect after there has been a lawful stop or arrest—without this, any search would be an assault. This can occur in several situations:

- under section 1, a search is permitted as part of a stop and search—if this is in public, it is limited to a superficial examination of outer clothing and of anything being carried. A more thorough search has to be out of public view[118]

- under section 32 a constable may conduct a limited search of an arrested person at a place other than a police station if there are reasonable grounds for believing there might be evidence or anything that might assist escape or present a danger. By section 32(4) the search is limited to the extent that is

---
[117] Ayres M., et al., *op. cit.*, p. 13.
[118] The conduct of such a search is regulated by Code A. 3.

reasonably required for discovering the article or evidence. The constable can also enter and search the premises where the accused was at the time or immediately before the arrest.[119]

- under section 53, once the suspect is at the police station, the arresting officer no longer has the power to search. Searches of detained persons, including a strip search if deemed necessary, must be carried out by an officer of the same sex, supervised by the custody officer under section 54. The Code of Practice regulates this procedure.[120] The custody officer must ascertain what personal property the person possesses and to that end may search him or her, including a strip search if deemed necessary but someone of the same sex must carry out the search. The custody officer may withhold any evidence of crime and also any personal effects if the officer believes that the person might cause harm with them. The details of the property will be entered on the custody record as well as the reason for withholding any item.

- under section 55, the police have the power to conduct intimate searches without the consent of the suspect. An intimate search is one of body orifices, other than the mouth.[121] It requires the authorisation of a superintendent who must have reasonable grounds for believing that a weapon or Class A drug is concealed. Only qualified doctors or nurses can carry out the search. During 2000/1, 172 intimate searches were carried out, 129 by or in the presence of a suitably qualified person but 43 by a police officer. 123 searches were made for Class A drugs—these were found in 25 cases. 45 searches were made for weapons—these were found in 2 cases.[122]

Even if there is a lawful stop or arrest, searches must not violate the guarantees against degrading treatment under Article 3 or the right to privacy under Article 8. PACE procedures conform to these requirements—Code A talks of the need to keep embarrassment to a minimum and, if there is more than simply surface search, this should not be in public view. Code C also talks of 'proper regard for the sensitivity and vulnerability of the person in these circumstances and every reasonable effort shall be made to secure the person's co-operation and minimise embarrassment'.

The European Court has considered the definition of 'degrading treatment'. Such treatment must be significant and attain a minimum level of severity.[123] Moving a prisoner in handcuffs in public was not degrading[124] nor were intimate body searches in *McFeeley v. UK*.[125] English courts already operate on a lower threshold than this—in *Lindley v. Rutter*[126] the police sought to remove the bra of a women detainee. The court held that such treatment was an affront to human dignity and quashed the conviction for assault on a constable, as the officer was not acting in the execution of her duty.

---

[119] s.32(2)(b) PACE.
[120] The conduct of such a search is regulated by Code C, Annex A.
[121] Hughes (1993), *The Times* November 12.
[122] Ayres M., et al., *op. cit.*, p. 16.
[123] *Hurtado v. Switzerland Application No. 17549/90, A 280-A (1994).*
[124] *X v. Austria Application No 2291/64, 24 C.D. 20 (1967).*
[125] *Application No 8317/78, 20 D.R. 44 at 85–6 (1980).*
[126] [1980] 3 W.L.R. 661.

3.8.4 *Searching Premises for Evidence*

The police have no general power to enter and search private premises in order to investigate criminal acts. They may do so under Part II of PACE, which provides the police with statutory powers to enter and search premises[127] for evidence. These powers can either be executed with or without a warrant: prior to PACE, only a small proportion (17 per cent) of searches were carried out under magisterial warrant[128] and post-PACE research suggests that the effect of sections 18 and 32 has reduced this to 12 per cent.[129] Searches of premises are governed by the Code of Practice,[130] which states that searches should be made at a reasonable time, that only reasonable force should be used and that due consideration for the property and privacy of the occupier should be shown. The extent to which these standards are observed might be doubted by those accustomed to news footage of police operations where the images of the sledgehammer through the door at 6 a.m., accompanied by TV cameras to record a bemused youth in boxer shorts, are scarcely conducive to the dignity of the individual.

3.8.4.1 SEARCHING PREMISES UNDER WARRANT

The general powers for justices of the peace to issue search warrants are contained in sections 8–16 of the 1984 Act. There will be a written application to the magistrate by a constable—it is *ex parte* which means that there is no right for the owner or occupier of the premises to be notified of or to be present at the application. The constable must state the grounds of the application, the premises to be searched and the articles being sought. The magistrate must act in a judicial manner and consider whether the evidence does show reasonable cause that a serious arrestable offence has been committed and that there is material[131] on the premises that is likely to be evidence in the investigation of the offence.[132] The magistrate must also be satisfied that entry by warrant is necessary to ensure access to the evidence.[133] This is a regime which conforms to Convention requirements as the interference with private space is in accordance with law, it is necessary, proportional and for the prevention of crime.[134] Although there are procedures to ensure the reliability of the information,[135] there are still suspicions that warrants are too easily obtained with the standard formula '... as a result of information received from a previously reliable source ...' being too hastily accepted by the magistrate.[136]

Part II of the Criminal Justice and Police Act 2001 has recently increased these powers. This operates in relation to seizure of material from premises or from the

---

[127] 'Any place' is the definition of 'premises' in s. 23 which seems sufficiently broad.
[128] Royal Commission on Criminal Procedure: *op. cit.*—supplementary volume on Law and Procedure Appendix 7.
[129] Bevan and Lidstone, *The Investigation of Crime*, (1991) para 4.07.
[130] Code B 5.
[131] Not being items subject to legal privilege, excluded material or special procedure material—s. 8(1)(c); Bevan and Lidstone, *op. cit.* 4.51–4.78.
[132] s. 8(1)(a) to (e).
[133] s. 8(3)(a) to (e).
[134] *Klass v. Germany* Application No. 5029/71, 2 E.H.R.R. 214 (1978).
[135] Code B 2.
[136] Bevan and Lidstone, *op. cit.* pp. 99–100.

person. These changes result from the judgment in *R. v. Chesterfield Justices and the Chief Constable of Derbyshire.*[137] The court addressed the problem that the police in executing a warrant have to decide what property they are entitled to seize and what they are not entitled to seize, because for example it might be subject to legal privilege. *Chesterfield Justices* made it clear that PACE does not entitle the police to seize material for the purposes of sifting it elsewhere. But there are circumstances where it is not practicable to establish on the premises subject to the search which material can be seized and which cannot—the sheer bulk of the material or because relevant material is contained within the same document or set of documents as material which is protected from seizure.

Sections 50(3) and 51(3) of the 2001 Act grants officers enhanced powers of seizure where it would not be reasonably practicable to make these determinations on the premises or to carry out any necessary separation. The police are only able to look at it to the extent necessary to determine whether it was material they had a legal entitlement to retain. Where it was clear that it did not fall into category, the material has to be returned under sections 53–55. Under section 53(4) there is the opportunity for interested parties to be present at any sift and ability to object to removal of items on grounds they fell into confidential categories and were not items police were empowered to retain. There is a further safeguard in the possibility of an application to a Crown Court judge under section 59 where it is suggested that the police have exceeded their powers. The government disingenuously argued for this reform on the basis that it does not give the police and other investigators excessive powers even if they are able to remove material from premises to examine it elsewhere as investigators will have no greater powers to examine such material than they currently have on premises.

3.8.4.2 SEARCHING PREMISES WITHOUT WARRANT

A search of premises without a warrant can be based either on the consent of the occupier, on the common law or on statutory powers. The police to a large extent rely on consent which need not be that of the owner but can be that of an occupier, including a squatter or a child of the family but probably not that of a mere visitor. The officer should explain the reason for the search and get the consent in writing, if that is practicable.[138] The advantage of consent is that it is not hedged in with the restrictions of the statutory powers and once a police officer is lawfully on any premises, under section 19 of PACE, he or she is able to seize and retain any item that is evidence of a crime.[139] Authority to enter and search without a warrant may be based on several grounds:

1. at common law—although other common law powers of search have been abolished, the power to enter and remain on premises 'to deal with or prevent a breach of the peace' was retained in PACE.[140] *Thomas v.*

---

[137] [2000] 1 All E.R. 411.

[138] Code B 4.

[139] ss. 19–23 spell out the broad powers that the police possess to seize and retain evidence. *Quaere* whether they can also retain goods with a view to returning them to their rightful owner—*West Mercia Constabulary v. Wagener* (1982) 1 W.L.R. 127.

[140] s. 17(6).

Sawkins[141] concerned a political meeting called to protest against the Incitement to Disaffection Bill. The police entered and remained in the hall, believing that there might be disorder, a belief based on their experience of previous similar meetings. The Divisional Court held that the police had a right to enter and remain on premises where they had reasonable apprehension of a breach of the peace. Whether this power was compliant with Article 8 was considered in *McLeod v. UK*.[142] The Court of Appeal had held that *Thomas v. Sawkins* was not limited to public meetings and that Parliament had accepted the validity of the power by accepting its retention in section 17(6).[143] Before the European Court the applicant argued that the power was 'not in accordance with law' as required by Article 8. The power is neither defined in statute nor is there judicial supervision. The Court considered the 'quality of the law' and held that the concept of breach of the peace had been clarified with sufficient precision to enable a person to foresee the consequences that a given act may entail. Although the decision in *McLeod* itself was that the officers' acts were a disproportionate response, the overall effect is to confirm that this common law power can, if properly exercised, be compliant with the Convention. Thus in domestic disputes, an officer could lawfully remain in the house even where the occupier insists he or she leave.[144]

2. under section 17, a constable has the power to enter and search premises without warrant and where no consent exists for various purposes: to execute a warrant of arrest; to make an arrest without warrant; to capture a person unlawfully at large; to protect people from serious injury or prevent serious property damage. This is a wide power to search for persons and any search of the premises should be limited to the extent reasonably required for the purpose. Following *McLeod*, this power is obviously in accordance with law and necessary, despite the lack of judicial involvement. Any violation of private space is undertaken for purposes which accord with Article 8(2). There would be a breach of convention rights if the officers lacked reasonable grounds for arrest or conducted a broader search that was reasonably required but even then the evidence would not be automatically excluded either under section 78 or under the Convention.[145]

3. under section 32, after an arrest for an arrestable offence, an officer can lawfully enter and search premises in which the person was when arrested or immediately before he or she was arrested if the constable reasonably suspects that there is evidence relating to the offence in question on the premises. As with section 17, the demands of effective law enforcement call for a power of immediate action and, following *McLeod*, section 32 is sufficiently precise as to the grounds for exercising that power. Prior judicial involvement is not a possibility. Officers can obviously go beyond their powers, for example, where reasonable grounds for the arrest do not exist or an officer seizes evidence of another offence which is neither

---

[141] (1935) 2 K.B. 249; Goodhart A.L., '*Thomas v. Sawkins*: A Constitutional Innovation' 6 *Cambridge Law Journal* 22 (1936–38).
[142] *supra.*
[143] [1994] 4 All E.R. 553.
[144] *Lamb v. DPP* (1989) 154 J.P. 381.
[145] *Schenk v. Switzerland* 13 E.H.R.R. 242 (1988).

relevant to the immediate offence nor connected with it. The same comments apply on exclusion of evidence as with section 17.

4. under section 18, after an arrest for an arrestable offence, an officer can lawfully enter and search premises occupied or controlled by the suspect if he or she reasonably suspects that there is evidence of the immediate offence or other offences on the premises. This is a broader and more significant power than those under sections 17 and 32. It normally has to be authorised by an officer with the rank of inspector or above.[146] Unlike the situations envisaged by sections 17 or 32, here the demands of effective law enforcement call for a power of prompt rather than immediate action. The question arises as to whether the exercise of this power should require judicial involvement and authorisation. Covert surveillance is an analogous situation and in *Klass v. Germany*[147] the Court said that it is in principle desirable to entrust the supervisory control of surveillance to a judge in accordance with the rule of law, but other safeguards might suffice if they are independent and vested with sufficient powers to exercise an effective and continuous control. Physical searches of houses involve a similar and significant violation of a person's private space. Although police inspectors are able to control their subordinates, they lack independence. There may well be an argument that such search powers should wherever possible require prior judicial authorisation.

3.8.5 *Powers of Arrest*

Arrest, 'the beginning of imprisonment', can be either under warrant from a magistrate[148] or without a warrant. The conditions for an arrest without warrant are laid down in PACE. The traditional requirements for a lawful arrest still apply: firstly that it requires 'reasonable suspicion' that an arrestable offence has been, is being or is about to be committed; secondly that there is a physical touching of the person to be arrested; thirdly this is accompanied by words indicating an arrest, which can be colloquial ('You're nicked.'). Section 28 makes it clear that not only must the suspect be informed of the fact of arrest but also the grounds for arrest either immediately or as soon as practicable. A failure to do this or the giving of the wrong reason can make the arrest unlawful.[149] Reasonable force can be used under section 3 of the Criminal Law Act 1967 and what is reasonable depends on such factors as the nature of the suspect's reaction, the gravity of the offence and the possibility of effecting the arrest by other means.

There are now four categories of arrest without warrant:[150]

1. the first or summary arrest power comes under section 24 which largely codifies the earlier law relating to arrestable offences so that an officer can arrest where there are reasonable grounds for believing that such an offence has taken place and that the suspect has committed it. Arrestable

---

[146] s. 18(4).
[147] *Application No. 5029/71*, 2 E.H.R.R. 214 (1978).
[148] Under Magistrates Court Act 1980, s. 1 for any offence.
[149] *Christie v. Leachinsky* [1947] A.C. 573.
[150] See Bevan and Lidstone, *op. cit.*, 5.06 ff for a detailed description of arrest powers.

offences in essence[151] are those for which a previously unconvicted offender over 21 could be sentenced to imprisonment for five years or more.

2. the second or general arrest power is provided by section 25 which gives a wider power of arrest for all criminal offences whether they are arrestable or not but where process through service of a summons is deemed inappropriate or impracticable. Under section 25(3) a 'general arrest condition' must be satisfied as where, for example, the police officer doubts that the suspect has given his correct identification or address. It is common practice for protestors such as animal rights activists to all give the same (false) name, a tactic which gives the police the power to arrest for offences such as obstruction.

3. the third category is under section 26 which repeals all statutory powers of arrest except those expressly preserved.[152] These are situations where a power of summary arrest is thought necessary and the approach through the general arrest conditions of section 25 inappropriate.

4. a fourth category, the power to arrest for breach of the peace still exists.[153] This is because PACE did not abolish existing common law powers of arrest. There is no substantive offence of breach of the peace[154] but a person may be taken in front of a magistrates' court and be bound over to keep the peace.

Do these powers comply with the Convention? The circumstances in which a person may be arrested and detained are provided for in Article 5(1) (a)-(f) but it is paragraph (c) that is of immediate interest. This permits,

the lawful arrest or detention of a person effected for the purpose of bringing him before the competent legal authority on reasonable suspicion of having committed an offence or when it is reasonably considered necessary to prevent his committing an offence or fleeing after having done so';

There is no requirement that arrest requires a warrant in all cases[155] and there is an obvious need for police officers to take immediate action in some circumstances. The powers of arrest in sections 24 and 25 comply with these requirements. In both cases, there must be reasonable suspicion of having committed an offence. These provisions are generally precise and accessible enough for people to be able to foresee the consequences of any given action.

However there may be some problems:

- section 24(7)(b) PACE permits a constable to arrest a person '*whom he has reasonable grounds for suspecting to be about to commit an arrestable offence.*' Common law authority from which this section derives empow-

---

[151] Although s. 24 includes some specially listed offences where the penalty is less.

[152] Police and Criminal Evidence Act 1984, Sched. 2.

[153] *DPP v. Orum* [1989] 1 W.L.R. 88; *Howell* [1982] Q.B. 416 for a definition of breach of the peace. This power is nearly co-terminous with the powers of arrest under the Public Order Act 1986, s. 4(3) and s. 5(4).

[154] There are several related offences for the imaginative prosecutor especially under the Public Order Act 1986.

[155] *X v. Austria* Application No. 7755/77, 9 D.R. 210 (1977).

ered arrest in circumstances that did not yet amount to a substantive crime or even an attempt.[156] The Human Rights Act 1998 would suggest that this section must now be interpreted to mean that the suspicious conduct amounts to an attempt or at least a breach of the peace.

- section 25(3)(a)-(c) covers the situation where the officer is unable to obtain the suspect's name or address. The offence is likely to be minor and to arrest the person a disproportionate response. But Article 5 does not appear to distinguish between arrest for serious or trivial offences so long as the purpose is to bring the suspect before a court.

- section 25(3)(d)(i) and (ii) permit arrest, *inter alia*, to prevent a person causing physical injury to himself or suffering physical injury. Such an arrest is obviously not to bring the person before a court and could only be justified under Article 5(1)(e) which permits lawful detention of persons of unsound mind.

- section 25(6) preserves the common law power which permits arrest for breach of the peace.[157] Although no offence need have been committed, the person may still be brought before a magistrates' court and be bound over. In *Steel v. UK*[158] the applicants had been involved in different demonstrations but in all the cases the police had arrested for breach of the peace. The European Court considered the 'quality of the law' in this area and held that the concept of 'breach of the peace' had been clarified with sufficient precision and confirmed that this common law power of arrest can, if properly exercised, be compliant with the Convention.

Can police arrest a suspect where the primary purpose is to further the investigation through questioning? Historically in England, the purpose of arrest was not for the purposes of interrogation, which was not seen as the constable's function. For the modern police, the power of arrest is consistently used not as a culmination of the inquiry and as a prelude to charging but as a technique of investigation. This practice was approved by the House of Lords in *Mohammed-Holgate v. Duke*[159] when it was held that an officer was not acting unlawfully when arresting someone against whom there existed reasonable grounds for suspicion and adequate grounds for arrest but where the objective of the arrest was to interview the suspect because it was more likely that he would confess in the police station than elsewhere.

Does this mean that the arrest is not for the purpose of bringing the suspect before a competent legal authority as required by Article 5? In *Murray v. UK*[160] part of the applicant's argument was that the reason for their arrest was not to bring them before a court but to gather information. Mrs Murray had been arrested, interviewed and released within a few hours. The Court found that her arrest itself was based on reasonable grounds, albeit by giving some credence to the government's assertion that the arrest was based on reliable but confidential information. The Court in *Murray* said that the fact that the interview lasted little over an hour did not mean that the arrest and detention were not for the purpose

---

[156] Criminal Law Revision Committee: Report (Cmnd. 2695) (1965).
[157] *DPP v. Orum. supra.*
[158] *supra.*
[159] [1984] A.C. 437.
[160] *Application No. 14310/88, Series A/300-A*, 19 E.H.R.R. 193 (1994).

of bringing her before a court—'*the existence of a such a purpose must be considered independently of its achievement*'. Her refusal to answer questions meant that the authorities could make no headway in pursuing its suspicions but that it could be assumed that, had those suspicions been confirmed, charges would have been laid. To this extent, the Convention does not exclude detention for questioning or 'helping the police with their inquiries'.

The police still rely heavily on this power of arrest, not as a prelude to charging necessarily but as a technique of investigation. In 2000/01 1.264m people were arrested for notifiable offences[161]—in 1988 this had been 1.44m. The majority of arrests, some 57 per cent in 2000/01, are for property offences. Between one quarter and one third of those arrested are released without charge. The reason for the release in most cases will be lack of evidence.[162] The decision to arrest, as with stop-and-search powers, is low-visibility and the law is sufficiently vague and flexible to allow an officer considerable discretion using police criteria, which are not necessarily legally relevant ones.[163] Factors such as previous involvement with the police, not recognising police authority[164] or general lifestyle will be significant. Such powers are 'not exercised randomly or representatively across society'[165] and it is the young adult working class male, frequently black, that is the likeliest object of police attention. Not surprisingly, the typical arrestee will be a young male—84 per cent of those arrested are male and 42 per cent are under 21. That in turn means that that group is more likely to be charged, prosecuted, convicted and imprisoned than other sections of society although crime is widely spread across age, gender, class and race.[166]

In 1998/99, 7 per cent of arrestees were black, 4 per cent were Asian and 1 per cent 'other'. The number of black people arrested for notifiable offences relative to the population was on average four times higher than the proportion of white people arrested.[167] The research shows that whites are more likely to be arrested for burglary and criminal damage, blacks for robbery and both blacks and Asians for fraud and drugs.

3.8.6 *Powers of Detention*

Arrest is the power to detain a person against their will. In origin it was the step immediately before charging and bringing before a court. That is no longer the case. Although the Royal Commission in 1981 recommended that a person should only be detained when it was 'necessary',[168] that threshold was never incorporated into law and is ignored by the police who regard arrest and detention as a prelude to gaining supplementary evidence, mainly through

---

[161] Ayres M. *et al.*, *op. cit.*, p. 2.
[162] The CPS will also discontinue cases—thus the attrition rate (*i.e.*, the proportion of those arrested not ultimately prosecuted) runs between 40% and 50% dependent on police force area
[163] McBarnett D., *Conviction* (1983) p. 36 ff., McConville M., *et al*, *op. cit.*, Chap. 2; Sanders and Young, *op. cit.*, Chap. 3.
[164] Piliavin I. and Briar S., 'Police Encounters with Juveniles' (1964) *Am. Jour. Social.* 70:206.
[165] McConville, *op. cit.*, p. 17.
[166] Box S., *op. cit.*
[167] *Statistics on Race and the Criminal Justice System* (Home Office, 2000) Chap. 5, p. 19.
[168] Royal Commission on *Criminal Procedure*, *op. cit.* para. 3.77.

interrogation.[169] On arrest a suspect must be taken to a police station.[170]

The arrested person is taken before the custody officer.[171] In brief the custody officer must decide whether sufficient evidence exists either to charge the person or to warrant further detention for the purpose of obtaining evidence through interview—in practice, detention is almost never refused.[172] In one SE force in 2000, there were 50,000 arrests—detention was refused in just 1.25 per cent of cases. The custody officer must ensure that the person is aware of their rights to legal advice, to notify someone of the fact of their arrest and to see the Codes of Practice. Throughout the period of detention, it is the custody officer's responsibility to monitor the conditions of the custody: how long and how often a person is interviewed; whether medical advice is required; whether proper sleep and refreshment has been provided. All of this should be recorded on the custody record[173]—typically there are 5 copies: for the station record, for the suspect, for case papers, a transit copy and finally for the local intelligence unit. The record is an essential source of information for the defendant and the court in the event of, say, a disputed confession. Proper documentation was seen by the Royal Commission to be a critical safeguard for police and suspect—documenting not just the events in custody but also the operation of police powers such as stop and search and, crucially, any interview with the suspect.[174] However research[175] has suggested that over 10 per cent of custody records may be falsely compiled.

The custody officer is initially responsible for the length of time that a person is detained in a police station. That detention must be periodically reviewed.[176] Prior to the Act, the police probably had to bring a suspect before a court within 24 hours.[177] Now, with some safeguards, they can hold people without charge for up to four days. Although section 41 lays down the principle that a person should not be held without charge for more than 24 hours, this can be derogated from in certain circumstances. Continued detention for a further 12 hours can be authorised by a senior officer (superintendent or above) if the detention is necessary to secure or preserve evidence, if the offence is a serious arrestable offence[178] and if the investigation is being conducted diligently and expeditiously'.[179] Further periods of continued detention up to 96 hours are possible with approval from the magistrates' court.[180]

---

[169] McConville, *op. cit.*, p. 39.

[170] This must be a designated police station under s. 30 PACE, s. 35 requires chief officers to designate certain stations to be used for the purpose of detaining arrested persons which will be stations which have the necessary personnel and resources for interviews, cells for detention, *etc.*

[171] s. 36 outlines the role of the custody officer; s. 37 defines the custody officer's duties before charge; s. 38 defines the custody officer's duties after charge and s. 39 outlines the custody officer's responsibilities to the arrested person. The custody officer will not be involved in the investigation.

[172] McKenzie I. *et al.*, 'Helping the Police with their enquiries,' [1990] Crim. L.R. 22.

[173] PACE, s. 37(4).

[174] A major complaint by the police has been the bureaucracy engendered by PACE—see Audit Commission: *Managing Crime Effectively* (Police Paper No. 12) Exhibit 17 'The Paper Chase' p. 29 indicates that some 40 forms need to be completed after arrest for even a minor offence.

[175] Sanders A. and Bridges L., 'Access to Legal Advice' in Walker C. and Sturner K. (eds): *Justice in Error* (1992).

[176] s. 40 PACE—the extent to which such reviews are carried out is doubtful—Dixon D. *et al.*, 'Safeguarding the rights of the accused . . .' 1 *Policing and Society*, p. 115 (1990).

[177] although in the 1970s there were several instances of the police holding suspects without access to legal advice for considerable periods before bringing them to court.

[178] These are listed in Sched. 3 PACE.

[179] s. 42 PACE.

[180] s. 43 PACE.

Although the custody officer is conceived in PACE as a quasi-judicial figure, removed from the immediate imperatives of the investigation, it is difficult for the officer to distance himself or herself from the dominant police objectives, collaborating and assisting the arresting officers.[181] Not to detain a suspect would mean undermining the authority of colleagues and authorising detention thus becomes a matter of routine. But prolonged detention is rare with perhaps 5 per cent detained for more than 18 hours. After 24 hours, the police require a warrant of further detention from the magistrates, unless the offence is a serious arrestable offence. In 2000/01,[182]

- 750 were held for more than 24 hours.

- 449 of these were released without charge within 36 hours.

- warrants for further detention were applied for in 326 cases and granted in 319.

- 243 of these were charged and 76 released without charge.

Code C, the Code of Practice for the Detention, Treatment and Questioning of Persons by Police Officers, establishes the regime for the detention of suspects, alongside the rights in the Police and Criminal Evidence Act 1984. This generally complies with the Convention. The detention must be in accordance with law—this will depend on the legality of the original arrest, discussed above. Under the Code of Practice, provisions in designated police stations for adequate heating, sanitation, sleep, recreation and food as well as access to medical treatment will normally conform to Article 3—this guarantees that no one shall be subject to torture or to inhuman or degrading treatment or punishment. This provision cannot be derogated from even in times of emergencies such as terrorist campaigns. The guarantee is against the most serious forms of mistreatment. For example, the Court in *Salih Tekin v. Turkey*[183] held that holding the applicant blindfolded in a cold, dark cell and inflicting treatment that left wounds and bruises on his body violated the prohibition on torture, inhuman or degrading treatment or punishment. Inhuman treatment is distinguished from degrading treatment, the latter involving humiliating and debasing conduct. This might include racially discriminatory treatment but it would not cover wearing prison uniform or appearing in public in handcuffs.[184] Intimate body searches were held not to be sufficiently humiliating in *McFeeley v. UK*.[185]

---

[181] McConville, *op. cit.* p. 42 although see Irving B. and McKenzie I, *Police Interrogation: The Effects of PACE* (Police Foundation, 1989).
[182] Ayres M., *et al.*, *op. cit.*, p. 14ff; See Maguire M, '*Effects of the PACE Provisions*' 28 Brit. Jour. Crim. (1988), p. 19; Irving and McKenzie, *op. cit.*; McConville et al., *op. cit.*, p. 46.
[183] *Application No. 22496/93* (1998).
[184] *Kaj Raninen v. Finland Application No. 20972/92*, 26 E.H.R.R. 563 (1997).
[185] *Application No. 8317/78*, 20 D.R. 44 (1980).

CHAPTER FOUR

The Investigation of Crime (2): Interviewing, Surveillance and Identification

4.1 INTERVIEWING—CONFESSIONS AS EVIDENCE

Interrogation is an essential investigative tool. Compared to other forms of acquiring evidence, it is cheap and the end result, a confession, is evidence that is seen by juries as reliable and convincing. Despite the right of silence and the privilege against self-incrimination, most suspects (especially those detained in the police station) talk to the police and many make complete or partial, verbal or written admissions of guilt.[1]

An admission of guilt by the defendant is crucial evidence. However the law would classify it as hearsay when the admission is repeated to the court by a police officer or other witness. Normally neither prosecution nor defence can rely on hearsay, that is, a witness repeating an out-of-court oral or written statement in order that the court should rely on the truth of that statement. The classic statement of the rule was formulated by Cross, '*an assertion other than one made by a person while giving oral evidence in the proceedings is inadmissible as evidence of any fact asserted.*[2]'

When a police officer repeats a defendant's confession (whether that confession has been taped, written down or merely remembered by the officer), this is hearsay. But there are a large number of exceptions to the hearsay rule which allow the evidence to be admitted—confessions (that is, statements by a party to

---

[1] Mitchell B. '*Confessions and Police interrogation of Suspects*' (1983) Crim. L.R. 596.
[2] This formula was approved by the House of Lords in *Sharp* [1988] 1 All E.R. 65 at 68b-c.

a case which are against that party's interest) have always been one of those exceptions. They do not have to be made to the police but usually are—indeed all statements made by a suspect to the police, whether exculpatory or inculpatory, are admissible into evidence.[3] Once admitted, such statements are deeply pre-judicial since juries will often not bother to look for other independent evidence that supports the confession.

The rationale for the rule excluding hearsay[4] is twofold: firstly it is unreliable and of less probative value; secondly it denies the defendant the opportunity to confront his or her accusers,[5] in other words to cross-examine those giving evi-dence which is adverse to the accused. Both justifications carry less weight when considering confessions: firstly, common sense tells us that confessions are reli-able evidence and therefore probative since people are unlikely to admit a state of affairs which is contrary to their own interests unless it is true; secondly, all the relevant people are in court so defendants are able both to confront the officer who took the statement and to testify on their own behalf.

Although confessions may be more reliable, they are not inevitably so and in practice unquestioning reliance on them is very dangerous. The young as in the Confait Case,[6] the disturbed,[7] the mentally ill or those with learning disabilities[8] let alone those subject to brutality and intimidation[9] are obviously vulnerable. But under hostile interrogation in the psychologically intimidating environment of a police station, even non-vulnerable people are also likely to make admissions which are not true,[10] not realising that once a statement had been made, there is great difficulty in retracting it. Stephen Downing's conviction, based on his own confession, was quashed in 2002 after he had served 27 years in prison.[11]

A central question for the Runciman Commission was whether independent corroborative evidence should be required for all confession cases. An indepen-dent study suggested that 95 per cent of such cases had such supporting evi-dence.[12] The consequences would be that a rule requiring corroboration would lead to few additional acquittals. Although three members of the Commission felt that there should never be a conviction based solely on a confession, the majority were satisfied with a recommendation that the judge in all cases should give a strong warning that care was needed before convicting on the basis of the con-fession alone,[13] explicitly referring to reasons why people might confess to crimes

---

[3] *ibid.*

[4] Zuckerman, A. The Principles of Criminal Evidence (1989) Chap. 11.

[5] See 6th Amendment to the United States Constitution.

[6] *Lattimore* (1976) 62 Cr. App. R.53.

[7] *Ward* [1993] 2 All E.R. 577.

[8] Timothy Evans confessed to killings of his wife and child committed by John Christie—Kennedy L., *Ten Rillington Place* (1961).

[9] The Birmingham Six were seriously assaulted before they made any statements—Mullin C., *Trial and Error* (1986).

[10] Generally Sanders and Young, *op. cit.* Chap. 5; Gudjonsson G., *Persons at Risk during Interviews in Police Custody* (Royal Commission on Criminal Justice Research Study No. 12 1992); McConville M. *et al* (1991). *op. cit.*, p. 56ff.

[11] *The Times* Jan 16, 2002; other disturbing cases are documented on www.innocent.org.uk.

[12] McConville M., *Corroboration and Confessions: The Impact of a Rule Requiring that no Con-viction be sustained on the Basis of Confession Evidence Alone* (Royal Commission on Criminal Justice Research Study No. 13 HMSO 1993). Corroboration is not the panacea against wrongful conviction—in the Birmingham Six case, there were confessions to the pub bombings and there was independent forensic evidence, later proved fatally flawed, that the defendants had handled explosives.

[13] Such a development does not need legislation and has been implemented in the case of identifi-cation evidence by the Court of Appeal in *Turnbull* [1977] Q.B. 224—see *infra*.

that they did not commit.[14] This recommendation has not been acted upon and the Auld Report[15] did not consider the issue, nor does the White Paper 'Justice for All' in 2002.

At common law, the judge had the discretion to exclude a confession if it was involuntary.[16] Substantial misconduct on the part of the interrogators was needed before confessions were excluded. Mere breaches of the Judges' Rules were insufficient. The overall attitude of the courts was that if the evidence was relevant and reliable, it should be admitted[17] since it was not the task of the courts to police the police.[18] This was illustrated in *Jeffrey v. Black*[19] when, having arrested the accused for the theft of a sandwich, the police illegally searched his flat for drugs. The evidence was admitted—the test was whether the evidence was relevant and reliable and the means by which it was procured, however unfair, was irrelevant.

Currently sections 76–78 of PACE regulate the position. Section 76(2) requires the prosecution to prove beyond reasonable doubt that a confession was not obtained:

a) by oppression—defined in section 76(8) as torture, inhuman or degrading treatment or the use or threat of violence or.

b) in circumstances likely to render the confession unreliable.

Section 77 lays down special provisions for those with a mental handicap and section 78 allows the court to refuse evidence (not simply confession evidence but of any kind) if it appears to the court that the admission of such evidence would have such an *adverse effect on the fairness of the proceedings* that the court ought not to admit it.[20]

It is these provisions that are used to test whether incriminating statements made by the accused, are sufficiently reliable to admitted into evidence and whether it is fair that they should be so admitted. As we have seen, Code C governs the detention, treatment and questioning of suspects. The police have been made to follow a set procedure in the Codes with strict conditions to be adhered to before the transcript of a police interview would become admissible evidence. This had been the concern of the Royal Commission in 1981 to ensure that the transcript was valid evidence both in terms of reliability and in terms of fairness.[21] Many other countries use a judicial intermediary to compile not only the record of any interview with the suspect but also the statements from witnesses, before these can be used as evidence. The Royal Commission was

---

[14] Royal Commission on *Criminal Justice, Report* Cm. 2263 (1993) paras 4.56–4.87.
[15] Lord Justice Auld,. *A Review of the Criminal Courts of England and Wales* (2001).
[16] *Ibrahim* [(1914) A.C. 599.
[17] *Sang* [1979] 2 All E.R. 1222.
[18] 'It is no part of a judge's function to exercise disciplinary powers over the police or prosecution. . .' *per* Lord Diplock in Sang *supra* at p. 1230. Perhaps that failure to realise that the reliability of evidence is immediately linked with police malpractices led directly to the self-inflicted wounds that the criminal justice system suffered in the 1980s.
[19] [1978] Q.B. 490.
[20] s.78 did not appear in the original bill but was the result of an amendment tabled by Lord Scarman enabling courts to exclude evidence on the basis of police malpractice. The government accepted the need for such an exclusionary clause but watered down the original with the eventual, rather obscure, text.
[21] Royal Commission on *Criminal Procedure: op. cit.,* paras 4.2ff.

unwilling to take this step towards a more inquisitorial role for the judiciary.[22] Instead it is the police who have been placed in a quasi-judicial role in interviewing suspects inside the police station and documenting the questions and answers for use in court proceedings. However the police still seem willing to use oppressive questioning with the recorder switched on.[23]

Tape-recording[24] of interviews back–up this process, again regulated by a Code of Practice. Prosecutors and defence lawyers rarely listen to the tapes and rely on summaries, which are prepared by police officers. Defence lawyers infrequently check these. From 2002, this has been taken further—section 76 of the Criminal Justice and Police Act 2001 provides for visual recording of interviews with suspects. This is to be welcomed as it offers an end to disputes in court about what actually happens during police interviews, by aiding the court's understanding of process and effective interpretation of the interaction between police and suspects. It provides extra reassurances that suspects are treated properly.[25]

Despite these reforms, tape and visual recordings of interviews and Codes of Practice have their limits:

- statements made outside the station or the interview room where Codes of Practice do not run are not automatically excluded. Prior to PACE, there was considerable concern about police 'verbals', the practice whereby a police witness would testify that the defendant had made an off-the-cuff incriminating remark. PACE sought to exclude such unverified and unverifiable police accounts. However the appeal court still admits in certain circumstances, testimony about 'spontaneous' admissions, which occurred at the scene or in the patrol car as it takes the scenic route to the station.[26]

- informal interviews,[27] perhaps making certain inducements, either in the cells or prior to the recorder being switched on can negate the reliability of any subsequent statement.

- the police are still responsible for taking witness statements and there is no judicial scrutiny of the police except through the trial process itself.

- breaches of the Codes in the station and in the interview room do not automatically lead to exclusion of the evidence.

A certain scepticism about the benefits of PACE may be justified but the first ten years after 1984 brought a sea change in appellate courts' attitudes to the admissibility of confession evidence. This change of attitude was remarkable in contrast to the previous strategy of 'crime-control', which had been adopted by the appellate courts for decades. The courts then accepted any relevant evidence regardless of its provenance or evidence of police malpractice—the objective was

[22] Such as the *juge d'instruction* in France—see the Royal Commission on Criminal Procedure, *op. cit.*, para 6.25ff; any move to an inquisitorial system was also rejected by the Royal Commission on Criminal Justice, *op. cit.*, paras 1.11–1.15. It was not considered by the Auld Report.
[23] *Paris* (1993) 97 Cr. App. R. 99—the Royal Commission on Criminal Justice, *op. cit.*, para 1.22 were concerned at the endless repetitive questioning that the tapes revealed.
[24] PACE s. 60—this is now nationwide practice.
[25] This new technique is being piloted in 5 police forces during 2002–2003.
[26] Sanders A., (1993), *op. cit.*, p. 91; Maguire M. and Norris C. *The Conduct and Supervision of Criminal Investigations*, Royal Commission on Criminal Justice Research Study No. 5 (1992).
[27] McConville et al.(1991), op. cit., p. 60.

to convict the guilty and this was given greater priority than the protection of suspects' rights. The Court of Appeal now adopts a pragmatic 'due-process' model whereby violation of the defendant's rights will in certain circumstances lead to the exclusion of evidence. This change has been driven in particular by the phrase '*adverse effect on the fairness of the proceedings*' contained in section 78 as well as by the miscarriage of justice cases which have so vividly illustrated the failings of the appellate system. It has been reinforced by the passage of the Human Rights Act 1998 and an acceptance that courts must take fundamental rights into account, especially the right to a fair trial enshrined in Article 6.

It is now common to argue that the evidence, however reliable, should be excluded if it was obtained in circumstances that would make it unfair on the accused to admit it. Although there is more concern with suspects' rights and more recognition that the police and prosecution should not profit from their own wrongdoing, this has not led to an automatic exclusion rule—that is, any breach of proper procedure by the police would lead to exclusion. It is far from a solely rights-based approach and any breach of the Act or Codes must be serious and substantial[28] so that the suspect's right to a fair trial would be put in jeopardy. Furthermore, if the trial judge has considered the issues arising under section 78 (that is, will the admission of the evidence jeopardise the fairness of the proceedings?) and concluded that it would not, the appellate courts are unlikely to intervene.

The accuracy of the description of the current position as a 'pragmatic' due process model may be shown by a confession that was the result of a surveillance operation. In *Khan*[29] the appellant was suspected of importing drugs. He visited the house of another man where, unknown to both of them, the police had installed a listening device from which they subsequently obtained a tape recording of a conversation, which clearly showed the accused's involvement. There were no statutory provisions that authorised such an action, which was both a civil trespass and also a prima facie breach of Article 8, which supports a right to respect for private life. There were Home Office guidelines on such surveillance, which had been complied with. At the trial and on appeal, the appellant argued that nevertheless the evidence had been improperly obtained and should be excluded. The House of Lords held that any breach of privacy was relevant to, but not determinative of, the trial judge's discretion to exclude evidence under the provisions of section 78 of PACE and that in this case, despite significant police malpractice, the facts were such that the judge had been entitled to hold that the circumstances did not adversely affect the fairness of the proceedings and did not require the exclusion of the evidence. Had the defendant been denied legal advice in the police station, any resulting statement would have been excluded. However a recording obtained from a trespass was admitted as evidence, despite the fact that it was legitimated only by government fiat. It is difficult to reconcile such divergent approaches but the European Court of Human Rights in Strasbourg came to a similar conclusion as the House of Lords in *Khan v. UK.*[30] The Court held that, although this was a breach of Article 8, there was no violation of the right to a fair trial.

---

[28] *Walsh* (1989) 91 Cr. App. Rep. 161—denying access to a solicitor would usually mean denial of a fair trial (*cf. Oliphant* [1992] Crim. L.R. 40) but a technical breach of detention rules would not.
[29] [1996] 3 All E.R. 289—such operations are now regulated by the Police Act 1997 or the Regulation of Investigatory Powers Act 2000.
[30] *Application No.* 35394/97, [2000] Crim. L.R. 684 (2000), [2000] H.R.C.D. 249.

4.1.1 *Police Interviewing Techniques*

There has been much criticism of police interviewing skills. John Baldwin's enquiry for the Home Office[31] examined four hundred interviews of suspects from four separate police forces and concluded that 'interviewing is a hit and miss affair' with just over a third of interviews being conducted not very well or poorly. The main weaknesses were identified as being lack of preparation, general ineptitude, poor technique, assumption of guilt, unduly repetitive, persistent or laboured questioning, failure to establish relevant facts and exertion of too much pressure. In 1993, the police introduced an interview model, PEACE, a mnemonic for planning and preparation, engage and explain, account, closure and evaluation. The training included tuition for interviewing witnesses, victims and suspects. In addition, provision was made for assessment and supervision of interviews. A further study in 2001[32] found an improvement in interviewing suspects when compared with previous criticisms, especially with regards to the provision of legal requirements and the use of questions. However, many of the basic communication skills, such as listening, were rated low. Indeed ten per cent of the interviews evaluated were considered as possibly breaching PACE. The only real difference between trained and untrained officers was interview length but supervision was associated with improved interviewing. In interviewing victims and witnesses, the standard was poorer than in interviews of suspects with no evidence of the techniques for enhancing witness recall being used. There were no differences whether or not the interviewer was trained, although again supervision did have an impact on performance.

4.1.2 *The Right to Silence*

Fundamental to discussion of interviewing is the concept of the right to silence. It remains a controversial issue. Until 1994, this right consisted of a conglomerate of different ideas:

1. there was the requirement of a caution—that is, that the police warned a suspect that he or she need not say anything and that whatever was said might be used in evidence. This had to be given initially when[33] the investigating officer had grounds for suspecting that that person had committed an offence and the purpose of the questions was to obtain evidence to use in court. A caution had to be given on arrest.[34] If the person was subsequently interviewed at a police station, the interviewer had to remind the interviewee at the start and after every break that he or she was still under caution. The caution was repeated at the point when the suspect was formally charged.

---

[31] Baldwin, J. *Video taping police interviews with suspects—an evaluation.* (1992) Home Office Police Research Series Paper 1.

[32] Clarke C. and Milne R., *National Evaluation of the PEACE Investigative Interviewing Course* (Home Office Police Research Award Scheme 2001); McGurk, B.J., Carr, M.J. and McGurk, D. *Investigative interviewing courses for police officers: An evaluation* (Home Office Police Research Series Paper 4).

[33] Code C 10.1—there is no need to caution a person if questions are being put prior to a search and in exercise of stop and search powers under s 1 PACE.

[34] Code C 10.3—unless it is impracticable or if the person has been cautioned immediately before in accordance with Code C 10.1.

2. there was the common law principle that the prosecution bore the burden of proof and had to prove the defendant's guilt beyond reasonable doubt.[35] In other words, there was a presumption of innocence and the underlying rationale was to be found in the maxim, *nemo debet prodere se ipsum*, no one can be required to be his own betrayer, or 'the right to silence'.

3. the most irksome aspect for the police and prosecution was that they were not permitted to comment on the defendant's decision to remain silent in the police station[36] or not to testify.[37] There were some limited exceptions—the prosecution could adduce evidence of silence when the accusation was made by victim[38] or parent[39] or where the accused was on 'level terms' with police.[40]

4. although the judge could comment on the defendant's failure to testify, he or she had to do so in measured terms and had to warn the jury that they must not assume guilt from the defendant's silence.[41]

5. there also exists a privilege against self-incrimination.[42]

Through the 1970s and 1980s, there were constant campaigns to reform the 'right to silence'. These started with the Criminal Law Revision Committee in 1972[43] whose arguments were rejected by the Royal Commission on Criminal Procedure in 1981.[44] It seems extraordinary that the debate was so active as, despite this 'right', most suspects talk to the police and furthermore unreliable confessions have frequently been identified as the cause of miscarriages of justice.

The safeguards introduced by PACE reinforced the right to silence. Within a few years, the police were arguing that the safeguards introduced, especially the suspect's access to legal advice, had tipped the balance in favour of suspects who would consistently refuse to answer police questions in 'no comment' interviews. The argument was that, as a result of the suspect's silence, more serious cases were being discontinued or else there were more acquittals, especially because of 'ambush' defences. This latter term meant that at trial the defence relied on significant facts which had not been mentioned to the police at the time of the investigation and which the prosecution were subsequently in no position to rebut. A Home Office Working Group[45] again favoured the idea of abolition, only for its arguments to be rejected in their turn by the Royal Commission on Criminal Justice in 1993, which commissioned two separate reports.[46] The

---

[35] *Woolmington* [1935] A.C. 462.

[36] *Hall* [1971] 1 W.L.R. 298.

[37] s. 1(b) Criminal Evidence Act 1898—the failure of any person charged with an offence to give evidence shall not be made the subject of any comment by the prosecution.

[38] *Horne* [1990] Crim, L.R. 188.

[39] *Parkes* [1976] 1 W.L.R. 1251.

[40] *Chandler* [1976] 1 W.L.R. 585.

[41] *Bathurst* (1968) 2 Q.B. 99; *Sparrow* [1973] 1 W.L.R. 488 though see Rupert Cross' forthright comments on 'gibberish' 'A Very Wicked Animal . . .' Crim. L.R. (1973) 329 at 333.

[42] Zuckerman, *op. cit.*, Chap. 15

[43] Criminal Law Revision Committee, 11th Report (1972) Cmnd. 4991 paras 28–52.

[44] Royal Commission on Criminal Procedure, *op. cit.* paras 4.33 ff.

[45] Zuckerman A., 'Trial By Unfair Means' [1989] Crim. L.R. 855.

[46] Leng R., *The Right to Silence in Police Interrogation*, Royal Commission on Criminal Justice Research Study 10 (1993); McConville M. and Hodgson J. *Custodial Legal Advice and the Right to Silence*, Royal Commission on Criminal Justice Research Study 16 (1993).

empirical evidence[47] put forward did not suggest that there was an unacceptable rate of either 'no further action' or acquittal for those few defendants, charged with serious crimes, who choose to remain silent.[48] The studies also dismissed the suggestion that there was any serious problem of 'ambush' defences.

The Royal Commission Report did suggest that the defence should be under an obligation to disclose aspects of its case[49] but stood firm against the wholesale abolition of the right to silence. Despite this, sections 34–37 of the Criminal Justice and Public Order Act 1994 were introduced, on the model of the position in Northern Ireland.[50] The Act allows juries, in certain circumstances, to use silence as evidence against the accused.

a) section 34 is aimed at 'ambush defences'. A judge is empowered to direct the jury that they may 'draw such inferences as appear proper' from a failure to mention a relevant fact relied on in the defence when it might reasonably have been mentioned during police questioning. The objective is to force the accused into disclosure of the defence. Such inferences can only be drawn where the prosecution have supplied substantial evidence linking the accused with the offence and on which a reasonable jury could convict. A jury would thus be told to attach less weight to a defence which has only been revealed at the trial and logically is correspondingly less credible. Such a provision will place pressure on the accused to disclose his or her defence at an early stage.

Section 34 is now redundant but not repealed. Advance disclosure of the defence case was a key recommendation of the Royal Commission Report.[51] Within two years of the passage of section 34, the Criminal Procedure and Investigations Act 1996 provides for disclosure by the accused in the form of a defence statement, a statement by the defence setting out the material lines of their case.[52] Yet section 34 still places great pressure on a suspect to make a premature statement to the police before there has been opportunity to reflect and take advice.[53]

b) section 35 is targeted on the defendant who remains silent in court. Where the prosecution have satisfied court that there is a case to answer and a defendant declines to testify in his or her own defence, the judge, in the presence of the jury, is empowered to tell the defendant that the stage has been reached at which he or she can give evidence and to issue a warning that if he or she remain silent, that it will be permissible for the jury to draw whatever inferences appear to be proper. Although this can only come into play once the prosecution have supplied substantial evidence, evidentially this seems suspect. It is arguable that there are valid evidential inferences to be drawn from the situations dealt with in sections 34, 36 or

[47] This is summarised in Leng, *op. cit.*, Chap. 2.
[48] Zander M., 'The investigation of crime: a study of cases tried at the Old Bailey' [1979] Crim. L.R. 203.
[49] Discussed in Chap. 7 para. 7.4.
[50] Criminal Evidence Order (No. 1987 of 1988); for its impact, see Jackson J. 'Curtailing the Right of Silence: Lessons from N. Ireland' [1991] Crim. L.R. 404.
[51] Royal Commission on Criminal Justice, *op. cit.*, paras. 57–73 but see note of dissent by Zander p. 221 paras 1–12.
[52] s.6.
[53] Youth Justice and Criminal Evidence Act 1999, s. 58, prevents a court from drawing adverse inferences where the suspect has not had the opportunity to consult a solicitor.

37: you could validly infer that a previously unmentioned defence was credible; you could validly infer guilty knowledge from a refusal account for one's presence or for one's possession of incriminating articles. The main result of a refusal to testify, whatever the reason, is not an inference about a specific item of evidence but instead is likely to be a general presumption of guilt.

There are strong arguments against this form of reasoning. These can be framed in constitutional terms since the right to silence is the final guarantee of the autonomy of the individual; there are also ethical considerations whether the state should ever use such evidence as the basis of a conviction. It undermines a principle of the rule of law that the prosecution should prove guilt and thereby the presumption of innocence. Technically, there is an old common law rule that if the prejudicial effect of a piece of evidence outweighs its probative value, then it should be excluded.[54] Here the prejudicial effect on the jury of the judge's direction about a failure to testify must far outweigh any probative quality and consequently section 35 infringes that rule. To an extent this has been recognised by the caution shown in Northern Ireland where failure to testify has been taken into account only where the prosecution case just rests on the brink of the necessary standard of proof.[55]

c) sections 36 and 37 are aimed at suspects who fail to give instant explanations to a police officer. Section 36 applies where the suspect gives no explanation to police about certain specific facts such as objects, substances or marks on clothing, which tend to suggest the accused's participation in the offence. Section 37 applies where the suspect gives no explanation to the police of his presence at a particular place, which again would tend to suggest participation in the offence. Both sections 36 and 37 require the accused to have been arrested and to be warned about the consequences of the failure to answer. Although this indicates that the objective threshold of 'reasonable grounds' for arrest should have been satisfied, as we have seen, the police often have a lot of suspicion and very little hard evidence. They already use arrest as a technique to gain that evidence by putting pressure on a suspect, through interrogation. These sections will encourage this practice, putting even greater pressure on the suspect since a refusal can be part of the prosecution's case, contributing to proof beyond reasonable doubt. Additionally both the latter sections will encourage the over-use of arrest by the police. Is this balanced by probative weight of the defendant's refusal to co-operate with the police?[56] It is possible to argue that a failure to account for your presence at a particular spot or your possession of a particular item has some probative weight: it raises an inference of guilty knowledge about a specific element of the offence. But the weight to be accorded to that inference is not necessarily that great. There are defendants who are confused and vulnerable, defendants who wish to protect others, let alone those who are just unwilling to co-operate. Can a jury ever regard silence as sufficient to quash a reasonable doubt they might harbour about the prosecution case?

[54] *Sang* [1980] A.C. 402.
[55] Jackson, *op. cit.*, pp. 410–412.
[56] Compare this with the U.S. Constitution, which has a 5th Amendment that provides a right against self-incrimination.

Sections 34, 36 and 37 have now been amended so that a court cannot draw such inferences where the accused has not had legal advice.[57] The essential framework remains and increases the pressure brought on people detained in police stations to answer questions. Although Bentham bears the burden of suggesting that the right to silence only protects the guilty and the criminally sophisticated when he wrote: *'Innocence claims the right of speaking as guilt invokes the privilege of silence.'* he did so at a time when the right to silence as we know it did not exist, when the defendant was not permitted to testify in his own defence and when interrogation by police officers did not exist. The pressure to answer police questions will necessarily bear on the innocent as well as the guilty. The controversy surrounding the right to silence encompasses empirical questions and evidential problems but ultimately it should be a decision based on concepts of due process of law and proper constitutional principles. It is another of those important markers that define the relationship of State and citizen, delineating constraints on the State and our moral choice that prosecution and punishment should not be based on evidence from the accused.

4.1.2.1 THE RIGHT TO SILENCE AND THE EUROPEAN CONVENTION

Provisions that place pressure on the suspect to answer police questions may infringe Article 6(2)—the right to silence was an integral part of the obligation on the State to prove the guilt of the accused. Northern Ireland provisions similar to sections 34 and 35 were considered in *Murray*,[58] which involved both a refusal to answer police questions and to testify. The European Court concluded that, where a prima facie case was established and the burden of proof remained on the prosecution, adverse inferences might be drawn. The Court saw the right to silence as a generally recognised international standard that lay at the heart of fair procedure but the requirement placed on the defendant to answer questions or to testify was not incompatible with the Convention. It would be if the conviction were based solely or mainly on any refusal to give evidence. As the legislation stands, the prosecution case must produce sufficient evidence, which could form the basis for conviction for a reasonable jury. It would be difficult to argue that any resultant conviction was solely or mainly based on adverse inferences drawn from the failure to answer questions or testify.

But *Murray* was distinctive—it concerned charges of terrorism, the independent evidence against the defendant was overwhelming and the trial took place before a Diplock court in Northern Ireland, which involved an experienced judge as the trier of fact, acting without a jury. There was substantial dissent in the European judgment and the concern about such provisions was echoed in *Averill v. UK*.[59] Incriminating fibres had been found on the accused who refused to account for them and contended that he was silent, not from the lack of legal advice, but from a policy of not talking to the RUC. The Court did not find that a sufficient justification and held that there was no breach of Article 6 but did say that the extent to which adverse inferences could be drawn must necessarily be limited and that there might be reasons why an innocent person might be unwilling to co-operate with the police.

The jury should be made aware of the accused's justifications for remaining

---

[57] s. 58 of the Youth Justice and Criminal Evidence Act 1999.
[58] (1996) 22 E.H.R.R. 29.
[59] *Application No. 36408/97*, (2001) 31 E.H.R.R. 36; [2000] Crim. L.R. 682.

silent and, were they to be satisfied that the reasons were cogent, should not draw adverse inferences from silence. In a non-terrorist case, *Condron and Condron v. UK*,[60] the applicants complained that their right to a fair trial under Article 6 had been violated by the trial judge's decision to leave the jury with the option of drawing an adverse inference from the applicants' silence during police interviews. The applicants had been tried on counts of supplying heroin and of possession of heroin with intent to supply. The Crown's case had relied on police surveillance of exchanges between the applicants, their co-accused and third parties. Before interview the applicants were cautioned. The applicants' solicitor had not considered that the applicants were fit to give interviews because they were suffering from heroin withdrawal. A police doctor found that the applicants were fit for interview. The applicants remained silent during the interviews on the advice of their solicitor but, at trial, they gave explanations for the exchanges observed by the police. The judge directed the jury in accordance with section 34. The Court of Appeal rejected the appeal, despite what they perceived as errors in the direction, because the conviction was safe given the almost overwhelming evidence against the accused.

At Strasbourg, the Court emphasised that the accused testified and gave an explanation for silence and that the trial was before a jury, all of which were distinguishable from *Murray*. The Court held that the right to silence was not absolute but that domestic courts required 'particular caution' before drawing adverse inferences. Convicting solely or mainly on such evidence would infringe Article 6 but the accused's silence, in situations which clearly called for an explanation, could be taken into account in assessing the persuasiveness of the prosecution evidence. In all the circumstances of this case, the jury should have been directed that silence could be taken into account but only if they were satisfied that the applicants' silence could not be sensibly attributed to their having no answer or none that would stand up to cross-examination.

There are other statutes that require persons to provide information that may be used as the basis for a criminal prosecution. For example, section 2 of the Criminal Justice Act 1987 requires any person under investigation by the Serious Fraud Office to answer questions, produce documents and furnish information.[61] The compatibility of such legislation with Article 6 was questioned in *Saunders v. UK*.[62] The defendant was convicted of fraud on the basis of answers that he had been compelled to give in the course of investigations by inspectors from the Department of Trade. The Court concluded that this infringed his freedom from self-incrimination and was in breach of the presumption of innocence and Article 6(2). Both *Saunders* and *Funke v. France*[63] establish that coerced 'cooperation' with the authorities in the pre-trial process may infringe the privilege against self-incrimination and jeopardise the fairness of any subsequent hearing, were the prosecution to use the product of that coercion as evidence. The British government response has been to restrict the use in evidence of answers given under such circumstances.[64]

---

[60] *Application No. 35718/97*, (2001) 31 E.H.R.R. 1.
[61] There are other statutes which compel the provision of information but where any statements made are inadmissible as evidence, Theft Act 1968, s. 31(1); Criminal Damage Act 1971, s. 9; Children Act 1989, s. 98.
[62] *Application No. 19187/91*, 23 E.H.R.R. 313 (1996).
[63] *Application No. 10828/84*, 16 E.H.R.R. 297 (1993).
[64] Youth Justice and Criminal Evidence Act 1999, s. 59 and Sched. 3 for a list of relevant statutes.

4.1.3 *Access to Legal Advice*[65]

Within the police station, PACE supports the right to silence by various provisions for assistance and legal advice. For example, an 'appropriate adult'[66] must be present in the case of a juvenile and in the case of a person who is mentally disordered or mentally handicapped—the value of the 'appropriate adult' cannot be underestimated particularly in the light of alleged confessions of suspects termed as 'vulnerable'. A detained person will be given a notice stating these rights as well as the opportunity to consult the Codes of Practice and a copy of the Custody Record:

- section 56 provides for a right for a person to be informed of the fact of your arrest.[67]
- section 57 provides additional rights for young persons.
- section 58 gives a right to legal advice.[68]
- section 59 provides for a duty solicitor scheme.

The right to legal advice was previously enshrined in the Judges Rules and has recently been acknowledged as a right in common law.[69] More recently the Human Rights Act ensures that a right to legal assistance is seen as a fundamental human right. It is implied in Article 5(4) which requires that a person is entitled to '*take proceedings by which the lawfulness of his detention shall be decided speedily by a court*'. This inference is reinforced by Article 6(3)(b) which provides that a person charged with a criminal offence should be provided with adequate time and facilities for the preparation of his or her defence and Article 6(3)(c) which provides a specific guarantee of the right to defend oneself or be legally represented and to be granted legal aid where appropriate. A failure to allow an accused legal advice in detention will be seen as a breach of a right to a fair hearing under Article 6.[70]

Prior to 1984 the right was more honoured in the breach[71] with few convictions being overturned as a result. The 1981 Royal Commission and subsequently the provisions in PACE recognised that the isolated suspect was vulnerable and able to be manipulated by interrogators even without malpractice on their part.[72] This was especially so given the police have no obligation to disclose the nature

---

[65] Royal Commission on Criminal Justice: paras 3.46–3.64; Baldwin J., *The Role of Legal Representatives at the Police Station* (1992) Royal Commission on Criminal Justice Research Study No. 3; McConville M. and Hodgson J. *op. cit.*,

[66] defined at C. 1.7(a).

[67] Previously s. 62 of the Criminal Law Act 1977.

[68] Access can be delayed (but never refused altogether) under s. 58(6) and (8) if the person is suspected of a serious arrestable offence and access might lead to interference with evidence, alerting of accomplices or hindering recovery of property. Similar provisions apply for s. 56.

[69] *R. v. Chief Constable of South Wales ex parte Merrick* [1994] 2 All E.R. 560—s. 58 does not apply to a prison held on remand in police cells but there is a common law right to legal advice which must be allowed by the police if reasonably practicable.

[70] Emmerson B., 'Crime and Human Rights' 150 *New L.J.* 13 (2000).

[71] Zander M., 'Access to a Solicitor in the Police Station' [1972] Crim L.R. 342; Baldwin J. and McConville M., 'Police Interrogation and the Right to See a Solicitor' [1979] Crim. L.R. 145.

[72] Softley P., *Police Interrogation* (Royal Commission on Criminal Procedure Research Study No. 4) (1980).

of the case against the suspect. Apart from the right to consult the custody record, there is at present no right for the legal representative to hear tapes of any prior police interviews with the suspect prior to advising them and nor are the police required to inform the adviser of the general nature of the case and the prima facie evidence against the suspect. Disclosure does happen but on a piecemeal basis although such disclosure seems essential for a representative to advise a client properly.[73] The police remain hostile to a solicitor's intervention which is seen as increasing a suspect's resistance to questioning and reducing their control.[74]

Everyone is entitled to free legal advice in the police station through the duty solicitor scheme. The Legal Services Commission (LSC) manages this—the LSC took over the public funding of defence work from the Legal Aid Board in April 2000.[75] The Commission established the Criminal Defence Service (CDS) and there is currently a mixed system by which criminal defence will be organised through, on the one hand, contracted private practitioners and on the other, public salaried employees. Despite the PACE provisions and the fact that custody officers did advise suspects of their rights,[76] there was a low take-up rate of legal advice of between 10–20 per cent in the immediate post-PACE years. However after the Codes were revised in 1991, take-up has risen to nearly 30 per cent.[77] The custody record contains a box with the printed alternatives 'I want a solicitor as soon as practicable' and 'I do not want a solicitor at this time'. Beneath the latter is space for the suspect's signature. Whichever option the suspect rejected is deleted. The format does not at present guard against the risk of the police falsely claiming that the suspect waived legal advice but also refused to sign. The extent of protection is still limited and it has been suggested[78] that defendants are not always given the leaflet advising them of their rights, that they are told to 'sign here' on the custody record without realising that they are waiving their right to see a solicitor or that they are told that a solicitor will not be available for some hours and it may be necessary to be detained in a cell. The alternative of a cosy chat and then going home seems attractive. The Royal Commission's recommendations included the video recording of events in a custody suite and interviewers both reminding suspects of their rights to advice at the beginning of an interview and asking for their reasons for waiving those rights. These reasons would be recorded on tape.[79]

Even where advice is given, it can be over the telephone. The police can interview before or after a lawyer's visit, thus negating the value of the advice. Further doubts have been raised[80] about the quality of the legal work and advice given, with solicitors or their representatives failing to obtain information from the investigating officers, often failing to acquire important facts from their own client and intervening in the interview on the client's behalf in less than one third of cases. To counter these criticisms, the Legal Aid Board introduced a Police

---

[73] Shaw G., 'Interviewing Techniques', *110 Police Review*, April 5, 2002 p. 25—this discusses the difficulties of pre-interview disclosure facing the police interviewer.

[74] McConville M., *et al.*, (1991), *op. cit.*, pp. 47–54.

[75] Access to Justice Act 1999; www.legalservices.gov.uk/, infra. Chap. 7, para. 7.3.

[76] Irving B. and McKenzie I. *Police Interrogation* (Police Foundation 1989), Sanders A. *et al.*, *Advice and Assistance at Police Stations* (Lord Chancellor's Dept. 1989).

[77] Sanders A. and Bridges L (1992), *op. cit.*

[78] Sanders *et al.* (1989), *op. cit.*

[79] Royal Commission on Criminal Justice, *op. cit.*, para 3.47.

[80] Royal Commission on Criminal Justice, *op. cit.*, paras 3.56ff, Baldwin J.(1992), *op. cit.*, McConville M. and Hodgson J.(1993), *op. cit.*,

Station Advisors' Accreditation Scheme in 1994. Only the advice from solicitors' representatives who are accredited will be eligible for payment under the Legal Aid Scheme.

But the provisions in PACE have proved a more substantial safeguard for suspects in police stations than those in the old Judges' Rules. Failure to observe the correct procedure in the Code of Practice, especially in relation to the provision of legal advice, can lead to the evidence obtained from the subsequent interview being excluded. In *Absolam*[81] the accused was arrested for threatening behaviour and taken to a police station. He emptied his pockets but the custody officer, knowing that the defendant had previously been arrested for possession of cannabis, said 'Put the drugs on the table'. The accused took a packet from inside his trousers and also admitted selling the drugs. Only then was he reminded of the caution but no written record was made until later when the accused refused to sign it. Nor was he advised of his rights under section 58 until a later stage. The conviction was quashed on appeal since not only was the defendant denied legal advice but also the custody officer's questions constituted an interview and Code C 3.1 specifies the sequence of events which should not be overridden. The Court of Appeal considered this to be a 'serious and substantial breach' and that the evidence ought not to be admitted as it produced an 'adverse effect on the overall fairness of the proceedings' under section 78.[82] Access to a duty solicitor was the issue in *Vernon*[83] where the accused nominated a solicitor who was unavailable as it was late at night. She agreed to be interviewed but was not told of the availability of the duty solicitor. The record of the interview was deemed inadmissible under section 78 as she would not have consented to be interviewed but for this breach.

The limits to exclusion were shown in *Walsh*,[84] which involved an allegation of robbery. There was an interview in the cell, which was not contemporaneously recorded, and there had been no legal advice. Again the conviction was quashed. But the appellate court made it clear that a breach of section 58 does not lead to the automatic exclusion of the statements—the breach must be significant and substantial which affects the reliability of the statement (section 76) or adversely affects 'fairness' (section 78). In *Dunford*[85] there was a breach of the Code in relation to provision of legal advice but the accused was seen as thoroughly conversant with his legal rights and the breach was thus not seen as significant.

The police are empowered to delay access to a solicitor under the serious arrestable offence provisions of section 58(8). Delaying access to a solicitor requires that the police believe that this individual solicitor would alert other suspects or hinder the recovery of evidence, albeit inadvertently. Such a belief could only be rarely held—access to legal advice is a fundamental right. The police cannot refuse to allow a suspect access to legal advice on the grounds that legal advice will be to remain silent. In *Samuel*,[86] there was an allegation of robbery. The suspect had asked for a solicitor but this was denied under section 58(8). After 24 hours, he admitted involvement in 2 burglaries and was charged with those. Relatives and lawyers were informed at this point but police continued questioning until the accused confessed to the robbery as well. The Court

---

[81] [1988] Crim. L.R. 748.
[82] See *Williams* [1989] Crim. L.R. 66; *Sanusi* [1992] Crim. L.R. 43.
[83] [1988] Crim. L.R. 445.
[84] [1989] Crim. L.R. 822.
[85] [1991] Crim. L.R. 370; also *Oliphant* [1992] Crim. L.R. 40.
[86] [1988] 2 All E.R. 135; see also *Parris* [1989] Crim. L.R. 214.

of Appeal quashed the robbery conviction under section 78 because although the initial refusal of access to a solicitor was justified, that refusal could not be justified after charging D with the burglaries.[87] Legal advice was seen as a 'fundamental human right'.

A different approach was seen in *Alladice*,[88] again an armed robbery case. While *Samuel* adopts a 'rights' approach, (so that the accused's rights should be protected by putting him into a position that he would have been in if his rights had been observed), *Alladice* displays a slightly harder Court of Appeal line. The nature of the right interfered with and the causal link between that interference and the evidence obtained are factors to be taken into account under section 78 in reaching a solution that reflects 'justice'. In *Alladice* the suspect was accustomed to police interviews and thus the court felt that a solicitor's presence would not have made a difference.

Such cases suggest that the Court of Appeal is weaving a rather uneasy road between the two rationales for excluding evidence. Although they have turned their backs on the strict 'reliability' approach (which would test the quality of the statement regardless of the infringement of the defendant's rights), they find it hard to embrace the full American 'fairness' model, which would lead to exclusion whenever the suspects' rights are infringed. The pragmatic approach in *Walsh* appears preferable as it seeks to measure the significance of the breach with the adverse affect on the fairness of the proceedings created.

Whether such a pragmatic approach can survive the passage of the Human Rights Act 1998 is doubtful. In *Murray v. UK*[89] the defendant was arrested under the Prevention of Terrorism (Temporary Provisions) Act 1989. Interviewed at Castlereagh Police Office, he was not given access to a lawyer for 48 hours. He refused to answer questions during this period and the trial judge drew adverse inferences from that refusal. The Court held that where such consequences from silence existed, it is of paramount importance for the rights of the defence that an accused has access to legal advice. The concept of fairness enshrined in Article 6 requires that the accused has the benefit of the assistance of a lawyer already at the initial stages of police interrogation. To deny access to a lawyer for the first 48 hours of police questioning—whatever the justification for such denial—was incompatible with the rights of the accused under Article 6.[90] A similar result was result was reached in *Magee v. UK*.[91] These affirmations of the right to legal advice must be seen in context. Both *Murray* and *Magee* involved people suspected of terrorism who were being interviewed in the coercive and intimidating atmosphere of Castlereagh. Although a police station interview room is less disagreeable, in principle this factor should not distinguish these cases from those accused of ordinary criminal offences. The strong statements from the Court on access to legal advice apply in all cases. The conclusion is that the *Murray* Case treats the right to advice as a fundamental right, attaching to all categories of suspect and which can only be restricted in extraordinary circumstances. If this is correct, it is difficult to see that the Court of Appeal can continue to regard the refusal of legal advice to suspects as not affecting the fairness of the trial, either

[87] The Court of Appeal is quite strict on further questioning once charged though if the suspect makes voluntary statement, then can be admitted—*Pall* [1992] Crim. L.R. 126.
[88] [1988] Crim. L.R. 608.
[89] *Application No. 18731/91*, 22 E.H.R.R. 29 (1996).
[90] In *Averill v. UK Application No. 36408/97*, [2000] Crim L.R. 682 (2000), the Court held that denial to access for the first 24 hours was also a breach.
[91] *Application No. 28135/95*, [2000] Crim. L.R. 681.

because they have a criminal record or because it would not have affected their behaviour in interview. In *Murray*[92] the Court explicitly rejected such an approach.

Although the Court has said that the right of access to a solicitor is fundamental to an accused's defence,[93] the Court has accepted that the right to legal advice may be subject to restriction for good cause. Section 58(8) PACE entitles the police to delay access to a solicitor under the 'serious arrestable offence' exception. *Murray* and *Magee* both show that the seriousness of the offence is not by itself enough to restrict the right. Relevant factors, which would justify delaying access to a lawyer, must be those that go to interference with the investigation in some way by the solicitor involved. The relevant factors for such restriction must relate to impeding the investigation away from the station and in such circumstances, it is difficult to conclude that delay of access would be often justified. Whether such access also means that a right to have your lawyer present at interview is a moot question under the Convention.[94] In the U.K., such a right is accepted but even here, under Code C, a lawyer may be asked to leave an interview if he or she is preventing the interviewer from putting questions properly.[95]

4.1.4 *Interviews Inside the Station*

The provisions of Code C regulate the interviews. An interview is defined[96] as the questioning of a person regarding his involvement in an offence and must be carried out under caution. There are general provisions regarding conditions of detention, relating to heating, lighting, proper food and exercise. Custody officers must be aware of the special provisions regarding the mentally handicapped, those with sight or speech impediments, the ill, foreigners and juveniles. The basic rights[97] of a suspect being interviewed allow for a minimum 8 hour continuous period of rest without interrogation in any 24 hour period with properly heated, ventilated and lit interview rooms, with no requirement to stand and with proper breaks for refreshment at recognised mealtimes. The interview will be tape-recorded under the provisions of Code of Practice E[98] and in the future may be visually recorded.[99]

When do breaches of Code C (other than those relating to legal advice) lead to the exclusion of evidence? Usually the evidence is an incriminating statement by the accused—a breach of the Code might lead to an argument that the statement should be excluded under section 76(2) because it was obtained by oppression or that it was obtained in circumstances that might render it unreliable. Even if the statement is considered to be reliable and not to have been obtained by oppression, there is a subsidiary argument that the statement should be excluded under section 78 because its admission would have an adverse effect on the

---

[92] *supra*, paras 67–68.
[93] *Bonzi v. Switzerland* Application No. 7854/77, 12 D.&R. 185 (1978).
[94] *Murray* (1996) *supra*, para 69.
[95] Code C 6.9.
[96] Code C 11.1A.
[97] Code C 12.
[98] The major problem with taping appears to be the inadequate summaries of the tapes produced by the police—Royal Commission on Criminal Justice, *op. cit.*, paras 3.73ff., Baldwin J., Preparing the Record of Taped Interview (Royal Commission on Criminal Justice Research Study No. 2) (1992).
[99] s. 76 of the Criminal Justice and Police Act 2001.

fairness of the proceedings. Any breach must be significant and substantial and not merely technical. For example, in *Taylor*[100] there was a breach of length of detention regulations as a result of delay in organising an ID parade. It was a minor delay and a technical infraction would not lead to the exclusion of evidence.

There was oppression in *Paris*[101] where the accused, on the borderline of mental handicap, made a confession having denied the offence 300 times. But merely discourteous behaviour is not oppressive.[102] But this can verge into oppressive conduct as in *Beales*[103] where the officer 'hectored and bullied' and fabricated evidence. When the police do act unethically, the Court of Appeal again fails to give a clear guide. In *Fulling*,[104] the police told the defendant that her lover had been unfaithful to her with another woman (being held in the next cell). The accused made a statement, which was not excluded since this was not 'oppressive' behaviour under section 76. The conviction was upheld but some questions remain. Could the statement be said to be 'reliable' in such circumstances beyond reasonable doubt—which is the burden placed on the prosecution in such cases? Or could it be said that deliberately (but not illegally) undermining the willpower of a suspect in this manner has an 'adverse affect on the fairness of the proceedings'? This can be contrasted with *Mason*,[105] a case which involved the arson of a car—the police alleged falsely that they had fingerprints of the defendant on a fragment of glass and as a result, he made incriminating statements. The conviction was quashed with the Court of Appeal stressing the need to balance the gravity of the charge, the public interest, the position of the defendant and the nature of the police illegality. This was regarded as a significant deception on a minor charge, not merely to deceive the defendant but also his lawyer.

Incriminating statements might also be excluded on the grounds of unreliability—this does not require any impropriety on the part of the police. Presence in the police station should mean that all the procedural safeguards are observed such as being interviewed in a proper room with recording or contemporaneous note taking. But in *Mathews*,[106] the accused was remanded in police cells where she was alleged to have made incriminating statements. These were given in evidence. The driving principles behind PACE meant that such unverified police statements should not be admitted but there is no automatic exclusion and section 78 leaves the issue to the trial judge's discretion—as long as the judge addresses his or her mind to the correct issues, the appellate court will usually not interfere with the decision. But in *Hunt*[107] the initial statements to officers were excluded as the defendant should have been cautioned and taken to the station for interview. An unsigned record of what was allegedly said placed a person in custody at a disadvantage. Similarly in *Sanusi*[108] the conviction was quashed where the suspect was questioned in the custody area of an airport without having been informed of his rights.

---

[100] [1991] Crim. L.R. 541.
[101] (1993) 97 Cr. App. R. 99.
[102] *Davison* (1992) (CA—unreported).
[103] [1991] Crim. L.R. 118.
[104] [1987] Crim. L.R. 492.
[105] [1987] Crim. L.R. 757 but *cf.*, *Bailey* [1993] Crim. L.R. 681 where play-acting by the police convinced the suspects that their cell had not been bugged and they made incriminating statements.
[106] [1990] Crim. L.R. 190.
[107] [1992] Crim. L.R. 582.
[108] [1992] Crim. L.R. 43.

A failure to caution is almost inevitably a substantial and significant breach.[109] Similarly if there are inducements held out to the accused, such as an offer of bail, the court will often conclude that any resulting statement is unreliable.[110] But the appeal courts allow wide latitude to the trial judge and as a result the decisions involving breaches of interview procedure are difficult to fit into clear factual categories—in *Trussler*[111] the Crown Court excluded the statements where the suspect was a drug addict who was arrested at 9 a.m. and he eventually made a statement at 2 a.m. the following morning. A doctor had been provided and the suspect had talked to his lawyer on the phone but there were long periods of questioning without adequate rest periods and the statements were eventually excluded as potentially unreliable under section 76(2)(b). But in *Crampton*[112] where the defendant was again suffering from withdrawal symptoms and made admissions after 19 hours in custody, the Court of Appeal emphasised that it is the function of the trial court to consider the issue of unreliability—although medical evidence at the *voire dire* accepted that answers in interview in these circumstances could be potentially unreliable, the trial judge could legitimately hold that the confession was in fact reliable.

The discretion to exclude evidence is exercised freely with regard to vulnerable defendants. There must be an appropriate adult present for young suspects as well as for the mentally handicapped.[113] Any exclusion of the evidence does not rely on police malpractice—even if they did not suspect that the suspect was mentally handicapped, the evidence would still be excluded.[114] In *Lamont*[115] the interrogation was of a mentally retarded suspect with an IQ 73 and acting under section 77 of PACE, the Court of Appeal excluded evidence of a confession, which provided the only evidence of intention in an attempted murder case. But in *Clarke*,[116] the accused admitted attempted theft while being taken to the police station. A record of the conversation was made and signed but at trial the defendant alleged that he was deaf and thus there had been a breach of the Codes.[117] On appeal, this argument was rejected. There was no breach of the Codes if the officer was unaware that the suspect was deaf but if shown as fact that the defendant was deaf, it could still be excluded under section 78. Exclusion of evidence is not predicated on proof of police misconduct as could be seen in *Brine*[118] where the suspect was properly interviewed but the interview was excluded after medical evidence that the accused was suffering from a mild form of paranoid psychosis.

4.1.5 *Interviews Outside the Station*

The Code of Practice regarding detention and interviews does not run outside the station and prior to PACE, there was concern about police 'verbals', the practice

[109] *Sparks* [1991] Crim. L.R. 128.
[110] *Barry* (1991) 95 Cr. App. R. 384.
[111] [1988] Crim. L.R. 447.
[112] [1991] Crim. L.R. 277.
[113] *Silcott* (1991), *The Times*, December 9.
[114] *Ham* (1995) CA unreported.
[115] [1989] Crim. L.R. 813.
[116] [1989] Crim. L.R. 892.
[117] Code C 13.5, which specifies that if a person appears to be deaf, he must not be interviewed in the absence of an interpreter.
[118] [1992] Crim. L.R. 122.

whereby a police witness would testify that the defendant had made an off-the-cuff incriminating remark. These are often unverified and unverifiable but are not automatically excluded as evidence in the trial. The appeal court still admits in certain circumstances, testimony about admissions at the scene or in the patrol car.[119] PACE and Code C were intended to eliminate this practice by focusing on the 'station interview' as the central stage where the authoritative record would be constructed. To achieve this, the central safeguards were the caution, the notification of the right to legal advice and the proper recording of interviews, initially by contemporaneous note taking and later by audio and visual recording.

Where practicable, the interview of an arrested person should always take place at a police station.[120] A suspect may be questioned outside the station if any delay might lead to interference or harm to evidence or other people, to alert others or to hinder the recovery of property but must stop as soon as the relevant risk has been averted. Suspects may also make a spontaneous statement and these may well be admissible. In *Parchment*[121] the suspect was discovered naked in the cupboard in a flat. Arrested and cautioned over some burglaries, he made spontaneous admissions. When there has been an arrest, there will have been a caution and any questions and answers must be recorded as soon as practicable with the suspect given the opportunity to read the record and sign it as correct.[122] Here the statements were only written up and shown to the accused later, at which point he was denied the offences. The Crown Court admitted the statements arguing that, while the police operated within PACE and its Codes, they could not be said to be operating unfairly under section 78. But that approach ignores the inherent unreliability of any such testimony where the record has not been taped nor contemporaneously noted. In addition it ignores the unfairness of relying on a defendant's statements where there has been no notification of any right to see a solicitor, let alone actual legal advice.

Despite this, an investigating officer must be able to ask questions which do not comprise an 'interview'. The answers might reinforce suspicions and provide grounds for arrest or conversely they might contain an innocent explanation and remove suspicion. An interview is defined[123] as the questioning of a person regarding his involvement in an offence. Questioning only to obtain information or an explanation or in the ordinary course of an officer's duties do not constitute an interview.[124] Nor do questions that are confined to the proper conduct of a search. In such cases, the requirement to make a contemporaneous note does not apply if it is impracticable. Again the Court of Appeal does not provide secure guidelines: in *Langiert*,[125] the trial judge held that it was not reasonably practical despite the presence of three officers. In *Chung*,[126] the court took a more robust approach and excluded the evidence where four officers were present.

Where the trial courts permit such statements to be admitted into evidence, the PACE safeguards are largely by-passed as 'verbals' will move from the police

---

[119] Sanders A. (1993), *op. cit.*, p. 91; Maguire M. and Norris C, *The Conduct and Supervision of Criminal Investigations* (1992), Royal Commission on Criminal Justice research Study No. 5.
[120] Code C 11.1.
[121] [1989] Crim L.R. 290.
[122] Code C 11.5 and C 11.10.
[123] Code C 11.1A.
[124] But seeking information might well constitute questioning about a person's involvement in an offence within Code C 11.1A—*Cox* [1993] Crim. L.R. 382; *Marsh* [1991] Crim. L.R. 455.
[125] [1991] Crim. L.R. 777; *White* [1991] Crim. L.R. 779.
[126] *Chung* (1991) 92 Cr. App. R. 314.

station to the scene of crime and police car, before the Code of Practice starts to run.[127] But the appellate decisions are far from clear. In *Maguire*[128] the officer advised the suspect in the police car to '*tell the truth*' and the suspect said that '... *we were only going in to have a look around ... for anything, for money, whatever.*' The charge was attempted burglary and the Court of Appeal held that, although Code did not apply only to interviews in police stations, in this case, this questioning did not constitute an 'interview' since there were no questions asked and thus the unverified police statement was admitted into evidence. *Maguire* should be compared with *Hunt*[129] where testimony about questioning in a police car was excluded. This approach was also taken in *Maloney and Doherty*[130] where a stipendiary magistrate excluded evidence of pocket book interviews undertaken at the scene, unseen and unsigned by defendants. In *Sparks*[131] there was an informal chat at the social services office, which an officer attended and yet the rules relating to recording and verifying still applied. But as *Maguire* shows, there is inconsistency and courts reach different conclusions admitting evidence in cases where substantial interviews have taken place outside the police station.[132]

The Royal Commission found that about 30 per cent of suspects report being questioned prior to arrest and there was evidence that negotiations took place off record as to what was to be said on the record.[133] Despite the dangers involved in the use of such unverified information obtained outside the police station, the Royal Commission did not consider its total exclusion but contented themselves merely with discussing the possibilities of extending tape-recording to all transactions between officer and suspect.

4.1.6 *Inadmissible Statement followed by Proper Interview*

If a statement is excluded because of a breach of the Codes, this does not automatically lead to exclusion of a second statement occurring in course of a properly conducted interview.[134] But if the grounds for impugning the first statement still exist, the second statement suffers the same fate. In *Canale*,[135] the officers deliberately broke the rules and consequently the court prevented the prosecution from gaining advantage. In *McGovern*[136] the suspect had IQ of 73 and it was felt that the impact of the first statement could not be excluded from affecting reliability of the second statement even though this latter was in the presence of a solicitor.

But does the inadmissibility of the confession mean that any evidence, which is discovered as a consequence of that confession, is inadmissible? In *Warwick-*

---

[127] Royal Commission on Criminal Justice, *op. cit.*, paras 3.7ff.; Moston S. and Stephenson G., *The Questioning and Interviewing of Suspects Outside the Police Station* (Royal Commission on Criminal Justice Research Study No. 22)(1993); McConville *et al.* (1991), p. 83ff.
[128] [1989] Crim. L.R. 815.
[129] [1992] Crim. L.R. 582.
[130] [1988] Crim. L.R. 523.
[131] [1991] Crim. L.R. 128.
[132] *Keenan* [1989] Crim. L.R. 720; *Brown* [1989] Crim. L.R. 500.
[133] Irving B. and Dunnighan C., *Human Factors in the Quality Control of CID Investigations* (Royal Commission on Criminal Justice Research Study No. 21) (1993).
[134] *Y v. DPP* [1991] Crim. L.R. 917.
[135] (1990) 91 Cr. App. R. 1.
[136] [1991] Crim. L.R. 124.

shall[137] the accused was charged as an accessory to handling. As a result of her confession, the stolen property was recovered having been hidden in her bedroom. But the confession had been obtained as a result of inducements and was held to be inadmissible. At common law this made no difference and the evidence of the finding of the property was admitted. This rule is preserved in section 76(4) of PACE—the fact that a confession is wholly or partly excluded shall not affect the admissibility in evidence of any facts discovered as a result of the confession. In *Warwickshall*, the discovery of the property in the accused's bedroom necessarily linked her with the crime without reference to the confession.

4.2 PRIVACY AND UNDERCOVER POLICING

Undercover policing, surveillance operations and interception of communications are all part and parcel of modern police work. Historically the police have never had any general statutory authority for such actions. Such authority as there was, has been based upon the common law principle that whatever is not expressly forbidden by law is permissible. Covert surveillance or undercover information gathering, not involving criminal or tortious conduct, were not forbidden because they did not, in general, infringe any right to privacy. Common law has never recognised a right to privacy as such. In *Malone v. Metropolitan Police Commissioner*[138] the plaintiff sued after the prosecution in an earlier criminal trial admitted to tapping his telephone. He claimed that telephone tapping, even authorised by the warrant of the Home Secretary, was unlawful. Sir Robert Megarry V.C. held that, 'No *new right in the law, fully-fledged with all the appropriate safeguards, can spring from the head of a judge deciding a particular case: only Parliament can create such a right'*.[139]

The European Convention does protect privacy in these circumstances—in *Malone v. UK*,[140] the applicant claimed that telephone tapping breached Article 8. The Court unanimously agreed—although the State can interfere with the right to privacy for the purposes specified in the Article, such interference has to be in accordance with the law. At that time, there was no legal authority for U.K. telephone tapping. The Court ruled that the law had to be sufficiently clear in terms to give citizens an adequate indication of the circumstances in which and the conditions under which telephone tapping could be carried out. The law had to indicate the scope of any executive discretion and the manner of its existence in order to give the citizen protection against arbitrary interference. These issues were addressed in the Interception of Communications Act 1985 which regulates interception of the post, telephone tapping and any communications sent by a public[141] telecommunications system.[142] The Regulation of Investigatory Powers Act 2000 now provides the regulatory framework.

But away from the interception of communications, in the absence of any common law right to privacy, there have been few legal constraints on police undercover operations until the Human Rights Act 1998. There is now protec-

---

[137] (1783) 1 Leach 263.
[138] [1979] 2 All. E.R. 620.
[139] *Malone*, supra, at 643a.
[140] *Malone v. UK* (1984) 7 E.H.R.R. 14 at 39–41.
[141] As defined s. 9 of the Telecommunications Act 1984.
[142] As defined in s. 4(1) of the Telecommunications Act 1984.

tion and accountability provided by recent legislation such as the Police Act 1997 and the Regulation of Investigatory Powers Act 2000.

4.3 UNDERCOVER AGENTS AND ENTRAPMENT

Intelligence-led policing can involve the targeting by the police of individuals suspected of involvement in criminal activities. The purpose is often to acquire evidence to be used in subsequent prosecution. Do the techniques of investigation threaten the fairness of the proceedings so that a judge might exclude that evidence in such circumstances? Undercover policing takes many different forms— informants, the agent provocateur, 'sting' operations, covert facilitation and, frequently, entrapment techniques.[143]

- 'Honeypot' Operations: these involve the police establishing bogus businesses. Common examples of this are phoney second-hand dealerships. In *Christou*[144] the police ran a jeweller's shop, buying stolen goods, recording transactions and ultimately trapping over 30 people. This took place over a period of time, which meant that the suspects were allowed to continue their offences without immediate police action.

- Integrity Tests: these involve placing tempting opportunities before targeted suspects. In *Williams v. DPP*[145] the police left a Transit van apparently loaded with cigarettes in public view, arresting the appellants when they attempted to take some of the cartons.

- Decoy operations: these involve police acting as a potential or actual victim. Female police officers might, for example, walk particular routes where sexual assaults have occurred. In the past male officers were known to loiter around public toilet blocks to bait the advances of homosexual men.

- 'Sting' or active participation operations: in such operations, police are active participants or conspirators with the suspected citizens they hope to trap. A common example (perhaps the most common) is police posing as drug buyers and often completing mock purchases from unsuspecting dealers. Statutory approval has now been given to the use of under age children by police officers to purchase alcohol.[146]

- Solicitation: there is often a fine line between the active participation of a police officer in a criminal transaction and solicitation, whereby the police officer actively encourages and coerces the commission of a crime. In *Wilson*[147] a police informer actively encouraged the accused into forging large quantities of American Express traveler cheques, even supplying the printing press!

---

[143] Stevens C., 'Covert Policing Techniques,' (Police Association of South Australia, Current Issues Working Paper 10); Cheney D, et al., *Criminal Justice and the Human Rights Act 1998* (2nd ed., 2001) p. 89; Billingsley R. et al., Informers (2001).
[144] [1992] 4 All E.R. 559.
[145] [1993] 3 All E.R. 365.
[146] Criminal Justice and Police Act 2001, s. 31.
[147] *The Guardian*, December 15, 1994—the Court of Appeal judgment was May 9, 1996 (Lawtel) Although the trial judge refused to exclude the evidence, he merely imposed suspended sentences, a clear comment on the propriety of the proceedings.

The undercover investigating officer might be regarded as the 'camera on legs' but acts, not simply as an observer but as a participant.[148] American law permits a substantive defence of entrapment,[149] so that, although *'artifice and stratagem may be employed to catch those engaged in criminal enterprises'*, government agents may not originate a criminal design—if the state does so, the defendant is entitled to an acquittal. In English common law, there is no such defence.[150] Any control over operations involving the participation of the police is exercised by the indirect (and less satisfactory) means of exclusion of evidence through section 78 of PACE or by staying the proceedings as an abuse of process.[151] The test for exclusion is whether the offence would have occurred but for the involvement of the police—an issue of causation rather than predisposition. *Smurthwaite*[152] involved allegations that the defendant had solicited another to murder his wife. Incriminating conversations were recorded by an undercover police officer, pretending to be a contract killer. These recordings were admitted into evidence. The Court of Appeal upheld this, asking *'Was the officer acting as an agent provocateur in the sense that he was enticing the defendant to commit an offence he would not have otherwise committed?'*[153]

English law will need to take into account the European Convention. The same issue has been raised in *Ludi v. Switzerland*[154] and in *Teixeira de Castro v. Portugal*,[155] in both of which undercover police officers made sample purchases of drugs. The issue was whether the admission of the testimony of the officers was in breach of the accused's right to a fair trial under Article 6. The outcomes were different. In *Ludi*, the operation was part of a judicial investigation and the drugs deal was already under way when the undercover officers arrived. The operation was not seen as a violation. In *Teixeira de Castro*, there was no real judicial supervision of the operation nor was there any pre-existing evidence to implicate the defendant. The Court stressed the issue as to whether the defendant was 'predisposed' to commit the offence.

The question of entrapment was reconsidered in *Looseley*[156] where the accused was telephoned by an undercover police officer who asked him if he could obtain 'a couple of bags' for him. The accused did so on this and on three further occasions. At his trial he submitted by way of a preliminary issue that the indictment should be stayed as an abuse of process on the ground of entrapment. The House of Lords reaffirmed that entrapment was not a substantive defence but the common law had remedies in respect of entrapment: first (and preferably) the court could stay the proceedings as an abuse of process and secondly the court could exclude evidence pursuant to section 78 of PACE as the admission of the evidence would adversely affect the fairness of the proceedings. A judge should consider whether the defendant would not otherwise have committed the offence, the nature of both the offence and the entrapment, whether the police had grounds for suspicion and were acting as part of a proper, supervised

---

[148] Maguire M. and John T., 'Covert and Deceptive Policing in England and Wales' *European Journal of Crime, Criminal Law and Criminal Justice* [1996] 316.
[149] *Jacobson v. U.S.* 503 U.S. 540 (1992): *Sorrells v. U.S.* 287 U.S. 435 (1932): *US v. Russell* 411 U.S. 423(1973).
[150] *Sang* [1980] A.C. 402.
[151] Choo A., *Abuse of Process and Judicial Stays of Criminal Proceedings* (1993).
[152] [1994] 1 All E.R. 898.
[153] *per* Lord Taylor C.J. at 903a.
[154] *Application No.* 12433/86, 15 E.H.R.R. 173 (1992).
[155] *Application No.* 25829/94, 28 E.H.R.R. 101, [1998] Crim L.R. 751 (1998).
[156] [2001] 4 All E.R. 897.

operation and how passive or active the police's role had been. The defendant's predisposition to commit the offence and his or her criminal record should rarely be factors. The limits of acceptable police behaviour include: whether the police had done no more than present the defendant with an unexceptional opportunity to commit a crime; and whether the police conduct was no more than might have been expected from members of the public in the circumstances. Ultimately the overall consideration was always whether the conduct of the police or other law enforcement agency was so seriously improper that it brought the administration of justice into disrepute. The House felt, perhaps disingenuously, that the jurisprudence of the European Court had not modified the judicial discretion conferred by section 78.

The issue for domestic law is that of judicial supervision of undercover operations. The Convention insists that any derogation from fundamental rights be 'in accordance with law'. In civil law systems, this is achieved by the supervision of an investigating judge. In the U.K. the promulgation of proper guidelines and the authorisation for operations have been in the hands of senior police management.[157] The appellate courts have laid down some principles on covert operations in cases such as *Smurthwaite* and *Looseley* but these scarcely amounted to a statutory framework. The lack of such legal authority for covert operations should be compared with detailed procedural framework for searching premises laid down by Part II of PACE. However reform has come with the Regulation of Investigatory Powers Act 2000, which introduced a structure for authorisation of undercover operations. The statute distinguishes between,

- directed surveillance which is undertaken for the purposes of a specific investigation, is likely to result in obtaining private information about a person. It does not include situations where the surveillance is an immediate response to events.

- intrusive surveillance which is carried out on residential premises or in private vehicles and which either involves an investigator on the premises or in the vehicle or the use of a surveillance device.

- covert human intelligence source which involves agents who establish a personal relationship to obtain information which is covertly disclosed.

In all these cases, the surveillance is regarded as lawful if an authorisation under the Act is obtained and subsequent actions are in accordance with that authorisation. There is a considerable difference in the nature of the authorisation required—directed surveillance and the use of covert human intelligence sources require the approval of a designated police officer, probably a superintendent under section 30. Intrusive surveillance, on the other hand, requires authorisation from a judicial commissioner. These are discussed later.

4.4 INTERCEPTION OF THE MAIL AND TELEPHONE TAPPING

The interception of communications can take place through phone taps or by the

---

[157] *Codes of Practice, Covert Law Enforcement Techniques* (Association of Chief Police Officers and HM Customs and Excise 1999).

cloning of mobile phones or pagers as well as through the opening of mail. The practice of intercepting letters under the Home Secretary's warrant is of very long standing although the authority for doing so is obscure.[158] Statutory authority arrived with the Interception of Communications Act 1985, which has now been replaced by Part I of the Regulation of Investigatory Powers Act 2000. Authorisation at the level of the Secretary of State is necessary for the police to conduct such intercepts of post or telecommunications. In contrast, lowly Crown Servants[159] such as officers from Customs and Excise have wide powers to make such intercepts under the Wireless Telegraphy Act 1949.[160]

It is now a criminal offence for a person intentionally to intercept a communication except under a warrant issued by the Secretary of State or where there were reasonable grounds to believe that the sender or recipient of the communication consented.[161] The Secretary of State can issue a warrant in the interests of national security; for the purpose of preventing or detecting serious crime or for the purpose of safeguarding the economic well being of the United Kingdom.[162] The total figure for warrants issued for telephone tapping and mail-opening in 2000 for England and Wales was 1,608. This represents a slight drop on the previous year (1,734) but is the third highest total in peacetime.[163] An executive power of this nature has considerable implications for individual privacy and although the Act conforms in a minimal sense with the requirements of Article 8, there are few controls, either through judicial or Parliamentary scrutiny. In this sphere, the passage of the Human Rights Act 1998 will not necessarily lead to any improvement in the protection of privacy.[164]

The Convention accepts that secret surveillance may be justified in order to counter threats from espionage, terrorism or serious crime. In *Klass v. Germany*,[165] German legislation permitted the State to open and inspect mail and listen to telephone conversations in order to protect against, *inter alia*, 'imminent dangers' threatening the 'free democratic constitutional order' and 'the existence or the security' of the State. The European Court provided the following general guidance as to the application of Article 8 to legislation authorising surveillance:

- the legislation must be designed to ensure that surveillance is not ordered haphazardly, irregularly or without due and proper care;

- surveillance must be reviewed and must be accompanied by procedures which guarantee individual rights;

- it is in principle desirable to entrust the supervisory control to a judge in accordance with the rule of law, but other safeguards might suffice if they are independent and vested with sufficient powers to exercise an effective and continuous control;

[158] The issue was considered by the Birkett Committee appointed in 1957—Report of the Committee of Privy Councillors (Cmnd. 283).
[159] The police are not Crown Servants—*AG for New South Wales v. Perpetual Trustee Co. Ltd* [1955] A.C. 457.
[160] Such powers are unlikely to comply with the requirements of the Convention.
[161] Regulation of Investigatory Powers Act 2000, s. 1.
[162] ibid. s. 5(3).
[163] Regulation of Investigatory Powers Act 2000, Report of the Interception of Communications Commissioner, October 2001, Cm. 5296.
[164] Mirfield P., *Regulation of Investigatory Powers Act 2000 (2), Evidential Aspects* [2001] Crim. L.R. 91.
[165] *Application No. 5029/71*, 2 E.H.R. 214 (1978).

- if the surveillance is justified under Article 8(2) the failure to inform the individual under surveillance of this fact afterwards is, in principle, justified.[166]

It is clear that there must be adequate and effective safeguards against abuse and thus proper machinery for supervision. This need not be in the hands of a judge and the machinery under the Interception of Communications Act 1985 (now under the Regulation of Investigatory Powers Act 2000) was considered adequate in *Christie v. UK*.[167]

Somewhat bizarrely, under section 17 of the Regulation of Investigatory Powers Act, evidence which is the product of telephone intercepts is not admissible as evidence: no evidence shall be adduced, question asked, assertion or disclosure made which discloses that there has been a telephone tap.[168] This does apply to mobile phones—*Effik*[169] suggested that these were not part of the 'public' telecommunications system and were not covered by the legislation but the decision in *Morgans* overturned this.[170] But section 17 does not apply to lawful foreign intercepts, despite the absence of formal regulations relating to the storage and use of the fruits of foreign intercepts.[171] Nor does the section cover the use of a listening device installed in the accused's car, which simply heard and recorded what he said into his phone.[172] The legislation also does not cover intercepts on internal networks—the phones in a prison, albeit connected with the national system, are not within section 1 since there were a number of features that were very uncharacteristic of a public system. The controls by the prison authorities were of great significance.[173] This might be compared with *Halford v. UK*[174] where the applicant was a senior police officer with the Merseyside Police who was pursuing an industrial tribunal claim against her employers on the grounds of sex discrimination. Her telephone calls made on the internal police network were intercepted and the Strasbourg Court held that these were not covered by the 1985 Act and were in breach of Article 8 as the interference was not 'in accordance with the law'.

4.5 COVERT SURVEILLANCE

Modern technology has brought in its wake more sophisticated mechanisms for observing people's lives than steaming open envelopes or listening to their phone calls. Policing now employs a range of special investigating methods, whether this involves the use of informants, undercover agents, surveillance, computer screening or advanced technical devices. Over the past decades, however, the devices available to the police for surveillance operations have become more specialised—new technologies have enhanced the ability not only to observe people through walls, overhear conversations, and track movement but also follow their computerised record trail. We are familiar with advanced micro-

---

[166] (1978) 2 E.H.R.R. 214 at 232–6.
[167] *Application No. 21482/93, 78A D.&R.*
[168] *R v. Preston* (1994) 4 A.C. 130; *Morgans v. DPP* (2000) 2 All E.R. 522.
[169] [1995] 1 A.C. 309.
[170] (2000) 2 All E.R. 522.
[171] *X, Y and Z* (2000) T.L.R. May 23, 2000.
[172] *Smart* (CA March 27 2002 Lawtel).
[173] *Allan* (2001) Crim. L.R. 739.
[174] *Application No. 20605/92, 24 E.H.R.R. 523, [1998] Crim. L.R. 75 3 (1998).*

phones and Closed Circuit Television Cameras (CCTV) but there are other, more esoteric, examples of surveillance technology:[175]

- BT has a system that can switch on the phone in your house in order to listen to any conversations in the vicinity.

- massive millimetre wave detectors use a form of radar to scan beneath clothing. By monitoring the millimetre wave portion of the electromagnetic spectrum emitted by the human body, the system can detect items such as guns and drugs from a range of 12 feet or more. It can also look through building walls and detect activity.

- Van Eck monitoring works on the basis that every computer emits low levels of electromagnetic radiation from the monitor, processor, and attached devices. Although experts disagree whether the actual range is a only a few yards or up to a mile, these signals can be remotely recreated on another computer.

- tracking devices of all kinds include cellular phones which transmit location information to the home system to determine call routing. This information can be used for automated tracking of the caller's movements. In 1993, fugitive Colombian drug kingpin Pablo Escobar was pinpointed through his cellular phone. Currently there is an effort to develop a system that would give location information for every cellular phone.

- Forward Looking Infrared (FLIR) was originally developed in the U.S.A. for use in fighter planes and helicopters to locate enemy aircraft. FLIR can detect a temperature differential as small as 0.18 degrees centigrade. FLIR is used to track people and cars on the Mexican border and search for missing people and fugitives. But law enforcement agents have also used it in residential neighbourhoods to obtain a thermal image of particular houses, because the high-pressure sodium lights used to grow marijuana indoors create huge amounts of heat. Where such surveillance has been undertaken without warrants, it raises the question whether the surveillance was an unlawful search in breach of the Fourth Amendment.[176]

Covert surveillance of one form or another is undertaken in order to obtain evidence of offences. In the U.K., until 1998, such surveillance was carried out under Home Office guidelines published in 1984[177] which required the personal authority of the Chief Constable for such an operation. The courts' approach to regulating surveillance operations can be seen in *Khan*[178] in which the appellant was suspected of importing drugs. He visited the house of another man where, unknown to both of them, the police had installed a listening device from which they subsequently obtained a tape recording of a conversation that clearly showed the accused's involvement. There were no statutory provisions that authorised such an action, which was both a civil trespass and also a prima facie breach of the right to respect for private and family life protected by Article 8 of

---

[175] These are drawn from Banisar D., 'Big Brother Goes High Tech' *Covert Action Quarterly* [Spring 1996]—see also Criminal Justice Matters, *Surveillance* No. 20 Spring 1995.
[176] Uglow S., '*Covert Surveillance and the European Convention on Human Rights*' [1999] Crim. L.R. 287 at 292.
[177] There were similar guidelines for Scotland, Northern Ireland and Customs and Excise.
[178] [1996] 3 All E.R. 289.

the European Convention on Human Rights. The Home Office guidelines, however, had been complied with. At the trial and on appeal, the appellant argued that nevertheless the evidence had been improperly obtained and should be excluded. The House of Lords held that any breach of privacy or of Article 8 was relevant to, but not determinative of, the trial judge's discretion to exclude evidence under the provisions of section 78 of PACE and that in this case the facts were such that the judge had been entitled to hold that the circumstances did not require the exclusion of the evidence.

This was reviewed by the Strasbourg Court in *Khan v. UK*,[179] which unanimously held that there was a breach of Article 8. The key issue was whether the surveillance was 'in accordance with law'. The Court said that this phrase required not just compliance with domestic law but also relates to the quality of that law, requiring it to be compatible with the rule of law. Domestic law must provide protection against arbitrary interference. The Home Office guidelines that existed were not adequate and the surveillance could not be considered to be in accordance with law. The Court also ruled that the Police Complaints Authority could not be an effective remedy for those with complaints against the police—it did not meet the requisite standards of independence need to constitute sufficient protection against abuse of authority. More surprisingly the Court went on to rule that, despite the admission of the evidence obtained by the breach of Article 8 and despite the fact that this was the main evidence against the accused, there was no violation of the right to a fair trial. The applicant did not suggest that there was an 'automatic exclusion' rule where a Convention right had been breached but argued that there must be an effective procedure to challenge admissibility of evidence, that the trial court must have regard to the nature of the violation and that conviction should not be based solely on evidence obtained by a breach of a Convention right. The Court reiterated the general principle that the essential issue was the overall fairness of the proceedings. The applicant had the opportunity to challenge the validity of the evidence (under section 78) at each stage and the Court gave weight to the fact that the domestic courts did not feel that the admissibility of the evidence had given rise to substantive unfairness. The weaknesses of this judgment are brought out by the one dissentient, Judge Loucaides, who defined 'fairness' as implying observance of the rule of law and suggested that, although there was no breach of domestic law, the U.K. courts ought not to admit evidence obtained in breach of the Convention. Effective enforcement of the Convention is otherwise hindered, as the police would not be deterred from repeating the conduct. Exclusion of the evidence or a stay for abuse of process are the only practical and effective remedies and should be a necessary corollary to Article 8 rights.

Covert surveillance is now governed by the provisions of the Regulation of Investigatory Powers Act 2000 and Part III of the Police Act 1997:

- the Police Act 1997 deals with a limited, but very important, area of police activity: namely those forms of police surveillance which involve some form of unlawful conduct on the part of the police. Normally the unlawfulness will involve civil trespass. Section 92 makes such conduct lawful under certain conditions. It does not provide a general scheme to regulate covert surveillance generally. The aims were more limited, namely to protect the police from civil actions on the grounds of civil trespass and the government

---

[179] *supra.*

from high profile actions in front of the European Court of Human Rights.[180] There must be some doubt whether the 1997 provisions satisfy the requirements of Article 8, in particular because there is no requirement for prior judicial approval in all cases.

● the Regulation of Investigatory Powers Act 2000 creates a parallel system of authorisations for undercover investigations which are not unlawful but although the police would not face domestic civil action, they may be acting in breach of the suspect's right of privacy. To that end, authorisation will be needed for 'directed surveillance', 'intrusive surveillance' and the 'use of covert human intelligence sources'.[181]

The Office of Surveillance Commissioners undertakes oversight of the authorisation of intrusive surveillance operations by the police, NCIS, the National Crime Squad and HM Customs and Excise. There will be a Code of Practice for covert surveillance operations but this still only exists in draft form.[182] The surveillance commissioners have rejected requests from the police for authorisations on the grounds that the offence did not constitute serious crime or where the surveillance was not likely to be of substantial value.

Table 4.1 Authorisations of Covert Surveillance 2001[183]

Regulation of Investigatory Powers Act		*Police Act 1997*	
Authorisations for intrusive surveillance by authorizing officer	299 (all U.K.)	Authorisations for property interference by authorizing officer	2565 (all U.K.)
Authorisations for intrusive surveillance requiring prior commissioner approval	285	Authorisations for property interference requiring prior commissioner approval	371

4.5.1 *The 1997 Police Act*

Prior to the passage of these Acts, U.K. police practices of visual and aural surveillance were in breach of this right to privacy as these practices were only regulated only by administrative guidelines which were not clearly formulated nor were they accessible for citizens.[184] The need for a statutory system of authorisation can be seen in *Klass*[185] where the European Court acknowledged the significance of the technical advances made in surveillance as well as the development of terrorism. Although the state must be entitled to counter terrorism with secret surveillance of mail, post and telecommunications under exceptional circumstances, this does not give it the right to adopt whatever

---

[180] *Justice*, Briefing on the Police Bill 1997 (1997).
[181] There are about 950 public authorities (including local authorities and health trusts) which are entitled to conduct covert surveillance under the provisions of the 2000 Act.
[182] As of July 2002—it can be seen at www.homeoffice.gov.uk/ripa/covsurv.htm.
[183] Report of the Chief Surveillance Commissioner (2002) Cm. 5360.
[184] See Joubert C., '*Undercover Policing—A Comparative Study*,' [1994] European Journal of Crime, Criminal Law and Criminal Justice 18.
[185] *supra*.

measures it thinks it appropriate in the name of counteracting espionage, terrorism or serious crime.

Part III of the Police Act 1997 establishes a system to authorise various methods of covert surveillance. Initially the government sought only to formalise the existing system of authorisation by chief officers but there was considerable opposition to this from inside and outside Parliament.[186] The Act as passed still relies upon senior police officers to give the initial authority to the investigating officers and for such authorisations to be retrospectively scrutinised by commissioners appointed under the Act. But, very significantly, where the surveillance is of a private dwelling or office or involves acquiring knowledge of confidential information of various kinds, it is necessary for the commissioners to give prior approval. The key argument advanced for judicial oversight of the authorisation procedure was that in a modern democracy, independent judicial scrutiny is required before interference with individual rights and that such interference should never be left simply to executive authorisation. A further strong argument was that any proposals permitting such surveillance simply on the authorisation of a senior police officer were likely to breach the right of the individual to respect for his or her home, personal privacy and private papers guaranteed by Article 8. The government eventually accepted this position, although the argument for judicial approval of every authorisation was rejected.

Many jurisdictions possess statutory schemes where the use of listening devices to intercept private conversations can only be on the basis of a judicial warrant. One survey[187] showed that prior judicial authorisation was the norm in Australia, New Zealand, United States, Canada, France and the Netherlands before there could be lawful interception of communications. The report concluded that such prior authorisation did not prejudice the operational effectiveness of the police in combating serious crime. Indeed such scrutiny raised standards by improving the internal screening of applications, ensuring that applications are supported by evidence and are not simply fishing expeditions. Scrutiny is cost effective as it reduces the number of unnecessary surveillance operations. In the United States, judicial authorisation is required even in the highly sensitive areas of foreign intelligence gathering.[188]

The key section of the Police Act 1997 is section 92, which states:

'No entry on or interference with property or with wireless telegraphy shall be unlawful if it is authorised by an authorisation having effect under this Act.'

This section is very broadly drawn—it makes lawful any entry or interference with property where the necessary authorisation has been given under sections 93 or 94. There are, however, many constraints:

- authorisation will normally be given by the chief officer of the force
- the criteria for interference with property are reasonably specific
- all authorisations will be scrutinised by the commissioners
- there are channels for complaint.

---

[186] Emmerson B., '*Crime and Human Rights*' 150 New L.J. 13 (2000).
[187] *Justice, op. cit.* (1997).
[188] Foreign Intelligence Surveillance Act, 50 U.S. 1801 ff quoted in *Justice, op. cit.* (1997)).

The section is overly broad in some senses but it is much too narrowly drafted: what was required was the legislation that provided an overall scheme for regulating the use of listening devices and all forms of covert surveillance. New technologies are emerging: the police require a system of authorisation which would legitimise their operations while individuals require assurance that fundamental freedoms are not being eroded. Further legislation was required for these purposes within three years.

Initial authorisation under section 93 of this Act is not usually by a judge but will be by a senior police or customs officer. The key criteria for authorisations are laid down in section 93(2). The authorisation should only be given where the authorising officer believes that:

- the action is necessary as it will be of 'substantial value' in the prevention or detection of 'serious crime' and;

- the objectives of the action cannot reasonably be achieved by other means.

Crime is to be treated as serious by virtue of section 93(4) if it involves the use of violence, results in substantial financial gain or is conducted by a large number of persons in pursuit of a common purpose[189] or it involves the commission of an offence for which a person over 21 without previous convictions could reasonably be expected to receive a prison sentence exceeding three years.[190]

Any belief that the criteria are satisfied is obviously a subjective judgment but the interpretation does not lie solely within the untrammelled discretion of an authorising officer and the surveillance commissioners do refuse and quash authorisations. If approval were needed for the authorisation, the officer would have to satisfy a commissioner that the belief was held on reasonable grounds.[191] If the officer were appealing against refusal of such approval or the quashing of an authorisation, the Chief Commissioner would also be in a position to evaluate the reasonableness of the decision.[192] The commissioners must hold or have held high judicial office and have been appointed for a period of three years. The Chief Commissioner acts under this statute and under the Regulation of Investigatory Powers Act 2000.

Under section 101 the Secretary of State shall issue a code of practice to regulate the work of the authorising officers. Such a Code should lay down the procedures and guidelines to ensure that authorising officers are aware of what is expected of them. As with the PACE Codes, a breach of a provision is a factor that the trial judge may take into account in deciding whether to exclude evidence under section 78.

4.5.2 *The Regulation of Investigatory Powers Act 2000*

The Police Act 1997 only affected those surveillance operations that required authorisation under the Act—namely unlawful conduct. Other U.K. police practices of visual and aural surveillance, lawful under domestic law, did not require statutory authorisation but are now regulated by Part II of the Regulation

---

[189] s. 93(4)(a).
[190] s. 93(4)(b).
[191] s. 97(4)—Report of the Chief Surveillance Commissioner *op. cit.*, p. 8.
[192] s. 104(3) and (4).

of Investigatory Powers Act 2000.[193] The Act applies to directed surveillance, intrusive surveillance and the use of covert human intelligence sources.

- directed surveillance is undertaken for the purposes of a specific investigation, is likely to result in obtaining private information about a person. It does not include situations where the surveillance is an immediate response to events.

- intrusive surveillance is carried out on residential premises or in private vehicles and which either involves an investigator on the premises or in the vehicle or the use of a surveillance device. This does not include tracking devices on vehicles but does include interception of communications where one party consents and there is no interception warrant. A surveillance device not on the premises is not intrusive unless it is providing information of the same quality and detail as would have been expected from a device on the premises. TV detector vans are specifically excluded!

- the use of a covert human intelligence source involves agents who establish a personal relationship to obtain information which is then covertly disclosed. This is undertaken in such a manner that the person is unaware of the surveillance or its purpose. This will cover undercover officers and other informants.[194]

In all of these cases, the surveillance is regarded as lawful if an authorisation under the Act is obtained and subsequent actions are in accordance with that authorisation.

The purposes of directed surveillance or of the use of covert human intelligence sources must be one of the following: the interests of national security, the prevention and detection of crime and disorder, the economic well-being of the state, public safety, public health or tax collection. The initial authorisation required by section 30 will be by a designated police or customs officer.[195] Authorising officers will be superintendents and authorisation should only be given where the action is necessary, proportionate to the objectives and proper supervision and control arrangements exist.[196]

The purposes that are accepted for intrusive surveillance are the interests of national security, the prevention and detection of *serious* crime and disorder or the economic well being of the state. The authorisation required by section 32 will be by a senior authorising officer—for the police that will be the Chief Constable of the force.[197] In urgent cases, it will be possible for the operation to be authorised by deputies of parallel rank. Authorisation should only be given where the authorising officer believes that the action is necessary and proportionate to the objectives. Crime is to be treated as serious[198] if it involves the use of violence, results in substantial financial gain or is conducted by a large number of persons in pursuit of a common purpose or it involves the commission of an

---

[193] Pt. II was brought into force on September 25 2000—S1 2000/2543.
[194] For these definitions, see Regulation of Investigatory Powers Act 2000, s. 26.
[195] Many other public authorities are included—sec Sched. 1.
[196] s. 29(5).
[197] For intelligence service operations, the Secretary of State must authorise the action. Elsewhere, as with ss. 28 and 29, many other public authorities as well as the police will need to use these provisions for their covert operations—see Sched. 1.
[198] s. 81(3).

offence for which a person over 21 without previous convictions could reasonably be expected to receive a prison sentence exceeding three years.

The authorisation does not take effect, except in cases of urgency, until notice of the intrusive surveillance has been given to a surveillance commissioner and been approved. Accountability is again provided by the appointment of surveillance commissioners as well as the Investigatory Powers Tribunal established under section 65—the jurisdiction of this body, *inter alia*, includes complaints by any person who believes that they have been subject to use of the investigatory powers under Part II of this Act or under Part III of the Police Act 1997.

4.6 IDENTIFICATION EVIDENCE

Investigators have always sought new methods to identify the culprit in a crime. In the 19th century, Alphonse Bertillon, a Parisian detective, invented a system of classifying people so that a number of features could be cross-checked. It consisted of a card, with two photographs on it, the person's place and date of birth, and a number of bodily measurements. There were four measurements of the right ear, and a 16-part coded description of its conch-like formation; four measurements of the forehead, five of the nose, one of the left foot, one of the left arm from middle finger to elbow, and measurements for height and bust. The blood group was noted, and the colour of the person's hair and iris were taken down according to a table of colours already prescribed by Bertillon. But the system had its racist overtones and was largely rejected and replaced by fingerprints and nowadays DNA testing. In the 21st century, the science of biometrics is making a comeback—the National Training Centre for Scientific Support to Crime Investigation are currently compiling a database of ear images, one of Bertillon's keys. A further body part—the iris—has been used by the Nationwide building society, which ran a successful six-month trial of iris recognition technology in the cash machine at its head office.

There are several methods which investigating officers might use to identify a suspect. Here we outline police powers in relation to the most important, namely fingerprints, DNA sampling and visual identification:

4.6.1 *Fingerprints*

The reliability of fingerprinting as a way of confirming a person's identity was established in the 19th century. The use of fingerprints by police started in earnest when Sir Edward Henry devised a classification system in the 1890s that enabled prints to be catalogued and retrieved based on their physical characteristics. The national collection of fingerprints was started at Scotland Yard in 1901 using the 'Henry System'. The first successful conviction using fingerprints was in a burglary case in 1902 when the burglar, Harry Jackson was jailed. In 1902, 1,722 fingerprint identifications were made at Scotland Yard using Henry's fingerprint classification system. This was compared to almost 400 identifications made by Bertillon's anthropometric system between 1894 and 1900, a system which recorded the dimensions of certain skeletal body parts. The original collection comprised paper records but technology has made it possible for fingerprint images to be stored digitally. Although over 4.6 million sets of fingerprints are still held on paper in the national collection, a fingerprint officer can now call up the images on a computer screen in seconds. The National Fingerprint Bureau is housed in Scotland Yard—in 2000, it made 10,000 identifications from marks found at crime scenes. The Bureau receives approximately 120,000 fingerprint sets each year. The National Automated Fingerprint Identification System (NAFIS) is operational in all English and Welsh police forces.

The police have various powers to take fingerprints without consent:

- Section 61 of PACE enables the police to fingerprint a person without consent if the person has been charged with a recordable offence or if the fingerprinting is authorised by an officer of at least the rank of superintendent—this is undertaken in order to confirm or disprove involvement of the person.

- Section 27 of PACE empowers the police to take fingerprints from those who had been convicted of recordable offences but had never been in custody—section 78 of the Criminal Justice and Police Act 2001 now extends that to enable fingerprints to be taken from those cautioned (or given a reprimand or final warning in the case of young offenders). Cautions are still not criminal convictions and people accept cautions for many reasons, not necessarily associated with guilt. Perhaps we need an additional caution— that if you accept this caution, you must realise that personal data about you will be held on police databases in perpetuity.

Section 64 required that prints be destroyed at the close of the investigation or if the person is acquitted. Under section 82(2) of the Criminal Justice and Police Act 2001, the police will be permitted to retain fingerprints of suspects taken in the course of an investigation even if the individual is not subsequently prosecuted or is acquitted. Further, section 82(4) allows for the retention of volunteer fingerprints given for elimination purposes. These cannot be used in connection with the investigation of another offence unless there is written consent but in that case, the prints can be used for the investigation of an offence and the conduct of a prosecution. Once given, that consent cannot be withdrawn.

4.6.2 *Intimate Samples and DNA*

Suspects will always leave traces of themselves by their very presence at the scene of a crime. These traces may be fingerprints, fabrics but also blood, saliva, semen or even breath. DNA reliability has been lauded nationally as the most reliable evidence known—this may be true but errors can occur. A sample taken from the scene of a burglary led to a suspect with advanced Parkinson's disease, who could not drive and could barely dress himself. He lived 200 miles from the site of the burglary. His blood sample had been taken when he was arrested previously, and then released, after hitting his daughter in a family dispute. He was arrested despite his protestations of innocence and alibi evidence that he was babysitting a sick daughter at home. Only after re-testing was the error recognised.[199] The overwhelming effect of DNA evidence meant that the police ignored all contrary indications as the DNA showed that 'it had to be him'. It is clear that police and lawyers should recognise that care needs to be taken during investigation and with statistical presentation in court.[200]

---

[199] This example was gathered from www.forensic-evidence.com.
[200] Redmayne M., '*Presenting probabilities in Court*' [1997] 1 I.J.E.P. 187.

Section 62 of PACE confers the right to take intimate samples from a suspect but only with consent in writing under the provisions of section 62.[201] A refusal to consent allows a court or jury to draw inferences, which may be used as evidence against that person and the suspect must be cautioned to that effect.[202] Non-intimate samples such as mouth swabs, hair or nail clippings can be taken from a suspect compulsorily under section 63 although again it must be authorised by a superintendent in writing and recorded on the custody record.

Under section 64 of PACE, fingerprints or samples should be destroyed if the person is cleared of the offence, cautioned or not prosecuted. In *AG's Ref. (No. 3 of 1999)*[203] a rape occurred in 1997 and DNA samples were taken from the scene. Nine months later, the defendant was arrested for burglary and a saliva sample taken. He was acquitted of the burglary but the sample was not destroyed and it was matched with the DNA from the rape. Could the police as part of the investigation of the rape use the (illegally preserved) sample? The House of Lords held that it could and this was confirmed by section 82(2) of the Criminal Justice and Police Act 2001 whereby the police will be permitted to retain DNA and fingerprints of suspects taken in the course of an investigation even if the individual is not subsequently prosecuted or is acquitted. This information can be used for the investigation of an offence and the conduct of a prosecution. Although the fingerprint and DNA databases are registered with the Data Protection Registrar and information stored on them is covered by data protection legislation, the retention of data on people who have not been convicted of any offence seems a disproportionate infringement of the individual's right to privacy and a small step on the way to the compilation of a mass DNA database. As explained earlier, section 82(4) allows for the retention of volunteer DNA samples and fingerprints given for elimination purposes.

4.6.3 *Eyewitness Identification*

The main sources of evidence for the police will be the examination of the crime scene, the interviewing of witnesses, the search of persons, vehicles and places for evidence and the interrogation of suspects. The eyewitness is a valuable source of information and one of the most obvious aspects of eyewitness testimony is the visual identification of suspects. A suspect description was used as a source of evidence in 43 per cent of 'primary detected' burglary cases.[204] In inter-personal crimes such as robbery, violence and sexual offences, eyewitness information is critical to the apprehension of a suspect.[205]

Identification testimony is treated in court as possessing considerable probative weight but, as with confessions, its true probative value is over-estimated. Identification evidence can be very strong, especially when it is recognition evidence of a person already known to the witness. This is commonly the case with offences of personal violence. On the other hand the identification of strangers, perhaps glimpsed for a moment at the scene of a crime can be extremely weak,

---

[201] The procedure is detailed in Code D 5.
[202] *Smith* (1985). *The Times* May 20; s. 62(10) of the Criminal Justice and Public Order Act 1994.
[203] [2001] 1 All E.R. 577.
[204] Coupe T., and Griffiths, M., *Solving Residential Burglary* (Home Office, 1996) Police Research Series 77.
[205] Phillips C. and Brown D., *Entry into the criminal justice system: A survey of police arrests and their outcomes.* (1998) Home Office Research Study 185: Pike G., *et al. The Visual Identification of Suspects: Procedure and Practice* (Home Office, 2002) Briefing Note 2/02.

depending upon a range of factors that may not be taken into account at trial.[206] Unfortunately the jury's and the judge's perception of the weight of identification evidence is less likely to be affected by 'scientific' factors (duration, range, visibility) than by the credence that is given to the witness (the witness's demeanour, the coherence of the testimony). The prejudicial effect of such testimony is strong since it is hard to doubt the impartial witness who clearly identifies the accused. Yet as psychological research has suggested, the odds on the witness being right are at best evens, odds that are difficult to square with proof 'beyond reasonable doubt'.[207]

Where the identification evidence is simply corroborative of other testimony implicating the accused, there is less concern. But often the conviction is based wholly or mainly on such evidence. Figures in this area are hard to come by. The Devlin Report[208] suggested that in 1973, there were 2116 identity parades, resulting in identifications in 45 per cent. 850 people were prosecuted, of whom 82 per cent were convicted. But 347 people were prosecuted and 258 convicted *solely* or *mainly* on identification evidence.

Naturally there have been many notorious cases of miscarriages of justice as a result of misidentification—the most famous of these was in the early years of the century when 12 women wrongly identified Adolf Beck.[209] The Devlin Committee itself was set up after the release of Luke Dougherty who was convicted of shoplifting.[210] Although Dougherty had been on a coach trip at the time and had a cast-iron alibi, he had only called two witnesses at his trial, his girlfriend and another friend who had previous convictions. The jury did not believe them and convicted. The initial appeal was rejected and it was only on a referral back to the Court of Appeal by the Home Secretary that additional alibi witnesses were heard. More recently John McGranaghan was sentenced to life imprisonment for rape after three women identified him. Routine scientific analysis of the semen stains would have proved that he could not possibly have committed those offences but he served ten years' imprisonment before the conviction was quashed.[211]

Safeguards can exist either at the point of trial (regulating the admissibility of identification evidence) or at the point of investigation (regulating the manner in which the police gather identification evidence).

4.6.3.1 IDENTIFICATION EVIDENCE: SAFEGUARDS AT TRIAL

Such safeguards require that a court impose conditions before admitting eyewitness identification testimony as evidence. What might such conditions involve?

[206] Clifford B., *'The Relevance of Psychological Investigation to Legal Issues in Testimony and Identification'* [1979] Crim. L.R. 153; Jackson J., *'The Insufficiency of Identification Evidence Based on Personal Impression'* [1986] Crim. L.R. 203; Wells G. and Loftus E., (eds), *Eyewitness Testimony* (1984).
[207] Loftus E., *Eyewitness Testimony* (1979, reissued 1996).
[208] Report to the Secretary of State for the Home Department of the Departmental Committee on Evidence of Identification in Criminal Cases, HC 338, (1976)—this committee was set up after the convictions of Virag and Docherty had been quashed—the former since the defendant had been on a coach trip at the time. Only calling two witnesses, one failed to turn up and the other failed to convince the jury!
[209] Glanville Williams: *'Evidence of Identification'* [1976] Crim. L.R. 407 gives several other examples as does www.innocent.org.uk.
[210] Discussed in the Devlin Report, *supra*, Chap. 2.
[211] Woffinden B., *Hanratty, The Final Verdict* (1997) at Appendix A.

- that there should be a legal requirement that there is other independent evidence linking the accused to the crime.[212] This would mean that there could be no conviction based solely on identification evidence. An alternative would be that the jury should be warned to look for other independent evidence but its absence should not necessarily be a bar to conviction.

- the Devlin Report's preferred option was that there should be legislation for a special warning which explained to the jury that identification alone did not comprise probable cause for a conviction unless there were special circumstances—namely: familiarity; where the accused was a member of a small group, one of whom had committed the crime; where the defendant had failed to counter evidence with his own story.

Neither of these materialised as a result of the Devlin Report. The significant controls were introduced at the point of trial by the Court of Appeal's decision in *Turnbull*.[213] The Court was against any rule that prevented convictions from being based on identification alone and argued that the crucial element was the quality of that identification. As a result the *Turnbull* judgment does not require other independent evidence. Instead the jury should be warned of the special need for caution before convicting the accused in reliance wholly or mainly on identification evidence and they should be told to examine closely the circumstances in which the identification came to be made. The impact of *Turnbull* has been considerable—where this warning has not been given, then the conviction will normally be quashed.

4.6.3.2 IDENTIFICATION EVIDENCE: SAFEGUARDS DURING INVESTIGATION

Initially some controls at the point of investigation were introduced, especially when the Home Office issued a 1978 circular to police forces tightening up procedures in identification parades. In 1981, the Report of the Royal Commission called for such procedures to be made statutory[214] but instead there is the PACE Code of Practice D. The courts always took a robust line with police improprieties in obtaining identification evidence. This approach has led to identification evidence being excluded under section 78 of PACE. The Code is statutory and the courts held that it was to be observed and not varied at the will of the police.[215] The courts placed high value on the parades as providing persuasive evidence for the Crown and as being a substantial safeguard for the suspect. Even where the difficulties of holding parades were considerable, they may still be required. In *Ladlow*[216] there were 21 suspects and 11 witnesses so the police held confrontations having decided that 232 parades were impracticable. The evidence of identification was excluded. Difficulty in finding volunteers for a parade does not make it impracticable unless the suspect's appearance was

---

[212] The common law traditionally used this concept of corroborative evidence but recent legislation has reduced the scope of such rules very significantly over the past 10 years. It is unlikely that they will be expanded again.
[213] (1977) Q.B. 224.
[214] Royal Commission on Criminal Procedure: *op. cit.*, para 3.138.
[215] *Quinn* [1995] *Crim. L.R.* 56.
[216] [1989] Crim. L.R. 21; *Gaynor* [1988] Crim. L.R. 242.

the reason for that difficulty.[217] The House of Lords in *Forbes*[218] reinforced this approach and the judgment emphasised that Code D imposed a mandatory duty on the police to hold a parade wherever the suspect disputed the identification. This was the case even where there has been an unequivocal identification. However, a breach of the Code does not lead to automatic exclusion of the evidence—in *Forbes* the House held that in order to assess section 78 fairness, you had to consider the proceedings as a whole and whether the accused's rights had been infringed.

Code D was significantly revised in April 2002[219] and the mandatory duty on the police to hold an identification parade was removed and much greater weight given to video identification. The need for suspects' consent disappeared and the police were givwen greater discretion over the choice of procedure to be used.

Under the revised Code there is a distinction between cases where a suspect is known and cases where a suspect is not known. For the first group, the police have a duty to hold an 'identification procedure' as soon as possible. The suspect's consent to the procedure is not required—although the suspect is told that he or she need not take part in the procedure, that procedure may still go ahead and can include a covert video identification or a covert group identification. The new code also confers discretion on the police not to hold a procedure where it would serve no useful purpose. Furthermore the police now have discretion to choose between the different methods of identification.[220] The methods that may be used are:

- a parade.

- a group identification.

- a video film.

- a confrontation.

No officer involved in the investigation may take part in these procedures. The police must consider each method in turn, although a procedure is not needed, for example, if the suspect has been clearly identified by witnesses at the scene.[221] Before all else, a record of the initial description given by the witness must be made before any other means of identification under the Code takes place.[222] This description is disclosable to the defence prior to any subsequent trial.[223]

- **identity parades**: where identification is disputed[224] or where the police feel it would be useful, the suspect shall initially be offered either a parade or a video identification. A parade may not be practicable because of the unusual appearance of the suspect or for some other reason, such as the suspects' refusal to participate. Identity parades have been in common use throughout

---

[217] *Jamel* [1993] Crim. L.R. 52; *Campbell and Marshall* [1993] Crim. L.R. 47.
[218] [2001] 1 All E.R. 686 overruling *Popat* [2000] 2 Cr. App. R. 208.
[219] S.I. 615/2002: Clover S. and Roberts A., '*Short-sighted or Forward-looking*' [2002] New L.J. 870.
[220] Code D 2.16.
[221] *Rogers* [1993] Crim. L.R. 386: deliberately engineering a street confrontation prior to an identity parade will lead to the exclusion of the evidence—*Nagah* [1991] Crim. L.R. 55.
[222] Code D 2.2
[223] *Fergus* (1993) 98 Cr. App. R. 313.
[224] Even where the witnesses claims to be acquainted with the suspect and thus to recognise rather than to identify—*Conway* [1990] Crim. L.R. 402.

this century. It was and remains a voluntary system and if the suspect chooses not to take part or to disrupt it (perhaps by refusing to wear some item of clothing or to speak certain words), there are no sanctions.[225] The arrangements for any form of identification must be conducted by a uniformed officer, inspector or above, not concerned with the case.[226] The suspect must be told of his rights not to participate and asked whether he wants a solicitor or friend present.[227] There is considerable documentation of the process—the parade has to be photographed or videoed. Everything said or done should take place in the presence or hearing of the accused but where the witness is behind a screen, a representative of the suspect must be able to see and hear everything. If there is no such representative, everything relevant should be recorded on video.

There should be a minimum of 8 others on the parade.[228] The Code requires that these resemble the suspect as far as possible,[229] although the disclosure to the defence of the eyewitness's initial description suggests that the other members of the parade should resemble that description rather than the suspect, whenever there is a discrepancy between the two. The places are numbered and if the witness makes a positive identification, it is by number. The suspect is able to make objections to the arrangements and such objections should be met, if practicable. The suspect is allowed to stand where he likes and to change position. The triers of fact will be in a position to assess the fairness of the composition of the parade for themselves because of the requirement that the line-up be photographed or videoed.

The witness should not be shown or reminded of his or her initial written description or shown photos or other descriptions prior to the parade and should be isolated from other witnesses.[230] A further source of error might be news coverage and after the procedure, the witness is asked whether he or she has seen any video films or photographs that might have been released to the news media by the police. The witness should be encouraged to look at each member of the parade at least twice and to identify by number. The witness can ask for particular clothing to be worn, gestures to be made or words to be spoken.

- **video identification**: the revised Code treats video identification on a par with ID parades. The police have discretion to proceed with this method of identification even if the suspect does not consent. The provisions in the Code provide greater scope for capturing images covertly. In essence this is an identification parade conducted on video and the provisions of Annex A must be complied with. The film must include at least eight other people under identical conditions who, as far as possible, resemble the suspect. The

---

[225] Although there is some authority that the judge can comment on the fact that the suspect has refused to take part in a parade, drawing on analogy from *Robert William Smith* (1985) 81 C. App. R. 286. It would appear in the U.S., the suspect can be forced to do this—*US v. Wade* (1967) 388 U.S. 218.

[226] Code D Annex B.

[227] Code D 2.21.

[228] Code D Annex B para. 9—a minimum of 12 is required if there are 2 aspects of similar appearance Normally separate parades should be held for each suspect.

[229] Clifford B., '*The Relevance of Psychological Investigation to Legal Issues in Testimony and Identification*' [1979] Crim. L.R. 153.

[230] Code D Annex B para. 14.

film should be shown to the suspect and his or her lawyer before it is shown to any witness and any objections, if reasonable, should be addressed. The suspect's lawyer should be present at the showing of the film and, in the absence of such a representative, the showing itself should be recorded on video. The provisions regarding the recording of initial descriptions as well as the prohibition of discussions between the witness and police officers or other witnesses remain the same as those with other methods of identification. Again the witness is asked whether he or she has seen any video films or photographs that might have been released to the news media by the police

- **group identifications**: these may take place with the suspect's consent or covertly. It is a form of identification that is seen as subordinate to a parade or video identification. Those forms may be impracticable or the group method may be more satisfactory than a parade.[231] A group identification takes place where the suspect is viewed by a witness amongst an informal group of people.[232] Many of the conditions under which group identification takes place replicate the safeguards for identity parades so that the officer in charge must give notice to the suspect, *inter alia*, of its purpose, how it will be carried out, of the suspect's rights as well as warning him or her that a refusal to take part or any significant alteration of appearance can be given in evidence at trial. Similarly any initial description by a witness must be recorded and officers who escort witnesses to the identification scene must not discuss the case or reveal whether any other witness has made an identification. Again the witness is asked whether he or she has seen any video films or photographs that might have been released to the news media by the police.

  The scene itself should be photographed or videoed where possible. The place where the group identification is held should be one where other people are passing by or waiting around informally so that the suspect can join them. The place for the identification should not be in a police station unless this is dictated by reasons of safety or security. Annex C gives examples of escalators, shopping centres or railway or bus stations. Such groups might be mobile (walking through a shopping mall) or stationary (in a bus queue). In either situation the suspect is allowed flexibility in joining the group or taking up position although unreasonable delay might be regarded as a refusal to co-operate. Anything done or said to or by the witness should be in the presence or hearing of the suspect's solicitor or friend. The witness should point out any person he thinks he saw at the earlier, relevant, occasion and if practicable, the officer in charge should arrange for a closer look and ask the witness if he or she can make a positive identification.

  It is possible for group identifications to be held covertly, without the suspect's consent. In such situations the identification necessarily takes place without the knowledge of the suspect who thus has no right to have a solicitor or friend present. The other provisions of Annex C should be adhered to.

- **confrontation**: as a last resort, when no other method of identification is

---

[231] One reason might be fear on the part of the witness.
[232] Code D Annex C. of Annex C should be adhered to.

practicable, the suspect can be confronted by the witness.[233] Before the confrontation, the suspect and his or her lawyer is provided with details of the first description given by the witness to the police. Any material released to the media by the police should also be provided, if this is practicable. The confrontation will be in a police station, possibly in a room equipped with a screen although this may only be used when a representative of the suspect is present or where the confrontation is recorded on video. The suspect shall be confronted by the witness who is asked 'Is this the person?' Identification evidence obtained from a confrontation in the precincts of the trial court should not be admitted even when this takes place at the behest of the accused.[234] The dock identification, that is, an identification at the trial itself without any preceding method of identification, is normally not admissible.[235]

As mentioned, under the Code there is a distinction between cases where a suspect is known and cases where a suspect is not known. For the second group, there are additional methods of identification, which may be used.

- **street identification**: after an incident it is common for the police to drive the victim or witness around an area to see whether they can identify the culprit. This is permitted under the Code[236]—again a written record of the description should be made prior to the tour and the officer should not draw the witness's attention to anyone. However a prior identification by the witness does not rule out a subsequent parade. In *Brown*[237] the victim of a robbery toured the area in a police car immediately after the attack and picked out the defendant. No parade was held but the Court of Appeal felt that the Code was mandatory and that a parade was not necessarily otiose. Once a suspect is in a police station, Code D applies and the police cannot decide simply to dispense with a parade. In *Powell v. DPP*[238] a suspect was arrested and brought to the station where he was identified by a police officer who had witnessed the original incident. The Divisional Court held that the police were obliged to hold a parade. However under the revised Code, the police may choose not to hold an identification procedure if it would serve no useful purpose.[239]

- **photographs**: if the identity of the suspect is not known, the witness may be shown photographs, photofits or similar pictures.[240] A written record of the description should be made prior to showing the photos. The witness shall be shown not less than twelve photos at a time, which should be of a similar type. He or she is told that the suspect may or may not be among the photos. No prompting or guidance should be given.

This raises a final question about the use made of a witness's description in

---

[233] The procedures are detailed in Annex D to the Code.
[234] *Joseph* [1994] Crim. L.R. 48.
[235] *Eatough* [1989] Crim. L.R. 289; *Horsham Justices, ex p. Bukhari* (1982) 74 Cr. App. R. 291.
[236] D.2.26—*Hickin* [1996] Crim. L.R. 584.
[237] [1991] Crim. L.R. 368.
[238] [1992] R.T.R. 270.
[239] Code D 2.15.
[240] Code D Annex E.

court. A witness may be asked to contribute to a photofit, or artist's impression of the suspect. In *Cook*[241] the photofit itself was permitted in evidence. But why? If a witness had made a written or oral statement describing the characteristics of, say, an assailant, such a statement would not have been admissible in evidence either of its facts (since it is hearsay) or as a prior consistent statement. Similarly a sketch produced by an artist following the directions of a witness is merely transforming words into images and must still be inadmissible.

Similarly the jury themselves can identify a defendant using a photograph or security video, although they may be warned of the perils of identification on such a basis.[242] Furthermore a witness who knows the identity of the person on the video can testify to this effect. This is illustrated in *Taylor v. Chief Constable of Cheshire*[243] in which a video was made of a shoplifter. Policemen were able to identify the accused from the video. Later the recording was erased by accident. The officers gave evidence of what they had seen on the video and Taylor was convicted. The video itself was direct evidence[244] and the court accepted the argument that there is no difference in principle between the evidence of witnesses who viewed the recording and those witnesses who claim to have seen the events by direct vision. Code D does not apply. However there are reasons why this form of identification should be regulated in a similar fashion to parades or video identifications by eyewitnesses. In *Caldwell and Dixon*[245] the robbery of an off-licence was captured on video and evidence of identification was admitted from police officers who had viewed the videotape. It is only too easy for one officer to recognise an accused and mention it to a colleague who might see a likeness, which had not previously occurred to him. This possibility was recognised by the Court of Appeal who felt that the Code D procedures should be adopted in such cases.[246]

[241] [1987] 1 All E.R. 1049.
[242] *Dodson and Williams* (1984) 79 Cr. App. R 220; *Downey* [1995] Crim. L.R. 414.
[243] [1987] 1 All E.R. 225.
[244] *Kajala v. Noble* (1982) 75 Cr. App. R. 149.
[245] [1993] Crim. L.R. 862.
[246] Elliott D., 'Video tape evidence: the risk of over-persuasion' [1998] Crim. L.R. 159.

CHAPTER FIVE

The Prosecution Process

5.1 PRE-TRIAL JUDICIAL SUPERVISION

There is a critical disjuncture between police investigation and prosecution of the offence. Once a suspect is identified, there are a series of decisions, which are shared between the police and the Crown Prosecution Service (CPS). This should imply collaborative systems of work between the two but this is rarely the case. The autonomy and culture of the police disrupts any coherent 'system' since they do not see themselves as part of the criminal justice system. The narrow philosophy of police officers frequently sees the courts simply as a mechanism that should validate police decisions. The attitude is that the police would only bring people before the court for valid reasons and acquittals are therefore defeats. Officers see little purpose and none of the values in 'playing by the rules' or in the intricacies of the judicial process, which are merely 'technicalities'. This is a blind spot as officers can see the public interest in the detection and punishment of offenders but fail to recognise the equally compelling public interest in ensuring that the power to prosecute is exercised in a manner constrained by social and moral values. Although the police constantly refer to their own accountability to the law, police culture possesses little belief in the principles of legality. Even the liberal police officer finds it difficult to excavate the values embedded in legal technicalities. Those values get hidden behind the formalities, which are the province of the lawyers, bureaucratic trivia of no interest to police or public.

Unlike most other jurisdictions, the police are not subject to independent supervision in the pre-trial process. Generally the police decisions are of great significance for both the victim and for the offender: whether to investigate[1] to take no further action (NFA), whether to caution or to prosecute; whether to charge or to summons; what offence to charge the suspect with; whether to grant

---

[1] The basic options are that a complaint may be investigated firstly over the telephone, secondly by the attendance of a uniformed officer or thirdly by mobilising CID. Alternatively the complaint may not be investigated at all.

bail. For the English police, the desired outcome will be an identified and charged suspect to pass to the CPS. This approach is adversarial in nature as the police build and strengthen their own case. They are unlikely to follow up possible lines of defence raised by an accused and will seek to undermine exculpatory state-ments.[2] The adversarial role can affect decisions: the level or number of charges might be designed to encourage negotiation over an eventual plea of guilty; it may be implied that police bail was contingent on making a statement. Yet English law sees no need for intervention or supervision by the CPS, judge or court[3] to ensure the quality of these decisions. In many other jurisdictions the police are under much stricter administrative and judicial control and adopt a more investigative strategy which would see the police gathering evidence for others to make the relevant decisions.

We justify the lack of pre-trial supervision by pointing to the adversarial nature of courtroom proceedings, the formal equality of the parties and the idea of the 'day in court' before a jury. All contribute to the illusion that the trial cures any pre-trial injustice. But by then it is too late for any consideration of whether the charges are at the right level of seriousness and of the appropriate number of reflect the events, whether there is adequate and admissible evidence to support those charges or whether it is in the public interest to proceed. Reformers such as Lord Scarman have argued for the introduction of an intermediate judicial offi-cer, supervising the decision to prosecute, the nature and level of charge or the need for remands in custody, while giving due weight to principles of legality, due process and the public interest. This reform is unlikely but the Auld Report recognised that the CPS had still to fill its proper role, closer to the Procurator Fiscal in Scotland. The prosecutor should take control of cases at the charge or, where appropriate, pre-charge, stage. They should take responsibility for char-ging, assume a more direct role than at present on disclosure and develop a more proactive role in shaping the case for trial, communicating appropriately with all concerned. Auld recommended that the CPS be given greater legal powers, in particular the power to determine the initial charge, and considerably more resources, in particular more trained staff and better information technology.[4]

5.2 ALTERNATIVE APPROACHES

This lack of supervision in England and Wales is unique and probably leads to an unnecessary number of formal prosecutions. The Scots have a procurator fiscal[5] who has responsibility at common law for the investigation of offences and may instigate and supervise police investigation, especially in cases of sudden death. The fiscal rarely gets involved in such primary investigation although statements will be taken from all witnesses in serious cases, even when the police has already seen these witnesses. The fiscal must be satisfied that there is a prima facie case for the prosecution. Although in 1981, the fiscal's approval was seen as simply a

[2] McConville M. *et al.*, *The Case for the Prosecution* (1991) p. 77.
[3] With the exception of bail decisions—some magistrates' courts also hold pre-trial reviews and all magistrates' courts hold committal proceedings for cases that are to be tried in Crown Court but the majority of these involve no consideration of the evidence and are merely 'paper' committals under Criminal Justice Act 1967, s. 1. See *infra*, Chap. 7
[4] Lord Justice Auld, *A Review of the Criminal Courts of England and Wales*, Chap. 8 (2001) Chap. 10, para. 12.
[5] Moody S. and Tombs J., *Prosecution in the Public Interest* (1982): Tombs J. and Moody S. L., '*Alternatives to Prosecution: The Public Interest Redefined*,' Crim. L. R. (1993) 35.

formality, ('*His is an extra door that has to be passed through in getting to court and in general it is readily opened*'[6]) a decade later the non-prosecution rate in Scotland had risen from 8 per cent to 47 per cent as part of a continuous process of what constitutes prosecution in the public interest.[7] Another ten years on, in 2000–2001, there were approximately 3,000 solemn disposals in the sheriff and jury courts, 42,300 summary disposals in the district courts. But 56,000 reports were dealt with by non-court means, including letters warning about future conduct, fixed financial penalties, fiscal fines and diversion from prosecution schemes. Following an evaluation of 18 pilot schemes, a national diversion from prosecution scheme was rolled-out across Scotland which will apply to people misusing drugs and alcohol, or experiencing mental health difficulties, and to young people aged 16 and 17 years and the female accused. Mediation and reparation schemes will continue to be available for use with all accused offenders. Furthermore procurators fiscal took no proceedings in some 44,000 cases.[8]

Many continental countries have an officer analogous to the French *juge d'instruction*,[9] in theory, a neutral figure representing the public interest. In eighteenth century France, the monarchy had at its disposal a centralised police force, regarded by Englishmen with horror.[10] That image of the French *mouchard* both delayed and shaped the form of the British police. But the Napoleonic reforms (which introduced the *juge d'instruction*) were a reaction to those self-same abuses of the *ancien regime* and the *juge* was to be a check on the police function, superior in power and status.[11] The role of *juge* was a natural focal point as a symbol of legalism, a concept of legalism that the French police with their links to despotic monarchy could not represent. In contrast in Britain, it was the local independent police that became that constitutional symbol, representing the limits of state power and public service.

In modern France,[12] the judiciary is a career choice for lawyers rather than a reward for distinguished or long-serving lawyers as it is here. This professionalism means that law school graduates progress through a competitive exam to the *Ecole Nationale de la Magistrature* (ENM) where a two-year course leads to qualification as a judge. The ENM graduate can choose initially between the prosecution service (*parquet*), being an examining magistrate (*juge d'instruction*) or a trial judge (*juge du siege*). The *juge d'instruction* in law can exert strong control over the police forces[13] and indeed there is a separate *police judiciaire* to carry out investigations into serious cases under the immediate direction of the *juge*. The *parquet/juge d'instruction* in France are frequently charismatic civil

---

[6] Royal Commission on Criminal Procedure: *Report* (1981) Cmnd. 8092 paras 6.35 ff.

[7] Tombs J. and Moody S. (1993), *op. cit.*

[8] Crown Office and Procurator Fiscal Service, Annual Report 2000–2001 (available at www.crownoffice.gov.uk/).

[9] Ploscowe M., '*Development of Inquisitorial and Accusatorial Elements in French Procedure*' 23 Journal of Criminal Law, Criminology and Police Science, pp. 372–390: Tomlinson A. '*Non-adversarial Justice: The French Experience*' 42 Maryland Law Review (1983) p. 131 at 146 ff.: Brouwer G.: '*Inquisitorial and Adversary Procedures—a Comparative Analysis*' 55 Australian Law Journal (1981) p. 207 at p. 212ff.

[10] For an excellent comparison of the French and English police between 1750 and 1850, see Emsley C, *Policing and its Context* (1983).

[11] For a short history of the French police, Le Clere M., *Histoire de la Police* (4th ed., 1973).

[12] Leigh L. and Zedner L., *Report on the Administration of Criminal Justice in the Pre-Trial Phase in France and Germany* (Royal Commission on Criminal Justice: Research Study No. 1 1992).

[13] In reality, of course, interference is limited, formal approval for police actions is readily forthcoming, often over the telephone. There is involvement in some 10% of cases—Royal Commission on Criminal Justice, *op. cit.*, p. 3 fn. 3.

heroes, initiating inquiries into anything that troubles *l'ordre publique* and pursuing the rich and powerful as well as the run-of-the-mill offender. The French often say of the '*juge*' that '... *il etait l'homme le plus puissant de France* ...'![14]

In the Netherlands, the public prosecutors' functions have wide ranging functions which include the following:[15]

a) they alone decide who shall be prosecuted in court and have the power to waive prosecution. The principle is that prosecutions should only take place when the public interest demands it.[16] There is a high level of such waivers.[17]

b) they have the power to release suspects on bail or indeed to extend periods of detention at their discretion.

c) they recommend to the court the level of sentence and the judge is bound to take this into account. Senior prosecutors issue national guidelines on both this and on waivers of prosecution.

Although there is an equivalent to the 'juge d'instruction', the Dutch public prosecutor exercises dominance across criminal justice.

In the U.S. as well it is the prosecutor, the District Attorney, who can exert influence over the course of investigations, making the decision whether to prosecute and on what charge. Several DA's offices have investigative teams attached to them.[18] Special prosecutors have conducted major investigations such as the Watergate allegations during Nixon's presidency; the Iran arms scandal during Reagan's; the Whitewater and Monica Lewinsky scandals during Clinton's. One might speculate that in the U.S., the history of law enforcement with its tales of gun-slinging sheriffs and rough-and-ready justice meant that the police were unlikely to fit comfortably into symbolic rule of law clothing. Violence and corruption is still linked in the American public imagination with law enforcement. It is the crusading District Attorney who plays the symbolic role. A classic example would be Rudolph Giuliani, appointed U.S. Attorney for the Southern District of New York, where he spearheaded the effort to jail drug dealers, fight organized crime, break the web of corruption in government, and prosecute white-collar criminals. He went on to become Mayor of the City of New York.

Here the CPS is in the position to exercise pre-trial supervision although it is unlikely to evolve in that direction in the short term. In 1981, the Royal Commission stressed the importance of different agencies being responsible for investigation and prosecution[19] and the consequence was the Prosecution of Offences Act 1985 which set up the CPS. Obviously the prosecutor has an immediate interest in the building of case files (interviewing witnesses and suspects, reports from the scene-of-crime officers and other experts) and the nature

[14] Larguier, J., *La Procedure Penale* (6th ed., 1987) p. 21.
[15] Downes D., *Contrasts in Tolerance* (1988) *passim*—in particular see pp. 13–15; also see Lensing H. and Rayar L., '*Notes on Criminal Procedure in the Netherlands*' (1992) Crim. L.R. p. 623.
[16] Here the Code for Crown Prosecutors (CCP) para. 7 could be interpreted in this way but the examples given in para. 8 go the other way, detailing negative factors where prosecution is not required and not positive factors indicating that prosecution is required.
[17] Nearly a half of burglaries and a fifth of rapes—see Downes, *op. cit.*, Tables 2.1 and 2.2 pp. 38–49.
[18] Royal Commission on Criminal Procedure: *op. cit.*, para. 6.33.
[19] Royal Commission on Criminal Procedure: *op. cit.*, Chap. 6 and para. 7.3.

of the charge. But the 1985 legislation did not give the service the power to supervise the investigation, make the original decision whether to prosecute or to decide on the nature and level of charges. The CPS does not even have the power to require the police to make further inquiries. The service does have statutory power to modify charges or to discontinue prosecution and certainly acts as guardians of the 'public interest' in making such decisions. But overall the 1981 Royal Commission's model of two autonomous agencies with overlapping powers and responsibilities has led to an uneasy relationship.

In 1993 the Royal Commission had the opportunity to clarify the relationship between the CPS and the police, either to move towards greater prosecutorial control or to reduce CPS interference in police decisions, emphasising their role as a junior partner. This nettle was not grasped and the status quo was affirmed. It was not desirable that the CPS should be put in charge of police investigations;[20] it was 'impracticable' that they should be responsible for the initiation of prosecutions;[21] there would be no fall-back power to require further inquiries but instead a formal system of consultation.[22] The Auld inquiry was less defeatist and supported a stronger CPS but was not specific about the relationship with the police.[23] Inevitably the interface between CPS and police will remain murky

5.3 PRE-TRIAL DECISIONS—CAUTION, CHARGE AND BAIL

We show remarkable haste, especially when a person has been arrested, in deciding whether to prosecute and, if so, the nature of the charge. An officer, not legally qualified and relatively junior, will take this decision at a very early stage of the proceedings, usually within hours of the suspect arriving at the station. Only rarely would the police seek CPS advice before charging.[24]

When a suspect has been brought to the station and interviewed, the options for the police are:

i) whether to prosecute and if so, whether to charge or to proceed by summons. If the outcome is to charge, then there are further decisions as to whether to release on bail.

ii) whether to caution the suspect that they do not intend to prosecute on this occasion but warn him or her about future conduct.

iii) whether to take no further action.

The police retain this discretion whether to prosecute in all cases, even for serious offences.[25] But the Auld Report recommended that the CPS take over responsibility for charging and the pilot schemes to evaluate this were set up in

---

[20] Royal Commission on Criminal Justice: Report (1993) Cm. 2263, paras. 5–16–5.17
[21] *ibid.* paras. 5–21.
[22] *ibid.* paras. 5–26.
[23] Lord Justice Auld: op. cit., Chap. 10.
[24] Crisp, D. and Moxon, D., *Case Screening by the Crown Prosecution Service: How and Why Cases Are Terminated*, Home Office Research Study. 137 (1994) suggests that national average is about 4%. Cited in Royal Commission on Criminal Justice, *op. cit.*, para. 5.17.
[25] In 2000, 1788 cautions were issued for offences triable only on indictment including rape (41) and attempted murder (1)—Criminal Statistics 2000 Cm. 5312. Table 5.11 ff., p. 122. Home Office guidelines state that cautions should **never** be used for the most serious indictable-only offences such as these.

2002. They have been hailed as a success and it is likely that plans to shift responsibility for the charging of suspects from the police to crown prosecution service lawyers will be implemented.[26]

5.3.1 *Cautioning*

It has been a penological truism for many years that one of the most effective and efficient disposals of offenders is to divert them from the courts altogether and if this is not possible, then to divert them from custodial sentences. This has been recognised in the growth of formal cautioning by the police, particularly when dealing with juveniles. This system was not based on any statutory power but on the recognition that the police were not legally obliged to prosecute each and every person whom they suspected of committing a criminal offence. The police had the discretion not to prosecute a person and might choose instead to caution.[27] There is now a statutory scheme for juveniles under the Crime and Disorder Act 1998 which replaced the old system of cautions with one involving reprimands and final warnings.[28] This does not apply to those aged over 18 and the legislation did not the old style caution for adults. The Home Office cautioning guidelines[29] lay down the criteria on which the decision to caution should be made. For adults:

- a caution can only be administered where there is a realistic prospect of a successful prosecution.

- the offender must admit guilt.

- the offender must consent to a caution being administered.

If these criteria are met, other factors to be taken into account are: the seriousness of the offence and the extent of the damage done; the interests and desires of the victim; the previous conduct of the offender; family background as well as the subsequent conduct of the offender such as a willingness to make reparation. The guidelines emphasise that, in respect of juveniles, prosecution is a last resort. Formal cautions are recorded and, if there is a subsequent conviction, can be cited as part of the offender's record. The risk of prosecution is not necessarily lessened since the development of diversionary techniques such as cautioning leads to the phenomenon of 'net-widening', that is, people are brought within the formal system when previously no formal action would have been taken.[30]

In 2000, 239,000 people of all ages were cautioned for crimes they committed, excluding motoring offences. 150,900 of these cautions were for offences which could be tried on indictment. Approximately a third of suspects were cautioned.[31] This is similar to a decade ago but represents a considerable increase from the 1980s—in 1982 when 160,600 were cautioned, 111,300 for indictable offences—at that point under a fifth of suspects were cautioned rather than

---

[26] *The Guardian* June 4, 2002.
[27] A formal warning by an officer of the rank of inspector or above as to the person's future conduct.
[28] This is discussed *infra* Chap. 11.
[29] Home Office Circular 18/1994.
[30] Pratt J., '*Diversion from the juvenile court*' 26 Brit. Jour. Crim. (1986) p. 212.
[31] *Criminal Statistics 2000* Cm. 5312. Tables 5.1–5.3 p. 109ff.

prosecuted. Over the past two decades, police cautioning has risen in both absolute numbers and in the percentage of offenders cautioned. The numbers peaked in the mid-1990s with over 40 per cent of offenders being cautioned. The then Home Secretary, Michael Howard, issued new guidelines in 1994 which in particular included warnings about multiple cautioning—cautions should not be administered to an offender in circumstances where there can be no reasonable expectation that this will curb his or her offending. It was only where the subsequent offence is trivial or where there has been a sufficient lapse of time that more than one caution should be considered. Cautions remain a significant technique of disposing of cases.

The cautioning rate varies considerably depending on the age and sex of the suspect. A young boy or girl aged 10 will be cautioned in 90 per cent of cases whereas the male over 21 will be cautioned in about 20 per cent of cases. The rate also varies according to police force area—whereas nationally 32 per cent of all offenders are cautioned, this goes up to 45 per cent in Surrey and down to 15 per cent in South Yorkshire.

Table 5.1 Persons Cautioned for Indictable Offences 1990 and 2000

Type of offender	1990	2000
All offenders	166,300 (33%)*	150,900 (32%)
All male offenders	124,200 (30%)	109,700 (29%)
All female offenders	42,100 (49%)	41,200 (47%)

In brackets, offenders cautioned as a percentage of offenders found guilty or cautioned

The rise in cautioning adult offenders over the past twenty years has also been remarkable. It is no longer an option reserved for juveniles. For adults, the cautioning rate varies according to the seriousness of the offence, gender and ethnicity. It also varies according to police force area—the male aged over 21 is seven times more likely to be prosecuted in South Yorkshire with a cautioning rate of only 5 per cent than in Surrey, where 35 per cent are cautioned rather than prosecuted.[32]

A caution cannot be administered unless the person admits the offence. A person might thus admit responsibility even when there is some doubt, for example the existence of the requisite criminal intent. Frequently the evidence on which a caution is based would not measure up to court scrutiny.[33] Despite this, the caution can be retailed to a court if the person is convicted of a subsequent offence, normally within three years. Cautioning is administrative justice, wholly within the control of the police and with no possibility of external challenge.[34] But the positive characteristics of cautioning are many: it keeps offenders out of

[32] *Criminal Statistics 2000, op. cit.,* Tables 5.4, p. 113.
[33] McConville M. et al. (1991): *op. cit.,* p. 78, 81–83.
[34] Although the decision *not* to caution a juvenile is reviewable—*R. v. Chief Constable of Kent, ex parte L* (1993) 1 All E.R. 756.

the courts, reduces the courts' workload with consequent economic benefits. The social benefits are significant as there is less stigmatisation and disruption to the person's life. It is also effective—87 per cent of those cautioned in 1985 were not convicted of a 'standard list' offence within 2 years of the caution. 80 per cent of those cautioned had no previous cautions or convictions but for those who had been previously convicted, there was a much greater likelihood that they would re-offend.[35]

Prosecution and conviction is the most expensive option in dealing with offenders. The value of diversionary schemes was recognised by the Runciman Commission, which felt that the limits of cautioning had yet to be reached for petty offenders. The disparities in cautioning rates across the country led them to recommend that cautioning should become statutory with national guidelines. The Commission recommended that the decision whether to caution should remain in the hands of the police although the CPS should be able to require the police to caution in lieu of prosecution.[36] This has not been implemented.

Even when the police choose not to caution but to prosecute, the CPS can review the case file to decide whether a caution would be a more appropriate course of action. In making such decisions, a Crown Prosecutor is governed by the Code for Crown Prosecutors (CCP), issued by the Director of Public Prosecutions and approved by the Attorney General.[37] The CCP lays down two criteria in assessing whether a prosecution is called for—that of evidential sufficiency and that of the public interest.[38] Where the Crown Prosecutor is not satisfied that a prosecution is appropriate, they can refer the case back to the police for them to administer a caution. If the police are unwilling to do this, the CPS can simply discontinue the prosecution.

> When deciding whether a case should be prosecuted in the courts, Crown Prosecutors should consider the alternatives to prosecution. This will include a police caution. Again the Home Office guidelines should be applied. Where it is felt that a caution is appropriate, Crown Prosecutors must inform the police so that they can caution the suspect. If the caution is not administered because the suspect refuses to accept it or the police do not wish to offer it, then the Crown Prosecutor may review the case again.[39]

5.3.2 Charging

A custody officer may authorise detention without charge where there were reasonable grounds for the initial arrest and for believing that detention without charge is necessary to secure or preserve evidence relating to that offence, or to obtain such evidence by questioning. But when an officer considers that there is enough evidence for a successful prosecution, the suspect should be taken before the custody officer who must decide whether the person should be charged.[40] Custody officers will rarely refuse to authorise detention—In one SE force in 2000, there were 50,000 arrests—detention was refused in just 1.25 per cent of cases. But in the same force, approximately a quarter of suspects were released

---

[35] Home Office. Statistical Bulletin (Issue 20/92).
[36] Royal Commission on Criminal Justice: *op. cit.*, para. 5.57ff.
[37] In accordance with s. 10 of the Prosecution of Offenders Act 1985—the most recent version can be found at www.cps.gov.uk/Home/CodeForCrownProsecutors/index.him.
[38] CCP para. 4.1 and 4.2.
[39] *ibid.* 6.12.
[40] PACE Code of Practice, C 16.1.

without charge, normally because of insufficient evidence.[41] The charging officer must identify clearly the offence that the suspect is alleged to have committed, both in factual and legal terms. The suspect will be cautioned[42] and asked if he wishes to say anything. The charge[43] will then be recorded in the police charge book.

Having been charged, the accused must not be questioned any further in relation to the offence with which he or she is charged[44] and must be brought before the court as soon as possible.[45] The Runciman Commission considered this former requirement as too restrictive and would permit further questioning provided that there has been a further caution and the opportunity to take legal advice.[46]

But what is a charge? Its legal significance is obscure. Sanders argues[47] that police charging is a nineteenth century development from their power to arrest and then to grant bail. The charge was simply the writing down of the allegation so that the court, police and the defendant could be sure of the precise nature of the allegation when the case came to court. As magistrates withdrew from investigation and interrogation, the police used the charge procedure more frequently. It took on a quasi-legal status as if it were the beginning of the legal process against the accused.

But does a charge 'institute proceedings'? If it does, then only a court may halt those proceedings. If not, the police can 'uncharge'. Although this is a technical issue, it highlights the obscurity of the boundaries between and the responsibilities of the police, the CPS and the courts. At common law it is only the bringing of suspects before magistrates and laying information as to an offence that initiates proceedings.[48] The legal implications of police charging were thus minimal since charging did not compel further proceedings. But within the police station, the charge was an important stage for the old Judges' Rules and is now more significant for PACE and for the PACE Codes of Conduct. Administering cautions and regulating periods of detention depended on it.

Its legal status appears to be changed under section 15(2)(c) of the Prosecution of Offences Act 1985 which states that proceedings are instituted when '. . . a person is charged with an offence after being taken into custody without a warrant, when he is informed of the particulars of the charge.' This would appear to limit police discretion to withdraw charges although the CPS still have statutory powers to discontinue prosecutions.[49]

The charge has a quality of being an irrevocable step. The police rarely

---

[41] But see McConville M. *et al.*, *op. cit.*, p. 118ff.

[42] The word 'caution' is used here in the sense of the PACE Codes of Practice that the suspect is warned that he does not have to say anything.

[43] The word 'charge' is open to several different meanings, dependent on context—Pearson J. in *R. v. Norfolk Quarter Sessions ex parte Brunson* (1953) 1 Q.B. 503.

[44] There are limited exceptions in PACE Code of Practice C.16.4 and 16.5—for example where the questions are necessary to prevent harm or loss, to clear up ambiguities or to comment on information which has come to light after charging.

[45] PACE, s. 46(2).

[46] Royal Commission on Criminal Justice: *op. cit.*, paras. 2.39–2.42.

[47] Sanders A. 'Arrest, Charge and Prosecution' 6 *Legal Studies*, 257 (1986).

[48] *Hill v. Anderton* (1982) 2 All E.R. 963, *per* Lord Roskill at 971.

[49] Prosecution of Offences Act s. 23(4) enables the CPS to discontinue prior to a court being informed. Sanders A., (1986) (*op. cit.*) regards this as conceptually irreconcilable with s. 15(2)(c).

'uncharge'.[50] It does mark the point at which the police cease to have an immediate interest and the papers are passed on to the Crown Prosecution Service. The issue of discontinuances by the CPS is discussed later. There have been recent changes in the responsibility for charging offenders. Ten years ago, the Runciman Report considered the suggestion that the CPS should have responsibility for framing the initial charge but saw practical difficulties in having prosecutors posted to police stations and felt it would add to delay.[51] In 1998, the Glidewell Report[52] proposed that criminal justice units be set up in police force areas which would be jointly staffed by the CPS and the police—this 'co-location' has been proceeding in all police forces. Further in 2001 the Auld Report recommended that the CPS take over responsibility for charging and the pilot schemes to evaluate this were set up in 2002. It is likely that plans to shift responsibility for the charging of suspects from the police to crown prosecution service lawyers will be implemented.[53]

5.3.3 *Bail*

After arrest, the defendant's liberty can only be restored by a decision of the police or the courts to grant bail. This is discussed later[54] but in outline, the police powers are as follows:

a) if the suspect is in police custody but has not been charged and if the custody officer is unwilling to authorise further detention for questioning, then the officer can release either unconditionally or conditionally on bail to report back to the police station at some point.[55]

b) if the suspect is in police custody and has been charged, the officer has the power[56] to release on bail subject to the condition that the suspect appear before the magistrates' court on a certain date. At present the police cannot impose other conditions.[57]

c) where the suspect has been arrested by magistrate's warrant, this warrant may already have the terms of bail endorsed on it—it is 'backed for bail'.

d) if none of these apply, the custody officer can detain the suspect and take him or her to the next sitting of the magistrates' court. Although the court may hear the case at the point, this is rare and the accused may make an application for bail.

---

[50] Sanders A., *'Police Charging and the Prosecution of Offences Act.'* 149 J. P., 662 (1985).
[51] Royal Commission on Criminal Justice. *op. cit.*, para. 5.21.
[52] Glidewell I., *The Review of the Crown Prosecution Service* (1998) Cm. 3972.
[53] *The Guardian*, June 4, 2002.
[54] *infra*, para. 7.2.
[55] PACE, s. 37(2) and s.40(8).
[56] PACE, s. 38. which also specifies the situations where bail may not be granted—that the name and address of the suspect cannot be ascertained, that custody is necessary to prevent harm to others or that there are reasonable grounds for believing that the suspect will not answer to bail.
[57] The power to impose conditions both for release on bail before and after charge is recommended by Runciman—Royal Commission on Criminal Justice, *op. cit.*, para. 5.22 and was introduced by s.27 of the Criminal Justice and Public Order Act 1994.

5.4 PERSPECTIVES ON PROSECUTION

Historically and culturally, prosecution and trial have more significance than the straightforward disposal of those identified by the police as committing a crime. In previous centuries the public interest in the detection of crime and the private interest of the victim were more interwoven and the prosecutor was far from an invisible figure. In the eighteenth century, he was the initiator and controller of events. It was a ritual that depicted, in a microcosm, the social relationships prevailing in that society. Hay[58] has demonstrated how class authority and legal ideology can be represented through the criminal prosecution. Through prosecution, a private citizen exercised a control over punishment (and thus over the life and death of others) that is extraordinary to modern eyes—'If I succeed, I shall certainly hang the culprit' wrote a 1796 prosecutor.[59] The power may have been indirect but nonetheless it was an important constituent in both personal and class relationships.

But the judicial process ensured that such prosecution and punishment were not seen too directly as the vengeance of an individual. Instead it was the law at work. The crime was represented as an attack on the 'body politic' and against the public good. It was not conceptualised as damage to specific and personal interests or to an individual's power or authority. The interests of the powerful may have been masked but not so obscurely as to prevent the message filtering through. In the eighteenth century, private prosecutors manipulated the pomp and ritual of the trial. The Assize was not just a set of trials as sittings of the Crown Court might be today—it was one of the social occasions of the year, to see and be seen and not merely by social equals. It was the visible representation of a class's cohesion, identity and characterization of themselves as rulers. Through the minutiae of punishment, through the capacity to use and abuse the bodies of others, the relationships of power and the pattern of social order were visibly and regularly re-enacted. Why? Foucault, among others, would argue that the use of the body as an object of punishment has always been a measure of individual and political power.[60] To humiliate, to flog, to maim or to kill are emphatic symbols of power. Allied to the legitimacy conferred by the processes of the court, these are the ultimate symbol of political authority.

In feudal times, the king and barons fought over the rights to hang thieves. In modern times, although we neither whip nor execute, the trial is still about what is to be done to the accused. The focus on the body means that the criminal trial can be seen as an important site for symbolic struggles. This is exemplified by the continuing campaign to restore capital punishment or by feminist groups who campaign to increase punishment for domestic violence or sexual assault. There is little evidence that murder or rape declines as a result of increasing judicial punishment. For such campaigners there is a hidden agenda, meanings to be communicated through the official rituals of trial and punishment.

The mounting of a trial, its abandonment or successful conclusion—all these have meanings, which are publicly negotiated. There is a significance that goes

---

[58] Hay, D., 'Property, Authority and the Criminal Law' in Hay. D. et al., (eds.), Albion's Fatal Tree (1975): 'Controlling the English Prosecutor' in 21 Osgoode Hall Law Journal, p. 165 (1983); 'The Criminal Prosecution in England' 47 M.L.R. p. 1 (1984).
[59] Hay. D., (1983), *op. cit.*
[60] Foucault M., *Discipline and Punish* (1977), Chaps 1 and 2

beyond the efficient processing of offenders.[61] Whether viewed by historians,[62] political scientists[63] or anthropologists,[64] the criminal trial becomes a complex social and political ritual, perhaps mystifying class relationships, perhaps symbolising constitutional ideals or, on a deeper level, a reaffirmation of order in the face of the irrational and the unknowable.

5.5 THE DEVELOPMENT OF THE PUBLIC PROSECUTOR

In eighteenth century England, the capacity to mobilise the criminal courts and to mould the punishment on your own behalf was a significant *private* right/rite. The state provided the legal and administrative mechanisms but the power to prosecute lay in the hands of private individuals who, in the main, were members of the propertied class. To the eyes of the working classes, the victims of the criminal justice system, the law was a mechanism of social discipline. The middle and upper classes had privileged access to and leverage over forms of punishment.

The criminal law was not just barely-concealed class aggression. The ideology of justice and of the 'rule of law' was of great importance. Nor was this mere rhetoric designed to mystify the masses: as Thompson has put it, men are not mystified by the first man who puts on a wig. '*If the law is evidently partial and unjust, then it will mask nothing, legitimise nothing, contribute nothing to any class's hegemony.*'[65] To be effective, substance had to be given to the values of neutrality, universality and equality. In that context, the nineteenth century should have witnessed the right of private prosecution withering away and a public prosecution service taking its place, alongside the parallel development of public police forces.

There were several moments in the nineteenth century[66] when it appeared as if this would happen. There were reports and parliamentary inquiries, all of which backed the idea. There was even government support. All that emerged was the 1879 Prosecution of Offenders Act and the new office of the Director of Public Prosecutions[67] (DPP). This initiative proved a damp squib and five years later the office was *de facto* merged with that of the Treasury Solicitor, and only re-emerged as a separate post in 1908. Even then there was neither a statutory definition of functions nor even public prosecutions to direct. The only identifiable group of day-to-day prosecutors were the Treasury counsel, retained by the DPP for prosecution work in the Central Criminal Court and Middlesex and Surrey Sessions. Yet they were merely barristers on whose services the DPP had first call and they also had large practices outside the prosecutorial function.

---

[61] *e.g.*, Garfinkel H., 'Conditions for Successful Degradation Ceremonies' 66 *American Journal of Sociology* (1956), p. 420; Carlen P., 'Remedial Routines for the Maintenance of Order in Magistrates' Courts' (1974) 1 *British Journal of Law and Society*, p. 101; McBarnet, D., *Conviction* (1983).

[62] Hay D. (1975), *op. cit.*

[63] Arnold T., *Symbols of Government* (1962), Chap. 6.

[64] *e.g.*, Gibbs J., 'The Kpelle Moot' 33 *Africa* (1963) p. 1: Ottenberg S, 'bo Oracles and Intergroup Relations' 14 *Southwest. Jour. Anth.* (1958): Bohannan P., *Justice and Judgement Among the Tiv* (1957).

[65] Thompson, E. P. *Whigs and Hunters* (1975).

[66] Although there were earlier possibilities of such developments especially in the 16th century with the Marian statutes—see Langbein. J. *Prosecuting Crime in the Renaissance* (1974).

[67] For a detailed account of these developments and the history of the DPP, see Edwards J.L.I.J., *The Law Officers of the Crown* (1964); for an outline, see Uglow S., 'Independent Prosecutions' *Jour. of Law and Soc.* (1984) p. 233.

Can we explain why there was no development of an autonomous prosecution service at that time or why such a service should materialise a century later? One explanation lies in the constitutionalist argument that it is necessary to impose constraints on the state and the executive at all times and to resist initiatives which expand government powers. Although the 'new police' had been accepted, it was done reluctantly and they provided a service which individuals, even wealthy individuals, could not provide for themselves. Private prosecution was another matter entirely. For the nineteenth century liberal, let alone the Tory squirearchy, access to the courts by the private subject signified that the law was not merely a weapon of the state and, to ensure that, its mobilisation should remain vested in private hands.

A complementary but contradictory answer lies in the development of the 'rule of law' conception later to be enshrined by Dicey. This stressed certainty, neutrality, universality and equality. These qualities were not part of the make-up of the private prosecutor who was to be found pursuing self-interest, discretionary and subjective justice, perhaps most notably with the Societies for the Prosecution of Felons.[68] But equally there was a seamier side to the public prosecutor. Parliamentary committees had heard of the 'low attorney' consorting with and bribing constables to obtain fees for prosecution. To what extent did this image tarnish reform movements pressing for public prosecutors? From the viewpoint of legal ideology of the 'rule of law', class conflict was to be masked and the working classes co-opted into the parliamentary road. Did the prospect of a new breed of corrupt public officials freeze the reforming zeal?

The private prosecution was neither abolished nor did it expand. It withered away with its tradition of private interest inimical to the rule of law. This process was aided by the practical problems of travel, cost and general inconvenience, which led to a deepening reluctance to become involved. It was a slow process as prosecution was regarded as an inalienable right of the citizen. Even after the First World War, the DPP, Archibald Bodkin, talked of the police's role as one of giving 'reasonable assistance by way of investigation to the prosecutor'.[69] Today, under the 1985 Prosecution of Offences Act, it still remains a possibility for the private citizen to undertake criminal prosecution.

It was the success of the 'new' police that must have contributed to the decline of the private prosecutor and the stillbirth of any public successor. All too easily the police were seen not only as investigators but also as prosecutors. Indeed the juridical basis for the prosecutions undertaken by the police was as if they were private citizens. From 1887, the Metropolitan Police routinely used a private firm, Wontners, to run prosecutions on their behalf. Outside London, where the control of the police was firmly vested in the local Watch Committees, the middle classes must have watched contentedly as prosecutions were *de facto* delegated to the police and their own responsibilities declined. Most police forces developed prosecuting solicitors' departments and they, although often referred to as 'County' prosecutors, looked to the Chief Constable as their 'client'. Furthermore, until the late 1980s, in many magistrates' courts, it was not the police agents who were the prosecutors but in many cases it was a uniformed police inspector.[70]

---

[68] Shubert, A., 'Private Initiative in Law Enforcement' in Bailey V. (ed.) *Policing and Punishment* (1981).
[69] Sir Archibald Bodkin, 'The Prosecution of Offenders', *1 Police Journal 353* (1928).
[70] Royal Commission on the Police: Report (1962), Cmnd. 1728, paras. 380–381.

5.6 THE MODERN PROSECUTION SYSTEM

Reform came about as the result of the Report of the Royal Commission on Criminal Procedure in 1981. The Report highlighted a range of problems:[71]

a) there was a lack of uniformity with differing procedures and standards applied across the country on such matters as whether to prosecute or caution so that while Cheshire cautioned 2 per cent or fewer of adults for indictable offences, Suffolk cautioned 22 per cent.[72]

b) the system was inefficient especially in the preparation of cases since many acquittals were the result either of the judge stopping the trial at the end of the prosecution case or directing the jury to acquit.

c) in principle, investigation and prosecution should be separate processes[73]. It was wrong for the prosecuting lawyer to have the investigating officer as a client. The goals of investigation and of prosecution were incompatible although a complete separation was in practice impossible.

d) there was no executive or democratic accountability or control over the existing system.[74]

The Commission recommended that a Crown Prosecution Service be established. The recommended structure was decentralised and modelled on the police, with a separate CPS for each police force area with a Chief Crown Prosecutor responsible locally to a supervisory body and nationally to the Director of Public Prosecutions (DPP).[75] But the government rejected this local option[76] and in the Prosecution of Offences Act 1985 created a national structure. Although the new service was independent of the police, only 31 areas were set up compared to 43 police forces. The areas are directly answerable to the DPP[77] whose role is to provide national guidelines and procedures, to intervene in difficult or complex cases, to appoint and supervise personnel and to manage resources generally. The Attorney General is responsible in Parliament for general policy but not for individual cases.

These areas were reorganised, firstly in 1992 when they were reduced to thirteen but in 1999 were increased to 42 so that each CPS area was co-terminous with a police force area. A Chief Crown Prosecutor heads each area. Financially the planned expenditure for CPS is £416m in 2001–2002–£304m is spent on salaries and accommodation and £100m on prosecution costs which are mainly counsel fees but also witnesses' expenses.[78] Currently the service employs over 7000 staff, including more than 2000 lawyers. Has the new system addressed the problems identified by the RCCP in 1981?

i) One of the central objections to the old system was the lack of objective

[71] Royal Commission on Criminal Procedure, *op. cit.*, Chap. 6
[72] *ibid.*, para. 6.40.
[73] *ibid.*, para. 6.23ff.
[74] *ibid.*, para. 6.48ff.
[75] For further discussion, see Uglow S. (1984), *op. cit.*, (1984) pp. 237–238.
[76] *An Independent Prosecution Service*, Cmnd. 9074 (1983).
[77] In 2002, this was Sir David Calvert-Smith.
[78] CPS Annual Report 2000–2001, p. 22—the expenditure has increased from £329m in 2000–2001.

fairness. The police were responsible for both investigation and prosecution. The creation of the CPS now means that there is a clear separation of these functions but the relationship between the police and CPS remains ill-defined, particularly in relation to charging and the gathering of further evidence. The Runciman Report did not resolve this.[79] In itself, such ambiguity does not affect the objectivity of case review by the CPS. But they are reliant on the police for the quality of the evidence supplied[80] and for co-operation.[81] This lack of a clear identity for the CPS is a major weakness for the criminal justice system since there is a residual sense of subordination to the police.

Recent initiatives have blurred the institutional boundaries between investigation and prosecution. The Glidewell report[82] recommended that the police should remain responsible for investigation and charging and the preliminary preparation of case papers, and that the CPS should be responsible for the prosecution process immediately following charge, advising as to any further investigation and the preparation of the case file, arranging the initial hearing in the magistrates' court and witness availability, warning and care. The report also recommended the creation of combined Crown Prosecution Service and police 'criminal justice' units headed by a Service lawyer, which were also to have sole conduct of fast-track cases and to be responsible for case management in magistrates' courts.[83] They also recommended the creation of what are now called criminal trial units consisting of lawyers with support staff, to be responsible for all prosecutions in the Crown Court and to act as advocates in trials of either way cases in magistrates' courts. The Narey report[84] reiterated the need to bring police and the Service closer together in the preparation of cases for trial by locating prosecutors in police stations to advise their administrative support units. These recommendations have been acted upon—most forces now have Glidewell criminal justice units, CPS areas have trial units (including a police presence) for the preparation and presentation of more serious cases[85] and, following recommendations in the Auld Report,[86] there are pilot areas where the CPS is taking more responsibility for initial charging.

ii) the second problem was one of disparities in standards, especially in cautioning rates in different parts of the country. Cautioning remains the province of the police and the unfairness inherent in the discrepancies, as discussed earlier, still exists.

iii) the third problem was the inefficiency of the system, both in terms of non-jury acquittals (this issue is explored below) and also in terms of

---

[79] Royal Commission on Criminal Justice, *op. cit.*, paras 4.3.1 and 4.3.2.
[80] See McConville M. *et al.* (1991), op. cit. and McBarnet D. *Conviction* (1981) for discussions on the police 'construction of a suspect population'.
[81] This is sometimes not present—see Block B., Corbett C. and Peay J., *Ordered and Directed Acquittals in the Crown Court* (Royal Commission on Criminal Justice Research Study No. 15) 1993, p. 14 and Royal Commission on Criminal Justice, *op. cit.* Chap. 6 Recommendation 1.
[82] *op. cit.*, Chap. 1. paras 27–28.
[83] *ibid.*, Chap. 8, paras 11 and 12.
[84] Narey M., *Review of Delay in the Criminal Justice System* (1997) Chap. 3. pp. 10–11.
[85] CPS Annual Report 2000–2001, pp. 10–11.
[86] Lord Justice Auld, *op. cit.*, Chap. 10, paras 42 ff.

delays. One of the agency's key targets was to reduce the average processing delay. It has made little impact in this area. There is still a problem of delay in criminal courts. Delay may be ascribed to many causes and the lack of urgency and overwork in the Crown Prosecution Service may be merely one.[87]

- For those tried at Crown Court, waiting times between committal and trial tend to vary according to the plea entered and whether the defendant is on bail or in custody. On average, defendants who pleaded guilty during 2000 waited 10.8 weeks whilst those who pleaded not guilty waited 19.6 weeks. Defendants committed on bail waited an average of 16.0 weeks in 2000 and for those committed in custody the average was 9.8 weeks. Waiting times also vary by circuit. Such figures do not include the period from first appearance to committal that can add at least 8–10 weeks on to the overall length.
- For those tried in magistrates' court, in 2000 it took 108 days on average to process an indictable case from offence to disposal—this was the shortest period since 1986 and was due to less delay between laying the information and the first listing, one of the measures designed to speed up the progress of cases through the system. A summary non-motoring case took 127 days on average while a summary motoring case took 150 days.[88]

iv) the lack of accountability, identified by the RCCP, remains. Although there is ministerial responsibility to Parliament through the Attorney-General for the performance of the CPS, there is a notable absence of any form of local accountability for prosecution policies and performance. It illustrates again the lack of cohesion in the system. The Police Act 1996 obliges police authorities to produce policing plans, identifying areas of concern and key objectives. Such plans necessarily impinge on the work of the CPS but there is no local body with whom the police authority can agree a joint strategy. The agencies, be they the police, CPS, courts, probation officers or prison governors, all work autonomously at a time when there is an obvious need on a local level for broad and co-operative strategies to be developed.

One development is the CPS Inspectorate, established in 1996, which conducts inspections in each CPS area to promote the efficiency and effectiveness of the Crown Prosecution Service through a process of inspection and evaluation; the provision of advice; and the identification and promotion of good practice. The CPS Inspectorate became an independent body as a result of the Crown Prosecution Service Inspectorate Act 2000, and will inspect and report on the CPS as a whole, covering all aspects of performance including interagency co-operation, diversity and resource management.[89]

---

[87] *infra*, Chap. 6.
[88] *Criminal Statistics 2000*, *op. cit.*, Table 6.4, p. 146.
[89] It is possible to access their regional and thematic reports at www.hmcpsi.gov.uk/.

5.7 THE CROWN PROSECUTOR

The state prosecutor is still not twenty years old and still far from the lynchpin around which the system of criminal justice rotates. Sandwiched virtually to vanishing point between the two symbolic reference points of the police and the judge, the new Crown Prosecutors or even senior Treasury counsel are faceless, certainly in terms of personal identity[90] and status. In Germany as well, although the prosecutor has theoretical mastery over pre-trial process, he has no discretion as to whether to prosecute and cannot engage in plea-bargaining[91]. As in the U.K. it is a low status office. Such anonymity also reflects an equivalent public ignorance of their function. What, after all, do prosecutors do? The functions of the CPS are to:

- Prosecute people in England and Wales who have been charged by the police with a criminal offence.

- Advise the police on possible prosecutions.

- Review prosecutions started by the police to ensure the right defendants are prosecuted on the right charges before the appropriate court.

- Prepare cases for court.

- Prosecute cases at magistrates' courts and instruct counsel to prosecute cases in the Crown Court and higher courts.

- Work with other agencies such as the police and the courts to improve the effectiveness and efficiency of the criminal justice system, for example through the Trials Issues Group (TIG). This latter group began life as the Working Group on Pre-Trial Issues. In 1990 it produced a Report containing recommendations designed to improve co-operation between the Police, the Crown Prosecution Service and the Courts, in particular, ways of improving the timeliness and quality of case files and improving court proceedings. It was enlarged and renamed the Trials Issues Group and its role is not limited to matters of administrative efficiency or to the working relations between the agencies represented but the focus of TIG is on the 'nuts and bolts' of the criminal justice system. Its effectiveness has been achieved by securing consensus between the wide range of criminal justice interests represented.[92]

The CPS receives files of individual cases from the police. On a day-to-day basis, these may require immediate action as the files refer to people arrested, charged and detained by the police who wish to see the accused remanded into custody. The prosecutor will present the case for remand to the magistrates, often with little time to consider whether remand into custody is justified. Once

---

[90] For example, there is a dearth of information or research on the Treasury counsel but see Tudor Price J. '*Treasury Counsel at the Old Bailey* . . .' Crim. L. R. (1985) p. 471. Even the DPP has had a low profile, although recently Sir Alan Green brought some unwelcome notoriety to the job. His successor, Barbara Mills, as the first woman DPP, has had a higher profile. The current DPP is Sir David Calvert-Smith.

[91] Langbein, J., *Comparative Criminal Procedure: Germany* (1977), pp. 11–13, 87 ff.

[92] www.lcd.gov.uk/criminal/backgfr.htm which also links to its publications and Newsletter.

immediate problems are resolved,[93] the file is handed to the team leader for the court concerned who assigns it to a prosecutor to review the information contained in it. A case file will contain details of the offender, of the offences with which she or he has been charged, details of witnesses and arresting officer, witness statements. The prosecutor will ask a number of questions:[94]

a) is the nature and level of charge appropriate given the evidence? This might involve discussion with the investigating officer who might have sought advice prior to charging as well as defence lawyers.

b) in the case of mixed offences,[95] what mode of trial (magistrates' or Crown court) would be suitable? The seriousness of the offence and whether magistrates possess sufficient sentencing powers are factors but the prosecutor's preference for summary trial might be overridden either by the magistrates or the defendant.

c) what is the quality of the evidence? Is there relevant, credible and substantial evidence going to all the facts in issue? Is there a realistic prospect of conviction? Again discussions might be needed with the police about additional evidence. The role of collaborative criminal justice units and trial units has been discussed. Such units not only provide the prosecution with evidence against the accused but also to deal with issues such as disclosure of all unused material to the defence.[96]

d) is there any reason in the public interest why this prosecution should not proceed?

The case is prepared for the first hearing at the magistrates' court. If it is a summary offence and the accused pleads guilty, the prosecutor reads out brief facts and that is the end of the matter. The CPS may use agents (local private lawyers) in some magistrates' courts sittings[97] but they now have designated caseworkers—these are non-legal staff that are designated under section 7A of the 1985 Act so that they may review cases and present in magistrates' courts.[98] If there is no plea or an indication of a not guilty plea, there will be an adjournment to prepare the case for trial, allowing time for obtaining witness statements and exhibits. There may be several preliminary hearings and the prosecutor at some stage will need to disclose the prosecution case.[99] A legally qualified Crown Prosecutor will present the case in court.

If the matter is triable only on indictment, prior to 1998, the prosecutor used to prepare for committal proceedings, which were a preliminary check that the prosecution case was strong enough and that there was a 'case to answer'. Committal proceedings for offences triable only on indictment have now been

---

[93] Here and elsewhere in this section. I draw upon the valuable summary of CPS operations in Block B., Corbett C. and Peay J. *Ordered and Directed Acquittals in the Crown Court* (Royal Commission on Criminal Justice Research Study No. 15, 1993), Chap. 2.

[94] These are given in outline here and considered in more detail, infra.

[95] *i.e.*, offences triable either summarily in the magistrates' court or on indictment in the Crown Court. See *infra*, chap. 6 para. 6.3.1.

[96] *Maguire* (1992) 94 Cr. App. R. 133; *Ward* (1993) 96 Cr. App. R. 1; *Edwards* (1991) 1 W.L.R. 207—this is discussed, *infra*.

[97] Royal Commission on Criminal Justice, *op. cit.*, para. 5.7.

[98] Guidelines are prepared by the DPP—these are published as Annex C to the CPS Annual Report 2000–2001—at that time there were 222 caseworkers.

[99] Magistrates' Courts (Advance Information) Rules 1985 (S.J. 85/601).

replaced as a result of section 51 of the Crime and Disorder Act 1998. From January 2002, offenders charged with such offences (together with any related either way and summary offences) will be 'sent' to the Crown Court for trial with no further hearing.[100] Where the matter is triable either way and jury trial has been chosen, committal proceedings still take place. These proceedings dated from 1848[101] since which date justices of the peace had to hold a preliminary hearing to ascertain whether there was a *prima facie* case against the accused. If there was, the defendant could be 'committed for trial' to a higher court, nowadays the Crown Court.

Until July 2000, after a successful committal, the Crown Prosecutor or, more likely, a law clerk would have to prepare the brief (consisting of all statements, interviews, tape transcripts, exhibits) for independent counsel. CPS barristers or solicitors did not have rights of audience in the higher courts. It was a flaw in the system that responsibility for a serious prosecution is transferred not just once (from the police to the CPS) but inexplicably for a second time from the CPS to a private barrister. There were obvious weaknesses: there was no machinery in barristers' chambers for allocating cases to appropriately experienced counsel;[102] there was no requirement for a preliminary written assessment by counsel of the strengths and weaknesses of the prosecution case;[103]; counsel would rarely offer advice to the CPS without first being asked; although counsel would be selected for particular cases, it was possible that on that day, they would not be available; at the trial itself, the CPS was often represented by an unqualified law clerk so that counsel assumed full responsibility for the conduct of the case, even offering no evidence on his or her own initiative (although such a course of action is more likely to be after CPS instructions or pressure from the judge.[104]) The lack of a proper line of responsibility at this point can only be wondered at. The trial is a natural focal point of the whole process where investigators, prosecutors, defenders, the courts and penal measures intersect. The criminal justice system suffers from the diffusion of responsibility and the lack of authority, which exists at the heart of the English criminal process.

The situation has improved—the CPS still employ independent counsel but since section 36 of the Access to Justice Act 1999, CPS lawyers are able to become Higher Court Advocates. The Act gave full rights of audience to all employed lawyers who meet the standards of their professional bodies. In 2001, the CPS had over 270 qualified advocates.

5.8 THE DECISION TO PROSECUTE AND THE CPS CODE

The prosecutor's first action is to review the police case, not simply to decide whether to take court action but also to confirm the nature and level of the charge against the accused and whether the mode of trial is appropriate. We have seen

---

[100] This is modelled on the legislation relating to the transfer for trial of cases involving serious or complex fraud (Criminal Justice Act 1987, s. 6) and of sexual cases and cases involving violence to children (s. 53 of the Criminal Justice Act 1991).

[101] Indictable Offences Act 1848, although the use of committal hearings can be traced back to the Marian statutes in 1554.

[102] Royal Commission on Criminal Justice. *op. cit.*, para. 5:39.

[103] The Royal Commission would require counsel to inform the CPS in writing that the case meets the criterion of the Code of Crown Prosecutors that there is a realistic prospect of conviction or that further evidence be required or that the case be discontinued—*op. cit.*, para. 5.39.

[104] Block *et al.*, *op. cit.*, p. 22.

the police acting as a preliminary filter, removing cases from the conveyor-belt of justice, by decisions either to take no further action or to caution. The CPS acts as a second filter using their power to discontinue prosecutions. The criteria they use are to be found in the Code for Crown Prosecutors (CCP).[105]

There are two basic issues, the first evidential and the second a matter of public interest. The first question is sufficiency of the evidence.[106] The Crown Prosecutor or designated caseworker reviewing the files must be satisfied that there is a realistic prospect of conviction. This is an objective test, namely whether a jury or bench of magistrates, properly directed in accordance with the law, would be more likely than not to convict the defendant of the charge alleged. The Crown Prosecutor must consider whether there is admissible, substantial and reliable evidence that an identifiable person has committed the offence. The prosecutor should be satisfied that there is no realistic expectation of an ordered acquittal or a successful motion of 'no case to answer'. He must have regard to obvious lines of defence. The Code details the issues that the prosecutor should consider,

    i) Is there evidence which might support or detract from the reliability of a confession? Is the reliability affected by factors such as the defendant's age, intelligence or level of understanding?

    ii) What explanation has the defendant given? Is a court likely to find it credible in the light of the evidence as a whole? Does it support an innocent explanation?

    iii) If the identity of the defendant is likely to be questioned, is the evidence about this strong enough?

    iv) Is the witness's background likely to weaken the prosecution case? For example, does the witness have any motive that may affect his or her attitude to the case, or a relevant previous conviction?

    v) Are there concerns over the accuracy or credibility of a witness? Are these concerns based on evidence or simply information with nothing to support it? Is there further evidence which the police should be asked to seek out which may support or detract from the account of the witness?

The 2000 Code is much less detailed than earlier versions, which directed the prosecutor to consider:

    i) the conduct of the police inquiry and interrogation especially with regard to breaches of the provisions of PACE Codes of Practice.

    ii) in particular the reliability of the accused's admissions, having regard to the age and understanding of the suspect.

    iii) the possibility of exaggeration, unreliability or bias on the part of a witness.

    iv) the possibility of a witness lying.

    v) matters which might undermine credibility of witness.

---

[105] Provided by the DPP in accordance with s. 10 of the Prosecution of Offenders Act 1985. The revised version was issued in 2000 and is published as Annex A to the CPS *Annual Report* 2000–2001.
[106] CCP, para. 5.

vi) the quality of the witness—the impression that might be made, the ability to stand up to cross-examination and any physical or mental disability.

vii) conflicts between eye-witnesses, and whether there is a suspicion that a false story might have been concocted.

viii) availability and competence of witnesses.

ix) the reliability of identification evidence.

x) whether the public would consider the proceedings oppressive?

xi) if separate trials be ordered for joint defendants, would there still be a realistic prospect of convictions?

Having considered the evidential aspects, the prosecutor should consider whether the public interest requires a prosecution.[107] It is not the case that every suspected crime should automatically be prosecuted. In 1951, Lord Shawcross, who was Attorney General, made the classic statement on public interest, which has been supported by Attorneys General ever since: '*It has never been the rule in this country—I hope it never will be—that suspected criminal offences must automatically be the subject of prosecution*'.[108] Bluntly this is rhetoric. Reading the revised Code leads to the conclusion that there is a presumption in favour of prosecution. Under the old versions of the Code, the prosecutor was urged that, if undecided, he or she should abide by the spirit of the cautioning guidelines. That injunction has now been removed. Again the old version stated '*... the police decision to institute proceedings should never be met with passive acquiescence but must always be the subject of review.*' That positive exhortation also has been removed.

The prosecutor is enjoined that, broadly speaking, the graver the offence, the more likelihood that the public interest requires prosecution. The Code's constant refrain is the 'seriousness' of the offence. As we shall see, this is consistent with the sentencing criteria laid down in the 1991 Criminal Justice Act.[109] With a serious offence, even where there are public interest factors against prosecution, the prosecution should often go ahead and those factors should be put to the court in sentencing.[110] The Code outlines the factors in favour of prosecution:

i) the prospect of a significant sentence.

ii) the use of weapons or violence.

iii) whether the victim was in public service.

iv) whether the accused was in a position of trust or authority.

v) whether the offender was the ringleader.

vi) was there premeditation?

vii) whether the offence was carried out by a group.

---

[107] Ashworth A., '*The "Public Interest" Element in Prosecutions*' Crim. L.R. (1987), p. 595.
[108] House of Commons Debates, volume 483, column 681, January 29, 1951 quoted in CCP, para. 6.1.
[109] See Chap. 9.
[110] *ibid.*, para. 6.2.

viii) was the victim vulnerable and was there significant harm or loss.

ix) did the motive involve discrimination.

x) was there a difference in ages between victim and defendant or any evidence of corruption?

xi) was the offence committed while the defendant was under a court order.

xii) is the offence likely to be repeated or is it prevalent in the area.[111]

The factors to be taken into account[112] in considering waiver of prosecution are:

i) would the likely penalty to be imposed by the court be purely nominal?

ii) was the offence committed as the result of a misunderstanding.

iii) was the harm minor and the result of a single incident.

iv) does the delay in bringing the case to court make the case 'stale'? The rule of thumb was 'was the offence committed 3 years before the date of trial?' This is less relevant where there is likely to be a substantial custodial sentence, the investigation has been complex or the accused has contributed to the delay.

v) is the defendant old or infirm? In such cases there should be prosecution only if the offence is very grave or there is a real danger of repetition.

vi) was the accused mentally disordered at the time of the offence or would prosecution have an adverse effect on the mental health of the accused? In such cases prosecution is rarely appropriate.[113]

vii) has the defendant put right the loss caused?

viii) could disclosure at the trial harm sources of information or national security?

Where the public interest factors are in favour of waiving prosecution, the CPS have statutory power[114] to discontinue. Discontinuance should involve consultation with the police but the final decision rests with the prosecutor exercising an independent judgement as guardian of the public interest. The Runciman Committee found that the CPS did exercise that judgment appropriately citing one study,[115] which suggested that nearly a third of discontinuances were dropped on public interest grounds. Of these, nearly a half were discontinued because of the triviality of the offence or of the likelihood of a nominal penalty. The factors were the youth, age, previous good character or mental state of the accused, the attitude of the complainant or the offer of compensation.

---

[111] *ibid.*, para. 6.4.

[112] *ibid.*, para. 6.5.

[113] See Home Office Circular: *Provision for Mentally Disordered Offenders*, No. 66/1990.

[114] s. 23 of the Prosecution of Offences Act 1985, but there is also a common law power to withdraw or offer no evidence even at a late stage—*Grafton* (1992) Crim. L. R. 826—even at Crown Court the judge cannot interfere even where this power is exercised after the trial has commenced. In such circumstances the judge can only direct an acquittal.

[115] Moxon D. and Crisp D., *op. cit.*

To prosecute only where there is an identifiable need should be central. Ethically we should make only a minimal use of punishment. But in resource terms, alternative strategies to prosecution are invariably cheaper and more effective. However assessment of public interest is only possible where the necessary information has been collected. The police are unlikely to consider this in detail nor do the CPS have resources available for such investigation. An encouraging development has been that some probation services run schemes to expand the quantity and quality of that information. There has been a growth of public interest case assessment (PICA) schemes and that the Royal Commission recommended that these be put on a country-wide systematic basis.[116]

Discontinuance of all charges is not the only option since the defendant may well wish to plead guilty to a lesser charge while maintaining a plea of not guilty to more serious charges. The CPS can accept such 'deals' but the Code's strictures are that the overriding consideration in considering acceptance of guilty pleas is that the court must not be left in the position where it is unable to pass a sentence consistent with the gravity of the actions. But having accepted a plea, the CPS should not then argue that the case is more serious than appears in the charge. Administrative convenience should not take precedence over interests of justice.[117]

The review process should also ensure that the number of charges should be as few as possible so as not to obscure the nature of case. Specimen charges can be used where appropriate. The CPS should not use multiplicity of charges as a lever to put pressure on the defendant so that he or she pleads guilty to a few charges in exchange for others being dropped. The charges laid should reflect the gravity of conduct but again as long as the court's sentencing powers are adequate, then factors such as the speed of trial and the mode of trial might permit a charge of lesser gravity.[118]

5.8.1 A Reviewable Discretion?

Earlier we examined the court's power to review police decisions not to enforce the law.[119] A CPS decision not to prosecute is subject to judicial review. In *Lewin v. CPS*,[120] a person left a drunk adult friend in a car on a hot day. The friend later died in the car and the CPS chose not to prosecute because it could not have been foreseen that the friend was being exposed to the risk of death. The Divisional Court held that the CPS had been entitled to decide not to prosecute. But in *R. v. DPP, ex parte Andre Joseph*[121] the decision not to prosecute for assault was unreasonable and the CPS were ordered to review it. There are three grounds for judicial review of decisions not to prosecute: (i) unlawful policy; (ii) the DPP had failed to act in accordance with settled policy; and (iii) perverse decisions.[122]

Reviews of a decision to prosecute are fewer but in *ex parte L*,[123] the applicant

---

[116] Royal Commission on Criminal Justice, *op. cit.*, para. 5.61.
[117] CCP, para. 9.1.
[118] CCP, paras. 7.1–7.3.
[119] supra, Chap. 2.
[120] May 24, 2002—Lawtel.
[121] (2001) Crim. L.R. 489.
[122] *B. Director of Public Prosecutions, ex parte C* (1995) 1 Cr. App. R. 136.
[123] *R. v. Chief Constable of Kent ex parte L* (1993) 1 All E.R. 756—see Uglow S., Dart A., Bottomley A. and Hale C. 'Cautioning Juveniles—Multi-Agency Impotence' (1992) Crim L.R. 632; Osborne P. 'Judicial Review of Prosecutors' Discretion' (1992) N.I.L.Q. Vol. 43, p. 178.

had been regarded as a suitable case for a caution by the local multi-agency juvenile offender liaison team but this was ignored by the police who chose to prosecute and were supported by the CPS. The juvenile sought to review this decision. Lord Watkins accepted that it was the decision of the CPS that was judicially reviewable and not any prior decision of the police:

> '[The CPS] has unquestionably the sole power to decide whether a prosecution shall proceed. It is entirely dominant in that very important respect and all the erstwhile corresponding power of the police has been stripped away . . .'

But can a CPS decision to continue proceedings against an individual be impugned in the Divisional Court at all? Some authorities[124] suggest that any body subject to statute such as the CPS was subject to judicial review while others indicate that the prosecuting powers of the Attorney General, under whom the DPP and CPS operate, cannot be controlled or supervised by the courts.[125] Since the lower criminal courts had the power to stop proceedings as an abuse of process,[126] judicial review was unnecessary but Watkins L.J. accepted that this power was too limited. A criminal court of trial was not an appropriate forum to test the merits of a decision to prosecute: firstly because there was the general policy aimed at keeping juveniles out of the criminal courts; secondly because individual juvenile defendants can scarcely argue that prosecuting them was an abuse of process since they had admitted guilt in order to be eligible for a caution. Judicial review was more appropriate and a CPS decision not to discontinue was open to challenge. The Divisional Court concluded that in this instance there had been a proper exercise of discretion. It also restricted its decision to the discretion to prosecute children and stated that judicial review of decisions to prosecute adults was not reviewable.

5.9 ATTRITION, DISCONTINUANCE AND NON-JURY ACQUITTALS

In the past, one of the major concerns was inefficiency. The Royal Commission in 1981 reviewed the old system of County Prosecuting Solicitors.[127] In 1978 43 per cent of Crown Court acquittals were the result either of the judge ordering an acquittal (19 per cent) or directing the jury to acquit (24 per cent),[128] a figure which suggested that cases were not properly reviewed prior to trial to check that there was sufficient evidence or that, where the evidence was present, there was a poor level of preparation of cases. A closer analysis was less damning since the commonest factors leading to a non-jury acquittal[129] were unforeseeable because either witnesses fail to attend court or fail to testify satisfactorily.

Reform brought the creation of the CPS, along with section 23 of the Prosecution of Offences Act 1985, which empowered the CPS to discontinue cases,

---

[124] *R. v. Panel for Take-overs, ex parte Datafin* (1978) Q.B. 815.
[125] Following Lord Dilhorne in *Gouriet v. Union of Post Office Workers* (1978) A.C. 435.
[126] See *R. v. Derby Crown Court, ex parte Brooks* (1985) 80 Crim. App. Rep. 164 at 169 and *R. v. Bolton JJ, ex parte Scally* (1991) 2 W.L.R. 239 at 256.
[127] Weatheritt M., *The Prosecution System: Survey of Prosecuting Solicitors' Departments* (Royal Commission on Criminal Procedure Research Study No 11 1981).
[128] Royal Commission on Criminal Procedure, *op. cit.*, para. 6.18 drawing on McConville M. and Baldwin J., *Prosecution, Courts and Conviction* (1981).
[129] Block *et al.*, *op. cit.*, p. 42.

which they do where there was no realistic prospect of conviction. Despite this, research for the Royal Commission on Criminal Justice in the early 1990s suggested that about 20 per cent of directed acquittals ought to have been foreseen and avoided because a proper review of the evidence would have revealed doubt as to whether there was sufficient evidence to justify the initial decision to prosecute. By use of their powers of discontinuance,[130] these non-jury acquittals could have been avoided.

Have matters changed? Attrition starts at an early stage—the CPS received 1.35m cases from the police in 2000/01. The initial review decision leads to the rejection of approximately twelve per cent of the cases submitted by the police, most commonly because there is insufficient evidence to proceed. There are local variations in this rate. Surveys have shown that the police are consulted about decisions to discontinue in over ninety five per cent of cases where consultation is possible, and object in around four per cent of cases.[131] The inspectorate tend to be highly satisfied with the standard and found that over ninety eight per cent accorded with the tests in the Code. However there is a lack of a positive and evidenced initial review when undertaken by lawyers rather than the caseworkers. The HMCPSI attributes this to a lack of positive case ownership as it is only in those instances when a full file is eventually received from police that a lawyer would examine the case carefully. By this time, it may be too close to the trial date or committal hearing to deal properly with disclosure or to enable further evidence gathering by police.[132]

The rate of subsequent discontinuance before cases get to court also is approximately thirteen per cent.[133] The HMCPSI considered a relatively high proportion of decisions to discontinue to be wrong in principle—some seven per cent. The inspectors have estimated that this would, if replicated across the whole spectrum of casework, represent in numerical terms around 11,000 decisions and would often be a source of distress to the witnesses and victims.[134]

Adverse cases are those, which are terminated or fail prematurely at court without a decision being made upon their merits by the magistrates or jury. They include cases in the magistrates' court lost at half time on a submission of no case to answer, a very small number of committals discharged after evidence has been read to the court, judge ordered acquittals where the prosecution drops the case before a jury is empanelled, and judge directed acquittals where a judge directs a jury to acquit. This is less of an issue in magistrates' courts where the CPS completed 949,400 cases in 2000 with fewer than six per cent involving a 'not guilty' plea and with the accused being acquitted in 31 per cent of these.

The CPS surveyed discontinuances in magistrates' courts in November 1993.[135] Of the prosecutions discontinued, forty-three per cent were for insufficient evidence and in a quarter of these cases, weak identification evidence was the reason for discontinuance. Thirty-one per cent were for public interest reasons,[136] nine per cent were where the defendant had eventually produced the relevant motoring documents and seventeen per cent were where the prosecution

---

[130] Under s. 23 of the Prosecution of Offences Act 1985 but also at common law—*Grafton* (1992) Crim. L.R. 826.
[131] National Audit Office, *The Crown Prosecution Service* (HC 400 1997/97) (1997).
[132] HMCPSI Annual *Report* 2000/01 (HC 801 2001/2002) (2002).
[133] CPS Annual *Report* 2000–2001, p. 26.
[134] HMCPSI, *op. cit.*, para. 4.5—the inspectorate work on a sample of cases from each CPS area.
[135] CPS Annual Report 1993–94, *op. cit.*, para. 3.3.
[136] These results resemble those in Moxon D. and Crisp D., *op. cit.*

were unable to proceed mainly because an essential witness was missing but also were the offence had been taken into consideration by another court or simply the prosecution were not ready.

At Crown Court, the attrition rate is much higher:

Table 5.2 Acquittals in Crown Court 1978–2000[137]

Year	% of all defendants acquitted	% acquittals after 'not guilty' pleas	% non-jury acquittals	Ordered*	Directed
1978	16	47	43	19	24
1980	18	50	42	22	20
1990	15	57	58	40	18
2000	26	67	63	49	15

Table 5.2 shows a detailed breakdown for 2000 when 72,800 adult defendants were dealt with, of whom 41 per cent pleaded 'not guilty'. About two thirds, 66%, of the 'not guilty' pleas were acquitted.

Table 5.3 Defendants acquitted after a plea of not guilty showing manner of acquittal 2000[138]

Plea	Outcome	Number	Percentage
Not guilty to all counts	Discharged by judge	9,563	54
	Acquittal directed by judge	2,549	14
	Jury verdict	5,588	32
	Total acquittals	17,700	100
Not guilty to some counts	Discharged by judge	169	7
	Acquittal directed by judge	410	18
	Jury verdict	1,682	74
	Total acquittals	2,261	100

Over the past two decades, there has been a steady rise in the number of non-jury acquittals and this is accounted for by the rise in number of ordered acquittals while directed acquittals have fallen slightly. Block[139] suggests that the

[137] Block B., *et al.*, *op. cit.*, p. 12; Zander M, '*What the Annual Statistics Tell Us about Pleas and Acquittals*' (1991) Crim. L.R. p. 252; *Judicial Statistics* 2000, Chap. 6.
[138] *Judicial Statistics* 2000, *op. cit.*, Table 6.10, p. 67.
[139] Block B. *et al.*, *op. cit.*, p. 13.

ordered acquittal is much more likely to be CPS-initiated when a weakness in their case has been identified between committal and trial. Despite recognising this, the prosecution cannot be dropped since once a defendant has been committed for trial, all parties have attend even where the CPS is not intending to offer evidence.[140] The rise in the numbers of 'ordered acquittals' suggests that pre-trial assessment of the relative strength of cases has improved markedly. Block's study looked at 100 cases of non-jury acquittals and concluded that in only forty five per cent was that acquittal unforeseeable and that twenty seven per cent were clearly foreseeable with evidential deficiencies. They also noted instances of inadequate advice from prosecuting counsel.

HMCPSI also assess CPS performance on the basis of a sample of cases—inspectors consider whether the adverse outcome was foreseeable by a reasonable prosecutor on the evidence and information available at the time. If it was, should some further action have been taken by the prosecution to try to remedy the problem or defect or should the case have been dropped sooner? In 2000, the conclusion was that some thirty four per cent of adverse outcomes were foreseeable, and that some nineteen per cent of adverse outcomes should have been the subject of some remedial action.[141] It is difficult to compare with the Block study but the HMCPSI figures do not suggest any significant improvement. Recent changes might affect the rate of adverse outcomes—CPS charging initiatives, the co-location of CPS with police criminal justice units, the rights of audience for CPS lawyers and consequently greater 'ownership' of the case.

Cracked trials are where a case is listed for a contested trial but on the day of the trial, it is disposed of in some other way, often because of the accused deciding to plead guilty. In 2000, 17,328 cases in Crown Court (approximately twenty three per cent) were classified as 'cracked.[142]

- Sixty per cent involved the accused pleading guilty.

- Fifteen per cent involved the prosecution accepting a plea of guilty to an alternative charge.

- Twenty per cent involved the prosecution offering no evidence.

In such cases, witnesses and victims have been put to the inconvenience and upset of attending. Many such cracked cases are foreseeable and the increase in CPS advocates taking responsibility for cases at court and engaging positively with the defence may have an impact in overcoming the late proffering of pleas and acceptance of these at court

5.10 SENTENCING AND APPEALS

Prior to the trial, the CPS does have a quasi-sentencing role since it has the power to discontinue and recommend that the police administer a formal caution. The procurator fiscal in Scotland can go further and make an offer to the accused to discontinue proceedings if the offender pays a fixed penalty.[143] It is an alternative

---

[140] Royal Commission on Criminal Justice, *op. cit.*, para. 5.37, recommends that the CPS be given the power to discontinue proceedings up to the beginning of trial in both magistrates' and Crown courts.
[141] HMCPSI, *op. cit.*, para. 4.6.
[142] *Judicial Statistics, op. cit.*, Table 6.7.
[143] Under s. 56 of the Criminal Justice (Scotland) Act 1987.

to prosecution that the Royal Commission would like to see introduced in England and Wales.[144]

After trial and conviction, it has always been a convention that the prosecution's job was over and there was no involvement in the sentencing of the offender. It is still the case that the CPS does not make any recommendation as to type or length of sentence. This can be affected indirectly—the decision on the nature of the charge or the acceptance of plea of guilty to an alternative offence may impact on the sentence. There have been proposals for reform in this area but the only change has been under section 36 of the Criminal Justice Act 1988, which permits the CPS to ask the Attorney General to refer cases to the Court of Appeal where a defendant has been convicted but in the eyes of the prosecution has been given an 'unduly lenient' sentence. The Court of Appeal may quash the sentence and substitute a more appropriate sentence which they see fit and which the court below had the power to impose.[145] The provision applies to sentences passed for offences triable only on indictment and such other offences or 'descriptions' of case as may be specified by order. This order-making power has been used to apply the provisions to matters such as the smuggling of drugs and indecent or obscene material; the production, cultivation or supply of controlled drugs; indecent assault; unlawful sexual intercourse with a girl under 16 and serious fraud cases.[146] The figures available for 1999 are that, of 78 references, the sentence was increased in 55 cases (70.5 per cent). There have been such references when courts have imposed non-custodial sentences for rape[147] and for conspiracy to supply drugs[148]. In some driving cases where death has been caused, fines have been replaced by prison sentences.

Generally the prosecution has no right to appeal against acquittal but there are a series of mechanisms that give the prosecution a limited right of appeal. Firstly the prosecution can appeal on a point of law by way of case stated to the Divisional Court of Queen's Bench either from a summary acquittal or from a successful appeal to the Crown Court following a summary conviction.[149] Secondly, in serious fraud or long and complex cases, there are pre-trial hearings and both parties can appeal against adverse findings on such matters as admissibility of evidence.[150] It is proposed that the prosecution should, in some circumstances, be able to appeal rulings before trial, during the hearing of the prosecution case and of no case to answer as well as other 'terminating rulings'.[151] Thirdly there is a right of appeal where a person has been convicted of intimidating or interfering with a juror or witness in another trial and that interference has led to an acquittal.[152] This has never been used. A fourth mechanism is the Attorney-

---

[144] Royal Commission on Criminal Justice, op. cit., para. 5.63.
[145] Criminal Justice Act 1988, ss. 35–36; SC Shute. '*Who Passes Unduly Lenient Sentences? How Were They Listed?*', *A Survey of Attorney General's References Cases*, 1989–1997 [1999] Crim. L.R. 603.
[146] Criminal Justice Act 1988 (Reviews of Sentencing) Order 1994 (S.I. 1994 No. 119): Criminal Justice Act 1988 (Reviews of Sentencing) Order 1995 (S.J. 1995 No. 10); Criminal Justice Act 1988 (Reviews of Sentencing) Order 2000 (S.I. 2000 No. 1924).
[147] A-G's Reference (No. 3 of 1993), (1993) Crim. L.R. 472.
[148] A-G's Reference (No. 16 of 1992), (1992) Crim. L.R. 456.
[149] s. 111 of the Magistrates' Courts Act 1980.
[150] Criminal Justice Act 1987, s. 9(11). Criminal Procedure and Investigations Act 1996, s. 35(1). This is discussed in *Law Commission Report*, No. 267, 'Double Jeopardy and Prosecution Appeals' (2001), para. 2.32 ff.
[151] White Paper, *Justice for All* (Cm. 5563) (2002) para 4.68.
[152] Criminal Procedure and Investigations Act 1996, ss. 54–57.

General's Reference was introduced in 1972 by section 36 of the Criminal Justice Act, this permits the Attorney-General to refer to the Court of Appeal any point of law even though it arose in a case where the defendant has been acquitted. This does not affect the status of the original verdict and the defendant remains acquitted. It is infrequently used—the first reference was made in 1974. In the 25 years since then, there have been a total of 41.

The key issue has always been whether there should be a general right of appeal for the prosecution. The argument against this has been the concept of double jeopardy. In recent years, this principle has come under attack—the MacPherson Report into the death of Steven Lawrence[153] suggested that '*consideration should be given to the Court of Appeal being given power to permit prosecution after acquittal where fresh and viable evidence is presented.*'[154] The Law Commission proposed[155] giving the Court of Appeal power to set aside an acquittal where there is apparently reliable and compelling new evidence of guilt but only for murder. The Auld Report argued for the abolition of the rule and would go further to allow a prosecution right of appeal where the jury verdict was seen as 'perverse'.[156] It is argued that the European Convention protects the rights of defendants who have been 'finally' acquitted in accordance with the law and that this does not preclude the re-opening of cases in exceptional circumstances.[157] The government has welcomed these recommendations and intends to introduce legislation to allow the Court of Appeal to quash an acquittal where there is significant new evidence. This would apply in serious cases such as murder, manslaughter and rape.[158] The double jeopardy rule, following in the footsteps of the right to silence, is to be significantly limited.

[153] *The Stephen Lawrence Inquiry, Report of an Inquiry by Sir William* (1999) Cm. 4262.
[154] *ibid.*, Recommendation 38.
[155] Law Commission Report No. 267, 'Double Jeopardy and Prosecution Appeals' (2001).
[156] Auld Report, *op. cit.*, Chap. 12, paras 47ff.
[157] Pattenden R., 'Prosecution Appeals' [2000] Crim L.R. 971.
[158] White Paper, *Justice for All* (Cm. 5563) (2002) para 4.63 ff; Home Office, *Criminal Justice: The Way Ahead* (2001) Cm. 5074 paras 3.53–3.56;

CHAPTER SIX

Courts and Trials

6.1 HISTORICAL ORIGINS OF ADVERSARIAL SYSTEM

As a representation of moral and rational government, the trial is one of the major constitutional institutions of the common law. Naturally the composition, jurisdiction and procedures of the modern courtroom are significantly the product of its history. Although settling disputes through court hearings was familiar to Anglo-Saxon and Norman England, the formal mechanisms for mobilising the law were amorphous. Some shape to the process came with the reforms of Henry II in 1166 through the Assize of Clarendon. This legislation provided for a 'jury of presentment',[1] which was a group of local people put on their oath to tell the truth about local crimes. This was not a jury of trial but one of accusation. Then as now a central question of any hearing lies in discovering the truth of an accusation.[2] But the mechanisms for uncovering truth have changed radically. In

---

[1] This was later known as the grand jury which was not abolished in England until 1933 to be replaced by committal proceedings but it still survives in the U.S.
[2] Milsom S.F.C., *Historical Foundations of the Common Law* (198) 1 Chap. 14; Plucknett T.F.T., *A Concise History of the Common Law* (5th ed. 1956).

the medieval trial, truth was not a matter of witnesses and evidence but instead was sought through ordeal, trial by battle[3] or by compurgation.[4] The only means of proof for those indicted by the presenting jury under the Assize of Clarendon was through the ordeal of water.[5]

There were other forms of ordeal through fire or ingesting a holy wafer. The result was a judgment of God, the *judicium dei*, and its legitimacy came from God. As such the proceeding required the presence of a priest. But at the Lateran Council in 1215 the Church declared the ordeal to be mere superstition.[6] Without the religious imprimatur, other methods of proof had to be found. Continental Europe turned to the Roman-canonical law of proof[7] with its calculus of evidence. This required 'full' proof and that might be obtained from a confession, from the evidence of two eyewitnesses, from eight items of circumstantial evidence or *indicia* or from a combination of these. These mathematics did not appeal to the English who instead turned to a familiar institution, the jury, expanding its functions from accusers to decision-makers. While the jury of accusation was the 'grand' jury, the trial jury was the 'petty' jury. Initially the mode of trial was apparently the choice of the accused. However the royal courts slowly adopted the jury as the means to decide on the truth of the allegations and after the Statute of Westminster in 1275, those who refused to 'put themselves upon the country' could be imprisoned. The thirteenth century trial was still not a fact-finding forum in the modern sense since the jurors were people who already knew directly or indirectly the circumstances of the accusation.[8]

In small, rural, homogenous communities, juries may well have been an effective means for the determination of the truth. Furthermore jurors were mainly male landholders, who could be relied on to uphold royal interests. The king had a significant interest in the operation of the courts—when justices were dispatched to the provinces, they were to inquire into matters affecting royal interests, including felonies, conviction for which involved the forfeiture of the felon's property to the king. There was increasing use of these royal courts and the jurisdiction exercised by local communities, by feudal landowners and by the church withered away. But, as we have seen,[9] any monopoly claimed by the state to investigate and prosecute crime was rejected, whether by accident, design or by an 'insular dislike for things foreign'.[10] Criminal prosecution became very much a matter for private individuals to mobilise the machinery of the law through accusation. How the accused was to confront or refute this (except through the knowledge of the local jury) remains shrouded in mystery:

'Of the actual conduct of a trial we know almost nothing before the sixteenth century,

---

[3] Initially introduced after the Conquest for appeals of felony where a Norman was the accused.
[4] Suspicion was often the basis of accusation and proof by compurgation involved the accused producing a set number of neighbours to swear to his or her overall good character.
[5] The accused was bound and lowered by a rope into a deep pool—if he sank to the level of a knot tied in the rope at the distance of his hair, he was declared innocent but if he floated, the water would not receive him and he was judged guilty. Warren W.L., *The Governance of Norman and Angevin England 1086–1272* (1987) p. 109.
[6] Warren, *op. cit.*, p. 213.
[7] Langbein J., *Torture and the Law of Proof* (1977).
[8] Milsom, *op. cit.*, p. 411 It is not until after the 17th century that personal knowledge of the case becomes a disqualification for a juror. Lord Justice Coke talked of trial being by jury and not by evidence.
[9] *supra* Chap. 1.
[10] Spencer J., *Jackson's Machinery of Justice* (8th ed. 1989) p. 19.

not nearly enough until the eighteenth. How the jury informed itself or was informed, how rules of evidence emerged, when and in what detail directions were given by the justices, these are things we do not know.'[11]

There was formal control of the criminal process by the king with his increasing monopoly of jurisdiction and thereby of punishment, especially over serious offences. Contrasted with this, however, is a local quality to justice, both through the jury system and by gentry acting as magistrates and influencing criminal courts. Legal doctrine remained unsophisticated and the extent of moral blame was dealt with by jury verdict rather than by technical rules of law. This is illustrated by the misconception that all criminals would face the death penalty throughout the thirteenth and fourteenth centuries—relatively few were executed and composition in cases of violence was common.[12]

It was the growth of the absolutist monarchies of the Tudors and Stuarts that led not only to greater centralised control of the courts and innovations in procedures but also to more savage punishments. The 'prerogative' court of Star Chamber, for example, operated without juries, on a basis of unidentified accusation and with the defendant interrogated by the judges under oath and perhaps under torture.[13] Political and popular opposition in the seventeenth century to such courts was to delineate the conditions under which the monarch or state has the power to restrict a person's freedom and to inflict punishment. That great characteristic of the common law, the adversarial form of trial, has to be understood in the context of these constitutional conflicts in the seventeenth century.

The two basic building blocks were the principles of natural justice. Progress was slow. In 1610 Chief Justice Coke might declare the first of these: that a man should not be judge in his own cause, *nemo iudex in suam causam*.[14] But even in the nineteenth century we find Lord Brougham citing the case of the Duke of Buckingham who heard a charge against a neighbouring farmer brought by his own gamekeeper and decided in the Duke's own home.[15] The second cardinal principle, that of *audi alteram partem*, was also recognised by the early 18th century.[16] But the criminal defendant had no means of getting his or her story heard since it was not possible to compel witnesses to testify (although they might do so voluntarily) nor was there professional assistance to examine witnesses or to speak on the accused's behalf until 1836. Furthermore the defendant could not give sworn testimony until 1898.[17] Even the 'bulwark of freedom', the jury, could not be relied on to be impartial.[18] It was not until the end of the nineteenth century that the central elements of the adversarial trial—legal representation, cross-examination of the prosecution witnesses, the ability to call and examine

---

[11] Milsom, *op. cit.*, p. 412.

[12] Given J., *Society and Homicide* (1977).

[13] Radcliffe and Cross, *The English Legal System* (5th ed. 1971) p. 107; Milsom, *op. cit.*, pp. 418–9; Holdsworth W.S., *History of English Law (1936–72)*, Vol. V p. 155 ff.

[14] *Dr. Bonham's Case* (1610) 8 Co. Rep. 113b.

[15] Quoted in Manchester A.H., *Modern Legal History* (1980) pp. 161–162.

[16] *The King v. University of Cambridge* (1723), 1 Str. 557 cited in Wade H., *Administrative Law* (1961) Chap. v 'Natural Justice'.

[17] Criminal Evidence Act 1898, s. 1.

[18] After the trial of the Quakers, Penn and Mead, in 1670, for a 'conspiratorial gathering', the jury were fined and imprisoned until eventually released by the Chief Justice who declared 'the right of juries to give their verdict by their conscience'. Harman H. and Griffith J., *Justice Deserted* (1979) p. 11.

your own witnesses, to testify on your own behalf and to address the jury—were in place. Nor was there a system of appeal until the early twentieth century.[19] Even then we lacked proper regulation of pre-trial investigation until 1984 under the Police and Criminal Evidence Act, there was no independent prosecution system until 1985 when the Crown Prosecution Service was inaugurated under the Prosecution of Offences Act and no body to investigate miscarriages of justice until the Criminal Cases Review Commission was created by the Criminal Appeal Act 1995.

The modern adversarial trial has had a long period of development. It is a system that places great significance on the day in court. It is only at this point that the information and argument from both sides is placed before the judge and jury, both of whom come to the courtroom with no prior knowledge or opinions. This might be contrasted to the inquisitorial method where there is a continuing judicial process of collecting evidence and interviewing witnesses. The common law trial is regarded as the single, public proceeding, both the beginning and end of the affair. It is difficult to explain why the adversarial process rather than the investigative process should have emerged in England: the relatively short period of absolutist monarchy and the impact of the puritan revolution in reaction to undiluted state power is one factor; the historical dominance of the local state over the national is another. Private prosecution correlated with the image of a society that was the product of the actions of its more powerful members, not of an interventionist government.

To modern eyes, adversarialism is not just a representation of the rule of law but of government itself: the agent of the state (the judge) sits above and apart from the individuals below. The competition of the courtroom mirrors the competition of the market place. But it was also the forum where the rights of the citizen should be at their most inviolable.

6.2 CHARACTERISTICS OF THE COMMON LAW TRIAL

Article 6 of the European Convention on Human Rights provides that:

> 'In the determination of ... any criminal charge against him, everyone is entitled to a fair and public hearing within a reasonable time by an independent and impartial tribunal established by law.'

The Human Rights Act 1998 provides that all public authorities, including the courts, take into account the convention and its jurisprudence. Common lawyers would argue that the accused has always been accorded a fair trial and that Article 6 merely encapsulates those elements that have always been characteristic of common law trial, namely, the independence of the court, its adversarial nature and the priority given to procedural fairness.

6.2.1 *Independence*

Constitutionally there must be independence for the court and the judge from the executive. Decisions can be challenged through appeal and review procedures,

---

[19] Manchester, *op. cit.*, p. 180 ff.—often execution of sentence was often carried out within a few days.

but there should be no interference by national[20] or local government. Although the judiciary are appointed by the Lord Chancellor, a member of the Cabinet and a head of a government department, it is very difficult to remove judges[21] or magistrates[22] except for extreme misconduct. Even in relation to the other agencies and institutions of the criminal justice system itself, the courts operate autonomously and guard their independence jealously.

Under Article 6 of the European Convention, a fair trial requires an independent and impartial tribunal. In determining whether a judge is independent, the criteria taken into account by the Court are the manner of appointment, the length of tenure, the existence of guarantees against outside pressure and the question whether the tribunal has the appearance of being independent.[23] The court must be an '*independent and impartial tribunal established by law*'. In *Lauko and Kadubec v. Slovakia*,[24] the accused were prosecuted and punished by a local administrative office for public order offences. The Court held that the office could not be seen as independent of the executive within the meaning of Article 6—administrative bodies could adjudicate but there had to be an opportunity to challenge before an independent and impartial tribunal. In *Lauko* there was no opportunity for review.

The trial is separated from all the previous events and the judge, in common with the jury and the spectators in the public gallery, is hearing the evidence for the first time. It is solely on the evidence that is retailed in court, usually by formal oral testimony, that the decision is based. It is an autonomy which verges on quarantine: the court's decision is not allowed to be infected by information that derives from any source other than the formal rules of evidence, except the assistance that the court can obtain in interpreting the law from appellate court decisions. The jury are instructed not to discuss the case with anyone else and once they have retired, they remain together[25] and incommunicado and their discussions are absolutely privileged.[26] It is contempt of court to discuss the case with a juror.[27]

Within the Crown Court itself, the judge is king. Once the case has been transferred to the court, discontinuance of the action (*e.g.*, by offering no evidence) or amendment of the indictment is subject to the consent of the judge.[28] Although there is an over-riding power of the Attorney-General to stop a prosecution by entering a '*nolle prosequi*', this control over the indictment empha-

---

[20] The extent to which this is valued by J.P.s can be seen in the Magistrates' Association's adverse response to the Home Office: *Scrutiny of Magistrates' Courts*, which suggested a rationalised and centralised system under the Home Office.

[21] Superior judges can only be removed after an address presented to the Queen by both Houses of Parliament. Circuit judges can be dismissed by the Lord Chancellor under powers given by the Courts Act 1971 for 'incapacity or misbehaviour'. See Spencer J., *op. cit.*, p. 368 ff. for some entertaining examples.

[22] Magistrates can be removed from the commission by the Lord Chancellor—Spencer *op. cit.*, pp. 410–412.

[23] *Campbell and Fell v. UK Application No. 7819/77*, A 80, 7 E.H.R.R. 165 (1984).

[24] *Application No. 26138/95*, (1998) H.R.C.D. 838.

[25] *Alexander* (1974) 1 W.L.R. 422.

[26] *Thompson* (1962) 1 A.E.R. 65.

[27] s. 8 of the Contempt of Court Act 1981. This prevents research into juries and any informed reform of the system.

[28] *Broad* (1979) 68 Crim. App. Rep. 28 but see *Grafton* (1992) Crim. L.R. 826. The Crown Prosecution Service is able to discontinue prosecutions before they have reached this stage under s. 23 Prosecution of Offences Act 1985. In magistrates' courts, however, they appear to be able to halt proceedings at any time *R. v. Canterbury Justices, ex parte Klisiak* (1981) 3 W.L.R. 60.

sises the role of the judge as representative of the monarch and of the conceptualisation of crime as an offence against the state: the Queen appears as the wronged party in the indictment and the juror swears an oath to try the issues between the Queen and the prisoner. The form of trial belongs as much to constitutional history as to a modern democratic state.

In France the trial judge will have a full *dossier* prepared by the *juge d'instruction*, including witness statements and the interrogation of the defendant. The examination of witnesses will be on the basis of these documents. Thereis judicial supervision of the process from the beginning of the investigation to the decisions in the prison itself on length of time to be served. This is the province of the *juge de l'application des peines*. The process, to common law eyes, inevitably seems less public and to possess a significant linkage between the State through the prosecution on one hand and the judiciary on the other.[29] In contrast, the English judge will usually know nothing about the case before the trial, will not have been engaged in supervising any investigation, taking statements from witnesses or the accused or making bail decisions. Nor, except in rare circumstances, would he or she be consulted over decisions to release from prison.

Formal independence of the courts from the state is an essential check on the power of executive government. Independence from the other criminal justice agencies also makes the courts a neutral forum, which is a key part both of the adversarial system and of due process. But the costs of such isolation are that the judiciary were reluctant to be involved in formulation of criminal justice policy,[30] especially over sentencing policy, although this is slowly changing. In 1991, the Criminal Justice Consultative Council (CJCC) was formed together with 23 local committees known as Area Criminal Justice Liaison Committees. These Area Committees have the objective of keeping under review the operation of the criminal justice system and working to improve co-operation between the various agencies and departments. In 1999, Ministers approved proposals that their role should change to that of a strategic one and be re-named Area Criminal Justice Strategy Committees. In addition, the Committees were increased to 42 to match the police force areas—many of the key criminal justice agencies are now organised on a similar geographical basis. Lord Auld's review of the criminal courts calls for further rationalisation of these bodies.[31]

6.2.2 *Adversarialism*

The language of Article 6 in many ways reflects the common law, adversarial, method of trial rather than the investigative system favoured in civilian jurisdictions. The common law court (judge and jury in the Crown Court or the magistrates) in making decisions, does not act as an investigative body, calling and examining witnesses on its own initiative. The hearing is structured, as with civil hearings, as a debate (or maybe battle) between the two parties, namely the prosecution and the defence. The case is prepared for trial by the CPS or defence lawyers and, in court, the lawyers decide which evidence is to be produced and which witnesses are to be called. In the courtroom they appear as equals, rein-

---

[29] New reforms for the French system are in the pipeline—West A. *'Reform of French Criminal Justice'* 150 New L.J. 1542 (2000).
[30] Senior judges are more likely to be involved in debates on criminal justice reform. This was much rarer in the past.
[31] Lord Justice Auld, *A Review of the Criminal Courts of England and Wales*, Chap. 8 (2001)

forced by the language of the 'defendant' and the 'prosecutor or prosecutrix' as if they were private individuals. That equality is illusory—there is a huge imbalance between the power and resources available to the prosecutor/state as opposed to the individual accused. The court plays a passive role,[32] listening to evidence which is advanced by the parties, who only call those witnesses likely to advance their cause and who are permitted to attack the credibility and reliability of the witnesses testifying for the other side. The judge should not interfere or act as an investigator and this is the major difference between common law countries and other European jurisdictions.[33]

One rationale for adversarialism lies in the right to confront the accuser and the evidence. Cross-examination as a technique of confrontation is well grounded in the common law and it is guaranteed by Article 6(3)(d).[34] Confrontation implies that the witness should be there in person in order that the reliability of the evidence and the credibility of the witness can be tested. The requirement for the physical presence of witnesses can lengthen trials because even where the evidence is uncontroversial, the witness is normally present. Criminal trials do not use pre-trial written pleadings,[35] as occurs in civil cases, although this process would reduce trial length by concentrating on those matters in dispute. There are nowadays more opportunities for pre-trial hearings to resolve issues that may arise during the trial.[36]

The judge acts as umpire, ensuring that the rules on procedure and evidence are followed. After the parties have presented their evidence and made their arguments, the judge directs the jury on the law to be applied and reminding them of the evidence that they have heard. The jury is expected firstly to decide questions of fact—that is, to make up their minds between conflicting accounts as to what happened—and then to decide on the guilt or innocence of the defendant. Right at the start of the trial they are plunged into the argument with the opening speech by prosecuting counsel and have to make the best sense they can of the issues until the judge comes to their rescue at the end. An American judge compared the experience to, 'telling jurors to watch a baseball game and decide who won without telling them what the rules are until the end of the game'.[37]

One glaring omission from the trial continues to be the victim: there is neither the right to speak, to be represented nor necessarily a place to sit. This is perhaps the consequence of the adversarial process on one hand and on the other, the conceptualisation of the crime as a wrong against society. Once the complaint has been made, control is relinquished. The victim still has many legitimate interests: firstly the need for information but there are still no statutory rights to

---

[32] Interventions by the judge during a trial may lead to the quashing of a conviction: *Hulusi and Purvis*, 58 Cr.App.R. 378; see also *Frixou* [1998] Crim.L.R. 352, and *Roncoli* [1998] Crim.L.R. 584.
[33] Tomlinson E.A. *'Non-Adversarial Justice: The French Experience'* in Maryland Law Rev. (1983) Vol. 42 p. 131. In Europe, several jurisdictions are considering reforms which would allow the defence lawyer to question prosecution witnesses directly—at present questions have to be asked indirectly through the presiding judge. This was one of the reforms in Italy's new Code of Criminal Procedure in 1989.
[34] It is also one of the rights granted in the 6th Amendment of the American Constitution, which provides for a fair and unbiased trial.
[35] One reason for this is that the plea of not guilty puts the entire prosecution case in issue. s. 10 of the Criminal Justice Act 1967 provides for formal admissions but is rarely used.
[36] *Infra* Chap. 7 at para. 7.5.
[37] Quoted in the Auld Report (*op. cit.*) that recommended that the judge should give a review of the charges and issues to the jury at the start of the case—Chap. 11 paras 15–24.

be informed about the course of the trial;[38] secondly the right to a role in the decision whether to prosecute or not but the victim's wishes are not decisive and may or may not be taken into account by the police or the prosecution;[39] thirdly the right to respect in presenting evidence in court where treatment of the victim in the witness box verges on the scandalous; finally there are issues of compensation.

The lack of protection of the victim-witness was demonstrated for many years in sexual assault cases where the defence was often a thinly veiled attack on the sexual morality and character of the victim, particularly when the defendant cross-examined the rape victim on her past sexual history. In such situations, the tactical interests of the prosecutor did not necessarily overlap with those of the victim.[40] Recent legislation[41] has introduced greater protection for the vulnerable witness as well as preventing those accused of rape from intrusive questioning of the victim.[42] There are other examples still exist: in homicide cases, a plea of provocation may well involve an attack on the deceased victim's character and the victim's relatives might wish to be independently represented in order to examine witnesses or should they be entitled to object to the acceptance of a plea of 'guilty' to manslaughter but of 'not guilty' to murder?

In certain European jurisdictions the victim has a right to legal representation. In France the victim can be joined to an action as *'une partie civile'* and has *locus standi* in all preliminary matters and at the trial, able to argue that the charge is insufficient, to object to a certain line of questioning or to ask that certain questions be put to a witness. Some even treat the victim as an auxiliary prosecutor, notably Germany. However the practical impact may be limited and the role is largely symbolic as the conduct of the prosecution being left entirely or almost entirely to the public prosecutor. Such reforms have been considered but rejected.[43]

6.2.3 *Fairness*

A fight model of dispute resolution requires rules of engagement, which are essentially based on the idea of fairness. But fairness itself is not a single or simple idea. First, it may be that the content of the law itself might be seen as unfair or unjust, as favouring one group above another or as infringing a fundamental right. Traditionally the doctrine of sovereignty of Parliament meant that from the seventeenth century[44] the courts would not interfere in the substantive quality of a statute.[45] This has been and will continue to be affected by the Human Rights

---

[38] Despite recommendations to the contrary by the Glidewell Report (*The Review of the Crown Prosecution Service* Cm. 3972 1998) or in the MacPherson Report on the Stephen Lawrence Inquiry (Cm. 4262 1999).

[39] *Code for Crown Prosecutors* (CPS 1994) para. 6.7 '. . . Crown Prosecutors should always take into account the consequences for the victim.'

[40] Temkin J., *Rape and the Legal Process* (1987) p. 162 ff.

[41] Pt II of the Youth Justice and Criminal Evidence Act 1999.

[42] *ibid.*, s. 41 but see *R. v. A. (No. 2)* [2001] 2 W.L.R. 1546, where the House of Lords held that on ordinary principles of statutory interpretation, section 41 is incompatible with the right to a fair trial.

[43] The Auld Report (*op. cit.*) recommended against giving victims, as some have suggested, a formal role in the trial process similar to that of the continental partie civile or auxiliary prosecutor, or any outwardly special position inrelation to the prosecutor. Chap. 11 paras 68–75.

[44] Wade, op. cit. pp. 128–129.

[45] Again this can be compared to the U.S., not least the current debate on the constitutionality of various states' abortion laws.

Act 1998 which requires that courts must, if possible, interpret statutes to be compatible with the European Convention on Human Rights or, if this is not possible, to make a declaration of incompatibility.[46] Courts now have to assess the 'fairness' of an offence against the fundamental rights laid down in the Convention. This has led to doubts as to the continued existence of the doctrine of reasonable chastisement as a defence for a parent charged with assault on a child[47] or the maintenance of discriminatory treatment between homosexual and heterosexual conduct.[48] The guarantee of freedom of expression under Article 10 will lead to further challenges to offences of obscenity and blasphemy. Even where the rule itself is seen as fair, its enforcement must be proportionate in order to safeguard other rights.[49]

Even if the content of the rule is fair, the decision itself may be challenged as unfair. In the common law, the decisions of the trier of fact are sacrosanct—the triers of fact are either the magistrates or the jury. There can be appeal by way of re-trial in Crown Court from a magistrates' decision and the Court of Appeal can order a re-trial if it believes the verdict to be unsafe. In both cases, the facts are re-heard. But there is no general system of appeal by which the appellate court substitutes its verdict, its assessment of the evidence, for that of the original trier of fact. Interference with the jury, before, during or after their deliberations is a criminal offence.[50]

We can talk about the fairness of the rule or the fairness of the decision but in the courtroom, fairness is about the procedure. Justice and fairness are to be found in the interstices of process. The assumption is that truth is more likely to emerge from due process of law. This is reflected in the system of appeals. This is a review of process rather than of the decision—the appeal court does not ask whether the lower court came to the correct decision; instead it asks whether it followed the correct procedure in arriving at that decision. Section 2 of the Criminal Appeal Act 1968[51] allows for convictions to be set aside where they are 'unsafe'. If, on the evidence, a reasonable jury properly directed could have reached that decision, the Court of Appeal will not interfere, even though they themselves might not have arrived at the same conclusion.

The root values of procedural justice are encapsulated in the House of Lords' decision in *Woolmington*[52] where Lord Sankey talked of the 'golden thread' of justice that the prosecution had to prove every element in a criminal charge and that proof had to be beyond reasonable doubt. The defendant had to prove nothing. Nowadays these common law values are mirrored in Article 6(2): '*Everyone charged with a criminal offence shall be presumed innocent until proved guilty according to law.*'

The key element of a criminal trial is the presumption of innocence—in other words, the obligation is on the State to prove each and every element of the offence charged. The accused should not be coerced into providing evidence for

---

[46] Human Rights Act 1998, s. 2 and s. 4.
[47] *A v. UK Application* No. 25599/94, 2 F.L.R. 959, [1998] Crim. L.R. 892, 27 E.H.R.R. 611 (1998).
[48] *ADT v. UK* (2001) 31 E.H.R.R. 33, [2000] 2 F.L.R. 697.
[49] *McLeod v. UK Application* No. 24755/94, 27 E.H.R.R. 493, [1999] Crim. L.R. 155 (1998)—the law relating to arrest for breach of the peace conforms with the ECHR but any arrest must be proportionate and bear in mind other rights such as the right to privacy or freedom of expression.
[50] Possibly perverting the course of justice or intimidating a juror under s. 51 of the Criminal Justice and Public Order Act 1994 or s. 8 of the Contempt of Court Act 1981.
[51] As amended by Criminal Appeals Act 1995.
[52] (1935) A.C. 462.

the prosecution. This raises issues not only in relation to the right to silence but also about the reversal of the burden of proof or the imposition of strict liability.[53] In addition Article 6(3) provides specific rights for defendants:

Everyone charged with a criminal offence has the following minimum rights:

(a) to be informed promptly, in a language which he understands and in detail, of the nature and cause of the accusation against him;
(b) to have adequate time and facilities for the preparation of his defence;
(c) to defend himself in person or through legal assistance of his own choosing or, if he has not sufficient means to pay for legal assistance, to be given it free when the interests of justice so require;
(d) to examine or have examined witnesses against him and to obtain the attendance and examination of witnesses on his behalf under the same conditions as witnesses against him;
(e) to have the free assistance of an interpreter if he cannot understand or speak the language used in court.

Such rights underpin our perception of a 'fair trial'. Furthermore they take precedence over more pragmatic aims such as the determination of truth or law enforcement. Frank[54] argues that Anglo-American criminal procedure detracts from the discovery of the truth. Were we to invent from scratch a mechanism to find out facts and allocate blame, the solution would not be an adversarial system, with its partisan advocates, untrained judges, reliant heavily on cross-examination and where the final decision is left to 12 people plucked arbitrarily off the street. The goal of discovering the truth and making a reliable decision might require a trained chairperson with investigative powers, sitting with assessors expert in the relevant field and with the parties' representatives having a much lower profile.

Some commentators[55] support this goal and attack the ritual formality of the trial especially when the 'guilty' are released because of some perceived technicality such as the non-disclosure to the jury of an accused's previous convictions. A trial, they argue, should keep its eye on the ball—that is, convicting the guilty and regarding unjustified acquittals as much as miscarriages of justice as unjustified convictions. Such arguments focus on one aspect of fairness—that is, the substantive justice of the decision itself. It is an interesting empirical question whether any reform would be able to deliver a lower 'error' level—the baseline is difficult as there is only anecdotal information about unjustified acquittals although we have considerable recent evidence on wrongful convictions. Restrictions on procedural safeguards may reduce the level of such acquittals but it invariably will increase the risk of wrongful convictions.

But justice is more than simple truth and we must not ignore the symbolic force of the trial. There is a distinction between the trial as a logical function and the trial as a symbol. In its outward form, the trial is about the determination of truth and the application of that truth to legal rules. This simple instrumental model of a trial is not sufficient. Compare the courtroom with a police station: what would

---

[53] *R v. Lambert* [2001] 3 All E. R. 577; *R v. DPP, ex parte Kebeline* [1999] 4 All E. R. 801—infra Chap. 8, para. 8.1.3.
[54] Frank J., *Courts on Trial* (1949).
[55] Such commentators are frequently police officers such as Robert Mark, ex-Commissioner of the Metropolitan Police. See Mark R., *Minority Verdict* (BBC—Dimbleby Lecture 1973) or Sir David Phillips, Chairman of ACPO in 2002 and Chief Constable of Kent.

be the public reaction if a court were to interrogate a defendant over days and nights with limited rest, no legal assistance, perhaps using the threat of violence or the inducement of release to obtain responses to questions?[56] That reaction would be one of horror. The trial must pay meticulous attention not simply to detail but to process. In the court, the accused's rights are paramount because of the covert function of the trial. The self-evident constraints on the prosecutor and the state, illustrate, rightly or wrongly, that we live in a society that treats its citizens in a fair and just manner.

6.2.4 *Rational Decision-Making*

It is not merely the due process aspects of criminal procedure that detract from the discovery of the truth. The predominant image of the courtroom is a plea of 'not guilty' followed by trial by jury.[57] The imperfections in pre-trial process can be swept away by the 'day in court', which will ascertain the truth, ascribe responsibility and impose proper and proportionate punishment. The trial is portrayed as rational decision-making within the overall values of the rule of law. But we should be cautious in accepting trial outcomes in these terms—there are elements in the management of the courts and trials, which directly contradict and undermine this.

6.2.4.1 EFFICIENT MANAGEMENT

Rational management techniques influence the courtroom as much as rational decision-making. Offenders are processed and disposed of as efficiently as possible in terms of time and resources. Key performance indicators relate to such issues as cost per case, the time taken between first appearance in magistrates' court and committal or between committal and trial or the backlog of cases for a particular court or petty sessional division. The publication of such KPIs creates pressure to maintain efficiency.[58] This leads to pressure to speed up cases and to the negotiation of outcome.[59] The defendant's role can be reduced to passivity especially where there are on-going professional relationships between the defence and prosecution lawyers, the police, probation services, court administrators and judges. Thus there is a divergence between the official and articulated ideals of the courtroom and the organisational reality that exists behind them. Central values can be too easily ignored and the quality of the decision reached becomes of lesser significance.

6.2.4.2 RITUAL

Even when there is a contested trial, rational decisions can take a backseat to the high level of ritual in the formal procedures, dress and language which regulate the parties. On one level these elements are anachronisms, relics of history that

[56] Only since the PACE Codes of Practice could defence lawyers be reasonably confident that a court would exclude confessions obtained in such circumstances.
[57] Although a popular image, most cases are heard by magistrates acting without a jury. As well, most cases are disposed of by guilty pleas—over 90% in magistrates' courts and around 70% in Crown Courts. Perhaps less than 5% of cases that are eligible to be heard by a jury actually are so heard.
[58] This is well illustrated by the approach taken in the Narey Report: *Review of Delay in the Criminal Justice System* (1997).
[59] *e.g.*, the importance of a high percentage of guilty pleas to reduce delays.

we are relatively comfortable with. The ritual also contributes to the sense of the authority of the court and towards the acceptance of its decisions. Ritual is maintaining the function of the law as a secondary reality,[60] establishing the authoritative version of the events and interpreting and explaining those events not merely in the courtroom but also for the outside world.[61] In many ways it is neither a formally rational nor very human process. For example, one American sociologist[62] has suggested that the trial is a process of recasting the defendant, away from his own identity and into a stereotyped social role (mugger, hooligan, drunk, vagrant). The trial becomes a degradation ceremony that reduces the defendant to a lower status. Through this process, broader patterns of social authority and of social power are once again demonstrated.

6.2.4.3 WORLD OF AUTHORITY

The courtroom is an imposed and imposing 'world of authority'[63] with dominance and subordination clearly signposted. There is the deference shown by all the personnel towards the bench as well as those elements of 'majesty': the elevated bench, private access to judge's 'chambers' and the judge's throne-like chair. The geography of the court carries this on: in the dock, the defendant is raised but on a lesser level; there is a rail surround, not to stop an escape attempt but representative of captivity. The public are well to the back of the court, segregated so that we are allowed to observe but not to participate. Carlen suggests that the organisation of space is such as to impede communication, especially for those who are not part of the routine cast and who are unfamiliar with a courtroom. Distances are much greater than one would normally use for disclosure of private or traumatic incidents or indeed for effective intervention. Communication is through the lawyers and there is also the sense of a play being carefully stage-managed, again maintaining the sense of domination, of the inexorability of the law.

The language employed, with its technical vocabulary and flowery and archaic forms of address, again puts the uninitiated at a disadvantage. The defendant becomes 'Smith' or 'this person'. The court insists upon the precise technical words,[64] again marginalising the accused. Any involvement by the defendant is essentially passive, responding to questions. Indeed the mode of discourse in the courtroom involves either interrogation or monologue, both of which are extraordinary (and resented) when they occur in day-to-day conversation.[65] Even the intelligent and articulate defendant is ill equipped to deal on an equal basis. Defendants feel confused, alienated and by-passed so that even the practice of asking the defendant if he has anything to say before sentence is now delegated to the lawyer.

Through the ritual, the geography and the language, there is a high level of situational control by the court and the lawyers. *'After all, they're near enough mates in the same play. They're the cast of the play, you're just the casual one-*

---

[60] Berger P. and Luckman T., *The Social Construction of Reality* (1967).

[61] Mansell W., Meteyard B. and Thomson A., *A Critical Introduction to Law* (2nd ed. 1999).

[62] Garfinkel H., 'The Trial as a Degradation Ceremony' 66 *American Journal of Sociology* 420 (1956).

[63] Carlen P., 'Remedial Routines for the Maintenance of Control in Magistrates Courts' 1 *Brit. Jour. of Law and Society* (1974) p. 101.

[64] Carlen *op. cit.*, p. 107—although this is less observed in youth courts or with vulnerable witnesses.

[65] Atkinson J.M. and Drew P., *Order in Court* (1979).

day actor. It's just another day's work to them'.[66] All defendants experience this control but the (legal) workforce in a court is mainly white, middle-aged, middle-class and male. Defendants are often coloured, young and working-class. There is an inevitable clash of conflicting beliefs, attitudes and of social realities. In this context, the perception of the courtroom as imposing a social authority is as valid a perspective as rational decision-making.

6.2.4.4 TRIALS AS NARRATIVE

We might also think about the trial as story telling. It is the party that puts together the most credible narrative that often wins. Narrative plays an important part in imposing order on our lives.[67] We see our own selves in terms of a biographical narrative, with the events of our lives moving in a connected flow, linked to some central theme. Similarly, narrative helps us to impose order on the external world. Thus we do not believe poor storytellers since their narrative is often internally inconsistent, jumps from one point to another and does not link to central action. Whether we believe or disbelieve what people tell us is more related to their abilities as storytellers than it is to the truth or otherwise of their story. This raises interesting questions about the human 'need' for order and how narrative satisfies that need. Put into the context of the trial, the reliance that is placed on narrative values further erodes the dominance of 'legal rationality' as well as requiring re-assessment of the role of the lawyer and of the decision-making by the judges or jury.

6.3 SUMMARY AND INDICTABLE TRIAL

There are currently two systems of courts that hear and decide criminal cases: the magistrates' courts for minor, summary, cases and the Crown Courts for more serious cases heard on indictment. Decisions in these courts can be challenged through a number of channels. These structures can be seen in Figures 6.1 and 6.2

The Auld Report[68] recommended that the two court systems should be replaced by a unified Criminal Court consisting of three divisions: the Crown Division, constituted as the Crown Court now is, to exercise jurisdiction over all indictable-only matters and the more serious 'either-way' offences allocated to it; the District Division, constituted by a judge, normally a District Judge or Recorder, and at least two magistrates, to exercise jurisdiction over a middle range of 'either-way' matters of sufficient seriousness to merit up to two years' custody; and the Magistrates' Division, constituted by a District Judge or magistrates, as magistrates' courts now are, to exercise their present jurisdiction over all summary matters and the less serious 'either-way' cases allocated to them. Auld also recommended a single centrally funded executive agency as part of the Lord Chancellor's Department responsible for the administration of all courts, civil, criminal and family (save for the Appellate Committee of the House of Lords), replacing the present Court Service and the Magistrates' Courts' Committees.

Quantitatively 95 per cent of all criminal cases will be dealt with in the

---

[66] Baldwin J. and McConville M., *Negotiated Justice* (1977) p. 85.
[67] Bennet W. and Feldman M., *Reconstructing Reality in the Courtroom* (1981).
[68] *op. cit.*, Chap. 7.

Figure 6.1 Trial on Indictment

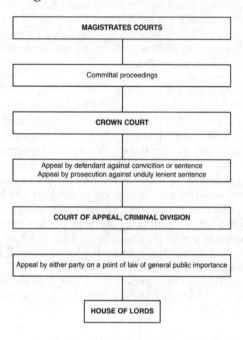

Figure 6.2 Summary Trial

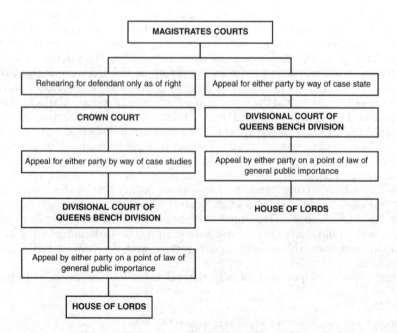

magistrates' courts. Even the remaining 5 per cent, the more serious cases, will normally start there with an initial hearing known as committal proceedings.[69] In magistrates' courts, the justices of the peace who hear cases are local people with no legal background, taking time from their jobs to serve as unpaid judges.[70] In contrast the Crown Court has a judge who will have been a lawyer of some experience before being appointed to the judiciary.[71] The trial takes place in front of a jury, a body of twelve people randomly selected from the local community.

6.3.1 *Classification of Offences and Mode of Trial*

Magistrates and Crown courts deal with different levels of offence. There are three different categories:[72]

a) **Summary offences:** these are the most minor crimes and are only triable 'summarily' in the magistrates court. 'Summary' does not refer to the speed or the lack of quality of justice in magistrates' courts (although often dozens of cases will be dealt with in a morning) but to the process of ordering the defendant to attend the court by summons, a written order usually delivered by post. This is the most frequent procedure adopted in magistrates' courts. McBarnett[73] suggests that too little concern is shown about summary justice and that the safeguards, which exist in the higher courts, are often absent. This is justified by an 'ideology of trivia' and a belief that the law and facts of such cases is very simple. Although summary offences involve a wide range of trivial matters, often relating to road traffic or perhaps not possessing a TV licence, this category also encompasses other more serious crimes such as driving with excess alcohol, assault on a police officer or indecent exposure. Redistribution of business from the Crown Court to the magistrates' courts, especially of offences of dishonesty and of public order crimes, has often been controversial. The most recent attempt to limit a defendant's right to opt for jury trial was in 1999 when the government introduced a Mode of Trial Bill with this objective. Again the criticism it attracted meant that this reform was quietly dropped in January 2002.[74]

b) **Indictable offences:** these are the most serious crimes, triable only on indictment in a Crown Court in front of a judge and jury. This category includes homicide, serious assault, rape, kidnapping, robbery, conspiracy and Official Secrets Acts offences. Magistrates will never try these cases. Prior to 1998, the accused always appeared in front of the magistrates' court in committal proceedings, which were a preliminary check that the

---

[69] The Crime and Disorder Act 1998, s. 51, has effectively abolished committal proceedings for offences triable only on indictment. It provides for offenders charged with such offences (together with related either way and summary offences) to be 'sent' to the Crown Court for trial.

[70] There are paid and legally qualified stipendiary magistrates in major conurbations.

[71] *infra* para. 6.3.3.1.

[72] This was the result of rationalisation brought about by the Criminal Law Act 1977, following recommendation of the James Committee—Report of the Committee on the Distribution of Criminal Business between the Crown Court and the Magistrates' Court (HMSO 1975) Cmnd. 6323.

[73] McBarnett D., *Conviction* (1981) Chap. 7.

[74] The Guardian January 22 2002; the controversy goes back to the James Committee's Report (*op. cit*). Its recommendation to make minor thefts only triable in magistrates' courts attracted great opposition during the debates on the Criminal Law Act 1977.

prosecution case was strong enough and that there was a 'case to answer'.[75] Committal proceedings for offences triable only on indictment have now been replaced as a result of section 51 of the Crime and Disorder Act 1998. From January 2002, offenders charged with such offences (together with any related either way and summary offences) will 'sent' to the Crown Court for trial with no further hearing. Once the case is at the Crown Court, an application may be made by the defendant for the dismissal of any charge upon which he has been sent for trial.[76]

c) **Triable either way:** these are triable either in magistrates' court or in Crown Court. The most common examples are theft and burglary but the category also includes indecent assault, arson and criminal damage.[77] There is no clear conceptual boundary here: theft is triable either way whereas social security fraud is a summary offence.

Summary trial is only possible if both the accused and the magistrates[78] assent to it. The defendant has the right to insist on jury trial and if the magistrates consider summary trial inappropriate, they too can elect for trial on indictment. Most defendants opt for summary trial,[79] not least because of the speed of the proceedings and the ceiling placed on the punishments that magistrates' courts can impose: the maximum term of imprisonment is six months imprisonment or twelve months if the accused is convicted of more than one offence; the maximum fine is £2000. Often either the magistrates decline jurisdiction or the defendants exercise their right to trial by jury. Where there is a doubt as to forum, the magistrates will hold a 'mode of trial' hearing[80] to decide whether the case is suitable to be heard summarily or not. The Lord Chief Justice, Lord Lane issued national mode of trial guidelines in 1990.[81] The guidelines have been revised and reissued by the Criminal Justice Consultative Council (CJCC). Both parties can address the court. Although the prosecutor's preference cannot bind the court, magistrates tend to follow the CPS recommendation.[82] The general issue is the seriousness of the offence and whether a magistrates' court would have sufficient sentencing powers to deal with it. For example, if the charge is one of theft or fraud, the court would con-

---

[75] Committal proceedings frequently take some months to be heard. Magistrates also make certain preliminary decisions, especially on the question as to whether the suspect was to be remanded in custody or released on bail. Where the accused was held in custody awaiting trial, then there would be regular hearings to renew the remand decision. Such functions will still be undertaken.

[76] This is modelled on the legislation relating to the transfer for trial of cases involving serious or complex fraud (Criminal Justice Act 1987, s. 6) and of sexual cases and cases involving violence to children (s. 53, Criminal Justice Act 1991).

[77] Under Sched. 2 to the Magistrates' Courts Act 1980, offences of criminal damage which do not amount to arson must be tried summarily if the value of the property damaged or destroyed is £5,000 or less.

[78] The hearing (like committal proceedings) can be before a single magistrate—although it is more common to have a full bench.

[79] In 2000, 272,000 people were found guilty in magistrates' courts of indictable offences; 70,000 (20%) were committed for trial—*Criminal Statistics 2000* (2001) Cm. 5312 Fig. 1.1 p. 18.

[80] ss. 18–21 of the Magistrates' Courts Act 1980 lays down the procedure.

[81] Practice Note (Mode of Trial: Guidelines), 92 Cr.App.R. 142; (1990) 1 W.L.R. 1439.

[82] Riley D. and Vennard J., *Triable-Either-Way Cases: Crown Court or Magistrates' Court?* (Home Office Research Study No. 98) (1988) where research showed that the magistrates disagreed with the CPS on 23 out of 623 occasions; Hedderman C. and Moxon D., *Magistrates' Court or Crown Court? Mode of Trial Decisions and Sentencing (HMSO 1992)* (Home Office Research Study No. 125).

sider the following characteristics to merit trial on indictment: where there was a breach of trust by a person in a position of substantial authority, or in whom a high degree of trust is placed; where the theft or fraud has been committed or disguised in a sophisticated manner; where the theft or fraud was committed by an organised gang; where the victim was particularly vulnerable to theft or fraud, *e.g.*, the elderly or infirm; where the unrecovered property is of high value.

Prior to 1997, magistrates had to decide on mode of trial in triable-either-way cases without the defendant being given the opportunity to plead. Since then there has been a 'plea before venue' procedure under section 17A of the Magistrates Courts Act 1980. This enables the defendant to indicate their plea in the magistrates' court before the mode of trial decision is taken. Defendants who indicate a guilty plea, will be convicted following summary trial and they may be committed for sentence to the Crown Court if magistrates consider that the offence warrants a more severe sentence than they have power to impose. Where a defendant indicates a not guilty plea the magistrate considers the appropriate mode of trial. The broad effect of plea before venue has been to redistribute the caseload of triable-either-way cases between magistrates' courts and the Crown Court. Magistrates' courts now deal with defendants pleading guilty for triable-either-way offences who would have been previously dealt with at the Crown Court. The downside is that they commit more cases to the Crown Court for sentence. In *Warley Magistrates' Court ex p. DPP*,[83] the court stated that magistrates should take into account any discount for early guilty pleas before deciding whether they have the power to sentence in a particular case. This effectively gives magistrates the power to sentence up to nine months for either-way offences where the offender pleads guilty, thus reducing the likelihood of committal for sentence.

In 2000 magistrates' courts committed 87,400 persons to the Crown Court either for trial or sentencing: 17,200 were committed for sentencing and 70,200 were committed for trial. Of these, approximately 20 per cent were indictable-only offences. Of the triable-either-way cases, it is the magistrates who are responsible for the case going to the senior court—70 per cent of those tried at the Crown Court were committed because magistrates had declined jurisdiction and in only 30 per cent of cases had the defendant elected trial.[84]

The criticism is that many cases are still unnecessarily tried on indictment. Magistrates are unwilling to accept jurisdiction despite the evidence that suggests that in many cases in which magistrates commit the defendant for Crown Court trial, the judge imposes a sentence that would have been within the power of the magistrates.[85] Many of such cases are not sufficiently serious or difficult to warrant the use of what is a relatively slow, cumbersome and expensive process. The overlap between the work of the Crown Court and that of the magistrates can be seen from the fact that 54 per cent of *all* adult custodial sentences are of six months or less. The Crown Court accounts for about 25 per cent of those and, in addition, imposed nearly 26,000 non-custodial sentences. If the latter were treated as six months or less, the Crown Court accounts for a high percentage of

[83] [1998] 2 Cr. App. R. 307.
[84] Johnson K. and colleagues, *Cautions, Court Proceedings and Sentencing—England and Wales 2000* (Home Office Statistical Bulletin 20/01).
[85] Hedderman C. and Moxon D., *op. cit.*

cases that need not have left the magistrates' courts. These are figures that are used to support the creation of a unified court system.[86]

Although defendants' elections have declined as a proportion over the past decade,[87] they may opt for Crown Court trial for various reasons. If they are remanded in prison and a custodial sentence is inevitable, prolonging the period spent on remand has advantages since conditions for the remand prisoner are more favourable.[88] Even though Crown Court judges are more likely to impose a custodial sentence and that that sentence may be longer than magistrates would have imposed in a similar case,[89] defendants consider that the trial at Crown Court is fairer and that there is more chance of acquittal.[90] The impact of the 'plea before venue' procedure has meant that more defendants who plead guilty have their cases disposed of in the magistrates' court. This in turn has reduced the proportion of defendants who finally end up pleading guilty to all or some of the charges in Crown Court. Overall 59 per cent of defendants pleaded guilty in 2000 although this figure varies—73 per cent of those charged with burglary pleaded guilty whereas only 31 per cent of those charged with sexual offences did so.

The ineffectiveness of the mode of trial hearings is apparent. Despite the automatic transfer of indictable-only cases and the 'plea before venue' procedure, there are defendants who intend originally to contest the allegations before a jury but eventually plead guilty and there are magistrates who decline jurisdiction only for the Crown Court to impose a penalty within the magistrates' own powers. The pressure on the workload of the Crown Courts remains with delays in processing cases.[91] There are also financial costs—a case involving 'not guilty' plea to an indictable offence in a magistrates' court will cost around £1,700 whereas a case involving a 'guilty' plea will cost around £550. Where a case is committed to Crown Court, the average cost of committal alone is £1,050—a case involving 'not guilty' plea will cost around £17,550 and an uncontested case will cost £2,600.[92]

In Scotland the choice of venue is a decision of the procurator fiscal, an equivalent of a crown prosecutor within the CPS. The Runciman Report rejected that simple option but recommended that if the prosecution and defence agreed on venue, that would be sufficient. If there was a disagreement, there would be a mode of trial hearing as at present but that, if the magistrates were to choose summary trial, defendants would no longer have the right to elect trial by jury.[93] A different and more controversial option would be to re-classify a range of

---

[86] Auld Report, *op. cit.* Chap. 7 para. 17. This proposal is not supported by the White Paper 'Justice for All' op. cit. ch. 4.

[87] Riley D. and Vennard J., *op. cit.*

[88] These include more visits, your own clothes and more money. The time spent on remand counts towards the eventual sentence.

[89] Hedderman C. and Moxon D., *op. cit.* (see Royal Commission on Criminal Justice: *op. cit.*, para. 6.8).

[90] 68% of all those pleading 'not guilty' at Crown Court are acquitted as opposed to 30% in magistrates' court—Johnson K. and colleagues, *op. cit.*; Vennard J., 'The Outcome of Contested Trials' in Moxon D., (ed.) *Managing Criminal Justice* (HMSO 1985).

[91] In 1998, the average time between the date of committal to the Crown Court at magistrates' courts and the start of the hearing at the Crown Court was 9.9 weeks for defendants who pleaded not guilty and 18.4 weeks for those who pleaded guilty. The average time for custody cases was 9.4 weeks and 14.4 weeks for bail cases.

[92] Harries R., *The Cost of Criminal Justice* (Home Office Research Findings 103; 1999)—the figures are for 1997 and do not include the cost of any sentence.

[93] Royal Commission on Criminal Justice; *op. cit.*, paras. 6.12–6.14.

minor property offences as summary offences. The Runciman proposal occupies the middle ground whereby the right is not automatically excluded and allows a defendant to argue that it is the appropriate form of trial in the circumstances of this particular case. Critics have argued that the derogation of this right to election is driven by economic considerations.[94] Further there is a widespread perception that the quality of Crown Court justice is more thorough and fairer than that in magistrates' courts. The Commission did not address this sense of dissatisfaction nor did it prevent their recommending an increase in magistrates' courts work.

The *Auld Report*[95] took a more radical stance. It criticised the two systems of criminal courts: first, the fact that cases have to commence in the magistrates' court before being sent or committed to the Crown Court for trial or sentence means that there are unnecessary delays inherent in our current system. Second, there is unnecessary confusion in our current system by allowing the separate courts to operate under different procedural codes, even though they are dealing with a 'continuum' of criminal work. Third, the separate administrations mean that there is no electronic sharing of information between the two that results in duplication of work, delay and increases the risk of error. For *Auld*, the answer was a unified Criminal Court which would enable the appropriate court to take control of a case at the earliest opportunity, thus keeping delays to a minimum. Allied to this there should be the adoption of a single criminal code. Auld suggested a single criminal court consisting of three Divisions: the Crown Division, constituted as the Crown Court now is, to exercise jurisdiction over all indictable-only matters and the more serious 'either-way' offences allocated to it; the District Division, constituted by a judge, normally a District Judge or Recorder, and at least two magistrates, to exercise jurisdiction over a mid range of 'either-way' matters of sufficient seriousness to merit up to two years' custody; and the Magistrates' Division, constituted by a District Judge or magistrates, as magistrates' courts now are, to exercise their present jurisdiction over all summary matters and the less serious 'either-way' cases allocated to them. The courts would allocate all 'either-way' cases according to the seriousness of the alleged offence and the circumstances of the defendant, looking at the possible outcome of the case at its worst from the point of view of the defendant and bearing in mind the jurisdiction of each division. In the event of a dispute as to venue, a District Judge would determine the matter after hearing representations from the prosecution and the defendant. The defendant would have no right of election to be tried in any division. In addition there should be a single centrally funded executive agency responsible for the administration of all courts, replacing the present Court Service and the Magistrates' Courts' Committees. The concept of a unified system has been rejected by the government in 2002.

6.3.2 *Magistrates and Clerks*

The unqualified, unpaid justice of the peace may be seen, alongside the jury, as an exemplar of the 'active community' with the ordinary citizen's input into the processes of justice.[96] It was not always so—the origins of the office of 'justice of

---

[94] Ashworth A., '*Plea, Venue and Discontinuance*' Crim. L.R. (1993) 830.
[95] *op. cit.*, Chap. 7.
[96] www.magistrates-association.org.uk/.

the peace' (J.P.)[97] can be found in 1195 when Richard I nominated country gentlemen as 'keepers of the peace' but their duties appear to have expanded in. the middle of the fourteenth century at the time of the Black Death. In 1361, the Justices of the Peace Act provided for the appointment of JPs in every county. Their function was the enforcement of the strict labour laws, which prevented free movement of labour around the country as well as wage freeze legislation. Their role as the Crown's representatives meant not merely judicial activity but also a range of administrative functions, a role that only disappeared in the nineteenth century with the emergence of democratically elected local councils.

The forefathers of the modern magistrate were less content to sit passively in a courtroom but operated in a more proactive role empowered to 'pursue, arrest … and chastise' offenders. In 1554, the Marian statutes cast them as public prosecutors while in the eighteenth century, the Fielding brothers who were London magistrates, showed most unjudicial activity by organising the Bow Street Runners. The restriction of the J.P.s functions to ones that are predominantly judicial comes about with the Summary Jurisdiction Act 1848, which established the procedure to be followed by justices' courts.[98] Outside court, magistrates exercised a supervisory role over the police either directly in the shire counties (until 1888) or through the Watch Committees in the boroughs.[99]

In 1949, the title of the court was formally changed[100] to 'magistrates' court' whereas before they were known as 'summary courts' or, worse, as 'police courts'—a title that suggested undue influence! There are approximately thirty thousand Justices of the Peace in England.

Table 6.1 Justices of the peace in England and Wales as at 1 April 2001 and selected years since 1978[101]

Year	Total	Men	Women
1978	23,483	14,633	8,850
1983	25,934	15,606	10,328
1988	27,926	15,992	11,934
1993	29,686	16,087	13,599
1998	30,361	15,713	14,648
1999	30,260	15,561	14,699
2000	30,308	15,544	14,764
2001	28,735	14,639	14,096

---

[97] Moir E., *The Justice of the Peace* (1969); Milton F., *The English Magistracy* (1967) Chap. 1.
[98] Manchester A. H., *Modern Legal History* (1980) pp. 74–79 and p. 162.
[99] Under the Police Act 1964 (now the Police Act 1996) J.P.s still sit on police authorities.
[100] Justice of the Peace Act 1949.
[101] *Judicial Statistics 2000* (Cm. 5223) p. 94.

Magistrates are normally[102] appointed by the Lord Chancellor who acts on the advice of local advisory committees. There are over 100 of these. The membership is mainly magistrates but one third should be local people who are not magistrates.[103] The committee is left to devise its own methods of generating applications.[104] Individuals and organisations can put forward candidates for consideration. Local political parties often nominate candidates. The bench should 'reflect the community it serves'[105] but the problem that occurs is one of balance, less in terms of gender[106] than of age, race and class. It has proved very difficult to appoint sufficient working class magistrates and less than 10 per cent of J.P.s are manual workers.[107] Magistrates are unpaid, although they do receive expenses. There is compulsory training before they are allowed to adjudicate as well as continuing refresher courses.[108]

Sitting part-time and normally in benches of three, magistrates deal with over 90 per cent of all criminal cases. They also deal with some civil cases, in the main family and licensing matters. Typically, they serve for between ten and twenty years. They are unpaid, receiving only a modest allowance for financial loss and subsistence. They are required to sit for a minimum of 26 half-day court sittings each year, but on average sit 40 or more times a year. In addition they will spend about a week a year on training activities.[109]

The J.P.s main work is crime—in 2000, 1,911,600 defendants had proceedings completed at the magistrates' courts whereas merely 95,300 had proceedings completed in the Crown Court.[110] J.P.s sit in groups of three in court for most hearings. The 'clerk to the court' assists them.[111] The clerk is the focal point of the court—with the justices simply as a superior form of jury. Nowadays justices' clerks are fully trained and paid lawyers, either a solicitor or barrister.[112] Their appointment is by the magistrates courts committee but has to be approved by the Lord Chancellor. A justices' clerk is responsible for legal advice tendered to the justices and the effective delivery of case management and the reduction of unnecessary delay. It is their job to manage the administration of the courthouse: listing cases for hearing; summoning witnesses; handling adjournments; collecting the fines; as well as managing the personnel of the court. In court, the legal adviser has the duty to provide justices with any advice they require to properly

---

[102] The legislative framework for appointments is in Pt 1 of the Justices of the Peace Act 1997. The Lord Chancellor is responsible in all areas except in Manchester, Liverpool and Lancashire where the appointments are made by the Chancellor of the Duchy of Lancaster

[103] The names of the members (save for the secretary) traditionally were not published, but nowadays can often be found in pamphlets seeking to recruit magistrates and on the Internet.

[104] The Lord Chancellor does issue guidelines for committees and there are training packs through the Judicial Studies Board.

[105] *Judicial Statistics 2000, op. cit.*

[106] In April 2001, 51% of J.P.s were men and 49% were women.

[107] Morgan R. and Russell N., *The Judiciary in the Magistrates' Courts* (Home Office RDS Occasional Paper 66); Darbyshire P., *For the New Lord Chancellor—Some Causes for Concern about Magistrates* [1997] Crim. L. R. 861.

[108] Spencer, *op. cit*, p. 408 ff.

[109] The range of training can be seen at the Judicial Studies Board website at http://www.jsboard.co.uk/

[110] Johnson K. and colleagues, *Cautions, Court Proceedings and Sentencing—England and Wales 2000* (Home Office Statistical Bulletin 20/01) at p. 2 and p. 4.

[111] Darbyshire P., *The Magistrates' Clerk* (1983).

[112] s. 43 Justices of the Peace Act 1997—a candidate must have a 5 year magistrates court qualification within the meaning of s. 71 Courts and Legal Services Act 1990—in other words, a right of audience in relation to all proceedings in magistrates' courts.

perform their functions on questions of law or of mixed law and fact, on matters of practice and procedure, on the range of penalties available and any relevant decisions of the superior courts or other guidelines. The adviser should assist in formulating reasons. In this process, a justices' clerk or legal adviser must not play any part in making findings of fact although they may ask questions of witnesses and the parties. The overall duty is to ensure that every case is conducted fairly. Problems can arise when clerks are seen to be too involved in the decision-making, for example, retiring with the magistrates when they leave to consider their verdict. They should take care to give their advice in open court wherever possible.[113]

In the major conurbations, a legally qualified and paid magistrate supplements the work of the J.P.s.[114] Originally known as a stipendiary magistrate, from August 2000, they became known as district judges. They are appointed by the Queen on the advice of the Lord Chancellor and are drawn from the ranks of practising lawyers with relevant background.[115] They normally sit alone. In 2001, there were 105 such judges with a further 150 deputy district judges who sit part time.[116] Under the Access to Justice Act 1999, there is now a single national service under the Lord Chancellor's department with a senior district judge. The judge is not limited to one commission area but shall sit where and when as determined by directions given by the Lord Chancellor. The Auld Report recommended building on these reforms by the creation of a district division, constituted by a district judge with at least two magistrates, to exercise jurisdiction over a mid range of 'either-way' matters of sufficient seriousness to merit up to two years' custody. But the implications of and opposition to such a change would be far-reaching, not least from the Magistrates' Association that has been a powerful force in resisting change to one of the oldest common law institutions. The policy of successive governments has been to maintain the institution of J.P.s:

'The government is wholeheartedly committed to the concept of summary justice provided by law people drawn from their local communities.'[117]

The Webbs cite Sidney Smith:

What in truth could we substitute for the unpaid magistracy? We have no doubt but that a set of rural judges, in the pay of government, would very soon become corrupt jobbers and odious tyrants, as they often are on the continent. But magistrates, as they now exist, really constitute a bulwark of some value against the supreme power of the state. They would not submit to be employed for base and criminal purposes. They are tools, perhaps, in some cases, but tools that must be respected.[118]

---

[113] *R. v. East Kerrier Justices* (1952) 2 Q.B. 719 though this has been held too restrictive. Where matters of law and fact are inextricably intertwined, the clerk may withdraw with the justices for virtually the whole period of their retirement—*R. v. Consett Justices, ex parte Postal Bingo* (1967) 2 Q.B. 9. There are Practice Directions on the role of the clerk—[1954] 1 W.L.R. 213 and *The Times* 11 October 2000.

[114] Seago P., Walker C. and Wall D., '*The Development of the Professional Magistracy*' [2000] Crim L. R. 631.

[115] This procedure is laid down by s. 78 Access of the Justice Act 1999. A candidate must have a 7 year general qualification within the meaning of s. 71 of the Courts and Legal Services Act 1990.

[116] The Auld Report at p. 73.

[117] *A New Framework for Local Justice* (1992) Cm. 1829 para. 8, p. 4: 'Justice for All' (2002) also rejects the idea in ch. 4.

[118] Quoted in Manchester, *op. cit.*, p. 77.

The alternative would be to create a career judiciary similar to France or Germany. In France, for example, law graduates take a competitive public examination to enter the *Ecole Nationale de la Magistrature* where they undergo a two-year period of training. Graduating from the ENM, they might start as examining magistrates, prosecutors or trial judges. Their career would involve promotion to the higher courts and offices. Such a system might easily be introduced in this country. While developing judicial training courses, it would not be difficult to expand the number of district judges and, furthermore, in the justices' clerks, there is a highly qualified group that already fulfils many quasi-judicial functions. Giving more judicial functions and higher status to the career of clerks is a viable option. The need for full time judicial officers at a local level is becoming more pressing. The jurisprudence of the European Convention consistently stresses the need for the investigation and prosecution of offences to be undertaken in 'accordance with law'. There is a clear need for proper regulation of the investigatory powers of the police and for preliminary judicial involvement in the preparation of cases for court.

The high profile cases involving miscarriages of justice suggest that the need for a properly trained, professional judiciary is more apparent in the higher courts than in the magistrates' courts. Criticisms of the justices of the peace are quite rare and their mistakes are more easily rectified through re-hearings in the Crown Court and by the supervision of the Divisional Court. But studies[119] would suggest that there is a level of routine injustice, which attracts little attention because of the perception of magistrates' courts as dealing with trivia: '... *the lower courts remain something to be laughed at or yawned over for the pettiness of their crimes, not watched with care for the marginality of their legality.*'[120]

6.3.2.1 THE ORGANISATION OF MAGISTRATES' COURTS

In the 1980s, executive responsibility for the system was split between the Home Office who to an extent controlled the finance, organisation and management of the courts while the Lord Chancellor's department arranged the appointment and training of J.P.s. All responsibility was transferred to the Lord Chancellor in 1992. Currently the organisation of the magistrates' courts is contained in the Justices of the Peace Act 1997[121] and their jurisdiction and powers in the Magistrates' Courts Act 1980. The building blocks of the system of magistrates' courts are as follows:

a) the central element is the '**commission area**', the name of which comes from the 'Commission of the Peace' which is the formal document from the Lord Chancellor setting out the powers and duties of the justices in a given area and authorising them to act. The commission areas are the shire counties and divisions of metropolitan districts. A court's jurisdiction is limited to offences allegedly committed within the area for which the court acts.[122]

b) the commission area is divided into '**petty sessional divisions**' or benches. There are over 600 of these—this represents a reduction from 1,000 forty

---

[119] McBarnett D., *Conviction* (1981) Chap. 7; Carlen P., *op. cit.*
[120] McBarnett D., *op. cit.*, p. 147.
[121] As amended in the Access to Justice Act 1999.
[122] Magistrates Courts Act 1980, s. 2(1).

years ago. Each bench has its own courthouse and (normally) justices'
clerk to which magistrates are assigned. Each bench is required to elect a
chairman and deputies. Petty sessional divisions will vary considerably in
size from a dozen J.P.s to over 100, some with only one weekly sitting
while others have several courts sitting daily. The Magistrates' Courts
Committee must regularly review petty sessional areas.[123]

c)　each commission area is administered by a **Magistrates' Courts Committee**[124] (MCC) which appoints justices' clerks and other staff, of which
there are over 10,000. The MCC provides court rooms and equipment and
advises on the organisation of petty sessional divisions. The MCC is a
committee of magistrates elected by their colleagues. Most shire counties
have one MCC, which manages all the courts in the county, whereas some
metropolitan boroughs have their own MCC and some other boroughs
have a combined MCC. The number of MCCs has reduced from 73 in
April 2000 to 42 in April 2001, in line with the Government's policy of
amalgamation to achieve greater alignment of boundaries with other
criminal justice agencies.

　　　The MCC will meet regularly to decide major management issues and
policy for the courts. They employ all the staff that work for the magistrates. Civil Servants answerable to the Lord Chancellor staff all other
courts. The most senior member of staff is called the Justices' Chief
Executive (JCE). The old term was Clerk to the Magistrates' Courts
Committee and in some areas this term is still being used. The JCE may
also be a Justices' Clerk, particularly in the smaller MCC areas. In the shire
counties, it is usual to have a JCE plus several Justices' Clerks. There are,
of course, meetings of representatives of MCC's and Justices' Clerks both
at local and national levels. The magistrates' courts receive an annual
budget. The system costs about £330m a year to run.[125] 80 per cent of this
budget is received direct from central Government—that is from the
Treasury via the Lord Chancellor's Department. Local authorities provide
the other 20 per cent. The amount of grant is determined by a formula and
varies from year to year. There is no representation of local politicians on
the MCC or any other means of accountability to the local authority.[126]

d)　there is also the **Magistrates' Courts Service Inspectorate**. This was
established under Part VII of the Justices of the Peace Act 1997. It provides
independent inspections of the magistrates' courts as well as thematic
reviews and advice on the system to the Lord Chancellor.[127]

How did this system evolve? Historically there has been (and still is) considerable local autonomy for both benches and Magistrates' Courts Committees.
This independence led to a range of problems. First, there were divergent standards between courts: in the award of legal aid to defendants; in the use of bail as
opposed to remanding in custody; most seriously, in sentencing—in 1985 one

[123] Justice of the Peace Act 1997, s. 33.
[124] *ibid*. Pt III.
[125] These figures are from the *Auld Report* Chap. 3, para. 18. The total income from fines, fees and
fixed penalties collected by magistrates' court in 1990/91 was £269,088,000.
[126] The model for the future is the Greater London Magistrates Courts Authority which came into
being in 2001, much more akin to a Police Authority.
[127] A description of their work can be found at www.mcsi.gov.uk/.

research study showed that Brighton imprisoned 30 per cent of those convicted of indictable offences whereas only a few miles away in Lewes, the comparable figure was 14 per cent.[128] In 2002, a study showed that just over 20 per cent of people charged with house burglary on Teesside receive an immediate custodial sentence compared with 41 per cent in Brighton.[129] Secondly many court centres are still inconveniently sited, have less than 12 J.P.s and sit infrequently. The separate existence of small benches is a waste of resources. Thirdly, there is often lack of communication and distrust between magistrates and other agencies. Magistrates often commented that collaboration with the police or prosecution compromises their independence. Finally, there remain difficulties in recruiting properly qualified staff. Local organisation meant that staff are not interchangeable and that career prospects remain limited. Many have chosen to move into the CPS where pay and promotion prospects are better.

Many of these issues were considered in a 1989 review.[130] At that time the magistrates' courts' system still reflected its historical roots, looking anachronistic and with no clear management structure. The 1989 review concluded that it was impossible '... to locate clear management, responsibility or accountability anywhere in the structure'; that there was little evidence of a planned relationship between work and resources, of any review of performance or of any scrutiny of efficiency and that the arrangements were not delivering value for money. The Scrutiny pointed to the increase in the unit costs of dealing with cases and enforcing fines as well as to the delays and backlog of cases. What was suggested was a centralised Government responsibility for the magistrates' courts service with the establishment of a 'Magistrates' Courts Agency' responsible to ministers but operationally independent. The Council of the Magistrates' Association rejected these proposals. They argued that J.P.s should continue to play a substantial role at every level of the service, that magistrates and their clerks should remain independent and superior to the administration of the service. These criticisms were reflected in the government's White Paper[131] and the subsequent legislation[132] which:

a) enabled the Lord Chancellor to streamline the system by giving him the power to reduce unilaterally the number of commission areas. From 105, there are now 42 in April 2001, in line with the boundaries with other criminal justice agencies. The Lord Chancellor may by statutory instrument make general regulations about the constitution, procedure and quorum of the MCC.[133] These committees are now much smaller with an upper limit of 12 with the power to co-opt up to 2 non-JP members.[134] The new style MCC has needed to adjust to the performance targets and other management measures encountered by other criminal justice agencies.

b) provided each of the new commission areas with a head of all paid staff.[135]

[128] Spencer J.R., *op. cit.*, p. 188 fn. 2.
[129] *Observer* May 5, 2002.
[130] Le Vay J., *Magistrates' Courts—Report of a Scrutiny 1989* (Home Office, 1989).
[131] *A New Framework for Local Justice* (1992) Cm. 1829.
[132] Police and Magistrates' Courts Act 1994 but now contained in the Justices of the Peace Act 1997.
[133] Justices of the Peace Act 1997, s. 29.
[134] *ibid.*, s. 28(2).
[135] *ibid.*, s. 40.

This justices' chief executive had a dual role of lawyer and manager—a justices' chief executive could not be appointed unless he or she was eligible for appointment as justices' clerk. This was removed in 1999 by the Access to Justice Act,[136] which defined the role of the chief executive to reinforce the distinction between his or her administrative role compared with the legal role of the justices' clerk.

c) provided greater accountability through a magistrates' courts' inspectorate,[137] independent and reporting directly to the Lord Chancellor. Extending the Audit Commission's remit to include the magistrates' courts provides further transparency.

These reforms have attracted criticisms,[138] not least because of the new funding arrangements which initiate a 'value for money' regime. The courts will be funded on a formula basis[139] which contains two main elements: around 75 per cent of grant based on unit costs for actual workloads, and around 25 per cent for accommodation and ancillary costs. In addition, a fixed amount is set aside for performance incentives, to be awarded on an annual basis. Although the White Paper restated the independence of magistrates and legislation[140] makes it clear that the chief clerk is not subject to direction in respect of any legal advice given to the benches, such funding arrangements and the introduction of performance targets presages a shift towards a managerial culture that must affect decisions, if income is related to cases processed. It has been suggested, for example, that the cost has made courts unwilling to order psychiatric assessments of defendants.[141] It is suggested that these arrangements could provide indirect control over other issues—for example, if the government were to wish to restrict the granting of legal aid.

6.3.2.2 THE WORK OF THE MAGISTRATES' COURTS

Much of the criminal work[142] of a J.P. is done either hearing cases summarily in the magistrates' court (including the Youth Court[143]) or sitting with a judge hearing appeals in the Crown Court. Their involvement goes beyond that and is varied:

a) during the investigative stage, JP's issue warrants to search premises,[144] to arrest,[145] or to authorise continued detention in a police station.[146]

---

[136] ss. 87 and 88.
[137] *ibid.*, Part VII.
[138] Raine J. and Willson M., *Reforming Magistrates Courts: A Framework for Injustice?* Justice of the Peace (1993) Vol. 157 p. 661: Editorial in The Magistrate (1994) Vol. 50 p. 2; *The Guardian* July 7, 1993.
[139] Lord Chancellor's Department, *Review of magistrates' courts revenue grant allocation formula* (Consultation Paper 2000).
[140] Justices of the Peace Act 1997, s. 48.
[141] *The Guardian*, July 1, 1996.
[142] Away from criminal work, magistrates also sit as a Family Proceedings Court, ordering husbands and fathers to pay maintenance to wives and children but also able to make separation orders. There is a range of bureaucratic work—licensing pubs, betting shops.
[143] see Chap. 11.
[144] Police and Criminal Evidence Act 1984, s. 8.
[145] Magistrates' Courts Act 1980, s. 1.
[146] Police and Criminal Evidence Act 1984, s. 43.

b) where the offence is serious enough to warrant trial in the Crown Court,[147] J.P.s sit as examining magistrates in committal proceedings. This is not a trial but a hearing to decide whether the prosecution evidence is substantial enough to justify the accused standing trial. There are two modes of committal proceedings *per se* as well, in certain cases, as transfer to the Crown Court without committal proceedings:

i) Under section 6(1) of the Magistrates' Courts Act 1980, there is active consideration by the bench of the evidence. The Criminal Procedure and Investigation Act 1996 radically reformed this. Previously the prosecution would outline its case and produce its witnesses who would be subject to cross-examination by the defence. At the close of the prosecution case, the defence would probably make a submission of 'no case to answer' or would have the opportunity to call evidence. Now all the evidence is written and will be either read through by the court or summarised for them. The defence can tender no evidence although the accused may still make a submission of 'no case to answer' inviting the magistrates to reject the charge at this point. However the standard of proof placed on the prosecution is not high and is merely whether the evidence discloses a *prima facie* case—that is, whether a reasonable jury *could* convict the defendant. Such full committal proceedings are rare—probably less than 7% of cases heard at the Crown Court will have had a committal proceeding where the evidence was considered.

ii) Under section 6(2) of the Magistrates' Courts Act 1980,[148] the court can commit to trial without consideration of the evidence. This is known as a paper committal. This form, which can take just a few moments, requires that the evidence consists of written statements, that the defendant is represented and that there is no submission of 'no case to answer'. Such proceedings are a formality[149] and over 90% of committals are of this type.

iii) Committal proceedings for offences triable only on indictment have now been replaced as a result of section 51 of the Crime and Disorder Act 1998. From January 2002, offenders charged with such offences (together with any related either way and summary offences) will 'sent' to the Crown Court for trial with no further hearing. Once the case is at the Crown Court, an application may be made by the defendant for the dismissal of any charge upon which he has been sent for trial. This is modelled on the legislation relating to the transfer for trial of cases involving serious or complex fraud (section 6 of the Criminal Justice Act 1987) and of sexual cases and cases involving violence to children (section 53 of the Criminal Justice Act 1991).

What purpose do committal proceedings serve? They are supposed to act as a further filter to ensure that evidentially weak cases do not come to

---

[147] *i.e.*, it is an indictable offence or is an offence triable either way and where either the magistrates have decided to commit for Crown Court trial or where the defendant has elected for Crown Court trial.

[148] This reform was first introduced by s. 1 of the Criminal Justice Act 1967.

[149] Once the mode of trial hearing has decided on Crown Court trial, then there will be a period for both sides to prepare papers for a s. 6(2) committal. When the parties return for the formal committal, a justices' clerk can make the necessary order—S.I. 1993/1183.

trial. At most 10 per cent of committals are 'old style' committals, presumably where the defendant considers that the prosecution evidence is flawed. 80 per cent of such old committals result in the defendant being committed for trial. That would mean, on current workload, that approximately 1,500 out of 77,000 cases would be thrown out at committal stage. In 2000, some 19,000[150] defendants were acquitted at Crown Court. Of that 19,000, some 36 per cent were non-jury acquittals[151] of which a high proportion should have been picked up by an effective filtering system.

Such figures suggest that committal proceedings are an inefficient way of screening out weak cases[152] and are an irrelevance, a false focus.[153] The alternative is simple transfer to Crown Court with the option for preliminary argument before the judge that there is no case to answer. Both Phillips and Runciman, embraced this reform.[154] The latter recommended that there should be an opportunity for the defence to argue that the prosecution's case is demonstrably inadequate. But such argument would be solely on the papers with no opportunity to cross-examine the prosecution witnesses orally. The Criminal Procedure and Investigation Act 1996 introduced these reforms. But the process is still time wasting and expensive. The unified criminal court preferred by the Auld Report would avoid this unnecessary stage and has much to recommend it.

c) the traffic court takes up much of the J.P.s time. In 2000 792,200 people were proceeded against for summary motoring offences, the lowest figure since 1963. The decline is the result of the use of fixed penalty notices— once mainly for parking offences, they can be used for speeding, going through a red light, not wearing seat belts or crash helmets. Offenders make payment direct to the court without any formal proceedings. These notices are an operational matter for the police and the extent of their use is hard to quantify but in 1998, 781,016 fixed penalty notices were issued for speed limit offences and in the same year, the London Boroughs alone issued nearly 3.6 million parking penalty notices.

d) J.P.s will try cases, both offences that are only triable summary offences as well as offences that are triable either way. Such offences comprise small property offences (frauds, thefts, burglaries, vandalism), minor assaults and woundings and a bewildering array of regulatory crime.

e) In 2000, there were 14,359 appeals against conviction by or sentence of the magistrates' court. These are heard by the Crown Court. This shows a considerable decline from the mid–1990s when there were over 25,000

---

[150] I have derived these figures from the overall committal figures given by Jones P., Tarling R. and Vennard J., *The Effectiveness of Committal Proceedings as a Filter in the Criminal Justice System*' in Moxon D. (ed.), *Managing Criminal Justice* (1985) and applying the overall acquittal rates in Crown Courts and the non-jury acquittal rates in Crown Courts given in Block B., Corbett C. and Peay J *Ordered and Directed Acquittals in the Crown Court* (RCCJ Research Study No. 15) (1993) p. 12 Table 2.

[151] Johnson K. *et al.*, *op. cit.*, p. 4.

[152] Jones P., Tarling R. and Vennard J., *op. cit.*

[153] Block et al., *op. cit.*, p. 64ff.

[154] Royal Commission on Criminal Procedure: *Report* (HMSO 1981) Cmnd 8092 para 8.24; Royal Commission on Criminal Justice: *Report* (HMSO 1993) Cm. 2263 paras. 6.20–6.32.

such hearings.[155] On the other hand, the 'plea before venue' reform[156] has meant a considerable increase in the number of committals for sentence—28,713 such cases were dealt with by the Crown Court in 2000. Whether it is an appeal against conviction or sentence or a committal for sentence, J.P.s are required to sit in the Crown Court,[157] although there are proposals to remove these requirements.[158] In these cases, the court must consist of a professional judge and between 2 and 4 J.P.s.

Magistrates are also permitted to sit with the Crown Court judge, when there is a guilty plea. If they do so, they must play (and be seen to play) a full part in the decisions.[159] But J.P.s do not take part in the Crown Court when the case involves a contested first instance trial.

f) the youth court has its own group of J.P.s and its own procedures. The rules and procedures are different from the adult court as is its philosophy, based as it is on the welfare of the child.[160]

6.3.2.3 THE COURSE OF SUMMARY TRIAL

The course of trial in a magistrates' court is the same whether the offence is a summary offence or one able to be tried either way. Jurisdiction requires that the accused is brought to court—this may be in answer to bail or in the custody of police or prison officers. Most frequently it is through the issue of a summons. The summons is issued by the court officers in response to an 'information'—this document contains the allegations against the accused and may originate by the prosecutor delivering a written accusation to the court or secondly by attending court and making the allegation orally so that it is written down by the clerk or thirdly by a copy of the police charge sheet being delivered to the court. The information is not only the justification for issuing a summons to the accused to attend court; it also forms the charge or charges on which the accused is to be tried. In that sense, it is like the count of an indictment and must ensure that there is a statement of the offence (that is, the name of that particular offence and, if statutory, the statute contravened) and the particulars of the offence (that is, a statement of the facts supporting the accusation). Once an information is laid, the court is under a statutory duty to hear the evidence and decide whether to acquit or convict.[161]

Unlike trial in the Crown Court, an accused does not have to be present for summary trial. Cases can take place in the absence of the accused who may have pleaded guilty by post[162] or simply have failed to turn up.[163] The CPS will normally conduct the prosecution. The accused may be legally represented, either by a barrister or solicitor, although one may represent oneself. The clerk should assist an unrepresented defendant in explaining the procedure and perhaps sug-

---

[155] *Judical Statistics 2000, op. cit.* Table 6.1, p. 64.
[156] Magistrates Courts Act 1980, s. 17A.
[157] Supreme Court Act 1981, s. 74 (1).
[158] Lord Chancellor's Department, *Magistrates sitting as Judges in the Crown Court* (Consultation Paper 1998).
[159] *Newby* (1984) 6 Crim. App. Rep. (S) 148.
[160] This is discussed further in Chap. 11.
[161] Magistrates' Courts Act 1980, s. 9(2).
[162] *ibid.*, s. 12.
[163] *ibid.*, ss. 11 and 13 which allow the court to hear the case in the defendant's absence in certain circumstances.

gesting the sort of questions that may be asked in cross-examination.

The course of the trial will be very similar to that in the Crown Court[165A]—the key difference is that the magistrates are judges of both law and fact whereas in the Crown Court those functions are split and the jury is the trier of fact. The case will start with the taking of the plea, guilty or not guilty. If the accused pleads guilty, the sentencing procedure follows (discussed in chapter 9). If the accused pleads 'not guilty', the prosecution may make an opening speech, outlining the case that the state intends to prove. The prosecution will call any witnesses[164] and examine them—they may then be cross-examined by the defence. In addition there may be other forms of admissible evidence such as documents or real evidence.

At the conclusion of the prosecution case, the defence may make a submission of 'no case to answer'. This is an argument that the state has failed to adduce sufficient evidence to prove one or more of the elements of the offence with which the accused is charged. The court must decide whether there is admissible evidence on all elements and also whether that evidence is sufficiently reliable that a tribunal could reasonably convict. If the submission is made out, the defendant is acquitted.

The defence has a right to either an opening or closing speech but will almost invariably opt for the latter. The defence case will follow the same pattern as the prosecution's—the calling and examination of witnesses and adducing other relevant evidence. Following the close of the defence case, the magistrates are likely to retire to consider their verdict—it need not be unanimous and if there are two or four magistrates who are evenly split, the case will have to be adjourned for re-hearing by a different bench.

6.3.3 *The Indictment and the Crown Court*

When an offence is too serious for magistrates' court, an indictment is drawn up for trial in Crown Court. The Crown Court is more formal and traditional than magistrates' courts—at the front of the court will be the raised bench where the judge sits beneath the Royal coat-of-arms. A private door will lead to the judge's room. Below the judge sits the clerk to the court, a less qualified and influential figure than the justices' clerk. Facing the judge will be the dock where the accused stands and in front of the dock will be the benches for the lawyers. At one side is the jury box with two rows of six seats and on the other is the witness box where witnesses enter to testify. There will be a public gallery at the back. There may be an area for probation officers or police officers.

A criminal trial in the Crown Court cannot start until there is a valid indictment. The indictment is a formal document containing the alleged offences against the accused, supported by the briefest of facts.[165] This document supersedes all other accusations (the police charge or the information laid before the magistrates) and it is to the indictment that the accused pleads guilty or not guilty. It is the indictment that should provide the starting point for the judge and the jury.

There can be more than one offence specified in an indictment but each offence must be contained in a separate 'count' or paragraph with a statement of the

---

[164] Witnesses may be compelled to attend—Magistrates' Courts Act 1980, s. 97.
[165] Indictments Act 1915, s. 3.
[165A] To be explored in chs. 7 and 8.

offence (that is, the name of that particular offence and, if statutory, the statute contravened) and the particulars of the offence (that is, a statement of the facts supporting the accusation). A count of the indictment should not charge the defendant with having committed more than one offence—this will make the indictment bad for 'duplicity'.[166] The rationale is based on the principle of specificity. Fairness requires that any accusation should be clear and specific in order that a defendant is able to answer it[167]—the European Convention talks of informing the accused of the *'nature and cause of the accusation against him'*.[168] An allegation that the defendant has 'shoplifted in Canterbury High Street constantly' is more difficult to counter than one that specifies the time and place of the offence.[169]

Joining together more than one offence or more than one defendant in a single indictment may derogate from the principle of fairness. The accused can be prejudiced by an indictment with several offences, especially where there is evidence that may be admissible on one count but be inadmissible on another. Similarly, evidence may be admissible against one accused but not another. For example, an offender charged with sex offences on small children may be entitled to a judge's direction to the jury to the effect that the evidence from one child is not to be taken into account on the other charge. However fair the judge may be, it is extremely difficult to counter the prejudicial effect of that evidence on the jury.[170] But separate trials for each defendant on each count is not practical and charges for any offences may be joined in the same indictment if those charges are founded on the same facts, or form or are a part of a series of offences of the same or a similar character.[171] The judge does have discretion to 'sever' the indictment and order separate trials, either on the different charges or for different defendants. This often involves difficult decisions as to the relevance and probative weight of the evidence proffered on one charge, especially when balanced against the prejudice it might engender against the accused generally.

The formality and brevity of the modern indictment has been criticised by the Law Commission[172] who felt that there should be more and clearer factual allegations so that the document can act as a 'practical agenda' for the jury in its deliberations. The Runciman Commission also felt that a 'system of particularised indictments would be of benefit to the clearer and more efficient conduct of trials'.[173] The Auld Report recommended that, in trials by judge and jury, the judge, by reference to the case and issues summary, copies of which should be provided to the jury, should give them a fuller introduction to the case than is now conventional.[174]

---

[166] *R. v. Greenfield*, 57 Cr. App. R. 84; *R. v. West* [1948] 1 K.B. 709, 32 Cr. App. R. 152; *R. v. Davey and Davey*, 45 Cr. App. R. 11.
[167] Ashworth A., *Principles of Criminal Law* (3rd ed. 1999) p. 76.
[168] Art. 6(3)(a).
[169] Conspiracy charges often suffer from and can be criticised for this lack of specificity about the precise acts complained of.
[170] Evidence that a defendant has committed other offences or is of bad character is not proof that he has committed this particular offence—Chap. 8.
[171] Indictment Rules 1971, r. 9.
[172] Law Commission: *Counts in an Indictment* (1992).
[173] Royal Commission on Criminal Justice: op. cit. para. 8.5.
[174] op. cit. pp. 518–523.

6.3.3.1 THE CROWN COURT

There is a unified Crown Court with a single administration, which was created by the Courts Act 1971 and which replaced the old system of Quarter Sessions and Assizes which was swept away in the Beeching reforms.[175] Only the Crown Court has the jurisdiction to hear criminal trials on indictment following committal proceedings.[176] There is an alternative to indictment known as a Voluntary Bill of Indictment that means that a High Court judge orders that the accused be tried on indictment.[177] In practice these bills are sought when:

- committal proceedings have been held and the defendant discharged—in which case, the judge is being asked to rule on the correctness of the magistrates' decision;[178] or

- where there are some policy reason why committal proceedings should not be held.[179]

Presiding in the Crown Court is a single 'professional' judge who will be a lawyer of at least ten years' experience. He or she sits with a randomly selected jury. There are different categories of judge:

a) High Court judges: these would normally be attached to the Queen's Bench Division and when in Crown Court would hear only the most serious cases. There are just over 100 High Court judges, of whom there may be up to 20 sitting in the Crown Court at any point.

b) Circuit judges: along with recorders, these handle 95 per cent of the work of the Crown Court. The office was created by the Courts Act 1971. In 2001, there were 574 full-time circuit judges.[180] It is a full time appointment and only barristers of at least ten years standing or recorders who have held the office for at least three years can be appointed. The Beeching Report recommended a mix of criminal work with civil work in the County Court but judges tend to specialise.

c) Recorders: along with circuit judges, these handle the routine work of the Crown Court. They are equivalent to circuit judges but their appointment is only part-time. In 2001 there were 1335 recorders.[181] They can be appointed, not only from the ranks of barristers, but also from solicitors of 10 years' standing. Recorders of 3 years experience can be appointed as circuit judges.

d) The Lord Chancellor may appoint deputy circuit judges and assistant recorders for fixed periods especially when backlogs of cases have arisen.

---

[175] Royal Commission on Assizes and Quarter Sessions (1969) Cmnd. 4135.
[176] Committal proceedings for offences triable only on indictment have now been replaced by direct transfer as a result of section 51 of the Crime and Disorder Act 1998.
[177] 'Practice Direction (Crime: Voluntary Bills)' [1990] 1 W.L.R. 1633.
[178] *Brooks v. DPP* [1994] 1 A.C. 568.
[179] *R. v. DPP, ex p. Moran and others* [1999] 3 *Archbold News* 3 where there was a deliberate attempt to frustrate committal proceedings.
[180] At 1.1.01—*Judicial Statistics 2000*, op. cit. Table 9.1, p. 91.
[181] *Judicial Statistics 2000*, op. cit.—including assistant recorders.

Technically the Crown Court is a single court that sits in 78 permanent and 15 satellite centres around the country These centres are divided into six circuits (Midland and Oxford, North-Eastern, Northern, South-Eastern, Wales and Chester, Western). Each circuit will have a High Court judge as a 'presiding judge'.[182] As far as management is concerned, all judges of the Crown Court are headed by the Lord Chief Justice who is responsible, in consultation with the Lord Chancellor, for their deployment and allocation of judicial work, and for advice on judicial appointments. In exercising these responsibilities, he acts largely through the Senior Presiding Judge for England and Wales, the Presiding Judges of each of the six judicial circuits and the Resident Judges—the latter term applies to the senior circuit judge at the major court centres. Save for those constitutionally important responsibilities and their involvement in a consultative capacity in various bodies concerned with the administration of justice, the judges have no formal role in the management of their courts. Administrative responsibility is exercised through the Courts Service[183] and a Circuit Administrator in each of the circuits heads Court Service staff.

Each centre will be designated as a first, second or third tier centre. The first tier is attended by High Court and such centres will also hear High Court civil work. Second tier centres will have regular visits from High Court judges hearing criminal but not civil work. Third tier centres are not visited by High Court Judges. Circuit judges, Recorders and Assistant Recorders will sit at all three classes of centre.

The jurisdiction of the Crown Court is less varied than the magistrates:

- The major work is hearing criminal trials on indictment, both for offences that are indictable only and for those that are triable 'either way'. The court has exclusive jurisdiction over such trials. There is a wide diversity in the complexity and seriousness of cases and the division of work between High Court judges and circuit judges rests on a Practice Direction by the Lord Chief Justice.[184] By this, offences are divided into four classes:

  a) Class 1 offences (*e.g.*, murder and Official Secrets offences) can only be tried by a High Court judge unless a particular case is released on the authority of the presiding judge to a circuit judge approved by the lord Chief Justice.

  b) Class 2 offences (*e.g.*, other homicides, rape) must be tried by a High Court judge unless a particular case is released by the presiding judge for trial by a circuit judge.

  c) Class 3 offences (those not in the other classes such as aggravated burglary or causing death by reckless driving) may be listed by the listing officer for trial by any category of judge.

  d) Class 4 offences (*e.g.*, all offences triable either way, robbery, serious assaults) will normally not be listed for trial by a High Court judge but will be tried by a circuit judge. This is by far the largest group—87 per cent of committals for trial are for Class 4 offences.

- The work of circuit judges also includes hearing committals for sentence

---

[182] Formalised in Courts and Legal Services Act 1990, s. 20.
[183] www.courtservice.gov.uk/.
[184] The Lord Chief Justice is empowered to make such directions by s. 75 of the Supreme Court Act 1981 and this direction is reported in (1987) 1 W.L.R. 1671.

from the magistrates' court. This occurs where the magistrates have tried a case summarily but have decided that their sentencing powers are insufficient. This area of work has increased significantly because of the introduction of the 'plea before venue' procedure.[185] In 2000, there were 27,591 committals for sentence, double the number in 1997. The judge conducts such hearings sitting with two lay magistrates.

● Circuit judges also hear appeals against conviction or sentence from the magistrates' courts. The judge conducts such hearings sitting with two lay magistrates. In 2000, there were 14,355 appeals against a decision of a magistrates' court disposed of by the Crown Court.

The amount of work going to the Crown Court has fallen over the past ten years—as is shown in Table 6.2, over 100,000 people were committed for trial in the early 1990s but by 2000 this figure had fallen by 30 per cent to just over 70,000. The great increase in Crown Court work has been in the area of committals for sentence.

Table 6.2 Committals for trial, committals for sentence, and appeals: Number of cases received and disposed of, 1989 to 2000[186]

Year	Committals for trial		Committals for sentence		Appeals	
	Receipts	Disposals	Receipts	Disposals	Receipts	Disposals
1989	98,668	101,232	13,718	13,689	17,223	16,860
1990	103,011	100,005	15,270	14,988	17,801	17,557
1991	104,754	101,999	16,554	15,995	19,150	18,433
1992	100,994	100,742	14,883	15,546	20,783	19,765
1993	86,849	85,566	11,088	10,956	24,531	23,722
1994	89,301	86,980	11,485	11,226	25,262	25,644
1995	81,186	88,985	11,718	11,726	25,240	26,062
1996	83,328	83,274	12,002	11,762	18,981	20,304
1997	91,110	90,096	14,871	13,378	16,269	16,196
1998	75,815	77,794	29,774	28,224	16,278	16,473
1999	74,232	73,539	31,928	30,641	15,413	15,381
2000	71,022	72,762	27,591	28,713	13,902	14,359

[185] Magistrates Courts Act 1980, s. 17A.
[186] *Judicial Statistics 2000*, op. cit., Table 6.1, p. 64.

6.3.4 *Waiting Times and Hearing Times*

There is no restriction on the time that may elapse between offence and prosecution although the prosecutor should take the staleness of the offence into consideration when exercising their discretion to prosecute. The CPS Code suggests that a factor against prosecution is where there has been a long delay between the offence taking place and the date of the trial, unless the offence is serious; the delay has been caused in part by the defendant; the offence has only recently come to light; or the complexity of the offence has meant that there has been a long investigation.[187] There are some statutory time limits: for a summary offence the information must be laid within six months of the offence.[188] Apart from these exceptions, legally there is no bar on proceedings for indictable or triable either way offences being commenced at any time.

Considerable delay might be regarded as abuse of process[189] but also Article 6 of the European Convention entitles a person charged with a criminal offence to a 'fair and public hearing within a reasonable time'. This period starts when the accused is charged and finishes when there has been a conviction or acquittal. Reasonableness must be judged on the complexity of the issues, whether other charges are pending, the conduct of the defendant and whether there are valid reasons for delay.[190] In *Howarth v. UK*[191] there was a delay of over two years between an original non-custodial sentence being given and a review under section 36 of the Criminal Justice Act 1988 which resulted in a heavier custodial sentence. This failed to satisfy the 'reasonable time' requirement. The Court found a violation of Article 6 and held that an assessment of the reasonableness of the delay should include an assessment of the conduct of the case authorities.

There are, however, 'custody time limits'. These were introduced[192] experimentally in 1987 but from 1991 have covered the whole country. These limits apply only to defendants held in custody and denied bail. If the prosecution is not started within these limits, the prosecution is not dismissed but the defendant should be released on bail unless the court agrees to an extension. The basic limits are:

a) for summary trial, 56 days from first appearance in magistrates' court to trial. This may be extended to 70 days if the choice of mode of trial has not been made within 56 days.

b) for trial on indictment, 70 days from first appearance to committal and 112 days from committal to arraignment.[193]

---

[187] Code for Crown Prosecutors (CPS 2000) para. 6.5—but the accomplices who aided the escape of George Blake, a Russian spy, were prosecuted (and acquitted) over 25 years later!

[188] Magistrates Court Act 1980, s. 127—for other statutory time limits, see Sprack J., *Emmins on Criminal Procedure* (8th ed. 2000) pp. 73–74.

[189] There is discretion for the examining magistrates to refuse to commit for trial—*R. v. Derby Crown Court, ex parte Brooks* (1984) 70 Crim. App. Rep. 164; *R. v. Grays JJ. ex parte Graham* (1982) Q.B. 1239.

[190] *Portington v. Greece* Application No.28523/95, [1998] HRCD 856.

[191] (2001) 31 E.H.R.R. 37; see also *Darmalingum v. The State* [2000] 2 Cr. App. R. 445 and *Flowers v. The Queen* [2000] 1 W.L.R. 2396.

[192] By the regulations made under s. 22 of the Prosecution of Offences Act 1985.

[193] Arraignment is the start of the Crown Court trial when the clerk reads the indictment to the accused and asks whether there is a plea of guilty or not guilty.

There is still a problem of delay in criminal courts.[194] This is of particular importance for those defendants remanded in custody awaiting trial.

- waiting times of defendants between committal and trial tend to vary according to the plea entered and whether the defendant is on bail or in custody. On average, defendants who pleaded guilty during 2000 waited 10.8 weeks whilst those who pleaded not guilty waited 19.6 weeks. Defendants committed on bail waited an average of 16.0 weeks in 2000 and for those committed in custody the average was 9.8 weeks. Waiting times also vary by circuit: in 2000 the shortest average waiting time was in the Wales and Chester circuit—9.4 weeks—while the longest was 17.1 weeks in the Northern circuit.[195] Such figures do not include the period from first appearance to committal that can add at least 8–10 weeks on to the overall length.

- in 2000 in magistrates courts, it took 108 days on average to process an indictable case from offence to disposal—this was the shortest period since 1986 and was due to less delay between laying the information and the first listing, one of the measures designed to speed up the progress of cases through the system. A summary non-motoring case took 127 days on average while a summary motoring case took 150 days.[196]

Delay may be ascribed to many causes. The lack of urgency and overwork in the Crown Prosecution Service may be one. Decisions by the defence may be another especially where there is a late change of plea from 'not guilty'. The system depends on a high proportion of 'guilty' pleas and changes in that rate affect 'productivity'. But the very organisation of the system induces delays. Aspects of pre-trial procedure are absurdly over-elaborate, especially mode of trial hearings and committal proceedings. A formal system of pre-trial review that would identify the substantial issues between the parties still does not exist. Worst of all is the practice whereby a legally-qualified Crown prosecutor prepares all the factual and legal aspects of a case but, as a result of a wholly unjustified restrictive trade practice, has to transfer responsibility to a barrister in private practice. Many of these were addressed in the Narey Report.[197] The main recommendations were:

- a closer working relationship between the police and the CPS, including the permanent location of prosecutors in police stations—this was intended to speed up cases which end in a guilty plea. At present, these are subject to the same separate procedures as contested cases, and the first court appearance is seldom less than four weeks after charge even in the most straightforward of cases. Narey felt that files could be ready for court within 24 hours, and the defendant convicted the next day. While co-location is happening, it has less effect on delay than anticipated.

---

[194] The position is regarded as 'most unsatisfactory' by the Runciman Commission (*op. cit.* para. 5.53) but the author's discussions with French and German judges would suggest that the position is considerably worse on mainland Europe.
[195] *Judicial Statistics 2000, op. cit.*, p. 70.
[196] *Criminal Statistics 2000, op. cit.*, Table 6.4 p. 146.
[197] *Review of Delay in the Criminal Justice System* (Home Office, 1997); for the evaluation, see www.homeoffice.gov.uk/cpd/pvu/delay1.htm.

- speeding up early administrative hearings—to achieve this Narey suggested that likely guilty plea cases would be listed for hearing the next sitting day after charge, and the abbreviated file would be made available to the duty solicitor, whose services those defendants needing legal advice would generally be expected to use. On the issue of excessive adjournments, the suggestion was that justices' clerks be given additional administrative powers to run early administrative hearings to bring cases to completion more promptly and save on unnecessary witness attendance. The presumption should be that cases would not be put before magistrates until they were ready to proceed, and that they should then proceed to early completion without unnecessary adjournment. The Crime and Disorder Act[198] went some way towards this goal by providing that a defendant's first appearance before a magistrates' court may take the form of an early administrative hearing at which eligibility for legal aid may be determined and arrangements made to obtain it. A single justice or a justices' clerk may conduct such hearings.

- the distribution of business—Narey found that a large majority of defendants electing trial plead guilty at the Crown Court and election for trial was little more than an expensive manipulation of the criminal justice system and not concerned with any wish to establish innocence in front of a jury. The main recommendation was the removal of the automatic defendant veto on the magistrates' decision on mode of trial—although this has not come about, offences triable only on indictment are now sent at the outset to the Crown Court rather than spending considerable time in the magistrates' court.[199] Furthermore the 'plea before venue' procedure (discussed earlier) was introduced in October 1997.

- pre-trial preparation at the Crown Court—Narey recommended that CPS prosecutors should be given rights of audience at plea and directions hearings in the Crown Court. In August 1998, CPS Higher Court Advocates began to present cases in the Crown Court, principally plea and directions hearings and pleas of guilty.

Once a trial in Crown Court begins, in 2000 the average hearing time is 2.6 hours for a not guilty plea and 0.9 hours for a guilty plea. A case where the defendant is committed for sentence takes 0.6 hours while the average hearing time for an appeal is 1 hour.[200]

6.3.5 *Appeals from the Magistrates Court*

The right of appeal is an essential element of any criminal justice system—however it is not enshrined within Article 6 of the European Convention. The review of decisions allows justice to be done to individual defendants, to bring finality to the process and enhance public confidence. But the appellate system in England and Wales is far from straightforward and has mixed and overlapping routes. This is demonstrated by the process of appeal from a magistrates' court: a

---

[198] Crime and Disorder Act 1993, s. 50.
[199] *ibid.*, s. 51.
[200] *Judicial Statistics 2000, op. cit.*, Table 6.21, p. 72.

defendant can appeal in two[201] ways from the decision of a bench of justices:

a) *Crown Court regular.* The defendant can appeal as of right against con-
    viction or sentence. It is only the defendant who has pleaded 'not guilty' or
    who is appealing against sentence that has this right. The defendant who
    has pleaded 'guilty' cannot appeal against conviction unless the plea is
    shown to be equivocal or to be entered under duress.[202] If the defendant
    appeals on the grounds of an equivocal plea, the Crown Court can remit
    the case to the justices for re-hearing on the basis of a 'not guilty' plea. The
    prosecution has no right of appeal against an acquittal.

    The procedure is the same as for summary trial. The appeal takes the form
    of a complete re-hearing of the entire case, calling the original witnesses
    (although additional witnesses may be called) and hearing the legal
    arguments again. The case is heard before a circuit judge or recorder who
    is assisted normally by two J.P.s. They can uphold or quash the conviction
    or vary the sentence, including increasing it but only up to the maximum
    that could have been imposed in the original hearing.[203] After a re-hearing
    in Crown Court, a defendant has a further avenue of appeal on matters of
    law to the Divisional Court of Queen's Bench by way of case stated or by
    judicial review—this is discussed below.

    In 2000, there were 14,355 appeals dealt with by the Crown Court,[204] less
    than 0.01 per cent of all cases heard by magistrates, a very low level. Of
    those appeals, 3,090 (21.5 per cent) were allowed, 4,485 (31 per cent)
    were dismissed, 3,268 (22.7 per cent) were varied and 3,512 (24.5 per
    cent) were abandoned or otherwise disposed of.[205]

b) Divisional Court of Queen's Bench

    > ... any person who was a party to any proceedings before a magistrates' court or
    > is aggrieved by the conviction, order, determination or other proceeding of the
    > court may question the proceeding on the ground that it is wrong in law or in
    > excess of jurisdiction by applying to the [magistrates] to state a case for the
    > opinion of the High Court on the question of law or jurisdiction involved.[206]

    This allows either the prosecution or the defence an appeal by way of 'case
    stated' to the Divisional Court of the Queen's Bench Division. This is an
    ancient jurisdiction by which the Queen's Bench controls the actions and
    decisions of inferior administrative and quasi-judicial bodies. It is a jur-
    isdiction that can be exercised by a single judge or by a Divisional Court
    comprising a Lord Justice and a Queen's Bench Division judge. It is a
    supervisory jurisdiction and this means that there is no rehearing of the
    evidence or the facts of the case. Indeed there is no dispute about the facts

---

[201] A third way is to apply for judicial review (as opposed to appeal) of proceedings in magistrates'
courts, seeking one of the prerogative orders—certiorari, mandamus or prohibition.
[202] This would include cases where the defendant who pleads 'guilty' but at the time or later in the
proceedings mentions matters that would have been the basis of a valid defence—e.g. a guilty plea to
shoplifting followed by '. . . but I thought I'd put it in the basket' or '. . . but my husband threatened
to beat me up'. Emmins C., *op. cit.*, pp. 352–353.
[203] The powers of the Crown Court are defined by s. 48 of the Supreme Court Act 1981.
[204] *Judicial Statistics 2000, op. cit.*, Table 6.13, p. 69.
[205] *ibid.*, Tables 6.14.
[206] Magistrates' Courts Act 1980, s. 111(1); *Practice Direction* [1972] 1 W.L.R. 4.

that are presented to the Divisional Court—the 'statement of the case' from the magistrates' court contains the facts as found by that court. It also contains any questions of law on which the opinion of the court is sought, the parties' contentions and the opinion of the magistrates. Thus no evidence will be called at the hearing, which will consist of legal argument that the magistrates applied the law wrongly, failed to apply it or acted in excess of jurisdiction. In one sense this procedure can overlap with the Crown Court's jurisdiction as the defendant might argue that the finding of fact was one which no reasonable bench could have made—or indeed that the sentence was so far outside normal sentencing limits as to be regarded as an error of law. The court can 'reverse, affirm or amend' the magistrates' decision,[207] replacing the conviction with an acquittal (or *vice versa*), changing or imposing a sentence, remitting the case to the magistrates with a direction to acquit or convict or ordering a retrial.[208] A decision of the Divisional Court may be appealed to the House of Lords.

In 2000 there were 95 appeals from magistrates' courts and 24 appeals from Crown Court by way of case stated received by the Divisional Court. 152 appeals were disposed of—83 were allowed, 65 were dismissed and 4 were withdrawn.[209]

Appeal to the Crown Court and case stated to the Divisional Court are the two main routes of appeal. There is also judicial review by the Divisional Court. These are overlapping, tortuous and with differing procedures and time limits. The Auld Report criticised the right to a re-hearing in the Crown Court, pointing out that the appeal tribunal (with the exception of the judge) was similarly constituted to the tribunal of first instance. The extension of the system of district judges and the improvement in the training of magistrates rendered such a right redundant.[210] Furthermore, a challenge on an issue of law or jurisdiction could arise in the Crown Court or the High Court. The recommendation was that there should be a single channel of appeal from a decision of the magistrates, namely a right of appeal against conviction or sentence to the Crown Court, similar to the grounds that would support an appeal from the Crown Court to the Court of Appeal. A judge sitting alone would hear this. The right to a re-hearing would disappear, as would the appeal by way of case stated or a claim of judicial review.

6.3.6 *Appeals from the Crown Court*

The defendant who has been convicted in the Crown Court or who has been sentenced in the Crown Court after committal from the magistrates' court may appeal against that conviction or sentence to the Criminal Division of the Court of Appeal and, following that, to the Judicial Committee of the House of Lords. Where the defendant has appealed from the magistrates' court to the Crown Court, that decision may be challenged by way of case stated to the Divisional Court of Queen's Bench.

The Auld Report criticised the existence of two routes of appeal and recom-

---

[207] Summary Jurisdiction Act 1857, s. 6.
[208] There is some controversy as to whether the Divisional Court has the power to order a re-trial but it has exercised this power in the past—*Jeffery v. Black* (1978) 1 Q.B. 490.
[209] *Judicial Statistics 2000, op. cit.*, Table 1.14, p. 18.
[210] Auld Report, *op. cit.*, Chap. 12 para. 26.

mended the abolition of the appeal by way of case stated or by a claim of judicial review. In its place would be a single channel of appeal to the Court of Appeal—where that appeal was from the Crown Court sitting as a court of first instance, it would be an appeal as of right against conviction and/or sentence but where it was a challenge to a decision of the Crown Court sitting as an appeal court, the appeal would be subject to the leave of the Court of Appeal which should only be given where there was an important point of law or principle.[211]

6.3.7 *The Criminal Division of the Court of Appeal*

The Court of Appeal (Criminal Division) sits mainly in London although recently it has sat for short periods in other major cities. The Lord Chief Justice acts as its President.[212] In 2002 there were 19 Lords Justices of Appeal as well as 46 High Court judges and 26 circuit judges who sit regularly.[213] It is divided into the civil and criminal divisions. Until 1907 there was no formal appeal court for defendants who wished to appeal against their conviction or sentence.[214] In that year the Court of Criminal Appeal was set up, consisting of the Lord Chief Justice and puisne judges[215] of the Queen's Bench. This jurisdiction was transferred in 1966 to the new Criminal Division of the Court of Appeal.[216] Both Queen's Bench Division judges and circuit judges[217] are still able to sit in the reformed court. The administrative side of the court is under the auspices of the Registrar of Criminal Appeals who must be a lawyer of ten years standing. For hearing appeals, the court normally consists of at least three judges[218] who can hear appeals against conviction and sentence. The Auld Report has suggested that a two-judge court should hear straightforward cases.[219]

The rule of binding precedent is less strictly applied in criminal matters. In *Taylor*,[220] Lord Goddard C.J. said,

'This court however, has to deal with questions involving the liberty of the subject, and if it finds, on reconsideration, that in the opinion of a full court assembled for that purpose the law has been either misapplied or misunderstood in a decision which it has previously given, and that, on the strength of that decision, an accused person has been sentenced and imprisoned it is the bounden duty of the court to reconsider the earlier

---

[211] Auld Report, *op. cit.* Chap. 12 para. 37.

[212] In 2002 this was Lord Woolf.

[213] Auld Report, *op. cit.* Chap. 12 para. 78.

[214] Although from 1848, there was the Court for Crown Cases Reserved designed to hear issues which were specifically reserved for it by judges on assize or by the chairmen of quarter sessions—Radcliffe and Cross, *The English Legal System* (5th ed. 1971) p. 353.

[215] High Court judges are known as 'puisne' judges. It means 'younger' and lesser in rank to the chief justices.

[216] Criminal Appeal Act 1966. The jurisdiction, powers and procedure are now governed by the Criminal Appeal Act 1968 as amended by the Criminal Appeal Act 1995. The membership and composition for different sorts of hearing is governed by the Supreme Court Act 1981.

[217] Criminal Justice and Public Order Act 1994, s. 52.

[218] Five judges occasionally sit—in *Vickers* (1957) 2 Q.B. 664, the old Court of Criminal Appeal sat with five members to decide on the interpretation of s. 1(1) of the Homicide Act 1957. More recently, a five member court laid down guidelines for the receipt of identification evidence in *Turnbull* (1977) Q.B. 224. Where an appeal against conviction is argued before a court of three judges who are not unanimous, there used to be a practice of relisting the appeal for argument de novo before a differently constituted court of five judges. This practice described in *Shama*, 91 Cr. App. R. 138, as 'well-established' has fallen into disuse.

[219] *Auld Report, op. cit.*, Chap. 12 para. 90.

[220] [1950] 2 K.B. 368; *Gould* [1968] 2 Q.B. 65.

decision with a view to seeing whether that person had been properly convicted.'

A defendant can appeal against conviction either with the leave of the Court of Appeal or if the trial judge issues a certificate that the case is fit for appeal.[221] Even where a defendant has pleaded guilty, he or she can appeal against conviction if there has been a misunderstanding as to the nature of the charge or the plea or where on the admitted facts, the defendant could not have been legally convicted of the offence.[222] Before the trial proper starts, it is possible to appeal from rulings made by the judge at a pre-trial hearing.[223]

On conviction, lawyers should not wait to be asked for advice by the defendant but should express a view, final or provisional, as to the prospects of a successful appeal. Where an appeal is advised, the procedure for applying for leave to appeal requires:[224]

a) notice of application for leave to appeal to be served on the Crown Court, along with the grounds on which the appeal is based (though these are provisional at this point). This is forwarded to the Registrar for Criminal Appeals.

b) the Registrar may either: refer it to the Court for summary dismissal, without a hearing[225] if the notice shows no substantial grounds; or directly to a full court for an expedited hearing; or normally he will refer it to the 'single judge'.[226]

c) the appellant can request a transcript of those parts of the original trial that are deemed necessary. This is usually the charges, summing up and relevant parts of the evidence. With this transcript, counsel (or the applicant in person) can redraft the grounds of appeal and these will be put in front of a single judge of the Court of Appeal—in the Criminal Division, this will often be a puisne judge.

d) the single judge, on consideration of the papers, will grant or refuse leave to appeal, along with ancillary matters such as bail or legal aid. If the application is refused, the application can be renewed in front of the whole court. In 2000, 28 per cent of those initially rejected, renewed their application and approximately 30 per cent of these were granted by the full court. Even where it is renewed, the case is normally decided without argument and on the papers.

e) where the appeal is of right or leave is granted, there will be a hearing in front of the full court. The appellant will normally be represented and, if in

---

[221] Criminal Appeal Act 1968 s. 1 as amended by the Criminal Appeal Act 1995. The trial judge's certificate is granted very rarely—in 1986, 10 appellants out of 1846 had such a certificate.
[222] Avory J. in *Forde* (1923) 2 K.B. 400. Thus in *Clarke* (1972) 1 All E.R. 219, the defendant pleaded guilty to shoplifting, having been told that her defence of lack of mens rea due to depression was a plea of insanity! Her conviction was quashed on appeal, despite the plea of guilty.
[223] Criminal Procedure and Investigations Act 1996, s. 35.
[224] The Registrar has issued 'A Guide to Proceedings in the Court of Appeal, Criminal Division' (1997) which is available through the Courts Service website: www.courtservice.gov.uk.
[225] Criminal Appeal Act 1968, s. 20.
[226] *ibid.*, s. 31. Faced with 7574 applications for leave to appeal between April 2000 and March 2001, the Court of Appeal would be faced with an unmanageable task without this procedure. See the Auld Report *op. cit.* Chap. 12 para. 37ff and also Malleson K., *A Review of the Appeal Process*, Royal Commission on Criminal Justice Research Series No. 17 (HMSO 1993).

custody, has a right[227] to be present unless the appeal involves an issue of law alone. If the appeal is against conviction (but not if it is against sentence) the Crown will also be represented.

Table 6.3: Court of Appeal (Criminal Division): Summary of results of appeals and applications during 2000[228]

	Appeal against conviction	Appeal against sentence	Total
Received	2,068	5,672	7,740
Allowed by single judge	508	1,597	2,105
Dismissed by single judge	1,351	3,892	5,243
Applications* for leave to appeal against conviction renewed	551	932	1,483
Granted	144	291	453
Refused	407	641	1,048
Appeals heard by the full court	483	1,806	2,289
Allowed	150	1,284	1,434
Dismissed	333	522	855
Re-trials ordered	72	na	72

*These are renewed applications to the Full Court following refusal by the Single Judge

Over 20 per cent of those convicted after a 'not guilty' plea appeal against that conviction. In 2000, there were such 9,682 convictions at Crown Court. In the same year, 2,068 appealed against conviction, although the figures are not directly comparable. Only 150 of these were ultimately successful—although this is nearly 30 per cent of those heard by the full court—and 72 then faced a re-trial. In the early 1990s it was not uncommon for there to be a two-year wait for an appeal against conviction to be heard. Currently the average waiting time is between eight and nine months.

Fewer than 7 per cent of those convicted appeal against sentence. In 2000, there were some 85,000 sentenced in the Crown Court, either after conviction or after committal for sentence. 5672 appeals against sentence were received—again the figures are not directly comparable. 1434 of these were successful—a quarter of all those who appealed and two thirds of those heard by the full court.[229] A decade ago it was not uncommon for there to be a 15-month wait for an appeal

---

[227] Criminal Appeal Act 1968, s. 22.
[228] *Judicial Statistics 2000, op. cit.*, Tables 1.7 and 1.8 p. 12–13.
[229] *Auld Report, op. cit.*, Chap. 12 para. 99 suggests that the court should draw back from its tendency to 'tinker' with sentences.

against sentence to be heard. Currently the average waiting time is about five months. By section 11(3) of the Criminal Appeal Act 1968, the Court does not have the power to increase sentences—the court can quash any sentence and replace it with the sentence that it sees fit, provided that it is one that would have been within the power of the Crown Court and that the accused is not dealt with overall more severely than he or she was by the Crown Court. But the court does have the power to direct that the time spent in custody between the commencement and the hearing of an appeal shall not count towards service of a custodial sentence.[230] Even the fact that an application for leave to appeal against conviction or sentence is made on the advice of counsel will not prevent an order for loss of time. This is supposed to have the effect of discouraging unmeritorious appeals[231] but this is rarely exercised. In practice the maximum period lost is 28 days. The Runciman Commission recommended an increase in the deterrent effect of this 'time-loss' rule so that the maximum should be 90 days.[232]

At the appeal the defendant will invariably be legally represented. Legal advice should have been available immediately after the conviction and the defendant's legal representative should offer at least provisional advice on the possibility of appeal,[233] which has to be within 28 days from the date of conviction or sentence.[234] Plotnikoff and Woolfson[235] found serious defects in the pattern of provision with 9 per cent of prisoners not visited in the cells, 23 per cent not being advised about appeal and nearly 90 per cent not receiving anything in writing about an appeal. Lawyers often were ill informed about the powers of the Court of Appeal, believing, for example, that they had the power to increase sentences. Applicants who sought to appeal without the benefit of legal advice were, not surprisingly, less successful.[236]

Section 2 of the Criminal Appeal Act 1968 specified several criteria for overturning a conviction—that the conviction was *unsafe or unsatisfactory*, that there had been a *wrong decision on any question of law* or that there was *a material irregularity in the course of the trial*. Even when one of these had been established by the appellant, there was a proviso: the court could dismiss an appeal, even though they find the point of law to be in the appellant's favour, if they feel that no miscarriage of justice has occurred. The Runciman Commission highlighted this section as contributing to the weakness of the Court of Appeal's performance. They considered the paragraphs of section 2 over-complex and overlapping. The Report recommended a straightforward test of whether the conviction '*is or may be unsafe*'. Such phrasing was felt to make the proviso redundant.[237] If the Court feels that the conviction is unsafe, the conviction should be quashed. If it may be unsafe, a new trial should be ordered. The Commission felt that retrials should be used more extensively.

The grounds on which an appeal may be based were changed by section 2 of

---

[230] '*Practice Direction (Crime: Sentence: Loss of Time)*' [1980] 1 W.L.R. 270.
[231] Criminal Appeal Act 1968, s. 29—this was challenged (unsuccessfully) in the European Court of Human Rights in *Monnell and Morris v. UK* (1988) 10 E.H.R.R. 205.
[232] Royal Commission on Criminal Justice, *op. cit.*, para. 10.26.
[233] Bar Council, *The Crown Court—A Guide to Good Practice*.
[234] Criminal Appeal Act 1968, s. 18 (2).
[235] Plotnikoff J. and Woolfson R., *Information and Advice for Prisoners about Grounds for Appeal and the Appeal Process*, Royal Commission on Criminal Justice Research Series No. 18 (HMSO 1993).
[236] Malleson, *op. cit.*; Royal Commission on Criminal Justice, *op. cit.*, para. 10.9ff. argues for more legal advice for appellants.
[237] Royal Commission on Criminal Justice, *op. cit.*, para. 10.32.

the Criminal Appeals Act 1995, amending the 1968 legislation. By this provision, the Court of Appeal shall allow an appeal against conviction if they think that the conviction is unsafe and shall dismissal an appeal in any other case. The appellant must establish that the conviction should be quashed according to the sole criterion that it was 'unsafe'. The old proviso no longer exists.

The 'safety' of a conviction is a difficult concept. The court's practice is not to review the evidence in order to substitute their judgment for that of the jury. It is not a re-hearing of the case. Obviously an 'unsafe conviction' exists where the judge has made an error, in explaining the law to the jury, in allowing the introduction of inadmissible evidence or in some other significant procedural fashion. At the appeal hearing, the burden of proof is cast on the appellant to establish that the conviction was unsafe. The standard of proof that must be reached appears to be low. Lord Widgery suggested that the court should set aside a verdict if there was a 'lurking doubt' in the minds of its members as to whether an injustice had been done.[238] And yet for the appellant to create the necessary doubt appears quite a difficult task and the court frequently takes the view that what appears a flimsy prosecution when looked at through the case papers might well have appeared strong to a jury who had the opportunity to hear and assess the witnesses.

Prior to 1995, the court possessed a discretionary power to receive fresh evidence under section 23 of the 1968 legislation. This was exercised rarely—the Runciman Commission[239] saw the powers as adequate but judged the Court's interpretation of them to be too narrow and recommended that they should take a more flexible approach. In 1995 the Criminal Appeal Act sought to liberalise this practice. The Court must have regard to whether the evidence appears to be capable of belief, to afford any ground for allowing the appeal, to be admissible and whether there was a reasonable explanation for the failure to adduce the evidence in those proceedings. The extent to which this has changed the practice remains moot.[240] The court is free to assess the evidence as it sees fit—there is no rule of law in a fresh evidence case that requires the court to assess what the jury might have done if they had heard the fresh evidence. Such an approach would be reasonable and if the conclusion is that the jury might have come to a different verdict had they heard the evidence, it follows that the conviction is unsafe.[241]

It has been suggested that the change in wording has not brought about any change in practice but in *Chalkley*[242] the Court of Appeal accepted that the omission of the word 'unsatisfactory' had changed the law, and held that a conviction would not be liable to be quashed on account only of procedural irregularity, or abuse of process or a failure of justice to be done. Thus suggests a potential conflict with Article 6, which requires a court to look, not only at the safety of a conviction but at the fairness of the proceedings. European jurisprudence requires the Court of Appeal must directly address the issue of the fairness of the proceedings. In *Condron v. UK*[243] the judge directed the jury that they might draw adverse inferences from the accused's failure to answer police questions. The Court of Appeal had regarded this as a significant defect but held

[238] *Cooper* (1969) 1 Q.B. 267 at 271.
[239] Royal Commission on Criminal Justice, *op. cit.*, para. 10.51ff.
[240] Criminal Appeal Act 1995, s. 4; *Gilfoyle* [1996] 1 Cr. App. R. 302.
[241] *Pendleton* [2002] 1 All E.R. 524.
[242] [1998] 2 Cr. App. R. 79.
[243] *Application No.* 35718/97, (2001) 31 E.H.R.R. 1, [2000] Crim. L.R. 679.

that, given the weight of the prosecution evidence, the conviction was safe. The European Court of Human Rights stated that both trial and appellate judges must inquire into overall fairness and the finding that a conviction is safe is not a substitute for such an inquiry. This significant point must raise serious questions about section 2 of the Criminal Appeal Act 1995—that it is not compatible with the court's obligations under the Convention.

But the Strasbourg decisions are somewhat contradictory. In contrast to the judgment in *Condron* is the Court's decision in *Khan v. UK*[244] where the police entered a house as trespassers, planted a listening device and obtained incriminating recordings. The key issue was the fairness of proceedings and whether the recordings should have been admitted into evidence. The Court had no difficulty in finding that this was a breach of Article 8 but went on to rule that, despite the fact that the recording was the sole evidence against the accused, there was no violation of the right to a fair trial.

The 'safety' versus 'fairness' debate creates difficulties. Are the two ideas related? Presumably fairness is the primary value—the State has a dominant position that it must be prevented from abusing by ensuring that its agents observe the rule of law. This is an aspect of the doctrine beloved by the Strasbourg Court of equality of arms and where the disputed evidence is the only evidence, the State, by its breach of the Convention, has irredeemably altered that equality. Parity and fairness can only be achieved by refusing to allow the State to rely on evidence obtained by abuse of power, however compelling that evidence may be. Recently in *Togher*[245] the accused had pleaded guilty and yet the Court of Appeal said *obiter* that a conviction should be liable to be quashed on the ground of abuse of process even after a plea of guilty where the appellant had been unable to apply for a stay at trial because the facts constituting the abuse had not been disclosed by the prosecution, contrary to their duty of disclosure.

If the appeal is successful, the court can quash the conviction.[246] Another option for the Court of Appeal is to order a re-trial. Under section 7 of the Criminal Appeal Act 1968, the court could only order a re-trial where they had allowed an appeal on the basis of fresh evidence. The Criminal Justice Act 1988[247] now gives much greater discretion to the court to decide whether to order a re-trial or not. The Runciman Commission felt that there should be more use of re-trials—the number has been growing from 3 in 1990 to 72 in 2000.[248]

6.3.8 *The Court of Appeal and Miscarriages of Justice*

Wrongful convictions[249] can stem from police malpractice, from the prosecution withholding evidence, from trial judge bias, from faulty forensic evidence. It is the job of the Court of Appeal to ensure that such errors are rectified. They have

---

[244] *Application No. 35394/97*, [2000] Crim. L.R. 684 (2000), [2000] H.R.C.D. 249.
[245] [2001] 3 All E.R. 463.
[246] Criminal Appeal Act 1968, s. 2(2).
[247] s. 43.
[248] Royal Commission on Criminal Justice, *op. cit.*, para. 10.64; *Judicial Statistics 2000*, *op. cit.*, Table 1.8, p. 13.
[249] Greer S., '*Miscarriages of Justice Reconsidered*' 57 M.L.R. p. 58 (1994).

proved inadequate for this task.[250] In the past the Court has been obdurate in upholding convictions even when cases were referred back by the Home Secretary.[251] *Cooper and McMahon*[252] involved the murder of a Luton postmaster in the 1970s. They and a third man were convicted on the uncorroborated evidence of an accomplice. The accomplice was later shown to have been lying in the case of the third man but the Court still insisted that his evidence in relation to Cooper and McMahon was reliable. It was referred back to the Court of Appeal four times before eventually the Home Secretary had to remit the remainder of the sentences.[253]

In the 1980s there was growing anxiety about the performance of the Court of Appeal. Again and again cases have had to be referred back to the court by the Home Secretary.[254] The Birmingham Six originally appealed in 1976. The Home Secretary referred the case in 1987 and the appeals dismissed. Referred again in 1990, the DPP decided not to resist the appeal, thus pre-empting the court. However the court went ahead with the hearing and quashed the convictions in 1991.[255] The 'fresh' evidence concerned the police methods of interrogation and the quality of the forensic evidence. In its essentials, that evidence had been heard by the court in 1987 but at that time the convictions were still upheld. It is hard to understand why the Lord Chief Justice, Lord Lane, and his colleagues were unable to discover a 'lurking doubt' that was patently obvious to everyone.[256]

In 1985, the murder of P.C. Blakelock at Broadwater Farm in North London was committed by a group of perhaps 30 people. Six persons went on trial, including Winston Silcott who was alleged to be the leader of the attack. The judge excluded confession evidence against three defendants and directed their acquittal. The other three were convicted, including Silcott although the sole evidence against him was unverified police evidence that he had made an incriminating statement ('You won't pin this on me ... nobody will talk'). Silcott had not signed this statement and denied making it. There was no identification evidence, no forensic evidence nor admissible evidence from alleged accomplices. Yet initially the court upheld the conviction feeling that presumably it was 'safe and satisfactory'.[257]

It is apparent that the Court of Appeal give due account to the fairness of the procedures at the trial. Malleson's study[258] showed that 80 per cent of successful appeals were on the basis of a wrong decision on the admissibility of evidence or alleged misdirection by the judge. Furthermore they have shown greater will-

---

[250] Thornton P., *et al.*, *Justice on Trial: Report of the Independent Civil Liberty Panel on Criminal Justice* (Civil Liberties Trust 1992): Woffinden B., *Miscarriages of Justice* (Coronet 2nd ed. 1989); Zuckerman A., 'Miscarriages of Justice and Judicial Responsibility', (1991) Crim L.R. 492; Zuckerman A., 'Miscarriages of Justice: A Root Treatment' (1992) Crim. L.R. 323; Buxton R., 'Miscarriages of Justice and the Court of Appeal', (1993) L.Q.R.

[251] Criminal Appeal Act 1968, s. 17—there was rarely a reference back without compelling reasons. This power was repealed by the Criminal Justice Act 1995 which established the Criminal Cases Review Commission.

[252] (1975) 61 Cr. App. R. 215.

[253] For the full story, see Woffinden, *op. cit.*, p. 171.

[254] In 1989–92, 28 cases involving 49 appellants had been referred, a sharp rise over the average of 5 cases a year since 1968.

[255] *McIlkenny* (1992) 2 A.E.R. 417.

[256] For a disturbing account of this case, see Mullin C., *Error of Judgement* (revised ed. 1989).

[257] The conviction was eventually overturned—*The Times*, December 9, 1991.

[258] Malleson, *op. cit.*; Royal Commission on Criminal Justice, *op. cit.*, para. 10.35 ff.

ingness to deal with pre-trial malpractice.[259] Despite this there has recently been substantial injustice. It is difficult to isolate the factors that seem to lead the court to such results:

a) the legal system has always placed considerable faith in jury verdicts, has been unwilling to lift the veil on how they are arrived at or to interfere with them.[260] If the jury has reached its verdict having heard all the relevant evidence and with no material irregularities, the Court of Appeal has been unwilling to substitute their verdict for that of a jury who have seen and heard the witnesses. However this has often placed too great a value on the truth-revealing qualities of the adversarial forum. There has been an unwillingness to accept that an analysis of the evidence, away from the emotion of the trial, often reveals its circumstantial nature and its true probative value.

b) until recently the prevailing belief, judicial and non-judicial, has been to take identification evidence and confessions at their face value. Jurors will still accord considerable weight to these items of evidence. Courts do not stress the need for independent supportive evidence.

c) although the standard of proof required is proof beyond reasonable doubt, this barrier seems somewhat easy to cross and the appellate courts pay little attention to the sheer lack of weight of the evidence against defendants. In a conspiracy to murder case in 1988, the evidence included driving licences in false names, a list of prominent public figures, a second-hand car, a radio and a woolly hat. This scarcely compelled the conclusion that the accused had plotted to kill. In this case, the Appeal Court freed the accused in 1990.[261]

d) as discussed earlier, although the court has a discretion to receive fresh evidence, it has been reluctant to receive fresh evidence, seeing decisions as to the facts as the jury's function and unwilling to turn a process of review into a form of rehearing.

e) finally the Court of Appeal appear to give considerable weight to maintaining public confidence in the police, the courts and the criminal justice system as a whole over and above those of justice in the individual case.

The Runciman Commission highlighted two weaknesses of the Court of Appeal's performance, the first being technical and the second cultural. The technical issue was the drafting of section 2 of the Criminal Appeal Act 1968 as was discussed earlier. The cultural problem was that the Court should be willing to substitute its judgment for that of the jury. In reaching its verdict, the jury can err in assessing the true probative weight of circumstantial evidence, of confessions, of accomplices, of unverified police statements, especially in the publicity spotlight and emotion generated by terrorist and other high profile cases. What is required is recognition by the Court that there are cases where the evidence

---

[259] Especially where there have been breaches of PACE Codes of Practice—*supra* para. 3.8.7.2 ff; Royal Commission on Criminal Justice, *op. cit.*, para. 10.47ff.
[260] Royal Commission on Criminal Justice, *op. cit.*, para. 10.40ff.
[261] Woffinden R., '*The Case of the Winchester Three*', 140 *New Law Journal* (1990) p. 164.

advanced does not reach the standard of proof required and a willingness to intervene.

6.3.9 *The Criminal Cases Review Commission*

The Runciman Commission rightly felt that its recommendations on fine-tuning aspects of the Court of Appeal were unlikely to ensure that wrongful convictions would always be rectified.[262] What was often required is the ability to instigate and supervise further investigation, a function which is ill-suited to a court. At the time of the Royal Commission the Home Secretary could refer cases to the Court under section 17 of the Criminal Appeal Act 1968. The relevant Home Office department attracted considerable criticism over its record—in 1990, the division was asked to sift some 790 cases of alleged miscarriages of justice but between 1989 and 1992, the Home Secretary's power to refer back was used on only 28 occasions. Applicants were given the barest of information why their application had been turned down. However this practice was ended by the High Court in *Hickey*[263] so that applicants had to be given both reasons for the refusal and disclosure of any new evidence that had emerged.

The Runciman Commission recommended that an independent Criminal Cases Review Authority[264] be set up which would take over this work and be responsible for referring cases back to the Court of Appeal. The body was set up by Part II of the Criminal Appeal Act 1995 and it commenced work in 1997.[265] It deals with miscarriages of justice in summary cases as well as those triable on indictment, and refers them to the appropriate court where it considers that there is a 'real possibility' that a conviction would not be upheld. It is an investigative body and reports to the Court of Appeal on any matter in an appeal referred to it by the Court.[266] It also advises the Secretary of State on the exercise of the Queen's prerogative of mercy. There have been an enormous number of applications following its establishment—it had received 3,995 applications by March 31 2001.These consisted of 279 transfers from the Home Office and Northern Ireland Office, 1,103 new cases in 1997–98, 1,037 in 1998–99, 777 in 1999–2000 and 799 in 2000–01. There was an initial surge of new cases after March 31 1997, when the Commission assumed responsibility for casework. More recently, the annual intake has been roughly 800 cases. By the end of 2001, it had referred 128 cases to the Court of Appeal, over 65 of which the Court has considered and, in 47 cases, quashed the conviction or reduced the sentence.[267]

---

[262] The BBC's series *Rough Justice* publicised worrying cases. The Carl Bridgewater killing is one see as well as the 1977 'torso' murder case—Greer, *op. cit.*, p. 71, *fn.60*.
[263] *The Guardian*, November 29, 1994, p. 1.
[264] Royal Commission on Criminal Justice, *op. cit.*, Chap. 11; Thornton P., *'Miscarriages of Justices: A Lost Opportunity'* (1993) Crim. L.R. 926.
[265] www.ccrc.gov.uk/.
[266] Criminal Appeal Act 1995, s. 5.
[267] Auld Report, *op. cit.*, Chap. 12, para. 105.

6.3.10 *Appeals Against Acquittal*

Generally the prosecution has no right to appeal against conviction or sentence on acquittal.[268] There are a series of mechanisms that give the prosecution a limited right of appeal:

a) **Case stated**—the prosecution can appeal on a point of law by way of case stated to the Divisional Court of Queen's Bench either from a summary acquittal or from a successful appeal to the Crown Court following a summary conviction. This can have the effect of remitting the case to the justices for re-trial.

b) **Pre-trial hearings**—in serious fraud or long and complex cases, there are pre-trial hearings and both parties can appeal against adverse findings on such matters as admissibility of evidence.[269]

c) **Tainted acquittals**—there is a right of appeal where a person has been convicted of intimidating or interfering with a juror or witness in another trial and that interference has led to an acquittal.[270] This followed a recommendation by the Runciman Commission that there should be the possibility of an appeal and a retrial where the jury can be shown to have been bribed or intimidated. The Commission did not recommend such a course in cases of a 'perverse' acquittal or in situations where the accused is convicted because of a mistake by a prosecution witness.[271] This has never been used.

d) **Attorney-General's Reference**: introduced in 1972 by section 36 of the Criminal Justice Act, this permits the Attorney-General to refer to the Court of Appeal any point of law even though it arose in a case where the defendant has been acquitted. However this does not affect the status of the original verdict and the defendant remains acquitted. It is infrequently used—the first reference was made in 1974. In the 25 years since then, there have been a total of 41. There are no reported references for some years (for instance, 1993 and 1997). In 1995 there were two; in 1996, one; and three for each of 1998 and 1999.

e) **'unduly lenient sentences'**: where a defendant has been convicted but in the eyes of the prosecution has been given an 'unduly lenient' sentence, the Attorney-General may refer that sentence to the Court of Appeal who may quash the sentence and substitute a more appropriate sentence which they see fit and which the court below had the power to impose.[272] The provision applies to sentences passed for offences triable only on indictment

---

[268] The prosecution can appeal on a point of law by way of case stated to the Divisional Court of Queen's Bench either from a summary acquittal or from a successful appeal to the Crown Court following a summary conviction—s. 111 of the Magistrates' Courts Act 1980.

[269] Criminal Justice Act 1987, s. 9(11), Criminal Procedure and Investigations Act 1996, s. 35(1). This is discussed in Law Commission Report No. 267, 'Double Jeopardy and Prosecution Appeals' (2001) para. 2.32 ff.

[270] Criminal Procedure and Investigations Act 1996, ss. 54–57.

[271] Royal Commission on Criminal Justice, *op. cit.*, para. 10.72ff.

[272] Criminal Justice Act 1988, ss. 35–36; SC Shute. *'Who Passes Unduly Lenient Sentences? How Were They Listed?: A Survey of Attorney General's Reference Cases, 1989–1997'* [1999] Crim. L.R. 603.

and such other offences or 'descriptions' of case as may be specified by order. This order-making power has been used to apply the provisions to matters such as the smuggling of drugs and indecent or obscene material; the production, cultivation or supply of controlled drugs; indecent assault; unlawful sexual intercourse with a girl under 16 and serious fraud cases.[273] The figures available for 1999 are that, of 78 references, the sentence was increased in 55 cases (70.5%).

Although the Runciman Commission rejected the idea of a general right of appeal for the prosecution, the MacPherson Report into the death of Steven Lawrence[274] suggested that *'consideration should be given to the Court of Appeal being given power to permit prosecution after acquittal where fresh and viable evidence is presented.'*[275] The Law Commission proposed[276] giving the Court of Appeal power to set aside an acquittal where there is apparently reliable and compelling new evidence of guilt but for murder It also recommended that the prosecution should, in some circumstances, be able to appeal rulings before trial, during the hearing of the prosecution case and of no case to answer as well as other 'terminating rulings'. The government has welcomed these recommendations.[277] The double jeopardy rule, following in the footsteps of the right to silence, is to be significantly limited. It is argued that the European Convention protects the rights of defendants who have been 'finally' acquitted in accordance with the law and that this does not preclude the re-opening of cases in exceptional circumstances.[278] The Auld Report would go further and allow a prosecution right of appeal where the jury verdict was seen as 'perverse'.[279]

The government has accepted many of these suggestions. In 2002, the White Paper, 'Justice for All'[279A] proposes that the Court of Appeal should have the power to quash acquittals in serious cases where there is compelling new evidence of guilt. There would then be a re-trial. Furthermore there is a proposal that the prosecution be given a right of appeal against a judge's ruling that effectively terminates the case.[279B]

6.3.11 *The House of Lords*

This is not the legislative body acting as a whole but merely the Judicial Committee of the House of Lords. It is the supreme appellate court. It deals with little criminal work—from 1998–2000, it dealt with ten criminal appeals only. House of Lords judges are senior judges who have been given honorific titles for life,

---

[273] Criminal Justice Act 1988 (Reviews of Sentencing) Order 1994 (S.I. 1994 No. 119); Criminal Justice Act 1988 (Reviews of Sentencing) Order 1995 (S.I. 1995 No. 10); Criminal Justice Act 1988 (Reviews of Sentencing) Order 2000 (S.I. 2000 No. 1924).
[274] *The Stephen Lawrence Inquiry: Report of an Inquiry by Sir William* (1999) Cm. 4262.
[275] *ibid.*, Recommendation 38.
[276] Law Commission Report No. 267, *op. cit.*
[277] Home Office, *Criminal Justice: The Way Ahead* (2001) Cm. 5074 paras 3.53–3.56; also see the Auld Report, *op. cit.*, Chap. 12 paras 47–65.
[278] Pattenden R., 'Prosecution Appeals' [2000] Crim. L.R. 971.
[279] Auld Report, *op. cit.* Chap. 12 paras 66–67.
[279A] Cm. 5563 para. 4.63.
[279B] *ibid.* para. 4.68.

entitling them to sit as members of the House of Lords but really to form the membership of this committee. A House of Lords panel will consist of five of such judges. Appeals from the Court of Appeal must involve a point of law of general public importance. The procedure involves the Court of Appeal certifying that it is a point of general public importance. Either the Court of Appeal or the House of Lords must give leave for the appeal to take place.

6.3.12 *Pardons*

After all these appeals have been exhausted, then the defendant can apply to the Home Secretary for a pardon[280] which is granted by the Crown under the royal prerogative of mercy. This is rarely used after convictions on indictment since the Home Secretary may refer to the Criminal Cases Review Commission any such matter. Similarly the Commission may refer cases to the Secretary of State for consideration.[281] No such matters were referred in 2000–2001.

6.3.13 *The European Court of Human Rights*

There are also the remedies through the European Court of Human Rights.[282] The basis of any individual application to the Court is that a State has acted in breach of its obligations under the Convention. A judgment upholding such an application does not overturn a domestic judgment or invalidate government action. It remains for the government to amend the domestic law so that it is compatible with the European Convention on Human Rights. Mostly the government does pass amending legislation.

To an extent applications to Strasbourg will become less significant with the passage of the Human Rights Act 1998. Although this does not make the European Convention part of English law, it obliges public authorities to act in a manner, which is compatible with Convention rights.[283] Furthermore it requires courts to give effect to all primary and subordinate legislation in a way that is compatible with Convention rights, if this is possible. If it is not possible, a superior court may make a 'declaration of incompatibility'. Furthermore courts must take account, not merely of the Convention itself, but of the body of jurisprudence that has been built up through the decisions of the European Court of Human Rights. But it is still a matter for the government to amend the law—or not! The impact of this for the criminal justice system is considerable—the guarantees against humiliating and degrading treatment, against loss of liberty, of a fair trial or respect for privacy have implications for the legislature, for the police and for the courts. These are considered in detail in the relevant sections.

---

[280] The effect of the pardon is to free the person from the imposed penalties. The conviction still stands until it is quashed by the Court of Appeal.
[281] ss. 15–16 of the Criminal Appeal Act 1995.
[282] Cheney D. *et al.*, *Criminal Justice and the Human Rights Act* (2nd ed. 2001).
[283] Human Rights Act 1998, s. 6.

7.1 SETTING THE SCENE FOR TRIAL

Proceedings against an accused start with his or her appearance in the magistrates' court. This will be as a result of:

a) the accused being arrested by the police and either being brought to the court in police custody or being bailed by the police to appear at court.

b) the prosecutor laying an information[1] before the magistrates which results either in the issue of a summons to attend the court or the issue of a warrant for arrest.

The whole process may be concluded in the magistrates' court—a minor case with a guilty plea may be heard and determined by the justices at this point. However, a case of any complexity is likely to be adjourned, especially if it is to be contested. Before the trial, there are further preliminary issues to be considered—whether the accused is to await trial in custody or at liberty; whether the accused is legally represented; the extent to which the prosecution (and the defence) will disclose their evidence and arguments before trial; whether there are to be preliminary hearings of any kind.

7.2 THE REMAND DECISION

An early decision will have to be taken about the liberty of the accused. If the case

---

[1] All information must be laid by a named and identified informant, with brief particulars of the offence and the statutory provision contravened.

is disposed of quickly or is minor, this is not a problem. In other cases, the police or the court will have to decide whether to remand on bail or in custody. The phrase 'remand on bail' indicates that the accused has been released and will surrender to the custody of the court for the trial. If bail is not granted, the defendant is 'remanded in custody'—in other words, he or she is sent to prison to await trial.

Where a defendant has been arrested with or without a warrant, his or her personal liberty has been curtailed. It can only be restored by a decision of the police or the courts to release on bail. Technically the person on bail remains under arrest but is under a duty to surrender to custody at an appointed time and place. Release, even under conditions, is important, both personally and for purposes of employment but also for the greater ease that the accused has in preparing a defence. Furthermore, conditions for those held in remand prisons are among the worst in the penal system.

Bail can be granted by a court or police officer in the following situations:

a)   if the suspect is in police custody but has not been charged, the custody officer can release on bail either unconditionally or on a condition to report back to the police station or under the normal conditions of bail under section 3 of the Bail Act 1976.[2]

b)   if the suspect is in police custody and has been charged, the custody officer can detain the suspect and take him or her before the court. However the officer has the power[3] to release on bail subject to the condition that the suspect appears before the magistrates' court on a certain date. The police can impose other conditions.[4]

c)   where the suspect has been arrested by magistrate's warrant, this warrant may already have the terms of bail endorsed on it—it is 'backed for bail'.[5]

d)   where the accused is brought from the police station to the magistrates' court, the court may hear the case at that point but this is relatively uncommon.[6] Normally the hearing is adjourned prior to a summary trial or committal proceedings but there will be a remand hearing. The accused will either be remanded on bail or in custody during this period. The Bail Act 1976 provides that a defendant should be granted bail unless the prosecution show that one of the exceptions under Schedule 1 applies— these would require that the prosecution shows that the accused is likely to abscond, commit a further offence, interfere with witnesses or otherwise obstruct the course of justice.[7] The 1976 legislation has been amended several times—for example, section 25 of the Criminal Justice and Public

---

[2] s. 37(2) and s. 40(8) of PACE 1984. This is known as DCB—'deferred charge, bail'.
[3] *ibid.*, s. 38 as amended by s. 28 of the Criminal Justice and Public Order Act 1994—this also specifies the situations where bail may not be granted: that the name and address of the suspect cannot be ascertained, that custody is necessary to prevent harm to others or that there are reasonable grounds for believing that the suspect will not answer to bail.
[4] s. 27, Criminal Justice and Public Order Act 1994.
[5] s. 117, Magistrates Courts Act 1980.
[6] 25% (22% in 1990) of defendants charged with indictable offences are dealt with on first appearance in magistrates' courts. On average cases are listed 3.3 times. 70% of those charged with summary non-motoring offences are dealt with at that time—*Criminal Statistics 2000* Cm. 5312 Table 6.4, p. 146.
[7] s. 4, Bail Act 1976.

Order Act 1994 prohibits the granting of bail to defendants accused of rape or murder if they have previously been convicted of one of those offences. Furthermore, section 26 gives magistrates the right to refuse bail if it appeared to them that the offence was committed while the accused was on bail for a previous crime.

The court not only has to give reasons for withholding bail but also must give reasons for granting it in relation to certain serious offences. Where bail is granted, it can be subject to conditions: the court may require that the defendant provide security of some form to guarantee that he or she will surrender to custody for trial; other conditions may involve surrender of passport or agreement not to go near certain areas or persons.

For many years the court could initially remand in custody for no longer than eight days and thus the defendant had to be brought to court each week.[8] As the accused has only limited rights to make repeated bail applications, such constant trips from prison to court had little purpose. The Criminal Justice Act 1982 permitted defendants to be remanded in custody for up to a month without attending court as long as they consented but even in these circumstances the case would still need to be formally listed each week. In 1988 the Criminal Justice Act went further and permitted remands in custody for up to 28 days whether or not the accused consents.[9] This only applies, not at the original hearing, but only at the second or subsequent remand hearing. The power has been available for all magistrates' courts since 1991. But the courts must be aware of the custody time limits introduced in 1985 and discussed earlier.

The defendant has only a limited right to make repeated argued bail applications. In *R v. Nottingham Justices, ex parte Davies*,[10] it was held that the defence were only permitted to make two fully argued bail applications. After those, a fresh hearing will be heard only if new considerations arise. This was given statutory effect by section 154 of the Criminal Justice Act 1988.

e) the Crown Court has jurisdiction to grant bail where the defendant has been refused bail by the magistrates' court, where he or he has been committed for trial or sentence or where he or she is appealing against conviction or sentence by the magistrates' court. The High Court also has jurisdiction where the person is appealing by way of case stated or seeking judicial review. Furthermore the Court of Appeal can grant bail where the accused is appealing against conviction or sentence. This latter power is exercisable by the single judge.

f) from 1994, the CPS were also given a right to appeal against a decision by magistrates to grant bail in cases which carry a maximum sentence of imprisonment of five years or more. The defendant would remain in custody until the hearing in front of a Crown Court judge who must decide within 48 hours of the original decision.[11]

---

[8] s. 128(6) and s. 128(A), Magistrates' Court Act 1980.
[9] s. 155.
[10] (1981) Q.B. 38.
[11] Bail (Amendment) Act 1993.

7.2.1 *Remand and the European Convention*

Article 5(3) of the European Convention lays down that a person is entitled to trial within a reasonable time or release pending trial. This implies a right to bail, which has been vigorously applied by the Court of Human Rights in Strasbourg. To what extent do the procedures in the 1976 Act conform to these requirements?[12] The Court's starting point is a strong belief in the presumption of innocence. There must be relevant and sufficient reasons to justify continued detention and it should not be prolonged beyond a reasonable time.[13] The prosecution must adduce persuasive[14] evidence that relevant reasons exist—these include the risk that the accused will fail to appear at trial, interference with the course of justice, the prevention of further offences, a need for further investigation, the defendant's own protection and the preservation of public order. Not only must the prosecution adduce evidence, it is likely that they will need to make earlier and fuller disclosure than is currently the case. The Court insists on the 'equality of arms' principle at this early stage as much as it does at the trial itself.[15] The Court will consider whether the weight of such a relevant factor is sufficient to justify continued detention. The seriousness of the offence or the likelihood of a severe sentence are not in themselves sufficient to conclude that the accused is likely to abscond. Other factors such as character, morals, home, occupation, assets, family ties and links with the country need to be considered. In *Letellier v. France*[16] a wife was accused of complicity in her husband's murder. Initially granted bail, she was later put into custody by a higher court. The Court held that this was a breach of Article 5(3) and that the seriousness of the charge was not in itself sufficient—here was a mother of 8 children who had already been on remand and not absconded.

The prospect of further offending is also a relevant factor but this should not be presumed from the fact of previous convictions. Those convictions should raise a plausible risk in the circumstances of the case. This issue is also raised by provisions such as section 25 of the Criminal Justice and Public Order Act 1994 which prohibited bail for those facing a murder, manslaughter or rape charge where the accused has previously been convicted of a similar offence. In *CC v. UK*[17] the Commission held that section 25 breached Article 5(3)—any tribunal must consider the merits of the issue, a process which the Act expressly prohibited. Burrow argues that the amendment of section 25 by section 56 of the Crime and Disorder Act 1998 so that bail may be granted in 'exceptional circumstances' still breaches the Convention as it proceeds from a presumption of guilt rather than a presumption of innocence.[18] A similar difficulty arises with provisions which provide that a defendant need not be granted bail if he was already on bail at the time of the alleged offence.[19] This assumes that the first

---

[12] This draws on Burrow J., *Bail and the Human Rights Act 1998* (2000) *New L.J.* 673, 736 and 903. Also relevant is the Law Commission, *Bail and the Human Rights Act 1998* (Consultation Paper 157).

[13] *Wemhoff v. FRG Application No. 2122/64, Series A/7*, 1 E.H.R.R. 55 (1968).

[14] This is a high standard—*Stogmuller v. Austria Application No. 1602/62, Series A/9*, 1 E.H.R.R. 155 (1969).

[15] *Lamy v. Belgium Application No.10444/83*, 11 E.H.R.R. 529 (1989).

[16] *Application No. 12369/86 A 207*, 14 E.H.R.R. 83 (1991).

[17] *Application No. 32819/96*, [1999] Crim. L.R. 228 and comment [1999] Crim. L.R. 300.

[18] *op. cit.* at 903.

[19] Para. 2A of Pt 1 of Sched. 1 of the Bail Act 1976.

offence was in fact committed and that there is an automatic likelihood of further offending.

The continuance of detention has to be kept under review at short intervals[20] as lapse of time itself is a relevant factor—this must raise the question whether section 154 of the Criminal Justice Act 1988 (which allows magistrates not to hear repeat arguments in bail applications unless there is a fresh argument of fact or law) is compliant with Article 5(3). Furthermore, at the end of the hearing, the Court insists that reasons for the decision are given, without which it is difficult to decide whether there has been a violation of the Convention.[21] Standard form reasons such as the 'requirements of the investigation' are not sufficient.[22] This presents problems for magistrates who rarely give fully reasoned decisions in the court record—indeed there is a *pro forma* decision sheet. Again practices will need to change.[23]

7.2.2 *Remand Practice*

In 2000:

2,082,000 were directed to appear at magistrates' courts

- 1,167,000 (56%) were summoned.
- 916,000 (44%) people were arrested and charged by the police.
- 774,000 (37%) were bailed by the police to appear at court.
- 142,000 (7%) were held in police custody until their first court appearance[24] In 1992 the figure was 100,000.

2,082,000 were directed to appear at magistrates' courts

- 1,493,000 (72%) were dealt with immediately or not remanded. Of these 21 per cent were acquitted, 72 per cent convicted and 7 per cent failed to appear.
- 505,000 (24%) were remanded on bail. Of these 29 per cent acquitted, 49 per cent convicted, 9 per cent were committed to Crown Court for trial or sentence and 13 per cent failed to surrender to bail
- 84,000 (4%) were remanded in custody. Of these 20% were acquitted, 45 per cent convicted, 49 per cent were committed to Crown Court for trial or sentence and 5 per cent (of those remanded in custody for part of the time) failed to surrender to bail.

84,000 defendants were remanded in custody by magistrates:

54,900 defendants were subsequently tried in magistrates' court, of whom 37,900 were sentenced:

- 2,800 received a discharge.
- 4,700 received a fine.
- 10,000 received a community sentence.

[20] *Bezicheri v. Italy Application No.11400/85*, A 11 64, 12 E.H.R.R. 210 (1989).
[21] *Neumeister v. Austria (No. 1) Application No. 1936/63*, 1 E.H.R.R. 91 (1968).
[22] *Clooth v. Belgium Application No. 12718/87*, A 225, 14 E.H.R.R. 717 (1991).
[23] This point is taken by the Law Commission, *op. cit.*
[24] *Criminal Statistics 2000, op. cit.*, Tables 8.1 and 8.3 pp. 203 and 205—the quality of the statistics in Chap. 8 is variable and only express an order of magnitude.

- 17,800 received either a suspended or immediate sentence of imprisonment.
- 20,800 were committed for trial or sentence and remanded in custody.
- 4,300 were committed for trial or sentence on bail.
- 3,900 failed to appear.[25]

28,300 were committed for trial and remanded in custody. At Crown Court;

- 4,700 (17%) were acquitted.
- 400 were discharged.
- 200 were fined.
- 3,100 were given a community sentence.
- 18,200 received either a suspended or immediate sentence of imprisonment.[26]

6,200 were remanded in custody awaiting sentence by the Crown Court:

- 800 were given a community sentence.
- 5,300 (77%) were given an immediate custodial sentence.[27]
- 100 failed to appear.

These figures demonstrate that courts are still too willing to use pre-trial custody—of those remanded in custody by magistrates, under a quarter were convicted and sentenced to imprisonment. Despite the 'right to bail' and statutory time limits, the use of pre-trial custody is still high as is demonstrated by the statistics on remands into custody:

Table 7.1 Remands in Custody 1990–2000[28]

		1990	1995	2000
Untried male prisoners	Annual receptions	50,431	52,347	50,866
	Average daily population	7,324	8,008	6,701
	Average number of days in custody	53	56	49
Untried female prisoners	Annual receptions	2,704	2,940	4,026
	Average daily population	300	344	396
	Average number of days in custody	40	43	36
Unsentenced male prisoners	Annual receptions	19,229	30,261	40,116

[25] *ibid.*, Table 8.5, p. 207.
[26] ibid., Table 8.7, p. 209.
[27] *ibid.*
[28] *Prison Statistics 2000* (Home Office 2001) Cm. 5250, Table 2.2, p. 46.

	Average daily population	1,731	2,807	3,873
	Average number of days in custody	33	34	35
Unsentenced female prisoners	Annual receptions	1,181	1,778	3,773
	Average daily population	84	147	304
	Average number of days in custody	26	30	30

In 2000 the daily average prison population of unconvicted and unsentenced prisoners was 11,270, constituting 17 per cent of the average prison population of 64,600. This is exactly the same proportion as in 1982 when the average daily number of remand prisoners was 7,432 or 17 per cent of the average prison population of 43,772.[29] The most significant change in the figures in recent years has been the rise in the number of unsentenced prisoners, explained perhaps by the introduction of the 'plea before venue' procedure that has meant that the accused must plead to a charge before any mode of trial decision. This results in many more guilty pleas being heard before the magistrates who, finding their powers of sentencing too limited, commit to the Crown Court for sentence and simultaneously remand the defendant into custody awaiting that sentence.

Is it justified to hold such numbers on remand? Recent comparative figures are not available[30] but in 1990 it was estimated that remand prisoners accounted for over 25 per cent of the prison populations in 12 of the (then) 23 member nations of the Council of Europe. The highest proportions were in Belgium (50.7%) and Malta (68.6%), whilst only three countries recorded figures of less than 10 per cent—namely, the Republic of Ireland (5.3%), Cyprus (7.8%) and Iceland (7.9%). In the U.S., the figure is approximately 20 per cent.

In 2000, the outcome of the trial of the 84,000 people remanded into custody was that 26 per cent were acquitted or proceedings were dropped, 25 per cent received fines or community sentences and 43 per cent received custodial sentences. The rest either failed to appear or the outcome is unknown. Such figures do not quite speak for themselves—the decision to remand in custody is not necessarily to be criticised when there is an acquittal or where a custodial sentence is passed. It is a different matter when defendants are fined or given a community sentence—if the facts and nature of the offence and the circumstances of the offender did not justify a custodial sentence at the end of the trial, is it likely that they would have done so at the start of the proceedings?

The remand process tends to favour women: men are more likely to be remanded in custody in magistrates' courts proceedings (4%) than women (2%). However taking account of the type of offence and offending history, gender appears to have only a marginal effect on remand decisions.[31] The daily average

---

[29] NACRO Briefing No. 32, *Remands in Custody* (December 1993).
[30] Individual countries are available through the International Centre for Prison Studies, www.kcl.ac.uk/depsta/rel/icps/.
[31] Home Office, *Statistics on Women and the Criminal Justice System 2001* (2002) Chap. 4.

population of unconvicted and unsentenced female prisoners was 700, constituting 21 per cent of the average female prison population of 3,350 which is slightly higher than the male proportion. 36 per cent of women remanded in custody will receive a custodial sentence compared to 48 per cent of their male counterparts—furthermore that sentence will on average be shorter.[32] They will spend just 36 days on remand compared with an average of 49 days for men. The proportion of ethnic minorities remanded in custody is similar to that of whites—20 per cent of whites and blacks are remanded in custody and 17 per cent of Asians.[33]

Much of the difficulty with bail comes with a lack of information in front of the court about the defendant. The VERA Institute of Justice[34] in New York has developed bail information schemes which are now being widely copied in this country. Many magistrates' court and some local prisons are now serviced by such schemes. Such schemes provide the court with information about the character of the accused or the conditions under which he or she would be living if bailed. This information seems to encourage courts to release on bail more often, without any increase in the breach of bail conditions.

7.3 LEGAL REPRESENTATION FOR THE DEFENDANT

Defendants were not permitted professional assistance to examine witnesses or to speak on their behalf until 1836 but legal representation nowadays is a central part of the due process model. The suspect in police custody is entitled to the advice of a lawyer as well as access to a duty solicitor scheme.[35] Outside court, an accused can consult a lawyer either privately or, much more likely, under the Green Form scheme[36] or under the legal aid scheme for representation in criminal proceedings. But it remains difficult to get full representation at public expense. The Benson Commission[37] argued for a statutory right to legal aid for bail applications, committal proceedings and trial of 'either way' offences. These recommendations were rejected.

For most defendants, the cost of legal advice and representation would be prohibitive. The legal aid scheme allows for the costs of conducting the defence to be borne by the state and not by the defendant. In 2001–2002, the cost of criminal legal aid was approximately £896m from a total budget of £12.8 billion for the criminal justice system. The management of this has been recently reformed—the Legal Services Commission took over from the Legal Aid Board the public funding of defence work in April 2000.[38] The Commission established the Criminal Defence Service (CDS)—this will introduce a mixed system by which criminal defence will be organised through, on one hand, contracted private practitioners and on the other, public salaried employees. There will be a contractual scheme by which private solicitors will be accredited and publicly

[32] Hedderman C. and Gelsthorpe L., (eds) *Understanding the Sentencing of Women* (HORS 170) (1997).
[33] Home Office, *Statistics on Race and the Criminal Justice System 2000* (2000) Chap. 7.
[34] www.vera.org.
[35] ss. 58 and 60 of the PACE 1984; *supra* 3.8.7.2.
[36] This is a scheme allowing two hours' worth of legal advice on any legal issue. It is normally used for giving initial advice to a client. It can also be used to take steps to apply for full legal aid. It does not cover representation in court.
[37] Royal Commission on Legal Service: *Final Report* (1979) Cmnd. 7648.
[38] Access to Justice Act 1999; www.legalservices.gov.uk/.

funded. At present the Commission is responsible for CDS services up to and including representation at the magistrates' courts.[39] The Lord Chancellor's Department manages these services in the Crown Court, although responsibility for these services is to be transferred to the Legal Services Commission in April 2003. Negotiations are also under way with the Bar Council over the extension of franchising arrangements to barristers' chambers.

But the radical departure is the introduction of salaried public defenders. The scheme in England and Wales is currently being piloted.[40] Such schemes are common in North America and Australia and a review of research[41] found that research in Canada consistently shows that the average case costs of staff lawyers are cheaper than private lawyers and that, despite the lower average costs, staff lawyers were found to achieve broadly similar or slightly better outcomes for their clients than private lawyers. Clients of staff lawyers were neither more nor less likely to be convicted than the clients of private lawyers. Where the client was convicted, those represented by a staff lawyer were less likely to be given a custodial sentence. Surveys of criminal justice actors (judges and prosecutors) as well as the clients themselves identified a general and equal satisfaction with the work of both staff and private lawyers. A key factor explaining why salaried lawyers cost less was that staff lawyers tended to spend less time on a case compared to their private colleagues—this applied to all the individual elements of cases such as research, preparation and advocacy as well as spending less time in court waiting rooms. Other differences in working practices of staff lawyers included the finding that staff lawyers achieved the withdrawal of charges or plead their clients guilty at earlier stages than private lawyers with the result that, overall, staff lawyers were able to conclude cases at earlier points and were involved in fewer trials.

For private lawyers, the CDS lays down a flat fee in all cases for hearings in magistrates' courts involving a guilty plea. There is a graduated payment for most trials. Longer and more complex cases are subject to the taxation procedure.[42] The defence solicitor, who holds the budget, runs the case as he sees fit and, if he instructs counsel, pays him from that budget. For Crown Court cases, solicitors and barristers are paid separately. For guilty pleas and short trials, solicitors are paid standard fees for preparatory work including securing proper prosecution disclosure, taking instructions from the defendant and preparation and service of the defence statement. For longer trials, solicitors' bills are subject to taxation. In the longest of trials the CDS enters into a specific contract with solicitors and counsel for the work that is to be undertaken.

Counsel are paid on the basis of standard graduated fees but there are no identifiable fees for any preparatory work, such as advising on prosecution disclosure, holding a conference with the defendant and advising on the form of the defence statement, on evidence and the general conduct of the case. The expectation is that counsel instructed for the trial will attend the plea and directions hearing. The reality is that other counsel attend them. They will have had little or no part in such preparation of the case as there has been, and no authority to advise or commit the defendant to any critical matters needing resolution. It is no

[39] In 2002, there were some 2,800 solicitors offices working under such contracts.
[40] This is a 4 year pilot which started in 2001—the pilots are in Birmingham, Liverpool, Middlesbrough, Cheltenham and Swansea.
[41] Scottish Office: *A Literature Review of Public Defender or Staff Lawyer Schemes* (Legal Studies Research Findings 19) 1998.
[42] Scrutiny after the event by court staff of what has been done in the case.

wonder that defendants, who have yet to see their trial counsel, are reluctant to enter pleas at that stage or to commit themselves to a firm strategy for the trial. The Auld Report regards the system of public funding as fundamentally flawed in that it does not provide an adequate reward or incentive for preparatory work.[43] The CDS have argued that this is due not to the payment system but to the working practices of the Bar and the listing practices of the courts.

In magistrates' courts a substantial proportion of defendants will be unrepresented.[44] However the Narey reforms[45] have provided for an enhanced court duty solicitor scheme and defendants who might formerly have been unrepresented are now getting advice. For those who remain unrepresented, magistrates' courts are much less adversarial than higher courts and both the bench and the clerk often question the defendant to obtain the information that they need, whether for the purpose of the plea itself, mitigating circumstances before sentence or working out a suitable payment plan for the fine. In provincial courts, this may come over as benevolent paternalism but elsewhere,

'To enter the lower courts is to be taken aback by the casualness and rapidity of the proceedings. The mental image of law carried into courts is shattered by observation. The solemnity, the skills of advocacy, the objections, the slow, careful precision of evidence, the adversarial joust, none of these taken-for-granted legal images are in evidence.[46]'

It is only the defendant who is unrepresented. The CPS lawyer normally will be present, although the service is increasingly used lay personnel in uncontentious matters. McBarnet charts the difficulties of the defendant attempting to refute the prosecution version of events, especially in the formulation of suitable questions for witnesses, as opposed to making statements.

'Accused: (to the magistrate) Well, all I can say is...
Magistrate: It's him you ask the questions
Accused: No questions then.'[47]

The unrepresented defendants are baffled both by such linguistic traps or else by legal terms that convey nothing.[48]

7.4 DISCLOSURE OF EVIDENCE

Disclosure by the prosecution of the evidence against the accused contributes to the efficiency of the pre-trial and trial process but it is also a major element of a fair hearing. Several notorious cases in England involving miscarriages of justice have emphasised the need for the accused to have access to information necessary for the proper preparation of the defence. In *Taylor*[49] a senior policeman with-

---

[43] Lord Justice Auld: *A Review of the Criminal Courts of England and Wales*, Chap. 8 (2001) Chap. 10, para. 17.
[44] Figures are somewhat imprecise—Zander M., '*Unrepresented Defendants in Magistrates' Courts*' (1972) *New L.J.* 1042 suggests less than 25% are represented; Riley D. and Vennard J., *op. cit.*, in a study of 909 cases triable either way suggested that 20% were unrepresented.
[45] *Review of Delay in the Criminal Justice System* (Home Office, 1997).
[46] McBarnet D., *Conviction* (Macmillan, 1981) p. 123 and Chap. 7.
[47] McBarnet, *op. cit.*, p. 132.
[48] McBarnet, *op. cit.*, p. 127.
[49] Reported in *The Independent*, June 15, 1993.

held information from the CPS that a witness identifying the defendants had made an earlier statement that one of the girls he had seen might have been black (neither defendant was) and that he had claimed a reward. The officer withheld the information fearing that it would be disclosed to the defence. The convictions were quashed. Precedent and statute have significantly altered the regulation of prosecution and defence disclosure in the past five years.

By 1996, the common law had developed to the extent that:

- in trials on indictments, common law required that there was full disclosure of prosecution information prior to trial, not only of the evidence on which the prosecution were intending to rely but also of 'unused material'.

- in magistrates' courts:
  - with regard to summary offence, there was no obligation on the prosecution to disclose their case. This did not occur until guidelines by the Attorney General in 2000[50] which require advance notice to the defence of all proposed prosecution evidence in 'sufficient time' to allow proper consideration. Prior to 1996 there was no advance disclosure of unused material,
  - there was a statutory obligation[51] on the prosecution to disclose their case in regard to triable-either-way offences which were being tried summarily. Prior to 1996 there was no advance disclosure of unused material,

By 1996 it was now recognised that there was a general duty on the court to ensure a fair trial, which would require the prosecution to produce all the material evidence or else face a stay of prosecution for abuse of process.[52] The major problem for the police and prosecution was the decisions in *Maguire*[53] and *Ward*[54] to give the defendant access to 'unused material' collected during the investigation. They also had to disclose any matters that might be held against prosecution witnesses—for example, that the witness had been subject to police disciplinary hearings.[55]

There has never been a common law obligation on the defendant to disclose the nature of the defence. It has been introduced in some circumstances by statute

- for alibi defences by the Criminal Justice Act 1967.

- for expert evidence under section 81 of the Police and Criminal Evidence Act 1984.

- for preparatory hearings in serious fraud cases.[56]

---

[50] *Attorney General's Guidelines on Prosecution Disclosure* (November 29, 2000).
[51] s. 48, Criminal Law Act 1977 and Magistrates Courts (Advance Information) Rules 1985 (S.I. No.601).
[52] *R. v. DPP, ex parte Lee* [1999] 2 All E.R. 737; *Liverpool Crown Court, ex parte Robinson* [1986] Crim. L.R. 622.
[53] (1992) 94 Cr. App. R. 133.
[54] [1993] 2 All E.R. 577.
[55] *Edwards* [1991] 2 All E.R. 266—see *Edwards v. UK Application No. 13071/87*, 15 E.H.R.R. 417 (1992).
[56] s. 9 of the Criminal Justice Act 1987.

Obviously, the shorter the notice that the prosecution have of a defence witness or item of evidence, the less able they are to counter the impact of such evidence. One argument for defence disclosure is that the principal function of the court and a jury is to determine the truth and they should be entitled both to an indictment which lays out an agenda of the issues to be decided and also to both parties putting forward their own evidence as to those issues and how they intend to answer the other's evidence. Concealment of evidence until a late stage by either side necessarily leads to the jury being unable to assess the weight or probative quality of such evidence. Such principles of proof argue for joint disclosure and Scotland has operated such a practice for several years with little dissent.[57]

Runciman[58] felt that the common law in England had swung too far in the direction of the defence. The Report saw practical problems in the sheer volume of material especially since many major investigations would use computerised databases. But there were also issues of principle. Should confidential and sensitive information contained in the material be so readily disclosed? This was seen as particularly acute where informants or undercover police officers were involved and the Attorney General's guidelines left considerable discretion to the prosecution. As far as the defence were concerned, the Report recommended that in all contested trials, the defence would have to indicate the substance of the defence or the fact that no evidence would be called. The arguments employed were pragmatic: defence disclosure would prevent the 'ambush' defence; it would encourage better preparation as well as guilty pleas or prosecution discontinuances where appropriate; it would facilitate better estimates of length of trial and thus more efficient use of resources. Opposition to the proposal points to the lack of any evidence of the widespread use of defence 'ambushes',[59] to the diminution of the burden of proof on the prosecution and argue that the 'reform' would in fact increase delay and waste resources.

The Criminal Procedure and Investigations Act 1996 put the recommendations on a statutory basis.[60] There is a three-stage process:

- primary disclosure by the prosecution which is automatic. A police officer known as a disclosure officer records all information gathered in the investigation, prepares a schedule of the material for the prosecutor. The prosecution would be under a duty to supply the defence with copies of all material relevant to the offence, the offender and the circumstances of the case. This would include material which may undermine the credibility of defence witnesses as well as those appearing for the prosecution.[61] Schedules of other information held by the police or other key participants such as expert scientific witnesses would be supplied at this point. The only potential problem here is the lack of formal judicial scrutiny over this procedure.

---

[57] Glynn, *'Disclosure'* [1993] Crim. L.R. 841 at 842.
[58] Royal Commission on Criminal Justice, *op. cit.*, para.6.41ff.
[59] Zander M. and Henderson P., *Crown Court Study* (Royal Commission on Criminal Justice: Research Study No. 19) (1993 HMSO) suggests that prosecution counsel see such ambushes in 7% of case whereas for the CPS and the police, the figures are 10% and 23% respectively. Counsel only considered them a serious problem in 3% of cases.
[60] Sharpe S. *'Article 6 and the Disclosure of Evidence'* [1999] Crim. L.R. 273.
[61] *Brown* [1997] 3 All E.R. 780.

- following prosecution disclosure, there is disclosure by the defence in the form of a statement by the defence setting out the material lines of their case. In the case of proceedings in the Crown Court, this is compulsory. Disclosure of the defence is not compulsory in the magistrates' court but the accused may give a defence statement to the prosecution and to the court on a voluntary basis.[62] Whether the disclosure is compulsory or voluntary, the absence of flaws in the defence statement can lead to adverse consequences for the accused as the jury may draw such inferences as they think proper from a failure to give a defence statement or where the defence in court differs from the one set out in the statement. The question remains whether these provisions infringe the presumption of innocence as the decision of the European Court in *Funke v. France*[63] suggests.

- under section 7, where the accused has given a defence statement to the prosecution, the prosecutor is under a duty to make any additional disclosures that become necessary. The prosecutor remains under a continuing duty to keep under review the question whether there is prosecution material which might undermine the prosecution case and which has not been disclosed to the accused and, should such material exist, it should be disclosed to the accused as soon as reasonably practicable.[64] The defence would be obliged to establish the relevance of the material sought, relating it to their disclosed case. Where the parties disagree on this aspect, the court could rule, after weighing the potential importance of the material to the defence.

The effectiveness and efficiency of the statutory scheme has come under scrutiny.[65] The studies suggest that disclosure officers are junior and inadequately trained, that there is insufficient time for prosecutors to review the material or to make sound decisions. This should improve with the CPS and police working together in co-located criminal justice units. The requirements for defence disclosure are seen as either unfair, and a breach of the accused's right of silence, or inadequate, in that there is no obligation to reveal proposed evidence or to state how he or she intends to controvert the prosecution case. The Crown Prosecution Service Inspectorate found that the Act did not command the confidence of criminal practitioners and highlighted:

- the failure of police disclosure officers to prepare full and reliable schedules of unused material;

- undue reliance by the prosecutors on disclosure officers' schedules and assessment of what should be disclosed;

- the awkward split of responsibilities, in particular between the police and the CPS in the task of determining what should be disclosed.

Both the Inspectorate and the Auld Report recommend greater involvement of

---

[62] s. 6, Criminal Procedure and Investigations Act 1996.
[63] (1993) 16 E.H.R.R. 297.
[64] s. 9, Criminal Procedure and Investigations Act 1996.
[65] Plotnikoff J. and Woolfson R., *A Fair Balance? Evaluation of the Operation of Disclosure Law* (Home Office RDS Occasional Paper No. 76) (2001); CPS Inspectorate, *Report on the Thematic Review of the Disclosure of Unused Material* (2000); Auld Report, *op. cit.*, Chap. 10 para. 115ff.

prosecutors, if not in the collation process, in identifying disclosable unused material. There should be more involvement of counsel in fulfilling the prosecution's duty of continuing review of unused material and the Inspectorate would like to see firmer reaction by prosecutors to no or inadequate defence statements. But Auld suggests that the requirements for the defence statement should remain as they are.

Under the Convention, Article 6(3)(a) requires that the accused is entitled to more detailed and specific information than notification of the charge itself. This must be given before the trial in order to permit a reasonable period for the preparation of the defence. The amount of detail required remains unclear—the Court has suggested that a judicial notification did not identify *'in detail ... the nature and cause of the accusation'*.[66] Such phrasing does not necessarily include the evidence against the accused let alone all material uncovered during an investigation. But *Rowe and Davis v. UK*[67] suggests a broader obligation to disclose any material which may 'assist the accused in exonerating himself',[68] to ensure equality of arms. The margin of appreciation accorded to States means that the 1996 Act in all probability satisfies such criteria in respect of time scale and detail

7.4.1 *Disclosure, Police Informers and Confidential Material*

The police and prosecution resent extensive disclosure, not simply because of the inconvenience of the procedures but because of the nature of the information. They were faced with the dilemma of either having to disclose sensitive and confidential material, especially the identity of informants, or having to discontinue prosecution. But the prosecution are entitled to seek immunity from disclosure on the grounds of public interest immunity (PII) because the information would, for example, reveal the identity of informants or details of police operational practices. Normally the defence would be aware of an application to decide on a PII claim and be entitled to make representations in open court. But such decisions as *Keane*[69] and *Davis*[70] approved an *ex parte* procedure so that such material could be placed before the court for a ruling on whether it should be disclosed without compromising its confidentiality. The prosecution can approach the court for an order for immunity from disclosure without informing the defence at all.

The Criminal Procedure and Investigations Act 1996 does not significantly affect these procedures. Section 3(6) allows the prosecutor, on application to the trial court, not to disclose information where it would not be in the public interest to do so. Where the trial is in the Crown Court, there is a duty on the judge to keep the issue under review at all times without the need for an application.[71]

This common law position is at odds with requirements of the Convention that takes the position that if material is relevant, it should be disclosed and the extent to which a domestic court has discretion to withhold such evidence is questionable.[72] The significant point is that it is normally a violation of Article 6 for a

---

[66] *Brozicek v. Italy Application No. 10964/84*, A 167, 12 E.H.R.R. 371 (1989).
[67] (2000) 30 E.H.R.R. 1.
[68] *Jespers v. Belgium* (1981) 27 D.R. 61.
[69] [1994] 2 All E.R. 478.
[70] [1993] 2 All E.R. 643.
[71] ss. 14 and 15, Criminal Procedure and Investigations Act 1996.
[72] *Jespers v. Belgium supra.*

court to hear the prosecution in the absence of the accused.[73] If this is the case, the common law rules relating to public interest immunity infringe Article 6. In *Rowe and Davis v. UK*, the Court held that the procedures had done so,

> '...it is a fundamental aspect of the right to a fair trial that criminal proceedings, including the elements of such proceedings which relate to procedure, should be adversarial and that there should be equality of arms between the prosecution and defence. The right to an adversarial trial means, in a criminal case, that both prose-cution and defence must be given the opportunity to have knowledge of and comment on the observations filed and the evidence adduced by the other party. In addition Article 6 (1) requires, as indeed does English law that the prosecution authorities should disclose to the defence all material evidence in their possession for or against the accused. However ... the entitlement to disclosure of relevant evidence is not an absolute right ... only such measures restricting the rights of the defence which are strictly necessary are permissible.'

During the applicants' trial at first instance the prosecution decided, without notifying the judge, to withhold the fact that prosecution witness was a paid police informer on grounds of public interest. Such a procedure, whereby the prosecution itself attempts to assess the importance of concealed information to the defence and weigh this against the public interest in keeping the information secret, cannot comply with Article 6. The Court of Appeal review of the undi-sclosed evidence (again in *ex parte* hearings) was not sufficient to remedy the unfairness caused at the trial by the absence of any scrutiny of the withheld information by the trial judge. A different result was reached in *Fitt and Jasper v. UK*[74] where the European Court, albeit on a majority of 9–8, drew significant differences with *Rowe and Davis* because the defence were kept informed and permitted to make submissions and participate in the above decision-making process as far as was possible without revealing to them the material which the prosecution sought to keep secret on public interest grounds. Furthermore the non-disclosed material played no further role in the case.

These decisions should clarify the role of the judge in PII decisions. Article 6(3)(a) is intended to ensure that an accused has sufficient information to prepare his or her defence[75] and not full disclosure of all the material gathered. Where information has not been disclosed, the 1996 Act requires the judge to keep this decision under review in the light of the nature of the defence. It is unlikely that these procedures infringe the right to a fair hearing. As has been noted, the rights guaranteed in Article 6(1) may be derogated from in the interests of public order and national security. The Court has recognised that a police informer need not be called as a witness as such a system is necessary to the administration of justice and to require such people to testify would undermine that system.[76] However there still remains the need to protect the interests of the accused in *ex parte* hearings and Auld recommends the use of independent counsel for this pur-pose.[77]

---

[73] *Neumeister v. Austria (No. 1) Application No. 1936/63* [EHRR 9] (1968).
[74] *Application No. 27052/95* (2000) and *Application No. 29777/95* (2000).
[75] *Bricmont v. Belgium Application No. 10857/84*, 48 D.R. 106 (1986).
[76] *Kostovski v. Netherlands Application No. 11454/85*, A 166, 12 E.H.R.R. 434 (1989).
[77] The Auld Report, *op. cit.*, Chap. 10 para. 191ff.

7.5 PRE-TRIAL REVIEW AND CASE MANAGEMENT

Arguments about disclosure reflect the emphasis on adversarialism in English courts. Parties are unwilling to cede tactical advantages to the other. Does a better truth emerge from this process of presenting a jury with opposing and contradictory accounts? Regardless of the answer to this question, the finder of fact, whether judge or jury, is entitled to a proper definition of the issues and clear exposition of the evidence. Pre-trial hearings should be essential in achieving this.[78] The opportunities for holding these have multiplied over the past five years.

in magistrates' courts in cases where it is needed there can be a 'pre-trial review'[79] of different sorts. They have developed piecemeal, and differ in practice and procedure from area to area.:

- *'early first hearings'*—are listed for a case which is likely to be an early guilty plea. If it turns out not to be so, the court will put it over to an 'early administrative hearing'.
- *early administrative hearing*—the court takes a plea before venue, determines mode of trial and sets pre-trial review and trial dates as necessary. This can be heard before a justices' clerk
- *pre-trial review*—this held where needed to assess the state of readiness.

in the Crown Court, there are four separate forms of procedure

- non-statutory *'plea and directions hearing'*—in which the judge can make non-binding rulings before the start of trial.[80] The magistrates' court should commit the defendant to appear in the Crown Court on a specific date fixed in liaison with the Crown Court listing officer for an initial plea and directions hearing where pleas will be taken and, in contested cases, prosecution and defence will be expected to assist the judge in identifying the key issues, and to provide any additional information required for the proper listing of the case. Local practice varies but Auld described these as *'in the main, they are perfunctory proceedings'*.[81]
- *'pre-trial hearing'*—under Part IV of the Criminal Procedure and Investigations Act 1996 which gives judges power to make binding rulings on points of law before the start of a trial. For example, the judge might be invited to make a ruling in law as to whether or not the facts support a particular charge. The trial judge will be able to discharge or vary any such ruling if he considers it in the interests of justice to do so.
- *'preparatory hearings'*—under the Criminal Justice Act 1987, as the start and part of the trial, for serious or complex fraud cases, in which the judge can make binding rulings on any issue of the admissibility of evidence or law which relates to the case.
- *'preparatory hearings'*—introduced by Part III of the 1996 Act for cases in which the indictment reveals 'a case of such complexity, or a case

---

[78] See Court of Appeal, dicta, in *Thorn* (1977) 66 Crim. App. Rep. 6.
[79] For a study of pre-trial review in magistrates' courts, Baldwin J., *Pre-Trial Justice* (Blackwell, 1985).
[80] Described in Royal Commission on Criminal Justice: *op. cit.*, para. 7.12ff. *'Practice Direction (Crown Court: Plea and Directions Hearings)'* [1995] 1 W.L.R. 1318.
[81] Auld Report, *op. cit.*, Chap. 10, para. 209.

whose trial is likely to be of such length, that substantial benefits are likely to accrue' from such a hearing. Again the judge can make binding rulings and appeal from such rulings lies to the Court of Appeal.

The Runciman Commission recommendations have brought about a crucial change with the statutory proceedings in that the preliminary hearings are treated as part of the trial, with the judge able to rule on such matters as the admissibility of evidence and that the trial judge, if different, should be bound by such rulings. These change signal a move towards a system by which criminal trials will be properly and judicially supervised from the moment when proceedings are instituted. But, as Auld puts it:

'...there are no fewer than four separate, but largely similar forms of preliminary hearing for Crown Court cases. They are a good example of the unsystematic and overlapping way in which the legislature, when it intervenes in matters of criminal law, burdens and confuses its procedures. In all of them arraignment may take place and, if there is an acceptable plea of guilty and the case is ready for it, the judge can proceed to sentence. Where the matter is to be contested and there are substantial outstanding issues, the hearings can be of real utility, for example as to the adequacy of mutual or third party disclosure or in ruling on claims of public interest immunity or on matters of law on agreed facts. But in all of them, there is little difference in effect between the 'binding' orders made in the statutory procedures and those made in the non-statutory plea and directions hearings. And, in all of them the court has little effective sanction to enforce its directions if the parties are unable or unwilling to comply.'[82]

7.6 THE PLEA AND PLEA BARGAINING[83]

The formal start of a trial at Crown Court is the public arraignment of the defendant, against whom a bill of indictment has been preferred and signed. It consists of three parts: (1) calling the defendant to the bar by name; (2) reading the indictment to him; (3) asking him whether he is guilty or not. At the magistrates' court, the information is put to the defendant who is asked to plead guilty or not guilty. Immediately apparent is the all-pervasiveness of pleas of guilty. Table 7.2 shows cases completed by the CPS at magistrates' court in 2000. Fewer than 6 per cent involved a not guilty plea and the accused was convicted in 69 per cent of these. Even so, there has been a decline in the number of guilty pleas in all categories of offences tried in magistrates' courts.

---

[82] *ibid.*, para. 211.
[83] *ibid.*, para. 91ff; Royal Commission on Criminal Justice, *op. cit.*, para. 7.41ff; Ashworth A., *The Criminal Process* (2nd ed. 1998) p. 276 ff; Darbyshire P., 'The Mischief of Plea Bargaining' [2000] Crim L.R. 895.

Table 7.2 Guilty Pleas, Convictions and Acquittals in Magistrates' Courts 2000[84]

Outcome	Magistrates' Court	Percentage
Guilty pleas	777,400	82
Proof in absence	116,000	12
Convicted after trial	39,300	4
Dismissal	16,600	2
Total	949,400	100

As is shown in Table 7.3, in the Crown Court, 72,800 defendants were dealt with, 59 per cent of whom pleaded guilty.[85] Ten years earlier, 70 per cent of defendants pleaded guilty. To an extent this decline is the result of the introduction of the 'plea before venue' procedure in 1997 which means that many more defendants pleading guilty will be dealt with initially in the magistrates' courts and only be sent to Crown Court for sentence, if necessary. The acquittal rate (66 per cent of contested cases) will be discussed later in relation to the jury.

Table 7.3 Guilty Pleas, Convictions and Acquittals in Crown Courts 2000

Offence group	Total Number	Percentage pleading guilty	Percentage of those pleading not guilty convicted
Violence	18,000	48	30
Sexual offences	5,100	31	33
Burglary	9,000	73	36
Robbery	5,900	60	40
Theft and handling	7,900	63	33
Fraud and forgery	3,400	60	37
Criminal damage	1,900	60	23
Drugs	9,400	71	52
Motoring	1,300	70	49
Other	10,900	62	29
Total	72,800	59	34

[84] *Criminal Statistics 2000, op. cit.*, Chap. 6; figures from CPS.
[85] *ibid.*, Table 6C, p. 141.

There is nothing sinister in a high rate of guilty pleas. Suspects are apprehended and charged because they are caught red-handed, are known to the victim, are easily identified by him or her or there has been a statement admitting some or all of the allegations. In such cases, a plea of 'guilty' is to be expected. But for many defendants the choice between guilt and innocence is not straightforward. For some, this may involve a cynical assessment of the strength of the prosecution case and the consequent risks of conviction after pleading not guilty measured against the benefits of a possible jury acquittal. For others, the interpretation of the events and the consequent responsibility for those actions is likely to be much more complex. Often the defendant is unwilling to accept the bald statement of 'facts' as advanced by the prosecution[86] or would like to introduce material which is legally irrelevant but which expresses the defendant's understanding of the incident.

To what extent is the plea the untrammelled choice of the defendant and to what extent does it rely on hidden pressures and informal negotiations? There are, of course, pressures from the start of the process—during police interrogation, pressure to 'get it off your chest' or 'clear the matter up' which may lead to admissions that will be hard to refute later and will lead to pressure from legal advisors to plead guilty. But our concern here is the pre-trial pressure which may affect choice of plea.

Early research showed that there are inconsistent pleaders: those who have pleaded guilty but still assert their innocence. Susan Dell's[87] study of 527 women in Holloway Prison, convicted in magistrates' courts, suggested that over 10 per cent (n=56) still alleged innocence despite having pleaded guilty. Baldwin and McConville[88] identified 150 defendants, about 10 per cent of the total guilty pleas and about 7 per cent of their sample overall, who had changed their pleas from not guilty to guilty at a late stage. The study discovered 121 late plea changers in their study. The defendants gave the following reasons for pleading guilty:[89]

Guilty as pleaded 35 (28.9%)
Plea bargain 22 (18.2%)
Tacit bargain 16 (13.2%)
Pressure from counsel 48 (39.7%)

What is significant from these figures are the large number of defendants who experience pressure from their own counsel to plead guilty. Such pressure is at a very late stage:

'There were a million and one things that I wanted to say to the barrister if I only could have had the time. There was a lot to say but when the barrister only comes in a few minutes before you go into court there's not a lot you can say and, anyway, he just didn't want to know.'[90]

---

[86] Baldwin J. and McConville M., *Negotiated Justice* (1977), p. 87 ff, where they give examples of the defendants who wish to plead guilty to the offence but challenge the prosecution's version of events.
[87] Dell S., *Silent in Court* (Bell, 1971).
[88] Baldwin J. and McConville M., *op. cit.*
[89] Baldwin and McConville (1977), *op. cit.*, p. 28.
[90] Baldwin and McConville (1977), *op. cit.*, p. 55.

Zander and Henderson's study[91] revealed a similar order of magnitude, concluding that each year there were some 1,400, possibly innocent, persons whose counsel felt that they had pleaded guilty in order to achieve a reduction either in the charges faced or in the sentence. There are other factors to consider, not least that the defendants may be alleging innocence as long as possible in order to gain maximum advantage from the system.

This research has identified the phenomenon of 'cracked' cases—ones that are listed for a contested trial but on the day are disposed of in another fashion. The largest percentage of such cases occur when the defendant pleads guilty on the trial date—this was the reason in 61 per cent of cracked trials in 2000. Other reasons include the prosecution accepting a plea of guilty to an alternative charge (15.2%), the prosecution offering no evidence ((20.6%) or the defendant being bound over to keep the peace (3.1%).[92] The numbers involved are large—13,206 defendants are either late pleaders or plead guilty to a lesser charge. The inefficiency of this is obvious but so is the cost to defendants in terms of continuing uncertainty and, more worryingly, the possibility that some will be pleading guilty against their wishes.

In managerial terms the courts need to process a large number of defendants annually. Without guilty pleas, the backlog of trials would be intolerable. The figures above suggest that there is a covert system of plea-bargaining as a means of encouraging defendants to plead guilty but at the expense of unacceptable pressures being placed on defendants. Plea-bargaining means that the defendant enters a mutually acceptable plea of guilty in return for some concession. These concessions were recognised by Newman in the U.S.[93] and would typically be a sentence concession on length of time to be served or the reduction or dropping of some of the charges. In the U.S. plea-bargaining is officially recognised whereas in England, it has remained much less obvious, perhaps due to the difference in role and status of the prosecution agencies and to the lack of a public defender system.

In addition, in England the judge retains control over the indictment and also has wide discretionary powers of sentencing.[94] Were the prosecution able to recommend a particular sentence,[95] this would significantly change the balance of power in plea negotiations. At present any bargain requires the active co-operation of the judge but the Court of Appeal has consistently set itself against any such involvement. In *Turner*,[96] the defendant was indicted for theft and pleaded 'not guilty'. His counsel strongly advised him to change his plea on the grounds that he might well go to prison if convicted but otherwise was likely to receive a non-custodial sentence. Counsel went to see the judge and on his return repeated his advice. Turner changed his plea but the Court of Appeal quashed the

---

[91] Zander M. and Henderson P., *op. cit.*

[92] *Judicial Statistics 2000, op. cit.*, Table 6.7, p. 66.

[93] Newman D.J., '*Pleading Guilty for Considerations: A Study of Bargain Justice*', *Journal of Criminal Law, Criminology and Police Science* Vol. 46 (1956) pp. 780–90.

[94] In England, the judge normally can make an order ranging from an absolute discharge to the maximum prison term specified in the statute. However in the U.S., many states have an indeterminate sentencing system so that the statute specifies a set sentence, say 3 to 5 years, for a particular offence and conviction for an offence automatically requires the judge to impose that sentence.

[95] This is already common practice in many civilian jurisdictions—see Downes D., *Contrasts in Tolerance* 1988 pp. 13–14 for the position in the Netherlands.

[96] (1970) 2 All E. R. 281. For an account of other Court of Appeal decisions, see Baldwin J. and McConville M., '*Plea Bargaining and the Court of Appeal*' 6 *British Journal of Law and Society* p. 200 (1979); Darbyshire P., '*The Mischief of Plea Bargaining*' [2000] Crim. L.R. 895.

conviction on the grounds that, since the defendant felt the views had emanated from the judge, it was idle to feel that there had been a free choice. The court stressed that though there should be freedom of access between the judge and counsel and that counsel could advise a client in strong terms, yet any such discussion should involve both prosecution and defence, that it should be limited to matters that counsel cannot, in his client's interests mention in open court and that the judge should never indicate what sentence he had in mind unless he is able to say that, regardless of plea, the sentence will not take a particular form.

The pressure is largely effective because of the sentencing discount. This practice is now recognised in legislation—in determining what sentence to pass on an offender who has pleaded guilty, a court shall take into account the stage in the proceedings at which the offender indicated his intention to plead guilty and the circumstances in which this indication was given.[97] This reform was the recommendation of the Runciman Commission who were concerned with the 'cracked' trial—to avoid this and to encourage early pleas of guilty they suggested the 'graduated' discount so that only the accused who pleaded guilty at a relatively early stage would be entitled to the full discount whereas the accused who changed his or her mind at the trial would only receive minimal advantage. The legislation is designed to allow the judge to pursue this policy.[98]

A guilty plea attracts a lesser sentence with the discount amounting to 25–30 per cent. The Court of Appeal has accepted that it was proper for the judge to ensure that the defendant was aware of the discount[99] although the same court has said[100] that it would be improper to extend a sentence because the defendant has pleaded not guilty or has run a defence in a particular way. The rationale for the discount is that a guilty plea shows contrition but since defendants rarely speak on their own behalf, this is more of a convenient presumption than a reality.

Late changes of plea can be regarded as the result of realistic and practical approaches, being adopted by the police, defence and prosecution lawyers, judges and the defendants themselves. Such agreements were expeditious and economical and were a confrontation with 'hard facts and realism'.[101] Others are less convinced since the existence of the sentencing discount means that defendants receive a lower sentence that they do not deserve—other jurisdictions, including Scotland, do not have this practice. It may also be indirectly discriminatory, as defendants from ethnic minorities tend to maintain a plea of not guilty and in consequence face risks of heavier sentences. Overall it is improper pressure, as defendants are never confronted with a free choice. All defendants, guilty or innocent, experience the pressure of the discount.

Both the Runciman Commission[102] and the Auld Report[103] rejected these arguments. Runciman envisaged what is in effect a plea bargaining hearing although it is called a 'sentencing canvass'. For Auld, it is an advance indication of sentence that would enable the defendant to know in advance where he would

---

[97] s. 152, Powers of Criminal Courts (Sentencing) Act 2000.
[98] This process had already been recognised by the Court of Appeal—*Hollington and Emmens* (1986) 82 Crim. App. Rep. 281.
[99] *Cain* (1976) Crim. L.R. 464.
[100] *Harper* [1967] Crim. L.R. 714.
[101] McCabe S. and Purves R., *By-passing the Jury* (Blackwell) 1972; Purves R., *'That Plea Bargaining Business: Some Conclusions from Research' Criminal Law Review* (1971), p. 470.
[102] Royal Commission on Criminal Justice: *op. cit.*, paras. 7.48 ff.
[103] The Auld Report, *op. cit.*, Chap. 10, para. 91 ff.

stand if he or she pleaded guilty. This derogates from the *Turner* rule that the judge should not engage in such negotiations. Auld specifically sees this as a bargain between the defendant and the court. Furthermore the parties could discuss the possibility of the accused pleading guilty to a lesser charge so that there could be a 'full and realistic discussion about plea and especially sentence.'

Whether a criminal justice system should have elements of discretion and covert negotiation that legitimate past processes and future actions against the defendant is not a question to which the Runciman Commission addressed itself. Similarly, neither is the straightforward issue as to whether a defendant should receive a more severe sentence just because he or she chooses to plead not guilty addressed. Ashworth castigated this section of the Runciman Report as its 'nadir' in its inability to distinguish issues of principles from managerial expediency. It is a position that applies equally to the Auld recommendations.[104]

7.7 THE JURY

The public generally regards the jury as a cornerstone in the criminal justice system, an important element in legitimating the system and ensuring public acceptance. A jury will pass verdict in any trial at Crown Court where the defendant has pleaded 'not guilty' to a charge in the indictment and where that plea has not been accepted by the prosecution. This will consist of 12 people between the ages of 18 and 70, registered as electors and resident in the United Kingdom for at least 5 years since the age of 13.[105] The function of the jury will be to listen to all the evidence relating to the charge, listen to the judge's direction on the law to be applied and then to make up their collective mind as to what they consider to be the facts of the case and to bring in a general[106] verdict of 'guilty' or 'not guilty' on the charge.

A majority of cases in Crown Court do not involve a jury but a plea of guilty—in 2000, 59 per cent of Crown Court defendants pleaded guilty. There were about 72,800 indictable cases heard which means that there were jury trials in some 29,850 cases.[107] The jury is not numerically significant in the criminal justice system as a whole—perhaps 1 per cent of cases end in jury trial. The magistrates' courts' jurisdiction has been expanded and the 'right' to jury trial has been slowly eroded. In other common law jurisdictions, there is an entrenched right to jury trial[108] but, as the Auld Report was at pains to point out, neither Magna Carta, the Bill of Rights nor the Human Rights Act provide such a constitutional right.[109] In consequence the demarcation of jurisdiction between summary and indictable trial has been on the political agenda for some time—in 1977, the Criminal Law Act[110] removed the right to jury trial for some drink/driving offences, for public order offences under section 5 of the Public Order Act

---

[104] Ashworth A., 'Plea, Venue and Discontinuance' [1993] Crim. L.R. 830.
[105] Juries Act 1974, s. 1.
[106] There can be a special verdict in certain cases such as an insanity plea.
[107] *Criminal Statistics 2000, op. cit.*, Chap. 6; Table 6C, p. 141—the total is for defendants aged 18 or over.
[108] In the U.S. this is where the offence involves at least 6 months custody on conviction; in Canada where it involves at least 5 years custody.
[109] The Auld Report, *op. cit.*, Chap. 5 para, 7 ff.
[110] ss. 15–17.

1936 and for assault on a police constable. In the 1970s, the James Committee[111] made more far-reaching recommendations, for example that theft under £20 would become a summary offence. This was resisted at the time although Runciman recommended taking away the defendant's right to elect for jury trial subject to review by the magistrates.[112] In 1999 a Mode of Trial bill was introduced to reduce that right of election but was dropped. The Auld Report has taken up that challenge again and recommended that defendants should not have the right to elect for jury trial but that magistrates should make this decision.[113] This recommendation has been opposed among others, by Liberty who argued for the need to support a jury system within a liberal and democratic society but also practically that the process of converting either-way offences into summary offences had reduced the incidence of jury trials and furthermore that '... *70% of cases committed to the Crown Court for jury trial were committed by magistrates themselves and only 4% of defendants actually exercised the right.*'[114]

In 2002 the government accepted these arguments and decided to retain the defendant's right to elect for jury trial.[114A] However they intend to introduce legislation to allow the accused to opt for trial by judge alone—a sensible approach where an offence has attracted wide and prejudicial publicity.[114B] More controversially they also are proposing to do away with juries in serious fraud trials, although it is estimated that only 1-20 of these occur annually.[114C]

The jury is not a democratic part of the trial. Jurors are randomly selected, untrained amateurs from all sections of the population and are, in theory, the least controlled aspect of criminal justice. They are unpaid.[115] Trial by jury has been regarded as a paradigm of English criminal law, described by Blackstone,

> 'The liberties of England will abide as long as this palladium remains sacred and inviolate; and will be secure against all open attacks and secret machinations, which might undermine it, by the introduction of new and arbitrary modes of trial by justices of the peace, commissioners of the revenue, and courts of conscience.'[116]

Whether the jury live up to this ideal is moot.[117] It has been said that the only cure for admiration of juries is to read Howell's State Trials, for example, the account of the conviction by a jury in 1792 of Thomas Paine for writing *The Rights of Man*. What is undoubted is that it is the most ancient element of 'the most ancient relic in any modern legal system',[118] dating from Anglo-Saxon and Anglo-Norman times. While the continental legal systems devised complex systems of logical proof, the English used the jury.[119]

---

[111] *Report of Committee on the Distribution of Business between the Crown and the Magistrates Courts, op. cit.*
[112] This issue on classification of offences and mode of trial is discussed *supra* at 5.2.1; Ashworth (1993), *op. cit.*, at p. 832.
[113] The Auld Report, *op. cit.*, Chap. 5 para. 119ff.
[114] Liberty, *Response to the Auld Review of the Criminal Courts* (2002).
[114A] 'Justice for All', *op. cit.*, para. 4.22.
[114B] *ibid.*, para. 4.26.
[114C] *ibid.*, para. 4.28.
[115] Although there is a financial loss allowance, wholly inadequate for the self-employed—Royal Commission on Criminal Justice, *op. cit.*, para. 8.56.
[116] Sir William Blackstone's 'Commentaries on the Laws of England', Book IV, Chap. 27, p. 905, para. V.
[117] See discussion in Spencer J., *op. cit.*, p. 390ff.
[118] Milsom H.F.C., *op. cit.*, p. 413.
[119] Milsom, *op. cit.*, p. 410.

7.7.1 *Composition and Selection of the Jury*

Until the Criminal Justice Act 1972, there was a property qualification imposed by statute before a person could act as a juror. This meant that juries were predominantly middle-class, middle-aged, middle-minded and male. The Morris Committee reporting in 1965[120] found that only 22.5 per cent of those on the electoral roll were entitled to be called up for jury service and that 95 per cent of women were ineligible. This was despite the fact that rate revaluation and inflation had increased numbers of those eligible to be jurors fourfold, to the extent that the Metropolitan Police Commissioner, Waldron, was already talking of a deterioration in the quality of jurors. The first reform of the jury system was the abolition of unanimous verdicts and the introduction of majority verdicts by the Criminal Justice Act 1967.[121] From that time, it was possible to convict or acquit if ten jurors agree where the jury consists of eleven or twelve jurors; alternatively if nine jurors agree where the jury consists of ten or eleven jurors. In 2000, some two thousand defendants were convicted by majority verdict, 21 per cent of all jury convictions.

Morris recommended that eligibility for jury service should be co-extensive with the franchise. This change was brought about in 1972 so that the qualification to be a juror was that you were aged between 18 and 70, had been ordinarily resident in the country for a period of at least 5 years since the age of 13 and were registered to vote. About 8 per cent of those eligible to vote are not registered on the Electoral Register.[122] Those excluded from jury service by the Jury Act 1974 include:

a) *ineligible by virtue of work*—this mainly concerns those involved in the administration of justice but also including the clergy. Runciman and the Auld Report both were critical of ineligibility based on occupation. But Auld went further, recommending that everyone should be eligible for jury service.[123]

b) *disqualified*—this may be by virtue of a criminal record. The disqualification can be for life or ten years depending upon the seriousness of the offence. Those disqualified also include the mentally ill and anyone on bail in criminal proceedings.[124]

c) *excusable as of right*—those over 65, MPs, servicemen, doctors and vets. Auld has recommended that nobody should be excusable as of right because of their occupation.

d) *discretionary excusal or deferral*—if you have served as a juror within the last two years or have been excused by a judge for a longer period; if there is any physical or mental disability; if there is an insufficient command of English. There is a general discretion to excuse for good reason,[125] with

---

[120] *Report of Interdepartmental Committee on Jury Service*, Cmnd. 2627 (1965).
[121] s.13 (now incorporated in s. 17 of the Juries Act 1974); s. 11 of the same Act introduced the 'alibi warning' designed to protect jurors from being deceived by 'ambush' defences.
[122] Airs J. and Shaw A., *Jury Excuse and Deferral* (Home Office Research Findings No. 102) (1999).
[123] The Auld Report, *op. cit.*, Chap. 5 para. 27ff; Royal Commission on Criminal Justice, *op. cit.*, para. 8.57.
[124] s. 40 Criminal Justice and Public Order Act 1994.
[125] s.9 Juries Act 1974.

the initial decision being made by the Crown Court Officer with the possibility of an appeal to the judge.[126]

A 1999 study[127] showed that of a sample of jurors, 13 per cent were ineligible, excused as of right or disqualified, 15 per cent failed to attend and 38 per cent were excused. This left 34 per cent available for jury service of whom half had that service deferred to a later date. The most common reasons for excusal were medical or involved care of children. The most common reasons for deferral were work (especially the self-employed) or holidays. One consequence is that generally men outnumber women on juries.

From 2000, jurors are summoned by a Central Summoning Bureau, using a computer system to select jurors at random from electoral rolls, issue summonses and deal with jurors' responses. There is a link with the Police National Computer which permits an automatic check on each person summoned. It was argued that this would ensure that all jurors are treated equally and fairly, and the rules enforced consistently, by centralising at the Bureau all decision-making on requests to be excused from jury service or have it deferred; it was regarded as more efficient as it would be possible to identify more accurately the number of jurors needed by the courts so fewer jurors are summoned only to be stood down and jurors would spend more time sitting on trials and less time waiting around.

The new system may well have an impact on ethnic minority representation on juries. Traditionally an official would select the panel for any particular week from the electoral roll by reading through the register picking each name. A consequence of this was discrimination. One early study[128] discovered that only 1 per cent of Birmingham jurors were of Asian or West Indian origin whereas the proportion in the population as a whole would be at least 12 per cent. It is also true, that ethnic minorities are less likely to be registered electors than whites.[129]

The gender and racial balance of juries has improved. Zander and Henderson found that women were slightly underrepresented and that non-white jurors made up 5 per cent of jurors as compared with 5.9 per cent of the total population.[130] But this does not address the problem of ethnic balance in individual cases. It has been suggested that where there are defendants from ethnic minorities, judge and prosecutor should use their powers to 'stand by' jurors to establish balance on the jury. In *Bansal*,[131] the judge in a case involving an anti-National Front demonstration ordered the jury panel to be drawn from an area which had a large Asian population. However in *Ford*,[132] the Court of Appeal held that a judge has no power to influence the composition of the jury by directing that a multi-racial jury be empanelled or by the use of his power of discretionary discharge, or by directing that the panel should be drawn from another jury catchment area. Any such change should be by statute. Recent research suggests that juries do not discriminate against black defendants[133] and

---

[126] Practice Direction (1988) 1 W.L.R. 1162.
[127] Airs J. and Shaw A., *op. cit.*
[128] Baldwin J. and McConville M., *Jury Trials* (1979).
[129] Airs J. and Shaw A., *op. cit.*
[130] Zander M. and Henderson P., *Crown Court Study* (Royal Commission on Criminal Justice: Research Study No. 19) (1993).
[131] (1985) Crim L.R. 151.
[132] (1989) 3 W.L.R. 762.
[133] Bridges L., Choongh S. and McConville M., *Ethnic Minority Defendants and the Right to Elect Jury Trial* (Commission for Racial Equality 2000).

that for black defendants there is a slightly higher acquittal rate than for whites.

Despite this, there is a perception that white juries are less fair to black defendants. The Commission for Racial Equality has argued that, where there is a racial dimension that results in a defendant believing that he or she cannot receive a fair trial from an all-white jury, there should be a specific procedure. The defence (or the prosecution on behalf of the victim) should apply to the judge to show that such a belief was reasonable because of special features in the case and that the judge should have the power to order that three jurors should come from the same ethnic minority as the defendant or the victim.[134] This recommendation has been echoed by Auld who recommended that a scheme be devised so that when the defendant and the complainant were of different ethnic origin, the judge's ruling would be for a racially diverse jury.[135]

7.7.2 *Vetting the Jury*

A further factor, which reduces the randomness, is the vetting of jurors by the police and the security services. This is an honoured tradition.[136] The ABC Official Secrets trial[137] in 1978 showed that it still continued when it was disclosed that the whole panel had been vetted, two members of the jury had signed the Official Secrets Act and the foreman of the jury was a former member of the Special Air Services (SAS). In November 1978, there was a trial of some Welsh Language demonstrators in Carmarthen. In a Welsh-speaking area, 10 out of 12 jurors had to listen through headphones since the defendants spoke Welsh and 11 out of 12 jurors had English surnames. The Home Office admitted that a junior officer had 'without authority' conducted a check.

There were strong words, both for and against, by the Court of Appeal in *Brownlow*[138] where Lord Denning dubbed vetting 'unconstitutional' and *Mason*[139] where Lord Lawton described it as 'just common sense'. Vetting jurors to obtain some tactical advantage in a minor case was an abuse of power. It was finally addressed by the Attorney-General in 1988 when a revised set of guidelines were published.[140] In these, the Attorney reiterates the principle of random selection and that only ineligible or disqualified jurors should be excluded. But in cases of terrorists and national security, jurors' names will be checked at the Criminal Records Office, also against Special Branch records and through local investigation. Such authorised checks require the personal authority of the Attorney General acting on the advice of the DPP. CRO checks may be carried out in any case and in an annexe to the guidelines, the Attorney General specifies such cases: where there is reason to believe that a juror is disqualified; where there has been an attempt to interfere with a juror in a prior and related trial; where the DPP or Chief Constable considers it important that no disqualified person serves on this particular jury. But random, and apparently routine, sample

---

[134] This proposal was made by Royal Commission on Criminal Justice, *op. cit.*, para. 8.63.
[135] Auld Report, *op. cit.*, Chap. 5 para. 60–62.
[136] Thompson E.P., '*The State versus its enemies*' New Society 19/10/78; Roberts S., '*Jury Vetting in the 17th Century*' 32 History Today (1982). Issue 2, p. 25; Findlay M. and Duff P., '*Jury Vetting— The Jury Under Attack*', [1983] *Legal Studies* 159.
[137] Spencer, *op. cit.*, p. 387; White, *op. cit.*, p. 117.
[138] *R. v. Sheffield Crown Court, ex parte Brownlow* (1980) Q.B. 530.
[139] (1981) Q.B. 881.
[140] (1988) 3 A.E.R. 1086—the earlier version are in (1980) 3 A.E.R. 785.

checks are still continuing.[141] Since the essence of any check is its secrecy and since the information is passed only to prosecution counsel, there is considerable capacity for the manipulation of the jury, a clear abuse of due process.[142] The most recent development is the Central Summoning Bureau, using a computer system to select jurors. As mentioned there is a link with the Police National Computer that permits an automatic check on each person summoned. The implications of this were considered neither by the Runciman Commission nor by Auld.

7.7.3 *Challenging Jurors*

In the courtroom, the clerk selects 12 cards. The juror comes forward and is sworn. There is some capacity to affect the composition of the jury through challenge, although that is now very restricted and to all intents and purposes was abolished in 1988:[143]

- *challenge for cause*—either party can now challenge for cause although the prosecution had no right of challenge whatsoever until 1307. Overall the defence is in a poor position to affect the composition of the jury since they will have little information. Nor are they able to gain much at the trial itself. Prior to 1973, jurors' occupations were included on the jury list but the Lord Chancellor, Lord Hailsham, used his responsibility for the jury list to abolish this practice.[144]

- *questioning jurors*—one means of gathering information was the 'voir dire' examination of jurors before they took the oath. In the U.S., both prosecution and defence lawyers examine prospective jurors and there is no limit to the number that can be rejected. In England, the right to question jurors has been restricted since 1973. In the 'Angry Brigade' trial of that year,[145] the judge permitted questioning of jurors to discover whether there was likelihood of bias. Later a Practice Direction[146] laid down guidelines so that defence lawyers cannot question jurors except regarding connections with institutions in the case but not on the juror's beliefs or possible bias.

- *peremptory challenges*—until January 1st 1988, the defence had the opportunity to make a peremptory challenge to the potential juror and arbitrarily reject a number. This was originally 35 but in modern times had been reduced to seven. The 1977 Criminal Law Act reduced it to three before the right was abolished altogether in 1988.

The curtailment on the right to challenge jurors has not affected the prosecution who have never had a right of peremptory challenge but have established the right to 'stand by for the Crown'. The 'stood by' juror only gets to serve on the jury if the entire panel has been used up. The Attorney General issued

---

[141] Royal Commission on Criminal Justice, *op. cit.*, para. 8.60 which does not mention the Attorney-General's guidelines or whether such checks are in line with them.
[142] Harman H. and Griffith J., *Justice Deserted* (NCCL 1979); East R., '*Jury Packing: A Thing of the Past?*' (1985) 48 Modern L.R. 418; White R., *op. cit.*, p. 117ff.
[143] s. 118(1), Criminal Justice Act 1988.
[144] Harman H. and Griffith J., *op. cit.*, p. 15.
[145] Dashwood A., '*The Jury and the Angry Brigade*' 11 W.A.L.R. 245.
[146] Practice Note (1973) 1 W.L.R. 134 now superseded by Practice Direction (1988) 1 W.L.R. 1162.

guidelines[147] that the power should be used sparingly and never in order to gain a tactical advantage. The defence have never had the right to 'stand by' jurors[148] and now can only challenge for cause.

7.7.4 *Juries and Acquittals*

Do juries play the legal game or do they operate on different criteria? There are plenty of recent examples of juries who have acquitted against the weight of the evidence, especially in cases involving the Official Secrets Acts or drink/driving charges.[149] This undermines the tidy structure of the judge directing the jury as to the legal rule to be applied and then the jury applying that rule to the facts as they decide them. One ex-juror[150] suggests that juries operate on other than purely legal criteria, in one case rejecting the evidence of the chief prosecution witness who was a 'tin pot dictator' and 'pipsqueak of a civil servant' and in another ignoring the fingerprint evidence before it. One of the main criticisms directed at juries' performance[151] is in regard to the acquittal rate.

Table 7.2 showed that the CPS at magistrates' court completed 949,400 cases in 2000. Fewer than 6 per cent of these involved a not guilty plea and the accused was acquitted in 31 per cent of these. Table 7.4 shows that in the Crown Court in 2000, 72,800 adult defendants were dealt with, of whom 41 per cent pleaded 'not guilty'. About two thirds, 66 per cent, of the 'not guilty' pleas were acquitted. A high acquittal rate such as this requires further analysis.

Table 7.4 Defendants acquitted after a plea of not guilty showing manner of acquittal 2000[152]

Plea	Outcome	Number	Percentage
Not guilty to all counts	Discharged by judge	9,563	54
	Acquittal directed by judge	2,549	14
	Jury verdict	5,588	32
	Total acquittals	17,700	100
Not guilty to some counts	Discharged by judge	169	7
	Acquittal directed by judge	410	18
	Jury verdict	1,682	74
	Total acquittals	2,261	100

---

[147] (1988) 3 All E.R. 1086.
[148] *Chandler v. DPP* (1964) A.C. 763.
[149] Zuckerman A.A.S., *The Principles of Criminal Evidence* 1989, p. 36.
[150] Ely Devons, 'Serving as a Juryman in Britain' 28 *Modern Law Review* (1965), p. 561.
[151] Assessing performance for researchers is particularly difficult since s. 8 Contempt of Court Act 1988 makes it an offence to disclose or publish what goes on in a jury room.
[152] *Judicial Statistics 2000, op. cit.*, Table 6.10, p. 67.

These figures for earlier years show that acquittal rates have risen in both magistrates and Crown Courts. In 1993, the acquittal rate in the magistrates' courts was much lower at 14 per cent. In Crown Court, the statistics produced by the 1981 Royal Commission[153] for 1978 showed that 47 per cent of defendants pleading 'not guilty' in the Crown Court were acquitted. In 1993 the acquittal rate was 58 per cent. Prima facie juries still look generous in comparison with magistrates. But as Table 7.4 shows, the figures must be treated with considerable caution. Where the accused pleads 'not guilty' to all counts, the jury is responsible for less than one third of subsequent acquittals—the acquittal rate is the result of the prosecution offering no evidence or the judge directing the jury to return a verdict of 'not guilty' at the conclusion of the prosecution's case.[154]

When guilty pleas are taken into account, this figure means that the jury are responsible for under 10 per cent of all Crown Court acquittals. Furthermore many of the acquittals will be justified given the nature and the weight of the evidence. Thus the number of 'perverse' verdicts by juries (that is, verdicts which are against the weight of the evidence) is relatively small. McCabe's study of 173 acquittals in Oxford suggested that only 15 (9%) could be described as perverse.[155] Baldwin and McConville[156] suggested that their respondents (judges, police, prosecution and defence lawyers) considered as many as 25 per cent of jury acquittals as being 'questionable'. They also found that the same respondents found 5 per cent of convictions also 'questionable'. Juries in the main play the legal game, following the judge's directions as to the law and finding the facts to apply to that law.

7.7.5 *Functions of Juries*

Devlin called them a bulwark against oppression, a safeguard of our liberties since the common sense of the ordinary person prevails when all else fails.[157] But how far can the jury go in ignoring the law or acquitting in disregard of the evidence that has been put in front of them? Such jury 'nullification' is known in the USA[158] and cases such as the acquittal of Clive Ponting indicates that juries may still regard 'justice' as separate from the technicalities of the law. Ponting was a senior civil servant who had sent documents to an opposition MP, which related to the sinking of the Argentinean battleship, the Belgrano, during the course of the Falklands conflict. Prosecuted under the Official Secrets Act 1911, he admitted passing the documents. The judge virtually instructed the jury to convict yet they still acquitted.[159] Jury nullification was considered but rejected by Auld who described it as '... *a blatant affront to the legal process*' and recommended that juries should have no right to acquit in defiance of the law or in disregard of the evidence.[160]

The more mundane functions of the jury include listening to the testimony and other evidence provided by the prosecution or defence, the argument of counsel

---

[153] Royal Commission on Criminal Procedure, *op. cit.*, para. 6.17ff.
[154] Royal Commission on Criminal Procedure, *op. cit.*, para. 6.18.
[155] McCabe S., *The Jury At Work* (Blackwell, 1972).
[156] Baldwin and McConville, *op. cit.*
[157] Devlin P., *Trial By Jury* (Stevens 1956).
[158] Freeman M., 'Why not a Jury Nullification Statute Here?' (1981) 131 *New Law Journal* 304.
[159] *The Times*, February 12, 1985.
[160] The Auld Report, *op. cit.*, Chap. 5 para. 99ff.

and the summing up and directions of the judge. Perhaps we should remember Mr Justice Swallow:[161]

'Gentlemen of the jury, the facts of this distressing and important case have already been put before you some four or five times, twice by prosecuting counsel, twice by counsel for the defence, and once at least by each of the various witnesses who have been heard; but so low is my opinion of your understanding that I think it necessary, in the simplest language, to tell you the facts again.'

It is their function to assess the credibility of a witness, the measure the weight that should be given to any piece of evidence and to determine the existence or non-existence of the facts in the case. The jury then have to apply their determinations as to the facts to the legal elements in the case. It is the judge's job to explain what those legal elements in any offence are. This clear demarcation between facts and law often becomes clouded—the definition of many offences include as 'facts' concepts that are relatively imprecise in their definition. The key elements of theft, for example, are the dishonest appropriation of property belonging to another. Often the key question is whether the defendant acted 'dishonestly'—should the judge leave this to the good sense of the jury or should she give a direction expanding on the single word and developing a legal definition?

Brutus v. Cozens[162] is authority for the proposition that it is for the jury to decide upon and apply the meaning of ordinary English words, such as dishonesty. In *Brutus*, the defendant had interrupted Wimbledon by blowing whistles and distributing leaflets. He was charged under section 5 of the Public Order Act 1936 with insulting behaviour and it was held that it was not for the judge to interpret 'insulting', but to leave it for the jury to decide. But juries are rarely left to their own devices in this regard—a judge will tell the jurors that they must consider whether community values would regard the accused's acts as 'dishonest' and whether the accused realised that other people would see his actions in that light.[163] It only takes a cursory glance around the criminal law to see that common sense concepts are frequently circumscribed by quite detailed definitions—in *Caldwell*,[164] the House of Lords took it on themselves to lay down the definition of 'recklessness' for the jury to follow. We can see the same process in the appellate courts' definition of 'intention' in *Hancock*[165] and *Nedrick*.[166]

7.8 THE ROLE OF THE JUDGE

Within the adversarial trial, the judge is the umpire ensuring that the procedural rules are followed. He or she exercises control over the indictment, over the taking of the plea, over the admission of evidence; acts as the ultimate arbiter of any issue of law; summarises the evidence for the jury; explains the law and draws their attention to the issues that have to be decided. Judges do not normally call or question witnesses. This can mean that the jury do not hear sig-

---

[161] Herbert A., *Uncommon Law* (quoted in the Auld Report, op. cit., Chap. 5 para. 5).
[162] (1972) 2 All E.R. 1297.
[163] *Ghosh* (1982) Q.B. 1053.
[164] (1982) A.C. 341.
[165] (1986) A.C. 455.
[166] (1986) 3 All E.R. 1.

nificant witnesses. Zander and Henderson found that in 19 per cent of trials, judges knew of one or more important witnesses who had not been called by either side.[167] The prosecution might not call an eyewitness because he is a friend of the accused. The accused might not call him because the witness has previous convictions which, when revealed in cross-examination, would harm the defendant's case. Adversarialism necessarily brings such considerations into play at the expense of a clear picture for the jury. The Royal Commission recommended a more proactive approach but spent little time on considering the philosophy of the trial that brings such a situation about.[168]

7.8.1 *Admission and Exclusion of Evidence and the Voire Dire*

The judge exercises a general supervisory function over the trial but in particular needs to address the question as to whether the evidence adduced by one or other of the parties is admissible and whether it can be placed in front of a jury.[169] The judge acts as a preliminary filter of the evidence, initially considering whether the conditions for admissibility exist. Even when those conditions exist, judges can still exclude admissible evidence by use of their discretionary powers. However, although they can exclude otherwise admissible evidence, judges do not have the discretion to admit otherwise inadmissible evidence.

That discretion may be exercised where the probative value of the evidence is negligible in relation to the time and trouble caused by its admission or, more significantly, where its prejudicial effect is so great as to outweigh the probative value. This was the result of the decision in *Sang*.[170] However that case also held that there was no discretion to refuse evidence solely on the grounds that it was obtained improperly, by a trick or by use of an agent provocateur. In such situations the prejudicial effect is not outweighed by its considerable probative quality.

The decision as to whether evidence is admissible is normally quite straightforward. Sometimes the judge will have to conduct a hearing to determine the question. This is called a '*voire dire*', taking its name from the special oath sworn by any witness. This hearing often needs to be conducted in the jury's absence although the defendant and his counsel will be present. Often the argument as to admissibility is purely legal but sometimes the judge will have to conduct a factual inquiry. For example with a young child or a person with learning difficulties, there may be an examination, a competency hearing, to decide whether the person can be a competent witness.

More importantly a judge might be called upon to rule upon the admission of a piece of evidence such as an incriminating statement by the accused. If the accused alleges that it was obtained in breach either of section 76 or section 78 of PACE 1984, there are conditions precedent before it can be admitted into evidence, namely for the prosecution to prove beyond reasonable doubt that the statement was obtained without oppression and in circumstances that would not render the statement unreliable. The judge will hold on admissibility hearing and

---

[167] Zander M. and Henderson P., *op. cit.*.
[168] Royal Commission on Criminal Justice, *op. cit.*, para. 8.18; for consideration of adversarialism, see para. 1.11ff.
[169] This is examined in more detail in Chap. 8.
[170] (1980) A.C. 402—although *Sang* is still good law, its effect has been lessened since judicial discretion to exclude evidence is largely governed by s. 78 PACE 1984—*supra* Chap. 4.

make such a decision in the absence of the jury. It is likely that a defendant would give evidence as to the circumstances in which the statement was made, testimony that might be very prejudicial. The defendant is protected in such hearings since he or she cannot be cross-examined on the truth or falsity of the alleged confession during the *voire dire*[171] nor are statements made at the *voire dire* admissible in the trial proper.[172]

If the judge admits the evidence, then it is a matter for the jury as to what weight might be given to it. The judge might consider a confession admissible but the defendant could still adduce evidence (already advanced at *voire dire*) to seek to persuade the jury that it was not reliable. Tactically the defence must decide whether to reveal their hand at the preliminary *voire dire* in order to exclude the evidence altogether or to wait for the trial proper and thus not alert the prosecution.

7.8.2 *Withdrawal of Issues*

The judge also exercises control by his ability to withdraw issues, or the whole prosecution, from the jury. This can affect both prosecution and defence. At the end of the prosecution case, the defence might argue that there is no case for the defence to answer since the prosecution had failed to satisfy the burden of producing enough evidence for a particular element of the offence so that there is not enough evidence for a conviction. Although, as has been seen, under the Criminal Appeal Act 1995, convictions can be quashed if they are in all the circumstances 'unsafe', the trial judge must not ask that question but:

    i) is there any evidence that the accused committed the crime?

    ii) is there sufficient evidence for a jury properly directed properly to convict?

The judge is not permitted to look ahead to the appellate process.[173]

However the judge may also withdraw a single issue from the consideration of the jury. For example, a defendant charged with murder might be arguing for a conviction for manslaughter on the grounds of diminished responsibility. The judge might well refuse to allow the issue of whether the defendant was suffering from diminished responsibility to go to the jury—the judge must ask whether a reasonable jury properly directed could reasonably conclude on the evidence presented that the defendant was suffering from diminished responsibility.[174]

7.8.3 *Summing Up*

After closing speeches from the prosecution and the defence, the jury will hear from the judge who should remind the jury of the evidence that has been put before them and explain to them the nature of the charge. He or she must put all aspects of the defence that have been disclosed by the evidence and must explain

---

[171] *Wong Kam-Ming* (1979) 1 All E.R. 939.
[172] *Brophy* (1982) A.C. 476.
[173] *Greenfield* (1981) 2 All E.R. 1060; Pattenden R., '*The Submission of No Case to Answer*' (1982) Crim. L.R. 558.
[174] *Galbraith* [1981] 2 All E.R. 1060.

to the jury about the burden and standard of proof that must be applied. The judge cannot direct the jury to accept his version of any disputed facts nor can he direct a verdict of guilty. There may be directions as to evidential law, for example, a warning to be cautious where the prosecution rests wholly or mainly on identification evidence.

Alhough judicial direction as to the substantive and evidential law is required, should judges sum up the facts?[175] The argument is that this inevitably influences the jury in one way or another.[176] Jurisdictions such as New York have written jury charges which seek to avoid reference to the facts of the case.

---

[175] *Wilson* (1991) Crim. L.R. 838 where the judge told the jury that it was unnecessary (after a short case) for him to review the facts. The Court of Appeal did not interfere but disapproved of this course in *Gregory* (January 14, 1993 unreported) which said there must be a reminder of facts in all cases.
[176] Wolchover D., '*Should Judges Sum Up on Facts?*' (1989) Crim. L.R. 781.

CHAPTER EIGHT

Evidence, Witnesses and the Course of Trial

8.1 INTRODUCTION

We now turn to the rules of evidence and procedure that govern the contested trial—this is where the defendant enters a plea of 'not guilty' to the charge and the prosecution intend to offer evidence. In the Crown Court, a jury is empanelled to hear the evidence and decide on guilt. In the magistrates' court, the justices of the peace (or, perhaps, the district judge) carry out this function. In a trial on indictment, there will be an opening speech by the prosecution, an overview of the evidence,[1] which would support the allegations in the indictment

---

[1] Omitting reference to any evidence where the defence has given notice that it will be contested as inadmissible, especially confessions—*Swatkins* (1831) 4 C. & P. 548.

but in an impartial manner. Whether such, often lengthy, openings are necessary was questioned by the Runciman Commission.[2] This supported the Law Commission's proposals for particularised indictments,[3] which would remove the need for opening speeches in routine cases, a reform which has also been supported in the Auld Report.[4] Although Runciman accepted a need for an opening address in more complex cases, best practice should be to review the issues involved in the trial and not a comprehensive rehearsal of the evidence to be given by each witness. Auld went further to suggest that it was for the judge to review the issues and for both parties to provide an agreed summary of the issues for the jury.

Currently, it is rare for there to be an opening speech for the defence. At the close of the prosecution case, this is an option but only where defence counsel intends to call witnesses as to facts in addition to the testimony of the accused and not otherwise.[5] At the close of the defence case, both prosecution and defence make closing speeches—although the defence does have the right to the last word[6] (other than the judge's summing up).

After the opening speech, the prosecution will advance witnesses and other forms of evidence such as written statements in order to persuade the jury of the correctness of the case against the accused. The defence in its turn can advance evidence in disproof. Cases are decided on the evidence presented in the courtroom. The only information on which the trier of fact can make a decision is that presented either by the prosecution or defence and tested by cross examination by the opposing party. Thus the rules of evidence are central to the outcome of any contested trial and, indeed, also affect pre-trial decisions to plead guilty or to discontinue. These rules are concerned with how 'truth' is established in a courtroom[7] because the adversarial system allows both parties to present information and interpretation to the court[8]—the 'truth' is seen as emerging from this counterpointing of differing accounts by interested parties rather than from scientific investigation by a disinterested adjudicator. The rules of evidence constrain the prosecution and the defence by considerations of relevance, probative force and the need not to create undue prejudice as well as excluding to a certain extent evidence of opinion, character and hearsay.

Police officers especially perceive procedural and evidential rules as merely technical devices to allow the guilty to go free. But these rules embody principles that are central to concepts of justice. One example is the highly complex rules of hearsay, which in essence prevent a witness from telling the court, what another person, not present at court, had seen or heard. On occasion the rule excludes relevant information and significantly affects the outcome. But the concept of a fair trial requires that the accused has the fundamental right to confront and test the quality of the evidence against him or her—admitting hearsay evidence negates that right by allowing an absent witness to testify through the mouth of another.

---

[2] Royal Commission on Criminal Justice (1993), Cm. 2263, paras. 8.7f.
[3] Law Commission, *Counts in an Indictment* (1992).
[4] Lord Justice Auld, *A Review of the Criminal Courts of England and Wales*, Chap. 11, para. 22ff (2001).
[5] Criminal Evidence Act 1898, s.2.
[6] Criminal Procedure Act 1865, s.2.
[7] As opposed to uncovering or 'constructing' facts during investigation—McConville M., Sanders A. and Leng R., *The Case for the Prosecution* (1991) p. 65ff.
[8] McEwan J., *Evidence and the Adversarial Process* (2nd ed. 1998).

8.1.1 *Relevance and Reasoning*

Confronted with an item of information, we might ask, 'Is it evidence?' This question contains within itself two issues. The first concerns the logic of proof: is the information relevant and probative of whatever issue that needs to be decided? Secondly, even if we answer 'yes' to that first question, there are the lawyers' issues: are there other reasons why we should not allow that information to be presented to the jury?

Items of information are presented to the court: oral testimony by witnesses; written documents; 'real' evidence such as material objects or fingerprints; automatic recordings; a witness's demeanour; even a jury visit to the site of the crime. Such information is not proof but it is data from which we can draw inferences and come to conclusions. Conclusions as to what? This is easily answered since it is a key principle of due process that an accused can only be tried for a recognised and specific offence. There must be proof of all of the legal elements required in that offence and only evidence that is relevant to those elements can be used.

When is evidence relevant? This is the central question and a simple definition is that evidence is relevant when it tends to make another fact more or less probable. In a shoplifting case,[9] there may be testimony from the store detective that she saw the accused put the goods into her own shopping basket rather than a wire basket provided by the store. The prosecution must show that the accused took the goods and did so dishonestly. Our witness's testimony is clearly relevant to those issues as the jury might believe the witness that the accused did take the goods and might also infer from the fact of concealment that she was dishonest.

This definition of relevance can encompass not just direct eyewitness testimony or confessions but also a wide range of circumstantial evidence. Runciman felt that the criterion of relevance was too widely interpreted by judges, allowing time-wasting by counsel and forcing juries to sit through evidence which adds little to what was already before them. A more robust approach would be encouraged by imitating the powers under Rule 403 of the U.S. Federal Rules of Evidence which empowers judges to exclude evidence if:

> 'although relevant, its probative value is substantially outweighed by the danger of unfair prejudice, confusion of the issues or misleading the jury, or by considerations of undue delay, waste of time, or needless presentation of cumulative evidence.[10]'

For juries, it is not just a simple matter of deciding which witnesses to believe but embraces the process of drawing inferences from evidence. This is one of common sense logic: people who put supermarket goods into their own baskets normally are not intending to pay for those goods. But there may be a conflicting interpretation put forward by the defence: 'I like to keep the washing powder separate from the food and use my shopping basket. I forgot it was there.' Often there are many relevant items of evidence, some supporting and others contradicting a particular inference and jurors must assess the weight that they are willing to place on any such inference. Furthermore they may have to deal with

---

[9] With theft, the prosecution must adduce evidence to prove each of five elements—the defendant appropriated property belonging to another, dishonestly and with the intention to permanently deprive.

[10] Royal Commission on Criminal Justice, *op. cit.*, para. 8.13.

chains of inferences. Evidence leads the jury to an inferred fact from which a further inference can be drawn and so on through a series of intermediate stages until we reach the ultimate issue that has to be decided.[11]

Overall this is inductive reasoning, drawing conclusions from established facts. But we do not draw inferences in a vacuum and juries often use generalisations, which are often not articulated: shoppers who hide goods in their own bags tend to be dishonest. In this case and many others, to use such generalisations is justifiable but it is moot how far courts go to uncover such generalisations and to assess their validity as opposed to their prejudicial quality. The shoplifter's previous convictions for theft, although relevant, are excluded. Any probative value such evidence might have is outweighed by the prejudicial generalisation it would create in the minds of the jury, namely 'once a thief, always a thief'. There is less protection from other stereotyping, perhaps based upon assumptions about age, race or nationality. The disproportionate numbers of young blacks prosecuted, convicted and given custodial sentences illustrates this.

8.1.2 *Proof*

Having heard the evidence, the trier of fact must come to a conclusion on the ultimate issue of guilt or innocence. This is a two-stage process:

a)   who has to prove anything? Must the accused satisfy the jury of her innocence or for the prosecution to convince them of her guilt? This is the question of the burden of proof. In a criminal trial, it rests upon the prosecution.

b)   what level of proof is needed? People's expectation of the court process is that the trial will reveal the truth. Yet it is impossible to reconstruct the past and to say with total certainty what happened. The courtroom is not about truth but about proof. Proof is about establishing the probability that a state of affairs did exist. In a criminal trial with an individual's liberty is at stake, a high standard is required and that occurs when the jury is satisfied 'beyond reasonable doubt'. In theory this seems a proper formula but in practice there are significant inadequacies. For example, juries have been allowed to convict on the basis of a confession, a single identification or statements by an accomplice without corroborating evidence. The jury is not necessarily to blame. In many cases where justice has miscarried, the quality of evidence, accepted by the judge as evidence on which a reasonable jury might convict, has nowhere approached 'proof beyond reasonable doubt'. The ready acceptance of circumstantial evidence has meant that sometimes not only the quality but also the quantity of the evidence is wanting.[12] The English legal system has always prided itself on its rules on proof of guilt but there remain real problems as to whether judicial supervision over the sufficiency of evidence is adequate.

---

[11] An excellent short story illustrating this is Kemelman's 'The Nine Mile Walk' in Anderson S. and Twining W., *Analysis of Evidence* (1991) p. 9. On the logic of proof, see Anderson and Twining, *op. cit.*, Chaps. 2 and 3.

[12] For example, Woffinden R., '*The Case of the Winchester Three*' 140 New Law Journal (1990) p. 164.

8.1.3 *The Burden of Proof*

The first question for a court is who has to prove anything? If no evidence is adduced, no arguments made, who wins and who loses? This is the question of the burden of proof. There are two types of burden: an evidential burden and a legal burden:

- the evidential burden could be described as setting the agenda for the court. What issues have to be decided? At the start of the trial, the charge facing the defendant will identify the basic issues—for example, in a murder trial, those issues are first whether the accused caused the death of the victim and secondly whether she did so with the necessary intent. The prosecution will produce evidence relevant to these issues but the judge will have to be satisfied that there is enough evidence for the issue to be left to the jury. The accused might wish to raise other issues—for example, that she acted in self-defence. She would have to produce enough evidence to satisfy the judge that there was an issue here to be decided by the jury. This evidential burden might be referred to as the problem of 'passing the judge'.

- while the evidential burden dictates who has to establish the issues to be decided by the trier of fact, it does not state which party has to *prove* a particular issue, that is, to persuade the trier of fact that their proposition is correct. This is the legal burden of proof. In a criminal trial the prosecution to prove all the elements of an offence for the defendant to be found guilty but also to disprove any defences, such as self-defence, raised by the accused. The defendant normally has to prove nothing.

8.2 ADMISSIBILITY

Not all evidence that the parties may wish to introduce will be admissible. Which witnesses can be heard, what questions can be asked, what documents introduced, what objects seen by the jury? Is the evidence admissible? Admissibility is a key concept. The basic rule is that all relevant evidence is also admissible evidence unless there is a rule that excludes it. This is a problem for the judge who has to decide whether evidence is relevant and whether an exclusionary rule applies. Since 1997 such questions may be decided at a preparatory hearing.[13] If the trial has started and there is an objection to certain evidence, (usually by the defence), the judge will hear argument in the absence of the jury and make a ruling.[14] In some cases it will simply be a matter of law but in others there will be a dispute as to whether the factual conditions for admitting the evidence have been met—a common example would be a dispute about the conditions under which a confession statement has been taken. The judge may hold an admissibility hearing or trial within a trial (known as a *voire dire*) with witnesses and argument. The burden is on the party seeking to admit the evidence to show that the precedent factors exist.[15] If the burden is on the prosecution it is proof

---

[13] Under ss. 28–32 Criminal Procedure and Investigations Act 1996, but appeals may be limited by the principle in *Gunawardena* [1990] 2 All E.R. 477; see chap. 7 at 7.5.
[14] See the comments of the Court of Appeal in *Hampshire* [1995] 2 All E.R. 1019 at 1028j.
[15] *Yacoob* (1981) 72 Crim. App. Rep. 313.

beyond reasonable doubt.[16] Where the defence is seeking to adduce evidence, the judge merely needs to be satisfied that the conditions for its inclusion are satisfied on the balance of probabilities.

8.3 ORAL TESTIMONY AND WITNESSES

Historically the common law adversarial trial relies upon oral testimony rather than written statements obtained at earlier hearings. By observing and listening to a witness, it is believed that the trier of fact can assess the weight to be attached to the witness's evidence more effectively than by reading a written statement.[17] The physical presence of a witness is seen as an integral element of a fair trial—Article 6 of the European Convention embraces the principle of a public trial and the accused's right to confront one's accusers through cross-examination.[18] The practice of the anonymous accusation adjudicated in secret is perceived as the hallmark of totalitarian societies.

Adversarial trial might encapsulate constitutional and human rights principles but its second and parallel aim is to elicit reliable information.[19] Yet the very adversarialism that underlies our ideas of fair adjudication inhibits the ability to get at the truth effectively: the atmosphere of the court bewilders the witness; lawyers coach witnesses so that their testimony will support a particular perception of the facts; cross-examination as a technique leads the honest witness into error rather than into elucidation; tactics and surprise play a major part; there is still inadequate pre-trial disclosure and insufficient acceptance of affidavit evidence on non-controversial issues.

We frequently over-estimate the quality of evidence put before juries and their ability to assess that evidence. Too much weight may be placed on an identification, a confession or eye-witness testimony.[20] Witnesses' ability to assess the passage of time or speed or to recall colours, events or statements varies considerably. Good powers of perception and recall are not related to the coherence and demeanour of a witness and these latter factors are key ones in a jury's assessment of the reliability of their testimony.[21] Whether we believe or disbelieve what people tell us has as much to do with their abilities as storytellers as with the truth of their story. Juries adopt unscientific standards to evaluate the probative quality of what is put before them.

More mundanely, the witness has to recall, without any assistance, actions, which are likely to have occurred several months ago. A statement has been made within a few days of an incident is inevitably more accurate but if the witness is available, that statement can normally not be introduced into evidence. In other European jurisdictions, that statement, taken under judicial supervision, would

---

[16] *Ewing* [1983] 2 All E.R. 645. Where the prosecution wish to rely on the accused's confession, they must prove beyond reasonable doubt that it was obtained in accordance with the conditions under s. 76(2) of PACE 1984.

[17] Oral testimony is often given even where there is no dispute. Formal admissions are possible under s. 10 of the Criminal Justice Act 1967 but this is significantly under-used.

[18] *Unterpertinger v. Austria* (1986) 13 E.H.R.R. 175—although the European Court recognises circumstances where witnesses may remain anonymous or written statements may be accepted into evidence.

[19] Frank J., *Courts on Trial* (1949).

[20] Clifford B., 'Eye-witness Testimony' in Farrington D. *et al.*, *Psychology, Law and Legal Process* (1979); Lloyd Bostocks (1983) (ed.) *Evaluating Witness Evidence*.

[21] Bennet W. and Feldman M., *Reconstructing Reality in the Courtroom* (1981).

be put into evidence and at trial the witness would be questioned on it. Our refusal to use such statements as evidence perhaps reflects a suspicion of statements taken by the police, unsupervised by any judicial process. There has been much criticism of police interviewing skills. John Baldwin's enquiry for the Home Office[22] examined four hundred interviews of suspects from four separate police forces and concluded that 'interviewing is a hit and miss affair' with just over a third of interviews being conducted not very well or poorly. Ten years later these findings were supported in a further study in 2001.[23] In such circumstances, courts will remain reluctant to accept the written record as an adequate substitute for the presence of the witness. It is a further argument for a professional magistracy.

In general everyone can be compelled to attend court[24] and is competent to give evidence; everyone is under an obligation to disclose the truth. But in the 18th and 19th centuries, a range of potential witnesses was disqualified because of first, a fear of manufactured evidence arising form the self-interests of the witness—whether the parties themselves, their spouses or people with other interests in the outcome of the proceedings—and secondly, a fear of evidence being unreliable due to the moral or other characteristics of the person giving evidence. Thus heathens, atheists, convicts, the mentally ill and children were excluded from the witness box.

Nowadays there are few restrictions on testifying. At every stage of the proceedings, all persons, whatever their age, are competent to testify unless they are unable to understand questions put to them as witnesses and give answers that can be understood.[25] This is a drastic simplification of the old law, which at times stressed understanding of the solemnity of the proceedings, the duty to tell the truth or the capacity to give intelligible testimony. For young children or the mentally disabled, it is a low threshold of their ability to give understandable answers to understood questions. If there is any question about this, the judge will hold a competency hearing in the absence of the jury and may receive expert evidence and question the witness.[26]

The defendants (and their spouses) have provided a longer lasting problem.

8.3.1 *The Defendant as Witness*

At common law, the accused was incompetent as a witness. Not only was there the fear of perjury but also the fear that the judiciary might compel the accused to incriminate himself or herself. Only in 1898[27] did the accused become a competent witness in all criminal proceedings, although only for the defence. The defendant cannot be compelled to testify for the prosecution but section 35 of the Criminal Justice and Public Order Act 1994 enables the judge to call on the accused to testify with the sanction that the jury could draw adverse inferences in

[22] Baldwin, J., *Video taping police interviews with suspects—an evaluation.* (1992) (Home Office Police Research Series Paper 1).
[23] Clarke C. and Milne R., *National Evaluation of the PEACE Investigative Interviewing Course* (Home Office Police Research Award Scheme 2001); McGurk, B.J., Carr, M.J. and McGurk, D., *Investigative interviewing courses for police officers: An evaluation.* (Home Office Police Research Series Paper 4).
[24] Criminal Procedure (Attendance of Witnesses) Act 1865.
[25] Youth Justice and Criminal Evidence Act 1999, s. 53.
[26] *ibid.,* s. 54.
[27] Criminal Evidence Act 1898 s. 1.

the event of a refusal. Once the defendant enters the witness box, he or she can be cross-examined notwithstanding the fact that the answers may incriminate.[28] The accused cannot normally be cross-examined on previous convictions or bad character.[29]

1. the accused may be a witness for the prosecution in very restricted circumstances. Where there are multiple defendants, one of the accused might choose to testify for the prosecution against another defendant. Under the Youth Justice and Criminal Evidence Act 1999, this can only occur if the accused-witness is no longer liable to be convicted of any offence in the proceedings.[30] Those situations are first where the accused has pleaded guilty to all charges; secondly where the accused has pleaded guilty to some charges and the plea of not guilty to the other charges has been accepted by the prosecution. The defendant should be sentenced after giving evidence;[31] thirdly where the accused has been acquitted through the prosecution offering no evidence or through the submission of a successful 'no case to answer' plea at the close of the prosecution case or through a '*nolle prosequi*' being entered by the Attorney General; finally where the prosecution has successfully requested severance of the indictment—although it seems to be a rule of practice that in such circumstances, accomplices should not be called to testify unless the prosecution has agreed to discontinue the case against them.[32]

   Allowing co-defendants to testify against each other is fraught with risks because of the self-interest involved. The limitations above aim at situations where the co-defendant no longer has any interest in understating his or her own involvement and exaggerating that of another defendant. But many miscarriages of justice have arisen from reliance on accomplice evidence.[33] The risks of such evidence will be accentuated by the abolition of the need of the corroboration warning in such cases[34] and would become even higher were the Runciman proposals for the extension of plea bargaining became law.

2. the accused may always testify for the defence: the accused is competent at every stage of the proceedings, whether at committal, trial or *voire dire*. An accused should give evidence before other defence witnesses[35] although this is a matter of judicial discretion. Having elected to testify, the accused is subject to cross-examination like any other witness.[36] Even if the accused only testifies about his or her own involvement, he or she can still be cross-examined by the prosecution about any co-defendants' involve-

---

[28] Criminal Evidence Act 1898 s. 1(2).

[29] *ibid.* s. 1(3).

[30] s. 53(4).

[31] *Weekes* (1982) 74 Crim. App. Rep. 161.

[32] In *Pipe* (1966) 51 Crim. App. Rep. 17, the defendant was prosecuted for theft—an accomplice, about to be tried separately for handling the stolen goods, was called to testify. Whether he should be permitted to testify is a matter of discretion.

[33] *e.g.* the Luton post-office murder—Woffinden B., *Miscarriages of Justice* (2nd ed. 1989) p. 172ff; Kennedy L., *Wicked Beyond Belief* (1980).

[34] s. 32, Criminal Justice and Public Order Act 1994; *infra.* para. 8.4.

[35] s. 79, Police and Criminal Evidence Act 1984.

[36] There are safeguards under s. 1(3), Criminal Evidence Act 1898 in relation to cross-examination about the defendant's character.

ment.[37] Further where an accused gives evidence on his or her own behalf, he or she can be cross-examined by the co-defendant, even though no evidence adverse to that co-defendant has been given. There is a limited right against self-incrimination and the accused can refuse to answer questions if those questions are likely to expose them to another criminal charge.[38]

Until 1994, the prosecution were not permitted to comment on the defendant's decision not to testify[39] although this was possible for a co-accused's counsel. Although the judge could comment,[40] he or she had to do so in measured terms and had to warn the jury that they must not assume guilt from the defendant's silenced. As we have seen, section 35 of the 1994 Act places pressure on the defendant to testify as there is a risk that the jury might draw adverse inferences from a failure to testify. Silence can thus be evidence for the prosecution.

3. the accused may always testify for a co-accused: defendants are unlikely to give evidence for a co-accused when they have not given evidence on their own behalf, since they would open themselves up to cross-examination on their own involvement. However they might do this on *voire dire*, for example, where a co-accused is seeking a ruling on the admissibility of a piece of evidence such as a confession.

8.3.2 *The Defendant's Spouse as Witness*

There was great reluctance to allow an accused's husband or wife to give evidence against their spouse. The 1898 legislation permitted spouses to testify for the defence but whether a spouse was a competent witness for the prosecution remained obscure. At common law, the spouse was a competent witness in cases of personal violence and treason but was probably not compellable.[41] There were also discrete statutes that made the wife a competent but not a compellable witness. But this confusion was blown away by the Police and Criminal Evidence Act 1984, which made the spouse[42] a competent witness in all criminal proceedings and a compellable witness in a small number of such cases. Section 80 contains the following provisions:

a) for the prosecution: the spouse is always competent but can only be compelled to testify where: i) there has been physical violence on a spouse or person under 16; ii) where there has been sex with a person under 16 or iii) where there has been an attempt or conspiracy at such offence. Why is

---

[37] *Paul* (1920) 2 K.B. 183.

[38] *Blunt v. Park Lane Hotel* (1942) 2 K.B. 253.

[39] What used to be s. 1(b) of the Criminal Evidence Act 1898—the failure of any person charged with an offence to give evidence shall not be made the subject of any comment by the prosecution.

[40] *Bathurst* (1968) 2 Q.B. 99; *Sparrow* (1973) 1 W.L.R. 488 although see Rupert Cross' forthright comments on 'gibberish' in [1973] Crim. L.R. 329 at 333.

[41] This issue was still being argued in 1978 when it was decided by the House of Lords in *Hoskyns* [1978] 2 All E.R. 136 that, even where the husband was charged with an offence of violence against the wife, the wife was still not a compellable witness against the husband.

[42] Husbands and wives are those who are *de jure* married to the defendant—*Khan* (1986) 84 Crim. App. Rep. 44 where the woman had gone through a Moslem ceremony of marriage with an accused who was already married to another woman under English law. The marriage was bigamous and void and the witness was not a spouse for these purposes.

there a greater public interest in these offences than in others? Is the protection of children more important than the protection of other people? The changing nature of marriage has made this immunity somewhat anomalous and it is difficult to see why a spouse should be entitled to withhold information from the court, once the prosecution has been initiated. Furthermore, if it is repugnant to see a wife being compelled to testify against her husband, there are other levels of relationship to which this argument would apply such as a mother against her son or unmarried couples.

b) for the defence: the spouse is both competent and compellable on behalf of the defendant although if husband and wife are jointly charged, then neither is competent nor compellable. The failure of a spouse to testify cannot be made the subject of comment by the prosecution.

Spouses are those who are *de iure* married to the defendant. In *Khan*[43] the woman had gone through a Moslem ceremony of marriage with an accused who was already married to another woman under English law. The marriage was bigamous and void and the witness was not a spouse for these purposes. If a person is no longer married that person is competent and compellable to testify as if that person and the accused had never been married. 'No longer married' would include divorce or annulment but certainly not judicial separation or just non-cohabiting.

8.3.3 *Children and other Vulnerable Witnesses*

The number of prosecutions for the sexual and physical abuse of children has led to concern about the manner in which children can give evidence.[44] These concerns encompass not just the question of their competence as witnesses,[45] but whether they should give sworn or unsworn evidence, the appropriateness of children testifying in an adversarial setting, the extent to which there should be independent corroboration of their testimony[46] as well as the extent to which relevant and reliable evidence was excluded through the hearsay rule.[47] These were problems that not only faced the child witness but in whole or in part other vulnerable witnesses, particularly those with learning disabilities or mental handicap or those who had been victims of sexual assault.

Many of these problems have been resolved.

- The formality of taking the oath was removed so that the evidence of children under 14 and mentally disabled witnesses could be given unsworn.[48]

- The competence test was simplified so that children, whatever their age, are competent to testify as long as they are able to understand questions put to

---

[43] (1986) 84 Crim. App. Rep. 44.
[44] These concerns are thoroughly examined in Spencer J. and Flin R. *The Evidence of Children* (2nd ed., 1993).
[45] *Hayes* [1977] 2 All E.R. 288.
[46] *infra* pp.
[47] *Sparks* [1964] 1 All E.R. 727 but see s. 54 Criminal Justice Act 1991.
[48] Originally provided for by s. 52 Criminal Justice Act 1991; s. 55 Youth Justice and Criminal Evidence Act 1999 now separates out the test of competence from the test for giving sworn testimony.

them as witnesses and give answers that can be understood.[49] This is a drastic simplification and for young children or the mentally disabled, it is a low threshold. If there is any question about this, the judge will hold a competency hearing in the absence of the jury and may receive expert evidence and question the witness.[50]

- A matrix of special measures provisions for vulnerable witnesses was brought together in the Youth Justice and Criminal Evidence Act 1999. These measures may be used where witnesses are eligible under sections 16 or 17—witnesses eligible for special measures include children, the mentally or physically disordered or those the quality of whose testimony is likely to be diminished by fear or distress. The court must inquire into the circumstances taking account of the views of the witness and may make a special measures direction. This may include screening the witness, giving evidence by live video link, evidence given in private, the use of video recording of evidence in chief, the use of video recording of cross examination and the examination of the witness through an intermediary.[51] Furthermore the accused may no longer cross-examine in person certain child victims or victims of sexual assault.[52]

8.4 SUPPORTIVE EVIDENCE AND CORROBORATION

One unacknowledged weakness of the common law is its attitude towards supporting evidence. The testimony of a single witness is legally sufficient for a conviction, and a jury might decide that the weight of such testimony is sufficient to resolve their reasonable doubts. Historically there were situations where law has required additional supportive evidence either because of the nature of the witness (where there is a motive for lying or the court distrusts the intellectual faculties of the witness) or the nature of the evidence (such as identification evidence) or the gravity of the complaint. This was known as corroboration.

What is corroborative evidence? Corroborative evidence must be relevant, admissible and credible. It must be independent and emanate from a source other than the original witness. The common law has never required that such evidence should confirm the whole of the original witness's account but it must verify a material part of that evidence and implicate the defendant. In *Baskerville*[53] Lord Reading said that corroborative evidence is evidence '... *which confirms in some material particulars not only the evidence that the crime has been committed but also that the prisoner committed it.*'

These requirements wete criticised as being highly technical and resulting in complexity and rigidity. Can the corroboration derive from the accused?[54] Are lies corroborative?[55] Can such lies be outside or inside the court? Is silence

---

[49] s. 53 Youth Justice and Criminal Evidence Act 1999.
[50] *ibid.*, s. 54.
[51] *ibid.*, ss. 23–29—see McEwan J. 'In Defence of Vulnerable Witnesses' [2000] 4 *Int. Jour. Evid. and Proof* 1; Birch D. '*A Better Deal...*' [2000] Crim. L.R. 223.
[52] *ibid.*, ss. 34–39—see the case of Ralston Edwards discussed in Uglow S. *Evidence* (1997) p. 355.
[53] (1916) 2 K.B. 658.
[54] *Dossi* (1918) 13 Crim. App. Rep. 158—the accused was charged with indecent assault. While giving evidence, he admitted some 'innocent' fondling and this could be treated as some corroboration of the child's testimony
[55] *Lucas* (1981) Q.B. 720.

corroborative if outside the court?[56] Such subtleties in a summing up could tax the most assiduous juror. However the scope and impact of these rules has now been greatly reduced:

1. There still remain a few offences,[57] all statutory, where the jury *must* find corroboration in the form of independent evidence. This is required as a matter of law and if there is no such corroboration, they must not convict.[58]

2. The greatest criticism[59] of corroboration rules centred not on the *mandatory* requirement for corroboration but on the corroboration *warnings* that had to be given to the jury in cases of sworn children, accomplices and sexual complainants. The warning was to make the jury aware of the dangers of convicting on uncorroborated evidence. They could still convict if, after consideration, they felt sure of the accused's guilt. But, if the judge has failed to warn the jury of such dangers, any conviction would almost inevitably be quashed. These have now all been repealed.

    a. The common law required actual corroboration in the case of children's unsworn evidence and a mandatory warning in the case of children's sworn evidence, a position which rested on assumptions about a child's suggestibility, the powers of observation and memory, the predilections towards fantasy, the egocentricity and children's evil nature.[60] The need for corroboration was removed in 1988 in the cases of both unsworn testimony[61] and sworn testimony.[62]

    b. If a witness was an accomplice to the crime, the judge also had to warn the jury that, although they may convict the defendant on the basis of the accomplice's evidence, they should recognise that it is dangerous to do so unless that evidence is corroborated. If no warning is given, then the conviction would be quashed.[63] The rationale behind the rule is that accomplice evidence is highly suspect since the witness has every reason to dissociate himself even after his acquittal. But in other ways, it may be argued that an accomplice who incriminates himself at the same time as incriminating the defendant is presumably more to be trusted. The substantive question that the court should be asking is about the witness's motives in giving evidence and whether those motives are such as to make the testimony unreliable and in need of

---

[56] *Cramp* (1880) 14 Cox C.C. 390 the accused was charged with inducing a miscarriage and was silent when taxed by the woman's father about certain pills.

[57] s. 89(2), Road Traffic Regulation Act 1984, s. 1, Treason Act 1795, s. 168(5), Representation of the People Act 1983 and s. 13 of the Perjury Act 1911.

[58] The unsworn evidence of children required corroboration as a matter of law but this was dispensed with by s. 34(1), Criminal Justice Act 1988 as did ss. 2, 3, 4, 22 and 23, Sexual Offences Act 1956 (procuring women for sex in various ways) but this requirement will be dispensed with by s. 33 of the Criminal Justice and Public Order Act 1994

[59] *e.g.,* Law Commission, *Corroboration of Evidence in Criminal Trials* (Working Paper No. 115 1990).

[60] The criticisms of the old law are forcefully put in Spencer J. and Flin R., *op. cit.,* Chap. 8.

[61] s. 34(1), Criminal Justice Act 1988.

[62] s. 34(2), Criminal Justice Act 1988 but only in trials on indictment—magistrates still need to warn themselves of the dangers of convicting on the uncorroborated but sworn evidence of a child.

[63] *Davies* [1954] 1 All E.R. 507.

corroborative evidence. This requirement was abolished by section 32 of the Police and Magistrates Court's Act 1994.

c. A similar and more objectionable rule that the judge must warn the jury of the dangers of convicting on uncorroborated evidence of a victim of sexual assault. The rationale here is less justified than with accomplices. There were two assumptions, firstly that there was a strong risk of false accusation and secondly, that, especially with child victims, the jury would be strongly prejudiced against the accused. But there was never any justification in assuming that rape victims are more prone to lie than victims of other crimes nor that juries convict more in such cases than in other cases.[64] This requirement was also abolished in 1994.[65]

3. These reforms mean that a judge no longer has a mandatory duty to warn juries about the need for supportive evidence in such cases. But the judge still has a duty to ensure a fair trial and may still, at his or her discretion, warn the jury about the dangers of convicting on uncorroborated evidence of suspect witnesses. If the judge chooses not to do so, the conviction may be quashed but not inevitably. An example where such a warning is desirable would be where an accomplice gave evidence in own defence that implicated a co-accused.[66] In *Kilbourne*,[67] Lord Hailsham said that a judge would be wise to warn about any principal witness where that witness has some purpose of his or her own to serve. Witnesses' motives can vary considerably and discretionary warnings should not be a question of closed categories.

The question remained whether judges would develop discretionary corroboration warnings to cover area that were previously covered by the old rules. In *Makanjuola*[68] the defendant was convicted of a sexual assault on a female fellow worker. The appeal argued that the judge should have given a full direction about corroboration regardless of the 1994 reforms. The Court of Appeal held that, where there was some evidentiary basis that the witness might be unreliable, the judge might warn the jury about the dangers of relying on unsupported testimony. Such a warning would not be in terms of corroboration—it might be a simple caution or might be in stronger terms suggesting that the jury look for some supportive evidence. But this should not be done on the basis that the witness belonged to a particular class such as accomplices or sexual complainants. With this decision many of the problems in this area should be a thing of the past.

8.4.1 *Warnings: Identification and Confession Evidence*

Questions about a need for supportive evidence arise in relation to identification evidence and confessions. In *Turnbull*,[69] the Court of Appeal held that when a prosecution is founded wholly or mainly on the identification testimony of a

---

[64] Temkin J., *Rape and the Legal Process* (1987) p. 133ff.
[65] Law Commission, *op. cit.*
[66] *Knowlden* (1983) 77 Crim. App. Rep. 94.
[67] (1973) A.C. 729.
[68] [1995] 3 All E.R. 730.
[69] *Turnbull* (1977) Q.B. 224.

single witness, the jury should be warned, as a matter of law, of the risks of convicting on identification evidence but the warning is not couched in terms of the need for supportive evidence. The Court rejected the idea that convictions should never be based on identification alone and argued that the crucial element was the quality of that identification. As a result the *Turnbull* judgment does not require other independent evidence. Instead the jury should be warned of the special need for caution before convicting and they should be told to examine closely the circumstances in which the identification came to be made. The impact of *Turnbull* has been considerable—where this warning has not been given, the conviction will normally be quashed.

There is no need for any warning at all in relation to confessions. A jury may still convict solely on the basis of the accused's confession. The Runciman Commission considered whether supportive evidence should be required before a confession became admissible. Were a significant number of defendants to be acquitted as the result of such a requirement, it was felt this would have an adverse effect on the public perception of the criminal justice system. The Commission's research[70] suggested that, in most cases that rested on confessions, there was supportive evidence. Perhaps 5%[71] of current confession cases might end in an acquittal because of the lack of supporting evidence of any kind.

The Commission's majority recommendation[72] was that there should be a judicial warning, on analogy with identification cases, so that jurors should be aware of the dangers of convicting where the prosecution is based wholly or mainly on confession evidence. This would not mean that, in law, the jury would not be prevented from convicting in such cases. The jury would be told to look out for 'supporting evidence', which would not be equivalent to corroborative evidence in the *Baskerville* sense. Instead it would be evidence, the effect of which is to make the jury sure that the contents of the confession are true and as such is similar to the Scottish 'special knowledge' provisions.[73] The recommendation has not been acted upon.

The repeal of rules requiring mandatory warnings was to enable judges to tailor any warning more flexibly to the particular circumstances of any case. But it is predictable that fewer warnings will be given with the consequent risk of more unjustified convictions. The criticisms of the old corroboration rules have obscured the primary question of whether convictions should ever rest wholly or mainly on evidence from a single source? Our experience of wrong identifications, of false confessions and of the fallibility of eye-witness evidence and even expert scientific testimony leads to the answer that the trier of fact should not just be warned of the danger of convicting but should not convict without supporting evidence. What is needed is the development of more appropriate forms of supporting evidence. Scottish law has a general rule that the evidence of a single witness cannot establish guilt but accepts a broad and flexible definition as to what can amount to additional evidence.[74] The principles of fairness embodied in the standard of 'proof beyond reasonable doubt' requires clearer recognition that

---

[70] McConville M., *Corroboration and Confessions* (Royal Commission on Criminal Justice Research Study No. 13) (1993).

[71] This figure might be less since the police would devote more resources to uncovering additional evidence.

[72] Royal Commission on Criminal Justice, *op. cit.*, para. 4.76 ff.

[73] *Manuel* (1958) J.C. 41; Choo A., '*Confessions and Corroboration*' (1991) Crim. L.R. 867 at p. 873.

[74] *Meredith and Lees* (1992) S.C.C.R. 459; Choo A. *op. cit.* at 872.

conviction on the word of a single witness or on a single item of evidence is inherently dangerous.

8.5 IMMUNITIES FROM TESTIFYING

All persons, if competent, may testify and can be compelled to do so. Other items of information, such as documents, if relevant and not subject to any exclusionary rule, can be introduced as evidence. There are no general immunities for any category of person—any principle of fairness should require that everyone disclose all relevant information to a court. But there are categories of information that cannot be revealed even if the information is relevant and probative. There are three of these:

1. A person does not have to answer questions that might incriminate him or her. A witness may, if he or she so wishes, decline to answer a question where such answers might expose the witness to subsequent criminal proceedings.[75] The principle of access to evidence is displaced by the need for fairness to the accused and to minimise the risk that they would be convicted out of their own mouth. Such a restrictive judicial attitude is undermined by the numerous statutory exceptions, which require persons to provide information that may be used as the basis for a criminal prosecution.[76] Examples are sections 434 and 436 of the Companies Act 1985 which require company officers to answer questions put by Board of Trade inspectors appointed to investigate fraud within the company; environmental legislation requires compulsory provision of water quality information by self-monitoring which can provide evidence for subsequent prosecutions. Section 2 of the Criminal Justice Act 1987 requires any person under investigation by the Serious Fraud Office to answer questions, produce documents and furnish information. *Saunders v. United Kingdom*[77] questioned whether such legislation was compliant with human rights principles. The defendant was convicted of fraud on the basis of answers that he had been compelled to give in the course of investigations by inspectors from the Department of Trade. This infringed his freedom from self-incrimination and was in breach of the presumption of innocence and Art 6(2) of the European Convention on Human Rights. This is consistent with the approach of the European Court of Human Rights that any legal compulsion to produce incriminating evidence infringed the right of silence.[78] Restrictions on the use of evidence obtained in such ways were enacted in 1999.[79]

2. A witness should not reveal in court information, which would be injurious to the public interest, were it to be publicly revealed. This is known as public interest immunity (PII). Even if neither party to the proceedings object to the evidence being introduced, the court or another person, such

---

[75] *Blunt v. Park Lane Hotel Ltd* [1942] 2 All E.R. 187.
[76] There are other statutes which compel the provision of information but where any statements made are inadmissible as evidence, s. 31(1), Theft Act 1968; s. 9, Criminal Damage Act 1971; s. 98 Children Act 1989.
[77] (1997) 23 E.H.R.R. 313.
[78] *Funke v. France* (1993) 16 E.H.R.R. 297.
[79] Youth Justice and Criminal Evidence Act 1999 s. 59 and Sched. 3.

as the government, is able to do so. Until the 1960s government ministers excluded information from courts at will—where such public interest was claimed by the requisite certificate from a minister, that claim would be accepted by the court.[80] More recently[81] courts have been reluctant to accept ministerial fiat and judges have assumed discretionary power to inspect documents and to decide whether the interests of the administration of justice outweigh the effects of disclosure on the State. In *Burmah Oil*,[82] Lord Scarman suggests that there is no class which is automatically excluded from inspection—'*I do not accept that there are any classes of document which ... may never be disclosed*' Even cabinet minutes ought not to be automatically protected, '*... what is so important about secret government that it must be protected even at the price of injustice in our courts?*' Although there is a recognised public interest in relation to governmental and administrative matters and a presumption in favour of a minister's judgment, there is a conflicting presumption in favour of disclosure of all information,[83] which is necessary for the proper administration of justice. The conclusion is that the court can always question a claim to withhold disclosure, inspect the relevant documents and balance the different public interests involved.[84] That balance of interests will normally be exercised in favour of the accused in a criminal trial,[85] unless the documents are of extreme sensitivity.

PII is very significant in the rules concerning the disclosure of material by the prosecution. One long-standing rule has been that no question may be asked which would reveal the identity of a person who has given information for the detection of crime.[86] This rule encompasses other areas of police activity. In *Rankine*[87] the police refused to answer questions as to the location of their observation post since the owner of the house might be at risk of reprisals. The common law developed a procedure, in cases such as *Davis*[88] and *Keane*,[89] for placing sensitive material before the court for a ruling on disclosure without compromising its confidentiality. More recently the Criminal Procedure and Investigation Act 1996 established a framework for disclosure to the defence of prosecution material.[90] But the issue as to whether material is protected by PII is still a matter of common law and this procedure may be still be *ex parte* and may involve no notice to the defence that an application is being made. This procedure was criticised by the European Court of Human Rights in *Rowe and Davis v. UK*.[91]

---

[80] *Duncan v. Cammell Laird* (1942) A.C. 624; *Asiatic Petroleum v. Anglo-Persian Oil* (1916) 1 K.B. 822.

[81] *Conway v. Rimmer* (1968) A.C. 910.

[82] *Burmah Oil v. Bank of England* (1980) A.C. 1090; see also *Air Canada v. Secretary of State for Trade* (1983) 2 A.C. 394.

[83] *Campbell v. Tameside Council* (1982) Q.B. 1065.

[84] *R. v. Chief Constable of the West Midlands Police ex parte Wiley* [1994] 3 All E.R. 420.

[85] See the *Matrix Churchill affair—Report of Scott Inquiry* (HCP 1995–96 115); *ex parte Osman* (1992) 1 W.L.R. 281.

[86] *Marks v. Beyfus* (1890) 25 Q.B.D. 494; *D. v. NSPCC* (1978) A.C. 171; *Slowcombe* (1991) Crim. L.R. 198.

[87] (1986) Q.B. 861.

[88] (1993) 1 W.L.R. 613.

[89] (1994) 2 All E.R. 478.

[90] s. 3.

[91] February 16 2000; Application No. 28901/95; *supra* chap. 7 at 7.4.1.

Away from the criminal trial, PII has been important where plaintiffs have launched civil actions against the police and have sought to rely on documents related to inquiries into police misconduct under Part IX Police and Criminal Evidence Act 1984.[92] Such decisions as *Neilson v. Laugharne*[93] had led to immunity from disclosure becoming almost automatic for documents coming into existence as a result of a police investigation. But this view was reconsidered and rejected by the House of Lords in *ex parte Wiley*[94] holding that a class claim to public interest immunity did not attach generally in such circumstances.

3.   There is a privilege not to disclose information within the lawyer/client relationship although not for other confidential professional relationship.[95] The objective is to encourage candour between the lawyer and the client so as to enable the lawyer to represent the client effectively. It is a privilege of the client and once the privilege has been waived, the lawyer cannot refuse to disclose the information. Confidential communications passing between a client and his legal adviser need not be given in evidence by the client nor can they be given in evidence by the client's legal adviser without the client's consent as long as:

a)   the communication was made in order to enable the client to obtain and the adviser to give legal advice.

or

b)   the communication was made with reference to litigation that is actually taking place or was in the contemplation of the client.[96]

This is a privilege about communications and not facts. A defendant can avoid disclosure of any instructions to the lawyer and any advice received. The defendant cannot hand over pre-existing documents, which would be open to seizure by the police if they remained in his own hands to a solicitor for safekeeping. But if the communications are privileged, they are also immune from search and seizure.[97] There were two exceptions to this:

- communications before a crime are not privileged if their purpose was to guide the commission of a crime.[98]
- it was generally thought that the privilege is overridden where the information is required by an accused person to prove his innocence—

---

[92] Previously s. 49 Police Act 1964 and now replaced by ss. 65–88, Police Act 1996.

[93] [1981] 1 All E.R. 829.

[94] [1994] 3 All E.R. 420.

[95] Such communications might be protected from seizure by the police at an earlier stage—ss. 8–14, PACE 1984. Under s. 10, Contempt of Court Act 1981 journalists need only disclose sources if 'necessary' for interests of justice, national security or prevention of crime—see *Secretary of State for Defence v. Guardian Newspapers* (1985) A.C. 339; *Insider Dealing Inquiry under Company Securities Act* (1988) A.C. 660 and *Maxwell v. Pressdram* (1987) 1 All E.R. 656.

[96] In *Waugh v. British Rail* (1980) A.C. 521, the widow of an employee killed in an accident sought internal reports on the accident—the House of Lords held that the dominant purpose was not litigation but to inform BR about the cause of the accident in order to prevent recurrence. Thus the reports were not privileged.

[97] ss. 8–10, PACE.

[98] s. 10(2), PACE; *Francis & Francis* (1988) 3 All E.R. 775 gives this a wide interpretation going beyond the common law of *Cox and Railton* (1884) 14 Q.B.D. 153.

in *Ataou*,[99] the accused and a co-defendant, H, shared the same solicitor. H made a statement to the solicitor that the accused was not involved but later changed his mind, pleaded guilty and gave prosecution evidence implicating the defendant. Could the defendant cross-examine H on this inconsistent statement? At trial, the judge held that the statement was privileged. The Court of Appeal held that it was for the defendant to show on the balance of probabilities that the defendant's interest in seeking to breach the privilege outweighed that of the client in seeking to maintain it. Since H here no longer had any interest, the line of questioning should have been allowed. Accordingly the accused's conviction was quashed. But this decision was overturned in *R v. Derby Magistrates' Court, ex parte B*[100] when the House of Lords held that the privilege was absolute. The width of this judgment is extraordinary. To hold that the court is never justified in undertaking a balancing exercise to compare the public interest in the lawyer/client privilege with the public interest in, for example, the liberty of an individual seems unnecessarily wide. Lord Taylor called in aid Article 6 of the European Convention on Human Rights to justify the assertion that legal professional privilege is a fundamental condition on which the administration of justice rests. But Article 5 of the same convention asserts the right to liberty, which is an equally fundamental concept. If a person's liberty is dependent upon the disclosure of communications between a third party and his or her lawyer, it seems bizarre to state that legal professional privilege must in all circumstances outweigh the injury that would occur if an innocent person received a lengthy prison sentence. The European Court of Justice's position would appear to differ, seeing it as '*a right not lightly to be denied, but not one so entrenched that, in the Community, the Council could never legislate to override or modify it.*'[101]

8.6 EXAMINATION OF WITNESSES

The parties decide what witnesses to call and what evidence to present. Prosecution and defence have the opportunity to call and examine witnesses favourable to their case. This is known as examination-in-chief. The parties also have the opportunity to test the strength of the other side's evidence by examining their witnesses and this is known as cross-examination. At the close of the defence case, the judge does have discretion to allow the prosecution call further evidence. Although the prosecution cannot seek to remedy defects in its own case after the close of the defence, if a line of defence has emerged that could not have reasonably been foreseen, rebuttal is permitted.[102] In *Milliken*,[103] the defence was that the police had fabricated evidence. The judge allowed the prosecution to call evidence in rebuttal and this was upheld by the Court of Appeal.

[99] (1988) Q.B. 798; also *Barton* (1972) 2 All E.R. 1192.
[100] [1995] 4 All E.R. 526.
[101] *AM&S Europe Ltd v. EC Commission* [1983] 1 All E.R. 705 at 721d-f *per* Advocate- General Warner.
[102] *Hutchinson* (1986) 82 Crim. App. Rep. 51.
[103] (1969) 53 Crim. App. Rep. 330.

8.6.1 *Leading Questions*

One of the myths of oral testimony is that the testimony of a physically present witness, recollecting the relevant events is the most reliable form of evidence. Thus the first 'rule' for examining-in-chief is that counsel must not ask questions which prompt the witness by suggesting the answer. These are known as 'leading questions'. This is not a cast-iron rule and it is possible to lead the witness on formal and introductory matters and on those where there is no dispute between the parties.

The myth rests on the fact that the witness will have given a statement to whichever party is calling him or her. Counsel will be aware of the contents of the statement and there is great temptation to ensure that all the necessary facts emerge rather than allowing the witness to recollect them freely. This archaic rule could be easily avoided and trials speeded up by allowing the witness's written statement to be admitted into evidence, copies to be supplied to the jury and examination being mainly confined to the opposing party.

8.6.2 *Refreshing the Memory*

This insistence on oral testimony can reduce a trial to a test of memory and counsel are recommended to show their witnesses their statements before they go into court to avoid this. Once in the witness box, there is still one means for witnesses to remind themselves of the events to which they will be testifying. This is known as 'refreshing the memory'.

This practice is commonly seen with police officers who, once sworn, produce and proceed to read from their notebooks. The problem here is that notebooks and other such documents are hearsay evidence and not admissible. Police witnesses are permitted to do this, not because they are constables, but because they have written up the notebook at the time of the incident. As a result of this 'contemporaneous recording', the witness can review the document in order to jog the memory. The witness testifies and it is this oral testimony that is evidence and not the notebook.

This bizarre process is more an avoidance of the consequences of the hearsay rule than an aid to recollection. In *Maugham v. Hubbard*,[104] the issue was whether the witness had received money. The witness had no recollection whatsoever of the transaction but was shown his written acknowledgment of receipt and swore that must be accurate and that he had received the money.

The chief condition, before a witness can 'refresh the memory', is contemporaneity. The witness must have 'made' the document (or at least verified it) at the time of the incident or soon after. Thus the police officer who observes an incident and later writes up the observations in a notebook can refer to that notebook. The document does not have to be written by the witness. If a witness dictates a car number plate to a police constable who writes this down and repeats it back to the witness, the witness can look at the notebook to refresh his memory, even though he did not look at it at the time.[105] Nor does it matter that the note is a result of collaboration. In *Bass*,[106] the constables wrote a joint note and both could refresh their memory from it. The requirement of con-

[104] (1828) 8 B. & C. 14.
[105] *Kelsey* (1982) 74 Crim. App. Rep. 213.
[106] (1953) 1 Q.B. 680.

temporaneity is not strict and days if not weeks can pass between the incident and its recording in a document.

The documents used for these purposes must be produced for the other party and for the jury to inspect. The opposition is allowed to cross-examine the witness on the relevant parts of the document, without making the document part of the evidence but if counsel chooses to examine on other parts of the document, the document can be admitted into evidence. But the document is merely evidence of the credibility of the witness. In *Virgo*,[107] the witness in a police corruption trial was Humphries, a man whose business interests involved Soho sex shops. He was permitted to use his diaries to 'refresh his memory' as to dates of payments made to Virgo and was cross-examined extensively by the defence on other aspects of his diaries which were admitted into evidence. Humphries was an accomplice to the corruption whose evidence at that time required corroboration. The diaries could not be used for that purpose and could only go towards Humphries' credibility as a witness.

Even if a witness looks at a document outside the courtroom, if the prosecution is aware of that, they must inform the defence and allow the defence to see the document. In *Richardson*,[108] the witness made a deposition to the police a few weeks after the burglary. This statement could not have been used as a 'refresher' in the trial but was shown to the witness before the trial. The defence appealed on the grounds that the witness's evidence was thus tainted and inadmissible. The Court of Appeal held that any such rule preventing witnesses from reviewing their statements would be unenforceable but that the prosecution had a duty to disclose this fact.

There are now provisions under sections 23 and 24 Criminal Justice Act 1988 which permit a prior statement by a witness to be admitted under certain conditions.[109]

8.6.3 *Previous Consistent Statements*

Counsel cannot ask their own witnesses about earlier oral or written statements made by the witness, which are consistent with current testimony. In *Roberts*,[110] the defendant was charged with murder. In his evidence, he wished to testify that it had been an accident and that, two days after the killing, he told his father that it had been an accident. In Court, he was not entitled to retail his statement to his father. At first this appears to be another illustration of the impact of the rule against hearsay. But, as we shall see, hearsay statements are not admitted as evidence of the facts contained within them. Here the witness wished to relate the prior statement, not as evidence of the facts, but as evidence of consistency and credibility. Despite this, such statements are still excluded. The rationale for such exclusion takes various forms: there is a danger of manufactured evidence to bolster the credibility of a witness; such statements add little weight to a witness' testimony and are superfluous and there is a danger of irrelevant side issues as to whether this prior consistent statement was actually made.

There are several exceptions to this rule:

---

[107] (1978) 67 Crim. App. Rep. 323.
[108] (1971) 2 Q.B. 484.
[109] For discussion, see *infra*.
[110] (1942) 1 All E.R. 187.

a) The prior consistent statement may be used to rebut an allegation of 'recent fabrication'. This does not permit a witness to retail previous occasions on which the same story was told just because the witness has been attacked on cross-examination but only where counsel has accused the witness of recently inventing the story. In *Oyesiku*,[111] it was put to the defendant's wife that she had colluded with the defendant, charged with assault on a police officer, in making up the story that the police officer was the aggressor. The conviction was quashed after the judge did not allow the defence to show that the wife had made such a statement to the solicitor before she had even visited the defendant at the police station.

b) Complaints made by the victim of a sexual assault soon after the attack are admissible in support of the victim's testimony.[112] Perhaps this exception is a relic from the rule that a woman should raise the hue and cry directly after an attack as a preliminary to an appeal of rape. It applies to all sexual offences, including indecent assault on a male.[113] The details of the complaint can be given in evidence although those details are not evidence of the facts or corroboration of the victim's testimony but merely reinforce the victim's credibility.[114] The complaint must be voluntary and not in response to a leading question. In *Osborne*,[115] it was accepted that questions such as 'What's the matter?', 'Why are you crying?' or 'Why didn't you wait for us?' were all acceptable but not 'Did X assault you?'. The complaint must be made at the first opportunity that reasonably offers itself.

c) Crucially statements, which are made on accusation or on discovery of incriminating articles, are admissible. Normally these are statements made by an accused to a police officer. Often it is an admission of some kind and is admissible as evidence of the facts it contains (although procedurally it must conform with the provisions of PACE).[116] This exception does not just apply to incriminating statements. Everything said to the police is admissible evidence.[117] This includes not only inculpatory statements but also exculpatory or self-serving statements. In *Duncan*,[118] the defendant told the police that he had lost his temper when the victim teased him. There was thereby both an admission and some evidence of a possible line of defence. The admission is treated as evidence of the facts contained. Is the self-serving statement to be treated in the same way or merely as supportive of the accused's credibility? The trial judge said that this was not evidence of facts but the Court of Appeal disapproved of this. In *Sharpe*[119] the House of Lords held that the whole statement was admis-

---

[111] (1971) 56 Crim. App. Rep. 240.
[112] Temkin, *op. cit.*, p. 144ff.
[113] *Camelleri* (1922) 2 K.B. 122.
[114] *Wallwork* (1958) 42 Crim. App. Rep. 153—a 5 year old was assaulted by the father and complained to her granny. The victim could not give evidence—could the granny testify as to the complaint? The testimony cannot be used as evidence of the facts contained but only to bolster the credit given to the testimony of the victim—since there was no such testimony, the granny's evidence was wrongly admitted.
[115] (1905) 1 K.B. 551.
[116] *supra* Chap. 3 para. 3.8.7.
[117] *Pearce* (1979) 69 Crim. App. Rep. 365.
[118] (1981) 73 Crim. App. Rep. 359.
[119] (1988) 1 All E.R. 65.

sible as evidence of the facts it contains, whether the statement is an admission or is self-serving.

d) Identification evidence is often treated exceptionally. When a witness identifies an accused, evidence of a previous identification is admissible. This is not simply to add weight to the witness's consistency but the evidence of the previous identification is evidence in its own right. In *Osbourne*,[120] the witness could not identify the defendant or remember that she had identified him previously at a parade. The police officer who had been in charge of the parade was permitted to testify to the fact of the identification. This was admitted despite a strong argument that such testimony was hearsay—that is, the officer's testimony was not simply reinforcing the witness's testimony but was significantly replacing it.

e) A more esoteric rule is that statements, which are made as part of the *res gestae*, are also admissible. This Latin phrase encompasses everything which comprises the event itself and these can be rehearsed in court, even though they are a repetition of testimony already given. In *Fowkes*[121] the accused was charged with murder. The son of the dead man was sitting in the room with his father and a policeman when a face appeared at a window and the fatal shot was fired. The son testified that he thought that the face was that of the accused (known as Butcher) but also that on seeing the face at the window, he shouted 'There's Butcher'. The policeman also testified as to what the son said.

8.6.4 *The Hostile Witness*

A prosecution or defence witness may not give the expected testimony; it may be actively hostile or just less favourable than was hoped for. The general rule is that counsel cannot question their own witness' character or credibility or produce prior statements that are inconsistent with the witness's testimony. However in some circumstances it is possible to impeach your own witness.

a) at common law, the judge has discretion if the attitude and demeanour of the witness is hostile, to allow leading questions and to put any prior inconsistent statements to the witness.

b) by statute under section 3 of the Criminal Procedure Act 1865, if (in the opinion of the judge) the witness's 'present testimony' should prove adverse, then counsel can contradict by proving prior inconsistent statements, providing that those have been put to the witness.

The statute does not nullify the common law, which gives latitude to the judge over the issue of mode of examination. In *Thompson*,[122] the defendant was accused of incest with his daughter. She refused to answer questions. The judge gave permission for her to be treated as a hostile witness and for previous statements to be put to her. Eventually she agreed that these statements were true. It was argued on appeal that, since she had stayed silent, there was no

---

[120] (1973) Q.B. 678; *Christie* (1914) A.C. 545; *McCay* (1991) 1 All E.R. 232.
[121] *The Times* March 8, 1856.
[122] (1976) 64 Crim. App. Rep. 96.

'present testimony' and section 3 could not apply. The Court of Appeal held, regardless of section 3, that the common law gave the judge discretion as to what questions could be put to the witness.[123]

What happens if, although confronted with the earlier statements, the witness still adheres to the initial testimony? In *White*[124] a witness gave a statement to the police implicating the accused but gave different testimony in court. Confronted with the prior statement, the witness insisted the sworn evidence was the correct version. The judge told the jury that they had to decide which story to believe. The conviction was quashed since the prior statement could only be introduced as casting doubt on the witness' credibility. It was not evidence of the accused's guilt.

8.7 CROSS-EXAMINATION

Cross-examination is the questioning of any witness by the opposing party and has been seen as the *'greatest legal engine ever invented for the discovery of truth'*.[125] The underlying purpose is to detract from the value of the testimony given by the witness by seeking to suggest contradictions, to undermine confidence and to cast doubt on the witness' credibility and veracity. A failure to cross-examine any witness on any part of the testimony can be taken as an acceptance of that evidence.[126]

Witnesses can be cross-examined on any relevant matter that either goes to the issue in front of the court or to the credibility of the witness. Prior statements, which are inconsistent with the testimony in chief, can be put to the witness.[127] Questions are not restricted to matters raised by direct examination although a witness cannot be asked about inadmissible matters. In *Treacey*,[128] the accused's confession was ruled inadmissible but when the accused testified, prosecution counsel sought to cross-examine him on that confession. The Court of Appeal held that the defendant could not be questioned on it as a prior inconsistent statement. This rule does not apply to co-defendants and in *Rowson*[129] an accused was permitted to cross-examine a co-accused on the latter's inadmissible confession in order to contradict his sworn evidence. The judge must warn the jury that the confession is not evidence of the co-accused's guilt. The relevance is to test the credibility of the co-accused who is giving evidence.

8.7.1 *Finality of Answers to Collateral Issues*

Witnesses can be cross-examined not just on matters which directly impinge on the trial but on their credibility—that is, whether they are worthy of belief. Such questioning might include suggesting that the witness has made other statements away from the court about the incident, which differ from the sworn testimony— these are known as prior inconsistent statements. It might also involve ques-

---

[123] Had the witness denied making these earlier statements, they certainly could be proved under s. 3. But it is a moot question whether they could have been proved at common law.
[124] (1922) 17 Crim. App. Rep. 59; see also *Golder* (1960) 1 W.L.R. 1169.
[125] Wigmore, *Evidence* (revised ed., 1974) para. 1367; for opposite opinions, see Uglow, *op. cit.*, p. 857.
[126] *Bircham* (1972) Crim. L.R. 430.
[127] under ss. 4–5, Criminal Procedure Act 1865.
[128] (1944) 2 All E.R. 229.
[129] (1986) Q.B. 174; *Myers* [1997] 4 All E.R. 314; *Lui Mei Lin* (1989) A.C. 288.

tioning the witnesses about their prejudices, criminal records or physical and mental disabilities.

In cross-examining there is thus a distinction to be drawn between those questions that are relevant to issues that need to be decided in the case and cross-examining on facts that merely go to the witness's credit. This distinction becomes important when counsel wants to introduce evidence in rebuttal of a witness' testimony. If that testimony concerns the issues that the court has to decide, this is usually permissible. But if the rebuttal concerns a collateral issue, such as the credit of a witness, counsel is bound by the answer given by the witness and cannot call independent evidence in rebuttal.

A classic example of this distinction is *Hitchcock*,[130] where the defendant was charged with unlawful use of a cistern. A witness testified that the cistern had been used. In cross-examination, the witness was asked (and denied) whether he had been paid to testify. Was the witness bribed to give evidence against the accused? Although this seems a central question, the defence were not permitted to contradict his denial by other independent evidence. Zuckerman argues[131] that this distinction between questions that go to the issues and questions that go to the credit of the witness is unfounded. If the witness testifies to seeing a car number plate at 30 metres and then denies that he has poor eyesight, *Hitchcock* makes it impossible to call the witness' optician in rebuttal. But the weight of the witness' testimony and its probative force depends completely on the quality of his eyesight—as was the case in *Hitchcock* where the value of the witness' testimony relies on whether he has been bribed to give evidence or not.

Particular problems arise within rape cases.[132] The common law rule was that the victim might be asked about sexual relationships with other men but that once an answer has been given, counsel have to accept it.[133] Nowadays we would see that common law rule as flawed—intimate details of a witness's private life are not relevant to any issue before the court. However the law creates a problem as the issue in rape cases is frequently not just the consent of the victim but the accused's belief in that consent.[134] As soon as the legal issue is defined in that way, the accused's beliefs about the victim's prior sexual history may have bearing. In *Bashir*,[135] the defence was that the victim was a prostitute. If the defendant knew this, it can be argued that there was a greater possibility that he believed that the victim was consenting.

Such questioning is at the very least a humiliating experience for the victim and was regulated by section 2 of the Sexual Offences Act 1976 which permitted such cross-examination only with the leave of the judge and he should allow this where it would otherwise be 'unfair' on the defendant. But the impact of *Morgan* meant that relevance was only too easy to establish.[136] Further reform was brought about in 1999,[137] which limits cross-examination on the victim's sexual behaviour to incidents that occurred at the same time as the alleged rape or where

---

[130] (1847) 1 Exch. 91.

[131] Zuckerman, *op. cit.*, pp. 94 ff.

[132] Temkin J., *op. cit.*, p. 119ff.; Temkin J., '*Sexual History Evidence—the Ravishment of Section 2*' (1993) Crim. L.R. 3.

[133] *Holmes* (1871) L.R. 1 C.C.R. 334.

[134] *Morgam* (1976) A.C. 182.

[135] (1969) 1 W.L.R. 1303.

[136] *Viola* (1982) 3 All E.R. 73; Temkin J., (1993) *op. cit.*

[137] s. 41, Youth Justice and Criminal Evidence Act 1999.

the behaviour was so similar to the alleged rape that the similarity could not reasonably be explained as a coincidence.

The experience of the rape victim in the witness box is extreme but not different in kind from the bullying and intimidation that many witnesses face when testifying. Although the court has the power to restrain such tactics,[138] courts often do not intervene.[139] Yet there is a public interest in encouraging people to report offences and to testify. Victims and witnesses have rights to the protection of their own personal dignity and privacy and these are recognised by the European Convention on Human Rights. These are rights that must be balanced against those of the accused. But the adversarial quality of trial gives overwhelming priority to the right of the accused to make a full defence that these other, equally compelling, public interests are overlooked.[140] Through the 1980s, there was piecemeal protection introduced, especially for child witnesses but a full review took place through an interdepartmental government group in 1998.[141] Many of the recommendations were implemented in Part II of the Youth Justice and Criminal Evidence Act 1999 with its matrix of protective measures for vulnerable victims and witnesses.

8.7.2 *Exceptions to the Finality Rule*

Evidence in rebuttal can be brought even on matters of credit when:

a) a witness denies making a prior inconsistent statement. These can be proved under sections 4 and 5 of the Criminal Procedure Act 1865.

b) a witness denies previous convictions. These can be proved under section 6 of the Criminal Procedure Act 1865 (although it must always be remembered that defendants who attacks a prosecution witness in this way, puts their own character at risk under section 1(3)(ii) of the Criminal Evidence Act 1898, should they choose to testify).

c) a defendant denies bias. In *Mendy*[142] the wife was charged with assault and the husband was due to give evidence on her behalf. He got a man to take notes of other testimony before he himself went into the box. He denied this but the prosecution were permitted to rebut this. In *Busby*[143] a constable denied threatening a witness. When the witness was called, the defence were not allowed to ask whether he had been threatened by the police officer as the judge said this only went to the officer's credit. The Court of Appeal quashed the conviction since it indicated that the policeman was prepared to cheat to secure a conviction.

d) a witness is suffering from a mental or physical disability. In *Toohey*,[144] the accusation was assault with intent to rob. The defendants argued that the victim had been drinking and that they were trying to get him home

---

[138] *Sweet-Escott* (1971) 55 Crim. App. Rep. 316.
[139] Royal Commission on Criminal Justice, *op. cit.*, para. 8.12.
[140] *e.g.* the short and discursive treatment of such issues by Runciman—Royal Commission on Criminal Justice, *op. cit.*, para. 8.36ff.
[141] *Speaking Up For Justice* (Home Office, 1998).
[142] (1976) 64 Crim. App. Rep. 4.
[143] (1982) 75 Crim. App. Rep. 79.
[144] (1965) A.C. 595.

when he became hysterical, alleging the accused were attacking him. A doctor examined the victim soon afterwards but although allowed to testify whether the victim was drunk or hysterical, was not allowed to give evidence as to whether drink would exacerbate hysteria or whether the victim was more prone than normal to hysteria. The House of Lords held that this had been wrongly excluded.[145]

e)   a witness has a reputation for untruthfulness.[146]

8.8 EXCLUSIONARY RULES

Even when there is a competent, compellable witness in the witness box, there may be some questions which are prohibited because of an 'exclusionary rule'. The most significant of these rules is that against hearsay but there is also a ban on witnesses expressing their opinions and on the prosecution advancing evidence about the accused's bad character, especially any previous convictions or crimes that might have been committed in the past.

8.8.1. *Hearsay*

The hearsay rule is commonly regarded as meaning that a witness cannot repeat in court what another person told them. This is too broad—witnesses are expected to testify as to the evidence of their own perceptions such as sight, hearing, taste, smell or touch. A witness can certainly testify to what another person said in their hearing—but only for certain purposes and but not for others. For example:

- in a criminal deception case, the witness/victim can testify that the accused told her that the watch was a genuine Rolex.

- but in a street robbery case, the witness/victim could not testify that a third person had told her the mugger was wearing a Rolex.

What's the difference? In the former, the prosecution must show that the accused lied—evidence that the witness heard the untrue statement is admissible because the court is not being asked to rely upon any fact in the accused's deceptive statement but is being asked to find as a fact that the statement was made and contained these words. This is within the direct perceptions of the witness who can be cross-examined on whether she heard and remembered the statement accurately.

In the street robbery scenario, the prosecution must show that the accused was the mugger and possession of the Rolex is (limited) circumstantial evidence of that. But the witness did not see this and is telling the court what the third party saw—the court is being asked to rely on a fact in the statement that is outside the experience of the witness. She may be cross-examined on whether she heard the third party's statement accurately but not whether the mugger was wearing a Rolex rather than another brand. The witness in court has testified about another

---

[145] But this might be compared with *MacKenny* (1981) 72 Crim. App. Rep. 78 where the defence were prevented from leading evidence from medical experts who had watched the chief prosecution witness and had formed the opinion that he was a psychopath very likely to be lying.
[146] *Richardson* (1969) 1 Q.B. 299.

person's perceptions and the accused is unable to cross-examine the real witness. This is hearsay and is by and large inadmissible in criminal proceedings. Witnesses cannot testify to out-of-court statements if the purpose of the testimony is to rely on the truth of the contents of that statement. If the prosecution wishes to prove a fact, they have to call the person who directly perceived it.

This applies not just to repeating other people's statements. Witnesses cannot testify as to what they themselves said. 'I told my wife that the mugger was wearing a Rolex' is not admissible as evidence. The fact that the witness told his wife does not prove anything about the defendant's watch. If the witness has already testified that he saw the watch on the mugger, it does show the witness's consistency but as we saw above, it is a prior consistent statement and thus not admissible for this purpose either. All out-of-court statements are excluded: whether they were sworn or unsworn; whether the person making the statement is a witness or not; whether the statement is oral or in writing or by conduct. Furthermore, the rule does not merely exclude those statements which expressly state another's perceptions but also those statements which imply what those perceptions were.

The rule against hearsay is broad,[147] its boundaries are indefinite[148] and there are a range of common law and statutory exceptions. But it is a rule and the judge has no discretion to admit a hearsay statement simply on the grounds that, as evidence, it is relevant, reliable and probative. The classic statement of the rule was formulated by Cross; '*a statement other than one made by a person while giving oral evidence in the proceedings is inadmissible as evidence of any fact stated therein*'.[149]

The critical aspect of the rule is that the statement is only inadmissible as evidence of any fact or opinion contained in it. If the statement is introduced for a separate and different purpose, it may be admissible. For example, where a witness's truthfulness has been doubted, a prior consistent statement may be introduced, not as evidence of the facts but as evidence that the witness is consistent and therefore more credible.[150] Another example of this can be seen where the witness testifies that the defendant had stated that there were pink elephants in the road. Although the witness is repeating another's words, such a statement is not hearsay because it is introduced, not as evidence that the elephants existed but that the defendant was drunk or mad.[151]

8.8.2 *Common Law Exceptions and Res Gestae*

Many exceptions to hearsay are common law although the list has recently been significantly amended by statute.[152] These varied exceptions are linked in that they are more reliable and probative than other types of hearsay statement. Since reliability has not been the core test for the exclusion of hearsay, pragmatism is a more convincing explanation for the piecemeal nature of these exceptions.

---

[147] *Kearley* (1992) 2 All E.R. 345. The rule's significance is now largely limited to criminal trials as a result of the Civil Evidence Act 1968.

[148] *Woodhouse v. Hall* (1981) 72 Crim. App. Rep. 39.

[149] Tapper C., *op. cit.*, p. 46.

[150] *Oyesiku* (1971) 56 Crim. App. Rep. 240.

[151] *Ratten* (1972) A.C. 378.

[152] Admissions and confessions in criminal law are now governed by s.76, PACE ss.23 and 24 Criminal Justice Act 1988 have also made substantial inroads into the scope of the hearsay rule concerning the admissibility of documents.

There were many exceptions at common law, including statements made in public documents and statements by deceased persons.[153] Many of these are now dealt with under sections 23 and 24 of the Criminal Justice Act 1988. The significant exception was the rule relating to confessions and admissions: a statement made by a defendant, adverse to his or her own case, is admissible as evidence of the truth of what it contains. This is now also regulated by statute.[154] The major exception still existing under common law is the rule that allows hearsay statements to be admitted if they are part of the *res gestae*. If a statement is made spontaneously as an intrinsic part of the action or event, that statement is admissible as evidence of the truth of what it contains. All acts and statements, which are part of the whole event, are admissible and this exception overrides all other exclusionary rules.[155] The critical question is what is 'part of the action' as opposed to statements preceding or subsequent to the event?

The normal *res gestae* situations consist of statements by participants or observers at events.[156] When a participant makes an uncalculated outburst in the heat of the moment, this is felt to be more reliable and less likely to be an invention. The critical elements are that the statement was spontaneous and contemporaneous with the events. In early cases, these elements were often seen as technical rules. *Bedingfield*[157] was a case where the defendant was charged with murder by cutting the victim's throat. There was evidence that the accused was in a room with the victim who emerged with her throat cut and said, 'Oh dear, Aunt, see what Bedingfield has done to me!' The evidence of that statement was held inadmissible because it occurred after the throat cutting and the '*res*' had been completed.

Such a strict approach to contemporaneity has long since disappeared. In *Ratten*,[158] the phone call by a sobbing woman was made at 1:15pm and the wife was dead by 1:20pm. If we interpret her statement 'Get me the police' as containing an inference, namely 'My husband is attacking me', that implied assertion is hearsay and inadmissible. The Privy Council held that, even if this was the correct interpretation, that statement itself was part of the *res gestae*, was made under the overwhelming pressure of the situation and thus admissible as an exception to hearsay. Lord Wilberforce said that the approach was not purely technical in the sense of lapse of time or change of venue—these were factors but were not decisive. The judge must be satisfied that the statement was made in circumstances of spontaneity or of involvement so that the possibility of concoction could be disregarded,

'. . . if the drama, leading up to the climax, has commenced and assumed such intensity and pressure that the utterance can be safely regarded as a true reflection of what was unrolling or actually happening, it ought to be received.'

This approach was accepted by the House of Lords in *Andrews*[159]where the

---

[153] Only where these were against interest, in the course of a duty, as to pedigree or as to public rights or in the settled and hopeless expectation of death. Statements by murder victims are not automatically admissible.

[154] S.76, PACE—this issue is discussed, *supra* Chap. 4.

[155] *Ellis* (1826) 6 B. & C. 145.

[156] Cross discusses statements accompanying relevant acts, statements concerning physical sensation and statements concerning the maker's state of mind—Tapper, *op. cit.*, pp. 723 ff.

[157] (1879) 14 Cox C.C. 341.

[158] (1972) A.C. 378.

[159] (1987) 1 All E.R. 513.

victim was attacked and stabbed in his own flat, made his way a few minutes later to the flat below and made statements to an extent identifying the defendant. Although factually similar to *Bedingfield*, the evidence was admitted. Lord Ackner said that the judge should be satisfied that the event was so unusual or startling that the victim's utterance would be an instinctive, spontaneous reaction without opportunity for reasoned reflection, and that the possibility of concoction could be disregarded.

8.8.3 *Statutory Exceptions to Hearsay*

The major statutory exceptions to the hearsay rule, apart from confessions, come under the provisions of the Criminal Justice Act 1988 admitting certain categories of documentary hearsay. Further exceptions were consolidated in Part II of the Youth Justice and Criminal Evidence Act 1999 which in certain cases permits a court to receive a videotape not only of the evidence in chief of a child or other vulnerable witness but also the cross-examination.

The first steps were tentative: the effect of *Myers*[160] was to exclude all business documents. The Criminal Evidence Act 1965 went a little way towards overturning this so that records compiled within a trade or a business were admissible and these provisions were broadened through section 68 of PACE in 1984.[161] The pace of change was fast and sections 23 and 24 of the Criminal Justice Act 1988 replaced section 68.

For the first time, section 23 provides a general exception to the hearsay rule in criminal proceedings for first-hand documentary hearsay:

'...a statement made by a person in a document shall be admissible in criminal proceedings as evidence of any fact of which direct oral evidence by him would be admissible...'

A document written by a person not able to be a witness is now admissible in evidence but only under certain conditions. Those conditions are to be found in section 23(2) and (3). The document is only admissible where the maker of the statement is unavailable because he or she is dead or mentally or physically unfit;[162] or where the maker is outside the U.K. and it is not reasonably practicable to secure his attendance;[163] or where reasonable steps have been taken but the maker of the statement cannot be found. In 'Justice for All' the government propose to make witness statements more widely admissible at trial.[164]

However, even where the maker of the statement is available to testify, section 23(3) creates a more controversial situation where a document can be used. This is where the statement is made to a person charged with investigating offences and where the maker of the statement is in fear or being kept out of the way. The Home Office Report in 1998, *Speaking Up For Justice*, highlighted the position of the intimidated witness alongside other vulnerable witnesses and Part II of the

---

[160] (1965) A.C. 1001.
[161] This followed recommendations in the 11th Report of the Criminal Law Revision Committee (Cmnd. 4991 1972).
[162] *Cole* (1990) 2 All E.R. 108.
[163] *Iqbal* (1990) 3 All E.R. 787; *Bray* (1988) Crim. L.R. 829, the prosecution cannot make such a claim where they only realise at the date of trial that the witness is abroad when he has been away 7 months.
[164] *op. cit.*, para. 4.6.1.

Youth Justice and Criminal Evidence Act 1999 provides a range of measures to protect such witnesses. Section 23(3) provides a fallback if all else fails. It is widely drawn and has attracted, on one hand, criticism[165] and, on the other, a desire to see the term 'fear' interpreted more widely, especially in the context of domestic violence when the section might be used to protect victims from direct court confrontation with their attackers.[166] It might be argued that, although a primary witness is not available for cross-examination, this can be seen as the defendant's own fault.

A statement is any representation of fact whether made in words or otherwise. The statement must be made by a person. This does not mean that the maker has to write it down but that it must be checked or accepted by the person.[167] It must be a statement of fact and not an expression of opinion. This exception is also limited to 'direct' hearsay: that is, where a witness has directly perceived some fact and recorded this in writing.[168]

For section 23 generally, the statement of the witness must be made in a document. There is no restriction here (unlike previous legislation) about documents created in the course of as trade or business and thus can encompass not just trade records, business letters but all forms of maps, plans, discs, tapes, films, diaries and, indeed, shopping lists.

This provision only cures the vice of hearsay. The statement is admissible as evidence of any fact of which direct oral evidence would be admissible. Thus the incompetent witness's statement does not become admissible because it is written down and signed.[169] Nor would evidence be admissible about the accused's character or which was in breach of the public policy provisions. Equally under section 28(1)(a), section 23 does not prejudice the admissibility of hearsay statements that might be admissible under the common law or other statutory exceptions. In other words, if a confession is admissible under section 76 of PACE or expert testimony under section 30 of the Criminal Justice Act 1988, the prosecution do not have to satisfy section 23 conditions as well.

Section 24 is the successor to section 68 for trade and business records. Such documents can be readily used as evidence and whereas section 23 only applies to first-hand hearsay, section 24 applies even where the hearsay is indirect hearsay and where the information has been passed down a chain. Section 24 requires that the document must have been created or received by a person in the course of a trade, business, profession or other occupation, or as a holder of a paid or unpaid office and that the information was supplied by a person reasonably be supposed to have had personal knowledge. The information can have been

---

[165] Wolchover D., 'Keeping Witnesses Out of the Way' (1988) New L.J., 461.

[166] Edwards S., 'What shall we do with a frightened witness?' (1989) New L.J. 1740; McEwan J., 'Documentary Hearsay Evidence—Refuge for the Vulnerable Witness' (1989) Crim. L.R. 629 at 637; Renshaw (1989) Crim. L.R. 811.

[167] This would still seem to exclude the client's statement to the solicitor in Re D. (1986) 2 F.L.R. 189 where the lawyer made notes and did not show them to the client. As a result the statement was inadmissible under s. 2, Civil Evidence Act 1968 and this would also be the case under s. 23, Criminal Justice Act 1988.

[168] Professor Birch has suggested that the section allows any statement to be admitted if the person creating or verifying the document could have testified as to the contents of that statement—this would go beyond 'direct hearsay' since this might include the witness recording a statements made by third parties which would have been admissible under another exception to hearsay (res gestae, for example)—see (1989) Crim. L.R. 603.

[169] H. v. H. (1989) 3 W.L.R. 933—a 5 year old would not be competent to testify and her statements to social worker, written down, do not become admissible as a result of s. 23.

supplied directly or indirectly. In such cases the document can be received into evidence and there is no requirement that the maker of the statement be unable to testify unless the statement was made for the specific purpose of a criminal investigation or criminal proceedings. If this is the case, section 23(2) or section 23(3) applies, although there is an additional possibility—that the person who made the statement cannot reasonably be expected to have any recollection of the matters dealt with in the statement. In *Farrand v. Galland*,[170] the charge was supplying a car with a false odometer reading. The evidence consisted of record cards of a previous owner, a car hire firm. The person who compiled the record was available but not called and the justices threw out the case. But the provisions have to be read disjunctively so that as long as one condition applies, then that is sufficient. Here it would be unreasonable to expect the person who filled out the card to have any recollection of the mileage.

The Act does provide certain safeguards in the form of judicial discretion. Whenever a document is admissible under sections 23 or 24, under section 25, the court has the power to exclude evidence, if in the interests of justice, it ought not to be admitted. Section 25(2), while not detracting from the generality of that discretion, directs the court to look particularly at several elements: at the nature and source of the document, to the extent to which other evidence on the issue is available, to the relevance of the evidence or to the risk of unfairness. It would appear that the burden of persuading the court that the document should be excluded rests on the party objecting to admission.

But if a document is admissible under sections 23 or 24 but it is one prepared for the purposes of criminal investigation, leave from the court is required under section 26 before the evidence is admitted. In this situation, section 25 has no part to play.[171] The provisions of section 26 are less generous to the party tendering the statement who bears the burden of persuading the court that the admission of the statement is in the interests of justice. The government are proposing to make such statements automatically admissible rather than depend on judicial direction.[172]

8.9 OPINION EVIDENCE

Witnesses give evidence of what they have seen, heard, smelt, felt or touched— direct evidence of their own perceptions. A witness's opinions, beliefs or inferences are not their perceptions but conclusions drawn from those perceptions and are not admissible to prove the truth of what is believed or inferred. Opinions are seen as having little probative weight and as usurping the function of the finder of fact whose task it is to draw the necessary inferences from the evidence unless:

> i) the matter calls for special skill or knowledge which a judge or jury does not possess in which case an expert witness will be allowed to express an opinion. In *Mason*,[173] the defence to a charge of murder was that the victim had committed suicide and the issue was whether the doctor could be asked whether the injuries could have been self-inflicted. The Court of Appeal held the answer admissible. However, even experts are not per-

---

[170] (1989) Crim. L. R. 573—although decided under PACE, it is relevant to s. 24.
[171] This is not always recognised by the courts—*Jennings and Miles* [1995] Crim. L.R. 810.
[172] 'Justice for All' *op. cit.*, para. 4.60.
[173] (1911) 7 Crim. App. Rep. 67.

mitted to give their opinion on the ultimate issue or issues that are within the competence of the ordinary juror.

ii) it would be impossible to separate observed fact from inference. Witnesses are allowed to express their opinion on issues which do not call for specialist knowledge and where the perceptions and statements of 'fact' are conclusions in themselves or mixtures of inference and facts, such as the speed of a car. Even in such cases, the non-expert is not permitted to testify as to the ultimate issue that has to be decided or as to those issues which are within the competence of the trier of fact.

8.9.1 *Expert Evidence*

The common law always has accepted expert evidence[174] in a range of matters: scientific, architectural, engineering, ballistics, blood, foreign law,[175] literary merit, handwriting, fingerprints, DNA,[176] voice identification,[177] ESDA,[178] market value among others.

The expert witness must establish credentials, which may be practical experience or professional qualification. The opposing party might inquire into these. If there are some credentials, the evidence is likely to be admitted and the rest would be a matter of weight.[179]

The facts on which an expert may form an opinion should be proved by admissible evidence. This is normally on the basis of his or her own perceptions: the pathologist who performs a post-mortem may give an opinion as to the cause of death. However it can also be on the basis of facts supplied by others: the pathologist might be asked whether, given certain marks on the body, what might be the likely cause of death. In such cases the expert should state the assumed facts on which the opinion is based so that the trier of fact can assess the weight of the opinion. But the expert witness may rely on facts of which he or she has no first-hand knowledge and which would be hearsay. In *Abadom*[180] the charge was robbery. The accused had some glass splinters in his shoe. Did they come from the scene of the robbery? The expert witness measured the glass's refractive index and then referred to Home Office statistics as to how common this kind of glass was. It occurred in only 4 per cent of glass samples investigated and the presence of such glass in the accused's shoe was, at the least, a coincidence. The expert witness was relying on inadmissible hearsay contained in the Home Office statistics but was entitled to rely on such material in forming his expert opinion.[181]

The courts have always sought to prevent the expert witness from expressing an opinion on the very point that the jury has to decide, the ultimate issue in the case, although the rule is often evaded so that the expert witness is allowed to

---

[174] In *Folkes v. Chadd* (1782) 3 Doug. K.B. 157, the opinion of an engineer was admitted on the issue of whether an embankment had caused the silting up of a harbour.
[175] *Bumper Development v. Metropolitan Police Commissioner* (1991) 4 All E.R. 638.
[176] Farington D., 'Unacceptable Evidence' *New L.J.* (1993), p. 806 and p. 857.
[177] *Robb* (1991) 93 Crim. App. Rep. 161.
[178] *Wellington* (1991) Crim. L.R. 543.
[179] *Silverlock* (1894) 2 Q.B. 766, a solicitor was accepted as an expert on handwriting although his experience had been picked up as an amateur. See *Robb* (1991) 93 Crim. App. Rep. 161 where the evidence was still accepted although there was doubt as to the techniques used.
[180] (1983) 1 All E.R. 364.
[181] See also *Bradshaw* (1985) 82 Crim. App. Rep. 79.

express an opinion on the final issue so long as he uses different language to that employed by the court.[182] The rationale here is that the finder of fact might be unduly influenced by an expert but in many trials, any expert evidence for one party is likely to be countered by expert evidence from the other side, not surprisingly often coming to diametrically opposed conclusions favouring the party by whom they are retained. The weight given by juries to expert testimony will inevitably vary: while juries should not be directed to accept inevitably the evidence of an expert witness, neither should they be invited to disregard it in favour of unaided lay opinion.

Nor should witnesses express opinions on matters within the competence of the jury—although courts draw fine distinctions. In *ABC Chewing Gum*[183] the issue was whether the 'battle cards' sold with the gum might deprave and corrupt children contrary to the Obscene Publications Act 1959. Parker L.C.J. suggested, although expert psychiatric evidence in general was admissible, that it would be wrong to ask whether the cards would 'deprave and corrupt'. This was not the case in *Stamford*[184] where the issue was whether an indecent or obscene article had been sent through the post. The Court of Appeal held that this was a matter for the judge and jury and that the judge was right in preventing the accused from calling evidence on current moral standards.

The expert witness rules raise problems especially in the area of psychiatric and psychological testimony. This can be raised not merely with specific defences such as insanity, diminished responsibility and provocation but generally with *mens rea* issues. In *Chard*,[185] the defendant was accused of murder. The defence was neither diminished responsibility nor insanity but the defendant sought to introduce the testimony of a psychiatrist as to his mental state at the time of the killing. The Court of Appeal upheld the trial judge's rejection of this since the issue of intent was a matter within the ordinary experience of the jury. A similar conclusion was reached in *Turner*[186] where the accused raised the defence of provocation and wished to call evidence of a psychiatrist as to how he would have reacted when confronted with his girlfriend's confession of infidelity. Since no issue of mental illness was involved, the court held that the jury did not need experts to inform them how ordinary people reacted to the stresses and strains of life. Lord Lawton said,

'If on the proven facts a judge or jury can form their own conclusions without help, then the opinion of an expert is unnecessary. In such a case if it is given dressed up in scientific jargon it may make judgement more difficulty. The fact that an expert witness has impressive qualifications does not by that fact alone make his opinion on matters of human nature and behaviour within the limits of normality any more helpful than that of the jurors themselves; but there is a danger that they may think it does.'

Zuckerman defends this approach,

'A judge deciding whether expert opinion should be accepted as an arbiter of a certain

[182] In *Rich v. Pierpoint* (1862) 3 F. & F. 35, the issue was medical negligence—a doctor who had been present in court throughout the proceedings could not be asked whether the defendant was guilty of any want of skill but might be asked whether anything he heard suggested improper conduct on the defendant's part.
[183] (1968) 1 Q.B. 159.
[184] (1972) 2 Q.B.
[185] (1971) 56 Crim. App. R. 268.
[186] (1975) 1 All E.R. 70.

matter has to consider the state of public opinion on the point. If the community has come to defer to professional standards on the matters in question, the courts will normally follow suit. Medical evidence is admissible on matters of health because we accept the authority of the medical profession in this regard. Psychiatry has not yet obtained a like acceptance. Psychiatric evidence is admissible on the issue of insanity but not … on the mental state of a normal person. It is argued that the distinction is irrational; for to understand abnormality psychiatry has first to master the normal mental processes. However, as long as the community does not defer to psychiatry on matters such as intention and credibility, the scope for expert evidence on such matters must remain limited … Only when public opinion is clear one way or another can we demand consistency from the courts.[187]"

Turner was followed in *Roberts*[188] where the defendant was profoundly and pre-lingually deaf. The court refused to permit psychiatric evidence as to the likely effect of physical abuse by the father of the accused. *Chard* was followed in *Reynolds*[189] where evidence was excluded that the defendant was emotionally disturbed and living in a fantasy world. There has been one exception to *Turner* in *Lowery*[190] where the Privy Council came to a different conclusion when faced with two defendants charged with a sadistic murder. One of the accused wished to call a psychiatrist to testify that the other was more predisposed to the crime. In the circumstances of the case, the jury might be seen to need assistance in relation to the relative aggression of the two accused?

Thus expert evidence:

- is admissible if it concerns an issue outside the knowledge and experience of the jury.

- is inadmissible if it concerns an issue of human nature and behaviour within the bounds of normality.

- is inadmissible if it concerns the personality of a witness or the accused.

Such restrictions on the accused's ability to mount a full defence seem unjustified. If there is professional opinion to go before a jury, there is little reason to reject it. The common sense of the jury led to many wrongful convictions in cases involving identification evidence and confessions. Similarly, with issues of responsibility, there is no clear division between the normal and abnormal.[191] People's reactions and behaviour are often counter-intuitive, especially in the areas of provocation and criminal intent. There might be a strong case for departure from the *Turner* approach.

---

[187] *Zuckerman*, op. cit. p. 67
[188] (1990) Crim. L.R. 122.
[189] (1989) Crim. L.R. 220; *Masih* (1986) Crim. L.R. 395 where on a charge of rape, the accused had an IQ of 72—expert evidence was inadmissible on issue of consent although it would have been if the defendant had been a mental defective with an IQ <69; *Wood* (1990) Crim. L.R. 264; *Toner* (1991) 93 Crim. App. Rep. 382.
[190] (1974) A.C. 85.
[191] Mackay R.D. and Colman A., '*Excluding Expert Evidence; A Tale of Ordinary Folk and Common Experience*' (1991) Crim. L.R. 800; Sheldon D. and MacLeod M., '*From Normative to Positive Data: Expert Psychological Evidence Re-examined*' (1991) Crim. L.R. 811.

8.9.2 *Non-expert Opinion*

The non-expert can give an opinion in relation to those matters where it is almost impossible to separate out the inferences from the perceived facts on which the inferences were based—age, speed, weather, handwriting, identity might all be given as examples. The condition of objects or indeed general value might also come in. In *Davies (No. 2)*[192] there was a court martial where the charge was driving a vehicle while unfit through drink. The witness testified that the accused had been drinking and was in no condition to handle the car. While the first part of this was admissible (a non-expert can testify as to whether somebody has been drinking), the latter part was not (only an expert could testify as to whether the accused was fit to drive).

8.10 THE ACCUSED'S CHARACTER

The character of the defendant, whether churchgoer or sinner, at first sight seems irrelevant and thus inadmissible as evidence as to whether he or she committed an offence. After conviction, of course, prior convictions are relevant to the issue of sentence. Yet even during the trial, it has not been feasible to treat the biography of the accused as a blank sheet. Evidence relating to the accused's character can be admitted in several contexts:

a) good character as evidence for the defence that the accused is not the sort of person likely to commit such an offence.

b) bad character which needs to be proved by the prosecution as an element of the offence.

c) prior offences which the prosecution alleges are evidence that the accused has committed the offence charged. Although the principle is that a person should only be tried for the crime charged, if a person has acted in a dramatically similar way previously, it can be argued that this tends to make it more likely that they have acted in the same manner this time. This is known as the 'similar facts' rule. The prejudice aroused when a jury hears of previous crimes is considerable and there is a difficult juggling act for the judge who must decide whether the probative weight of the previous actions exceeds the prejudicial effect.

d) if the accused decides to testify, the problem of previous discreditable acts arises again. A normal witness can be cross-examined as to credit. However this would be very prejudicial for the defendant. When the defendant was made a competent witness on his or her own behalf by the Criminal Evidence Act 1898, section 1(f) provided a shield which protected the accused from such questions. There are situations when that shield can be lost such as where the accused alleges good character, gives evidence against a fellow defendant or attacks the character of prosecution witnesses.

---

[192] (1962) 1 W.L.R. 1111.

8.10.1 *The Accused's Good Character*

A defendant can adduce evidence of his own good character, either by testifying himself or through witnesses. In *Rowton*,[193] the defendant was charged with indecent assault and was permitted to introduce such evidence of good reputation. This evidence was confined to general reputation and could not extend to detailing specific creditable acts nor could a witness be asked as to the accused's disposition, *i.e.*, whether he would be likely to commit the acts with which he was charged.[194]

The accused is entitled to a direction on evidence of good character.[195] The purpose of such testimony appears primarily to go to the credibility of the accused who has testified, giving his or her denials more weight.[196] However, whether or not the defendant has testified, he or she is entitled to a direction that good character is an indicator of innocence.[197] One final problem is where there are co-accused, one with good character and the other with bad character. The accused with good character is entitled to a direction that good character is relevant to both credibility and to innocence. However the judge should either not mention the other defendant's character or direct the jury not to speculate about it.

8.10.2 *Bad Character as an Element of the Offence*

Bad character, in the shape of a previous conviction, can be an element of another offence. In such circumstances, this prior conviction can be proved as part of the prosecution case—for example, to convict a person of driving while disqualified, it is necessary to prove the prior conviction and sentence; under section 21 of the Firearms Act 1968, a person sentenced to a term of imprisonment of three years or more shall not possess a firearm—it is obviously necessary to prove the earlier conviction and sentence in order to obtain a conviction under section 21—this 'double jeopardy' rule is under review.[198]

The accused may raise the earlier trial—there are the special pleas of autrefois acquit and autrefois convict which are based on the double jeopardy rule that a person should not be prosecuted twice for the same offence. It would be a complete defence for the accused to show that he or she had been tried before for this offence.

8.10.3 *Bad Character and Similar Fact Evidence*

The extent to which the prosecution may refer to or adduce evidence about the accused's character is controversial. The common law rule is quite restrictive: the prosecution is not allowed to adduce evidence-in-chief of the defendant's bad character or to cross-examine defence witnesses with a view to eliciting such evidence. If it is inadvertently referred to, the jury may be discharged and a new

---

[193] (1865) Le. & Ca. 520.
[194] See also *Redgrave* (1981) 74 Crim. App. Rep. 10.
[195] *Berrada* (1989) 91 Crim. App. Rep. 131.
[196] In medieval England the accused could escape liability by such means through compurgation—producing sufficient neighbours to swear to your honesty and credibility.
[197] *Vye* (1993) Crim. L.R. 602.
[198] 'Justice for All' (2002) *op. cit.*, para. 4.54ff.

trial ordered. The Law Commission has published proposals[199] to reform this area but these have scarcely satisfied the police or prosecuting authorities who would prefer to see the introduction of the accused's previous convictions as the normal approach.

As the law stands, this rule excludes adducing evidence of bad character. There are two situations where there can be exceptions to this rule—first when the prosecution are leading their evidence-in-chief and secondly, when prosecuting counsel is cross-examining the accused.

In building the case against the accused, the prosecution can only use the accused's prior convictions if those convictions satisfy the criteria under two common law exceptions:

1.   where the defendant puts his own character into issue, the prosecution can cross-examine the accused on prior disreputable conduct but also can advance evidence in rebuttal.

2.   where the previous acts or, normally, convictions are sufficiently similar to the offences charged that they are seen as having probative force. In such cases the prosecution is allowed to advance evidence of that conduct. This is known as the similar fact rule.

Rowton illustrates the situation where the prosecution are allowed rebuttal of good character evidence advanced by the accused — after the accused had put his own character into issue, the prosecution were able to call witnesses as to his reputation who testified that he was a man capable of the grossest indecency and the most flagrant immorality! Such evidence is restricted to reputation and not to specific discreditable acts. You do not assert your own good character by holding a Bible in your hand as you give his evidence[200] nor by wearing a regimental blazer.[201]

This right of rebuttal for the prosecution only applies where the accused makes character an issue by advancing evidence of good character. In *Butterwasser*[202] the accused cross-examined the prosecution witnesses on their bad character. The prosecution sought to counter this by calling a police officer to testify as to the accused's prior convictions. Although these convictions could have been put to him if he had testified,[203] he did not do so and there is no common law rule that permits the prosecution to counter defence imputations against prosecution witnesses by advancing evidence of the defendant's bad character. Once the accused's character is in issue, everything is in. In *Winfield*,[204] the charge was indecent assault and the accused led evidence of his sexual propriety. But the prosecution were permitted to counter this by advancing evidence of convictions for dishonesty.

The second common law exception is evidence of similar facts. This is an exception to the general rule that the prosecution are prohibited, at common law, from introducing evidence of the defendant's bad character or reputation and, by

---

[199] Law Commission, *Evidence of Bad Character in Criminal Proceedings* (Report No. 273) (2001).
[200] *Robinson* [2001] 3 Archbold News 2.
[201] *Hamilton* [1969] Crim. L.R. 486.
[202] (1948) 1 K.B. 4.
[203] s. 1(3)(ii), Criminal Evidence Act 1898.
[204] (1939) 4 All E.R. 164.

statute,[205] from cross-examining the defendant about his character. This general rule is justified on the grounds that it is an unwarranted inference that because the accused was a thief on a previous occasion, therefore he is also a thief on this occasion. This prohibition has been modified since the consistencies and patterns in people's behaviour mean that we are justified in treating previous conduct as a factor in deciding whether a person has committed an act. That previous conduct can have probative weight. At the same time, such testimony about an accused's previous offences is highly prejudicial.[206] The prejudice exists because the proof of the previous conviction detracts attention from the proof of guilt of this offence and tends to undermine the standard of proof required. The court must balance the prejudice against the relevance and probative weight of such evidence.

In *Makin*,[207] the defendants accepted children from their mothers, alleging that they would adopt them on payment of a small sum of money. A baby's body was found buried in the garden and the accused were charged with the murder. The prosecution sought to adduce evidence that other such bodies had been found in gardens of other houses occupied by the defendants in order to rebut any possible defence of accident. The Privy Council held that the evidence was admissible— although there is a general rule that evidence of disposition and bad character is in general inadmissible, it may be introduced where it is relevant to an issue before the jury. The key issue is relevance—does the evidence possess such relevance, such probative force that it outweighs any possible prejudice? For example, the evidence might relevant to rebut a defence as in *Makin* itself— evidence of the other bodies tended to rebut any defence of accident or natural causes. Similarly in *Smith*,[208] the defendant was charged with the murder of his third wife by drowning her in the bath. The prosecution were allowed to advance evidence that the first and second wives had died in identical circumstances.

The logic of *Makin* is powerful but this exception to the rule against bad character evidence is in general quite limited and trial courts are reluctant to allow any mention of previous convictions. In one area, this is not the case. The courts have used the banner of similar fact to allow deeply prejudicial testimony especially in cases involving what the courts regarded as sexual deviancy. In *Thompson*[209] the defendant was accused of indecent assault on two boys. They had taken the police to the place where the defendant had made a second assignation. The defendant was arrested without any further offence taking place. Could the police use evidence that the accused had two powder puffs on him and that he had indecent photographs in his flat? The House of Lords held that they could: although the accused's sexuality could be seen as confirming the boys' identification of him, that probative aspect must have been overwhelmed by the prejudice created in the minds of the jury. The failure of the appeal courts to recognise this is seen in *Sims*[210] where the accused was charged on counts of buggery and indecent assault against several men. He applied for severance of the trials but this was refused since the evidence relating to one complaint was

---

[205] s. 1(3), Criminal Evidence Act 1898.
[206] Lloyd-Bostock S., '*The Effects on Juries of Hearing About the Defendant's Previous Criminal Record: A simulation study*' [2000] Crim L.R. 734.
[207] (1894) A.C. 57.
[208] (1915) 11 Crim. App. Rep. 229.
[209] (1918) A.C. 221.
[210] (1946) K.B. 531.

admissible on the other charges. Sodomy, according to the Court of Appeal, was an especial category and cited Sumner in *Thompson*,

'Persons ... who commit the offences now under consideration seek the habitual gratification of a particular perverted lust which not only takes them out of the class of ordinary men gone wrong but stamps them with a hallmark of a special and extra-ordinary class as much as if they carried on their bodies some physical peculiarity.'

Homophobia of this nature illustrates the problems of inarticulated general-isations that can distort the process of proof.

The weakness of the *Makin* judgment was that the court did not address the question of how relevant the evidence should be—in the case itself, the evidence of the other bodies was overwhelming but in other subsequent cases, the impact has been more marginal. Appellate courts have struggled to provide a clear test for trial judges. The principle was that the relevance or probative force had to outweigh the prejudicial effect but courts sought less abstract test.

In *Boardman*,[211] the accused was a headmaster of a boarding school for boys charged with sexual offences on separate occasions on two pupils. The simila-rities in the accounts by the two pupils were striking but the defence was that the boys were lying and that the incidents never occurred. Were the accounts given by each boy admissible on the charge relating to the other? The House of Lords upheld the trial judge's decision to admit the evidence. Evidence of similar fact may be admitted if the judge views its probative force in relation to an issue in the trial as outweighing its prejudicial effect. Critically the House stressed that the strength of the probative force lies in any striking similarity between the prior conduct and the current charge. That similarity should be inexplicable on the basis of coincidence or concoction.

A common theme from the *Boardman* judgments was that the previous con-duct should possess a 'unique or striking similarity' to the offence charged. However in practice that approach proved less than easy to apply[212] and in addition the courts became fixated by 'striking similarity' and failed to see it simply as an illustration of the need to balance probative weight and prejudicial effect. The House of Lords addressed these issues in *R. v. P*[213] where the defendant was accused of incest with and rape of his two daughters. There was evidence that he had engaged in incest over a long period, using force and threatening both girls unless they kept silent. He had paid for abortions for both. At trial, he applied for the counts relating to each daughter to be tried separately. The judge refused, holding that the testimony of one daughter was admissible evidence on charges involving the other. The Court of Appeal quashed the conviction on the grounds that there was no feature of striking similarity. The House of Lords restored the conviction and held that the test of admissibility was whether the evidence was relevant and had probative value which outweighed its prejudicial effect. It was not necessary to single out 'striking similarity' as an essential element, although in some cases where identity was in issue a 'signature' might be looked for. This judgment reflects the principles propounded by Lord Wilberforce in *Boardman* while at the same time casting off the straitjacket of 'striking similarity'. 'Striking similarity' can have probative value—for example,

---

[211] (1975) A.C. 421.
[212] *Novac* (1976) 65 Crim. App. Rep. 107; *Johannsen* (1977) 65 Crim. App. Rep. 101; *Tricoglus* (1976) 65 Crim. App. Rep. 16; *Barrington* (1981) 1 W.L.R. 419.
[213] [1991] 3 All E.R. 337.

in *Straffen*[214] where the accused was confined in Broadmoor having strangled two young girls. He was charged with strangling another little girl. The killing took place during a period while he was at large from Broadmoor and the circumstances identical to the earlier killings. Evidence of those earlier killings was admitted.

Accusers' stories may derive from a common cause, collusion, coincidence or the fact that they are all telling the truth. The degree of probative weight increases where the court can rule out collusion or coincidence. This can be seen in *Roy*[215] where a doctor was accused of indecent assault on a number of patients. There was nothing 'striking' about the accounts with no bizarre elements but yet aggregated the stories had considerable probative weight, rebutting any suggestion that these assaults might have been *bona fide* medical examinations.

But although a valid principle underlies these cases, there are no criteria for determining the probative weight, let alone the prejudicial effect, of evidence of previous criminal conduct. As long as the trial judge addresses his or her mind to the balance between proof and prejudice, the appellate court will not interfere with any conclusion. Without guiding criteria, it becomes a lottery and abrogates the principle is that it is unfair that an accused should be answerable at a trial for anything other than the offence charged. It also infringes the concept of treating like cases alike because an accused with a criminal record will be treated differently from an accused without a record. The need is for the courts to take a less relaxed attitude to identifying and combating prejudice.

8.10.4 *The Accused as Witness*

As suggested above, there are two situations where there can be exceptions to the rule which excludes a court from hearing evidence of the accused's bad character—first when the prosecution are leading their evidence-in-chief and secondly, when prosecuting counsel is cross-examining the accused. The latter situation did not arise until 1898, when, under the Criminal Evidence Act, for the first time the defendant became a competent witness. The evidence-in-chief posed no problems but ordinary witnesses could be cross-examined on their character and credibility. What constraints were to be imposed on the prosecution?

The structure decided upon was that the prosecution, under section 1(2), was able to ask the defendant questions notwithstanding the fact that the answers might incriminate the accused as to the offence charged: '*A person charged and being a witness ... may be asked any question in cross-examination notwithstanding that it would tend to criminate him as to the offence charged.*'

But they could not attack the defendant's credibility, as they might other defence witnesses, by asking questions about prior convictions. This was achieved by section 1(3):

> '*A person charged and called as a witness ... shall not be asked ... any question tending to show that he has committed or been convicted of or been charged with any offence other than that wherewith he is then charged or is of bad character...*'

Section 1(3) enabled the accused to testify about the offence while keeping a

---

[214] (1952) 2 Q.B. 911.
[215] (1992) Crim. L.R. 185; *Laidman and Agnew* (1992) Crim. L.R. 428.

secret of any murky past. Only under certain circumstances would the prosecution be entitled to inquire into that past. But what is the relationship between section 1(2) and section 1(3)? The sections can be mutually contradictory since a question on a previous conviction can tend to incriminate (thus within section 1(2)) while at the same time showing that the accused has committed another offence (thus outside section 1(3)).

In *Jones*[216] the accused was charged with murder and rape of a young girl guide. Previously he had been convicted of the rape of another young girl. At his trial for murder, he gave an account of his movements that corresponded almost word for word with the account he had given in the previous trial. Could he be questioned about this with a view to showing that the account was false? It could be argued that section 1(2) permitted the question since it tended to show that his account was false but that section 1(3) prohibited it since it revealed a previous conviction. The minority judges, Lords Denning and Devlin took a broad view that the line of questioning was permissible under section 1(2) because it tended to persuade the jury that the alibi was false and thus incriminated the defendant. This interpretation has logical weight but undermined the protection afforded by section 1(3). Any shield for the accused was secondary to probative value.

The majority in the House of Lords held that section 1(3) prohibited any question '... tending to show that he has committed ...' This meant 'reveal such offences'. On the face of it, they were supporting the human rights of the accused over the probative force of the disputed evidence. However the defendant had also had testified in chief that he had 'been in trouble with the police'. The majority held that, since he had mentioned these problems, the prosecution were not 'revealing' prior offences and thus their questions were permissible. This approach subordinated section 1(2) to section 1(3) and construed section 1(2) narrowly to permit questioning only facts that directly link the accused with the offence. But this interpretation of section 1(3) was highly technical and the protection afforded to the accused easily avoided. The defendant had not revealed any specific prior offence and yet the seriousness of the previous incident must have been apparent to the jury.[217]

The logical argument, supported by common law authority such as *Makin*,[218] would permit any question which relevant and probative (whether directly or indirectly). That common law position is expressed in section 1(2). All section 1(3) aims to do is to prevent the questioning of the defendant as to credit. The mere fact that evidence tends to show other crimes should not make it inadmissible if it is relevant to a matter before jury. The prosecution are entitled to advance evidence-in-chief as long as the probative weight is sufficient to outweigh any prejudicial effect.[219] It is difficult to argue that the defence in *Jones* should be permitted to advance a complicated exculpatory story without the jury being made aware that the same story had been used before. The argument against this is that the accused is at a considerable disadvantage by having leading questions advanced in cross-examination, without prior argument and without foundation being laid by the prosecution. Procedurally it would be better if the prosecution advanced their own witnesses who could then be cross-examined by the

---

[216] (1962) A.C. 635.
[217] See a similar approach in *Anderson* (1988) 2 W.L.R. 1017.
[218] (1894) A.C. 57.
[219] *P* (1991) 3 All E.R. 337.

defence.[220] Although this would disadvantage the prosecution since they would be unable to cross-examine the defendant on the issue, the relevant facts could still be laid before the jury.

8.11 ESTOPPEL

The general principle is that a party to an action is not allowed to assert or to contradict certain facts which are either a matter of record, of deed or of conduct. This is largely a matter of civil law but in criminal cases, there are the special pleas of autrefois acquit and autrefois convict which are based on the double jeopardy rule that a person should not be prosecuted twice for the same offence. The 'same offence' means one for which the defendant could have lawfully been convicted at the original hearing. Thus if the accused is convicted of GBH, there is no bar to a homicide prosecution if the victim dies subsequent to the conviction.

In *Sambasivam*,[221] the defendant was charged with both possession of ammunition and carrying firearms. At the first trial he was acquitted on the first charge and a new trial was ordered on the second charge. At that trial, the defendant was convicted but the prosecution relied on a confession admitting both charges. The conviction was quashed since the court should have been told that the prosecution were bound by the acquittal and that made the confession less reliable. To an extent, the House of Lords in *R. v. Z* have qualified this principle.[222] This was a rape case and it was held that the prosecution could advance evidence of previous rape trials at which the accused had been acquitted. Provided that a defendant is not placed in double jeopardy, relevant evidence is not inadmissible because it shows or tends to show that the defendant was, in fact, guilty of an offence of which he had earlier been acquitted.

There are situations where the outcome of the previous proceedings is relevant. In *Ollis*,[223] the accused was acquitted of an offence involving passing a dud cheque. Subsequently he was charged with a similar offence and the prosecution adduced evidence of the earlier acquittal, arguing that it did not reopen that issue but that it showed the defendant's knowledge about the state of his bank account.

In civil law, once parties have fought and decided an issue, they are bound by that result. However issue estoppel appears to have no place in criminal proceedings. In *Humphrys*,[224] the defendant was acquitted of driving while disqualified in July 1972. Although a police officer gave evidence of identification, the defendant testified that he had not driven anything in 1972. He was later charged with perjury in relation to that statement—the prosecution had other witnesses as to his driving at that time but also sought to reintroduce the officer to give the same evidence. The House of Lords upheld the conviction—there is no such thing as issue estoppel in criminal law largely because of the difficulty of defining the issues in criminal cases in the absence of pleadings and a reasoned decision, because it would operate unfairly in the defendant's favour because of

---

[220] In *Cokar* (1960) 2 Q.B. 207 the prosecution were not allowed to advance similar fact evidence in cross-examination—a proper foundation had to be laid. be laid.
[221] (1950) A.C. 458.
[222] [2000] 3 W.L.R. 117; the double jeopardy rule is under review: 'Justice for All' *op. cit.* (2002) para. 4.6.3.
[223] (1900) 2 Q.B. 758 but see *G v. Coltart* (1967) 1 Q.B. 432.
[224] (1977) A.C. 1.

the burden of proof and if it operated on behalf of the prosecution, this might be equally unfair on the defendant. Thus in *Hogan*[225], the defendant was convicted of causing grievous bodily harm but the victim died and he was charged with murder. The trial judge refused to allow the defendant to argue lack of intent and self-defence since these issues had been determined at the original trial. *Hogan* is overruled in *Humphrys*.

8.12 S.74 PACE

To what extent can the prosecution use previous convictions as evidence of the facts on which they were based? The old common law rule was that in *Hollington v. Hewthorn.*[226] This was a negligence action between two drivers where the Court of Appeal held that the plaintiff was not entitled to use the prior conviction of the defendant for careless driving as evidence of the defendant's negligence. This would mean that the prosecution would need to prove the facts anew even in related trials. In *Spinks*,[227] the principal offender stabbed the victim and was convicted of GBH. The defendant was tried as an accomplice and it was held that prosecution could not use the principal's conviction as evidence that the offence had been convicted.

This position was changed by section 74 of PACE so that a conviction is admissible where it is relevant to an issue in the case. The problem is that of relevance to an 'issue'. In *Robertson and Golder*[228] the charge involved in one case was conspiracy to burgle and evidence of convictions for burglaries carried out by Robertson's alleged co-conspirators was permitted; in the other case Golder was charged with robbery and the convictions of his alleged partners was given in evidence against him. The burden of proving the convictions wrong would normally rest on the defence.

The prejudicial effect of proving convictions is obvious and the problem is one of fairness. Even where the conviction is admissible under section 74, it may be excluded under section 78 since it would have an adverse effect on the fairness of the proceedings.[229] In *Mattison*[230] the accused was charged with indecency with another person who was similarly charged with indecency with the accused. The other person pleaded guilty but the defendant pleaded not guilty. The conviction was quashed after the other person's conviction was admitted into evidence.

---

[225] (1974) Q.B. 398.
[226] (1943) K.B. 587.
[227] (1982) 1 All E.R. 587; *Hassan* (1970) 1 Q.B. 423.
[228] (1987) 3 All E.R. 231.
[229] *O'Connor* (1986) 85 Crim. App. Rep. 298.
[230] (1990) Crim. L.R. 117; see also *Turner* (1991) Crim. L.R. 57.

CHAPTER NINE

Issues in Sentencing

LISA DICKSON

9.1 INTRODUCTION

In the year 2000 1.42 million people were sentenced by the courts in England and Wales, an increase of 1 per cent on the previous year.[1] With the exception of offences which carry a mandatory sentence, those individuals imposing sentences have a range of options at their disposal, both custodial and non-custodial. While the choice of disposal in each case will be affected by a number of factors, for example the maximum penalty imposed by statute, and any mitigating circumstances or sentencing guidelines provided by the Court of Appeal[2], sentencers still retain a great deal of discretion in determining the sentence to be imposed in each case. The table reproduced below provides an indication of which sentences are

---

[1] *Criminal Statistics England and Wales 2000*, Cm. 5312 (HMSO 2001), p. 150.
[2] For information regarding practice directions, and the directions themselves, see http://www.courtservice.gov.uk.

being made use of within the courts, as compared to 1995, and to what degree.

Table 9.1 Types of Sentence 1995 and 2000[3]

Type of Sentence	1995	2000
Absolute Discharge	21,200	15,700
Conditional Discharge	106,200	106,100
Fine	1,070,100	1,017,100
Probation Order[4]	49,400	56,700
Supervision Order	10,100	11,600
Community Service Order[5]	48,300	50,200
Attendance Sentence Order	7,500	7,100
Combination Order[6]	14,600	19,300
Curfew Order	0	2,600
Reparation Order	n/a	4,000
Action Plan Order	n/a	4,400
Drug Treatment & Testing Order	n/a	300
S90–92, PCC(S) Act 2000[7]	400	600
Secure Training Order	n/a	100
Detention & Training Order	n/a	5,100
Young Offender Institution	18,800	20,200
Fully suspended imprisonment	3,200	3,100
Unsuspended imprisonment	60,300	80,600
Otherwise dealt with	19,300	24,900
ALL SENTENCES	1,429,400	1,429,600
Immediate custody	79,500	106,600
Community sentences	129,900	156,100

[3] *Criminal Statistics England and Wales 2000* Cm. 5312 (HMSO 2001) Table 7A, p. 155.
[4] Now called the Community Rehabilitation Order, see s. 41–45 of Powers of Criminal Courts (Sentencing) Act 2000.
[5] Now called the Community Punishment Order, see s. 46–50 of Powers of Criminal Courts (Sentencing) Act 2000.
[6] The Community Punishment and Rehabilitation Order, see s. 51 of Powers of Criminal Courts (Sentencing) Act 2000.
[7] s. 90–92 of the Powers of Criminal Courts (Sentencing) Act 2000 which replace the repealed s. 53 of the Children and Young Person Act 1933.

The sentence is the test as to whether justice has been done, both to the victim and to the defendant. A sentence by any court involves doing harm to the defendant in some way: it might be as limited as the humiliation and stigma associated with a court appearance followed by an absolute discharge; it might involve financial penalties; it might be a partial curtailment of personal liberty through weekend working on a community punishment order; it might involve extreme restriction on liberty of movement and major interference with personal, social and economic relationships through an immediate custodial sentence. With regard to public perception, it is possible to suggest that justice in sentencing involves the harm being meted out to the defendant having an equivalence to that suffered by the victim: in criminal justice terms this idea is reflected by the requirement that the punishment is proportionate to the seriousness of the offence[8]: fairness or justice exists in the act of balancing. It is easily stated, but far more difficult to achieve. It is this difficulty that has given rise, in part, to much debate and some fundamental questioning concerning sentencing. What aims should sentencing practice be attempting to achieve? Who should determine what the sentencing objectives actually are?

Today, in England and Wales, it is taken for granted that the courts are responsible for sentence. Historically this was not the case[9]: the development of 'broad band' criminal offences such as theft, replacing large numbers of more specific crimes, led to wide discretionary sentencing powers and this has been coupled with the development over time of a jurisprudence of sentencing by the Court of Appeal.[10] As recently as 1992 the importance of judicial control over sentencing was identified as one of the hallmarks of judicial independence.[11] Legislative reform and proposals for sentencing councils were greeted as an attempt by parliament to interfere with the judiciary's proper constitutional sphere of action. However, there is little constitutional basis for such far-reaching judicial control over sentencing policy especially where there is legitimate Parliamentary concern over sentencing policies and practices.[12] An attempt to redress the balance of discretion afforded the judiciary and achieve legislative dominance can be found in the Criminal Justice Act 1991 which laid down a very detailed sentencing framework for the courts, a framework which remains dominant today, albeit somewhat revised and arguably undergoing a process of erosion.

Should we permit judges this latitude, subject to their expressing in advance in open court what their criteria and objectives are? The judge has broad discretion in choosing between sanctions and determining the level of severity. Sentencers are guided in this by their own penal philosophy[13] or objectives, be it incapacitation of the offender, protection of society, belief in the reformative qualities of punishment, general or individual deterrence, compensation to the victim or some interpretation of retribution and just deserts'.[14] This freedom is inevitably a source of disparity because judges pursuing different objectives will treat similar

---

[8] As established by the Criminal Justice Act 1991 sentencing framework.
[9] Radzinowicz, Sir L. and Hood R., *The Emergence of Penal Policy in Victorian and Edwardian England* (Stevens, 1986) Chap. 22 and 23.
[10] Thomas D.A., *The Principles of Sentencing* (Heinemann 2nd ed., 1979).
[11] Ashworth A., *Sentencing and Criminal Justice* (Weidenfeld, 1992) Chap.2.
[12] Ashworth, *op. cit.*, p. 43.
[13] Hogarth J., *Sentencing as a Human Process* (University of Toronto, 1971).
[14] The traditional terminology employed for discussion of the philosophies underlying sentencing decisions is: deterrence, incapacitation, retribution and rehabilitation.

cases differently. The judge pursuing the objective of deterrence, for example, may consider a different type and severity of sentence than the retributively minded judge. Such disparity is a plain breach of equal treatment principles of due process and does not encourage the development of a consistent and coherent sentencing policy. All four[15] philosophies or objectives in sentencing possess some importance and that importance will vary according to the multiplicity of cases that come before the courts. But to adopt such free choice for the sentencer is a negation of equal treatment. Constitutionally penal policy should be a matter for government and legislature and not for the judiciary. Furthermore, though the objectives might all possess some importance, it is far from saying that they all possess equal importance or validity.[16] Although much is claimed empirically for, say, the deterrent effect of exemplary sentences, there are different ethical values which attach to different philosophies of punishment and we need to make social choices between these. Such choices should not, arguably, be left to the individual sentencer.

With such arguments in mind, this chapter seeks to consider some of the main areas pertinent to current sentencing policy and practice. It is not intended to provide exhaustive guidance on all possible sentencing disposals; rather this chapter seeks to highlight some of the developments and issues which are coming to the fore in criminal justice debate. Firstly, the changes in legislation which directly relate to sentencing and sentencing policy. Such an overview will provide a necessary background to the development of the current position and sentencing framework. This then leads on to elucidation on current sentencing practice and an overview of how sentencing decisions are taken and the information available to sentencers when determining the choice of disposal in each particular case. The remainder of this chapter provides an overview of the primary sentences in use today, firstly, custodial sentences and subsequently the various options that make up non-custodial sentences for adult offenders.[17] Given the government focus in the last 2 years on review of the criminal justice process and in particular potential changes to the sentencing framework, it is on this subject that the majority of this chapter will be concerned. It is likely that such broad and detailed reviews and reports will result very soon in a legislative overhaul of sentencing policy, and thus potentially practice, as such exhaustive discussion of existing sentencing procedures may prove, in a short period of time, to be of developmental or historical importance only.[18]

---

[15] Retribution, deterrence, incapacitation and rehabilitation.

[16] For interesting discussion of these ideals as sentencing aims, see Bagaric, M., 'Incapacitation, Deterrence and rehabilitation: Flawed Ideals or Appropriate Sentencing Goals' (2000) 24 *Criminal Law Journal* 19.

[17] Non-custodial sanctions available solely for young offenders will be considered separately in Chap. 11.

[18] For recent and more in-depth discussion of sentencing policy and existing procedures and practice, see Ashworth, A., (2000), *Sentencing and Criminal Justice* (3rd ed., Butterworths, London).

9.2 THEORIES OF SENTENCING AND THE EMERGENCE OF A POLICY FRAMEWORK[19]

Prior to 1991 sentencing policy operated in a piecemeal fashion, governed primarily by the individual sentencer's own sentencing or penal philosophy. The objectives of sentencing during this time arguably fell into the much-rehearsed categories, those of deterrence, incapacitation, retribution and rehabilitation. At this time no coherent stated objective existed,[20] which perhaps goes some way to explaining concerns raised later in the 1990's regarding inconsistent sentencing patterns.[21] Sentencing policy as such was directed to a degree by guideline decisions provided by the higher courts but was in effect a policy of judicial self-regulation.[22] The approach whereby the judiciary enjoyed relatively unfettered discretion had given rise to the problems noted above and resulted in the question of how best to ensure that coherent sentencing objectives were in place and applied consistently by all courts?

9.2.1 *The Criminal Justice Act 1991*

One alternative approach to judicial discretion is to define a principal objective through legislation, although shackling the judiciary is not an easy task. The 1991 Criminal Justice Act provides an authoritative primary rationale or philosophy, focusing on retribution and just deserts.[23] Secondary considerations (in certain circumstances) are incapacitation, in order to protect the public from risk of serious harm, and reform/rehabilitation since the court must decide which of various non-custodial options is most suitable for the offender.[24] Thus 1991 witnessed the beginnings of the new sentencing framework, a framework which attempts to prioritise the theories underlying sentencing and provide guidance on how sentencing decisions should be taken. Indeed, the Criminal Justice Act was welcomed as a platform from which coherent sentencing decisions could be made by providing a framework or process that must be followed by the courts.

The first basic decision in the process set out by the legislation is a selection from among categories of sentences. These are:

a)   custodial sentences.

b)   community sentence.

c)   fines.

d)   discharges, binding-over orders or other disposals.

---

[19] The provisions contained within ss. 1–15 of the Criminal Justice Act 1991 have, like much of the later legislation discussed, been consolidated within the Powers of Criminal Courts (Sentencing) Act 2000 (PCCSA). During the early part of this section below, the section provisions are noted with their 1991 Act references. However, when moving on to consider information available to sentencers, the PCCSA section numbers will also be provided.

[20] No direct sentencing policy/philosophy was expressly stated in statute.

[21] See Prison Reform Trust *Sentencing: A Geographical Lottery*, July 1997.

[22] von Hirsch, A. and Ashworth, A. [eds] (1992) *Principled Sentencing* (Edinburgh University Press, Edinburgh, Chapter 5.3).

[23] s. 1 of the Criminal Justice Act 1991.

[24] s. 6(2)(a) of the Criminal Justice Act 1991, though s. 6(2)(b) orders the court to ensure that the restrictions on liberty are also commensurate with the seriousness of the offence.

The 1991 Act lays down a framework for the first three of these.[25] The framework is a pyramid where the base is the fine which is the presumptive penalty in most cases.[26] If the court seeks to move up the pyramid, it must be satisfied that it has cleared certain thresholds:

- if the court wishes to move from a fine to a community sentence, it must to be satisfied that the offence is sufficiently serious to warrant this.[27]

- if the court is to take the next step and move from a community sentence to a custodial sentence, it must be satisfied that the offence (or a combination of the offence and others associated with it[28]) is so serious that only a custodial sentence can be justified.[29]

- a secondary decision is that of the tariff: the length of prison sentence, the content of the community sentence or the amount of a fine. Under the framework, this must be 'commensurate with the seriousness of the offence'.[30]

There are certain key concepts embedded in the 1991 sentencing framework. The foremost principle is that of proportionality and seriousness. Despite other factors,[31] the twin pillars of the 1991 sentencing framework are:

- that neither a custodial nor a community sentence should be imposed unless the offence is so serious that the imposition of the lower band of sentence could not be justified[32]

- that the length of the custodial sentence or the nature of the community sentence should be proportional to the seriousness of the offence.[33]

Such considerations became mandatory for the court, which must address the question of seriousness. However 'seriousness' was not defined, and this becomes relevant to a discussion on the objective or theories underlying sentencing decisions. In *Cox*[34] the defendant, aged 18, pleaded guilty to theft of some tools and reckless driving. He was sentenced to four months detention. The Court of Appeal relied on Lawton L.J. in *Bradbourne*[35] where he had indicated that the term meant,

'... the kind of offence which when committed by a young person would make right-

---

[25] Though this has been amended by the Criminal Justice Act 1993 and in the case of fines, wholly jettisoned.
[26] Ashworth (2000), p. 271–278.
[27] Criminal Justice Act 1991, s. 6(1).
[28] Under the 1991 Act, the rule was that the court could only decide on the seriousness of an offence based on the offence and one other associated with it. This has now been altered by s. 66(1) of the Criminal Justice Act 1993 which allows a court to consider any number of associated offences.
[29] Criminal Justice Act 1991, s. 1(2).
[30] Criminal Justice Act 1991, s. 2(2)(a), s. 6(2)(b) and s. 18(2) (this latter is the amended section introduced by s. 65 of the Criminal Justice Act 1993).
[31] Such as protection of society and the impact of multiple offences and past convictions.
[32] s. 1(2)(a) and s. 6(1) of the Criminal Justice Act 1991.
[33] s. 2(2)(a) and s. 6(2) of the Criminal Justice Act 1991.
[34] (1993) Crim. L.R. 152.
[35] (1985) 7 Crim. App. Rep. (S) 180 (interpreting similar provisions in s. 1(4A)(a) of the Criminal Justice Act 1982)

thinking members of the public, knowing all the facts, feel that justice had not been done by the passing of any sentence other than a custodial one...'

The court in *Cox* felt that the hurdle had been overcome in this case. Finding that an offence is sufficiently serious did not oblige a court to impose a custodial sentence. The court must subsequently take into account all information about the offence (including aggravating and mitigating circumstances) as is available to it.[36]

The focus on the seriousness of the offence should have prescribed considerations of general deterrence, prevalence of the offence or incapacitation. However in *Cunningham*,[37] a robbery case, Taylor L.C.J. made it clear that seriousness could not be interpreted in a vacuum. The prevalence of the offence was a legitimate factor: whereas one violent sexual attack on a woman gravely harmed the victim, a series of attacks put women in fear and limited their freedom of movement and accordingly such an attack might be viewed even more seriously. Seriousness is not an abstraction but is a factor rooted in the material circumstances of the community.[38]

Lord Taylor also felt that deterrence could enter into the determination of the length of a sentence. The aims of a custodial sentence are to punish and deter and the phrase 'commensurate with the seriousness of the offence' must mean commensurate with the punishment and deterrence that the offence required. However, section 2(2)(a) did prohibit the 'exemplary' sentence by which extra length is added to a sentence to make a special example of the offender.

One further factor was any failure of the offender to respond to previous non-custodial penalties. In 1991 the view was that the central principle in sentencing should be the seriousness of the immediate offence and not the offender's previous record. This was reversed in 1993[39] and courts were now permitted, in deciding on the seriousness of an offence, to take into account any failure of the defendant to respond to sentences for previous offences. The logical connection between the seriousness of the instant offence and the defendant's past behaviour is far from obvious[40] but this is a theme which has been developed by subsequent legislation, most notably provisions in the Crime (Sentences) Act 1997 introducing an automatic life sentence in certain instances (considered below).

9.2.1.1 THE TOTALITY PRINCIPLE

When a defendant is convicted of multiple offences, the court has the option of making the sentences on different offences concurrent or consecutive. Where the offences are broadly of the same type and at the same time, the sentences will be concurrent. However there are exceptions so that charges involving a firearms offence,[41] an assault on a police officer[42] or perverting the course of justice[43] will often be sentenced consecutively regardless of whether they took place at the same time as other offences.

---

[36] s. 3(3)(a) and s. 7(1). Additionally, s. 28(1) permits the court to mitigate the sentence by reference to any matters that the court feels are relevant to sentence.
[37] (1993) 2 All E.R. 15.
[38] See further Custodial Sentences in section 9.7
[39] s. 66(6) of the Criminal Justice Act 1993.
[40] Ashworth *et al.*, (1994), *op. cit.*, p. 105.
[41] *Faulkner* (1972) 56 Crim. App. Rep. 594.
[42] *Kastercum* (1972) 56 Crim. App. Rep. 298.
[43] *Attorney General's Reference No.1 of 1990* (1990) 12 Crim. App. R. (S).

This is affected by the 'totality' principle,[44] stated by Lawton L.J.

'When cases of multiplicity of offences come before the court, the court must not content itself by doing the arithmetic and passing the sentence that the arithmetic produces. It must look at the totality of the criminal behaviour and ask itself what is the appropriate sentence for all the offences[45]'.

Problems emerge: the logic of this would produce what Ashworth has called 'a discount for bulk offending' and yet sentencing a multiple burglar to the same term as a rapist offends moral sense. The sentencer is forced into compromises so that the final sentence should bear a recognisable relationship to the sentence that would have been passed for the single most serious offence and that no defendant should be faced with a crushing weight of sentence simply as a result of arithmetic. As such the totality rule is endorsed by section 28(2) Criminal Justice Act 1991 which states that nothing in the Act should prevent a court 'in the case of an offender who is convicted of one or more other offences, from mitigating his sentence by applying any rule of law as to the totality of offences'.

The issue of sentencing offenders who have committed multiple offences is affected by the requirement to assess the seriousness of an offence under the provisions of the Criminal Justice Act 1991. Under the original 1982 legislation, the Court of Appeal held that where there were multiple offences, these could not be aggregated to increase the seriousness of any single incident and thus warrant a custodial sentence.[46] An example of such practice is seen in *Choudhary*[47] where the defendent used a stolen credit card in a series of small offences obtaining an overall sum of £3,000 a custodial sentence was imposed at first instance. However this sentence was quashed on appeal as no single incident warranted an order for detention, in essence the court refused to allow single offences which would warrant non-custodial disposals to be aggregated to warrant the imposition of a custodial sanction.

This principle, focusing solely on the seriousness of the specific offence, was modified in 1991 so that the court, in assessing the seriousness of an offence, could consider that offence and one other associated with it. This applied not only in assessing seriousness in relation to custodial sentences but to community sentences also.[48] Despite the limited retreat, the prohibition on aggregating offences so as to increase overall seriousness still held. This has now been altered by section 66(1) of the Criminal Justice Act 1993 which allows a court in assessing seriousness to take into account '... *the offence, or the combination of the offence and one or more other offences associated with it ...*'. This reverses the previous policy and allows courts to aggregate offences, none of which would in themselves have been serious enough to warrant a custodial sentence, in order that a prison sentence can be imposed. It is doubtful whether the court in *Choudhary* would now reach the same result.

---

[44] Thomas (1979), *Principles of Sentencing* (2nd ed, Heinemann), p. 59.
[45] Quoted by Thomas (1979), *op. cit.*, p. 56.
[46] *Davison* (1989) 11 Crim. App. Rep. (S) 570.
[47] (1992) 13 Crim. App. Rep. (S) 290.
[48] s. 1(2)(a), s. 2(2)(a) and s. 6(1) of the Criminal Justice Act 1991.

9.3 FURTHER DEVELOPMENTS IN THE SENTENCING FRAMEWORK

The 1991 Act was a departure from a less interventionist governmental approach to sentencing policy and marked, as stated, the beginning of the new statutory sentencing framework. It was envisaged that the legislation would provide a solid basis on which consistent sentencing decisions could be formulated. While the Act heralded a new approach to sentencing theory or policy, the framework it developed has since been subject to development and revision. Why should this be necessary? The 1991 Act is perhaps best summarised as '*a partnership in which the legislature establishes the framework and the courts develop the more detailed numerical guidance; however ... the framework established by the Criminal Justice Act 1991 is less clear than one would have hoped for.*'[49] As such subsequent legislation has taken pains to reaffirm or clarify sentencing policy in order to ensure that the framework becomes *more* clear. The main pieces of legislation to embark on this policy are summarised below.

However, it must first be noted that while there has been much legislation in the intervening decade which affects sentencing policy, for example the Criminal Justice and Public Order Act 1994 and the Human Rights Act 1998, these will not be considered within this section. While each of these Acts is in effect part of the development of the sentencing framework the impact has not been as direct as that of the legislation considered below. Similarly, the Crime and Disorder Act 1998 and Youth Justice and Criminal Evidence Act 1999 would seem pertinent to a discussion on sentencing policy as both pieces of legislation created a number of new non-custodial disposals,[50] however, these disposals are limited in the main to young offenders, and as such lie outside the ambit of discussion in this section. Sentencing policy towards young offenders is dealt with separately under youth justice rationales[51] which can be stated simply by reference to the Crime and Disorder Act 1998 which provides:

> 37 (1) It shall be the principle aim of the youth justice system to prevent offending by children and young persons.

9.3.1 *Crime (Sentences) Act 1997*

The Crime (Sentences) Act 1997 was created to counter, in part, continuing criticism of sentencing policy as being still somewhat confused. Provisions of the Act were aimed at improving consistency and adding to the framework by providing more coherent and definitive guidelines to the process for determining sentence. However, unlike the 1991 legislation, which intended to provide a basic sentencing platform, the CSA 1997 was more specific on the offences that it targeted.[52] The Act sought to promote '*greater certainty in the sentencing of*

---

[49] von Hirsch, A. and Ashworth, A. [eds] (1992) *Principled Sentencing* (Edinburgh University Press, Edinburgh), p. 289. For a similar discussion of the White Paper which resulted in the Criminal Justice Act 1991, see Wasik, M. and von Hirsch, A., '*Statutory Sentencing Principles: The 1990 White Paper*' (1990) 53 M.L.R. 508.
[50] for example, the Reparation Order (s. 67) and the Action Plan Order (s. 69) in the Crime and Disorder Act 1998 and the Referral Order (s. 1) of the Youth Justice and Criminal Evidence Act 1999.
[51] For further discussion of the youth justice system see Chap. 11.
[52] For example, s. 2 which relates to the imposing of an automatic life sentence on conviction for a second time of certain offences. See s. 9.7.2 in Custodial sentences.

repeat offenders who commit serious crimes, class A drug trafficking and domestic burglaries'.[53] This was part of a government policy designed to ensure 'Honesty in Sentencing'[54] but was a further departure away from a strict interpretation of 'just deserts' promulgated by the Criminal Justice Act 1991 and further demonstrates a re-emergence of the ideals of deterrence and incapacitation, most notably in section 2 of the Act which makes provisions for the imposition of an automatic life sentence on conviction of a second legislatively specified offence.

9.3.2 *Powers of Criminal Courts (Sentencing) Act 2000*

This Act, in essence, provides for the consolidation of sentencing practice, incorporating the practice and policy which had come before it in many acts of parliament, into one statute. The Act itself divides sentencing powers and policy into 8 separate 'Parts' as follows:

Part I— Powers exercisable before sentence.

Part II— Absolute and Conditional Discharge.

Part III— Mandatory and Discretionary Referral of Young Offenders.

Part IV— Community Orders and Reparation Orders.

Part V— Custodial Sentences, *etc.*

Part VI— Financial Penalties and Orders.

Part VII— Further Powers of Courts.

Part VIII— Miscellaneous and Supplementary.

Within each relevant 'Part' the provisions fall into 'Chapters' which make provision for different types of offence or offender, for example, within Part V, Custodial Sentences, the Act separates custodial sentences applicable to young offenders and adult offenders. This is arguably another step towards a more coherent and easily navigable sentencing framework and is to be much commended. While not a codification of sentencing as such, the Act provides a much clearer picture of sentencing policy and how sentencing decisions should be reached, not least because the primary guidance for sentencers is now contained within one document.

9.3.3 *Criminal Justice and Court Services Act 2000*

The Criminal Justice and Court Services Act 2000 is a more recent affirmation of the government's commitment to a developing a rational and statutory sentencing policy. The opening sections provide unequivocal evidence of this.

1.—(1) This Chapter has effect for the purposes of providing for—

(a) courts to be given assistance in determining the appropriate sentences

---

[53] Jason-Lloyd, L. (1997) N.L.J., Vol. 147. 1070 at 1072.
[54] A popular government sound-bite used at the time of the introduction of the 1997 legislation.

to pass, and making other decisions, in respect of persons charged with or convicted of offences, and

(b) the supervision and rehabilitation of such persons.

(2) Subsection (1)(b) extends (in particular) to—

(a) giving effect to community orders,
(b) supervising persons released from prison on licence,
(c) providing accommodation in approved premises.

2.—(1) This section applies to—

(a) the functions of the Secretary of State under this Chapter,
(b) the functions of local probation boards, and officers of local probation boards, under this Act or any other enactment so far as they may be exercised for the purposes mentioned in section 1.

(2) In exercising those functions the person concerned must have regard to the following aims—

(a) the protection of the public,
(b) the reduction of re-offending,
(c) the proper punishment of offenders,
(d) ensuring offenders' awareness of the effects of crime on the victims of crime and the public,
(e) the rehabilitation of offenders.

Section 1 makes mention of the idea of rehabilitation of offenders, re-emphasising the remaining importance of this rationale to current sentencing policy. However, in addition the aims of the criminal justice process as a whole are stated in section 2. In this way it is possible to suggest that the traditional theories of sentencing are beginning to unite with stated aims of the criminal justice process, although with regard to this Act, those aims are actually laid out for the individuals listed in section 2(1) rather than the courts specifically.

9.4 REVIEW OF THE SENTENCING FRAMEWORK

Although the spate of legislation from 1991 onwards has attempted to create a coherent sentencing framework, the position of sentencing *policy* is currently in a state of flux. While the legislation allows the practice of sentencing to continue undisturbed, the recent government interest in the ideas or aims of sentencing have become a focus in the government programme for reducing crime.[55]

This focus by government on sentencing policy and underlying aims is an interesting topic for debate in itself. 2001 witnessed the publication of no less than three important papers and reports[56] which are directly concerned with the aims and objectives of sentencing, or at least have the ability to impact significantly on sentencing policy. Given the well-received White Paper on criminal justice of 1990[57] and subsequent 1991 Criminal Justice Act, the ethos of which

---

[55] For general information see http://www.crimereduction.gov.uk.
[56] *The Auld Review, The Halliday Report* and the Home Office paper *Criminal Justice: The Way Ahead*, Cm. 5074, 2001.
[57] *Crime, Justice and Protecting the Public* (Home Office, Cm. 965, 1990).

still governs sentencing policy, is it not surprising that such a broad review is seemingly necessary only ten years later? Perhaps not. One of the primary aims of the 1991 Act was to provide a firm and more coherent sentencing rationale, in fact a framework, which could guide the courts in determining which disposal to select within a stated structure of just deserts. While the aim of the legislation was to ensure that sentencing policy was directed by this idea of the sentence fitting the offence through the notion of 'just deserts' or proportionality, there is evidence to suggest that this was not always the case in practice. Indeed, as Ashworth comments, '*There is no shortage of evidence that actual practices may diverge from the formal rules and principles*'.[58] In addition, subsequent legislation detracted from this aim to a certain extent, most notably s2(2) of the Crime Sentences Act 1997[59] whereby automatic life sentences must be imposed for a second violent offence.[60] In effect section 2(2) of the 1997 Act requires the award of a sentence which is greater than would normally attach to the current offence before the court. This arguably undermines a strict interpretation of 'just deserts' which should ensure that an offender receives a sentence which is commensurate or proportionate with the offence before the court[61] by imposing a sentence which punishes not only for the current offence but allows a previous offence, for which a sentence has already been served, to trigger a more severe sentence, that of a life sentence.

Given the difficulties that have arisen in respect of ensuring a coherent and consistently applied rationale for sentencing it is perhaps of no great surprise that the current government has called for, and has begun instigating, a radical overhaul of the sentencing system. However, there may be another reason contributing to why sentencing policy has enjoyed such close scrutiny in recent years. The Labour government, like many before it, has made use of ideas for improving criminal justice as part of their electoral platform.[62] The recent strategy, encapsulated by the slogan '*Crime, let's bring it down*'[63] has been allied with what could be termed a 'promotional campaign' whereby Home Office websites provide a plethora of information regarding criminal justice policy in a number of easily navigable and simply titled websites.[64] The government is committed to its policy of crime reduction and of clear importance within this is a commitment to ensuring that public confidence in the criminal justice process as a whole is improved. In this objective sentencing policy has an important function. It is possible to suggest that a sentence becomes symbolic, in public perception, of the efficacy of the criminal justice process. Within the process many decisions are taken which are not necessarily readily identifiable by the public, for example, why the Crown Prosecution Service chooses not to prosecute in a particular case. Moreover, despite the government's attempts to render accessible much of their criminal justice policy, many of the procedures are too technical for easy public consumption. In contrast to this sentencing, both custodial and non-custodial,

---

[58] Ashworth (2000) p. 358.

[59] Now incorporated as s. 109 of the Powers of Criminal Courts (Sentencing) Act 2000.

[60] The Act itself provides a list of the offences included in such a category which will trigger the provision.

[61] Or any other offences which the defendant has asked to be taken into account.

[62] See, generally, The Labour Party (2001), *Ambitions for Britain: Labour's Manifesto 2001*.

[63] See http://www.crimereduction.gov.uk.

[64] For example, http://www.crimereduction.gov.uk, http://www.secureyourmotor.gov.uk, http://www.policereform.gov.uk, http://www.criminal-justice-system.gov.uk and http://www.fairer-sentencing.co.uk (although this last website citation has a 'co.' domain rather than the usual 'gov'. it links immediately to the Home Office website).

can be readily identified and understood. Public confidence in sentencing—both on a policy and operational level—may ultimately translate into confidence in the criminal justice process more generally. To this end changes in the names of some non-custodial sanctions,[65] while seemingly superficial, may have much greater impact than would be initially supposed.

One further point worthy of consideration in discussion of sentencing policy is that of vocabulary. The objectives underlying sentencing are often discussed in terms of rehabilitation, retribution, deterrence and incapacitation.[66] However, with the increasing political focus on sentencing policy and the need for a sentencing framework the vocabulary has undergone a change. As such, the traditional terminology for the discussion of sentencing rationale loses some of its currency. With the numerous government White Papers, reports and reviews and speeches concerning both the criminal justice system as a whole, and sentencing practice in particular, new ideas and terms have come to the forefront in statements regarding the actual aims of sentencing. In addition to the recognised philosophies of sentencing new terminology has infused the debate. This suggests that traditional ideas must at least share discussion space with these new focus points. The Home Secretary, in a speech to the National Probation Service provides a useful sound-bite encapsulating the government's current aims—'*We can summarise the aims of sentencing with the three Ps and the three Rs: prevention, protection, punishment; and reparation, reducing crime, and rehabilitation.*'[67] It is perhaps surprising, to anyone that reads the text of this relatively short speech, that the Home Secretary did not include an additional 'P' in his list, that of 'public confidence', given that this idea occurs time and time again throughout this speech. Indeed, the Home Secretary comments; '*the public are driven crackers with frustration ... and I am determined to hammer out what they deserve—a reformed, common-sense sentencing system. Because public confidence is key.*'[68]

Given the political impetus towards a more coherently developed sentencing 'system' the next section will attempt to navigate through some of the more important reports and papers which have emerged under the auspices of the Home Office in the last year. The Halliday review of sentencing policy and the Auld report on the criminal courts, both published in 2001, provide broad issues from which ideas of future sentencing aims, and the level of importance such aims will enjoy, relative to each other, can be gleaned. This is further augmented by the 2002 publication of the government White Paper *Justice for All* which seeks to translate recommendations and findings into concrete proposals for the criminal justice system.[69] We are currently awaiting the Bill/s which will inevitably arise from such a broad and far-reaching review and consultation, bills which will attempt to '*put sense back into sentencing*'.[70]

---

[65] ss. 43–44 Criminal Justice and Courts Services Act 2000—Probation Orders become Community Rehabilitation Orders; Community Service Orders become Community Punishment Orders.
[66] For further detail and history of such analysis, see Ashworth, A. (2000) *Sentencing and Criminal Justice*. (3rd ed., Butterworths, London), Chapter 3
[67] Speech by Home Secretary on sentencing reform, National Probation Service inaugural conference, July 5, 2001, para. 15.
[68] Speech by Home Secretary on sentencing reform, National Probation Service inaugural conference, July 5, 2001, para. 41.
[69] *Justice for All*, Cm. 5563, 2002, published July.
[70] Speech by Home Secretary on sentencing reform, National Probation Service inaugural conference, July 5, 2001, para. 3.

9.4.1 *Criminal Justice: The Way Ahead*[71]

The timing of the publication of Criminal Justice: The Way Ahead gives rise to comment. The Paper was presented to parliament in February of 2001 just a few months prior to the publication of both the Halliday Report on the review of the sentencing framework and Auld Report on the review of the Criminal Courts. Given that this Paper attempted to present a broad overview of plans for criminal justice process, including a proposal for a codified system,[72] it is perhaps surprising that it was not delayed long enough to allow a discussion, however brief, of the proposals made in the two commissioned reviews. Despite this curious choice of publication date, the Paper makes clear a number of proposals with regard to sentencing, some of a policy level and a number of suggested procedural reforms.

On a policy level, there is explicit acceptance that the current sentencing framework, provided under the auspices of the 1991 Criminal Justice Act, does not work.[73] As such it is likely that an overhaul of the sentencing framework is imminent, perhaps with a re-organisation of the priorities of sentencing aims. At a procedural level there is concern expressed about the feedback courts receive on the effectiveness of sentences that have been imposed and the lack of cohesion between various elements of the sentencing process—

> 'There is a sharp division of roles between sentencers, who confine themselves to the immediate offences and surrounding circumstances, and the prison and probation services who implement sentences passed. There is no requirement to work collectively in managing the sentences as a whole, nor take account of the offender's progress during sentence'.[74]

The Paper considers both custodial and non-custodial sanctions and proposes a 'way forward' in order that sanctions can better meet the aims of reducing re-offending and increasing reparation. In summary, with regard to sentencing, the Paper breaks down into a number of focussed components that include proposals for;

- The supervision of offenders post-release from a short-term custodial sentence (termed 'Custody Plus').[75]

- More transparency for victims of crime and communities.

- Sentences becoming more offender based rather than offence based—by this it is envisaged that greater weight may be afforded to previous convictions, previous sentences and the effect such a sentence had on the offender.

9.4.2 *The Halliday Report*[76]

In 2000 the Home Office announced the commission of a Review Of The Sentencing Framework. The communication making the announcement provides

---

[71] *Criminal Justice: The Way Ahead*, Cm. 5074, 2001, published 26 February
[72] For discussion see Editorial, *Reviving the Criminal Code*, [2001] Crim. L.R. 261.
[73] *Criminal Justice: The Way Ahead*, Cm. 5074, 2001, para. 2.61, p. 41.
[74] *Criminal Justice: The Way Ahead*, Cm. 5074, 2001, para. 2.64, p. 41.
[75] *Criminal Justice: The Way Ahead*, Cm. 5074, 2001, paras 2.73–2.75.
[76] Home office (2001) *Making Punishments Work: Report of a Review of the Sentencing Framework for England and Wales.*, published July 4, 2001.

elucidation of why such a task was being undertaken: '*Public confidence in our system of justice is too low. There is a feeling that our sentencing framework does not work as well as it should and that it pays insufficient weight to the needs of victims* ... *There is insufficient consistency or progression in sentencing and sentencers receive insufficient information about whether their sentencing decisions have worked*'.[77] Further, the announcement suggested that an appropriate sentencing framework should '*deliver the twin aims of public protection and a reduction in re-offending*'.[78] By 2001 when the Report was delivered, this twin aim was not as evident, with a letter from the Home Secretary stating that the review '*was tasked with considering what principles should guide sentencing decisions and what types of disposal should be made available to the courts so as to reduce re-offending more effectively*'.[79] Moreover, given that the announcement of the Review was made in the year that the Human Rights Act 1998 took effect it is perhaps surprising that no mention is made of human rights in the announcement communication. Such a failing is particularly unexpected given the number of appeals to the European Court of Human Rights regarding sentencing in the last decade.[80] However, the final Review report, the Halliday Report, does make reference to human rights. Thus the introduction to chapter 2 recognises that principles of justice and fairness require, amongst other things, that sentences comply with human rights. The Report makes clear that its subsequent proposals for a new framework have been tested to ensure compliance with the Human Rights Act 1998.[81]

The Halliday Report was published in July 2001 and the review proved to be both far-reaching and broad, considering a wide variety of sentencing issues. As has been noted, '*the contents of the Report leave virtually no stone of the sentencing system unturned*'.[82] The Report document, which extends to 164 pages, makes a great number of recommendations and proposals many of which echo the aims of *Criminal Justice: The Way Ahead*. Though a full analysis of the document is out with the ambit of this chapter, not least as there are over 50 key recommendations made by the Report,[83] the primary exhortations of the Report pertaining to the sentencing framework and sentencing aims can perhaps be summarised as follows:

- The framework under the 1991 Act '*needs to address more directly than at present the purposes of crime reduction and reparation, as well as punishment*'[84] rather than focus solely on the notion of proportionality.

- While the Report recommends the retention of much of the 1991 frame-

---

[77] Home Office Communications Directorate, CCN077828, C. 4000, May 2000, p. 1.
[78] Home Office Communications Directorate, CCN077828, C. 4000, May 2000, p. 2.
[79] Letter from the Home Secretary requesting consultation on the published Halliday Report, July 5, 2001, p. 1, see http://www.homeoffice.gov.uk.
[80] For a discussion of sentencing policy/practice and human rights see Cheney, D *et al.* (2001) *Criminal Justice and the Human Rights Act 1998* 2nd ed, Jordans, Bristol, Chap. 5.
[81] Home Office (2001) *Making Punishments Work: Report of a Review of the Sentencing Framework for England and Wales*, July 2001, para. 2.4, p. 12.
[82] Baker, E. and Clarkson, CMV. '*Making Punishment Work? An Evaluation of the Halliday Report on Sentencing in England and Wales*', (2002) Crim. L.R. 81 at p. 83.
[83] For excellent discussion of the Report, see Baker, E. and Clarkson, CMV, '*Making Punishment Work? An Evaluation of the Halliday Report on Sentencing in England and Wales*,' (2002) Crim. L.R. 81.
[84] Home Office (2001) *Making Punishments Work: Report of a Review of the Sentencing Framework for England and Wales*, July 2001, para. 1.71, p. 10.

work, most notably the idea of proportionality and the totality principle,[85] this is in a subtly altered framework 'package'. The report proposes that the idea of proportionality, or the sentence being commensurate with the offence committed, should set the parameters of the sentencing decision, a sentencer should then pay more heed to previous convictions in an effort to tackle potential re-offending and ensure protection of the public. What this would mean in practice is a policy of bifurcation. The Report recommends that for non-violent and less serious crimes the presumption should be that the offender is punished in the community through means of more effectively monitored and implemented community sanctions. Contrasted to this is the policy to be adopted towards more serious crimes and persistent offenders where perhaps more serious sanctions should be imposed in order to take account of previous convictions.

- The Report asserts that sentencing can make an important contribution to both increasing public confidence and crime reduction. This may be achieved through improving public awareness of sentencing practice and policy.

- The notion of 'seriousness of criminal conduct' should be clarified and should be governed by a number of principles including the seriousness of the offence, the offender's criminal history, and offender's culpability and sentencing guidelines should be created to explain how to account for such factors.[86]

- The Report, like the government paper considered above, recommends 'Custody plus'.[87] Indeed, in conclusion of its findings on prison sentences of less than 12 months, the Report recommends that a 'compulsory supervision in the community' period be introduced in order to ensure such short custodial sentences can prove to be effective in reducing crime.

- New sentencing guidelines should be created and set out 'entry points' for considering severity of sentence in conjunction with graded definitions of seriousness of offences.[88]

- The reasons for sentencing decisions, including any grounds for mitigation, should be recorded for subsequent retrieval, preferably electronically.[89]

Overall, the Report aims at making proposals which are designed to ensure a greater consistency in sentencing practice, generally through the provision of greater guidance and a perhaps more formulaic approach to sentencing decisions, and a clearer sentencing framework or philosophy. In terms of clearer framework, this does not only mean, according to the Report, clearer for sentencers, but also more easily accessible to the public so that the recommended philosophies underlying decisions can be more readily understood. Public confidence in sentencing is an idea which is evident throughout the Report's many recommendations. It is perhaps understandable therefore that comment on this subject

---

[85] Home Office (2001) *Making Punishments Work: Report of a Review of the Sentencing Framework for England and Wales*, July 2001, para 2.9, p. 13.
[86] *ibid.*, para 2.8, p. 13.
[87] *ibid.*, see paras 3.12–3.19, p. 24.
[88] *ibid.*, p. 21.
[89] *ibid.*, p. 21.

has been made which notes that '*The Halliday report will appeal to the Action Man approach that has come to characterise New Labour's policy formulation. The temptation may be, as the recommendations are debated, to impose an even more executive will upon the courts*'.[90] It remains to be seen how far the many recommendations of the Halliday are implemented. While the Report findings were welcomed by the government, the Home Secretary swiftly made clear that it cannot be assumed that the recommendations will be imported wholesale into legislation: '*It will act as a catalyst for us to examine what we do, and above all why we do it, in preventing, tackling and punishing offending behaviour. But it is not—and was not intended to be—a blueprint*'.[91] The government has chosen to take time to consider both the Report findings in-depth and the responses that the Report precipitated. While a White paper on the subject of sentencing and possible codifying of the sentencing framework was initially expected in the early months of 2002,[92] publications was delayed until July,[93] perhaps reflecting the government concern regarding the criminal justice process. As the Home Secretary noted in 2001: '*We need to get this right: we need a sentencing system built to last, and one which is radical enough to have a real impact on both offending behaviour and public perception*'.[94]

9.4.3 The Auld Report[95]

With regard to the traditional motivations or objectives of sentencing, incapacitation, deterrence, rehabilitation and retribution, the difficulty involved in establishing a framework which delivers such ideals is made evident in the Auld Report of 2001 where it is noted that

> 'we should not expect too much of the criminal justice system, the courts in particular, as a medium for curing the ills of society. Courts undoubtedly have deterrent, rehabilitative and reparative roles, but they are all too often the last resort after all other attempts to deter and/or reform have failed. In their present sentencing role they are a blunt instrument of social repair'.

However, Auld remains confident that the process can be made more effective— '*with development of new and constructive combinations of punishment and rehabilitation—one form of 'restorative justice'—they may have more of a role, with other agencies, in diverting people from crime before recidivism sets in*'.[96] The Report of the Review of Criminal Courts of England and Wales, the Auld Report, was published in October 2001. While not specifically aimed at sentencing policy, being more broad in nature, the Report makes a number of pertinent suggestions regarding overall sentencing policy and practice which add to the morass of current debate. Of interest within a sentencing context is the

[90] Louis Blom-Cooper and Terence Morris, *Leave law to Courts*, Society section, *The Guardian*, September 2, 2001.
[91] Speech by Home Secretary on sentencing reform, National Probation Service inaugural conference, July 5, 2001, para. 5.
[92] See Lords Hansard, vol. 628, November 11, 2001, Column WA 140, *Written Answers*, where Lord Rooker anticipates the publication of the White Paper in Spring 2002.
[93] Justice for All, Cm. 5563, 2002, published July.
[94] Speech by Home Secretary on sentencing reform. National Probation Service inaugural conference, July 5, 2001, para. 11.
[95] Review of the Criminal Courts of England and Wales (2001) HMSO, published October 2001.
[96] Review of the Criminal Courts of England and Wales (2001) HMSO, Introduction, para. 9.

proposal made regarding a scale of graduated sentence discount for guilty pleas, allied with the concept of providing an advance indication of sentence to those defendants considering pleading guilty. The proposals made by the Review suggest that

> 'there should be introduced, by way of a judicial sentencing guideline for later incor-poration in a Sentencing Code, a system of sentencing discounts graduated so that the earlier the tender of plea of guilty the higher the discount for it, coupled with a system of advance indication of sentence for a defendant considering pleading guilty'.[97]

Such a recommendation, if implemented, is another step towards a formalised and more rigid sentencing structure, including the much debated notion of codification of sentencing procedures. Moreover, like the Halliday Report which preceded it, the Auld Report encourages the use of information technology, designed to ensure any new sentencing framework is transparent both for sen-tencers and the general public. To this end the Report recommends the possible creation of an on-line sentencing information system.

One of the most important recommendations made relates to the creation of a Unified Criminal Court structure which amalgamates the existing Magistrates Courts and Crown Courts.[98] Within this another tier should be created, the Divisional Court. While such a proposal would seem relevant to a discussion on court structuring, rather than sentencing, it is of interest that the Auld Report considers that the factor determining which court should hear the case is to be determined by reference to the seriousness of potential sentence, with the Divi-sional Court taking cases where the expected sentence is of between 6 months and 2 years duration and further, potentially determining the mode of trial for all cases. Such a structure would go some way to assisting any sentencing infor-mation/advance indication of sentence systems but remains a contentious subject given that the new Divisional Court would be responsible for determining in which court triable either-way offences should be heard. An attempt to further reduce a defendant's right to elect mode of trial for such offences will prove unwelcome if the government's previous attempts to do so are to be used as a measure. The Mode of Trial Bill progressing through parliament was quietly 'dropped' in January 2002 after meeting widespread opposition. This particular recommendation may indeed face the same treatment.[99] The government response to the recommendations of the Auld Report has mirrored that afforded the preceding Halliday Report. The welcome accorded the Report is tempered with caution. The Lord Chancellor notes *'Sir Robin makes some radical recommendations which will need the most careful consideration. The Govern-ment has taken no decision on his Report and we are keen to encourage wide debate on these issues before we reach decisions'.*[100]

---

[97] Review of the Criminal Courts of England and Wales (2001) HMSO, Chap. 10, para. 114.
[98] See Chap. 7 of the Review of the Criminal Courts of England and Wales (2001) HMSO.
[99] See responses to the Auld Report, in particular that by Michael Zander Q.C., *Lord Justice Auld's Review of the Criminal Courts: A Response.* Available at http://www.homeoffice.gov.uk.
[100] News Release 'Radical Review of the Criminal Courts', Attorney-General's Chambers, October 8, 2001.

9.4.4 *Justice for All*[101]

The most recent government publication concerning the criminal justice process is the White Paper, Justice for All, published in July of 2002. The Paper is the culmination of the review work conducted in the previous few years and subsequent consultation process, and the document lays out government proposals for the criminal justice process in its entirety. Within the document, chapter 5 focuses on sentencing, and echoing previous government sound-bites is entitled 'Putting the Sense back into Sentencing'. The proposals made are, in light of the *Auld* and *Halliday Reports*, entirely expected, as is the concern regarding public confidence in the sentencing process. The Paper recognises that the

> '*public are sick and tired of a sentencing system that does not make sense. They read about dangerous, violent, sexual and other serious offender who get off lightly, or are not in prison long enough or for the length of their sentence. There is no real clarity for magistrates and judges in sentencing and the system is so muddled the public do not always understand it or have confidence in it.*'[102]

To this end proposals are made to establish, through legislation, a Sentencing Guidelines Council, which will augment the work done by the Sentencing Advisory Panel. The new Council will seek to improve public confidence and ensure greater consistency in sentencing practice by formulating and disseminating sentencing guidelines for all criminal offences. In line with earlier discussion on who should determine what sentences are and how they should be determined[103] the document takes great pains to reassure readers that the creation of such a Council is not an attempt to remove discretionary power from sentencers, noting '*We fully recognise the importance of an independent judiciary, and do not seek to infringe upon its independence. Our intention is to strengthen and broaden the current guidelines.*'[104]

The first steps towards ensuring greater clarity in sentencing decisions are taken by the document itself, whereby the proposed sentencing scheme is laid out in table format, followed by a brief discussion of what each of these sentences entails.[105] The ideas of the Custody Plus[106] and Custody Minus[107] sentences are included as is a proposal for a sentence involving Intermittent Custody, whereby the custodial element of a sentence could be served at weekends while the cumminty element is performed during weekdays. Of interest within the proposals for concrete sentences is the planned Customised Community Sentence. The current structure of community sentences allows for the imposition of one, or a certain combination of, community sentence, such as the Community Punishment Order. Justice for All suggests that community sentences should all come under one umbrella and in future sentencers should be permitted to select elements from available community sentences in order that the can be '*matched to*

---

[101] *Justice for All*, Cm. 5563, 2002, published July.

[102] *Justice for All*, Cm. 5563, 2002, para. 5.2, p. 86.

[103] See section 9.1.

[104] *Justice for All*, Cm. 5563, 2002, para. 5.15, p. 90.

[105] See *Justice for All*, Cm. 5563, 2002, para. 5.19, p. 91.

[106] Defined in para. 5.19 as 'a short prison sentence followed by a community programme'.

[107] Defined in para. 5.19 as 'a short prison sentence will be suspended and the offender will undertake a community sentence'.

the individual offender[108]. In their words, community sentences should, in future be tailor made for each case in an attempt to achieve *'effective sentences in the community which are flexible enough to meet the particular needs of a case, where the courts are not forced to choose between options'*.[109]

While such proposals are not surprising there is a proposal which does perhaps seem a little out of place, given the focus on make sentences more clear, understandable and accessible. Chapter 5 notes the government proposal to create an indeterminate sentence of offenders who commit violent or sexual offences. The idea put forward is that

> *'We want to ensure that the public are adequately protected from those offenders whose offences do not currently attract a maximum penalty of life imprisonment but who are nevertheless assessed as dangerous. We believe that such offenders should remain in custody until their risks are considered manageable in the community'.*[110]

While such a proposal would seem to follow on from concerns regarding public safety and public confidence, it is particularly interesting given the recent judicial concern regarding indeterminate sentences, in particular the mandatory life sentence, which would seem on the face of it to involve procedures of a similar type to the proposed new sentence. Indeterminate sentences of this nature have come under the scrutiny of both domestic judges and the European Court of Human Rights[111] with regard to whether the operation of these sentences breach human rights legislation, in particular issues arise concerning the role of the Home Secretary in determining whether and when such offenders should be released. While much of the concern has focused on which body should be responsible for assessing release, and the White Paper makes specific mention that for this new sentence it should be the Parole Board[112], it would seem prudent to ensure that judicial uneasiness is allayed prior to implementation of another form of indeterminate sentencing.

With regard to the philosophy underlying the sentencing process, the White Paper makes a bold step by claiming that *'For the first time, we will set out in legislation the purposes of sentencing'* and further that *'Sentencers will be required to consider these purposes when sentencing and how the sentence they impose will provide the right balance between the purposes'*.[113] Indeed, the document provides the purposes of sentencing which will be incorporated into legislation. These are

- *first and foremost protect the public. This is paramount;*

- *act as a punishment and ensure the punishment fits the crime;*

- *reduce crime. Sentencing must be an effective tool which leads to fewer crimes;*

---

[108] *Justice for All*, Cm. 5563, 2002, para. 5.20, p. 91.
[109] *Justice for All*, Cm. 5563, 2002, para. 5.20, p. 91.
[110] *Justice for All*, Cm. 5563, 2002, para. 5.41, p. 95.
[111] See *Stafford v. the United Kingdom*, Application No. 46295/99. Judgment given 28 May 2002. This case dicussed the recent domestic cases concerning mandatory life sentences, in particular, *R. (Anderson and Taylor) v. the Secretary of State for the Home Department*, BLD 1411013733. (see para. 46 of the European Court's decision in *Stafford v. the United Kingdom*)
[112] *Justice for All*, Cm. 5563, 2002, para. 5.41, p. 95.
[113] *Justice for All*, Cm. 5563, 2002, para. 5.8–5.9, p. 87–88.

- *deter (this includes both the general effect on the population at large and the specific effect on the offender);*

- *incapacitate, where offenders are physically prevented from committing crimes by removing them partly or entirely from society;*

- *reform and rehabilitate, so that the offender can learn new skills and attitudes which make him or her less likely to reoffend; and*

- *promote reparation. We must actively encourage offenders to make amends for the crimes they have committed.*[114]

Given the number of purposes listed by the document, and the requirement that sentencers balance all of these often competing interests, it will be interesting to see how such proposals translate into working practice in the coming years.

9.4.5 *A Word on Restorative Justice*

In January 1999 the government launched its Crime Reduction Programme.[115] One of the three main 'sentencing theme' topics was that of Restorative Justice. Such a theme is a development of one of the principal elements of the Crime and Disorder Act 1998[116] which promoted the concept of restorative justice within the youth justice system.[117] This theme has also been clearly evident in the recent reviews of the criminal courts and sentencing framework discussed above. As such restorative justice has become one of the platforms of crime reduction policy, albeit currently confined, in the main, to youth justice. Initial research conducted on behalf of the Home Office only reported in the closing months of 2001.[118] However, with the noted benefits of many of these evaluated pilot schemes, together with the success evident in the youth justice sector, it is possible that further use will be made of restorative justice measures for adult offenders in the future. Indeed, as part of the continuing Crime Reduction Programme, the government has continued to fund three schemes[119] which, it is hoped, will provide further empirical data with which future governments can evaluate the potential of restorative justice schemes and determine their place within the criminal justice process.

Restorative justice as a philosophy of sentencing operates as '*a problem-solving approach to crime which involves the parties themselves, and the community generally, in an active relationship with statutory agencies ... Restorative Justice may be seen as criminal justice embedded in its social context*'.[120] In this way the use of restorative justice may assist in encouraging pubic confidence in the criminal justice system as a whole, and perhaps more specifically in senten-

[114] *Justice for All*, Cm. 5563, 2002, para. 5.8, p. 88–89.
[115] See http://www.crimereduction.gov.uk.
[116] The Crime and Disorder Act 1998 talks of restorative justice in terms of reparation, for example, s. 67 introduces the Reparation Order for young people aged 10–17 years convicted of an offence other than one where the sentence is fixed by law.
[117] the youth justice system and its aims were established by s. 37 of the Crime and Disorder Act 1998.
[118] Miers, D *et al.* (2001), *An Exploratory Evaluation of Restorative Justice Schemes*, RDSD Crime Reduction Research Series Paper 9.
[119] Funding has been awarded until end of March 2003. The 3 schemes are Justice Research Consortium, REMEDI (a South Yorkshire mediation service) and NACRO/London Probation Area.
[120] Marshall, TF (1999) *Restorative Justice: An Overview*, Home Office RDSD, p. 5.

cing, as public participation, in what is effectively the administration of a sentence, is ensured. One such example of this comes from a recent initiative in promoting restorative justice, that of the introduction of the Referral Order.[121] Under the provisions of a Referral Order, young offenders, aged between 10–17 years, pleading guilty to a first time offence, may be referred to a Youth Offender Panel. The Panel consists of 2 volunteers from the local community and 1 member of a Youth Offending Team. The panel meets with the offender and family and, if possible, the victim of the crime, thus effectively recognising the twin aims of victim participation and, hopefully, increasing public confidence. After pilot studies had been completed and evaluated the Referral Order programme and Youth Offender Panels began work in April 2002. A Press Release from the Youth Justice Board[122] summarised the hopes for the scheme— *'Neighbourhoods and victims of crime will now have an even greater role in the youth justice system thanks to this new approach to first-time offenders, which will build on the principle of restorative justice'.*[123]

However, it would be premature at this stage to assume that restorative justice can offer any form of a panacea to the ailments of the sentencing process or indeed can adequately meet the complex aims of government concerning sentencing policy. One exploratory evaluation of the schemes referred to above has identified a number of difficulties which must be overcome for restorative justice schemes to operate effectively. Primarily, the research noted that the schemes were *'fragile, being vulnerable to funding cuts, and were often dependant on work "beyond the call of duty" by small numbers of exceptionally committed individuals'*. The report, despite a number of positive points, goes on to note:

> 'Whatever its precise form, "restorative justice" is a labour-intensive and time-consuming activity, beset by communication problems and delays. Particularly where direct mediation is contemplated, it can involve weeks of preparatory and exploratory work, and, even then, many cases do not reach the desired conclusion. This situation raises some doubts about the potential future potential of mediation as a mainstream service capable of "processing" large numbers of cases within (or outside) the criminal justice system'.[124]

Further to this, concerns have been raised regarding the perceived benefits to victims of restorative justice schemes, the difficulties to be encountered in determining the correct role or function of the actors involved[125] and the procedural safeguards which have been or will be put in place to govern the operation of such schemes.[126] The potential for restorative justice and the place such schemes will have in the criminal justice process must therefore await further research, evaluation and debate in order that concerns regarding their

---

[121] s. 1 of the Youth Justice and Criminal Evidence Act 1999.
[122] established by s. 41 of the Crime and Disorder Act 1998.
[123] Youth Justice Board Press Release, 'Youth Offender Panels Go Live' April 2, 2002.
[124] Miers, D *et al.* (2001) *An Exploratory Evaluation of Restorative Justice Schemes*, RDSD Crime Reduction Research Series Paper 9, p. (ix).
[125] For example, victims, offender, community members and agents of the state.
[126] For further discussion see Ashworth, A. (2002) *'Responsibilities, Rights and Restorative Justice'*. *British Journal of Criminology* 42: 578–595 and Wright, M. (2002) *'The Court as Last Resort: Victim-Sensitive, Community-Based Responses to Crime'*. *British Journal of Criminology*, 42:654–667.

effectiveness can be allayed and, to use governmental terminology, a way forward can be found.

9.5 INFORMATION FOR SENTENCERS

9.5.1 *Guidelines on Sentencing*

In 1990 the government's policy was that the new proposed legislation, guidance from the Court of Appeal and the Attorney-General's new power to refer over-lenient sentences, would contribute to the development of coherent sentencing practice which would be disseminated to the courts by the Judicial Studies Board.[127]

It is arguable that such confidence was misplaced, at least in respect of guidelines on sentencing. Guidelines on sentencing provide a broad overview of judicial policy on the formulation for sentences for particular offences and indications of aggravating and mitigating circumstances which may be taken into account in the determination of the specific sentence to be awarded in any given case.[128] Although the Court of Appeal had developed guidelines on sentencing through judgment in some areas,[129] there was often little or no guidance for lesser offences, for example offences involving theft and deception.[130] With regard to such broad offences it is arguable that it is crucial that firm and coherent guidelines exist as it is in such cases that the borderline threshold between custodial and non-custodial penalties cries out for definition.[131] However, in 1990 in the case of *Mussel*,[132] Lane L.C.J. declined the opportunity to lay down guidelines for sentencing in offences of domestic burglary on the grounds that there were too great a variety of possible situations. Thus, Court of Appeal guidance seemed to be reserved, in the main, for more serious and narrowly construed offences, arguably those types of offences where sentencing decisions involved less variables. However, theses particular reservations expressed by Lane L.C.J. in 1990 have since dissipated, resulting in guidelines for sentencing in cases involving domestic burglary which can be found in *R. v. Brewster and others*.[133] This does not mean that the difficulties associated with the provision

---

[127] Crime, Justice and Protecting the Public (HMSO 1990 Cm. 965). For further information concerning the work of the Board, see http://www.jsboard.co.uk.

[128] As an aid to definition, one commentator describes such guideline judgements as follows: '*The Court of Appeal's quantitative guidance in its guideline judgments offers, in effect presumptive tariffs. At their best, they will attempt to set out sentences appropriate to several sets of case circumstances for an offence*'. Lovegrove, A. *Writing Quantitative Narrative Guideline Judgments: A Proposal* (2001) Crim. L.R. 265 at 267.

[129] For example, *Billam* [1986] 8 Crim. App. Rep. (S) 48—provides sentencing guidelines for offences of rape. (The Sentencing Advisory Panel has proposed a revision of these guidelines in their advice of May 24, 2002). More recently, in *R. v. Toomer and others* [2001] 2 Cr. App. R. (S) 30 the Court of Appeal laid down general principles as guidance for sentencing in cases of offences involving child pornography.

[130] However, the Sentencing Advisory Panel has recently proposed that the Court of Appeal issue guidelines for sentencers for cases of domestic burglary (May 10, 2002) and also handling stolen goods (March 15, 2001).

[131] The difficulties arising from a lack of coherent sentencing guidelines have been recognised in the recent government White Paper, *Justice for All*, Cm. 5563, 2002. The Paper proposes the creation of a Sentencing Guidelines Council which will be responsible for the production of clear sentencing guidelines for the entire range of criminal offences. (See chapter 5, para. 5.13–5.18, p. 89–90).

[132] (1990) 12 Crim. App. Rep. (S) 607.

[133] (1998) 1 Cr. App. R. (S) 181.

for, or lack of, guidelines for these 'lesser' offences have also dissipated.[134]
Commenting on the guidelines established in *Brewster*, Ashworth makes the
point *'the result was nothing like other guideline judgments'*.[135]

Guideline judgments seek to set out a sentencing tariff, and custody threshold
if possible and appropriate, whereby sets of circumstances commonly associated
with the particular offence are described and the effect this may have on sentence
elucidated on. As a result guidelines on sentencing may require that, to be of real
and effective use in a particular case, the case in question must fit in to the set of
circumstances described. It has been noted that *'this approach to guidance
requires that for a particular offence, like robbery, there be at least some degree
of patterning associated with the commission of the offence'*.[136] Such patterning
is not always readily in evidence—how then to take into account the variables of
such a case? The answer comes in part through a departure from the guideline in
question, an action which surely undermines the aim of sentencing guidelines—
promoting a consistent and uniform approach to sentencing disposals. Comment
has been made:

> 'the sentencer is free to take other factors into account—unless the judgment has
> deemed them irrelevant to sentence—and to depart from the presumption, as justice
> would require in the individual case. But this guidance in respect of case circumstances
> associated with an offence is not without difficulties in principle and as practiced by the
> court'.[137]

Despite the improvement in guidelines for sentencing[138] it is possible to suggest
that even the increase in sentencing guidelines has not met criticisms or overcome
the difficulties and challenges raised due to the piecemeal nature of sentencing
practice. As Nicola Padfield comments:

> 'The Guidelines have no legal status, the justices' clerks and local liaison judges may
> well play a role in deciding the extent to which these guidelines are adopted in indi-
> vidual courts. Whilst fixed penalties for some minor offences are widely accepted, so is
> the need to individualise them at a more serious level.'[139]

It remains to be seen whether the proposed Sentencing Guidelines Council[140]
will, in practice, overcome these difficulties and concerns.

Sentencing guidelines do not encompass all of the advice available to those
involved in making the sentencing decision. Allied to the guidelines to sentencing
is the recent creation of the Sentencing Advisory Panel which assists the Court of

---

[134] For fuller discussion, see Ashworth, A. and von Hirsch, A., *'Recognising Elephants: The Problem
of the Custody Threshold'* [1997] Crim. L.R. 187 and Lovegrove, A., *'Writing Quantitative Narrative
Guideline Judgments: A Proposal'* (2001) Crim. L.R. 265.
[135] Ashworth (2000) p. 33.
[136] Lovegrove, A., *'Writing Quantitative Narrative Guideline Judgments: A Proposal'* (2001) Crim.
L.R. 265 at 267.
[137] Lovegrove, A., *'Writing Quantitative Narrative Guideline Judgments: A Proposal'* (2001) Crim.
L.R. 265 at 267.
[138] While this section has considered guidelines on sentencing with reference to those issued by the
Court of Appeal, in respect of Magistrates Courts, the Magistrates Association has been issuing its
own *Sentencing Guide for Criminal offences and Compensation Table* since 1989, with regular
updates. For discussion see Ashworth (2000) Chap. 2.8 esp. p. 55.
[139] Nicola Padfield (2000) *Text and Materials on the Criminal Justice Process* (Butterworths, London), p. 275.
[140] Justice for All, Cm. 5563, 2002, para. 5.13–5.18, p. 89–90.

Appeal in formulating guidelines, after a wide consultation process. While such a process is to be welcomed as a step towards ensuring a coherent and consistently applied sentencing rationale it is not the only information made available to sentencers, and indeed for many offences such guidance may not always be available. On a more practical and every-day basis, sentencers can make use of Pre-Sentence Reports and, in a narrow form and sense, victim personal statements.

9.5.2 *The Sentencing Advisory Panel*

Perhaps as a means of countering continued criticism surrounding inconsistent sentencing practice 1998 witnessed the creation of the Sentencing Advisory Panel,[141], an independent public body '*charged by the Home office with encouraging consistency in sentencing in the Crown Court and the magistrates' courts of England and Wales*'.[142] Section 80 and 81 of the Crime and Disorder Act 1998 make clear the intention of the legislature with regard to sentencing guidelines and the role to be played by the Sentencing Advisory Panel:—

80 (3) Where the Court decides to frame or revise such guidelines, the Court shall have regard to—

    (a) the need to promote consistency in sentencing;

    (b) the sentences imposed by courts in England and Wales for offences of the relevant category;

    (c) the cost of different sentences and their relative effectiveness in preventing re-offending;

    (d) the need to promote public confidence in the criminal justice system; and

    (e) the views communicated to the Court, in accordance with section 81(4)(b) below, by the Sentencing Advisory Panel.

81 (3) The Panel may at any time, and shall if so directed to do so by the Secretary of State, propose to the Court that guidelines be framed or revised under section 80 above for a particular category of offence.

In formulating or altering guidelines the Courts shall have regard to the views of the Sentencing Advisory Panel and at the same time recognise the need to promote consistency in sentencing. While this perhaps does not rectify all of the difficulties associated with inconsistent sentencing policy and practice, both the creation of the Panel and the statutory recognition of the need for sentencing guidelines do go some way to addressing concerns raised by unsystematic policy. Since the Panel began its work in July 1999 it has provided nine advice reports to the Court of Appeal,[143] with at least two reports as a direct result of a request

---

[141] S. 81 of the Crime and Disorder Act 1998, the Panel began work in July 1999. See http://www.sentencing-advisory-panel.gov.uk.

[142] http://www.sentencing-advisory-panel.gov.uk/about/index.htm.

[143] For a comprehensive list and the full text of the consultation process and reports/advice see http://www.sentencing-advisory-panel.gov.uk.

from the Court of Appeal as directed by the 1998 legislation.[144] Indeed, the Panel
was requested to provide advice on the subject of extended sentences[145] by the
Court of Appeal. The Court then issued a guideline for sentence on the subject of
extended sentences, basing the guidance on a proposal[146] from the Panel in the
case of *Nelson*.[147]

It is not only in the area of new sentencing guidelines that the Panel is concerned. The Panel also commissions its own independent research and can
recommend that revised sentencing guidelines be issued by the Court of Appeal.
This has been done with regard to the sentencing guidelines established for the
offence of rape,[148] current guidance on sentencing can be found on the case of
Billam.[149] Such recommendation from the Panel comes after research and consultation and was considered appropriate given the developments, both statutory[150] and in case law, since the *Billam*guidelines were created.

The Panel is working well alongside the Court of Appeal[151] such that the
Halliday Review, and the subsequent responses to the Report, recognised their
work and the Review proposed to extend their role.[152]

9.5.3 *Pre-Sentence Reports*

The probation service was founded in 1908[153] and has always prepared reports
on offenders for the court, initially on candidates for probation alone but later on
a broader basis. By the 1960s, there was a need to improve the quantity and
quality of information coming before the court. The Streatfeild Committee[154]
encouraged greater use of what was then termed Social Inquiry Reports (SIRs).
The Criminal Justice Act 1991 renamed SIRs calling them Pre-Sentence
Reports[155] (PSRs) and this term remains in current use. The PSR has had a

---

[144] Advice was sought by the Court of Appeal in regard to sentencing in cases involving the
importation and possession of opium (resultant advice, June, 2000) and also, in *Wild* (No. 1) [2002] 1
Cr. App. R. (S) 37 the Court of Appeal requested the Sentencing Advisory Panel's advice concerning
sentencing for offences involving child pornography. This followed on from the general principles
provided to guide sentencing in such matters by the Court of Appeal in *R. v. Toomer and others*
[2001] 2 Cr. App. R. (S) 30.

[145] S. 85 of the Powers of Criminal Courts (Sentencing) Act 2000 which makes provision for the
award of extended sentences on defendants who have committed a sexual or violent offence. The
'extension period' is an additional period during which time the offender will be subject to supervision
and licence.

[146] October, 2001.

[147] [2001] Crim. L.R. 498.

[148] Research report and proposals (May 24, 2002) available at http://www.sentencing-advisory-
panel.gov.uk.

[149] [1986] 8 Cr. App. R. (S) 48.

[150] By virtue of the Criminal Justice and Public Order Act 1994 the rape can now be committed
against a male victim.

[151] In March 2001 the Panel provided the Court of Appeal with a proposal for guidelines for the
offence of handling stolen goods. The Court of Appeal favourably considered this proposal in May
2001 in the case of *R. v. Webbe and others* [2001] E.W.C.A. Crim. 1217.

[152] The government's summary of responses received to the *Halliday* Report recognises, a p. 10, the
'*strong support for the guidelines to be made by a body like the Sentencing Advisory Panel which
drew on a wider knowledge and experience base and which consulted widely*'. See http://www.
homeoffice.gov.uk.

[153] Probation of Offenders Act 1907.

[154] *Report of the Interdepartmental Committee on the Business of the Criminal Courts*, Cmnd. 1289
(HMSO, 1960).

[155] Following the recommendations of the White Paper, *Crime, Justice and Protecting the Public*,
Cm. 965 (HMSO, 1990).

chequered development[156] since 1991 with legislative revisions being made as to when a PSR is required.[157] The current position is contained within the PCCSA 2000 where section 162 defines what is meant by a pre-sentence report.

'162 (1) In this Act "pre-sentence report" means a report in writing which—

    (a) with a view to assisting the court in determining the most suitable method of dealing with an offender, is made or submitted by an appropriate officer; and

    (b) contains information as to such matters, presented in such manner, as may be prescribed by rules made by the Secretary of State.'

The content of a PSR is currently governed by the *National Standards for the Supervision of Offenders in the Community 2000*, and the standards are revised and updated periodically. The bulk of the information to be contained within a PSR is set out by the *Standards* and includes analysis of:

● the offence or offences.

● the offender.

    ◆ this includes an assessment of the offender's character, family, employment and social background and any factors which may assist in explaining any motivation for the offence or offences. The current standards also look to evaluate offending patterns and an assessment of the outcome of previous court disposals if appropriate.

● Risk to public of re-offending.

● Proposal/recommendation for sentence.

However, the PSR is currently undergoing yet another metamorphosis. In line with current government policy which seeks to achieve a 'seamless'[158] criminal justice process, the PSR is becoming subsumed into the Offender Assessment System (OASys). OASys is the new common assessment process developed jointly by Prison and Probation service. This new scheme was piloted in Durham in 2000–2001 and four more areas have since begun to use the system. OASys is more broad and far-reaching than its PSR predecessor and is designed to include more extensive information about the offender. It has been described as '*a practical expression of seamlessness, linking probation and prison services, completed pre-sentence report, evaluated and updated on reception into custody for sentence plan and during the custodial period/sentence plan review, pre-discharge and again on licence*'.[159] While OASys, at the time of writing, is only in

---

[156] See Ashworth (2000) p. 312–315.

[157] Criminal Justice and Public Order Act 1994, Sched. 9 para. 40 inserted into the relevant sections of the 1991 legislation, requiring a PSR the imposition of a custodial or community sanction, the additional proviso that a PSR need not be sought if, in the court's opinion such a report would be unnecessary. However, see *R. v. Gillette* TLR December 3, 1999 where it was held that if the court was considering imposing a custodial sentence on an offender for the first time, unless the period of proposed custody was very short, obtaining a pre-sentence report should be the inevitable practice.

[158] This term has moved into common currency with the crime reduction arena. See for example, Home Office (2001) *Criminal Justice: The Way Ahead*, (Cm. 5074), para. 2.79, p. 44, and more generally the Halliday Review

[159] paper given by Sarah Mann, Head of Offender Assessment National Probation Directorate and Trish Wincote, Sentence Management Group, HMPS 'OASys—a common Offender Assessment System' at Criminal Justice Conference: Towards the Seamless Sentence, February 27–28 2001.

the fledgling stages of operation,[160] the new system, with its provision of updated information available to the courts, arguably embodies the proposals of the Halliday and Auld Reports which recommended that more information be made available to sentencers, including the response of offenders to any previous sentences handed down by the courts.[161]

9.5.4 *Victim Personal Statements*[162]

While victim statements do not have the direct impact on the award of a sentence that both sentencing guidelines and pre-sentence reports may have, their existence does qualify for mention within a discussion of sentencing and advice to those empowered with passing sentence. The current position within this jurisdiction is that victim statements can be taken into account by a court prior to sentencing in so far as the effects of the crime relate on the victim qualify as 'the circumstances of the offence'.[163] In practice the courts have adopted a process whereby victim personal statements have operated as a tool for 'compassion' to be shown by the courts, rather than as a means of increasing a sentence. In doing this the courts have recognised both the importance of ensuring that a victim has some form of role in the trial process while at the same time balancing this against allowing such statements to become a form of 'vengeance'.[164] What the courts have rightly refused to do is to entertain a role for victim personal statements whereby they influence the specific form of sentence and tariff level to be imposed through the actual suggestion of sentence or level of sanction within the statement itself.[165] Unlike many other jurisdictions which do recognise victim personal statements in this role, the courts in England and Wales remain concerned about the need to determine sentences objectively according to the criteria contained currently within the Powers of Criminal Courts (Sentencing) Act 2000. To this end a Practice Direction on this subject has been issued by the Lord Chief Justice which clearly establishes in what manner the courts should allow victim personal statements to have effect.[166] The Practice Direction clearly echoes the position adopted by the courts and is to be particularly welcomed in view of the inclusion of the recommendation that sentencers explain to victims that any declaration made in the statement concerning appropriate sentence will not be taken into account. In an evaluation made of the initial pilot projects of victim statements it was found that only approximately 30 per cent of victims made use of the opportunity to make a statement but one of the main concerns raised by those who took the opportunity to make a statement was that they felt their words had not achieved the hoped for affect on sentence.[167] It is to be hoped that

---

[160] and has not as yet moved from the written format to an IT process.

[161] See Halliday (2001) para. 1.47–1.48, which firmly places the OASys programme under the heading of 'What works'. See also para. 10.15 which recommends full implementation of OASys preferably in electronic form.

[162] Commonly known as Victim Impact Statements, this is distinguishable from a common American form of Victim Opinion Statement.

[163] s. 81(4)(a) and s. 36(1) of the Powers of Criminal Courts (Sentencing) Act 2000.

[164] For example, see *Roche* [1999] 2 Cr. App. R.(S) 105 and *Perks* [2000] Crim. L.R. 606.

[165] For discussion of victim statements see Sanders, A *et al.*, 'Victim Impact Statements: Don't Work, Can't Work' (2001) Crim. L.R. 447.

[166] Practice Direction—Victim Personal Statements. Issued by the Lord Chief Justice October 16, 2001.

[167] See C. Hoyle *et al.*, *Evaluation of the 'One Stop Shop' and Victim Statement Pilot Projects* (Home Office, 1998).

through clear explanation to those making victim statements, as recommended in the practice direction,[168] such concerns will decrease as understanding of the ambit of such statements becomes more widely understood.

9.6 THE DECISION TO IMPRISON—AN OUTLINE OF THE PROCESS

After conviction or a guilty plea, if the court is considering imposing a custodial or community sentence, before making up its mind, the court should:

a)   obtain a pre-sentence report[169] and to take it into account before making up its mind about whether a custodial sentence is justified, what the length of such a custodial sentence should be, whether a community sentence is justified and whether the offender is suitable for such a sentence.

b)   obtain information about the circumstances of the offence.[170]

c)   take into account any information about the offender which is before it. In deciding on a custodial sentence, this information is not relevant to the seriousness of the offence but is relevant to whether the offender presents a serious risk of harm to the public.[171] It is also relevant to whether the defendant is suitable for a community sentence.[172]

Having obtained and taken into account this information, the court must then ask itself the following:

If the answer to all these questions is **NO**, then the court must consider a non-custodial sentence, a discharge or fine.

If the answer is **YES** to any of these questions, the court may choose to impose a custodial sentence and if it does, it must explain to the offender in open court and in ordinary language why it is passing a custodial sentence.[173]

The length of sentence must be:

either:

a)   commensurate with seriousness of offence (or a combination of the offence and other offences associated with it).[174]

or:

---

[168] See also the comments of the court in *R. v. Perks* [2000] Crim. L.R. 606.

[169] s. 3(1) with regard to potential custodial sentences and s. 7(3) of the Criminal Justice Act 1991 with regard to potential non-custodial sentences. These provisions are now consolidated in s. 81(1) and s. 36(4) respectively of the Powers of Criminal Courts (Sentencing) Act 2000. However, if, in the court's opinion a pre-sentence report is not required, it need not obtain one.

[170] s. 3(3)(a) (custodial sentences) and s. 7(1) (non-custodial sentences) of the Criminal Justice Act 1991, now consolidated in s. 81(4)(a) and s. 36(1) respectively of the Powers of Criminal Courts (Sentencing) Act 2000.

[171] s. 3(3)(b) of the Criminal Justice Act 1991, now governed by s. 80(2) and s. 81(4)(b) of the Powers of Criminal Courts (Sentencing) Act 2000.

[172] s. 7(2) of the Criminal Justice Act 1991, now s. 36(2) of the Powers of Criminal Courts (Sentencing) Act 2000.

[173] s. 79(4) of the Powers of Criminal Courts (Sentencing) Act 2000.

[174] s. 2(2)(a) of the Criminal Justice Act 1991 (now consolidated in s. 80 of the PCCSA 2000).

Table 9.2

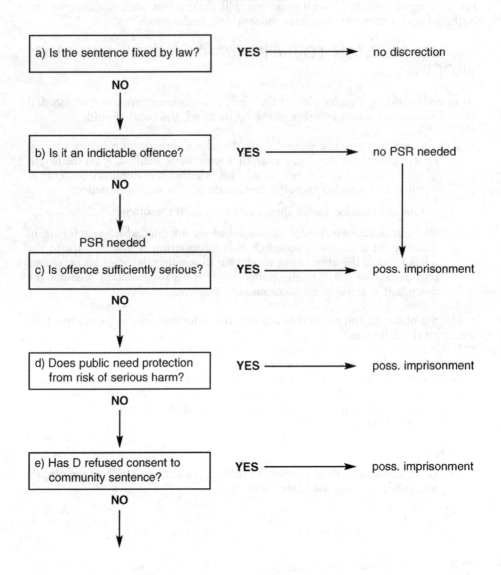

a) Is the sentence fixed by law?   YES ────────────►   no discretion

NO
│
▼

b) Is it an indictable offence?   YES ────────────►   no PSR needed

NO
│
▼

PSR needed *

c) Is offence sufficiently serious?   YES ────────────►   poss. imprisonment

NO
│
▼

d) Does public need protection   YES ────────────►   poss. imprisonment
   from risk of serious harm?

NO
│
▼

e) Has D refused consent to   YES ────────────►   poss. imprisonment
   community sentence?

NO
│
▼

---

* unless the Court is of the opinion that no such report is necessary.

b) necessary to protect public from serious harm from the defendant.[175] Where such a term is longer than that commensurate with the seriousness of the offence, then the court must state its reasons why this section applies and explain to the offender in open court and in plain language why the sentence is for this term.[176]

9.7 CUSTODIAL SENTENCES

'The number of offenders sentenced to immediate custody for all offences increased by one per cent to 106,200 in 2000. This is 34 per cent higher than in 1995. In 2000, immediate custody sentences given for indictable offences rose one per cent, for summary non-motoring offences fell by five per cent and for summary motoring offences rose by two per cent ... 76 per cent of all custodial sentences in 2000 were for indictable offences. 25 per cent of those convicted of an indictable offence received a custodial sentence, the highest percentage for over 40 years, and compares with 14 per cent in the early 1990s.'[177]

The use of custodial sentences has been increasing in recent years.[178] Perhaps part of the reason for this lies in the difficulties encountered in creating an effective working sentencing rationale and framework. The 1991 Act required that, in general, a custodial sentence be imposed only when necessary,[179] reflecting the philosophical notions of just deserts (and rehabilitation). However, a few provisions, to be discussed below, allow for the court to impose a sentence which is longer than the specific offence before it warrants, reflecting ideas of incapacitation and deterrence, philosophies which in a strict sense can lead to increased numbers of custodial sentences and increased lengths of custody. Allied to this is another possible reason for the increased use of custody. It is possible that the increase in custodial sentences may be attributable to a perceived lack of confidence in the criminal justice process as a whole and even, perhaps, the media attention afforded to particular crime. For example, the recent increase in the theft of mobile telephone has resulted in strong words from Lord Woolf C.J.[180] in the *Attorney-General's Reference Nos. 4 and No 7 of 2002*.[181] A report of the proceedings notes Lord Woolf's concerns:-

'The proportion of robberies involving telephones had risen from 8 per cent in 1998/9 to 28 per cent in 2000/01. Faced with that background, the courts had no alternative but to adopt a robust sentencing policy towards those who committed these offences. Those who did so must understand that they would be punished severely. Custodial

---

[175] s. 2(2)(b) of the Criminal Justice Act 1991 (now consolidated in s. 80 of the PCCSA 2000).

[176] s. 2(3) of the Criminal Justice Act 1991 (now consolidated in s. 80 of the PCCSA 2000).

[177] Criminal Statistics England and Wales 2000, Cm. 5312 (HMSO, 2001) Chap. 7, paras 7.15 and 7.16, p. 156.

[178] Magistrates' courts use of custodial sentences for indictable offences increased from 12 per cent in the first quarter of 1999 to 14 per cent in the last quarter of 2000. The Crown Court's use of these sentences also increased, to 64 per cent in 2000. The average length of Crown Court sentences for males aged 21 and over rose from 24.1 months in 1999 to 24.2 months in 2000, a return to the 1997 level. See *Criminal Statistics England and Wales 2000*, Cm. 5312 (HMSO, 2001) Chap. 7, paras 7.19 and 7.21 and Table 7B, p. 151.

[179] it must be proportionate with the seriousness of the offence or necessary to protect the public.

[180] Woolf C.J. made clear in his comments that he was not setting out a new sentencing guideline however, such guidelines would require consultation with the Sentencing Advisory Panel.

[181] *Attorney-General's Reference No. 4 of 2002 (Adrian Michael Lobban), Attorney-General's Reference No. 7 of 2002 (Christopher Sawyers), (Steven James Q)* [2002] E.W.C.A. Crim. 127.

sentences would be the only option available to the courts when these offences were committed, unless there were exceptional circumstances. That would apply irrespective of the age of the offender and irrespective of whether the offender had previous convictions'.[182]

In these words we see the ideas of retribution and deterrence moving to the fore, with the requirement that a custodial sentence be linked to the seriousness of the offence given the wide interpretation envisaged by *Bradbourne* and *Cox*.[183] Seriousness can be seen to take account of how prevalent the crime is in this jurisdiction. Such an example demonstrates the difficulties attached to the process for determining as to whether a custodial sentence is warranted and still remains. It is probable that legislation, which may assist, will soon be forthcoming following the proposals of the Auld Review and Halliday Report. Indeed, the recent White Paper, *Justice for All*, recommends how seriousness should be determined and the severity of sentence calculated, the first such towards achieving a legislative footing for such deliberations. It remains to be seen whether this process and terminology will be more clearly defined by such legislation. A point incidental to this discussion, but worthy of consideration, is the additional impact any changes in sentencing policy will inevitably have on the Prison system.[184] Any continuing increases in sentence length or use of incarceration will lead to a greater number of prisoners within the penal system. This in turn leads to a period of overcrowding and arguably a decrease in standards within prisons.[185] This issue has been considered by the courts to be one which is a valid consideration to be taken into account in determining whether a custodial sentence is warranted, and indeed the length of a custodial sentence.[186]

However, with regard to custodial sentences the difficulties for the courts lie not only in the area of determining when the threshold of seriousness between non-custodial and custodial sentences has been crossed, but also in the area of what form and duration of custodial sentence should be imposed. Such questions have arisen with regard to setting tariffs in cases involving the award of a life sentence, either discretionary or mandatory,[187] and also in relation to any discount which should be awarded for an early guilty plea.[188] Of particular interest are provisions concerning sentences which are extended beyond a period which is commensurate with the offence, either with regard to the period of custody or

---

[182] *Attorney-General's Reference No. 4 of 2002 (Adrian Michael Lobban); Attorney-General's Reference No. 7 of 2002 (Christopher Sawyers), (Steven James Q)* [2002] E.W.C.A. Crim. 127. Report taken from [2002] Crim. L.R. Case & Comment, 333.

[183] See s. 9.2.1 of The Criminal Justice Act 1991.

[184] Figures from the Home Office state, '*The general pattern in sentencing of indictable offences has changed little between 1998 and 1999 but continued to increase in severity at both courts. 23.4 per cent of those sentenced for indictable offences in 1999 were given a custodial sentence, the highest annual rate for over 40 years. 2,500 more persons were sentenced to custody for indictable offences*' Margaret Ayres and colleagues, Home Office Research, Development and Statistics Directorate, Issue 19/00, October 31, 2000, p. 1.

[185] See Chap. 10

[186] see *R. v. Mills* [2002] E.W.C.A. 26 where it was held that the increase in the female prison population was an acceptable consideration, amongst other issues, to be taken into account when determining whether a custodial sentence was necessary, and more generally *R. v. Ollerenshaw* [1999] 1 Cr. App. R. (S) 65.

[187] see practice direction on tariffs for life sentences by the Lord Woolf reported at [2000] 1 W.L.R. 1655, or more recently applied in *R. v. Mason & Anor* [2002] E.W.C.A. Crim. 699.

[188] see *R. v. Hussain* [2002] E.W.C.A. Crim. 67. If the recommendations of the sentencing review reports regarding the implementation of a graduated scale of discount are implemented these issues may become nothing more than a formulaic process.

licence, and the imposition of automatic life sentences, both of which are considered below.

9.7.1 *Extended Sentences*

Section 1(2) of the Criminal Justice Act 1991[189] states that a court should not impose a custodial sentence on an individual unless certain criteria are, in the court's judgment, met.[190] However, section 2 of the Act goes on to provide how a custodial sentence should be applied. The section states:

2) The custodial sentence shall be—

(a) for such term (not exceeding the permitted maximum) as in the opinion of the court is commensurate with the seriousness of the offence, or the combination of the offence and [one or more] offences associated with it; or
(b) where the offence is a violent or sexual offence, for such longer term (not exceeding the maximum) as in the opinion of the court is necessary to protect the public from serious harm from the offender.[191]

In other words, in order to protect the public from potential serious harm a court may be justified in imposing a custodial sentence which is longer than warranted in the by the circumstances of the offence. These provisions have been augmented by provision in section 58 of the Crime and Disorder Act 1998[192] which allow the courts to impose an extended sentence on an offender found guilty of committing a violent or sexual offence if in the courts opinion such extension is warranted by the belief an ordinary licence period 'would not be adequate for the purposes of preventing the commission by him of further offences and securing his rehabilitation'.[193] Under the auspices of section 58 of the 1998 Act the extended sentence is made up, usually, of a custodial element[194] and an extension period for which the offender will be subject to licence and thus potentially recall to prison, and it is to the length of extension period that the court must address its considerations of necessary to prevent further offending and securing rehabilitation.[195] While both disposals apply to offenders who commit violent or sexual offences there is an important distinction to be made between the purposes of longer than commensurate sentences available under section 2(2) of the 1991 Act and the extended sentence instituted by the 1998 Act. With regard to section 2(2)(b) the consideration which triggers the provision is that a longer custodial sentence is required to protect the public from potential

---

[189] Consolidated as s. 79 of the PCCSA 2000.

[190] For a discussion of the tests employed by the courts see Ashworth, A & von Hirsch, A, (1997) 'Recognising Elephants: The Problem of the Custody Threshold,' Crim. L.R. pp. 187–200.

[191] Violent offences are defined in s. 31(1) of the 1991 Act Now consolidated as s. 161 of the PCCSA 2000.

[192] now consolidated in s. 85 of the PCCSA 2000.

[193] s. 85(1)(b) of the PCCSA 2000.

[194] the normal term that the court is of a mind to impose for the offence, see s. 85(2)(a) of the PCCSA 2000.

[195] s. 85(4) expresses the requirement that extension periods should not exceed 10 years in the case of a sexual offence and 5 years in cases involving a violent offence.

harm from the offender.[196] This can be contrasted with the trigger for the provisions of the extended sentence which is that in the court's opinion a proportionate sentence (and applicable licence period of any) would be inadequate in preventing further offending by the defendant or achieving his rehabilitation.

With regard to section 2(2)(b) of the 1991 Act the courts have chosen to provide relatively general guidance on when such a sentence is warranted. Cases suggest that an appropriate way to proceed is to explain to the defendant what the commensurate sentence for the offence would be and then how much is being added on in the interests of protecting the public.[197] In addition the length of 'added' part of the sentence should be reasonably in proportion to the offence for which it is being imposed.[198] Beyond this not much guidance has been provided and there have been concerns about the efficacy of section 2(2)(b) and extended sentences generally. Ashworth has commented that the:

> 'power to impose a longer-than-normal sentence granted by section 2(2)(b) of the 19991 Act is fundamentally unsatisfactory. The legislative scheme is inadequate, incorporating few procedural safeguards ... Even the internal logic of section 2(2)(b) is doubtful: what degree of public protection is likely to be provided by adding an extra two or even three years to a sentence?'.[199]

Similar arguments can be advanced regarding extended sentence. The Court of Appeal has also acknowledged these difficulties, requesting advice from the Sentencing Advisory Panel on extended sentence. The resulting advice[200] and proposals have been relied upon in the recent case of *Nelson*[201] where general guidance with regard to extended sentences is provided. The court proposed a 3-stage test to be employed by sentencers which in essence reflects the previous practice of the courts. Firstly, a sentencer must determine what sentence would be commensurate with the seriousness of the offence. Secondly, consideration must then be afforded to the question of whether a longer period of custody is warranted to protect the public from risk of harm. Finally, the sentencer must, if the offence involves a violent or sexual offence,[202] determine whether an extended licence period is required in order to prevent re-offending and secure the rehabilitation of the offender.[203]

9.7.2 *Automatic Life Sentences*

The imposition of an automatic life sentence for conviction of a second serious

---

[196] While this would seem to be based on a rationale of incapacitation the European Court of Human Rights has declared that the sentence is based on a punitive and deterrent elements. See *Mansell v. United Kingdom* (1997) E.H.R.L.R. 666—the application claimed that continued detention after the tariff period had expired should be reviewed in a similar way to discretionary life sentences and failure to do so was in breach of Art. 5. The Commission declared the application on this ground to be manifestly ill-founded.

[197] See *Mansell* (1994) 15 Cr. App. R. (S) 844 and *Coull* (1994) 15 Cr. App. R. (S) 305.

[198] See *Crow and Pennington* (1995) 16 Cr. App. R. (S) 409.

[199] Ashworth (2000), p. 189.

[200] published November 2001.

[201] *R. v. Nelson* [2001] E.W.H.C. Crim. 2264.

[202] and the custodial sentence to be imposed is longer than 4 years.

[203] The court made note that it would not be appropriate to reduce the proposed custodial term just because an extended licence period is being imposed.

offence[204] was made possible by section 2(2) of the Crime Sentence Act 1997, now consolidated as section 109 of the Powers of Criminal Courts (Sentencing) Act 2000 which provides:

'109(2) The court shall impose a life sentence, that is to say—

(a) where the offender is 21 or over when convicted of the offences . . . a sentence of imprisonment for life;

(b) where he is under 21 at that time, a sentence of custody for life under section 94 above

unless the court is of the opinion that there are exceptional circumstances relating to either of the offences or to the offender which justify its not doing so.'

The difficulty for sentencers has been to determine the meaning of 'exceptional circumstances' which afford the courts the discretion to decide not to impose the automatic life sentence. Originally the meaning of 'exceptional circumstances' was considered in the case of *R. v. Kelly*[205] where the defence argued that, amongst other factors, the defendant's youth at the time of the first serious offence and the 10 year conviction free gap between that offence and the one before the court should qualify as 'exceptional circumstances'. Lord Bingham C.J. disagreed stating that to amount to exceptional circumstances the factors must be those which are not normally encountered. The presumption would seem to be that to qualify as exceptional circumstances the factors involved would need to be unusual and such factors as relative youth at the time of the first offence and the passage of time between offences would not, of themselves, justify the court in refusing to impose an automatic life sentence.

The question then becomes what will qualify as exceptional circumstances? Since the decision in *Kelly* the courts have provided guidance on this matter and have departed from the approach taken in that case. In *Buckland*[206] the defendant had attempted to rob a bank using an imitation firearm and through presenting a note of his demands to the cashier. The note also contained the defendant's name and address. On determining whether an automatic life sentence should have been imposed the Court of Appeal, while accepting that the provisions for the imposition of an automatic life sentence were appropriately triggered, found that the level of incompetence displayed in the attempted robbery could indeed amount to exceptional circumstances. The meaning to be attached to 'exceptional circumstances' has since been more clearly stated. In the case of *Offen*[207] Lord Woolf C.J. stated that the provisions of section 2(2) of the 1997 Act (now section 109 of the 2000 Act) clearly created a norm, that those who committed 2 serious offences posed a risk or danger to the public and it was thus proper to impose a sentence of indefinite custody. Thus, if the court was satisfied that the offender in question did not pose such a danger or risk to the public and therefore constituted an exception to this norm.[208] In such instances it would be appropriate for a court to determine that this exceptional circumstance

---

[204] The list of offences which for the purposes of the section amount to a 'serious offences' are listed in s. 109(5) of the PCCSA 2000 and include attempted murder, attempted or actual rape and offences under s. 18 of the Offences Against the Person Act 1861.

[205] (1999) 2 Cr. App. R. (S) 176.

[206] (2000) Crim. L.R. 308.

[207] (2001) 1 W.L.R. 253.

[208] *Offen* [2001] 1 W.L.R. 253, *per* Lord Woolf at para. 97.

existed and therefore not impose an automatic life sentence. This approach has since been followed in a number of cases[209] including a re-appraisal of the sentence imposed on Mr Kelly following a recommendation of the Criminal Cases Review Commission[210] and it is likely that it is this formula which will be followed in future.

9.8 SUSPENDED SENTENCES

Courts possess the power[211] to suspend a sentence of imprisonment of 2 years or less. The period during which it is suspended is between 1 and 2 years. If the offender re-offends during that period, the suspended sentence is activated unless the court feels that it would be unjust to do so.

Suspended sentences were introduced, along with parole, by the Criminal Justice Act 1967[212] against a background of a sharply rising prison population.[213] The pragmatic aim of the government was to reduce prison population. This proved shortsighted. 1968 saw an immediate drop of 20 per cent in the prison population as sentencers suspended all custodial sentences of under 2 years. The population then rose again. This was due to a combination of factors: firstly the suspended sentence was not being used purely as an alternative to imprisonment but was also employed in place of fines and probation orders;[214] secondly the courts gave longer suspended sentences than they would had custody been immediate and were also perhaps awarding suspended sentences when the offence committed was not serious enough to have warranted immediate custody. The effect was that the number of persons given either suspended or immediate sentences of imprisonment rose, and when they re-offended, their suspended sentences were automatically activated.

Although automatic activation was quickly removed, criticisms persisted that the suspended sentence was still used inappropriately. One such criticism was that the suspended sentence was disproportionately employed in favour of middle-class offenders.[215] More significantly for modern policy-makers, the suspended sentence, if completed successfully, lacked any element of punishment apart from the stigma of the court appearance. Following the recommendations of the White Paper,[216] the Criminal Justice Act 1991 restricted the conditions for suspending imprisonment: under section 5, the offence has to be one which is punishable by imprisonment and the suspension has to be justified by the 'exceptional circumstances' of the case[217] thus ensuring that the presumption became that suspended sentences would not be used unless such 'exceptional

---

[209] See *McDonald* [2001] 2 Cr. App. R. (S) 127 and *Turner* [2001] E.W.C.A. Crim. 2918.
[210] *Kelly No. 2* [2002] 1 Cr. App. R. (S) 85.
[211] ss. 118–121 of the Powers of Criminal Courts (Sentencing) Act 2000, originally, s. 22 of the Powers of Criminal Courts Act 1973.
[212] Partially suspended sentences were introduced s. 47 of the Criminal Law Act 1977. This was repealed by s. 5(2)(b) of the Criminal Justice Act 1991.
[213] Bottoms A., 'The Suspended Sentence in England 1967–78' (1981) 21 *Brit. Jour. Crim.* 1.
[214] Now called Community Rehabilitation Orders.
[215] *Moxon, op. cit.*, p. 35—especially for such offenders convicted in cases involving of breach of trust.
[216] *Crime, Justice and Protecting the Public*, Cm. 965 (HMSO, 1990) para. 3.20.
[217] It can be combined with fines or compensation orders—s. 118 of the Powers of Criminal Courts Act 2000.

circumstances' warranted a reversal of the presumption.[218] *Okinikan*[219] indicated that such circumstances should be exceptional and that good character, youth and an early plea are not exceptional by themselves or in combination. The use of the suspended sentence has declined sharply since the introduction of the 1991 legislation such that while in 1987, 29,200[220] offenders received a suspended sentence; the number in 2000 had declined to only 3100.[221] Current provisions for the process to be employed by the courts are contained within the relevant sections of the Powers of Criminal Courts (Sentencing) Act 2000, including those for the imposition of a suspended sentence supervision order[222] whereby an offender awarded a suspended sentence may be required to undergo a period of supervision by a local probation officer for a fixed period of time.

9.9 NON-CUSTODIAL PENALTIES

Throughout the 1980s,[223] the image of conservative criminal justice policy was that of strict social control: by 1990, expenditure on the criminal justice system had reached £7b per annum, a 77 per cent increase in real terms over 10 years and moving from 4 per cent to 6 per cent of total government spending; new offences had been introduced especially in the area of public order, football hooliganism and drugs and there had been no significant decriminalisation; police forces had been strengthened in terms of personnel, legal powers and resources; and a new, rationalised and 'streamlined' prosecution process had been initiated. Sentencers still remained committed to custodial sentencing despite a broad range of non-custodial options. Those options, introduced in a piecemeal fashion, bore no obvious relationship to each other or to the sentencing process in terms of severity of punishment. Non-custodial penalties might fairly be said to have been in some disarray.

However, at the start of the 1990s, the White Paper[224] and the Criminal Justice Act 1991 were concerned with reducing the prison population and developed a more coherent philosophy not solely for custodial sentences but also for non-custodial penalties. The latter were to be grouped as 'community sentences' with stress on reparation and punishment in the community. The rhetoric remained that of punishment[225] with the aim of attaching a more punitive image to non-custodial sentences and making them acceptable to the public as punishment and not as a 'slap-on-the-wrist'. The White Paper[226] talked of restructuring community services to reflect the concept of graduated restrictions on liberty, consistent with the just deserts principle, from probation to community service to curfew orders. In the midst of this, the legislation did not introduce any radically new measures. However, the hopes of the 1990 White Paper and subsequent legislation were not realised in that community sanctions remained embedded in

---

[218] However, see the recent government White Paper, *Justice for All*, Cm. 5563, 2002, which proposes a new sentence of 'Custody Minus' whereby the custody element of the sentence will automatically be suspended, see para. 5.30–5.32, p. 93–94.

[219] (1993) 2 All E.R. 5.

[220] *Criminal Statistics 1992*, Cm. 2410 (HMSO 1993) Table 7A, p. 137.

[221] *Criminal Statistics England and Wales 2000*, Cm. 5312 (HMSO, 2001) Table 7A, p. 155.

[222] s. 122 of the PCCSA 2000.

[223] Hale C. and Brake M., *Public Order and Private Lives* (Routledge, 1992).

[224] *Crime, Justice and Protecting the Public*, Cm. 965 (HMSO (1990).

[225] *ibid.*, para. 4.1.

[226] *ibid.*, para. 4.7.

public perceptions as a 'soft option'. In a further attempt to address this difficulty the Criminal Justice and Court Services Act 2000 has renamed a number of community sanctions: Probation Orders become 'Community Rehabilitation Orders';[227] Community Service Orders are now Community Punishment Orders[228] and Combination Orders become Community Punishment and Rehabilitation Orders.[229] The new names, reinforcing the terminology of the aims of sentencing, will, it is hoped, assist in finally altering how such sanctions are perceived. Since the 1991 legislation the range of community penalties have not only undergone some name changes, but the range of available disposals has altered with new orders, especially in the arena of youth justice,[230] being introduced.

To be fair, the use of community penalties has increased in recent years, but this has not been achieved at the expense of immediate custodial sentences. In this sense the hopes of the government, to reduce prison population, have not been realised. Rather the increase in the use and number of community sanctions has to be seen alongside a decrease in the use of fines and suspended sentence. The Halliday Report and recent White Paper, Justice for All, recognise the difficulties associated with non-custodial sentences,[231] especially in the areas of perception and adequate enforcement, and it is to be hoped any future legislation takes such recommendations, and subsequent comment, to heart in attempting to find a solution to these problems in order that non-custodial penalties can be used effectively and viewed as such.

9.9.1 *Fines*

Fines have traditionally been seen as the most common form of disposal within the Magistrate's Courts. However, since 1990 there has been a downward trend in the use or fines[232] such that in the year 2000 fines were used in only 31 per cent of indictable offences. Indeed, there has been a steep decline in the proportional use of the fine for indictable offences from 50.6 per cent in 1978 to 34 per cent in 1992.[233] The recent decrease from 1990–2000 correlates with an increase in the use of community sentences for indictable offences in Magistrates courts which have risen in 2000 to 31 per cent.[234] This compares with overall figures[235] for fines being used as the means of disposal for 70 per cent of offenders.[236]

A fine is a possible sentence in any case where sentence is not fixed by statute, and a court can award a fine in addition to another sentence.[237] At common law,

---

[227] s. 43, of the Criminal Justice and Courts Services Act 2000.
[228] s. 44, of the Criminal Justice and Courts Services Act 2000.
[229] s. 45 of the Criminal Justice and Courts Services Act 2000.
[230] See Chap. 11 on Youth Justice.
[231] See Chap. 6 of the Halliday Report, and chap. 5 of Justice for All.
[232] This has been coupled with a similar decline in the use of discharges.
[233] *Criminal Statistics 2000, op. cit.*, Table 7.3, p. 155.
[234] *Criminal Statistics 2000, op.cit.*, para. 7.19, p. 157, see also Table 7.2, p. 152.
[235] This includes both summary and indictable offences in both Magistrate and Crown Courts.
[236] *Criminal Statistics 2000, op.cit.*, para. 7.9, p. 155. This section of the Statistics provides further useful information:—*Use of fines for summary non-motoring offences rose by three percentage points to 80 per cent due to the increase in the number of cases under the Wireless Telegraphy Acts ... The use of fines for summary non-motoring offences rose by three percentage points to 80%, due to the rise in the number of cases (mainly TV licence evasion) under the Wireless Telegraphy Acts.*
[237] S. 127 of the PCCSA 2000.

the maximum is unlimited though magistrates have a ceiling of £5000.[238] With statutory crimes, the maximum will be specified by the legislation. The great advantage of the fine is its flexibility, enabling it to be related to the seriousness of the offence. The problem comes with the offender's means to pay. Prior to 1991, a court could mitigate the amount for offenders of limited means (*Fairbairn*)[239] but not increase it. In 1991, following a number of other jurisdictions which had introduced 'day fines',[240] the Criminal Justice Act created a new system of 'unit fines' in magistrates' courts.[241] The impact was a rise in the proportionate use of the fine, most apparent among the unemployed. Though the average fine remained the same, this masked a rise in the level of fines for the employed and a decline for fines for the unemployed.[242] But there was public criticism[243] and although the Magistrates' Association, among others, felt that such complaints confirmed a need for fine-tuning the system and not abolishing it, the entire commendable reform was swept away in 1993[244] and fining returned to its previous diversity.

Now the PCCSA 2000 lays out the steps to be followed in determining whether a fine is an appropriate disposal and if so, at what level the fine should be fixed. The court must ensure that the amount of the fine reflects the seriousness of the offence.[245] However the court is also obliged to inquire into the financial circumstances of the offender[246] and take this into account, along with the circumstances of the case, in determining the amount of the fine to be paid.[247] These financial circumstances can have the effect of reducing and increasing the fine[248] and this is an important change to the pre- 1991 law. In addition, the court has the power to remit either part or the whole of the fine if later enquiries into the offender's financial circumstances[249] satisfy the court that had the information been available at the time of sentencing a smaller fine would have been imposed, or no fine at all.[250] Courts have the power to allow time to pay fines[251] with the ultimate resort being imprisonment.[252] The table below provides comparative information regarding fine defaulters, the numbers received into custody and the average length of stay. The number of fine defaulters received into custody has fallen dramatically since 1992, this is due in part to recommendations from the Lord Chancellors Department that other options to custody be considered for

---

[238] The amounts payable as a fine by offenders under the age of 18 is lower than that of adults. The court also has the power to require a parent to pay their child's fine. See ss. 135–138 PCCSA 2000.
[239] (1980) 2 Crim. App. Rep. (S) 315.
[240] Grebing G., *The Fine in Comparative Law* (Cambridge, 1982).
[241] There were maximum units for each level of offence (2 for level 1 and 50 for level 5) and the offender would be sentenced to a set number of units. The amount was assessed by multiplying units by the offender's weekly disposable income.
[242] Home Office Statistical Bulletin, *Monitoring of the Criminal Justice Act 1991* (Issue 25/93).
[243] If offenders did not reveal their means, there was an assumption that they possessed the maximum disposable income—this led to some notorious cases of very large fines for dropping crisp packets.
[244] s. 65 of the Criminal Justice Act 1993.
[245] s. 128(2) of the PCCSA 2000.
[246] s. 128(1) of the PCCSA 2000.
[247] s. 128(3) of the PCCSA 2000.
[248] s. 128(4) of the PCCSA 2000.
[249] under s. 128(5) if the court has insufficient information regarding financial information, for reasons stated in the section, it may make 'such determination as it thinks fit'. The provisions regarding the remitting of a fine are triggered only if the fine has been made in circumstances described in s. 128(5).
[250] s. 129(2) of the PCCSA 2000.
[251] s. 139(1) of the PCCSA 2000.
[252] s. 139(2) of the PCCSA 2000.

fine defaulters[253] and to the Crime (Sentences) Act 1997 which provided for the imposition of various community sentences, including a curfew order, in cases of fine default.

Table 9.3 Population and Reception of Fine Defaulters 1992–2000[254]

Year	Average Daily population	Annual Receptions	Average time served (men/women)
1992	382	19,826	7.3/6.8 days
1996	141	8,555	7.0/5.0 days
2000	87	2,476	7.0/5.0 days

9.9.2 *Compensation Orders*[255]

Compensation orders are available where an offence has caused loss or damage. The offender may be required to pay compensation. It may be the only sentence or it may be in addition to another sentence. If the offender is under 16, a parent must pay. If the offender is over 16, the court may order the parent to pay. In determining the amount of compensation, the court should have regard to the offender's (or the parents') means.[256]

9.9.3 *Probation Orders*[257]

(Renamed as Community Rehabilitation Orders)[258]

Probation orders were first introduced for adults in 1908 and have a tradition rooted in reform of the offender and social work. In recent times the probation order has been viewed as a means of allowing an offender to confront his or her behaviour, and in which emphasis is placed on self-reliance and self-discipline, thus recognising and encouraging the individuality and autonomy of the offender.[259] It has been commented that the '*contemporary probation order is clearly conceived as a purposeful, flexible instrument of punishment in the community and creative engagement with the offender, intended to be enforced rigorously*'.[260]. The PCCSA 2000 lays out the requirements and process for the imposition of the probation order and the statutory provisions are augmented by the guidance provided in the *National Standards for the Supervision of Offenders*

---

[253] The courts reaffirmed this position in the cases of *Oldham JJ, ex p. Cawley* [1996] 1 All E.R. 464 and *Stockport JJ, ex p. Conlon* [1997] 2 All E.R. 204.

[254] Home Office (2001) *Prison statistics England and Wales 2000* (Cm. 5250) Table 1.13, p. 30.

[255] s. 130 of the Powers of Criminal Courts (Sentencing) Act 2000.

[256] s. 138 of the PCCSA 2000.

[257] ss. 41–45 of the PCCSA.

[258] s. 43 of the Criminal Justice and Courts Services Act 2000.

[259] See McWilliams W. and Pease K. 'Probation Practice and an End to Punishment' 29 *Howard Jour. Crim. Just.* 14 (1990).

[260] Stone, N., 'The Ambit of the "Standard" Community Rehabilitation Order' [2001] Crim. L.R. 214, p. 218.

in the Community.[261] In essence a probation order allows the courts to require an offender to undergo a period of supervision, of between 6 months and 3 years, imposed in an attempt to 'secure the offenders rehabilitation, protect the public from harm or prevent the commission of further offences'.[262] There can be conditions attached to the order[263] which can be used both to provide the punitive restrictions on liberty as well as ensuring that the order is tailored to the needs of the individual:

a) requirements as to residence including in an approved hostel.[264]

b) requirements as to activities—either participating or refraining from 'specified activities'[265] which include schemes and activities organised by the probation service.

c) requirements as to attendance at a probation centre.[266] Such centres have regimes which combine skills learning, discussion, counselling and therapy sessions with the objectives of confronting offenders with their offending and assisting them in tackling their problems.

d) requirements as to treatment for mental condition.[267] This can include psychological treatment either residentially or as part of a non-residential programme.

e) requirements as to treatment for drug or alcohol dependency.[268]

9.9.4 *Community Service Orders*[269]
(Renamed as Community Punishment Orders)[270]

Community service orders were introduced by the Criminal Justice Act 1972 after recommendations in the Wootton Report.[271] These are available only for offenders aged 16 and over and require the offender to undertake unpaid work in the community organised and supervised by the probation service.[272] The minimum number of hours is 40 and the maximum 240. The court must be satisfied on the general criteria for making a community sentence and that the offender is a suitable person for such work, and further that arrangements can be made in the offender's local area for provision of the work specified in the order.[273]

When the sentencing framework was established in 1991 the structure of the community service order remained relatively unchanged from its 1972 incarnation. However, there was a move away from any rehabilitative ethic and towards

---

[261] Home Office (2000).

[262] see s. 41(1) of the PCCSA 2000.

[263] s. 42 of the PCCSA 2000.

[264] PCCSA 2000, Sched. 2 (1).

[265] PCCSA 2000, Sched. 2 (2).

[266] PCCSA 2000, Sched. 2 (3).

[267] PCCSA 2000, Sched. 2 (5).

[268] PCCSA 2000, Sched. 2 (6).

[269] PCCSA 2000, ss. 46–50.

[270] s. 44 of the Criminal Justice and Courts Services Act 2000.

[271] Advisory Council on the Penal System, *op. cit.*

[272] or, if the offender is between the ages of 16–18, the work will be organised and supervised by a member of the youth offending team.

[273] PCCSA 2000 s. 46(4) and (6).

punishment so that the seriousness of the offence was matched by the number of hours of volunteer work. This theme has been continued by the re-naming of the order to Community Punishment Order in an attempt to solidify the recognition of the order as a sanction at the high tariff end of non-custodial measures.

9.9.5 Combination Orders[274]

The Combination Order is, as its name suggests, an amalgamation of two other non-custodial sanctions, the previously considered probation and community service orders. Originally created as a new sentencing option by section 11 of the 1991 Criminal Justice Act, the combination order has been directed at offenders whom the courts believe should make reparation through community service but who also need supervision to tackle their problems. The aim of the sentence is to provide another option of community sentence at the high end of the non-custodial sentence tariff scale. The minimum supervision period is 12 months rather than the usual probation minimum of 6 months and the maximum number of hours which can be imposed as the community service element is 100 as opposed to 240. It must be with the consent of the offender and the court must be of the opinion that the order will lead to the rehabilitation of the offender or will protect the public from harm from him or prevent the commission by him of further offences.[275]

9.9.6 Curfew Orders[276]

Curfew orders were introduced in 1991[277] and require the offender to remain at a specified place[278] for a specified time of between 2 and 12 hours per day. It may be imposed on its own or with the requirement of electronic monitoring.[279] There is flexibility to specify different lengths of time for different days and places. The overall maximum length is for 6 months with a maximum daily period 12 hours, either as a block or in sets of shorter periods totalling no more than 12 hours. The minimum period is 2 hours in one day. Additionally, curfew orders can be imposed as a single order or in combination with another appropriate community sentence.

   The curfew order is only practical if there is effective enforcement and the only realistic way that has been suggested has been through electronic tagging. Initial concerns raised concerning the practical difficulties of tagging, fears of equipment failure, have not been realised to any great extent and after pilot trials were completed, electronic monitoring is now available nationwide.

---

[274] s. 51 of the PCCSA 2000.
[275] s. 51(3) of the PCCSA 2000.
[276] s. 37 PCCSA of the 2000, see also s. 59 for imposition of a curfew order in the case of persistent petty offenders who have defaulted on fine payments.
[277] s. 12 of the Criminal Justice Act 1991.
[278] Under s. 37(8) of the PCCSA 2000 the court must consider the attitude of other people who will be affected by the offender's enforced presence, presumably at home. The court must also avoid impact on religious beliefs, work, school and the performance of other community orders (s. 36(5)).
[279] s. 38 of the PCCSA 2000.

9.9.7 *Drug Treatment and Testing Orders*[280]

The Drug Treatment and Testing Order was created under the auspices of the Crime and Disorder Act 1998[281] and provides an opportunity for the courts to impose a sentence which requires the offender to comply submit to a treatment programme for a specified period and undergo regular testing for drugs. The ideal underlying this order, which can be imposed for between 6 months and 3 years, is rehabilitation. Provided that the court is satisfied that the offender is indeed dependent on or misusing drugs, and that such dependency/misuse may be treated a DTTO may prove to be an appropriate non-custodial sanction. The consolidated provisions of the PCCSA 2000 provide detailed guidance on whether and how this order should be made and the application of these statutory provisions this has been discussed by the courts in *R. v. Tower Bridge Magistrates Courts, ex parte the Inner London Probation Service.*[282] As the DTTO is a relatively new form of disposal, with only 300 such orders made in the year 2000, it is difficult to evaluate its effectiveness as a means of either reducing crime or rehabilitating offenders. However, the DTTO does fit well within the framework outlined by the both the Halliday and Auld reports.[283] This order seeks to reduce crime by tackling what may be the cause of offending in the case of those receiving the sentence, that of drug use. In addition the DTTO also serves as a template for the type of sentences envisaged by the Halliday Report, sentences which allow the court to monitor the progress of offenders and evaluate the ways in which they respond to the imposition of such sentences in closer collaboration with relevant agencies such as the probation service. This vision becomes one step closer to being realised in the proposals and ethos of the White Paper, Justice for All. The statutory provisions relating to DTTOs provide the courts with the power to regularly review the offender's progress throughout the order, in the presence of offender and the individual charged with supervising the implementation of the sentence.

---

[280] ss. 52–58 of the PCCSA 2000.
[281] s. 61.
[282] [2001] E.W.H.C. Admin. 401.
[283] Indeed, *Justice for All*, Cm. 5563, 2002, singles out the DTTO to note that it is a recent improvement which provides a demanding and specialised form of sentence tackling the specific reasons behind offending, see para. 5.20, p. 91.

CHAPTER TEN

The Prison System of England and Wales

DR. DEBORAH CHENEY

10.1 INTRODUCTION

The aims and values found in the basic theories of punishment structure how the state uses prison as a punishment practice. The main theories of rehabilitation, deterrence, incapacitation and just desert, are all embodied within the process of punishment that is incarceration behind prison walls. An average day in the criminal justice workload sees 5,600 defendants sentenced, 375 offenders entering prison under sentence and 65,000 supervised in prison on remand or under sentence.[1] In January 2002 the prison population numbered 68,195 (compared with 63,403 in January 2001) and at the time of writing the prison population has reached in excess of 71,000[2], with the average cost of a prison

---

[1] Figures taken from *Criminal Justice: the way ahead*, Cm. 5074 (HMSO, February 2001).
[2] Pressures of numbers has forced the prison service to use police cells to accomodate the overflow.

sentence being £37,500 per year. It is estimated that by 2008 the population will be between 70,200 and 83,500.[3] Each year the Prison Service discharges around 90,000 prisoners and within 2 years of finishing a prison sentence over half of offenders, and nearly 80 per cent of those with more than 5 previous convictions, will be convicted and sentenced for further offences.[4]

In 'Criminal Justice: the way ahead', the Government outline their philosophy for dealing with offenders. This includes a sentencing philosophy based on the offender, not just the offence, thus paying attention to sentence outcomes, with sentences that include a punitive element together with elements of reparation, offending behaviour and proceeds of crime. This philosophy, translated into the terms in which prisons will offer these elements, is found in the stated objective of HM Prison Service: To protect the public by holding those committed by the courts in a safe, decent, and healthy environment; reduce crime by providing constructive regimes which address offending behaviour, improve educational and work skills and promote law-abiding behaviour in custody and after release'.

The wording of this objective makes clear that prisoners are committed to prison *as* punishment, not *for* punishment. The primary focus of the term of imprisonment is to turn around offending behaviour and release individuals back into the community who will not return to crime. The 'safe, decent, and healthy environment' is essential if prisoners are not to feel victimised and thus fail to acknowledge the victims of their crime. The concept of a 'healthy prison' has been well established by HM Chief Inspectorate of Prisons [HMCIP] as a necessary vehicle if the tasks of addressing behaviour and improving skills and education are to succeed. The elements of a healthy prison are that the weakest prisoners feel safe; all prisoners are treated with respect as individuals; all prisoners are busily occupied, are expected to improve themselves and given the opportunity to do so, and that all prisoners can strengthen links with their families and prepare for release. In addition all staff should feel safe; be treated with respect as individuals and be informed and consulted within their sphere of work; have high expectations made of them; be well led, and respect their own health.

The difficult balancing act which HM Prison Service need to accomplish on a day to day basis is one of protecting the public whilst incapacitating, acting as a deterrent and rehabilitating, the latter being an aim of paramount importance given that all but circa 25 of those currently behind prison walls will be released back into the community. It is unlikely that a penal system structured by only one theory of punishment would be either coherent or possible. As Walker states, legislators and sentencers draw variously on the philosophies of punishment with just deserts governing official policy, incapacitation ruling how to deal with violent offenders and a rehabilitative framework being adopted for certain groups; whilst the nature of the sanctions available may discount all or several of the general philosophical aims.[5]

Maintaining this difficult balance, across a diverse prison population, is sorely tested by changing political stances, public pressure and the aftermath of

---

[3] Figures taken from: C. Gray and M.Elkins, *Projections of long-term trends in the prison population to 2008*, Home Office Statistical Bulletin, May 23, 2001. See http://www.homeoffice.gov.uk/rds/index.htm.
[4] *Criminal Justice: the way ahead* Cm. 5074 (HMSO, February 2001).
[5] Walker, N., *Why Punish* (Oxford University Press, 1991).

escapes.[6] PS accountability to different agencies, recommendations of HMCIP establishment reports and Thematic Review findings, together with those of exhaustive research indicators, join with these elements of quality control and, in some instances, provide conflicting messages, which are difficult to juggle. A Governor can find himself in the position that: 'I am sitting at my desk contemplating two reports which have arrived on my desk almost simultaneously. The Inspectorate report says I am a decent bloke trying to run a prison on tuppence h'penny. The report of the Security Audit basically says I am the handmaiden of Satan.'[7]

The Prison Service of the twenty-first century is a far cry from those of other generations and is bound tightly by beaurocratic practices evolving from a host of Standards, Targets, Instructions and Orders. However in one respect it has not changed and that is, despite persistent calls to do so, the Service has failed to streamline the large number of instructions which engulf Governors on a daily basis. The Woolf Report in 1991 observed 'the confetti of instructions descending from headquarters' and the Learmont Report of 1995 described 'a blizzard of paperwork', in 2001 the Laming report identifies a 'paper mountain'.[8] The Annual Report of HMCIP 1999–2000 states of this situation 'What is most galling about much of this imposition is that it concerns the production of vast amounts of information, that are so meaningless as far as achieving the aim of the Prison Service is concerned.'

Table 10.1 Breakdown of communications and requests for action received by a Governor of a Category C prison over a twelve-month period.[9]

Notices to staff	39	Main actions required	83
Internal communications	5	Main actions required	5
Prison Service Standards	30	Main actions required	120
E mails	800	Main actions required	400
Prison Service Orders	34	Main actions required	786
Prison Service Instructions	73	Main actions required	310
Total communications 981			
Total actions required 1704			

[6] The Mountbatten Report emphasised security and control, *Report of the Inquiry into Prison Escapes and Security*, Cmnd. 3175, (HMSO, 1966); the May Committee adopted the approach of positive custody, *Report of the Inquiry into the U.K. Prison Services*, Cmnd. 7673, (HMSO, 1979); the Woolf Report recognised the elements of security, control and justice all had to be present, *Report of an Inquiry into Prison Disturbances April 1990*, Cm. 1456, (HMSO, 1991). *Review of PS security in England and Wales and the escape from Parkhurst prison on Tuesday January 3, 1995*, General Sir John Learmont, KCB, CBE, Cm. 3020, (HMSO, 1995); *The Escape from Whitemoor prison on Friday September 9, 1994*, Sir John Woodcock, CBE QPM, Cm. 2741, (HMSO, 1994).

[7] *Prison Governor Association Magazine*, September 2001.

[8] *Modernising the Management of the Prison Service*, An Independent Report by the Targeted Performance Initiative Group, chaired by Lord Laming of Tewin, CBE.

[9] *Modernising the management of the Prison Service*, An Independent Report by the Targeted Performance Initiative Group, chaired by Lord Laming of Tewin, CBE, p. 14. See http://hmprisonservice.gov.uk.

The Woolf Report of 1991, product of the investigation into the circumstances surrounding the Manchester Prison riot in 1990 [sparking off riots in nine other prisons across the country], provided a blueprint for the future of the Prison Service. It became the most far reaching examination of the PS since the publication in 1895 of the report of the Gladstone Committee, both reports establishing a vision of imprisonment where management obligations and objectives ran alongside purposeful activities, respect for family ties, justice and fairness. The 1895 report from the Departmental Committee of Prisons advocated that prisons should: 'turn prisoners out of prison better men and women physically and morally'.[10] Meaningful contact with the outside world, rather than an isolated and austere deprivation of it was stated in no uncertain terms: If extra visits to prisoners, or privileges to send or receive communications from friends or relations, would be beneficial to a prisoner and likely to assist in making him a better man, such relaxations would be desirable'.[11] These ideals were echoed by Lord Woolf.

Considerable weight was given to the findings by Lord Woolf, and in many ways the development of the prison estate since 1991 has adhered to the core ideals of his report. That said, the explosion of the prison population, increased beurocracy and political pendulums has rendered the future Woolf foresaw diluted by the pressures of these elements.

The current vision of a modernised prison estate, premised on addressing historic inadequacies, does however, reflect the 'stamp' of Lord Woolf. The community prisons he advocated in 1991 form a part of the blueprint for the future, with increased opportunities for prisoners to remain close to their home. Government proposals include 'campus style' prisons holding all types, gender and security category of prisoners in order to afford the least disruption to rehabilitation and settlement needs, currently the side-effect of moving through a sentence by moving prison and area. Further innovations will be necessary if proposals for an intermittent sentence are successful, as both the location of prisons and their facilities will need to be addressed if intermittent custody is to be adequately supported.[12]

10.2 A BRIEF HISTORY OF PUNISHMENT

The history of punishment of the body of the criminal is a well-documented account of severity.[13] Many punishments were undertaken within the community itself, a 'drama of punishment' in which 'punishment becomes a form of festivity; in a relatively small and enclosed city, it turns into celebration of communal feeling'.[14] As such, the forced procession of the shaven-headed, the use of whipping posts, ducking stools, branding irons and the pillory, and even the aftermath of executions, enabled public approbation to be displayed in its most physical form and, in the case of the pillory, become part of the punishment

---

[10] Prison Reform Trust, *Gladstone at 100*: essays on the past and future of the prison system, 1995.
[11] Prison Reform Trust, *Gladstone at 100*: essays on the past and present of the prison system, 1995.
[12] *Justice for All*, Cm. 5563, July 2002, 6.42–6.45 at p. 113.
[13] For detailed accounts see G.R. Scott, *The History of Corporal Punishment* (Luxor Press, London, 1959) and *The History of Capital Punishment* (Torchstream Books, London 1950), E.W. Pettifer, *Punishments of Former Days* (Waterside Press, 1992) and the excellent work *The Hanging Tree* by V.A.C. Gatrell, (Oxford University Press, 1994). For a history of the abolition of capital punishment in Britain see B.P. Block & J.Hostettler, *Hanging in the Balance* (Waterside Press, 1997).
[14] Ackroyd, P., *London: the biography* (Chatto & Windus, London, 2000), p. 65.

process. The display of punishment in this manner epitomised retribution and the societal censure of retribution as reprobation[15]; an expression of disapproval rather than a remedy to a problem.

The involvement of the public in executions themselves grew over time. The road travelled by the condemned from Newgate prison to the gibbet at Tyburn Hill invariably took on a carnival or holiday attraction atmosphere. This extended even after death when the heads of rebels and traitors were boiled and placed on London Bridge to become a paying attraction,[16] or the dissection of the bodies of those hanged could be seen for a few pennies.[17] In a similar manner both the cellar of Fleet prison and the chapel galleries of Newgate[18] afforded paying spectators the opportunity to view the condemned.

When in 1783 the gallows were moved from Tyburn, where they had stood since 1196, to outside Newgate prison, thus removing the traditional procession of the condemned through the streets, the diarist Samuel Johnson wrote indignantly to Boswell: 'Sir, executions are intended to draw spectators. If they don't draw spectators, they don't answer their purpose. The old method was most satisfactory to all parties: the public was gratified by a procession: the criminal was supported by it'.[19] With this move, Newgate itself drew closer to becoming a focus of both containment and punishment. The last public hanging outside Newgate was in 1868, and from that time took place behind prison walls.

The use of prisons as holding centres for those awaiting corporal or capital sentence to be carried out has a long history stretching back to medieval England. From the 17th century this role of 'warehousing' was used for those sentenced to transportation to the colonies, first in America and then, at the outbreak of the American War of Independence in 1776, to Australia.[20] As Shaw states: 'This at least satisfied the society from which the criminals were expelled, if no one else. There was no need to worry about their behaviour in future; the process was cheap; the receiving society could usually be ignored'.[21]

The use of prisons for confinement as punishment itself was a product of the 16th century and bridewells, established as houses of correction for vagrants, were virtually indistinguishable from prisons themselves. Newgate prison, rebuilt in 1670 after the Great Fire on its original 12th Century site, consisted of 5 stories with 5 sides for prisoner groups, underground dungeons with chains and stocks for the condemned and a press room for those who refused to plead (which operated until 1734).[22] The prison was rebuilt again in 1770, and in 1782

---

[15] From the Latin reprobation: rejection by God's decree, and therefore pre-destination or fore-ordination to eternal damnation.

[16] Ackroyd, P. *London: the biography*, *op. cit.* p. 65.

[17] Pettifer writes of the body of Mary Bateman, executed in York on March 20, 1809 and given to Leeds Infirmary, where 2,500 people were allowed to view it on payment of 3d, after which her skin was tanned and distributed. Pettifer, *Punishments of Former Days*, p. 37.

[18] Wednesdays and Thursdays between 12 and 3 Newgate became a 'theatre' open to visitors. After the final execution there in May 1902, and demolition in August, the auction of execution shed relics sold for £5 15s 0d and plaster casts of famous criminals for £5. Ackroyd, *London: a biography*, p. 154 and 256.

[19] Ackroyd, P., *London: the biography*, p. 295/6 *op. cit.* The first hanging to take place at Newgate after the move from Tyburn was on December 9, 1783.

[20] For a detailed account of penal transportation, see A.G.L.Shaw, *Convicts and the Colonies: a study of penal transportation from Great Britain and Ireland to Australia and other parts of the British Empire*, (The Irish Historical Press, 1998).

[21] Shaw, A.G.L., *Convicts and the Colonies: a study of penal transportation from Great Britain and Ireland to Australia and other parts of the British Empire*, *op. cit.*, p. 21.

[22] Ackroyd, P., *London: the biography*, *op. cit.*, p. 234, 247 and 249.

after being fired by rioters, yet official reports from prison inspectors in 1836 and 1843 nonetheless condemned the squalor and horror of the prison.

These early prisons of containment operated on a profit-making basis for the jailers. Unwaged, they earned their living by running brothels, charging entry to traders and the curious, selling food and alcohol and charging for chains to be removed, effectively creating a two-tier system based on the poverty or wealth of those incarcerated. Domestically organised under monopolistic rule, there was a vast difference in practices across the country. In 1777 John Howard published a damning indictment of the system entitled 'State of the Prisons', having visited every prison in the country and recorded a detailed account of his findings, even down to the weight of chains. Whilst this resulted in the passing of a Penitentiary Act, pressures of the Napoleonic wars meant that ongoing efforts in respect of penal reform was a priority for none other than individual reformers such as Elizabeth Fry, whose ministrations began in the early 1800s.[23]

It was not until the 19th century that the philosophy of combining the incarceration in cells with redeeming penitent souls became adopted in the design and organisation of what was to become the penitentiary. This was the singular move from an assault on the body of the criminal to a more sensory approach to their punishment, as envisaged by the words of John Howard: 'We have too much adopted the gothic mode of correction, viz. by rigorous severity, which often hardens the heart; while many foreigners pursue the more rational plan of softening the mind in order to [encourage] its amendment'.[24]

This philosophical move was given the practical tools of salaried jailers and secure and sanitary accommodation through the 1823 Gaol Act, which also set out basic rules for prisoners, and accountability through the creation of the first prison inspectors authorised by statute in 1835. In 1842 the first penitentiary was built at Pentonville with the emphasis on securing the penitence of those incarcerated at the core of the regime.[25] This meant that solitary confinement, physical exercise as a silent hooded figure and monotonous hard labour, ensured each individual had the time and silence in which to repent their sins.

Statutes in 1865 and 1877 resulted in all prisons being placed under the Prison Commissioners, headed by Du Cane, with the commissioners themselves being responsible to the Home Secretary and to Parliament. The Gladstone Committee of 1895 was highly critical of prison regimes implemented by Du Cane, criticising the failure to pay regard to the 'moral as well as the legal responsibilities of the prison authorities' and recommending sweeping changes that were then implemented in the 1898 Prison Act. The Act introduced classification of prisoners into three divisions wherein sentence could be served, limited corporal punishment, sentence remission for good conduct, and placed administration of the prison service in the hands of the Home Secretary.

Du Cane was replaced as chair of the Prison Commissioners by Ruggles-Brise, until his resignation in 1921, and during the inter-war years the commissioners, influenced by the social work background of one of their number, Alexander Paterson, developed open prisons, Borstal regimes and after-care for prisoners. It

---

[23] For an account of the early prisons and penal reform efforts, see M. Ignatieff, *A Just Measure of Pain*, 1978 and Morris, N., and Rothman, D.J., *The Oxford History of the Prison: the practice of punishment in western society* (OUP, 1995).

[24] 'John Howard, Prisons and Lazarettos', quoted in Bender, J., *Imagining the Penitentiary: fiction and the architecture of the mind in eighteenth century England* (The University of Chicago Press, 1987), p. 22.

[25] The tone having been set by the Carnarvon Committee which was created in 1863.

was to be called 'the essential period of penological "optimism" when imprisonment as an institution of social reform was at its most viable and some of the
ideals of the Gladstone Committee came closest to realisation'.[26]

In 1963 the management of the service was removed from the prison commissioners to the Prison Department of the Home Office, headed by a Director
General, and in 1992 the service was given agency status.

10.3 MODERN PRISONS—ADMINISTRATION

10.3.1 *State Prisons*

The Prisons Service Management Board [PSMB], chaired by the Director General[27] and comprising five non-executive directors (external to the PS) and seven
directors, is the senior management team of the service. The executive directors
have separate responsibility for security, high security, personnel, corporate
affairs, finance, regimes and healthcare. As an advisory and co-ordinating body,
the PSMB decide upon goals and performance targets for the work of the service
and monitor performance. The Board link with individual establishments
through Area Managers, who manage 13 geographical cluster groups of prisons,
and with the High Security and women's estate. The security categorisation of a
prison is designated Male Local, Cat B, C or D, Male Remand Centre, Female
Local, Closed or Open and Male Closed or Open Young Offender Institute
[YOI]. Prisoners enter the system at a local prison, spend the majority of their
sentence at a training prison and transfer to resettlement or open prisons prior to
release.

The Prison Service publish a Framework Document (responsibilities,
accountability and Key Performance Indicators), Corporate Plan (strategy to
achieve 3 year objectives) and Business plan (key targets and programmes within
the financial year), in line with their agency status, and an Annual Report.

In the 2001–2002 to 2003–2004 Corporate plan, the Service prioritise their
major work as follows:

- Maintaining security and preventing escapes.

- Delivering, in partnership with the National Probation Service, Youth Justice Board (YJB) and community and voluntary sector, improved regimes.

- Managing the prison populations safely, in particular through a long-term
  suicide prevention strategy.

- Improving prison healthcare, including problems relating to mental health,
  drugs and alcohol, in partnership with the NHS.

- Building upon YJB partnership in developing secure places for 15 to 17 year
  olds meeting vocational and educational needs.

- Increasing capacity, not least with a view to the increasing female estate.

- Increasing efficiency, developing human resources, and modernising infra-
  structure.

[26] Harding C., et al., *Imprisonment in England and Wales: A Concise History* (1985), p. 194.
[27] Promoted to Second Permanent Secretary in September 2002. See 'Prison Service Director General', Home Office press release, September 9, 2002 at www.homeoffice.gov.uk.

The basic statutory framework for the administration of prisons is the Prison Act 1952,[28] whilst the Prison Rules 1999,[29] and Young Offender Institution Rules 1988,[30] provide the detail which governs day to day operation of prisons and interaction with prisoners.[31]

Supplementing the legislated actions are Prison Service Orders [PSO] which are issued on an almost daily basis, to amend existing prison service manuals or outline mandatory action to be taken by governors and staff, and cover topics from Anti-bullying strategy to Zoonotic infections.[32]

PSOs also underpin[33] and provide the detail for Prison Service Performance Standards [PS] which are in place to outline policies and procedures on a specific area of prison life and thereby ensure consistency across the service, and provide key audit baselines to assess prison performance against an agreed standard.[34] At the time of writing there are 67 standards, ranging from Accommodation to Use of IT, applying variously to all prisons (including those contracted out), female prisons, open prisons, those holding convicted and sentenced males and females other than Cat A.[35]

Key Performance Indicators [KPI] form part of the Corporate Plan and the PS Annual Report records historic performance against each KPI. The KPIs for 2001–2002 are:

- To ensure no category A escapes.

- To ensure that the number of escapes from prisons and escorts undertaken by Prison Service staff expressed as a proportion of the prison population is lower than 0.05 per cent.

- To ensure that the number of escapes from contracted out escorts is no more than one per 20,000 prisoners handled.

- To ensure that the number of positive adjudications of assault on prisoners, staff and others expressed as a proportion of the average population is lower than 9 per cent.

- To ensure that the number of prisoners held two to a cell designed for one expressed as a percentage of the population does not exceed 18 per cent.

- To ensure that the number of minority ethnic staff in the Prison Service expressed as a proportion of the total workforce is at least 4.1 per cent by April 2002.

---

[28] Amended in 1991 by the Criminal Justice Act to take account of private sector prisons. The Prisons (Alcohol Testing) Act 1997 also operates as an amendment to the Prison Act 1952, incorporated in s. 16B (1–3) of that Act.
[29] As amended by the Prison (Amendment) Rules 2000.
[30] As amended by the Young Offender Institution (Amendment) Rules 1988, 1989, 1992, 1993, 1994, 1995, 1996, 1997, 1998, 1999 and YOI (Amendment) Rules 2000 and (No. 2) 2000.
[31] The Prisoners Earnings Act 1996 is not yet in force.
[32] For a complete list see M.Leech & D.Cheney, *The Prisons Handbook 2002* (Waterside Press, 2002), p. 541–543 and http://www.hmprisonservice.gov.uk.
[33] Together with, where relevant, Instructions, Statutory Instruments and Manuals.
[34] Audits of establishments, carried out by staff from PS headquarters, assess practice under the headings of security, safety, decency and health, organisational effectiveness and efficiency and regimes. A Key Performance Target is set for each establishment and they are graded acceptable, deficient, marginal or unacceptable.
[35] For a complete list see Leech, M. & Cheney, D., *The Prisons Handbook 2002* (Waterside Press, 2002), pxxvii-xxxiii and http://www.hmprisonservice.gov.uk.

- To ensure that the average staff sickness does not exceed ten working days per person by April 2002.

- To ensure that the average cost per uncrowded prison place does not exceed £35, 910.

- To ensure that the average cost per prisoner does not exceed £37, 418.

- To deliver 23,400 accredited educational or vocational qualifications in 2001–2, including 18,000 Level 2 Basic Skills awards.

- To ensure that prisoners spend on average at least 24 hours per week in purposeful activity.

- To deliver 8,100 accredited Offending Behaviour Programme completions in 2001–2, including 1,160 Sex Offender Treatment Programmes.

- To ensure the rate of positive results from mandatory drugs tests is lower than 12 per cent by April 2002.[36]

One of the major criticisms of KPIs is that they encourage a focus on, and measurement of, quantity rather than quality of service delivery, and that the appropriateness of what is chosen to be the subject of a KPI is wanting. There is no KPI for the amount of staff prisoner contact hours, for example, nor a self-injury/suicide focused KPI. On the subject of meaningful choices for KPIs, Sir David Ramsbotham, when holding the post of HM Chief Inspector of Prisons, remarked: 'I would find it much more meaningful if KPIs covered such aspects as recording the number of prisoners who could not read when they were received into prison, and the number who could not read when they left or when they were transferred, in other words measures of achievements in working to achieve the overall criminal justice system aim'.

The Chairman of the Prison Governors Association [PGA] identifies with this view. The PGA directly challenged the Director Generals claim that a prison delivering Key Performance Indicators and Targets was a prison that treated prisoners decently, on the grounds that the assumption they measure anything associated with decency was erroneous. The Chairman has also pointed out the dangers of an approach to performance measurement that believes it can be turned into an exact science by providing ever-increasing targets.[37]

10.3.2 *Private Prisons*

Private prisons were introduced into the United Kingdom in 1992 with the opening of a remand prison, The Wolds, in East Yorkshire.[38] This was followed in 1993 by Blakenhurst[39] and then in 1994 by the opening of Doncaster.[40] The concept of privatised prison management was explored in 1984, by the Adam Smith Institute[41], as a means to solve overcrowding. A Select Committee on Home Affairs

---

[36] For a list of key KPI data returns per establishment, 2001–2002, see M.Leech & D.Cheney, *The Prisons Handbook 2002* (Waterside Press, 2002), pxxxv-xxxvi.

[37] Newell, M., 'Performance Management: overused and misunderstood', *Prison Service Journal*, No. 141, May 2002, p. 10–14.

[38] Run by Group 4 Prison Services, in 1995 the prison was re-roled to take convicted prisoners.

[39] Since 2001, run under a Service Level Agreement after the success of a PS bid team.

[40] The prison continues to be run by Premier Prison Services Ltd.

[41] Omega Report on Justice Policy.

recommended privatisation proceed after visiting private prisons in the U.S.[42] and in 1988 a government green paper and feasibility study, by Deloitte Haskins Sell, set out the cost effectiveness of proceeding.[43] In 1990 the draft Criminal Justice Bill creating enabling legislation extended the remit to beyond the remand sector, in 1992 the Criminal Justice Act became law and in 1993 the Criminal Justice Act 1991 (Contracted Out Prison) (No. 2) Order 1992 was approved.[44]

Administration of a private prison is governed by a Service Level Agreement [SLA] between the State and the company, in which expected services and standards are outlined, together with agreed payment for the services.[45] A Controller[46] is employed by the State at each prison to ensure the contract is complied with, adjudicate in disciplinary proceedings, and authorise the use of prisoners' restraints. Failure by the company to meet standards and agreed regime services results in a financial penalty.[47] In all other terms private prisons are subject to Parliamentary scrutiny, Prison Service PSO and PSI and the accountability factors that are outlined below.

Supporters of privatisation lay stress on private prisons as agents of reform through good practices spreading throughout the system. Detractors highlight the 'commercial in confidence' status of the SLA and inherent problems of specifying all contractual contingencies, together with a moral repugnance of putting profit first and making money out of punishment. Regardless of the merits of such debate, privatisation is here to stay[48] and the ethos of private sector involvement now extends to a wider field including prison shops ('canteen') and prisoner escort services. With the increasing expansion of the prison population, it is less the matter of cost-effectiveness than that of sheer available containment space that solidifies the value of private prisons.[49]

10.4 MODERN PRISONS—ACCOUNTABILITY

The first step toward accountability for what happens behind prison walls can be traced to the inspectors authorised by statute in 1835. The Prison Act of 1952 made provision for an Inspectorate of Prisons in section 5 of the Act, however reports were confidential and an inspectorate independent of the prison department and reporting directly to the Home Secretary was not recommended until 1966. A renewed recommendation was made in 1979 by a committee of inquiry into the Prison Service (the May Committee)[50], and in 1981 the Home Secretary

---

[42] *Contract Provision of Prisons*, HC291, 1987.

[43] *Private Sector Involvement in the Remand System*, Cm. 434, (1998) and *A Report to the Home Office on the Practicality of Private Sector Involvement in the Remand System*, 1988.

[44] This extended private management to existing prisons, with only the private sector able to bid for newly constructed establishments.

[45] Payment is reduced if performance measures are not met.

[46] A civil servant of governor grade.

[47] For example, in 2001 The Wolds were fined £11,472.50 and Doncaster £30,000.

[48] There are now 9 private prisons, The Wolds, Doncaster, Parc, Altcourse, Lowdham Grange, Ashfield, Forest Bank, Rye Hill and Dovegate, with a competition current for a further 2 at Ashford and Peterborough.

[49] The Carter Report, an independent review of the private sector involvement in running prisons, finds that this sector has helped to drive down costs and improve public sector prison performance. A recommendation of the report is that all new prisons should be designed and built by the private sector, with the private and public sectors in a management partnership. See PS news release February 26, 2002 at http://www.hmprisonservice.gov.uk.

[50] *Report of the Inquiry into the United Kingdom Prison Services*, Cmnd. 7673 (Home Office, 1981).

appointed the first independent Prisons Inspector. That said, PS accountability is not solely a matter for the Chief Inspectorate of Prisons and Probation[51] [HMCIP], but attends also upon the ministrations of the Prisons and Probation Ombudsman, Boards of Visitors and voluntary agencies who have the interests of prisoners at the core of their work.

Proposed future developments within the prison estate are directed toward making governors more accountable for performance of their prison, with more delegated powers reinforced by locally monitored Service Level Agreements. The price of failing to demonstrate the necessary standards, in both performance and costs, will be closure or contract out to the private sector. It has also been proposed that all prisons, both public and private, should be open to market testing.[52]

10.4.1 *Her Majesty's Chief Inspector of Prisons and Probation*

HMCIP reports directly to the Home Secretary and is a member of the Home Office. The duty entailed in the role is to inspect and report to the Secretary of State on prison service establishments in England and Wales, and in particular on: conditions; the treatment of prisoners and other inmates and the facilities available to them. Inspections are undertaken by an inspectorate team, on an announced and unannounced basis, and findings of the inspections are published. Together with the inspection reports on individual establishments, and an annual report, the Inspectorate publish thematic reviews on various aspects of prison life.[53] The job of the Inspector is to inform and advise the Home Secretary in order to assist the Home Secretary to discharge his/her accountability for prisons. Resort to publicity, and recommendations within establishment reports to the Home Secretary, Director General, Area Managers and the governor of the establishment inspected, are the extent of the powers the role embraces.

The current HMCIP is Anne Owers, who succeeded General Sir David Ramsbotham GCB, CBE in 2001, at the end of his 5 year appointment. Sir David proved to be a controversial HMCIP, very ready to walk out of prisons and use the press to publicise extreme conditions. His term was characterised by publication of hard-hitting reports and in-depth thematic reviews covering such topics as suicide, women prisoners and the remand population.

Throughout his inspection reports Sir David took as a focus his conception of a 'healthy prison' and in his final annual report (1999/2000) during his term of office he expanded the healthy prison elements into 'Expectations', a criteria for assessing the treatment and conditions for prisoners. A stand-alone document, 'it focuses on the quality of outcomes, not the quantity of process, and the criteria are presented more in the form of a checklist than a table of what can be measured'.[54] This focus on outcomes for prisoners, is his practical response to the criticism of KPIs (stated earlier).

---

[51] So called since 2001 when the brief of HM Chief Inspector of Prisons was extended. The role of Prisons Ombudsman was extended to include probation in the same year.

[52] *Justice for All*, Cm. 5563, July 2002, 6.40 and 6.41 at p. 112 to 113.

[53] See http://www.homeoffice.gov.uk/hmipris/hmipris.htm.

[54] Sir David Ramsbotham, commenting upon his Annual Report in M. Leech & D. Cheney, *The Prisons Handbook 2002*. (Waterside Press, 2002), p. 592.

10.4.2 *Prisons and Probation Ombudsman*

The creation of the post of Prisons Ombudsman [PO] (since 2001 the Prisons and Probation Ombudsman) was a direct consequence of the Woolf Report. The improvement of standards of justice within prisons was a core recommendation of the report, which stated that:

> '*prisoners should know why a decision which materially adversely affects them is being taken. This is essential to achieve satisfactory relations within prisons. If prisoners consider they have a genuine grievance they should be able to have resort to a grievance procedure which has at its final stage the necessary degree of independence*'.

The first PO to be appointed (in November 1994), was Vice-Admiral Sir Peter Woodhead KCB and the current incumbent is Stephen Shaw. Whilst the post was originally intended to enjoy unfettered access to prison service documents, establishments and individuals, in April 96 the Home Secretary curtailed this brief. It was announced that the Ombudsman would not be able to review any decision made by PS Ministers, that the PS would be the sole arbiter of what documents the Ombudsman could see or not see, and that a copy of the report following investigation of a complaint must be sent to the PS before a copy was sent to the prisoner complainant. All three of these restrictions were deemed unacceptable by a Home Affairs Select Committee in May 1996, and in June 98 a working party considered amended terms of reference.

The present position is that the Ombudsman may investigate complaints by individual prisoners and individuals under the supervision of the National Probation Service (NPS) who have exhausted and failed to obtain satisfaction from the PS and NPS complaints systems. S/he can consider the merits of matters complained of, in addition to the procedures involved, and can investigate all decisions taken in relation to prisoners by all working in prisons with the exception of decisions involving the clinical judgment of doctors.[55]

The total number of complaints received by the Ombudsman during 2000–2001 were 2,176, and during 2001–2002 a total of 2,825 (1,202 eligible), 96 per cent of which concerned the PS. Investigations were completed in 1,107 cases, a rise of 112 per cent on the previous year. The trend of the highest number of complaints emanating from the high security estate remained the same, as did that of complaints relating to adjudications and prisoners' property forming the most significant number of complaints.

Table 10.2

Complaint Categories 2001–2002[56]	Number
Adjudications	490
Assaults	9
Security	81

[55] For full details of Terms of Reference, see *Prisons & Probation Ombudsman Annual Report 2001–2002: The Pursuit of Decency*, Cm. 5530 (June 2002) and http://www.ppo.gov.uk.
[56] *Prisons & Probation Ombudsman, Annual Report 2001–2002: The Pursuit of Decency*, Cm. 5530, (June 2002), p. 8. See http://www.ppo.gov.uk.

Food	10
General conditions	94
Regime activities	80
Links	73
Medical	16
Pre-release	29
Property	147
Race and religion	14
Segregation	13
Transfers and allocation	65
Miscellaneous	75

One of the main concerns raised by the Ombudsman is that 'Remand prisoners, short-sentence prisoners, women prisoners and young prisoners are all significantly under-represented in my caseload'. Writing in February 2001, he recorded the under-representation by young offenders as a 'particular personal anxiety, given that the two most worrying establishments I have visited in the past 12 months have both been young offender institutes'.[57] Prompted by these concerns a research study was undertaken by his office to review complaints from Young Offender Institutions and the report considered a number of factors that attend upon the lack of complaints from this section of the prison population. These included lack of information about and access to formal procedures, fear of being disadvantaged if a complaint is made and a need for a more immediate relief than the formal system based upon limited confidence in adult authority.[58]

A more general concern in respect of the effectiveness of the office of Ombudsman is raised by an overview of the complaints investigated since creation of the office. Between 1995 and 2002 the largest number of complaints have consistently arisen from the categories of adjudications, property and categorisation. Also consistent have been the themes within these categories of complaint. Adjudication complaints have focused on lack of fair hearing, incorrect procedures, failure to examine possible defences, sketchy recording of evidence and excessive punishments. Property complaints have centred on loss or damage with findings of improper procedures, inaccurate paperwork or non-recording of property and insufficient detail of property to value for compensation. Categorisation complaints have largely centred on improper reasons for recategorisation to a higher security category, on grounds of behaviour not warranting such a move, and even after misbehaviour or complaining, rather

---

[57] *Prisons & Probation Ombudsman, Annual Report 2000–2001.* See http://www.ppo.gov.uk.
[58] *Listening to young prisoners: a review of complaints procedures in Young Offender Institutions by the Prisons Ombudsman,* 2001. Overall, significant variations were found in the use of the request/complaints procedures, across establishments. Compared with adults, a higher proportion of complaints from young offenders concern property, with complaints against adjudications being much lower.

than recategorisation upward based upon any clear change of risk. Thus whilst the value of the Ombudsman's role to secure justice for individual prisoners is great, the fact that trends and themes remain consistent over time suggests that the value of the role to hold the PS accountable—and thereby change unacceptable practices—is demonstrably weak.

That said, Government proposals for changes to be made to the status and role of the PO may change this state of affairs. Currently the PO is an administrative Home Office appointment, but it has been acknowledged the importance of the role warrants a clear statutory basis. In 'Justice for All', the Government pledge: 'we will legislate to achieve this as soon as possible'. In addition, consideration is being given to extend the remit of the PO to investigate suicides.[59]

10.4.3 *Boards of Visitors*

Holding the PS accountable is a role which falls to ordinary members of the public in the form of Boards of Visitors [BOV], a principle of independent inspection having its roots in visiting committees of magistrates in Tudor times. Every prison establishment has a BOV made up of members of the public who have been appointed by, and are subject to triennial review by, the Home Secretary.[60] Under Sec 6 of the Prison Act 1952, BOV members have a right to enter their appointed prison unannounced at any time and, as keyholders and unescorted, have the right to unimpeded access to any part of that prison. Their duties are prescribed by the Prison Rules 1964 to inspect and satisfy themselves of the manner in which the prison operates; physical conditions; treatment of prisoners; staff and prisoner grievances; conduct of disciplinary hearings; conditions of segregation, and all aspects of prison life.

Prisoners may approach a BOV in person with a grievance or request a meeting in writing. Whilst in discussion with a BOV member the prisoner is entitled to be out of hearing of prison staff. In addition to attending to the problems prisoners are facing, BOV members are also called upon to monitor the use of physical restraints (such as body belts) and the holding of inmates in segregation. Written records must be kept of all matters investigated and a monthly meeting of all BOV members is required. An Annual Report must be submitted to the Home Secretary.

Historically, Boards were involved in adjudications upon prisoners. Their role as a disciplinary body came under strong criticism in the Woolf Report, which recommended this aspect of their work be abolished as inappropriate.[61] Adjudications, and the meting out of punishments thus became the province of prison governors from 1992. Whilst the role of the BOV in this respect was undoubtedly unacceptable, going in tandem with assisting prisoners with complaints, at least whilst adjudications were in their hands the courts were more willing to interfere with decisions, particularly in respect of challenging punishments given. With the move of adjudications into the hands of governors, adjudications have taken on the persona of a managerial task, thus one in which the courts are unwilling to intervene. This task now appears to rest largely with the Ombudsman (as raised above).

---

[59] *Justice for All*, Cm. 5563, July 2002, 6.39 at p. 112.
[60] For full details of the work of the BOV, see http://www.homeoffice.gov.uk/bov/main.htm.
[61] See Woolf, para. 12.169. In 1982 the EC held BOVs were not independent and impartial for the purposes of Art. 6 of E.C.H.R. but the E.C.H.R. held the contrary. See *Campbell & Fell v. UK* (1982) 5 E.H.R.R. 207 and (1984) 7 E.H.R.R. 165.

Criticism, much of it warranted, has always surrounded the work of the BOV. Not least, how representative they are of the prison population (in terms of age, background and ethnicity), the disparity between Boards and how they operate, the degree of their own accountability, the variable quality of annual reports and the effectiveness of these in holding the PS accountable, given the lack of notice which is taken of them. The Lloyd review of BOVs in 2001, whilst detailing these and other criticisms, nevertheless held it to be vital that lay monitoring of prisons continues as essential to such a closed system. The review also felt that 'regular contact with interested members of the local community, if they manage to project the best qualities of humanity and understanding which can be found in society outside, can of itself bring benefit to both prisoners and staff'.[62]

10.4.4 *Association of Prisoners*

A more recent move to inject some accountability has come from within the prison population itself with a move by ten prisoners in HMP Nottingham, on October 2, 2000, to form the Association of Prisoners [AOP].[63] One of the proposals of the Association, under the General Secretary John Hirst, a serving prisoner, is that every prison should have a representative who would air grievances before a committee, the decision of which the governor would be obliged to accept and act upon. Criticisms of the association largely centre upon the diversity of the prison population, lacking a common interest, rendering the association inappropriate, also the fact that the natural choice of long-term prisoners as the basis of the organisation would render the association non-representative.[64]

10.5 THE PRISON POPULATION AND REGIMES

Over and above particular regimes specifically tailored to categories of offenders, a prison is run on a day-to-day basis on the principle of dynamic security. The theoretical base for this has its roots, as have many PS developments, in the Woolf Report, and poses that where prisoners are occupied by routines and activities prison order will be maintained and an ordered and active prison will engender a safe prison. How staff integrate with prisoners on a daily basis is thus part of a regime designed to make prisoners feel safe and thereby less motivated to pose a control problem.

There has thus been a move away, in principle, from the 1980s tendency to lock prisoners in their cells for lengthy periods and provide them with sparse activity when unlocked. Regimes must meet minimum standards, such as an average of at least 24 hours per prisoner per week spent in purposeful activity enshrined in one of the published PS KPIs. That said, a report by the European Committee for the Prevention of Torture and Inhuman or Degrading Treatment or Punishment [CPT] on their visit to the U.K. in 2001, highlights just how 'flexible' entitlements are. They discovered at Feltham young offenders institute out-of-cell time of one hour per day with outdoor exercise was the exception

---

[62] *Review of the Board of Visitors: a report of the working group chaired by the Rt. Hon. Sir Peter Lloyd, MP*, Home Office, 2001, p. 27. There have been 5 reviews of BOVs since 1984.

[63] An official response from the PS in the matter of the AOP has yet to be formed.

[64] For arguments for and against an AOP, see John Hirst and Joan Aitken in Forum in M.Leech and Cheney, D., *The Prisons Handbook 2002*, p. 558–562.

rather than the norm. They identified that in order to ensure prisoners are guaranteed a basic requirement of at least one hour of daily outdoor exercise, rule 30 of the Prison Rules 1999 should be amended.[65]

How a prisoner serves his/her sentence, what is offered to them in their regime, is integral to the goal of breaking the cycle of re-offending. As the Prisons Minister has stated: 'The Prison Service receives people whom largely the other public services—education, health, employment—have already failed. Unless we get to grips with some of their problems that contribute to their offending, we will continue those failures'.[66]

10.5.1 *Incentives and Earned Privileges*

The establishment of an Incentive and Earned Privileged Scheme [IEPS] in June 1995 was a further step to introducing a national framework whereby regime specifics and incentives would be standardised, as recommended by the Woolf Report. The scheme links with the dynamic security equation, being designed to create a disciplined environment, and thereby a controlled environment, safe for both prisoners and staff alike. Three levels of regime are offered, basic, standard and enhanced, through which prisoners' progress via responsible behaviour and constructive work and activity and the national framework sets down seven key earnable privileges. These are: access to private cash; extra/improved visits; enhanced earning schemes; earned community visits; own clothes; time out of cell and in-cell television.

Examples of key earnable privileges:

	Disciplinary minimum	Basic	Standard	Enhanced
Convicted				
Private cash	Nil spends for 42(adult) 21(YO) days	£2.50per week	£10per week	£15per week
Visits (quantity)	Restrictable to basic level for 42(adult) 21(YO) days	Two half hour or one hour visits per 28 days.	At least 3 visits per 28 days.	Typically 4 or 5 one hour visits per 28 days.
Unconvicted				
Private cash	As above	£15per week	£30per week	£30per week

[65] R. 30 provides, 'weather permitting and subject to the need to maintain good order and discipline, a prisoner shall be given the opportunity to spend time in the open air at least once every day, for such a period as may be reasonable in the circumstances'. See the *CPT Report to the Government of the U.K. on the visit to the U.K. from February 4–16, 2001*, CPT/Inf (2002) 6, Strasbourg April 18, 2002, para. 58. The government Social Exclusion Unit have recorded that the average time spent in YOIs on purposeful activity remains lower than that in adult prisons and young prisoners are twice as likely to spend 23 hours or more in cell than their adult counterparts. See *Reducing Re-offending by ex-prisoners* (Social Exclusion Unit, Home Office, July 2002), p. 3.

[66] Prisons Minister Beverley Hughes, speaking at the PS Conference 2002, *Prison Service News*, No. 207, (March 2002), p. 8.

Visits (quantity)	As above	Total of 1.5 hours per week.	Higher than basic	Higher than standard

That said, it is not always possible for an establishment to offer all of these as local circumstances and the class of prisoner held will be the deciding factor in which are to be adopted and which, of necessity, rejected. For example, time out of cell and earned community visits are privileges where sentence criteria and risk assessment are important considerations that might render them being offered impossible or inappropriate. It is clear then that the ideal is tempered across establishments by such concerns and this is also the case in respect of available resources, for example, staffing levels will influence adoption of the full enhanced visit entitlement. Given that the system also has its very foundation in officer/ prisoner interaction, to monitor, measure and react to behaviour and reward accordingly, where staff resources are slim prisoners are at a disadvantage.

Further criticism of the IEPS lies in the fact that whilst there may be a standard system of incentives as Woolf envisaged, there is little in the way of standardisation of the ideals of behaviour required for basic, standard or enhanced. This has led to disparity between prisons with arbitrary regard to what behaviour warrants reward. On the flip-side, whilst withholding or removing privileges must not be associated with guilt or punishment, the Prisons and Probation Ombudsman has recorded instances where the system has indeed been used as a 'secondary disciplinary system'.[67] As a motivator to improved behaviour, IEPS has also been criticised as offering minimal distinctions between the three stages that affords little attraction for prisoners to make an effort. In addition, the criteria to 'trade visits' for conduct, is tantamount to penalising the families of prisoners.

10.5.2 *Security Categories*

Security categories govern the distribution of prisoners and their regimes and, with the exception of women (discussed later) these are:

Cat. A: those whose escape would be highly dangerous to the public or to State security.

Cat. B: those for whom the highest conditions of security are not necessary, but for whom escape must be made very difficult.

Cat. C: prisoners who are considered not to have the will or resources to make a determined escape attempt, but who cannot be trusted in open conditions.

Cat. D: prisoners who can be trusted in open conditions.

These categories were established by the Mountbatten Report, following the spectacular and highly publicised escapes of two of the Great Train Robbers, Charles Wilson from HMP Birmingham in 1964 and Ronnie Biggs from HMP Wandsworth in 1965, and from HMP Wormwood Scrubs in 1966 of the spy

---

[67] See for example, *PPO Annual Report 2001–2002*, pp. 69 and 71 at http://www.ppo.gov.uk.

George Blake. The day-to-day operation of categorisation is in many respects controversial (see criticisms raised in the annual reports of the PO) but there is no doubt that security, and threats to this and thereby order within prisons, have been catalysts for changes in day to day operation since the Woolf Report investigation of the prison riot in Manchester in April 1990. Two significant reports, those of Learmont[68] and Woodcock[69], delivered a disasterous blow to the far-reaching, reccommendations made by Lord Woolf. Both reports created waves of policy change in respect of privileges and practices, affecting both the quality of a prisoners' daily life and rehabilitation.[70]

The difficulty faced by the PS in offering valuable regimes to what is a disparate population, is immense. The basic skills of most prisoners are very poor with 80 per cent and 50 per cent respectively having the writing and reading skills of an 11 year old, and 65 per cent the numeracy skills of a child of that age. Young prisoners between 18–20 have basic skills over a third worse than older prisoners. Add to this the fact that 70 per cent of prisoners will be fighting a drug misuse addiction and the same number will be suffering from at least 2 mental disorders, and the enormity of the challenge is made clear.[71]

10.5.3 *Remand Prisoners*

Arguably the most comprehensive appraisal of regimes offered by the PS to the remand population takes the form of a thematic review undertaken by HMCIP.[72] The pen-picture of this section of the prison estate is of isolated and anxious individuals, who have experienced trauma in their domestic lives and who, prior to entering custody, were without work and dependent upon the State. A significant number were abusing drugs and alcohol, and many had children. As a group the remand population were identified as having more health problems, in particular mental health, than the sentenced population, with high levels of psychiatric morbidity.[73]

The most significant differences between the remanded and sentenced populations lie within the category of contact/communication in that both domestic visits and correspondence opportunities are more generous in respect of quantity and quality. Prisoners have higher limits on the use of private cash, are permitted to wear their own clothes (unless a unconvicted Cat. A prisoner and there is reason to believe there is a serious risk of the prisoner attempting escape), vote,

---

[68] Sir John Learmont, *Review of Prison Security in England and Wales and the escape from Parkhurst Prison on Tuesday 3 January 1995*, Cm. 3020, HMSO, 1995.

[69] Sir John Woodcock, CBE, QPM, *Report of the Enquiry into the escape of six prisoners from the special security unit at Whitemoor prison, Cambridgeshire on Friday 9 September 1994*, Cm. 2741, (HMSO, 1994).

[70] One direct result was the introduction of volumetric control limiting prisoners in cell possessions to those which can be fitted into two boxes measuring 0.7m × 0.55m × 0.25m, with a volume of 0.9625 cubic metres. This in particular affected the quality of life of long term prisoners. Another effect, attending directly upon efforts to rehabilitate prisoners back into the community prior to their release, was the immediate curbing of home leave and release on temporary licence and prohibitions with regard to the quality of visits.

[71] *Reducing re-offending by ex-prisoners* (Social Exclusion Unit, Home Office, July 2002), p. 3.

[72] *Unjust Deserts: A thematic review by HM Chief Inspector of Prisons of the treatment and conditions for unsentenced prisoners in England and Wales* (Home Office, December 2000). Fieldwork covered 11 establishments (raised to 37 by inclusion of findings from HMCIP reports of the previous 2 years) and 700 prisoner surveys.

[73] In 2001, 11,241 people were on remand, one in six of the overall population. *See Reducing re-offending by ex-prisoners* (Social Exclusion Unit, Home Office, July 2002), p. 143.

be treated by an outside doctor/dentist and are not required to work. The PS Statement of Principle in respect of this group states:

'Unconvicted prisoners are presumed to be innocent. Subject to the duty to hold them and deliver them to court securely and to the need to maintain order in establishments, they will be treated accordingly and, in particular, will be allowed all reasonable facilities to: seek release on bail, preserve their accommodation and employment, prepare for trial, maintain contact with relatives and friends, pursue legitimate business and social interests, obtain help with personal problems. They will receive health care appropriate to their needs. They will have opportunities for education, religious observance, exercise and recreation and, where possible, for training and work'.[74]

One of the major problems identified by the thematic review was in respect of bail and legal help, where the experience of prisoners was at variance with claims made by governors of establishments. Less than half of those who wanted to see either a Bail Information or Legal Services Officer had received contact, 75 per cent of young and 69 per cent of adult remands remained without such contact, and in one YOI no young prisoner had succeeded in seeing either officer. Time out of cell varied enormously between establishments from being unlocked virtually all day to being locked in cell almost all day and, when out of cell, there was a general paucity of opportunity for purposeful activity, work and education. In particular the allocation for physical training of one hour per week for an adult and two per week for a young prisoner, was considered far too low to meet the need for self achievement. The resettlement opportunities pledged by the Statement of Purpose were also found wanting in practice. Not least, 37 per cent of prisoners had lost their homes as a result of coming to prison and yet only 9 per cent of those who sought help on housing had received it. The Social Exclusion Unit have recorded that remand prisoners are half as likely to have participated in work whilst in prison, with young people 20 per cent less likely to have attended education classes. With regard to help with resettlement and release, they are half as likely as sentenced prisoners to have obtained such advice.[75]

What the review of the remand population particularly highlights is the acutely damaging effect of local prisons generally, on their prisoner complement. The review suggests this to be largely the result of a clash between a diverse prisoner population, inadequate physical facilities and overcrowding, and a prison officer culture of disengagement with prisoners and resistance to change.[76]

10.5.4 Women Prisoners

In recent years the experience of prison for women has been transformed in respect of their achieving a distinct status as 'women prisoners'. During the period of the early prisons there was no segregation of male and female prisoners and it was the Goal Act of 1823, which marked the beginning of the sexes being held separately and of women placed solely under the supervision of women jailers. This move toward an 'improvement' for women was largely the result of

[74] *Prisoners' Information Book: Male and Young Offenders*, HM PS & Prison Reform Trust, 1999, p. 17.
[75] *Reducing re-offending by ex-prisoners* (Social Exclusion Unit, Home Office, July 2002), p. 146.
[76] The review concludes with a statement of intention to follow up the report in two years and to monitor the conditions of unsentenced prisoners in the ongoing HMCIP inspection programme.

reformers such as Elizabeth Fry, less motivated by genuine concern for the women themselves than the affront to sensibilities of the scandal of pregnancies conceived during sentence. The 'penitent' approach adopted with women offenders was their re-education into a femininity they had broached by their (unfeminine) criminal behaviour. As such 'women's work' was their lot in terms of prison occupation, and it was only in the 1970s that vocational courses for women prisoners was introduced. The maternalistic and medicalised approach to women prisoners under the care of female officers was to change in 1976 when the Sex Discrimination Act ushered in their being placed under the supervision of both male and female prison officers.

That said, women have not until recent times been recognised as a distinct category of prisoner. The classic manifestation of this is the PS form on which to record injuries to prisoners, this adopts an outline of a body bearing no female characteristics. As a section of the prison population, they have been, to adopt the terms of Devlin, 'Invisible Women'.[77] The Prison Rules apply to men and women alike, the only specific reference to women being Prison Rules 12(1) and (2).[78] Virtually the only difference which traditionally existed between men and women was in respect of their being allowed to wear their own clothes[79] and to change their hair without prior permission[80].

In 1997 HMCIP published a thematic review, the subject matter of which was women prisoners.[81] It was a detailed and hard-hitting report. In January 1998 a Women's Policy Group [WPG] was established within the Directorate of Resettlement at PS headquarters, with a brief to ensure that the needs of women and female YOIs, criminogenic and other, should be reflected in the development of PS policy and regimes. In 1999 the WPG published a report on mothers and babies in prison, encompassing both appraisal of and recommendations for, the current practice.[82] In October 2000 a consultation document was published on the Government strategy on women offenders and in July 2001 a Women's Policy Team was established in the Home Office to co-ordinate policy and research in relation to women.

The characteristics of women prisoners have been clearly established by the 1997 HMCIP thematic review and the follow-up to this report undertaken by HMCIP in 2001.[83] Whilst their number in 1991 were 1,559, this had reached 3,940 by January 2002 and at the time of writing the women's estate is comprised of 3,738 adult females and 643 female young offenders, a total of 4,481.[84] A quarter of these women are held on remand and over 65 per cent do not go on to receive a custodial sentence.[85]

The findings of HMCIP in respect of the characteristics of women offenders have changed little since a Home Office study undertaken of 200 women pris-

---

[77] See A. Devlin, *Invisible Women: what's wrong with women's prisons* (Waterside Press, 1998).

[78] PR 12(1) Women prisoners shall normally be kept separate from male prisoners. PR 12(2) The Secretary of State may, subject to any conditions he thinks fit, permit a women prisoner to have her baby with her in prison, and everything necessary for the baby's maintenance and care may be provided there (YOI R. 22).

[79] A matter which operates to the disadvantage of women in respect of volumetric control.

[80] Males must seek permission before growing or shaving off a beard, for example.

[81] *HMCIP, Women in prison: a thematic review* (Home Office, 1997).

[82] *Report of a review of principles, policies and procedures on mothers and babies/children in prison* (HMPS, 1999).

[83] *Follow-up to women in prison: a thematic review by HMCIP* (Home Office, June 2001).

[84] http://www.hmprisonservice.gov.uk.

[85] Lyon, J., 'Women who Offend', *The Magistrate*, April 2002, p. 105.

oners between 1993 and 1994. They are relatively young, with little skills in paid employment and, prior to being imprisoned, will have lived solely off benefits. The majority are primary carers of children with 55 per cent of women prisoners having at least one child under 16 and over one third having a child under 5.[86] Only 25 per cent of their children will be being looked after by their biological fathers, compared with 90 per cent of the children of the male population. The educational level of women in prison is lower than that of male prisoners, one study finding 74 per cent had left school when they were 15 or 16.[87] The majority will have suffered abuse and have drug and alcohol problems, with sentenced women having a higher rate of previous psychiatric treatment and deliberate self-harm than the male population, with around two thirds of the population self-harming in custody.[88] That in many cases their high levels of social and economic deprivation which have led to their offending is not turned around by the prison experience, is evident: 'A recent NACRO survey found that 45 per cent of women leaving prison expected to be homeless and a Home Office study found that only 25 per cent of women interviewed a few months after release had got jobs'.[89]

Findings by HMCIP in the 2001 follow-up thematic review confirmed the significant improvements that have been made following the appointments of a Head of Women's Policy Group and subsequently Operational Manager of Women's Prisons. In particular the Inspector praised the improvement of health care regimes, increased awareness of abuse issues, developments in maintaining family contact and increased recognition of the needs of the foreign national women's population (of which the latter accounts for between 20–25 per cent). Concern remains, however, that security arrangements have not been relaxed, despite the fact women prisoners do not pose a major risk to prison order or the public. General conditions and treatment of juvenile and young adult female prisoners remains a concern, not least as conditions for this group have not reached the standard achieved for males since the introduction of the Youth Justice Board. Furthermore, the practice of holding young women alongside adult women continues.[90]

Categorisation for women takes a different form than that for the male population, being designated Open, Semi-open[91], Closed and Local, the exception being that a woman may be allocated Cat. A status. The majority in this latter category will be lifers and the manner in which the prison system treats women lifers has given cause for concern for a number of years, and was the subject of a Howard League briefing paper in 1999.[92] Their small number has worked against them, policy making no distinction between males and females serving life and only as recently as January 2002, with full amalgamation of the Review and Management Sections of the Lifer Unit, have the case working teams included one solely responsible for women lifers.[93] The establishment of an

[86] HMCIP, *Women prisoners: a thematic review* (Home Office, 1997).

[87] Hamlyn B. & Lewis, D., *Women prisoners: a survey of their work and training experiences in custody and on release* (Home Office Research Study No.208, 2000).

[88] Details compiled from research and thematic reviews.

[89] Lyon, J., 'Women who offend', *The Magistrate*, April 2002.

[90] For further discussion of reform for the women's prison population see D.Wedderburn, *Justice for Women: the need for reform, the report of the committee on women's imprisonment*, Prison Reform Trust, 2000.

[91] Prisoners who present a low risk to the public but who require a level of physical perimeter security to deter abscond, Prison Service Instruction 43/00.

[92] *Life in the Shadows: women lifers* (Howard League, 1999).

[93] 'All Change in Lifer Unite', *Prison Report*, Issue No. 58, Prison Reform Trust, July 2002, p. 5.

Operational Manager for Women's Prisons will surely impact upon what has been a marginalized group.

Of the 140 existing prisons, there remain only 17 for women, including one shared Cat. A status facility and four Mother and Baby Units [MBU]. Of the MBU facilities, two permit babies to remain with their mother until 9 months of age and two up to 18 months.[94] Of the 125,000 children affected by the imprisonment of a parent each year, it is estimated that 10,000 children every year are affected by the imprisonment of their mother.[95] Women are not automatically permitted to have their baby with them and demand is high and the criteria stringent, with the threat of babies being taken away from their mothers a (distasteful) potential control issue.[96] As a result of the increasing numbers of women going to prison, HMP Buckley Hall has been re-roled from a male to a female prison and two new prisons are planned,[97] however this paucity of number means that women will continue to be held further away from their families than the male population.[98]

With the recent recognition of a distinct women's estate, much of the nature of how women are currently dealt with behind prison walls promises to change and hitherto uncharted areas are being explored, not least a lifer programme for women and sex offender treatment programme for women. A new dialectical behaviour therapy to address the behaviour of women with borderline personality disorder is currently being piloted in 3 women's prisons.[99] As the WPG have been quoted as saying:

'We have been given a real "window of opportunity" to make a difference—to develop a better understanding of the needs of women; to provide regimes that will be better equipped to meet those needs; and also to build a culture and ethos in the women's estate as a whole that will support them'.[100]

The major difficulty resides in introducing these changes whilst there is a population explosion of the women's estate. Between 1993 and 2000 the female

---

[94] Prison Service Order 4801 refers. In May 2001 two cases before the Divisional Court challenged this policy, incorporating a challenge under Article 8 of the European Convention on Human Rights and UN Convention on the Rights of the Child. A judicial review before the Queen's Bench Divisional Court followed. See *R. (on the application of P) v. Secretary of State for the Home Department* [2001] All E.R. (D) 278 *(Jul) and R. (on the application of Q and another) v. Secretary of State for the Home Department* [2001] All E.R. (D) 278 (Jul).

[95] Lyon, J., 'Women who offend', *The Magistrate* (April 2002), p. 105.

[96] For further details of MBUs see, *Department of Health, Inspection of facilities for mother and babies in prison: a report on the third multi-disciplinary inspection conducted by the Department of Health,* (DofH, 1996), HMPS, *Mother and Baby Units* (1992), HMPS, *Working on a mother and baby unit: helping mothers care for their babies* (1993); *Imprisoned women and mothers* (Home Office Research Study 162), Research and Statistics Directorate, 1997; *In the best interest of babies?, the Howard League submission to the Prison Service review of mother and babies in prison* (Howard League 1999).

[97] In Ashford Middlesex, for 450 women, and in Peterborough for 360 women.

[98] In response to a parliamentary question on January 15th 2001, the Home Secretary Paul Boateng confirmed that 41,000 prisoners were held over 25 miles from their home, with 15,000 held between 50 and 100 miles from home. The result of questionnaires from prisons inspected by HMCIP between December 1, 1999 and November 30, 2000, 29% of women at Eastwood Park and 41% of women at Holloway, received less than one visit per month. By comparison, findings over five male local prisons recorded the highest number of male prisoners receiving less than one visit a month was 15 per cent (Brixton) and the lowest 3 per cent (Wandsworth).

[99] *Prison Service News* No. 208, (April 2002), p. 9.

[100] *Prison Service Journal* (November 2000).

population rose by an astounding 115 per cent and between April 2001 and April 2002, by just under a quarter.[101]

10.5.5 *Juveniles and Young Offenders*

The average young offender will have had a disruptive family life. They will probably have been in care (adult prisoners are 13 times more likely to have been in care than the average person) and will have experienced poor parenting interest, have truanted or been excluded from school (only 16% of 16 year olds in custody have previously been in mainstream education). All have a poor sense of their own future. A quarter of young offenders in custody are either parents or about to be, and young men with criminal parents are four and a half times more likely to offend than those without.[102] Their health will be poor, they will have abused drugs and alcohol, and be at risk of suicide and self-harm. They will have difficulty with relationships, be immature and impulsive and respond to frustration with violence, will fail to see the consequences of their actions and lack of empathy for their victims. In sum, being both volatile and vulnerable, they pose a demanding prison population.[103]

A number of reports catalogue the problems faced both by young prisoner and prison staff caring for them, in meeting the needs of this section of the population.[104] Not least it has been suggested that the street culture rules of young offenders may be solidified by prison subculture, leading them to indulge in bravado, bullying, and to challenge both the staff and the rules of the prison.[105] A central difficulty in dealing with them in a prison setting is achieving a balance between allowing them to be normal adolescents, whilst maintaining overall control. HMCIP has identified key elements staff should encourage, which include providing a significant adult role-model to ensure a positive adult relationship in their lives (one which respects and values them); providing a prosocial atmosphere, and opportunities to take responsibility.

A young offender is a prisoner aged 18–21 years and a juvenile, aged 17 years and under. In January 2002 there were over 8,000 young adults in custody, of which 7,500 were male, and 2,450 under 18 years of age, as of June 2002 there are 10,917 male and 643 female, young offenders, a total of 11,560.[106] England and Wales imprison more children and young people than any comparable European country, with an average of 10,000 plus 15–21 year olds locked up annually.[107] In March 2002 there were 2,915 juveniles being held in secure

---

[101] For an overview of how the PS is tackling the population explosion, see *Prison Service News* No. 209 (May 2002), p. 10–13.

[102] *Reducing Re-offending by Ex Prisoners*, Social Exclusion Unit 2002.

[103] See (Bryans), 'Viewpoint: young offenders', M.Leech & D.Cheney, *The Prisons Handbook 2002*, (Waterside Press), p. 386–387.

[104] HMCIP, *Young Prisoners: a thematic review* (Home Office, 1997); HMCIP, *Suicide is Everyone's Concern: a thematic review* (Home Office, 1999), J.Lyon & A.Wilson, '*Tell them so they listen': a message from young people in custody* (Home Office, 2000), A.Neustatter, *Locked in, locked out: the experience of young offenders out of society and in prison* (Calouste Gulbenkian Foundation, 2001), Prisons Ombudsman, *Listening to young prisoners: a review of complaints procedures in young offender institutions* (2001); HMCIP, *A Second Chance: a review of education and supporting arrangements within units for juveniles managed by HM Prison Service 2001–2002* (Home Office, 2002).

[105] HMCIP, *Young offenders: a thematic review* (Home Office, 1997), p. 17.

[106] http://www.hmprisonservice.gov.uk, (June 28, 2002).

[107] A.Neustatter, 'Viewpoints: young offender institutions', *The Magistrate*, (June 2002), p. 172.

accommodation, of which 334 boys and 84 girls were being held in non-Prison Service accommodation.[108] In July 2002 there were 2,740 15–17 year old males and 156 15–17 year old females in Juvenile Young Offenders Institutions.[109] Young offenders are held in either closed or open young offender institutions [YOI][110] (unless female in which case they are held alongside adult women) and, whilst instances of juveniles held in PS custody has given rise to concern in the past, they are also largely held in secure accommodation or local authority run supervised secure premises.[111] On the last visit to the U.K. in 2001 by the European Committee for the Prevention of Torture and Inhuman or Degrading Treatment or Punishment [CPT], Hillside Secure Centre and Medway Secure Training Centre were inspected. Both held girls and boys older than 12 and younger than 18, Hillside having a capacity of 18 and Medway 44. The CPT report emphasised the need for a positive and personalised environment and in particular, physical activity and intellectual stimulation. The CPT commended the aspirations to address offending behaviour, foster skills and attitudes, and build up the self-esteem of the minors by encouragement and recognition of achievement which was absent in their former environments.[112]

Separate prison rules govern the young offender population, but the regime elements to which they are subject remain essentially the same as those for adult males, distinguishing factors being differentiated awards for punishments and IEP categories. The distinction between YOI and adult establishments is instead on the overall philosophy, the input to specific needs of young males in order to prevent re-offending. Currently approximately 88 per cent (nine in ten 15–17 year olds) and 75 per cent (three in four 18–21 year olds), re-offend within two years of release.[113] Thus addressing educational shortcomings and offending behaviour directly, providing vocational training and strengthening family ties, is paramount to counter the social dysfunctionality that characterises this group. In sum, a much more imaginative approach now governs how young adults are dealt with, compared to their traditional 'warehousing'.

The introduction of the Detention and Training Order [DTO],[114] for offenders under 18, marked a clear distinction between young adults and juveniles. There were 5,500 DTOs made in a 9 month period in 2001, compared with 4,200 over the same period in 2000 and the probation union have stated that the rise in the number is such that positive work with young offenders is being threatened.[115] Concern has surrounded children under 18 being held in prison, expressed not least by HMCIP who, in his 1997 thematic review, recorded: 'The Prison Service is essentially an organisation for adults, neither structured nor equipped to deal with children ... More damage is done to immature adolescents than to any other type of prisoner by current conditions'. There are currently 13 PS establishments

---

[108] *Reducing re-offending by ex-prisoners* (Social Exclusion Unit, Home Office, 2002), p. 154.

[109] *Justice for All*, Cm. 5563, July 2002, p. 140.

[110] In accordance with the Criminal Justice Act 1988.

[111] Under s. 123(4) of the Criminal Justice Act 1988 the Home Secretary may require a young offender to serve his sentence in an adult male establishment.

[112] Report to the Government of the U.K. on the visit to the U.K. from February 4–16, 2001, CPT/Inf (2002) Strasbourg April 18, 2002, paras 100–117.

[113] Ross, I., *Viewpoint: Release*, M.Leech & D.Cheney, *The Prisons Handbook 2001* (Waterside Press, 2001), p. 363.

[114] Introduced in April 2000 to replace Detention in a YOI for 15–17 year olds and Secure Training Order for the 12 to 15 years age group.

[115] Fletcher, H., National Association of Probation Officers, *British youth jails at crisis point*, prisonact-list@prisonactivist.org, April 2, 2002.

in the under 18 estate and the regimes operated at these are outlined in PSO 4950. Inter-agency co-operation characterises the regime, given that the DTO combines a sentence served both in custody and under supervision within the community, and a 'seamless sentence' is the ultimate aim. The prison regime requires a busy individually tailored programme with dedicated staff building up a constructive relationship with the offender that enables them to feel both safe and secure.[116]

In their July 2002 proposals, the Government announced their aim to pilot a 'Going Straight Contract' for 18 to 20 year olds, a group for which there is currently no specific provision, based on the importance of effective rehabilitation, to reduce re-offending. Under this proposal prisoners will sign a rehabilitation contract covering the whole of their sentence, both in prison and in the community. Employing a system of award and sanctions, prisoners would be required to follow an individually tailored agreed programme and also make payments from prison earnings to make reparation to victims and contribute to the provision of post-release support mechanisms.[117]

10.5.6 Male Prisoners

As of June 2002, the adult male prison population was 55,935.[118] Their regime is that which forms the generic basis for all the groups set out above, with their own specific needs appended. In a system designed and organised for adult males, groups such as women and young offenders are only in very recent times being conceptualised as very distinct groups, for which the adult male approach falls short in delivery. The regime elements discussed here thus apply equally to the aforementioned groups.

The daily regime for all prisoners is structured from the moment they wake. Whilst specifics vary between prisons by virtue of the size of the population, security category and mix of prisoners, an average day might last from 0745 hs to 2100 hs. Between breakfast, lunch and evening meal prisoners should expect, as a basic day, opportunities for work,[119] education and training,[120] relaxed association with other prisoners,[121] physical exercise,[122] religious

---

[116] For a view on the necessity for specialised, targeted interventions for prisoners under 18, and a critique of the environment prisons offer such offenders, see C.Day, *Viewpoint: prisoners under 18,* Leech, M. & Cheney D., *The Prisons Handbook 2001* (Waterside Press), p. 390–391.

[117] *Justice for All,* Cm. 5563, July 2002, 6.28–6.31 at p. 110–111.

[118] http://www.prisonservice.gov.uk, June 28, 2002.

[119] Prison R. 31(1) requires convicted prisoners to do 'useful work' for a maximum of 10 hours per day whilst Prison R. 31(5) states that, whilst they may wish to do so, unconvicted prisoners do not have to work. Prisoners are not covered by minimum wage legislation (see s. 45 of the National Minimum Wage Act 1998), and work available and local rates of pay vary, subject also to IEP.

[120] Three out of five prisoners are excluded from 96 per cent of all jobs as a result of their poor basic skills. Improvement of these is at the centre of the partnership launched in April 2001, between the PS and Department for Education and Skill. A PS core education curriculum has been established to secure literacy and numeracy, social and life, and basic skills, as an essential foundation for reintegration into an offence-free lifestyle on release from prison. In 2001–2002, prisoners achieved 16,000 Level 2 basic skills qualifications that could help them find a job.

[121] Prisons differ in respect of the amount of time out of cell, association, and exercise offered, and Prison R. 30 which establishes a criteria of providing a 'reasonable time' in the open air every day, assures this is consistently variable. The provision is also, as many aspects of prison life are, subject to IEP.

[122] Health related physical activity is favoured by the PS, with a view to prisoners hopefully adopting a lifestyle change, in addition to awards for PE skills, which offer potential employment opportunities.

observance,[123] visits (both legal and family),[124] healthcare[125] and facilities to telephone[126] and correspond[127] with outside contacts. Restrictions on, and variations within, these activities, are subject to such elements as prisoner status, IEP, and strictures of punishment determined by adjudications for breach of prison discipline.

Constructive activity in the form of Offending Behaviour Programmes [OBP] are also available, but not throughout the prison estate. It is thus possible that a prisoner who requires such input as part of their sentence plan may wait some considerable time before transferring to an establishment where these are offered, and even then face a delay due to pressure of demand. Given that OBP forms an integral part of risk assessment and progress by a prisoner in this regard is essential to decisions such as parole or recategorisation to a different security category, delays can have damaging effects. Where courses are offered these include Reasoning and Rehabilitation, Enhanced Thinking Skills, Anger Management and Cognitive Self Change Programmes, in addition to a family of five Sex Offender Treatment Programmes.[128]

Opinion on the benefit of these programmes is mixed. Lack of practical relevance to lifers and long-term prisoners, disadvantage to short-term prisoners, inherent necessitated vulnerability for those taking part (which can be exploited as a weakness), and accessibility for prisoners whose standard of educational levels is not high, form just some of the criticisms. At the core however is the unpalatable truth that if a prisoner does not take part, because they feel there is nothing meaningful to gain or, indeed, if they are professing innocence, such failure will be seen as a refusal to address risk factors, thus impinging directly

---

[123] The PS is committed to accommodating all religious observance, as per Prison Service Order 7A. Whilst each prison Chaplain is required by the Prison Act 1952 to be a Church of England adherent, a Chaplaincy team of different religious observants normally shares the role of pastoral care. A PS Directory and Guide on Religious Practices is available to ensure that festivals and holy days (requiring excusal from work or fasting), religious diets and the requirement for religious artefacts, are catered for.

[124] The number of visits, plus matters as to whether a prior Visiting Order is needed and what, if anything, can be handed in on visits, are subject to unconvicted/sentenced status, IEP, and the multifunctional status of the prison itself.

[125] Prisoners are entitled to the same quality and range of healthcare as that afforded by the National Health Service, and have the same rights to accept or decline treatment as the general population. The Government is investing £42 million over three years in the improvement of healthcare facilities and, under the Mental Health-In-Reach Programme, 300 community psychiatric staff will be provided by the NHS to work in prisons. See Justice for All, Cm. 5563, July 2002, 6.14 at p. 107.

[126] The majority of prisons now operate a PIN phone system, established to prevent contact with victims. A definitive list of numbers for family, friends and legal contacts must be submitted and these will be the only numbers prisoners can call, with the addition of organisations such as the Samaritans and Criminal Cases Review Commission. The prisoners' designated PIN number must be entered before dialling the numbers and if there are reasonable grounds to intercept a call this is permitted under s. 2 of the Interception of Communications Act 1985. The level of PS monitoring of calls varies according to high/low risk prisoners and any information received which suggests a prisoner may be involved in criminal activities.

[127] Unwarranted interference with a prisoner's private life, freedom of expression, and access to the legal system, must be held in balance with the necessity to ensure that illicit content is not being despatched or received via correspondence. Legal correspondence, including that to the Prisons Ombudsman, is privileged and cannot be stopped or read without identifiable grounds, and then in the presence of the prisoner. Prison R. 39, YOI R. 14 and SO 5B 32(3) refer.

[128] For a full outline of these and their availability, see J. Parkin, *Offending Behaviour Programmes*, Leech, M., & Cheney, D., *The Prisons Handbook 2002* (Waterside Press, p. 295–301). There are plans for further programmes covering domestic violence, adult and youth acquisitiveness and booster programmes for all areas (the latter currently confined to SOTP).

upon progress through a sentence plan.[129] Of recent times, attention has also been drawn toward the paucity of women-centred OBP and this is a concern the women's estate is now beginning to address.

The issue of typical drug abuse amongst offenders prior to entering prison, and indeed of drug abuse within the prison setting, has ensured that treatment and prevention in this field forms a large part of a prison regime, for both prisoners and their visitors.[130] Male and female alike share the process, with the sole exception of select criteria for strip-searching of males and females. The Prison Service Standard on Drug Strategy states:

> 'Staff in all establishments will work to ensure a continuing reduction in the availability of drugs through a range of supply reduction methods, identify prisoners who are drug misusers, provide them with the opportunity for treatment and support to help them avoid drugs and reduce the risk of them committing drug related crimes after their release'.

Thus random drug testing by urine sample, voluntary drug testing compacts and rehabilitation and detoxification programmes form part of a massive PS strategy. In addition, in 1999, the PS introduced a Counselling, Assessment, Referral, Advice and Throughcare service [CARAT] to identify prisoners for referral immediately on reception to prison and thence assess and work toward detoxification and drug free release, which latter offers a maximum of 8 weeks post-release support.[131] In 2000–2001 there were 3,100 entrants to the 50 intensive treatment programmes for prisoners. The importance of the CARAT service cannot be underestimated, with drug users more likely to re-offend on release and also be at high risk of drug related death in the first few weeks following release.[132]

All prisoners are subject to prison rules and a list of disciplinary offences is contained in both the Prison Rules and Young Offender Institution Rules.[133] The most recent inclusions were four disciplinary offences relating to racist behaviour by prisoners, in July 2000.[134] When a charge is raised against a prisoner they appear for adjudication by a governor grade at which a prisoner should be given 'a full opportunity of hearing what is alleged against him and of presenting his own case'.[135] A great deal of criticism and controversy surrounds the operation of the disciplinary system and claimed justice and fairness. Not least complaints by prisoners about adjudications consistently top the list of those received by the Prisons Ombudsman and it is arguable that the process will face a great challenge

---

[129] For two views on OBP by serving prisoners see: T.Carrigan and L.Wicks in M.Leech & D.Cheney, *The Prisons Handbook 2001* (Waterside Press), p. 285–286 and 2002, p. 301–302. See also the investigation by the Prisons Ombudsman of the IEP scheme discriminating unfairly against prisoners who asserted their innocence, *Annual Report 2000–2001* at http://www.ppo.gov.uk.

[130] 80% of males and 75% of female remand prisoners admit prior drug use and 51% of males and 54% of females drug dependency. In 2000, 521 visitors were arrested for attempting to smuggle drugs into prison. Justice for All, Cm. 5563, July 2002, p. 131.

[131] For more detail on these topics, see Cheney, D., '*Drugs & Alcohol in Prisons*', *The Prisons Handbook 2002* (Waterside Press), p. 328–335.

[132] *Justice for All*, Cm. 5563, July 2002, 6.15 at p. 107 and 8.29 at p. 127.

[133] R. 51, *Prison Rules 1999*; R. 50, *YOI Rules 1988*.

[134] R. 51(A), 51(17A), 51(20A) and 51(24A) for racially aggravated assault, racially aggravated damage, threatening, abusive or insulting racist words or behaviour and threatening abusive or insulting racist words, drawings, symbols or other material.

[135] Prison R. 54 and YOI R. 52. A Prison Discipline Manual was produced by the PS in 1995 in an attempt to ensure consistency in the disciplinary system.

to retain legitimacy in the light of the Human Rights Act 1998 (discussed later).[136]

10.5.7 *Life Sentenced Prisoners*

The prison lifer population encompasses, over 21, the Mandatory and Discretionary lifer and, under 21, Custody for life, Detention during Her Majesty's Pleasure and Detention for Life. At any one time there are approximately 4–5,000 lifers in the system (predicted to rise to 7,000) and the average sentence served is 12–15 years. Of those natural lifers who are reviewed after 25 years, and thence every 3 years, a decision is taken in respect of whether they can be moved to a fixed tariff.

Cullen and Newell record that this group are distinguished by virtue of being likely to be unmarried white males between 20 and 30 who have a dysfunctional background, and that 90 per cent will have taken one life (in all probability of someone they knew). Around 1,400 lifers suffer from a psychiatric condition and in the last 10 years the rate of imprisonment for this group has doubled, with discretionary lifers serving longer than the mandatory 15year average. In the words of Cullen and Newell:

'Lifers make the best prisoners. Every Governor would like to hold lifers. They are generally sensible, mature, non-criminal, stabilising, quiet and intelligent. They understand the rules of the game and they accept them because it makes for a peaceful life inside, and it is the only sure way of earning release. Measured on the league table of risk as a prisoner, lifers represent the lowest risk'.[137] Given these characteristics, the positive and stabilizing influence of lifers renders them a useable 'control' tool in an establishment, arguably flying in the face of equitable and just containment.

The PS Standard with regard to the life sentence is that:

'All life sentenced prisoners will be managed with the aim of meeting their individual needs during sentence. The aim is to reduce risk so that release can take place on tariff expiry where the risk to public safety is assessed as manageable and continues to be manageable after release'.[138]

However the creation of their maximum dependence also makes the assessing of the group for their ability to survive independent freedom a bureaucratic nonsense. A similar hurdle to progression through sentence and their eventual rehabilitation is the unpalatable truth that the PS Lifer Manual describes those who maintain their innocence as 'undeniably difficult'. Treatment programmes (notably SOTP) require prisoners to take responsibility for the consequence of their (alleged) offending behaviour and actively acknowledge guilt, or worsen their situation.[139]

Allocation of lifers is undertaken centrally by the Lifer Management Unit

---

[136] Also for a full discussion of the issues see Cheney, D., *et al.*, *Criminal Justice and the Human Rights Act 1998* (2nd ed., 2001, Chap. 6 '*Prisoners' Rights*', especially 6.3.3.
[137] *Prison Service Journal* (1999) and Coyle, A., *The Management of Prisoners Serving Long Sentences*, ICPS address to the Department of Justice, Barcelona November 11, 2001.
[138] For the full PSN see http://www.prisonservice.gov.uk.
[139] A 'throffer', offer to reward/threat to punish. For a detailed account of lifers, see Cullen, E., & Newell, T., *Murderers and Life Imprisonment* (Waterside Press).

[LMU].[140] The aim is progression to lower security conditions and eventual release, through a structured sentence. Newly sentenced lifers are immediately assigned a Wing Lifer Personal Officer and their risk of self harming or attempting suicide is assessed. A Life Sentence Plan [LSP] is prepared and the prisoner should be moved to a First Stage prison [FSP] within 6 months. However for those convicted of sex-related offences, who must be placed at a FSP which offers a sex offender treatment programme [SOTP], it is often difficult to meet the 6 month criteria by virtue of the fact SOTP is not available nationally and the demand is great.[141]

The FS prison, High Security or Cat. B, will be home for the lifer for 18 months and upwards, and it is here that offending behaviour needs are addressed and future projections are decided upon. After being moved to their Second Stage prison [SSP], the lifer will be held until such time as they prove suitable to be transferred to a low security establishment. Time spent at the SSP will incorporate most of the necessary offending behaviour work and planning for release, and it is here that the prisoner must demonstrate significant and sustained progress, self-reliance and self-discipline. After full risk assessment, escorted absences from the prison are made available to assist in the prisoners' adjustment to life in the community. The prisoner reaches the low security Third Stage Prison [TSP] only after a Parole Board recommendation with ministerial and Lifer Unit approval, and even then an average of 2 years precedes release on Life Licence, to ensure final testing of the prisoner.[142]

This seemingly smooth process is however very different in design and practice. As the Prison Reform Trust have discovered: 'In theory a prisoner's progress through a life sentence is the result of careful, local and individualised planning and evaluation. In practice, the system often seems illogical, chaotic and perverse'.[143] The number of Parole Board Reviews alone, and time taken to complete them (each around 9 months), means large numbers of lifers are not released until 12 months or more after their tariff expiry date.[144]

The situation for young lifers,[145] and the support available to them during sentence to address offending behaviour whilst assisting them to adolescence, poses very specific management problems. Not least they are likely to move from a child centred establishment, through a YOI, to an adult prison and individual adult identity, all significant changes that raise their own psychological demands.

In September 2001 the European Committee for the Prevention of Torture and Inhuman or Degrading Treatment or Punishment [CPT] published their 11th

---

[140] As of July 2002 this comprised 8 case working teams, including one with sole responsibility for young lifers and women. See 'All Change in Lifer Unit', *Prison Report*, Issue n. 58, Prison Reform Trust, July 2002, p. 5.

[141] For details and availability see Parkin, J., '*Offending Behaviour Programmes*', in M.Leech & Cheney, D., *The Prisons Handbook 2002* (Waterside Press), p. 295–303.

[142] Life sentenced prisoners have lower reconviction rates on release. Of the 1,587 released between 1972 and 1994 in England and Wales, 9 per cent were reconvicted of an offence within 2 years, compared to 57 per cent of all prisoners discharged in 1996 who were reconvicted during the same period. *Prison Statistics for England and Wales* (Home Office, HMSO, 2000).

[143] *Prison Service Journal* (March 1999).

[144] In March 2002 *Prison Service News* reported that, in future, decisions on Parole Board recommendations for transfer of lifers to open conditions will be made by the Lifer Unit. The new arrangement is hoped to expedite the review process. *Prison Service News*, No. 207, (March 2002), p. 9.

[145] Between 10 and 17 years of age, sentenced under the Children and Young Persons Act after conviction for an offence that, in the case of an adult, would carry a sentence of 14 years or more.

General Report and included in this their concerns over the deleterious and desocialising effects of restrictions applying to life sentenced prisoners. They found that: 'the situation of such prisoners left much to be desired in terms of material conditions, activities and possibilities for human contact' and were particularly critical of restrictions being applied indiscriminately to all lifers, irrespective of individual risk.[146]

10.5.8 *The Therapeutic Community Prison*

In 2000 HMP Grendon celebrated its 40th anniversary as a therapeutic community [TC], a position it has uniquely held since opening.[147] However the same year saw an expansion of therapeutic places with the opening of Dovegate (places for 200 male adults) and a facility at Send (40 adult women). The ethos of the TC, as a democratised community, requires staff and prisoners alike to subscribe to common expectations in respect of duties and responsibilities, and prisoners to account for their behaviour to other prisoners. This would seem to be a contradiction in a prison setting, but Grendon have proven this wrong.

All prisoners who arrive at Grendon have volunteered to be there and have been interviewed and assessed prior to being accepted to ensure their intelligence is average or above and that they are of robust psychological fibre. Each wing of the prison is a self-contained community. The beliefs which inform how they are run are democracy, responsibility, tolerance and community, factors which in turn empower, confront and support. Therapy in every aspect of daily life is the all pervasive ethos of the prison whether it be through psychotherapy, aversion therapies, psychodrama, art therapy, or even through how community meetings examine publicly the actions of individuals or vote on whether one of their number should stay at the prison. The therapeutic work '... is about trying to unearth unconscious feelings, memories and attitudes that are involved in offending; trying to unearth things that may have happened many years ago, and which may be consciously forgotten, but which sit in the unconscious, silently controlling behaviour. The therapeutic community is in effect an environment designed to be sufficiently flexible and unstructured to allow the less logical and more primary process parts of the members to emerge'.[148] The success of this approach has been underlined by research findings that prisoners treated at Grendon have lower reconviction rates than would be expected had they not gone there.[149]

---

[146] *11th General Report on the CPT's Activities*, CPT/Inf (2001) 16, Strasbourg September 3, 2001, p. 17. For a detailed discussion of the problems faced by lifers, see A.Coyle, *The Management of Prisoners Serving Long Sentences*, ICPS, presentation to the Department of Justice, Barcelona, November 22, 2001, http://www.kcl.ac.uk/depsta/rel/icps/home.html.

[147] Grendon was the brainchild of Dr Norbert East and Dr W.H.Hubert whose 1939 report, *The Psychological Treatment of Crime*, recommended a specific type of prison to deal with 'abnormal and unusual types of criminal'. See B.Healey, *Grendon a History: 1939–2000* (HMP Leyhill, January 2000) and Dr E.Cullen (*Grendon and future therapeutic communities in prison*), (HMP Leyhill, January 2000) and within a series of Prison Reform Trust Reports, '*Achieving Prisons*'.

[148] Healey, B., *Grendon, a history: 1939–2000* (HMP Leyhill, 2000), p. 65.

[149] For a detailed account of the work at Grendon, see Genders, E., and Player, E., *Grendon: a study of a therapeutic prison* (Oxford University press, 1995); Cullen *et al.* (eds), *Therapeutic Communities for Offenders* (John Wiley & Sons, 1997) and Healey, B., *Grendon, a history*. For findings on reconviction rates see Marshall P., *A reconviction study of HMP Grendon Therapeutic Community*, Research Findings No. 53, HO Research and Statistics Directorate, 1997 at http://www. home-office.gov.uk/rds/index.htm.

10.6 RELEASE

A central aim of both the prison and probation services is the successful resettlement of offenders back into the community. This should be accomplished through regimes which promote responsible behaviour, address offending behaviour, work to acquire education and skills, involve both sentence planning and a proactive approach to resettlement needs.

As Pryor, a prison governor himself, states:

'... prisons are designed to remove responsibility. That is what the community asks the court to do; to limit the choice to break the law. And prisons to limit the choice to wander at will. And many prisoners show by their attitude and behaviour that this was entirely justified, often for more reasons than were apparent to the Court. The fact remains however that you can't lock people up just because they are unpleasant, or even because they are dangerous, if the sentence does not allow it. The fact is that people other than Lifers will be released, and the Prison Service has to make the best of the job in ensuring a proper resettlement plan'.[150]

Ideally, a prisoner should be working toward release from the first day of reception into a prison and offending behaviour courses are a large part of preparation for release, however few prisons offer an accredited 'pre-release course' and where they are offered, their effectiveness is questionable. In addition there is a tendency for short-term prisoners to be disadvantaged by virtue of the time and opportunity afforded to do meaningful work in preparation for release.[151] This is itself a grave cause for concern, given that 66 per cent of the national convicted population are short term prisoners serving less than 12 months.

Essential resettlement knowledge should include that in respect of housing, education and employment, support to counter addiction, benefits and, crucially, reintegration into the community. Reinforcing the importance of these areas, particularly for the short-term prisoner, are the findings of an inter-agency project. In a survey of one local prison, releasing 70 per cent of its population into the immediate community, 25 per cent of prisoners had over 31 previous conviction, 55 per cent 10 or more and the average number of offences committed before first conviction were 48. As a group, 61.2 per cent of the prisoners had no formal qualifications, 84 per cent had used drugs (77 per cent daily) and 75 per cent spent over £25 per week on alcohol.[152]

Morgan and Owers found that insufficient priority is given to both resettlement work and outcomes by the PS, and that provision was patchy and not needs-related. Results of their survey on preparation for release record that only about 10 per cent of those surveyed (9 per cent of the women) said they had attended a pre-release course, with 20 per cent stating they had chosen not to. Of the automatic unconditional release prisoners surveyed, 7 per cent had attended a

---

[150] Pryor, S., *The responsible Prisoner: an exploration of the extent to which imprisonment removes responsibility unnecessarily and an invitation to change* (Autumn 2001). Available at the website of HMCIP, http://www.homeoffice.gov.uk/hmipris/hmipris.htm.

[151] See Leech, M., & Cheney, D., *A Report into Inmate Development & Pre-release Courses at HM Prisons Wymott and Elmley*, available from UNLOCK, the National Association of Ex-Offenders and at http://www.tphbook.dircon.co.uk.

[152] Kent Police research found, of 134 offenders, they had been in custody 1,345 times, been charged with 674 offences and been linked as a suspect or offender to 1,783 offences. See *Short Term Prisoner Project: An inter-agency response to persistent offending* (HMPS, Kent Probation Service and Kent County Constabulary, HMP Canterbury).

course and 12 per cent chose not to. The remaining 70 per cent of those surveyed, and 81 per cent of those interviewed stated they had not attended a course because none was available or they did not know whether one existed.[153]

The crucial importance of preparing prisoners adequately for return to the community cannot be underestimated. The reality is that in many cases their sentence may make the factors associated with re-offending worse. For example 'a third lose their house while in prison, two-thirds lose their job, over a fifth face increased financial problems and over two-fifths lose contact with their family'.[154]

10.6.1 *Release on Temporary Licence*

Two specific types of release on licence are designed to assist prisoners toward a seamless release and encourage the pursuit of a future law-abiding life. These are the Facility Licence and Resettlement Licence, both privileges subject to risk assessment. The Facility Licence is available for a specific and not social purpose, to Cat. C or D prisoners who have served at least one quarter of their sentence. It is granted for attendance at job interviews, to obtain accommodation and to undertake paid employment. The Resettlement Licence has the core purpose of strengthening family and community ties and offering the opportunity to make arrangements for accommodation, work and training on release. The Licence is available to adult prisoners sentenced to four years or more after October 1, 1992, to be taken no earlier than their parole eligibility date and after a parole decision has been made. Those adult or young offenders who have been sentenced to less than four years, but a minimum of one year, may apply for the licence after a third of their sentence or four months after sentence (whichever is longer) has been completed.[155]

10.6.2 *Home Detention Curfew*

The Crime and Disorder Act 1998 introduced the Home Detention Curfew [HDC] scheme, which commenced on January 28, 1999. Eligible prisoners, who have reached the age of 18 and are serving sentences of under four years, but over three months, are considered automatically for the scheme, subject to risk assessment. HDC release, between two weeks and two months before the automatic release date, requires a prisoner to be electronically monitored through the wearing of a tag, and consent to remain at their address at specific times. If a prisoner breaches the conditions or is charged with an offence whilst on HDC, s/he will be recalled to prison and forfeit the opportunity to benefit from the scheme during a future sentence.[156] The Home Secretary David Blunkett announced that the introduction of presumptive HDC would commence at the beginning of May 2002. From that date prisoners serving sentences of between 3

---

[153] Morgan, R., and Owers, A. *Through the prison gate: a joint thematic review by HM Inspectorates of Prisons and Probation*, (2001), p. 48.

[154] *Reducing re-offending by ex-prisoners*, (Social Exclusion Unit, Home Office, 2002). The Government White Paper, Justice for All, Cm. 5563, July 2002 records that 43% of sentenced prisoners and 48% of remand prisoners state they have lost contact with their families since entering prison, see p. 85.

[155] Prison Reform Trust & HMPS, *Prisoners' Information Book: Male Prisoners and Young Offenders*, Chap. 5. See http://www.hmprisonservice.gov.uk; http://www.prisonreform.demon.co.uk.

[156] Prison Reform Trust & HMPS, *Prisoners' Information Book*, Chap. 6. http://www. hmprisonservice.gov.uk; http://www.prisonreform.demon.co.uk.

months and under 12 months will be released on HDC for the latter part of their sentence, unless there are compelling reasons not to do so. Those released will exclude those convicted of violent or serious drugs offences and prisoners who have any history of sexual offending.[157]

A study commissioned by the PS into the first 16 months of the operation of HDC records:[158]

Table 10.3

Total prisoners discharged	126,400
Number eligible for HDC	72,400
Eligibility rate per discharged population	57%
Number released on HDC	21,400
Release rate per those eligible	30%
Number recalled	1,100
Recall rate as per those on HDC	5%
Average number on curfew at any time	2,000

Between 1999 and 2001, over 44,000 prisoners have been released on HDC and less than 2 per cent have offended during their time under curfew.[159] As of June 28, 2002 there are 2,327 prisoners on HDC.

10.6.3 *Eligibility for Release*

Table 10.4

Sentenced before 1.10.92			
Parole date	*Parole granted*	*Parole refused*	YO supervised for
1/3 of sentence	Probation supervision up to 2/3 point	Unconditional release at 2/3 point	minimum of 3 months, even if beyond sentence expiry or to aged 22years. Additional days awarded set back release date and parole eligibility but not sentence expiry date

[157] *Prison Service News*, No. 208, (April 2002), p. 6.
[158] Dodgson et al., Home Office. Research Study 222: *Electronic monitoring of released prisoners: evaluation of the HDC*, 2001. For an analysis of the study see R.Morgan and A.Owers, *Through the Prison Gate: a joint thematic review by HM Inspectorates of Prisons and Probation*, Chap. 7.
[159] *Prison Service News*, No. 208, (April 2002), p. 6.

Sentenced on/after 1.10.92			
Under 12 months	*12 months to under 4 years*	*4 years or more*	Some sex offenders will be supervised until sentence expiry date.
If not released on HDC unconditional release at ½ way point.	If not released on HDC, conditional release at ½ way with supervision to ¾ point.[160] Since April 2001, local probation boards have a statutory duty to consult and notify victims about release arrangements for offenders serving 12 months or more for a sexual or violent offence.	Release on parole at ½ way or automatic release at 2/3 point and supervision to ¾ point.	All schedule one sex offenders must register with the police on release. All prisoners remain 'at risk' until end of sentence. Additional days awarded set back release date and parole eligibility but not sentence expiry date.

Discretionary [DL] and mandatory lifers [ML]

Sentencing	*Ist Parole Review*	*Parole Reviews*	*Tariff expiry*	If not released at tariff expiry, parole review every 2 years.
Minimum tariff set.	3 years before tariff expiry or 3 and a half years if in Cat C for 12 months.	Every 2 years or shorter period. Conducted on papers for ML and orally for all other lifers.	DL oral hearing before Discretionary Life Panel. ML interview with parole board member and review by parole board. (but see discussion of *Stafford v. the United Kingdom* discussed below)	If released, subject to life licence and risk of recall to prison for natural life. The release plan is subject to outcome of requirement that the Probation Service contact the victim or their family.

Creighton records that the Human Rights Act 1998 [HRA] has impacted upon the period between parole reviews for indeterminate prisoners who have completed their tariffs (other than mandatory lifers). Both the number of Parole Board Reviews and the time taken to complete the reviews, has resulted in severe delays to release. Judgments before the European Court have held that 2 year review periods do not satisfy the speedy review of detention required by Article

---

[160] The Government have proposed that for all prison sentences of 12 months and over, other than for dangerous offenders, automatic release would be at the halfway point, with licence conditions extending until the end of the entire sentence. *Justice for All*, Cm. 5563, 5.37 and 5.38 at p. 95.

5(4) of the Convention and also that the HRA requires a review take place promptly on expiry of tariff.[161]

A recent ruling in the European Court of Human Rights has exercised this very issue by holding, in *Stafford v. the United Kingdom*, that Article 5(4) of the HRA 1998 applies to mandatory lifers who have completed the tariff period of their sentence. Whilst the powers of the Secretary of State to set tariffs remains unaffected by the judgement, his or her power to veto Parole Board recommendations has been affected. In addition, prisoners whose tariff has expired will have an entitlement to oral parole hearings. The effects of the judgement, in May 2002, were immediately seen in the release on parole of Satpal Ram, who was released in June 2002 after having served 15 years of a life sentence handed down in 1987.[162]

10.6.4 *The Parole Board*

Parole has its historical origins in the Ticket of Leave given to transported convicts and which entitled them to work on their own account and have freedom within the colony. This was granted after a number of years during which the convict had demonstrated good behaviour. When penal servitude was introduced in 1853 for those who would have been transported, the system remained and the Penal Servitude Act 1857 introduced a formal scheme of earned remission and this was extended in 1898 to all prisoners.

In 1964 a Labour Party study recommended the establishment of a Parole Board[163] and a government white paper the following year supported the proposal of an earned period of freedom on parole, over and above the one third remission system.[164] The Parole Board was established in 1968 under the Criminal Justice Act 1967 and became an independent executive on July 1, 1996 by virtue of the Criminal Justice and Public Order Act 1994. Legislation governing their powers to consider release and recall of prisoners are entailed in the Parole Board (Transfer of Functions) Order 1998,[165] Criminal Justice Act 1991,[166] Crime (Sentences) Act 1997.[167]

At the heart of the decisions made by the Parole Board is the question whether, if a prisoner is released, will the safety of the public be put unacceptably at risk. To determine this, the Board must be satisfied that the prisoner has recognised, and carried out, the necessary work to deal with the features of his/her crime.[168] A large part of assessing this is to determine whether the prisoner understands

---

[161] See Creighton, S., 'Life Sentences', in M. Leech and D. Cheney, *The Prisons Handbook 2002* (Waterside Press), p. 391–392.

[162] See 'New Ruling', *Prison Report*, Issue No. 58, Prison Reform Trust, July 2002, p. 5; Vikram Dodd, 'Asian who killed man in race row freed after 15 years', *the Guardian*, 19 June 2002; 'Saptan Ram calls for unlawful imprisonment enquiry' *the Guardian*, 19 June 2002.

[163] As at July 2002 the Parole Board is comprised of a Chair, Judicial members (33), psychiatrists (22), probation staff (9), criminologists (5) and independents (51). See http://www.hmprisonservice.gov.uk, press release July 2002.

[164] *Crime: a challenge to us all* (1964); *The Adult Offender* (1965). The Criminal Justice Act 1967 gave prisoners entitlement for consideration for release on parole.

[165] To decide upon applications from prisoners serving under 15 years and for those serving over 15 years make a recommendation to the Secretary of State.,

[166] To decide on the early release of determinate sentenced prisoners serving 4 years or more and revoke licences.

[167] To release mandatory and discretionary lifers and those persons detained at Her Majesty's Pleasure and serving life sentence under s. 109 of the Powers of Criminal Courts (Sentencing) Act 2000, and to revoke licences.

[168] For example, the risk factors of alcohol, drugs, attitudes to women and anger management.

how personal attitudes and lifestyle at the time of the offence led to the crime, and whether attitudes and behaviour have been modified to the extent the prisoner can avoid similar situations on release. The importance of a realistic and supportive release plan is also taken into consideration.[169]

Government proposals for sentencing reform, announced in July 2002, would change the remit and role of the Parole Board, making the release of all juveniles sentenced for serious crimes subject to a Parole Board decision. If taken forward, discretionary release would apply only to dangerous, sexual and violent offenders, all other prisoners being subject to community supervision after serving the custodial part of their sentence.[170]

10.6.5 *Reducing Re-offending*

A report by the Social Exclusion Unit records that of those 58 per cent of prisoners (72 per cent young offenders) reconvicted in the 2 years following release, each will have received an average 3 further convictions, for each of which 5 recorded offences are committed.[171] Highlighting proven links between social exclusion and re-offending, the report recommends measures for the Prison Service to adopt to ensure a rehabilitative focus and to close this 'revolving door'. They identify 9 key factors that influence re-offending, all of which should be addressed during sentence: education, employment, drug and alcohol misuse, mental and physical health, attitudes and self-control, institutionalisation and life skills, housing, financial support and debt, and family networks. In sum, 'the task is not to resettle prisoners in society, but to settle them for the first time'.[172]

As part of this process the Government announced, in July 2002, their proposals for new innovative sentences, and reform of short custodial sentences, to combine custody with community activity and punishment with rehabilitation. The decision to seek reform of short sentences is prompted by the knowledge that high re-offending rates for this group suggests there has been little opportunity for meaningful behavioural or rehabilitation work to be done. Looking to offering more support on release, a new sentence of Custody Plus would require a prison sentence of up to three months, followed by compulsory supervision in the community for the entire 12 month sentence. Another proposal, that of Intermittent Custody, equally seeks to strengthen family and community ties, without compromising on punishment. Under this proposal, offenders would serve their custodial sentence either at weekends or during the week, whilst the remainder of their time would be spent in the community, enabling them to continue in employment and meet family responsibilities.[173]

These significant moves towards minimising recidivism are further evident in Government proposals to act upon criticisms of the archaic Rehabilitation of Offenders Act 1974 [ROA]. In July 2002 the Home Office issued a report reviewing the ROA with a view to making the act pro-active in reducing crime. The review found that hitherto the act has been limiting the prospects of the resettlement of ex-offenders, making it virtually impossible for them to put their

---

[169] For full details of the work of the Parole Board, see http://www.paroleboard.gov.uk.
[170] *Justice for All*, Cm. 5563, July 2002, 5.45 and 5.46, p. 96.
[171] *Reducing the risk of re-offending by ex offenders*, Social Exclusion Unit.
[172] Social Exclusion Unit, *Reducing re-offending by ex-offenders*, (July 2002), p. 4. See http://www.cabinet-office.gov.uk/seu/index.htm.
[173] *Justice for All*, Cm. 5563, July 2002, Chapter 5, in particular 5.37–5.38 and 5.33–5.36.

past behind them. The objective behind revising the Act is: 'to provide a clear and coherent balance between the interests of those who have been convicted of a crime, but now want to lead constructive and law-abiding lives, and those vulnerable people who deserve protection from those who may continue to pose a risk.[174] The main findings of the report concluded that over a quarter of the working age population has a previous conviction and that whilst employment can reduce re-offending by between one third and one half, a criminal record can seriously diminish employment opportunities. The very title of the review 'Breaking the Circle', suggests that review of the ROA will stand alongside measures proposed in 'Justice for All', to tackle re-offending proactively and decisively.

10.7 PRISONERS AND THE HUMAN RIGHTS ACT 1998

Historically the European Court has for a number of years impacted upon areas of prison life such as jurisdiction over prison administration, access to lawyers and the courts, disciplinary hearings, release procedures and living conditions. It is therefore not surprising that with the coming into force of the Human Rights Act, the PS would look to policies and practices with a view to deflecting challenges. Arguably, uncharacteristic proactive measures which have been set in train in the last 2 years—have been prompted in part by the HRA. These include the individualising of the women's and under 18 estates, focus on child protection measures, appointment of Race Equality and Muslim Advisors and new procedures for mother and baby units. A more direct identified innovation was the discontinuance of strip-searching procedures for prisoners identified at risk of suicide and self-injury on the grounds it was likely to be challenged under Article 3.[175]

The potential importance of the HRA for prisoners is summed up by the view of the current Director General that:

> 'Prisons are of their very nature inward-looking. Sometimes that inwardness makes them bleak and dangerous. Closed from outside influence they can degenerate and, at worst, prisoners can be abused and brutalised. This is a real and constant danger because for perfectly good reasons prisons are not easy to penetrate'.[176]

That said, the very pursuit of challenges under the Act will not be an easy task for prisoners. As Quin states: 'In the wider society the little person who stands up for their rights against the excesses of bureaucracy of the State is seen as something of a hero. If that person is a prisoner, they are likely to be seen as a nuisance, a subversive or a trouble-maker'.[177] That this statement has more than a ring of truth about it is suggested by the findings of the Prison Ombudsman of reprisals exacted against a prisoner who pursued a legitimate complaint to his office.[178]

---

[174] *Breaking the Circle: A Review of the Rehabilitation of Offenders Act 1974*, http://www.homeoffice.gov.uk/roareview, 10 April 2002.
[175] PSI 27/2000. Art. 3: Right to freedom from torture and inhuman or degrading treatment or punishment.
[176] Narey, DG Martin speaking at a conference at Huntercombe YOI, *Prison Service Journal*, No. 131, September 2000, p. 5.
[177] Quin, P., Perrie Lectures, 1998.
[178] *The case of Mr A (10001/00), Prison Ombudsman Annual Report 2000–2001*, Cm. 5170 (July 2001), p. 20. See http://www.ppo.gov.uk.

A brief consideration here of the areas of prison life where the HRA might make a considerable difference to prisoners, also highlights some of the main difficulties faced by the PS and areas in which they have attracted much criticism. These include the large numbers of suicide and self-harm cases, circumstances of deaths in custody, continued overcrowding, the conduct of disciplinary hearings, conditions for the disabled and mentally ill, discriminatory practices, and the effect of prison processes on family life.

10.7.1 *Vulnerable Prisoners*

According to Prison Reform Trust, too many mentally-ill young people are in prison with more than 9 out of 10 young offenders having at least one mental health problem and more than half on remand having a mental disorder. Conditions such as schizophrenia and manic depression are 50 times more common among sentenced male prisoners than 16 to 19 year olds in the community.[179] The European Committee for the Prevention of Torture and Inhuman or Degrading Treatment or Punishment have raised concerns in respect of the mental health of prisoners, not least with regard to how Close Supervision Centres tend to be an 'end of line' facility for some prisoners suffering from mental disorders, a highly unacceptable state of affairs.[180]

Over a quarter of male remand prisoners and half of all women prisoners have attempted suicide in their lifetime and the suicidal group are 4 or 5 times more likely to have several categories of mental disorder simultaneously. The majority of deaths take place in local prisons, in single cells, healthcare centres, and segregation units, by hanging using bedding as a ligature at a window ligature point. There were 72 suicides in prison in 2001, 81 in 2000 and 91 in 1999.[181] The highest number of self-inflicted deaths by sentence length, are found amongst lifers, and those serving up to 12 months, and (taking the local prison as an example), the majority will commit suicide after they have been at the establishment up to 7 days, between one week and 12 months, and between 2 to 6 months.[182] The PS recognised in an internal review in 2001 that under-emphasis on prevention, poor implementation of policies and resource problems are all factors in which they fell short and a 3 year implementation strategy to reduce suicides commenced in February 2000.[183]

Article 2 of the HRA, which protects the right to life, is a possible source of challenge to the manner in which documentation in respect of the suicidal is handled, care for the vulnerable, safety measures and adequate supply of healthcare.[184] The proactive responses of the PS to phase out the use of strip cells for the suicidal and to discontinue strip-searching of those at risk, both suggest the recognition by the Service of their vulnerability to challenge in respect of the

---

[179] Prison Reform Trust, *Troubled Inside* (2001).

[180] Report to the Government of the U.K. on the visit to the UK from February 4–16, 2001, CPT/Inf(2002) 6, Strasbourg April 18, 2002, paras 63 and 78.

[181] For a breakdown of the figures see Deaths in Custody in *The Prisons Handbooks 2000, 2001* and *2002*, Leech M. & Cheney D. (Waterside Press).

[182] Sources: *HMCIP, Suicide in Prisons: thematic review*, (1984), A.Liebling, *Suicide in Prison (1992), HMCIP, Suicide is Everyone's Concern*, (1999), HMPS, *Prevention of Suicide and Self-harm in the Prison Service*, Internal Review, 2001.

[183] *The Safer Local Prison Programme*, final evaluation due December 2003.

[184] See *R. v. Chief Constable of Dorset Police, ex parte (1) Josette Fuller (2) Amanda Wright (3) Tina Tarr (4) Julie Booth and Secretary of State for the Home Department (Interested Party)* 2002.

fact they have a duty to take reasonable care to prevent a deliberate act of self-harm and a suicide which is a forseeable consequence of a failure in that duty.[185] A similar duty extends to the actual effect of prison conditions on mental health[186] and the duty to protect prisoners from others who may wish to do them harm[187] and from bullying and abuse.[188] Perhaps it is as a result of the ackowledgement of the vulnerability of prisoners in these areas that, at the time of writing, the Government are considering giving the Prisons and Probation Ombudsman power to investigate suicides.[189]

10.7.2 *Prison Conditions and Overcrowding*

In *Ireland v. UK*[190] the Court held inhuman treatment to be that which deliberately causes severe mental or physical suffering and degrading treatment that which arouses in its victims feelings of fear, anguish and inferiority capable of humiliating or debasing them. Article 3 in respect of freedom from torture and inhuman or degrading treatment and punishment is applicable equally to matters such as the effect of prison conditions on mental health raised above.[191] In addition, procedures at visits and reception, during strip-searching and drug testing, during medical treatment and adjudications, and the conditions of prisoner transport and severity of segregation, are areas providing potential challenges.[192]

Conditions of detention specific to segregation units have already been challenged[193] but with the massive increase of the prison population, overcrowding (in itself) may yet give rise to a challenge on the grounds of inhuman and degrading treatment. The Council of Europe Committee for the Prevention of Torture [CPT] have recorded their concerns that overcrowding leads to cramped

---

[185] For breaches of duty by the police facilitating suicide see *Sheila Reeves (Joint Administratrix of the Estate of Martin Lynch Deceased) v. Commissioner of Police for the Metropolis* [1999] 3 W.L.R. 363; *Osman v. UK* [1999] 1 F.L.R. 193; *R. v. Secretary of State for the Home Department ex parte John McFadyen* [2002] Q.B.D. March 4, 2002. For a discussion of this issue see Cheney et al., *Criminal Justice and the Human Rights Act 1998*, Jordans, 2001, p. 200–203.

[186] See the findings of HMCIP in respect of Close Supervision Centres, HMCIP, *Inspection of Close Supervision Centres: August-September 1999: a thematic inspection* (Home Office, 2000).

[187] See *John Gill v. The Home Office* [2000] L.T.L. July 6 and in particular the Case of *Paul and Audrey Edwards v. UK, Application Number 00046477/99, REF00003449*, March 14, 2002 in which the European Court held violation of Art. 2 regarding both the circumstances of their son's death and the failure to provide an effective investigation. For a full account of the death of Christopher Edwards and the personal account of his parents, see Edwards A. and Edwards, P., *No Truth, No Justice*, (Waterside Press, 2002).

[188] A concern raised by HMCIP, Ford, R., 'Patrol shortages endanger prisoners', *The Times*, 2000.

[189] *Justice for All*, Cm. 5563, July 2002, 6.39 at p. 112.

[190] *Ireland v. UK* (1978) 2 E.H.R.R. 25.

[191] Actions which are such that they could 'destroy the personality and cause severe mental and physical suffering', have been considered actionable by Strasbourg. See *X v. UK* (1981) 21 D.R. 99 as quoted in Livingstone, S., and Owen, T., *Prison Law: text and materials*, (Oxford University Press, 1993), p. 107.

[192] *Hurtado v. Switzerland* (1994) has established that in some instances humiliation can qualify under Art. 3, see R. English in *Analysis of the Convention and the Human Rights Act 1998* (One Crown Row, Human Rights Interactive); handcuffing prisoners en route to court may be a contravention as claimed by the Magistrates Court Service, Gibb, F. 'Handcuffs breach human rights', *The Times* June 13, 2000.

[193] See *Ireland v. UK* (1978) Series A/25, p. 162 and *Delazarus v. UK* and *Windsor v. UK* (both unreported) quoted in Creighton S., and King V., *Prisoners and the Law*, (Butterworths, 1996), p. 219–220.

and unhygienic accommodation; a constant lack of privacy (even when performing such basic tasks as using a sanitary facility); reduced out-of-cell activities and an overburdenend health-care service.[194] Any PS claim of 'safe' overcrowding is likely to be countered by the CPT in the terms: 'It is a fundamental requirement that those committed to prison by the courts be held in safe and decent conditions. For so long as overcrowding persists, the risk of prisoners being held in inhuman and degrading conditions will remain ...' even if conditions [there] are 'safe' according to Prison Service criteria, in the view of the CPT they can hardly be qualified as decent.[195] The specifics were stated clearly by Coyle when addressing the Committee on Legal Affairs and Human Rights at the Council of Europe Parliamentary Assembly in 2002. Prison overcrowding can: violate the rights to life and security of the person, have potentially dangerous public health effects, seriously affect the ability to control crime and violence within the prison, and make it impossible to deliver international requirements on separation of prisoners such as men from women, young from adult and pre-trial from convicted.[196]

With the quite staggering increase in recent years of the population of female offenders, and lack of prisons available which has made the PS resort to re-roling a male prison, women-specific overcrowding challenges are equally an issue. The CPT have singled out a 'number of hygiene and health issues in respect of which the needs of women deprived of their liberty differ significantly from those of men' stating that 'the failure to provide such basic necessities can amount, in itself, to degrading treatment'.[197]

10.7.3 *Disciplinary Procedures*

As the annual reports of the Prisons and Probation Ombudsman make clear, by far the largest single component of the workload of the office, every year, are complaints concerning prison discipline and in particular the operation of adjudications (see the figures in the Prisons Ombudsman section). Not least, failure to keep a contemporaneous hand-written record of what has transpired during an adjudication, which disadvantages any effective appeal, and failure to enquire into the prisoner's defence, always figures highly.

Inappropriate punishments, given most decisions to charge prisoners are inherently discretionary, and harsh use of the punishment of added days to a sentence, were applied until July 2002 without thought being given to the European Court of Human Rights,[198] despite the fact that the Director General had gone on record stating the Service might be 'vulnerable in the area of adjudica-

---

[194] Report to the United Kingdom Government on the visit to the United Kingdom and the Isle of Man carried out by the European Committee for the Prevention of Torture and Inhuman or Degrading Treatment or Punishment from September 8–17, 1997 CPT/Inf (2000) 1 (Strasbourg, January 13, 2000).

[195] *Response of the United Kingdom Government to the report of the European Committee for the Prevention of Torture and Inhuman or Degrading Treatment or Punishment on its visit to the United Kingdom and the Isle of Man* CPT/Inf (2000) 7 (Strasbourg, May 11, 2000) para. 59.

[196] Coyle, A., ICPS, speaking in Paris on March 19, 2002. Available at http://www.kcl.ac.uk/depsta/rel/icps/home.html.

[197] European Committee for the Prevention of Torture and Inhuman and Degrading Treatment or Punishment, *10th General Report on the CPT's Activities* CPT/Inf (2000) 13 (Strasbourg, August 18, 2000) paras 30 and 31.

[198] See *Prisons and Probation Ombudsman Annual Report 2001–2002*, p. 78–83.

tion and additional days'.[199] For example, in the 2001–2002 annual report of the Ombudsman he records 7 added days and 7 days forfeiture of privileges for being in bed after 10 am on a Saturday, 3 added days for lending a beard trimmer, and 7 days for disobeying an order to remove a tray of pork from an oven due to religious objections. In all cases the Ombudsman recommended the punishment be remitted or suspended. The Home Office have estimated that on any one day, the prison population is increased by 1,050 as a result of additional days handed down by governors in disciplinary proceedings.[200]

The PS Instruction which was issued to provide guidance on the implications of the 1998 Act includes the warning that

> 'It is therefore very important that governors do not impose punishments which are disproportionate to what is necessary, taking account of all the circumstances of the case, to achieve their aim, namely to act as a deterrent to that prisoner and others in order to ensure good order and discipline in the prison'.

This Instruction formed part of the evidence considered by the European Court of Human Rights in July 2002, when reaching a decision in the case of *Ezeh and Connors v. the United Kingdom*.[201] The Court held that the nature of the charges against Ezeh and Connors, adjudicated upon by a governor, together with the nature and severity of the potential and actual penalties,[202] led to the conclusion that both applicants were subject to criminal charges within the meaning of Article 6(1) of the Convention and that Article 6 thus applied to their disciplinary proceedings.[203] Accordingly, the Court further held that denial by the Governor of a right to legal representation breached Article 6(3).[204] Whilst an appeal is planned, the Prison Service must now ensure that disciplinary proceedings, where added days are involved, must comply with the right to legal representation and an independent adjudicator, enshrined in Article 6.[205]

Historically, by far the most contentious areas of challenge in respect of adjudications have related to matters such as prisoners' access to information and legal representation, the opportunity for a prisoner to prepare a case and their procedural disadvantage. These, together with the very status of adjudications in respect of the impartiality and fairness of the proceedings, will surely continue to be tested, following the decision in *Ezeh and Connors*.[206]

---

[199] Gibb, F., and Ford, R., 'Prison chiefs are in the front line', *The Times*, September 12, 2000. In the same month the Service issued PSI 61/2000 providing guidance on the implications of the 1998 Act on the conduct of adjudications and the imposition of punishments.

[200] Levenson, J., 'Costly Mistakes', *Prison Report*, Issue No. 58, Prison Reform Trust, July 2002, p. 6.

[201] Application numbers: 00039665/98 and 0040086/98, Strasbourg, 15 July 2002.

[202] Ezeh faced adjudication for an offence contrary to Rule 47(17) of the Prison Rules 1964 and was awarded 40 additional days custody, 14 days cellular confinement, 14 days exclusion from associated work and 14 days forfeiture of privileges. Connors faced adjudication for an offence contrary to Rule 47(1) and was awarded 7 additional days together with 3 days cellular confinement, and fined £8.

[203] Application numbers: 00039665/98 and 00040086/98, Strasbourg, 15 July 2002, at para. 100.

[204] Application numbers: 00039665/98 and 00040086/98, Strasbourg, 15 July 2002, at para. 106.

[205] See 'Adjudications Review after European Ruling', *Prison Service News* No. 212, September 2002, p. 6 and 'Prison Governors Lose Power to Extend Prisoner's Sentences', *Prison Reform Trust Press Release*, 26 July 2002 at http://www.prisonreformtrust.org.uk.

[206] European case law challenging the impartiality and fairness of proceedings in respect of courts—martial, may assist. See *Findlay v. UK* (1997) 24 E.H.R.R. 221, for example. For a detailed discussion see Cheney *et al.*, Criminal Justice and the Human Rights Act 1998, Jordans, 2001.

10.7.4 *Family Ties*

Articles 8 and 12 protect the right to respect for private and family life, home and correspondence, and right to marry and found a family. The CPT have made clear the critical importance, particularly in the context of a prisoner's social rehabilitation, of the opportunity to safeguard relations with family and friends.[207] One hurdle faced by prisoners is the imposition of blanket bans simply because a privilege might be abused by someone, thus disadvantaging all, including families, when the result is prohibition of items being sent in to the prison, handcuffing and closed visits.[208] The Prisons Ombudsman has recorded his own concerns in this respect that 'I am deeply disturbed by the reduction in the number of visits in recent years, and suspect that closed visits may be one reason for it'.[209] Together with visits, personal correspondence issues, cell searches, distance from home and access to inter-prison visits are all potential case law challenges.

The importance of proximity to home and respect for family life, has already been held by the European court in the case of Wakefield,[210] in respect of a prisoner and his fiancee. It has yet to be tested in the context of a mother and child who, given there are only 4 MBU and women are more likely to be held further from their homes, is an area ripe for challenge. The PS have pledged their policy on mothers and babies/children in prison 'will reflect ... Article 8, save where it is necessary to restrict the prisoner's right for a legitimate reason, such as good order and discipline, or the safety of others including babies'.[211] With the rising numbers in the women's estate, pressure on the PS to meet demands will be great. In addition there may be more efforts such as those made in May 2001 to challenge the policy requiring separation of mothers and babies after 18 months,[212] and 2000 in respect of artificial insemination.[213]

10.7.5 *Discrimination*

In the last two annual reports in particular the Ombudsman has highlighted cases where prisoners have faced a disciplinary charge for alleging racism on the part of officers, and that the number of such cases have increased. The central issue, as identified by the Ombudsman, is that the PS response to allegations of racism with a disciplinary charge, and not the necessary investigation of the allegation, is highly inappropriate and damages both race relations and prisoner confidence in fair treatment. That said, his office has also identified serious flaws such as lack of

---

[207] Report to the U.K. Government on the visit to the U.K. and the Isle of Man carried out by the European Committee for the Prevention of Torture and Inhuman and Degrading Treatment or Punishment from September 8–17, 1997 (Strasbourg, January 13, 2000).

[208] For the concerns of the Ombudsman, see, for example, his *Annual Report 2001–2002*, pp. 48, 52–53 and 89.

[209] *PPO Annual Report 2001–2002*, p. 48. For complaints received in respect of problems maintaining family ties, see p. 47–53.

[210] *Wakefield v. UK* D 15817/89, (October 1, 1990).

[211] *Report of a Review of Principles*, 'Policies and Procedures on Mothers and Babies/Children in Prisons', HMPS, 1999.

[212] *R.* (on the application of P) *v. Secretary of State for the Home Department* [2001] All E.R. (D) 278 (Jul); *R.* (on the application of Q and another) *v. Secretary of State for the Home Department* [2001] All E.R. (D) 278 (Jul).

[213] *R. v. Secretary of State for the Home Department, ex parte Mellor* [2000] 2 E.L.R. 951 QBD.

the required vigour and impartiality when an internal investigation has taken place.[214]

The PS acknowledge they have a racism problem, highlighted not least by the findings at HMP Wandsworth and results of an inquiry into HMP Brixton.[215] Following the latter findings, the Director General stated: 'I have already acknowledged that the Service is not only institutionally racist, but that pockets of blatant racism still exist'.[216] Much effort has gone into attempting to resolve this problem but it is clear from complaints to the Ombudsman, and his own findings during investigations that entries in prisoners' history sheets have not reflected well on the authors or the Service for which they work,[217] that the potential for challenge under Article 14 (in attendance upon any of the other articles) remains. Similarly, discrimination in respect of gender,[218] sexual orientation,[219] religion[220] and against disabled prisoners fall within the ambit of this article. The latter in particular links strongly to the type of degrading experiences covered by Article 3.[221]

---

[214] See for example his Annual Report of 2001–2002, p. 38.

[215] Wright, O., 'Way of fear is still the rule, say inmates' *The Times*, July 4, 2000; Ford, R., 'Race-row prison faces private take-over *The Times*, July 6, 2000; '*Race Equality Advisor, Assessment of Race Relations at HMP Brixton*', RESPOND, (June 2000).

[216] PS press release, 'Prison Service recognises magnitude of poor race relations' (October 31, 2000).

[217] *Prisons Ombudsman Annual Report 1999–2000*, Cm. 4730, (2000).

[218] See 'Prisoners Rights' in Cheney et al., *Criminal Justice and the Human Rights Act 1998*, p. 230–231.

[219] For an account of issues in respect of gay, bisexual and transsexual prisoners, see Taylor, S., '*Gay and Bisexual Prisoners*', TPHB (2002), pp. 445–447 and Wells N., '*Viewpoint on Transsexual Prisoners*', TPHB, (2002), p. 447.

[220] The Ombudsman raises the issue of the importance of the needs of all religious groups being respected by the PS through a complaint of lack of flexibility and insensitivity to the religious needs of a Muslim prisoner to celebrate Eid, in his latest Annual Report. PPO, *Annual Report 2001–2002*, p. 60. Art. 9 is also relevant in respect of the right to religious freedom and pertinent issues include provision of multi-faith rooms, facilitating religious observance, diets and holidays and allowing religious artefacts necessary for worship in-cell.

[221] For accounts of harrowing experiences faced by serving disabled prisoners, see 'Viewpoints on disability in prison' by Sleightholme Y., Langton M. and Kulvinder Singh Mahal in Leech M. & Cheney D., *The Prisons Handbook 2001*, p. 401–403 and Langton M. in *TPHB 2002*, p. 422–423. For a discussion of the issues, see Parry J., 'Disability in Prison', *TPHB 2002*, p. 418–422.

CHAPTER ELEVEN

Youth Justice

KATHERINE DOOLIN

11.1 THE DEVELOPMENT OF YOUTH JUSTICE

During the eighteenth and nineteenth centuries juveniles who offended were generally dealt with in a similar manner as adult offenders in attributing blame and inflicting punishment. Treatment was harsh with children punished physically, transported, or sent to prison or the hulks (prison ships) under the same conditions as adults.[1] There was a gradual development in the nineteenth century of special measures directed to juveniles but any signs of a distinction being made between adult and child offenders came in the systems of punishment used rather than in the court process. In 1823 a separate convict hulk for juvenile offenders was established and in 1838 Parkhurst[2] was opened as a prison for boys aged between 10 and 18 years. There was some attempt at classification between younger and older boys and, as well as a punishment ward, there was also a probationary ward for newcomers. 'Parkhurst however did little to undermine the prevailing view that *all* offenders should be held fully responsible for their actions . . .'[3] The regime was still as repressive as that for adult offenders, with leg irons, whippings, and long periods of confinement to cells.

A critic of regimes such as Parkhurst, Mary Carpenter, was a principal advocate for reformatory schools. 'She was convinced that reformation depended on meeting the perceived needs of children for care and support as well as overt discipline.'[4] Her initiatives resulted in the Youthful Offenders Act 1854 which gave courts the discretionary power to send child offenders, known as the 'dangerous classes', to reformatory schools for a period between two and five years as an alternative to sending them to adult prisons. The Industrial Schools Act 1857 allowed deprived children, known as the 'perishing classes', to be sent indefinitely to industrial schools which provided some rudimentary education.[5] There were some reformatory and industrial schools in existence prior to this

---

[1] Berlins, M. and Wansell G., *Caught in the Act* (1974), Chap. 1.
[2] Parkhurst was converted to a women's prison in 1864 and then later became a high security prison for adult males.
[3] Muncie J., *Youth and Crime* (1999), p. 58.
[4] *ibid.*, p. 59.
[5] Musgrove F., *Youth and the Social Order* (1964), Chap. 3.

time but the 1854 and 1857 Acts gave formal and legal recognition to the schools. Further, the schools were run by voluntary agencies and, after the legislation was passed, the Government contributed towards the running costs.

The reformers believed that the causes of crime and social disorder lay in the 'deficiencies in working-class family life, in the low moral condition of parents and in parental neglect.'[6] Taking children away from what appeared to be a corrupted moral environment and placing them in reformatories and industrial schools allowed the state to intervene to control the young and try to ensure that they were moralised and disciplined. While the approach of the reformers was to encourage 'depraved' and 'deprived' children to show moral transformation, self-improvement and expiation for their crimes,[7] the reality often diverged starkly from the rhetoric. The schools were still rigid and disciplinarian and before entering a reformatory a 14-day prison sentence had to be served. By the 1880s there were more than 200 reformatory and industrial schools but there were also many thousands of children in adult prisons.

The Gladstone Committee set up in 1895 to look into the prison system was very concerned with the welfare and treatment of juveniles. The Committee recognised that attitudes to child offenders had changed with greater emphasis on viewing them as victims rather than upon their moral responsibility. The Prevention of Crime Act 1908 gave formal recognition to detention centres, known as borstals, for 16 to 21 year olds. But it was the Children Act 1908, enacted by the Liberal Government that heralded legislative recognition that children and young people who offended should be dealt with by a separate court process.[8] This Act set up special juvenile courts for predominately criminal cases but the court also had powers over care and protection cases. The juvenile court was still held in the magistrates' courts but sat at separate times from the adult courts. Further, the Act abolished the imprisonment of children under 14 years. The creation of separate courts for the young reflected the view that juveniles were less responsible than adults for their actions and that the law, both in attributing blame and inflicting punishment, should take into account their immaturity and lack of understanding of the consequences of their actions. As Fionda claims: 'In short, this new court was to recognise the nature of childhood (as it was then perceived) and structure its system of punishment accordingly.'[9]

In 1927 a *Report of the Departmental Committee on the Treatment of Young Offenders*[10] concluded that there was little or no difference in character and needs between the neglected and the delinquent child and it was the court's responsibility to look after the welfare of children, not to punish them. This welfare principle, that was also evident in earlier reforms, was given prominence in the Children and Young Persons Act 1933. Section 44 of the Act states that:

'Every court in dealing with a child or young person who is brought before it, either as being in need of care or protection of as an offender or otherwise, shall have regard to

---

[6] *supra* at n. 3, at p. 59.
[7] Pratt J., *Punishment in a Perfect Society* (1992), p. 116.
[8] There had been some movement before 1908 to distinguish between juvenile and adult offenders. Legislation in 1847 and 1879 meant that children would be dealt with summarily in magistrates' courts rather than in Assizes or Quarter Sessions.
[9] Fionda J., 'The age of innocence?—the concept of childhood in the punishment of young offenders' (1998) 10(1) *Child and Family Law Quarterly* 77.
[10] Home Office, *Report of the Departmental Committee on the Treatment of Young Offenders* (The Moloney Committee), Cmd. 2831 (1927).

the welfare of the child or young person and shall in a proper case take steps for removing him from undesirable surroundings and for securing that proper provision is made for his education and training.'

In addition to directing magistrates to give primary importance to the 'welfare of the child', panels of magistrates were to be specially selected to hear juvenile cases, court hearings were to be held in camera with restrictions placed on the reporting of cases in the press, and provisions were included to allow juveniles to be separated from adults at the police station, at court or on remand. The 1933 Act also abolished capital punishment for those offenders under the age of 18 and took away the distinction between reformatories and industrial schools reorganising them as 'approved schools' which provided education and training.

The welfare approach was not without its critics who advocated a more punitive stance towards delinquency. This conflict was evident in legislation at the time. The Children Act 1948 provided powers for local government to take children deemed in need of care and protection into local authority care, ending the need to place these children in approved schools along with juvenile offenders. But in the same year the Criminal Justice Act 1948 introduced remand centres, attendance centres (where juveniles would be required to attend centres mainly run by the police for a number of hours a week), and detention centres (short periods of custody where the regime was tough and disciplinary).

In 1960 the Ingleby Committee[11] pointed out the growing conflict that existed between the welfare and judicial functions of the juvenile court and proposed that the age of criminal responsibility should be raised to 14 years. Although the age of criminal responsibility was raised to 10, many of the Committee's views did not become law in the Children and Young Persons Act 1963 but they did influence later proposals. The new Labour administration was imbued by the Fabian philosophy which argued that 'depraved' children were often 'deprived' children. The Longford Report[12] illustrated this approach by arguing that juvenile courts should be abolished and replaced by a family service, if necessary a family court, where welfare concerns would be paramount. These proposals were adopted in the 1965 White Paper *The Child, the Family and the Young Offender*.[13] This approach was viewed by critics as too radical and the 1968 White Paper, *Children in Trouble*,[14] included a compromise that retained juvenile courts but adopted care and treatment provisions. The 1968 White Paper formed the basis of the Children and Young Persons Act 1969.

What was proposed by the 1969 Act is generally regarded as the high point of a welfare approach.[15] One of the main aims of the welfare model is the identification of a juvenile's needs and the provision of treatment to suit those needs,[16] with children in trouble or neglected children being dealt with by the same system. The focus is on the offender rather than any offending. The deviant behaviour is seen as symptomatic of an underlying disorder, such as maladjust-

---

[11] *Report of the Committee on Children and Young Persons*, Cmnd. 1191 (1960).
[12] Labour Party, *Crime—A Challenge to Us All* (1964).
[13] Home Office, *The Child, the Family and the Young Offender*, Cmnd. 2742 (1965).
[14] Home Office, *Children in Trouble*, Cmnd. 3601 (1968).
[15] Harris R.J., 'Towards Just Welfare' (1985) 25(1) *British Journal of Criminology* 31. See also Newburn T., 'Young People, Crime, and Youth Justice' in M. Maguire, R. Morgan, and R. Reiner (eds) *The Oxford Handbook of Criminology* (3rd ed., 2002), p. 551.
[16] Morris A. and McIsaac M., *Juvenile Justice?* (1978), p. 30. See also May D., 'Delinquency Control And The Treatment Model: Some Implications Of Recent Legislation' (1971) 11(4) *British Journal of Criminology* 359.

ment, immaturity, damaged or abnormal personality,[17] that needs treatment to
be rectified. There is an expanding bureaucracy of experts, for example social
workers, health and education professionals, who become the primary decision-
makers regarding the substance of treatment for the juvenile. The Act included
many reforms based on these welfare principles but a number were never
implemented:

- the juvenile court was retained but the age of criminal responsibility was to
  be raised to 14 (section 4). All children under 14 would have been dealt with
  in non-criminal proceedings. This was never implemented—the age of
  criminal responsibility remained at 10.

- decisions to prosecute 14–17 year olds were to be based on consultation
  between relevant agencies, not just the police (section 5). This was never
  implemented.

- approved schools were abolished and replaced by community homes with
  residential and educational facilities.

- it was also intended to phase out the use of borstals and detention centres
  for those under 17 (section 7). Borstals were not abolished until 1982[18]
  when they were replaced by 'youth custody centres'. Detention centres
  continued until 1988[19] when they were amalgamated with youth custody
  centres and renamed 'young offender institutions'.

- supervision orders (non-custodial) and care orders (social services to be
  given the power to place the child into some form of residential institution)
  were introduced. Magistrates' powers were reduced as the substance of
  these orders was decided by social workers who were given extensive discretion.

Despite a significant increase in the use of cautions, the 1970s saw a doubling
of the use of custody for juveniles and an accompanying decline in the use of
community-based sentences.[20] Much of the 1969 Act was never implemented by
the incoming Conservative government in 1970, but the legislation attracted
considerable criticism. The welfare philosophy came under increasing attack
from different political lobbies. Law and order proponents argued that the
approach was too 'soft' on juvenile offending, magistrates and police fought
against restrictions that reduced their powers, and civil libertarians raised concerns that the emphasis on treatment denied juveniles their full legal rights and
led to indeterminate and disproportionate sentencing. Even some of those
working within the treatment framework became disillusioned with the rehabilitative ideal. By the late 1970s such critiques had led to the emergence of a
'justice-based' approach to juvenile offending, with greater focus on the
offending rather than on the offender and emphasising certainty, due process,
legal rights and procedural safeguards, determinate sentences commensurate to
the seriousness of the offence, and punishment through the least restrictive
intervention.

---

[17] As stated in the 1968 White Paper, *Children in Trouble, supra* at n. 14.
[18] Criminal Justice Act 1982.
[19] Criminal Justice Act 1988.
[20] Newburn, *supra* at n. 15, at p. 552.

Applying justice-based principles, the Criminal Justice Act 1982 aimed to limit the use of custody for young offenders.[21] The Act introduced a sentencing framework for the juvenile court where custodial sentences could only be imposed where an offender was unable or unwilling to respond to non-custodial alternatives, where the custodial sentence was necessary for the protection of the public, or where the offence was so serious that a non-custodial punishment could not be justified.[22] Further the 1982 Act reduced the detention centre sentence, abolished borstals in favour of 'youth custody centres' with fixed-term orders replacing indeterminate sentences, and introduced more non-custodial penalties including community service for 16 year olds.

The Criminal Justice Act 1988 placed further restrictions on the use of custody for juveniles requiring the court to ask whether they would, given all the circumstances, pass a custodial sentence in the case of an adult and whether there was a history of failure to respond to non-custodial measures. Further, a custodial sentence could not be justified on the grounds that it would deter other potential offenders and the court had to specify on which criteria the decision to impose custody was based, giving reasons.[23] The 1988 Act also reorganised the system of custody for juveniles by amalgamating detention centres and youth custody centres to become 'young offender institutions' for 15–17 year olds.[24] Such provisions within the Criminal Justice Acts of 1982 and 1988, the increased support for diversion of young offenders from court, and the use of cautions for second and third offences all had a significant effect on the reduction of young offenders in custody in the 1980s. The number of juveniles in custody in prison service establishments fell from 10,510 in 1982 to 5,572 in 1992.[25] At the end of this decade the Children Act 1989 removed all care proceedings from the juvenile court signalling the separation of the child offender from the child in need of care and protection.

The Criminal Justice Act 1991[26] makes it clear that if the court wishes to impose a custodial or community sentence, for adult or young offenders, the threshold of 'seriousness of the offence' must be crossed and the sentence must be commensurate with the seriousness of the offence. When dealing with young offenders, this 'just deserts' approach must also be balanced with the welfare principle contained in section 44 of the Children and Young Persons Act 1933 referred to above. The Act also changed the name of the juvenile court to 'Youth Court'[27] and extended its jurisdiction to include 17 year olds.[28] The Youth Court is a magistrates' court specially constituted to deal with matters concerning 10 to 17 year old offenders. The magistrates who sit as the Youth Court are elected by their peers and must undergo specialist training. Benches are not normally single sex. Parents or guardians of children under 16[29] must attend the Youth Court and the court can also require the parents of older children to attend. The court operates its own special procedures, cases are not normally open to the public

---

[21] *ibid.*, p. 552.

[22] Criminal Justice Act 1982, s. 1(4).

[23] Criminal Justice Act 1988, s. 123(3).

[24] The Crime and Disorder Act 1998 introduced the detention and training order which replaced detention in a young offender institution for 15–17 year olds.

[25] *Prison Statistics 1992* Cm. 2581, Table 3.4, p. 59.

[26] Criminal Justice Act 1991, Part I.

[27] *ibid.*, s. 70(1).

[28] *ibid.*, s. 68.

[29] *ibid.*, s 56.

although there is a move towards greater openness especially with victims, and there are restrictions on press reporting but these can be dispensed with if it is in the public interest to do so.[30] When a child or young person is charged with homicide (murder or manslaughter) the matter must be dealt with in the Crown Court.[31] Other 'grave crimes' may be dealt with in the Crown Court if the court of first appearance believes the child or young person should be given a longer sentence than magistrates are authorised to do so.[32]

In the early 1990s there was a growing moral panic perpetuated by the Conservative government and the media about 'persistent young offenders' being out of control, with a more punitive response to juvenile offending being demanded. The tragic murder of two-year old James Bulger in 1993 attracted massive national press and 'provided the strongest possible evidence to an already worried public that something new and particularly malevolent was afoot.'[33] Section 1 of the Criminal Justice and Public Order Act 1994 introduced the 'secure training order' for persistent offenders aged 12 to 14 who had been convicted of three imprisonable offences and who had failed to comply with non-custodial penalties. The minimum sentence was six months and the maximum two years with half the sentence served in custody and the other half in supervision in the community.[34] Further, section 17 of the 1994 Act doubled the sentence of detention in a young offender institution for 15 to 17 year olds from one year to two years. At the same time the cautioning system, particularly the use of repeat cautions for second and third offences committed by juveniles, was coming under increasing criticism. The Crime (Sentences) Act 1997 extends the use of electronic tagging to juveniles under 16 to enforce curfews.[35]

The age of criminal responsibility in England and Wales still remains at 10, lower than most other European countries. A child under 10 is deemed *doli incapax*, incapable of criminal intent. For those aged 10 to 17, the term 'child' refers to those aged 10 to 13 and 'young person' refers to those aged 14 to 17. According to *Criminal Statistics 2000*, in 2000–2001 25 per cent of all recorded crime was committed by those under 18.

11.2 THE POLICE AND CODES OF PRACTICE

As has been seen in earlier chapters, the pre-trial process in England revolves around the police. The vulnerability of juveniles requires that the police meet higher standards in the investigation and prosecution of children and young people, taking into account their ages, needs and understanding. On the street, where decisions are of low visibility with little control over the individual officer, there is a problem of discrimination on grounds of race, colour, and class. The black, working class youth is more likely to be the subject of police attention than his white middle class counterpart.[36]

---

[30] Crime (Sentences) Act 1997, s. 45.
[31] Children and Young Persons Act 1933, s. 53(1).
[32] *ibid.*, s. 53(2).
[33] Newburn, *supra* at n. 15, at p. 556. See also Brown S., *Understanding youth and crime* (1998), Chap. 3; Hay C., 'Mobilization Through Interpellation: James Bulger, Juvenile Crime and the Construction of a Moral Panic' (1995) 4 Social & Legal Studies 197; Fionda, *supra* at n. 9.
[34] The Crime and Disorder Act 1998 introduced the detention and training order which replaced the secure training order for 12–14 year olds.
[35] Crime (Sentences) Act 1997, s. 43.
[36] McConville M., *et al.*, *The Case for the Prosecution* (1991), Chap. 2.

Police conduct is regulated by the PACE Codes of Practice. Code A deals with police powers to stop and search people. There is generally no special provision made for juveniles, although note 1E stipulates that juveniles should not be subject to a voluntary search. Code B deals with the searching of premises and the seizure of property found by the police on persons or premises and contains no special provisions pertaining solely to juveniles.

Code C pays considerable attention to the position of juveniles. It concerns the codes of practice for the detention, treatment and questioning of persons by police officers. Juveniles should not be arrested or interviewed at their place of education unless unavoidable and the principal or a nominee must be informed.[37] When brought to the police station, juveniles should not be held in a police cell unless there is no other secure accommodation available. When held in a cell, they must not be kept with a detained adult[38] and the reason for placing them in a cell must be recorded.[39] The key element is that the police should do nothing except in the presence of an 'appropriate adult'. This might be a parent, guardian, social worker, the care authority or voluntary organisation if the juvenile is in care, or failing these, another responsible adult.[40] The adult is not 'appropriate' if involved in the offence, of low intelligence[41] or is hostile to the juvenile. A solicitor acting in a professional capacity does not qualify.

The police are under an obligation to discover the person responsible for the juvenile's welfare and as soon as practicable inform him or her that the juvenile has been arrested, the reason for it, and where the juvenile is being held. This right is in addition to the juvenile's right not to be held incommunicado.[42] In the case of a juvenile subject to a supervision order, reasonable steps must be taken to notify the person in charge of supervision.[43] Juveniles may not wish their parents to be present, or parents choose not to attend, in which case the police must find another 'appropriate' adult. The juvenile must be made aware of the adult's presence. The adult's role is to ensure that the juvenile is aware of the right to legal advice and not to be held incommunicado. The adult should be present at the various stages of cautioning,[44] identification processes (under Code D) or intimate searches.[45] Unless in 'exceptional cases of need' as determined by a superintendent or above,[46] the 'appropriate' adult must be present at all times during the interviewing process and is told that his or her role is not just that of observer but as an adviser to the juvenile, ensuring that the interview is conducted properly and facilitating communication between the juvenile and the interviewer.[47] Some adults are so overawed that they are of little value as advisers

---

[37] Code C para. 11.15 and n. 11C.
[38] *ibid.*, para. 8.8.
[39] *ibid.*, para. 8.12.
[40] *ibid.*, 1.7 and nn. 1C, 1D.
[41] Morse [1991] Crim.L.R. 195.
[42] Code C, para. 3.7.
[43] *ibid.*, para. 3.8.
[44] *ibid.*, para.10.6. If the juvenile is cautioned in the absence of an 'appropriate' adult, the caution must be repeated again in the adult's presence.
[45] *ibid.*, Annex A. If the juvenile does not want the intimate search to be conducted in front of the 'appropriate' adult, and the adult agrees, a record shall be made of the juvenile's decision and signed by the adult.
[46] *ibid.*, Annex C.
[47] *ibid.*, paras. 11.14–11.16 and n. 11B.

and may even side with the interviewer.[48]

Code D deals with identification procedures and it can be assumed that the rules contained within this Code apply to juveniles. For example, when video identification is used an 'appropriate' adult must be given a reasonable opportunity to see the complete set of images before it is shown to any witness.[49]

11.3 NEW LABOUR'S YOUTH JUSTICE

The Labour Government came to power in May 1997 and immediately stressed that reforming the youth justice system would be a key priority for the incoming government. While in opposition they had already raised concern about the problem of youth and crime. In May 1996 the Labour Party published the consultation paper, *Tackling Youth Crime: Reforming Youth Justice*, in which they asserted that there was:

> 'an overwhelming need to regain public and professional confidence in a youth justice system that is seen as increasingly ineffective in dealing with persistent young offenders and is actually contributing to youth crime.'[50]

The consultation paper also outlined a number of proposals for 'a radical overhaul of the youth justice system'[51]—many of which subsequently became law. At the same time, the Audit Commission published its report, *Misspent Youth: Young people and Crime*,[52] which claimed that the youth justice system was expensive, ineffective and inefficient. The report included a number of criticisms, including the time taken to process juvenile offenders through the court which needed to be speeded up; the cautioning system, particularly the use of repeat cautions; the lack of programmes available to challenge a young offender's behaviour; and a lack of effective multi-agency working to tackle offending. While the report made it clear that services needed to deal much more effectively with offending behaviour, preventing the offending in the first place should be the aim. In breaking the cycle of anti-social behaviour, the Commission identified a number of risk factors including, inadequate parenting, unstable living conditions, drug and alcohol abuse, behavioural problems, peer pressure, truancy and exclusions, and lack of training and employment. The Commission suggested that local agencies should develop programmes to target these risk factors and pilot the schemes, evaluating them to learn what works. In summary, as Newburn states:

> '*The emphasis in the Commission's report was on clarity of objectives, consistency of approach, and targeting of resources. Central to this was the aim that resources be shifted from processing to prevention. Its central recommendations emphasized the need for: consistency of aims and objectives in youth justice; improved inter-agency cooperation in meeting these aims and objectives; the creation of appropriate performance indicators for all agencies involved in youth justice; and the monitoring of performance so as to improve the functioning of the system.*'[53]

---

[48] Brown D., Ellis T., and Larcombe K., *Changing the Code: Police Detention under the Revised PACE Codes of Practice*, Home Office Research Study No. 129 (1992), p. 72.

[49] Code D, Annex A, para. 7.

[50] Labour Party, *Tackling Youth Crime: Reforming Youth Justice* (May, 1996), p. 8.

[51] *ibid.*, p. 18.

[52] Audit Commission, *Misspent Youth: Young people and crime* (November, 1996).

[53] Newburn, *supra* at n. 15, at p. 559.

Within six months of being elected the Labour Government published a number of consultation papers dealing with reforming the youth justice system, including *Tackling Youth Crime,*[54] *Getting to Grips with Crime: A Framework for Local Action,*[55] *Community Safety Order: A Consultation Paper,*[56] *New National and Local Focus on Youth Crime: A Consultation Paper,*[57] and *Tackling Delays in the Youth Justice System: A Consultation Paper.*[58] The Home Secretary formed a Youth Justice Task Force in June 1997 comprised of a range of people with varied experience of the youth justice system and chaired by Lord Norman Warner. The role of the Task Force was to advise the Home Secretary on the development of youth justice policy and to provide a link with relevant agencies dealing with young offenders.

The White Paper *No More Excuses—A New Approach to Tackling Youth Crime in England and Wales*[59] was published in November 1997. It included many of the reforms proposed in the above consultation papers. As is evident from the title, the Government believed that an 'excuse culture' had developed within the youth justice system, one which excused itself for its inefficiency and too often excused young offenders. The White Paper reiterated the Government's pledge to be 'tough on crime' and 'tough on the causes of crime' and, in doing so, set out the aims of their programme of reform:

— a clear strategy to prevent offending and re-offending;

— that offenders, and their parents, face up to their offending behaviour and take responsibility for it;

— earlier, more effective intervention when young people first offend;

— faster, more efficient procedures from arrest to sentence;

— partnership between all youth justice agencies to deliver a better, faster system.

To give effect to these aims, many of the proposals included in the White Paper subsequently became law in the Crime and Disorder Act 1998. The Act includes:

— making preventing offending the principal aim of the youth justice system;

— abolishing the presumption of *doli incapax* for 10 to 13 year olds;

— creating a national, independent Youth Justice Board to monitor the operation of the youth justice system and advise on policy;

— creating Youth Offending Teams to co-ordinate the organisation and provision of youth justice services locally;

— replacing cautioning with a system of reprimands and final warnings;

---

[54] Home Office, *Tackling Youth Crime* (September, 1997).
[55] Home Office, *Getting to Grips with Crime: A Framework for Local Action* (September, 1997).
[56] Home Office, *Community Safety Order: A Consultation Paper* (September, 1997).
[57] Home Office, *New National and Local Focus on Youth Crime: A Consultation Paper* (October, 1997).
[58] Home Office, *Tackling Delays in the Youth Justice System: A Consultation Paper* (October, 1997).
[59] Home Office, *No More Excuses—A New Approach to Tackling Youth Crime in England and Wales*, Cm. 3809 (1997).

— introducing a number of new orders—action plan, reparation, detention and training, anti-social behaviour, child safety, parenting—as well as child curfew and truancy provisions.

Part I of the Youth Justice and Criminal Evidence Act 1999 is part of the continuing reform of the youth justice system by the current Government. The Act introduces the 'referral order'—a mandatory order for most young offenders who plead guilty on their first court appearance.

11.3.1 *The Aim of the Youth Justice System*

The 1997 White paper stated that:

'The Government believes that there has been confusion about the purpose of the youth justice system and the principles that should govern the way in which young people are dealt with by youth justice agencies. Concerns about the welfare of the young person have too often been seen as in conflict with the aims of protecting the public, punishing offences and preventing offending. This confusion creates real practical difficulties for practitioners and has contributed to the loss of public confidence in the youth justice system.'[60]

In response, section 37(1) of the 1998 Act makes preventing offending by children and young persons the principal aim of the youth justice system and all persons and bodies who carry out functions in relation to the youth justice system must have regard to that aim.[61]

In supporting the overall aim of preventing offending, the Youth Justice Task Force proposed the following objectives:

— the swift administration of justice so that every young person accused of breaking the law has the matter resolved without delay;

— confronting young offenders with the consequences of their offending, for themselves and their family, victims and the community;

— punishment, proportionate to the seriousness and persistency of the offending behaviour;

— encouraging reparation by young offenders for victims;

— reinforcing parental responsibility;

— helping young offenders to tackle problems associated with their offending and to develop a sense of personal responsibility.[62]

11.3.2 *Organisational Structure*

Section 41(1) of the Crime and Disorder Act 1998 creates a Youth Justice Board (YJB) for England and Wales. The Board consists of members appointed by the

---

[60] *ibid.*, para. 2.1.
[61] Crime and Disorder Act 1998, s. 37(2).
[62] Youth Justice Task Force, *Preventing Offending By Young People: The Final Report of the Youth Justice Task Force* (1998), para. 7.

Home Secretary[63] and includes those who have extensive recent experience of the youth justice system.[64] The main aims of the YJB are to monitor the operation of the youth justice system and the provision of youth justice services, to identify and promote good practice, to award grants to develop such practice, and commission research to evaluate the practice. Further, to advise the Home Secretary on the operation of that system, on national standards and the monitoring of such standards.[65] Section 41(6) of the 1998 Act allows the Home Secretary to expand the functions of the Board and, from April 2000, the YJB became the commissioning body for secure facilities for young offenders.

Section 38 of the Crime and Disorder Act 1998 places a statutory duty on all local authorities to ensure the provision of youth justice services in their area.[66] The local authorities must establish a Youth Offending Team (YOT) in their area, and formulate and implement an annual youth justice plan. The plan, which must be submitted to the YJB, must set out how youth justice services are to be provided and funded, the composition and funding of the YOT, and how the YOT will operate and what functions the team will carry out.[67]

Section 39 of the 1998 Act creates the duty for local authorities to establish a YOT, with co-operation from the Chief officers of police, probation and health authorities. The YOT must consist of at least one probation officer, a local authority social worker, a police officer, a health authority representative, and a person nominated by the chief education officer.[68] The main aims of this multi-agency team are to co-ordinate the provision of youth justice services for those in the local authority's area and to carry out the functions assigned to them in their local authority's youth justice plan.[69] YOTs have been in operation in all local authorities since April 2000. Prior to this a number of pilot schemes were set up to implement this new system and were subsequently evaluated.[70]

11.3.3 *Abolition of Doli Incapax for 10 to 13 year olds*

It used to be the law that children aged between 10 and 13 years inclusive were presumed to be *doli incapax*, incapable of criminal intent. This presumption had to be rebutted by the prosecution before a child could be convicted. The prosecution had to prove beyond reasonable doubt that the child knew that what he or she had done was seriously wrong, as opposed to merely naughty or mischievous. But the presumption of *doli incapax* for this age group came under increasing criticism in the 1990s. In March 1994 the divisional court in the case of *C v. DPP*[71] purported to abolish the presumption on the grounds it was outmoded and contrary to common sense. However, on appeal the House of Lords overruled the Divisional Court's decision and upheld the presumption of *doli incapax*

---

[63] Crime and Disorder Act 1998, s. 41(3).
[64] *ibid.*, s. 41(4).
[65] *ibid.*, s. 41(5).
[66] The youth justice services that the local authority are required to provide are detailed in s. 38(4) of the Crime and Disorder Act 1998.
[67] Crime and Disorder Act 1998, s. 40.
[68] *ibid.*, s. 39(5).
[69] *ibid.*, s. 39(7).
[70] Holdaway S., Davidson N., Dignan J., Hammersley R., Hine J., and Marsh P., *New Strategies to address youth offending: The national evaluation of the pilot youth offending teams.* Home Office RDS Occasional Paper No. 69 (2001).
[71] *C v. DPP* [1994] 3 W.L.R. 888.

but they expressed the view that the time had come for Parliament to review the presumption for 10 to 13 year olds.[72]

Section 34 of the Crime and Disorder Act 1998 abolishes the presumption of *doli incapax* for those aged 10 to 13 years. In stressing the need for young offenders to face up to the consequences of their offending and take responsibility for their actions, the Government asserted that the presumption 'flies in the face of common sense' and it is archaic, illogical and unfair in practice.[73] The abolition of the presumption for this age group has been heavily criticised, particularly since the age of criminal responsibility remains at 10—one of the lowest in Europe.[74]

11.3.4 *Reprimands and Final Warnings*

The previous practice of informal warnings and cautions for 10 to 17 year olds is replaced by a statutory system of reprimands and final warnings detailed in sections 65 and 66 of the Crime and Disorder Act 1998. For less serious offences, a police officer may reprimand a young offender if he or she has not been previously reprimanded or warned. Where the offender has already received a reprimand or the offence is too serious for a reprimand he or she will be warned. This is a final warning as it may be given only once; if the child or young person re-offends then, except in unusual circumstances, he or she will be prosecuted at court. As a result of the Criminal Justice and Court Services Act 2000, the reprimand or final warning no longer has to be administered at a police station.[75]

The Government's rationale behind introducing the new system is explained in the 1997 Consultation Paper, *Tackling Youth Crime*, which states:

'The police reprimand and Final Warning scheme is intended to provide a targeted and effective early response to offending. The Government believes that many young people can be successfully diverted from crime without recourse to court proceedings, provided the response is clear, firm and constructive. But when a child or young person fails to take the opportunity provided and offends again, there must be a penalty to pay and this requires swift and appropriate court action.'[76]

Young offenders who receive warnings are referred to a YOT who assess the offender and, unless considered inappropriate to do so, arrange for them to take part in a rehabilitation programme. These programmes can include reparation, mediation, victim awareness sessions, drug/alcohol awareness sessions, and other cognitive behaviour sessions.

The practice of 'restorative cautioning' has also developed for administering reprimands or warnings. The police hold a meeting or 'conference' at which the young offender, parents, and it is hoped, victims attend. As well as delivering the reprimand or warning, the police officer facilitates discussion about the harm

---

[72] *C v. DPP* [1995] 2 W.L.R. 383.

[73] *Tackling Youth Crime, supra* at n. 54, at paras 3 and 7.

[74] Cavadino P., 'Goodbye doli, must we leave you?' (1997) 9(2) *Child and Family Law Quarterly* 165. See also Bandalli S., 'Children, Responsibility and the New Youth Justice' in B. Goldson (ed.) *The New Youth Justice* (2000), Chap. 5.; Stokes E., 'Abolishing The Presumption of *Doli Incapax*: Reflections On The Death Of A Doctrine' in J. Pickford (ed.) *Youth Justice: Theory and Practice* (2000), Chap. 3.

[75] Criminal Justice and Court Services Act 2000, s. 56.

[76] *supra* at n. 54, at para. 54.

caused by the offence and how this could be repaired. The most well known practice of 'restorative cautioning' is the Thames Valley Police initiative launched in 1998[77] which has been the subject of an evaluation by researchers from the Centre for Criminological Research at Oxford University.[78]

11.3.5 New Criminal Orders

Detention and training order:
Section 73 of the Crime and Disorder Act 1998 creates the detention and training order (DTO). It is the new custodial sentence for offenders aged 10 to 17, replacing the secure training order (available for 12 to 14 years) and detention in a young offender institution order (available for 15 to 17 years) which now cease to have effect.[79] In order for the court to impose a DTO the threshold of 'seriousness of the offence', stipulated in the Criminal Justice Act 1991, must be crossed. Further, for those offenders aged 12 to 14, the DTO can only be made if he or she is a persistent offender. In the case of offenders aged 10 and 11, the DTO can only be made if it is believed that only a custodial sentence would be adequate to protect the public from further offending by the child.

The length of sentence imposed is four, six, eight, 10, 12, 18 or a maximum of 24 months. It is expected that half of the sentence be served in custody and the other half in the community under supervision of a probation officer, local authority social worker, or member of a YOT. The 1998 Act provides for early or delayed release from the custodial part in some cases. The rationale behind introducing the DTO was the Government's belief that:

> 'the new detention and training order will provide clearer, simpler, more flexible and more consistent custodial arrangements for young offenders. The increased emphasis on supervision after release, on a clear sentence plan to tackle the causes of offending and on continuity of supervision before and after release from custody should provide for a more effective custodial sentence, complementing the Government's proposals for more effective community penalties.'[80]

The most controversial aspect of the DTO is the potential for the courts to impose custodial sentences on offenders as young as 10. Critics claim that this seriously detracts from the Government's attempts to bring rehabilitation back into the system and is a negative aspect of the Crime and Disorder Act 1998.[81]

Action plan order:
The action plan is a new form of community order for offenders aged 10 to 17 introduced by section 69 of the Crime and Disorder Act 1998. As was explained in the 1997 White Paper, *No More Excuses*, the action plan order is 'a short,

---

[77] For more information on the Thames Valley restorative cautioning initiative see Young R. and Goold B., '*Restorative Police Cautioning in Aylesbury—From Degrading to Reintegrative Shaming Ceremonies*' [1999] Crim.L.R. 126; Young R., 'Just Cops Doing "Shameful" Business?: Police-led Restorative Justice and the Lessons of Research' in A. Morris and G. Maxwell (eds) *Restorative Justice for Juveniles* (2001), p. 195.

[78] Hoyle C., Young R., and Hill R., *Proceed with Caution: An evaluation of the Thames Valley Police initiative in restorative cautioning* (2002).

[79] Crime and Disorder Act 1998, s. 73(7). Long-term detention for 'grave' offences is still an available sentence for the Crown Court under s. 53 of the Children and Young Persons Act 1933.

[80] *No More Excuses*, *supra* at n. 59, at para. 6.20.

[81] Fionda J., 'New Labour, Old Hat: Youth Justice and the Crime and Disorder Act 1998' [1999] Crim.L.R. 36, 44.

intensive programme of community intervention combining punishment, rehabilitation and reparation to change offending behaviour and prevent further crime.'[82] The action plan order is a community order and therefore the threshold of 'seriousness of offence' stipulated in the Criminal Justice Act 1991 must be crossed. The order is for three months and requires the offender to comply with the conditions of the plan and places the offender under the supervision of a YOT member, probation officer, or local authority social worker. Requirements to be included in an action plan include any or all of the following things:

— to participate in specified activities;

— to present himself or herself to a person or persons specified in the requirements or directions at a place or places and at a time or times so specified;

— to attend an attendance centre (this is only if the offence is punishable with imprisonment in the case of an adult);

— to stay away from a specified place or places;

— to comply with any arrangements for education;

— to make reparation to a specified person or persons, or the community (reparative activity should be a part of action plans wherever possible);

— to attend any hearing fixed by the court, no longer than 21 days after the order is made, where a report will be given as to the effectiveness of the order and the extent to which it has been implemented.[83]

The action plan order cannot be combined with a custodial sentence, community rehabilitation order, community punishment order, community punishment and rehabilitation order, supervision order, or attendance centre order.[84] The action plan order is generally considered the first option for making a community order.

Reparation order:

Sections 67 and 68 of the Crime and Disorder Act 1998 introduce a new reparation order for offenders aged 10 to 17. The reparation order requires the young offender to make reparation to the victim or victims, or to the community for up to 24 hours within a three-month period. Victims' views must be sought before a reparation order is made. There is a presumption that the court will make a reparation order wherever possible and, under section 67(11) of the 1998 Act, must give reasons if it does not. The order was created as part of the Government's aim to encourage young offenders to take responsibility for their actions.

'*For a young offender to accept responsibility for his or her offence and face up to the harm which they have caused to the victim is both a valuable moral lesson and a first step to rehabilitation. Bringing home to them the effects of their offending both on themselves and on others will help to stop young offenders from offending again.*'[85]

[82] *supra* at n. 59, at para. 5.18.
[83] Crime and Disorder Act 1998, s. 69(5).
[84] *ibid.*, s. 69(4).
[85] *Tackling Youth Crime*, *supra* at n. 54, at para. 1.

The Government also stressed the potential for reparation to benefit victims who may receive compensation, an apology or the chance to ask offenders why they committed the offence and to say how it made them feel.[86] Reparation may take the form of a verbal or written apology, mediation, a restorative or family group conference,[87] repairing the damage, or work for the community. It is clear that, whatever form it takes, reparation should be in kind, rather than financial.[88] The reparation order cannot be made in conjunction with a custodial sentence, community punishment order, a community punishment and rehabilitation order, a supervision order, or an action plan order.[89]

The Government advocated in the 1997 White Paper, *No More Excuses*, that:

> '*it will be necessary to reshape the criminal justice system in England and Wales to produce more constructive outcomes with young offenders. Its proposals for reform build on principles underlying the concept of restorative justice.*'[90]

Restorative justice is a much-debated concept, but 'at the risk of over-simplification, the philosophy on which it is based can most helpfully be summarised in terms of the "three Rs" of Responsibility, Restoration and Reintegration.'[91] It is about engaging with the offenders to encourage them to take responsibility for their actions and its consequences, to make amends for the harm that has been caused, and reintegrating the offender and the victim back into the community. The new action plan and reparation orders, together with the potential for reparation as part of a supervision order or a final warning,[92] demonstrate the Government's commitment to their assertion made in the 1997 White Paper. But the extent to which these new reforms fully embrace the restorative philosophy is the subject of much debate. Dignan claims that:

> '*One of the most important effects of the Crime and Disorder Act ... will be to establish at least some elements of the restorative justice approach as part of the mainstream response to offending behaviour by young people for the first time in England and Wales.*'[93]

Morris and Gelsthorpe are critical of Dignan's sentiments. They feel that any emphasis on restorative justice is just one theme in a broadly punitive and controlling piece of legislation, claiming 'it would take a considerable leap of imagination'[94] to describe as one of the most important effects of the Crime and

---

[86] *No More Excuses*, *supra* at n. 59, at para. 4.13.
[87] For more on Family Group Conferencing in England see Dignan J. and Marsh P., 'Restorative Justice and Family Group Conferences in England: Current State and Future Prospects' in A. Morris and G. Maxwell (eds) *Restorative Justice for Juveniles* (2001), Chap. 5.
[88] Home Office, *The Crime and Disorder Act Guidance Document: Reparation Order* (2000), paras 6.1–6.2.
[89] Crime and Disorder Act 1998, s. 67(4).
[90] *supra* at n. 59, at para. 9.21.
[91] Dignan J., 'The Crime and Disorder Act and the Prospects for Restorative Justice' [1999] Crim.L.R. 48.
[92] See Evans R. and Puech K., 'Reprimands and Warnings: Populist Punitiveness or Restorative Justice' [2001] Crim.L.R. 794. As part of their evaluation of a warning clinic, many young offenders and YOT workers found the warning system 'arbitrary, unfair, and disproportionate'.
[93] *supra* at n. 91, at p. 50.
[94] Morris A. and Gelsthorpe L., 'Something Old, Something Borrowed, Something Blue, but Something New? A comment on the prospects for restorative justice under the Crime and Disorder Act 1998' [2000] Crim.L.R. 18, 19.

Disorder Act, the establishment of at least some elements of the restorative approach as part of the mainstream response to offending behaviour by young people. However, Dignan does warn that restorative justice 'might become subordinated to the more traditional and punitive approaches of the past'[95] and concludes that 'the reforms hardly amount to a "restorative justice revolution", let alone the "paradigm shift" that some restorative justice advocates have called for.'[96]

Referral order:

> 'Of all New Labour's restorative justice initiatives, arguably the most significant ... has been the creation of referrals orders as part of the Youth Justice and Criminal Evidence Act 1999.'[97]

This new order, created by Part I of the 1999 Act, is mandatory for 10 to 17 year olds who plead guilty and are convicted by the courts for the first time, unless the crime is serious enough to warrant a custodial sentence or the court proposes an absolute discharge.[98] The referral order is the sole sentence for the first conviction, although it may be accompanied by ancillary orders such as costs, compensation, forfeiture of items used in the commission of the offence, and exclusion from football matches. Once a referral order has been made, the young offender is referred to a Youth Offender Panel which consists of a YOT member and at least two members of the community who have undergone training provided by the YOT. One of the community members chairs the panel. The order requires the offender to attend all of the panel meetings. A parent or guardian of an offender under the age of 16 is required to attend the meetings. The offender can choose one other person over the age of 18 to accompany him or her. Other people may attend, such as the victim, a victim supporter, and anyone else the panel believes is capable of having a 'good influence' on the offender, although their attendance is voluntary.

The aim of the panel is to reach agreement with the offender on a programme of behaviour, with the principal aim of preventing re-offending. If the victim attends, the panel is an opportunity for him or her to talk to the offender about the offence. The programme of behaviour agreed, known as the 'youth offender contract', must not be for a period of less than three months or for more than 12 months.[99] The contract should always include reparation to the victim or to the community. It may also require the offender to attend mediation sessions with the victim or other person; to be at home at specified times, to attend school, or other educational establishment, or place of work; to attend specified activities such as those designed to address offending behaviour or drugs/alcohol awareness sessions; to present himself or herself to a specified person at a specified time and place; or to stay away from specified places and/or persons.[100] If the offender does not agree to a contract or breaches any terms of the contract, he or she will

---

[95] *supra* at n. 91, at p. 54.

[96] *ibid.*, p. 58.

[97] Newburn, *supra* at n. 15, at p. 567. For a critical review of referral orders, see Ball C., 'The Youth ^istice and Criminal Evidence Act 1999 Part I: A significant move towards restorative justice, or a ^ne for unintended consequences?' [2000] Crim.L.R. 211; Haines K., 'Referral Orders and Youth ^der Panels: Restorative Approaches and the New Youth Justice' in B. Goldson (ed.) *The New ^ustice* (2000), Chap. 4.

^ustice and Criminal Evidence Act 1999, s. 1.

^(1).

be referred back to court. Referral orders became available nationally from April 2002. Prior to this the orders were piloted in 11 areas and these projects were evaluated. The evaluation reported[101] high satisfaction levels from the young people; 72 per cent felt that the purpose of the meeting was fully explained to them, 91 per cent said that they had understood what was going on at the meeting, 84 per cent felt that they were treated with respect, and three-quarters responded that they did not feel pushed into anything in the meeting. Nearly all of the parents interviewed felt that they were treated fairly and with respect. Less encouraging are the numbers relating to victim involvement. A victim attended a panel in only 13 per cent of cases where there was at least an initial meeting held. Of those victims who did attend a panel meeting, a significant number of them expressed dissatisfaction about the limits to their involvement and participation in the whole panel meeting.

11.3.6. *New Non-criminal Orders*

The Crime and Disorder Act 1998 introduces a number of new orders that have been termed 'non-criminal' in the sense that they actively seek to prevent offending rather than react to it.[102] As a result of the focus on anti-social behaviour and poor parenting, rather than criminal activity, these orders have been the subject of much criticism and are viewed by some commentators as the most controversial aspect of the 'new youth justice'.[103]

Anti-social behaviour order:

The anti-social behaviour order (ASBO) was originally termed 'community safety order' and the September 1997 consultation paper of the same name stated the Government's rationale in creating the order.

> *'Anti-social behaviour causes distress and misery to innocent, law-abiding people—and undermines the communities in which they live ... The Government is committed to tackle this problem to allow people to live their lives free from fear and intimidation.'*[104]

The aim of section 1 of the Crime and Disorder Act 1998 is to target anti-social behaviour of those aged 10 and over; behaviour that is defined in section 1(1) as 'caused or was likely to cause harassment, alarm or distress to one or more persons not of the same household as himself.' The local authority or police can apply to the magistrates' court in the area where the complaint is alleged for an ASBO. It is a civil order. The court must decide, on the balance of probabilities, whether the defendant has behaved in an anti-social manner as defined by the statute and that an order is needed to protect the community from further anti-social acts. If granted, the ASBO, prohibits the defendant from doing anything described in the order. The order applies for a minimum of two years. Between April 1999 and September 2001 a total of 466 ASBOs were granted, 74 per cent were for those under the age of 21.[105]

Arguably, the most controversial aspect of the ASBO is the penalty for non-compliance with the order. While a civil matter in the first instance, if the

---

[101] Newburn T., Crawford A., Earle R., *et al.*, *The Introduction of Referral Orders into the Youth Justice System: Final Report*. Home Office Research Study 242 (2002).
[102] *supra* at n. 81, at p. 44.
[103] Newburn, *supra* at n. 15, at p. 563. See also Fionda, *ibid.*, pp. 44–46.
[104] *supra* at n. 56, at para. 1.
[105] Campbell S., *A review of anti-social behaviour orders*. Home Office Research Study 236 (2002).

defendant does not comply with the terms of the order it becomes a criminal matter. On summary conviction the maximum is six months imprisonment and/ or a fine; on conviction on indictment the maximum is five years imprisonment and/or a fine.[106] Gardner *et al.* have been very critical of the order, claiming that it involves 'a marriage of civil and criminal proceedings, in an attempt to get round the difficulties of both by combining a little of each.'[107] They conclude:

'*It strikes us as strange that a government which purports to be interested in tackling social exclusion at the same time promotes a legislative measure destined to create a whole new breed of outcasts.*'[108]

Child safety order:

Continuing the Government's theme of preventing offending and early intervention, section 11 of the Crime and Disorder Act 1998 creates child safety orders for those under 10 years old. These orders were proposed in the September 1997 consultation paper, *Tackling Youth Crime*, and carried through to the White Paper, *No More Excuses*, in November of that year. The rationale behind the reform is to 'prevent specific children slipping into the crime habit.'[109] The order is made in the family proceedings court and the civil standard of proof is applied. The order can only be made once one of the conditions in section 11(3) has been met, which includes if the child commits an act that would have been an offence if he or she had been over the age of criminal responsibility. Fionda is highly critical of this provision asserting that:

'*In this respect the Government have sought to abandon the minimum age of criminal responsibility without stirring up the political hornets' nest that would have ensued had they done so expressly. Further, to bring individual children directly into the youth justice system, when their delinquency falls short of behaviour prohibited by the criminal law, is reminiscent of the early Victorian attempts at welfare which have long since been discredited and abandoned.*'[110]

The effect of the child safety order is that it places a child under 10 under supervision, normally for three months but it may be up to a year in exceptional circumstances.

Local child curfew schemes:

Section 14 of the Crime and Disorder Act 1998 establishes local child curfew schemes. Local authorities and the police,[111] after receiving support from the Home Secretary, are able to impose a ban on children of specified ages (originally under 10 but now has been extended to under 16)[112] being in a public place in specified areas during designated times unless they are accompanied by a parent or responsible person over 18. The ban is for a specified period not exceeding 90 days. Children found breaking the curfew may be removed and taken home by the police. Contravention of the ban may also be considered grounds for imposing a child safety order. The Government's justification for introducing

[106] Crime and Disorder Act 1998, s. 1(10).
[107] Gardner J., von Hirsch A., Smith A.T.H., Morgan R., Ashworth, A., and Wasik, M., 'Clause 1— The hybrid law from hell?' (1998) 31 *Criminal Justice Matters* 25.
[108] *ibid.*, p. 27.
[109] *Tackling Youth Crime, supra* at n. 54, at para. 102.
[110] *supra* at n. 81, at p. 45.
[111] Criminal Justice and Police Act 2001, s. 49.
[112] *ibid.*, s. 48.

local child curfews can be found in the consultation paper, *Tackling Youth Crime*:

> '*Unsupervised young children gathered in public places can cause real alarm and misery to local communities and can encourage one another into anti-social and criminal habits.*'[113]

Parenting order:

In addition to children and young people facing up to the consequences of their actions, New Labour asserts that parents must also recognise their responsibility for the actions of their children.[114] Sections 8 and 9 of the Crime and Disorder Act 1998 enable the court to impose a parenting order on a parent of a child subjected to a child safety order, a child or young person on an anti-behaviour or sex offender order, and a young offender.[115] An order will require the parent to comply with the conditions in the order for a maximum of 12 months and to attend counselling or guidance sessions once a week for a period up to three months.[116] A parent will be liable for a fine if he or she, without reasonable excuse, fails to comply with the order. Some commentators have viewed the parenting orders as an extension of governmental control over private family life and are critical of the inclusion of parenting classes and guidance sessions within a statute that focuses on punishing offending behaviour.[117]

Sex offender order:

Section 2 of the 1998 Act enables the police to apply to the court for a sex offender order and, while unlikely to apply to a juvenile, nothing in the provision prevents it doing so. The person who is subject to the order must be a sex offender (as defined by the statute and can include someone who has been reprimanded or warned as a juvenile for such an offence) and has acted in such a way as to give reasonable cause to believe that an order is necessary to protect the public from serious harm. A sex offender order is for a minimum of five years. This is a civil order but breach of the order without reasonable excuse results in imprisonment for a maximum of six months and/or a fine for summary conviction and imprisonment for a maximum of five years and/or a fine for conviction on indictment.

11.4 OTHER EXISITING ORDERS

There are a number of other orders a court can make when dealing with young offenders. The aim of this section is to provide an overview of some of these orders that have not been previously discussed in this chapter.[118]

Discharges:

Discharges can be of two types, either absolute or conditional, and can be used for adults as well. An absolute discharge is where the court takes no further action, reflecting the triviality of the offence, the circumstances in which it came to be prosecuted or factors relating to the offender. A conditional discharge

---

[113] *supra* at n. 54, at para. 113.
[114] *ibid.*, para. 32.
[115] Crime and Disorder Act 1998, s. 8(1).
[116] *ibid.*, s. 8(4).
[117] *supra* at n. 81, at p. 46. See also Cavadino M., Crow I., and Dignan J., *Criminal Justice 2000* (1999), Chap. 7.
[118] Many of these orders have already been discussed in Chap. 9.

imposes no immediate penalty but the offender remains liable to punishment for the original offence if convicted of another offence within a set period, not exceeding three years. If a juvenile is sentenced within two years of receiving a final warning the option of a conditional discharge will not usually be open to the courts.

Fines:

This is a monetary penalty and can be used for adults as well. For those under 16, the parent will normally be ordered to make the payment. This is also possible for those aged 16 to 17. There are special maximum limits for fines given in the Youth Court.

Compensation order:

This is a monetary penalty imposed by the court and can be used for all ages. The compensation is paid to the victim, via the court, for all or part of the harm/ damage suffered. It may be the only sentence or it may be in addition to another sentence. If the offender is under 16, the parent must pay. For those aged 16 to 17, the court may order the parent to pay. When determining the amount of compensation, the court should have regard to the offender's (or the parents') means. The upper limit of the maximum amount to be paid is the same as in the adult court.

Binding-over order:

Binding-over orders involve the court requiring the offender to enter into a recognisance to be of good behaviour and to keep the peace. Failure to do so means the forfeiture of the sum stipulated by the court. This order applies to all ages. With the aim of preventing further offending, the court can order parents or guardians to enter into a recognisance to take proper care or exercise proper control over the juvenile (**parental bind-over**). Courts are able to add a condition to a parental bind-over to ensure the juvenile's compliance with a community sentence imposed on him or her.

11.4.1 *Community Orders*

There are eight community orders—an action plan order, a drug treatment and testing order, a curfew order, an attendance centre order, a supervision order, a community rehabilitation order, a community punishment order, and a community punishment and rehabilitation order.[119] The sentencing framework requires that community orders can only be imposed where the 'seriousness' threshold (parallel with that for custodial sentences but obviously less difficult to satisfy) has been crossed.[120] Having crossed the threshold, the court must then perform a balancing act by which the type and length of community order must be commensurate with the seriousness of the offence and also must be the most suitable for the offender.

Curfew order:

The curfew order was introduced by section 12 of the Criminal Justice Act 1991 and requires the offender to remain at a specified place for a specified time of between two and 12 hours per day for a period not exceeding six months. In the case of an offender aged under 16, this period is reduced to not exceeding three months.[121] Curfew orders are only available where the courts have been

---

[119] The action plan order is dealt with in s. 11.3—New criminal orders.
[120] Criminal Justice Act 1991, P. I.
[121] Powers of Criminal Courts (Sentencing) Act 2000, s. 37(4).

notified that monitoring arrangements are available in individual areas. The use of electronic monitoring, 'tagging', can also be part of a curfew order.

Attendance centre order:

The attendance centre order was first introduced in the Criminal Justice Act 1948 and is available for offenders under 21. The order requires the offender to attend a centre, usually run by the police, for a fixed number of hours. Normally, 12 hours attendance will be prescribed but this can be reduced for those aged under 14. The maximum time that can be prescribed is 24 hours for those offenders under 16 and 36 hours for those 16 to under 21. The timetable will consist of physical exercise of some kind, instruction on technical skills or crafts and discussion on topics such as citizenship.

Supervision order:

The supervision order was introduced by the Children and Young Persons Act 1969 and all offenders under 18 are eligible. The maximum period that can be spent under supervision is three years. The offender will be under the supervision of a local authority social worker, a probation officer, or a member of a YOT team. The role of the supervisor is to 'advise, assist and befriend the offender.'[122] The conditions of supervision may be specified by the court or the court may delegate this power to the supervisor. There may be conditions to live at a particular address, to attend at a specified place at specified times and to take part in specified activities. These activities are known as intermediate treatment and cannot involve more than 90 days during the duration of the order. Section 71 of the Crime and Disorder Act 1998 enables reparation, to the victim or community, to be a condition of a supervision order and it is subject to the same 90 days requirement.

There can be more restrictive conditions: the court may require the offender to remain at home for up to 10 hours between 6 pm and 6 am during the first three months of the order or to refrain from certain activities. If the court imposes any of these conditions, it must get the offender's consent and consult with the supervisor. The court may also include a residence requirement to live in local authority accommodation for up to six months or to comply with education requirements. The court may also specify people with whom the offender is not to live, if the offence is serious and the offending is due to the circumstances in which he or she has been living, and if the offender was already subject to a supervision order when the offence was committed.

Community rehabilitation order:

This order was formerly known as a probation order.[123] It is available for offenders aged 16 and over. If the offender is 16 or 17, he or she will be under the supervision of a probation officer or a member of a YOT. The minimum period of supervision is six months but it must not exceed three years. The statutory aim of the order is that the supervision will secure the offender's rehabilitation or will protect the public from harm from him or her, or prevent the commission by the offender of further offences.[124] There can be conditions attached to the order.

Community punishment order:

This order was formerly known as a community service order.[125] It is available

---

[122] *ibid.*, s. 64(4).

[123] The probation order was renamed 'community rehabilitation order' by the Criminal Justice and Court Services Act 2000, s. 43(1).

[124] Powers of Criminal Courts (Sentencing) Act.2000, s. 41(1).

[125] The community service order was renamed 'community punishment order' by the Criminal Justice and Court Services Act 2000, s. 44(1).

for offenders aged 16 and over and requires the offender to undertake unpaid work in the community. The order is usually overseen by a probation officer, but if the offender is 16 or 17 the order may be overseen by a member of a YOT. The number of hours which an offender may be required to work in the community will be specified in the order; the minimum number of hours is 40 and the maximum is 240 hours.

Community punishment and rehabilitation order:

This order was formerly known as a combination order,[126] created by section 11 of the Criminal Justice Act 1991, and applies to offenders aged 16 and over. The statutory purpose of the order is to secure the rehabilitation of the offender, or to protect the public from harm from him or her, or to prevent the commission of further offences by the offender.[127] The order requires the offender to be under supervision for a minimum of 12 months but no more than three years, and to perform unpaid work in the community for a minimum of 40 hours but no more than 100 hours.

Drug treatment and testing order:

This order was created by section 61 of the Crime and Disorder Act 1998. It applies to offenders aged 16 and over who are dependent on or have a propensity to misuse drugs and, as such, require or may be susceptible to treatment. The order, which lasts for a minimum of six months to a maximum of three years, includes a treatment requirement (either residential or non-residential) and identifies the treatment provider. Further, the order includes a testing requirement where the offender is to provide samples to ascertain whether he or she has any drug in the body during the period of the order.

---

[126] The combination order was renamed 'community punishment and rehabilitation order' by the Criminal Justice and Court Services Act 2000, s. 45(1).
[127] Powers of Criminal Courts (Sentencing) Act 2000, s. 51(3).

Index